Transcultural Concepts in Nursing Care

Transcultural Concepts in Nursing Care

SECOND EDITION

Margaret M. Andrews, Ph.D., R.N., C.T.N.

Chairperson and Professor
Department of Nursing
Nazareth College of Rochester
Rochester, New York

Joyceen S. Boyle, Ph.D., R.N., F.A.A.N., C.T.N.

Professor and Chair
Department of Community Nursing
School of Nursing
Medical College of Georgia
Augusta, Georgia

J. B. Lippincott Company

Philadelphia

Sponsoring Editor: Margaret Belcher
Coordinating Editorial Assistant: Kimberly Oaks
Cover Designer: Jerry Cable
Production Manager: Janet Greenwood
Production: Textbook Writers Associates
Compositor: Circle Graphics
Printer/Binder: R.R. Donnelley & Sons
Cover Printer: Lehigh Press

Second Edition

6   5   4

Library of Congress Cataloging-in-Publication Data
Andrews, Margaret M.
    Transcultural concepts in nursing care/Margaret M. Andrews,
Joyceen S. Boyle—2nd ed.
        p.   cm.
    Boyle's name appears first on the earlier edition.
    Includes bibliographical references and index.
    ISBN 0-397-55115-0 (pbk.)
    1. Transcultural nursing.   I. Boyle, Joyceen S.   II. Title.
    [DNLM: 1. Transcultural Nursing.   2. Nursing Care—psychology.
3. Nursing Assessment.   4. Cross-Cultural Comparison—nurses'
instruction.   5. Ethnic Groups—nurses' instruction. WY 87 A568t
1995]
RT86.54.A53   1995
362.1'73—dc20
DNLM/DLC
for Library of Congress   94-27740
                                                                                     CIP

Any procedure or practice described in this book should be applied by the healthcare practitioner under appropriate supervision in accordance with professional standards of care used with regard to the unique circumstances that apply in each practice situation. Care has been taken to confirm the accuracy of information presented and to describe generally accepted practices. However, the authors, editors, and publisher cannot accept any responsibility for errors or omissions or for any consequences from application of the information in this book and make no warranty express or implied, with respect to the contents of the book.

Every effort has been made to ensure drug selections and dosages are in accordance with current recommendations and practice. Because of ongoing research, changes in government regulations and the constant flow of information on drug therapy, reactions and interactions, the reader is cautioned to check the package insert for each drug for indications, dosages, warnings and precautions, particularly if the drug is new or infrequently used.

Contributing Authors

Margaret M. Andrews, Ph.D., R.N., C.T.N.
Chairperson and Professor
Department of Nursing
Nazareth College of Rochester
Rochester, New York

Joyceen S. Boyle, Ph.D., R.N., C.T.N.
Professor and Chair
Department of Community Nursing
School of Nursing
Medical College of Georgia
Augusta, Georgia

Patricia A. Hanson, M.S., R.N., C.
Associate Professor
Department of Nursing
Nazareth College of Rochester
Rochester, New York

Paula Herberg, Ph.D., R.N., F.N.P
Associate Dean (Nursing) and Director
The Aga Khan University
Karachi, Pakistan

Kathryn Hopkins Kavanagh, Ph.D., R.N.
Assistant Professor
Psychiatric Community Health and Adult Primary Care
University of Maryland at Baltimore
Baltimore, Maryland

Jana Lauderdale, Ph.D., R.N.
Assistant Professor
Parent Child Division
College of Nursing
University of Utah
Salt Lake City, Utah

Patti A. Ludwig-Beymer, Ph.D., R.N., C.T.N.
Senior Health System Consultant
Lutheran General Health System
Park Ridge, Illinois

Margaret A. McKenna, Ph.D., R.N., C.T.N.
Lecturer, Nursing Program
Adjunct Lecturer
Department of Health Services
University of Washington
Seattle, Washington

Foreword

Change is constant, and since the first publication of *Transcultural Concepts in Nursing Care* in 1989, multiple changes in the health care system have been taking place. With health care reform on the horizon, traditional roles and care settings are shifting to reflect increasing numbers of nurses providing primary care and an increasingly diverse array of care settings. International changes, too, have been significant, as new nations have emerged and old ones have undergone dramatic evolution, some even disappearing. The world in which we are now living is very different from the world of 1989.

The authors, Margaret Andrews and Joyceen Boyle, rightfully bring to nursing and to the health care profession a revised edition of their monumental textbook. The revised text reflects the dynamic changes that are transforming the decade that is carrying us into a new millennium.

Each chapter has been thoroughly updated with knowledge and research specific to the chapter's content area, and several chapters present suggested learning activities to engage the reader in pursuing further inquiry. These additions help crystallize how cultural concepts are applied in nursing practice. New subject matter about current issues, such as community and world health and international nursing, have strengthened the book.

Another important strength of the text is the authors' fearless attack on those concepts which threaten to weaken the field of transcultural nursing. Those damaging concepts, I believe, deal with categorizing groups of people as minorities. The authors prefer, instead, to explore and explain cultural diversity according to subcultures, religion, race, and combinations of all three. They rightfully chide those who continue to use such terminology as *minority* as limiting and labeling. They enlighten us by examining the role of ancestry, migration, and intermarriage in developing the dynamic, heterogeneous populations we now have in the United States, Canada, and other places in the world.

As Andrews and Boyle reconceptualize diverse health care, they give us a more comprehensive framework which encourages nurses to assess each client and client family and provide culturally meaningful care. Throughout the text, the authors remain true to their goal of improving care of the client through theory-based transcultural nursing practice. This revised edition brings us to a heightened level of knowledge, skill, and commitment in our role of changing health care into a more relevant, sensitive, and culturally competent system.

JoAnn Glittenberg, Ph.D., R.N., F.A.A.N.
Professor and Director
Division of Mental Health
College of Nursing
Research Professor
Department of Psychiatry
College of Medicine
University of Arizona

Preface

Initially published in 1989, this text began as a collegial effort among faculty and doctoral students at the University of Utah College of Nursing to help us expand and clarify our view of transcultural nursing. Because many of the contributors had strong clinical backgrounds and an interest in solving practice problems, we wanted a book that would apply transcultural nursing concepts to clinical practice. At the same time, we recognized that the practice of nursing is theory-based; thus we wanted to develop a research-based theoretical framework relevant to transcultural nursing practice.

It is not surprising, then, to discover that the second edition of *Transcultural Concepts in Nursing Care* strongly reflects the 1992 published recommendations of the American Academy of Nursing (AAN) that begin with a commitment to quality and culturally competent care, and go on to include a commitment to

- Foster the development and maintenance of a disciplinary knowledge base and expertise in culturally competent care.
- Synthesize existing theoretical and research knowledge regarding nursing care of different ethnic/minority, stigmatized, and disenfranchised populations.
- Create an interdisciplinary knowledge base that reflects heterogeneous health care practices within various cultural groups.
- Identify, describe, and examine methods, theories, and frameworks appropriate for utilization in the development of knowledge related to health care of minority, stigmatized, and disenfranchised populations.

In addition, similar commitments by the National League for Nursing and most state boards of nursing require or encourage inclusion of cultural aspects of patient care in the nursing curriculum and underscore the importance of the purpose, goals, and objectives for publishing the second edition of *Transcultural Concepts of Nursing Care*.

Purpose: To contribute to the development of theoretically based transcultural nursing and the advancement of transcultural nursing practice.
Goal: To elevate the level of delivery of culturally sensitive client care.
Objectives:

1. To develop a theoretical basis for using concepts from the natural and behavioral sciences for nursing practice.
2. To apply a transcultural nursing framework to guide nursing practice in diverse health care settings.

3. To analyze major concerns and issues encountered by nurses in providing trans-cultural nursing care to clients—individuals, families, groups, communities, and institutions.

Recognizing Individual Differences and Acculturation

When considering transcultural issues, nurses are, with increasing frequency, citing the federally defined population categories, i.e., white, black, Hispanic, Asian/Pacific Islander, and American Indian/Alaska Native. Historically, this classification was used by the U.S. and Canadian governments so that demographic data about traditionally underrepresented populations could be gathered in a systematic manner. Presumably, this was done so that decisions about public policies and allocation of resources for these five population groups could be made in a more equitable way, an outcome that we support. The creation of these five population groups has had a tremendous impact on our conceptualization of the various groups, as well as on how or even *if* we think about other cultural groups. A major impact is that unique characteristics of each of the five cultural groups have become hopelessly enmeshed with others in the same category. Thus, despite changing immigration and refugee policies and the responses to these policies, the creation of five population categories has become metaphorically set in stone. Individual differences, changes over time, and the impact of acculturation often are ignored. The outcome is reminiscent of the melting pot metaphor, only we now have five pots instead of one!

We believe that it is tremendously important to recognize the myriad of health-related beliefs and practices that exist among the dozens of cultural groups that are often called white (sometimes used synonymously with Caucasian, Anglo-American, Euro-American, or European American), those whose origins are traditionally traced to Europe. Nor is recognition being given to the differences among people who identify themselves as Hispanic/Latino: those from Puerto Rico, Mexico, Spain, Guatemala, or "Little Havana" in Miami have some similarities but many cultural differences. It is equally puzzling that members of the 510 federally recognized Native American tribes are treated homogeneously. Similarly, African Americans may trace their ancestry to literally thousands of different African tribes on a vast continent or, in more recent history, to South America or the Caribbean Islands. Of course, intermarriage, the effects of immigration, and other factors also must be considered by transcultural nurses.

We would like to comment briefly on the terms *minority* and *ethnic minorities*. These terms are perceived to be offensive by some because they connote inferiority and marginalization. Thus we prefer to make reference to a specific subculture or culture whenever possible. We refer to categorizations according to race, ethnicity, religion, or a combination, such as ethnoreligion (e.g., Amish), but we make every effort to avoid using the term *minority* for any group(s). In contrast, we believe the concept or term *minority* is limiting not only for those to whom the label is applied but also for nursing theory and practice.

New to the Second Edition

In the second edition we have updated content, integrated research throughout the text, and at the request of colleagues, added chapters on international nursing and nursing in the community. We also reconceptualized and expanded the chapter formerly called "Transcultural Perspectives in the Nursing Process" because of our belief in the epistemologic and ontologic bases of the "curriculum revolution" in nursing.

Cultural Assessment in Diverse Care Settings

Now called "Transcultural Nursing Care," Chapter 2 encourages nurses to use cultural assessment, both process and content, for gathering culturally relevant data about all clients (individuals, families, groups, and communities) in diverse health care settings.

Critical Thinking Linked to Delivering Culturally Competent Care

We believe that cultural assessment skills, combined with the nurse's critical thinking ability, will provide the necessary data (and culturally relevant, meaningful interpretations of those data) on which to base transcultural nursing care. Using this approach, we are convinced that nurses will be able to provide culturally relevant and contextually meaningful care for clients from a wide variety of cultural backgrounds, rather than simply memorizing the health beliefs and practices of any specific cultural group. We believe that nurses must acquire the skills needed to assess clients from virtually any and all groups that they encounter throughout their professional careers. We also have attempted to address transcultural nursing from a Canadian perspective when it seemed appropriate.

Chapter Pedagogy

Learning Activities. Several chapters contain selected learning activities that focus on the content of that particular chapter.

Current Research. Current research studies related to the content of the chapter are presented in Research Boxes. For those readers who wish to pursue additional transcultural nursing knowledge, we urge that you complete the learning activities and read about new research studies that relate to transcultural nursing.

Case Studies Based on Actual Experiences. Case studies based on the authors' actual clinical experiences are presented to make conceptual linkages and to illustrate how concepts are applied in the health care setting. (*Authors' note*: The case studies use pseudonyms to protect the confidentiality and anonymity of the authors' clients and research subjects.)

Using a Theoretical Framework in Transcultural Nursing

The text is divided into three sections. The first section focuses on the theoretical aspects of transcultural nursing. The development of a transcultural nursing framework that includes concepts from the natural and behavioral sciences is described as it applies to nursing practice. Because nursing perspectives are used to organize the content of this book, the reader will not find a chapter purporting to describe the nursing care of a specific cultural group. Instead, the nursing needs of culturally diverse groups are used to illustrate cultural concepts that are used in nursing care. For example, Chapter 2 discusses domains of cultural knowledge that are important in cultural assessment and describes how this cultural information can be incorporated into other aspects of nursing care. The emphasis is on critical thinking and processing cultural knowledge to develop strategies for excellent transcultural nursing care.

Applying Transcultural Concepts Across the Life Span

Chapters 3 to 6 use a developmental framework to discuss transcultural concepts across the life span. The care of childbearing women and their families, children, adolescents, middle-aged adults, and the elderly is examined, and information about various cultural groups is used to illustrate common transcultural nursing issues, trends, and problems.

Applying Transcultural Nursing Concepts in Diverse Clinical Settings

In the third section of the book, Chapters 7 to 13, selected clinical topics are used to illustrate the application of cultural concepts in nursing practice. The clinical application of concepts uses situations commonly encountered by nurses and describes how transcultural nursing principles can be applied in diverse settings. The selection of clinical topics varies widely and reflects the interests and diversity of the contributing authors. The chapters in this section are intended to illustrate the application of transcultural nursing knowledge to nursing practice. In this section, transcultural nursing care in chronic illnesses and in mental illnesses, as well as the transcultural aspects of pain, is examined. Transcultural nursing care in specific settings such as critical care and the community is described, and the importance of transcultural nursing concepts in selected practice settings is emphasized. The interrelationship between religion and culture is the focus of Chapter 12. In Chapter 13, ''International Nursing and Health,'' the nurse is introduced to global health issues and concerns and to the roles of nurses in the international practice settings.

A Final Note

Because some members of the original group were unable to continue with the project, we recruited other transcultural nursing colleagues. Their significant contributions have enriched this second edition, both in scope and content, and have assisted all who have worked on this text to achieve our stated purpose of contributing to the development of transcultural nursing theory and practice.

Margaret M. Andrews
Joyceen S. Boyle

Acknowledgments

We gratefully acknowledge the assistance of our families, friends, and colleagues in making this book possible. We also appreciate the help of the many nursing faculty, practitioners, and students who have offered their comments and suggestions.

A number of colleagues reviewed specific sections of the text and offered invaluable constructive criticism and suggestions. Special thanks to Dr. Roy C. DeLamotte, Dr. Lydia DeSantis, University of Miami School of Nursing, Dr. Bernadette Melnyk, University of Rochester School of Nursing, and Donna Moriarity, Medical College of Georgia, School of Nursing, for their reviews.

We are indebted to the many individuals who allowed us to take photographs of them, including members of our families. Particular appreciation is extended to Henry J. Andrews, Jr., Dr. William Arnold, Dr. Patti Ludwig-Beymer, Lutheran General Health System Media Center for Health Communications, Lydia E. McAllister, and Dr. Margaret A. McKenna, who took special photographs for us.

A special word of thanks to Margaret Belcher, Nursing Editor, Janet Greenwood, Senior Production Manager, and Kimberly R. Oaks, Editorial Assistant, J. B. Lippincott Company, who have supported and encouraged us throughout this project. We are grateful to Dana Norton, Project Manager, and Marty Tenney, Designer, Textbook Writers Associates, for assistance with editing and design and for their careful attention to detail during the final stages of production.

We acknowledge and thank our secretaries, Marilyn S. Brulé and Lisa M. Carrier, for their help in preparing this manuscript. Without their hard work and effort, this project would not have been possible.

We wish to express gratitude to our mothers, Virginia Andrews and Joyce Spencer, and to our fathers (now deceased), Henry Andrews and Harold Spencer, for teaching us to respect and value cultural diversity. Thanks also to Henry, Marilyn, Michael, Peter, and Suzanne Andrews and John Boyle for their interest and support. We are also grateful for the support of our friends, too numerous to list by name.

Lastly, we would like to thank each other for a friendship that has withstood the test of time (and two editions of this book). We have found our professional endeavors in transcultural nursing to be both satisfying and rewarding.

Contents

Foreword by JoAnn Glittenberg   vii

Preface   ix

Part I   Transcultural Nursing: Theoretical Perspectives   1

1   Theoretical Foundations of Transcultural Nursing   3
Introduction   3
A Transcultural Nursing Perspective   4
The Phenomenon of Culture   8
The Concept of Environment   19
The Concept of Health   21
The Concept of People   34
The Concept of Nursing   36
The Study of Transcultural Caring Concepts   42
Summary   44

2   Transcultural Nursing Care   49
Introduction   49
Critique of the Prevailing Nursing Paradigm   50
Transcultural Perspectives on Nursing Diagnoses   50
Transcultural Perspectives on Nursing Theories   52
Cultural Competence, Cultural Competencies, and Excellence
    in Transcultural Nursing Care   54
Cultural Assessment   55
Culture Values   55
Cross-Cultural Communication   62
Culture and Nutrition   73
Traditional Healers   78
Culture and Symptoms   79
Biocultural Variations in Health and Illness   80
Ethnopharmacology   90
Culture and Disease Prevalence   92

Clinical Decision Making and Nursing Actions   92
Evaluation   94
Summary   94

Part II   **A Developmental Approach to Transcultural Nursing**   **97**

   3   *Transcultural Nursing Care of the Childbearing Family*   **99**
Introduction   99
Pregnancy   100
Birth   107
Postpartum   111
Infant Care   113
Fertility Control   116
Summary   119

   4   *Transcultural Perspectives in the Nursing Care of Children*
and Adolescents   *123*
Introduction   123
Family and Culture   123
Normal Growth and Development   128
Health and Health Promotion   140
Illness   142
Culture and Adolescent Development   157
Special Health Care Needs of Adolescents   159
Communicating with Adolescents   160
Adolescent Health Care   162
Transcultural Nursing Care of Children and Adolescents   166
Evaluation of the Nursing Care Plan   169
Application of Cultural Concepts to Nursing Care   169
Summary   175
Learning Activities   175

   5   *Transcultural Perspectives in the Nursing Care of Middle-Aged Adults*   *181*
Introduction   181
Cultural Influences on Adulthood   181
Psychosocial Development During Adulthood   183
Health-Related Situational Crises   185
Summary   199
Learning Activities   199

   6   *Transcultural Perspectives in the Nursing Care of the Elderly*   *203*
Introduction   203
The American View of Aging   205
Growing Old and Becoming Sick: Cross-Cultural Variations in Illness
   Among the Elderly   210
Cultural Dimensions of the Developmental Aspects of Aging   216
A Transcultural Example: Assessment and Intervention with a Recently
   Migrated Family   223
Summary   228
Learning Activities   232

Part III   Clinical Topics and Issues in Transcultural Nursing   235

7   *Alterations in Lifestyle: Transcultural Concepts in Chronic Illness*   237
Introduction   237
The Nursing Management of Clients with Hypertension   238
African Americans and the Increased Risk for Hypertension   239
Lifestyle Changes in Chronic Illness   239
Cultural and Behavioral Factors: Influences on Lifestyle   242
Coping Behaviors in Health and Illness   244
Summary   250
Learning Activities   250

8   *Transcultural Perspectives in Mental Health*   253
Introduction   253
Mental Illness and Mental Disease   254
Diagnosis: Problems with Normality and Abnormality   255
Mental Health Needs, Beliefs, and Practices   259
The Challenge of Categories   260
Communication   268
Nurse, Know Thyself   270
Culture and Psychiatric/Mental Health Nursing   272
Culture-Specific Care   274
Ideologic Conflict in Psychiatric/Mental Health Nursing   276
Summary   278
Learning Activities   281

9   *Transcultural Concepts in Critical-Care Nursing*   287
Introduction   287
Patient Vulnerability   288
Family Issues   290
Culturally Congruent Care   292
Summary   297
Learning Activities   298

10   *Transcultural Aspects of Pain*   301
Introduction   301
Definitions of Pain   301
Measurement of Pain   302
Expressions of Pain   304
Nursing Subculture: Views and Attitudes About Pain   306
Applying Transcultural Nursing Concepts to People in Pain   308
Alternative Practices   312
Summary   318
Learning Activities   319

11   *Culture and the Community*   323
Introduction   323
Culturally Competent Nursing Care in Community Settings   323
A Framework for Providing Transcultural Care with the Community   324
Cultural Issues in Community Nursing Practice   325
Culture and Community   330
Health Care Practitioners and Cultural Issues   333

Communication and Culture   334
Cultural Assessment   336
Using Cultural Knowledge in Primary, Secondary, and Tertiary Preventive
    Programs   341
Summary   347
Learning Activities   349

12   Religion, Culture, and Nursing   *353*
Introduction   353
Dimensions of Religion   353
Religion and Nursing Care   356
Spiritual Care and the Phenomenon of Nursing   357
Religion and Childhood Illnesses   357
Nursing Care for the Dying or Bereaved Client and Family   359
Religious Trends in the United States and Canada   370
Listing of Select Religions   370
Learning Activities   407

13   International Nursing and Health   *411*
Introduction   411
Historical Overview   412
The World's Health   413
The World's Nurses   422
International Nursing as a Specialty   424
International Nursing as a Career   426
Preparation for International Nursing   426
Patterns of Cultural Adjustment   428
Going Abroad   431
Summary   435
Learning Activities   435

Appendix A   *Andrews/Boyle Transcultural Nursing Assessment Guide*   *439*

Appendix B   *Resources in Transcultural Health and Nursing*   *445*

Appendix C   *Significant Cultural Events and Holidays*   *447*

Appendix D   *Selected Agencies Sending Nurses Abroad*   *451*

Index   *455*

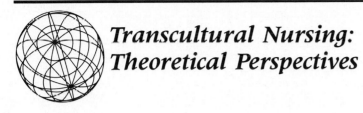

Transcultural Nursing:
Theoretical Perspectives

1

Theoretical Foundations of Transcultural Nursing

Paula Herberg

Introduction

Transcultural nursing is concerned with the provision of nursing care in a manner that is sensitive to the needs of individuals, families, and groups. Such individuals, families, or groups often represent diverse cultural populations within a society as well as between societies. Consider the following:

My mother was born in 1927. She had a myocardial infarction in 1987 and was admitted to the critical-care unit of a local hospital. On my first visit to her, after expressing the usual "daughter-type" concerns and questions, and being a nurse as well as a daughter, I asked her "how are the nurses?" She replied that they were all great, "except the night nurse. He's always talking and telling me things. I wish he would just leave me alone and let me rest. Why does he keep asking me if I have any questions?"

I currently live and work in Karachi, Pakistan. The latest debate in nursing services is whether or not the female nurses should be expected to catheterize male patients. Opinions vary, but there are many nurses who say "no" even though they personally and professionally feel that they should be able to catheterize male patients. They argue that patients do not expect them to do it and it perpetuates the stereotype of nurses as women of "loose morals."

My driver, who has a high school education, recently had a bad cold. His usual response to a cold is to go to a polyclinic and get an injection. What is in the injection is beyond me, but he does not expect to be "cured" of his cold without this ritual trip to the polyclinic, even though it is an expensive venture. This time I suggested that he needed to drink lots of fluids and recommended orange juice. He gave me the

Margaret M. Andrews and Joyceen S. Boyle: TRANSCULTURAL CONCEPTS IN NURSING CARE, SECOND EDITION. © 1995 J.B. Lippincott Company.

funniest look and said, "but juice is cold." He could not understand using a cold food to treat a cold condition.

There are certainly hundreds of other examples of the ways in which cultural beliefs and values color people's health care expectations. Leininger (1989b) commented that many nurses function as though the way they practice nursing is universally understood and accepted. In fact, as Leininger points out, there are no universal standards of nursing practice because of the wide range of cultural diversity among peoples and health care providers.

The purpose of this chapter is to introduce and discuss the theoretical concepts that form the foundation of transcultural nursing and the nursing care issues discussed in the chapters that follow. The use of transcultural concepts in clinical practice situations will facilitate nursing care that is culturally relevant and help nurses work more effectively with clients from different cultural groups. Nurses, who have more direct interactions with clients than any other health team member, should be especially aware of the cultural dimensions of nursing care. Application of transcultural nursing principles can lead to more effective and sensitive encounters between clients and nurses.

A Transcultural Nursing Perspective

A major aim of transcultural nursing is to understand and assist diverse cultural groups and members of such groups with their nursing and health care needs. A thorough assessment of the cultural aspects of a client's lifestyle, health beliefs, and health practices will enhance the nurse's decision making and judgment when providing care. Nursing interventions that are culturally relevant and sensitive to the needs of the client decrease the possibility of stress or conflict arising from cultural misunderstandings. There are often problems when persons from two cultural backgrounds with conflicting values meet, unless at least one of the persons is willing and able to recognize and adapt to the values of the other. One method of reducing potential misunderstandings is to sensitize nurses to their own cultural biases and behaviors as well as to those of their clients. Both the process of sensitization and the result, more sensitive and effective nursing care, are the concerns of transcultural nursing.

Development and Current Status of Transcultural Nursing

Madeleine Leininger (1970) observed that one of anthropology's most important contributions to nursing was "the realization that health and illness states are strongly influenced and often primarily determined by the cultural background of an individual." In addition to Leininger, several authors (McKenna, 1984; Dougherty and Tripp-Reimer, 1985; Lipson and Bauwens, 1988) have described transcultural nursing as a *synthesis* of anthropology and nursing.

The development of the theory of transcultural nursing can be traced to the work of a group of nurses with doctoral preparation in anthropology who were interested in applying concepts, primarily from anthropology, to nursing care (Clark, 1959; Leininger, 1967; Macgregor, 1960, 1967; Osborne, 1969) and who established the Council on Nursing and Anthropology (CONAA) within the American Anthropological Association in the 1960s. Leininger took that idea a step further in 1974 by founding the

Transcultural Nursing Society and gaining recognition for the new subspecialty that she called "transcultural nursing" (Andrews, 1992).

Today, contributions to theory building in transcultural nursing come from nurses with preparations in a variety of disciplines, including those with advanced degrees in nursing itself, who are prepared to advance the subfield of transcultural nursing in terms of theory development, research, practice, and consultation (Andrews, 1992; Morse, 1988; Ray, 1989; Wenger, 1992).

The evolution of transcultural nursing can be represented as a model (Fig. 1-1) in which concepts borrowed from disciplines such as anthropology, sociology, and biology are applied in conjunction with nursing concepts, such as caring and the nursing process, to nursing care issues involving clients' health beliefs, behaviors, and practices, as well as to the health care delivery system in general. The synthesis of ideas created from this conjunction constitutes the emerging discipline of transcultural nursing. Using these synthesized concepts, the nurse can improve the quality of care given by learning to focus on the ways in which illness and health are expressions of a particular culture and how culture influences patients' expectations of nursing care.

Several assumptions and propositions are basic to the practice of transcultural nursing (Leininger, 1978, 1988b, 1991). One is a belief that caring is a universal phenomenon that varies only in form and manifestations; that is, caring for others exists in all cultures, but the methods by which this is done and the meaning that *caring*

Figure 1-1. The development of transcultural nursing.

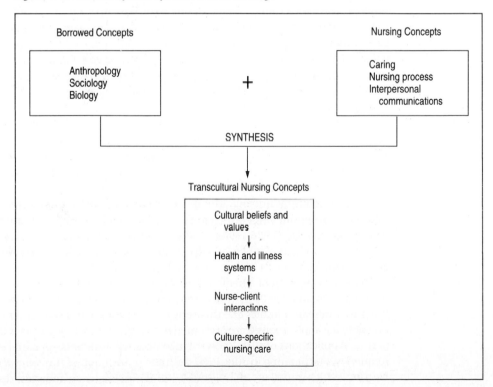

conveys are as diverse as the groups that define it. For example, in some cultures, all care may be provided only by members of the immediate family, by female relatives, by same-sex practitioners, or by specifically designated healers.

What is valued and judged as "good" care is culturally determined, culturally based, and culturally validated. Therefore, members of a cultural group can identify and define what is good care, but outsiders probably cannot do so in the same way. For nurses working with a variety of clients, the closer the nursing care matches the clients' values and expectations, the more accepted it will be. Client satisfaction with nursing care is tied to the degree to which expectations are shared and met.

Thus transcultural nursing is concerned with shared meanings and the degree to which nurse and client agree or disagree on the cultural symbols of health, healing, illness, disease, and caring. Such symbolic meanings influence all aspects of nurse-client interactions. How cultural groups define and treat various illnesses, promote and maintain health, prevent illness, and structure their health care system are basic knowledge requirements for effective transcultural nursing care.

Transcultural nursing can be defined as that field of nursing focused on the "comparative study and analysis of different cultures and subcultures in the world with respect to their caring behavior, nursing care, and health-illness values, beliefs, and patterns of behavior with the goal of developing a scientific and humanistic body of knowledge in order to provide culture-specific and culture-universal nursing care practices" (Leininger, 1978, p. 8).

Chrisman (1990) makes the point that transcultural nursing is a fundamental element of all nursing care, not just care given to minority groups and foreign populations. He states that transcultural nursing is the base of professional nursing practice and that "no matter how sensitive nurses may believe they are, when their sensitivity is based upon untrained common sense, one cannot speak of professional practice; only good, albeit idiosyncratic, personal practice" (p. 38). Professional transcultural nursing practice, according to Chrisman, contains sophisticated assessment and analytic skills, the ability to carry out culturally sensitive planning, and experience in designing and implementing culturally relevant nursing interventions.

Several themes emerge from these definitions. First, cultures can be compared and contrasted with respect to health beliefs, health behaviors, and nursing care measures. Second, the goal of such study is to identify, test, refine, and apply such knowledge to the provision of culturally relevant care. Third, the outcome of such study is a body of knowledge useful to the practicing nurse. Fourth is the idea that this body of knowledge defines transcultural nursing. The need for such a body of knowledge is validated by statements from nursing's professional bodies (Meleis, 1992), including the American Nurses Association (1986), which calls for nurses to include individual value systems and lifestyles in their plans for health care and which urges the profession to meet health and nursing care needs of a diverse and multicultural society.

The development of a body of knowledge in transcultural nursing became evident in the 1970s and 1980s as more and more articles began to appear in the nursing literature. Research studies and theoretical discussions of transcultural nursing concepts and practice applications were presented in the writings of many nurses during this time period. Applications of such knowledge to practice situations appeared with increasing frequency, culminating in July 1989 with the publication of the *Journal of Transcultural Nursing*, which aimed to "share transcultural nursing ideas, theories, research findings and/or practice experiences with other nurses/disciplines worldwide" and to "advance the knowledge base of transcultural nursing and promote humanistic care" (Leininger, 1989a, pp. 1–2). In her opening editorial, Dr. Leininger welcomed diverse viewpoints, theories, and research perspectives exploring the multifaceted aspects of transcultural nursing worldwide and encouraged nurses to expand their world views in relation to nursing, education, practice, and research.

In the 1990s, the field of transcultural nursing seems firmly established (Chrisman, 1990; Muecke and Srisuphan, 1990; Rothenburger, 1990; Camphina-Bacote and Ferguson, 1991; Dobson, 1991; Giger and Davidhizar, 1991; Spector, 1991; Weller, 1991; Hirschfeld and Holleran, 1992; Kavanaugh and Kennedy, 1992; Stevens, Hall, and Meleis, 1992; Bernal and Froman, 1993). Certification in transcultural nursing has been available since 1988 from the Transcultural Nursing Society (Roessler, 1990). Transcultural nursing concepts are reflected in the literature related to practice issues (Frye, 1990; Lawson, 1990; Blenner, 1991; Camphina-Bacote, 1991; Gates, 1991; Lopez and Hendrickson, 1991; Reeb, 1992), education (Lindquist, 1990; Eliason and Macey, 1992; Millon-Underwood, 1992; Rosenbaum, 1991; Meleis, Lispon, and Paul, 1992), management (Cliff, 1992; Davis, 1992; Harnar et al., 1992; Park, 1992), and care for specific cultural groups (Carbal et al., 1990; Kirkpatrick and Cobb, 1990; Phillips and Lobar, 1990; Calvillo and Flaskerud, 1991; Lane and Meleis, 1991; Meleis, 1991; Porter and Villarruel, 1991; Wuest, 1991; Adams, Briones, and Rentfro, 1992; D'Avanzo, 1992; Spangler, 1992; Villarruel and Ortiz de Montellano, 1992; Burkhardt, 1993).

A Transcultural Nursing Framework

In order to help develop, test, and organize the emerging body of knowledge in transcultural nursing, it is helpful to have a specific conceptual framework from which various theoretical statements can emerge. Such statements can be tested with a variety of research methods, including *ethnonursing*.* Perhaps the best known theoretical framework is that developed by Leininger (1991, pp. 41–43) and known as the *sunrise model* (Leininger's Fig. 1.1.5). Leininger's model is based on the concept of cultural care and presents three major nursing modalities that guide nursing judgments and activities to provide culturally congruent care, that is, care that is beneficial and meaningful to the people being served.

Leininger's model represents a specific transcultural nursing framework. The theoretical foundations on which that framework is based, which organize the discussions on which that framework is based, and which organize the discussions that follow in this chapter are shown in Figure 1-2. This theoretical foundation encompasses the concepts central to the discipline of nursing and uses the concept of culture as the integrating factor. The central concepts of the discipline of nursing have been identified as *people, environment, health,* and *nursing.* These four concepts focus and structure what is important in nursing.

Therefore, use of this theoretical base clarifies what is important in the development of theory in transcultural nursing. As the model shows, all four concepts must be

---

* *Ethnonursing* is the study of how a local culture perceives, knows, and practices caring or nursing care activities (Leininger, 1978).

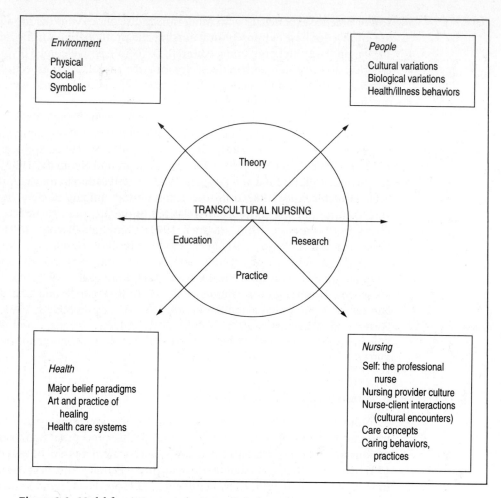

Figure 1-2. Model for components in transcultural nursing.

interrelated to understand transcultural nursing knowledge. Because the focus in transcultural nursing is on the *cultural dimension of care*, each component must be approached from that perspective. The details of the content areas contained in the framework are outlined in Table 1-1.

The Phenomenon of Culture

Although studied and analyzed thoroughly (see Kroeber and Kluckhohn, 1952, for a classic analysis), culture is a little-understood phenomenon. Yet cultural perceptions affect the way people are viewed and expected to act in various situations. A person's behavior is determined by cultural influences as well as by personal characteristics. However, these cultural influences are so subtle that people are rarely aware of their operation; most persons have only a very basic understanding of their own culture, although they function in it quite automatically.

Table 1-1. Theoretical foundations of transcultural nursing

Culture	Environment	Health	People	Nursing
Definitions	Physical environment	Concepts, definitions	Biologic variations	Professional nurse in
Characteristics	Climate	Health	Help/health-seeking	cultural encounters
Formation of values	Topology	Disease	process	Stumbling blocks
Value orienta-	Location	Illness	Health-illness behaviors	Building blocks
tions	Resources	Sickness	Cultural variations	Culturally competent
Cultural groups	Diet	Health belief systems	Individual/group	nursing care
Belief systems	Social environment	Magicoreligious	assessment	Nursing care concepts
Manifestations	Family systems	Biomedical	Lifestyle—activities of	Caring
	Definitions	Holistic	daily living	Nursing process
	Characteristics	Art and practice of	Beliefs, values	Cultural
	Orientation	healing	Health orientation	assessment
	Functions	Prevention and health	Health practices	Interpersonal
	Other systems	promotion	Taboos, rituals, rites	skills
	Education	Diagnosis and	of passage	Technical skills
	Economics	treatment		Cultural diagnosis
	Religion	Practitioners		Health planning
	Politics	Types of healing		Implementing care
	Technology	systems		plans
	Social welfare	Popular		Evaluation
	Roles and	Folk		Study of transcultural
	relationships	Professional		nursing
	Symbolic environment	Choice of healing		Theory development
	Art and history	systems		Research
	Music and literature	Health orientations		Education
	Language and			Practice
	communication			

It is not enough to define *culture* as either a special manifestation of the rich and educated or the body of folklore, legends, rituals, and customs of a traditional society. All people have culture, expressed in the attitudes and institutions unique to their particular group. Culture is a view of the world and a set of traditions used and transmitted from generation to generation. As Kumorek (1978) states, culture is "a closed system of questions and answers concerning the universe and man's behavior in it, which has been accepted as authoritative by a human society."

Culture is learned not only through formal study but also through a process of cultural "osmosis," in which the values, attitudes, roles, and behaviors acceptable to and expected by the cultural group are absorbed. This process begins in the family. Parents, through example, praise, and punishment, communicate to their children "correct" cultural behavior. Later, the whole community (through its social structures, such as schools) participates in delineating its cultural expectations. Consider the following situation (Kumorek, 1978):

The American child, seated with his family at dinner, reaches for the salt and pepper, which are in front of his mother. The father corrects: "Does the cat have your tongue? Ask your mother for what you want, and she will pass it to you."
The Afghan child, seated with his family at dinner, asks his mother for the salt and pepper. The father corrects: "Don't you have hands? Don't bother your mother; reach for what you want."

In both situations the child begins to learn what behavior is valued and expected. It is easy to see how ingrained these expectations become by thinking of any situation in which culturally expected behavior is not forthcoming. Typically, one's reaction is ingrained, automatic, subconscious, and negative, perhaps to the point of revulsion. For example, in Pakistan, it is rude to blow one's nose in public. Therefore, people are accustomed to sniffing instead. When a Westerner sniffs, the immediate public reaction conveys that the person is unmannered and inconsiderate. When Pakistanis cope with the miseries of a head cold by sniffing constantly, their Western colleagues often react with irritation ("She's driving me crazy; why doesn't she just blow her nose!").

Defining Culture

The first record of the term *culture* as used today is credited to Sir Edward Tylor, a British anthropologist who wrote in 1871 that culture is "the complex whole which includes knowledge, belief, art, morals, law, custom and any other capabilities and habits acquired by man as a member of society." Culture represents a way of perceiving, behaving, and evaluating one's world. It provides the blueprint or guide for determining one's values, beliefs, and practices.

Cultural Characteristics and Concepts

Culture has four basic characteristics:

1. It is *learned* from birth through the processes of language acquisition and socialization. From society's viewpoint, socialization is the way culture is transmitted and the individual is fitted into the group's organized way of life.
2. It is *shared* by all members of the same cultural group; in fact, it is the sharing of cultural beliefs and patterns that binds people together under one identity as a group (even though this is not always a conscious process).
3. It is an *adaptation* to specific conditions related to environmental and technical factors and to the availability of natural resources.
4. It is a *dynamic*, ever-changing process.

Humans do not exist without culture. It is a universal phenomenon. Yet the culture that develops in any given society is always specific and distinctive, encompassing all the knowledge, beliefs, customs, and skills acquired by members of the society.

It is erroneous to think that cultures follow an evolutionary path toward the "ideal" of modern, industrialized society. Such thinking reflects a self-centered bias common to many members of the Western world. All cultures are equal; those which are labeled "civilized" are simply different from those which are labeled "primitive," not more advanced or better.

Every culture defines the relationships and roles that people assume as members of society. Along with roles come prescribed rights and obligations. Although basic human relationships are universal, it is deceptive to think that roles and relationships are expressed similarly in different cultures. For example, siblings in our culture can be defined as two persons with either the same mother, the same father, the same mother and father, or the same adoptive parents. In some Asian cultures, siblings are also defined as any infants nursed by the same woman. In other cultures, certain kinship patterns, such as maternal first cousins, are defined as sibling relationships.

In addition, role responsibilities differ from culture to culture. For example, in Western countries such as the United States, the role responsibilities of parents are changing. In many families, the father's caretaking role in relation to children and the household has been expanded. In some traditional cultures, the role of the father does not include any caretaking or household responsibilities. Such roles and responsibilities are always based on the value system of the culture and are governed by established rules of conduct.

Culture and the Formation of Values

Values are personal perceptions of what is good or useful (Samovar and Porter, 1991). Values guide the differentiation of desirable from undesirable states of affairs. Values are a universal feature of all cultures, although the types and expressions of values differ widely. *Norms*, the roles by which human behavior is governed, flow from the cultural values of the group involved. Norms often provide direction for living up to values. If a woman's modesty is valued, norms for dress may include long-sleeved, loose-fitting garments. If males are valued, couples may have many children in an effort to have many sons.

All societies have rules or norms that specify appropriate and inappropriate behavior. Individuals are rewarded or punished as they conform to or deviate from established norms. Norms set limits within which persons may seek alternative ways of achieving their goals. Values and norms are learned in childhood along with the suitable behaviors that reflect them.

Values serve many functions. Potter and Perry (1993) list six such functions:

1. *One's perceptions of others are influenced by values.* Mrs. Jones comes to the clinic with her son, who is dirty and unkempt. Nurse Smith, who values the work ethic, perceives Mrs. Jones as a lazy, irresponsible mother. In contrast, Nurse Roberts, who places a high value on interpersonal relationships, notes that Mrs. Jones is loving and attentive toward her son. Mrs. Jones, who places a high value on cleanliness, is embarrassed because her son got dirty in an impromptu football game just before they had to leave home for the clinic.
2. *Values direct persons' responses toward each other.* Miss Howard, a student nurse, values self-directed learning. When she is assisting Dr. Tilly in surgery, she asks one question after another. Dr. Tilly values quiet so that he can concentrate on the procedure. He expects nurses to respond to his requests and maintain silence. He finds Miss Howard a nuisance and reacts accordingly. She finds him uncooperative, which goads her to ask even more questions.
3. *Values reflect a person's identity and form a basis for self-evaluation.* The student who values achievement views good grades as an indication of self-worth. When such a student's grades do not meet his or her expectations, he or she is likely to view himself or herself as a failure.
4. *Values serve as the foundation for a person's position on various personal, professional, social, political, and philosophical issues.* Every member of the health care team has values regarding life and death. A nurse who values "a woman's right to control her own life

choices'' may volunteer to work at the local family planning clinic or champion the pro-abortion candidate in the next election; in contrast, a nurse who places a high value on the "right to life" may elect to promote anti-abortion legislation.

5. *Values, which motivate behavior, are expressed through feelings, actions, and the knowledge a person pursues. Values are goals toward which behavior is directed.* Ami Lloyd has always valued human service endeavors. She feels that helping others is a social obligation and a self-rewarding activity. As a result of these values, Ami is investigating social work, nursing, and law as possible future careers.

6. *Values give meaning to life and provide self-esteem.* Perceptions of happiness and satisfaction are related to one's values. Persons find security in their values. These values influence the way persons interact, the way they make decisions, and the directions they follow in their lives.

Common Value Orientations

According to Kluckhohn (1979), value systems or orientations, because they are tied to the socialization processes of society, reflect the *personality of a culture*. Every society has a basic value orientation that is shared by the bulk of its members as a result of early common experiences; this is called the *dominant value orientation*. Kluckhohn proposes that there are a limited number of basic human problems for which all people must find some solution. She identifies five common human problems with respect to values and norms: persons' innate nature, their relation to nature, their time dimension, the purpose of their existence, and their relationships with others (Table 1-2).

Subcultures can be categorized by geographic region, religion, age and sex, social class, political party, ethnic identify, occupational role, or isolation from the dominant society by choice, discrimination, or locale. Subcultural groups are distinguished from one another and from the dominant culture by such characteristics as speech patterns, dress, gestures, etiquette, forms of worship, foods, eating habits, and lifestyles.

Ethnic groups usually share a common culture, but it is unwise to generalize that all members of any ethnic group are culturally identical without acknowledging individual factors such as education or geographic location. Spector (1991) defines an ethnic group as a social group within a larger social system given special group status on the basis of a trait complex of religious, linguistic, sex, lifestyle, ancestral, racial, physical, or national characteristics. Ethnic groups in the United States can be viewed as subcultures and as minorities. Orque and Bloch (1985) differentiate the two as follows:

Subculture: a large group of people who, although members of a larger cultural group (or in transition from one cultural identification to another), have shared characteristics that are not common to all members of the larger cultural group and that enable them to be thought of as a distinguishable subgroup.

Minority group: a group of people who, because of physical or cultural characteristics, receive different and unequal treatment from others in the society; minority group members see themselves as recipients of collective discrimination.

Cultural Groups in the United States

As the year 2000 approaches, the number of ethnic (minority) group populations in the United States continues to grow. Demographers project that by the year 2080, 51.1

Table 1-2. Cultural value orientations

Theme	Solution Types		
	A	B	C
What is man's innate human nature?	*Evil:* Either unalterable or perfectible only with discipline and effort	*Mixed:* A combination of good and evil; lapses in behavior are unavoidable, but self-control is possible	*Good:* Unalterable or corruptible
What is man's relationship to nature?	*Destiny:* Man is subjugated to nature; fatalism, inevitability	*Harmony:* Man and nature exist together as a single entity	*Mastery:* Natural forces are to be overcome and put to man's use
What is man's significant time dimension?	*Past:* Focus is on ancestors and traditions	*Present:* The time is "now"; little attention is paid to the past; future is considered vague or unpredictable	*Future:* Orientation is toward progress and change; not content with present; past considered "old-fashioned"
What is the purpose of man's being?	*Being* (Dionysian): Spontaneous expression of impulses and desires; nondevelopmental in focus	*Being-in-becoming* (Apollonian): Self-contained and inner controlled; detachment that brings enlightenment; development and self-realization paramount	*Doing* (Promethean): Active striving and accomplishment, competition against externally applied standards of achievement
What is man's relationship with his fellow men?	*Lineal:* Continuity through time; heredity and kinship ties; ordered succession	*Collateral:* Group goals primary focus; family orientation	*Individual:* Personal autonomy and independence; authority not absolute; group goals submerged; individual goals dominate

Kluckhohn, F. R. (1976). Dominant and variant value orientations. In P. J. Brink (Ed.), Transcultural Nursing: A Book of Readings, pp. 63–81. Englewood Cliffs, N. J.: Prentice-Hall. Reprinted by permission.

percent of the total U.S. population will be comprised of various ethnic minority groups: Hispanics, 23.4 percent; blacks, 14.7 percent; Asians and others, 12 percent (U.S. Bureau of the Census, 1990). With the constant influx of peoples from different societies coming to the United States each year as immigrants, refugees, tourists, students, and patients, it is easy to see the rich mix of ethnic and cultural groups represented in America. As many as 150 different ethnic groups and more than 500 tribes of Native Americans have been identified to date.

Ethnicity refers to the values, perceptions, feelings, assumptions, and physical characteristics associated with ethnic group affiliation or membership. Ethnicity influences one's sense of space and time and one's sense of belonging. It commonly develops through daily contacts with family, friends, and persons in one's neighborhood with whom one associates and lives.

In the United States and Canada, the dominant cultural group is that of white, middle-class Protestants who are descendants of northern European immigrants who came to this country at least two generations ago. A member of this group is often referred to as a WASP (*White Anglo-Saxon Protestant*). Common characteristics of this group include a high school education or even a college degree, a conservative outlook or value system, a family orientation, a sense of commitment to higher education for one's children as a way to financial stability, a "Protestant work ethic" (which dictates that persons ought to work and, conversely, that they are failures if they are unemployed), semitraditional sex/work roles (although increasing numbers of women are working outside the home), a materialistic outlook, an orientation toward the future, a personal faith in God (even among those who are not active church members), and an imperviousness to serious illness.

Major Value Orientations in the United States. In 1977, Massey presented an interesting comparison of generational value systems in the United States. He stated that value systems are tied to the historical, communal, shared events that occur during one's childhood and that basic values are established by the age of 10 years. Thus each generation develops its own value system. He identified four value systems for persons born in the United States between 1920 and 1980: the traditional, in-between, rejection, and synthesis groups. The major characteristics of persons from the traditional and rejection groups are compared in Table 1-3. Since his work, people maturing in the 1970s have come to be labeled the "me generation." The 1980s carried over the values of the me generation and refined them to include an emphasis on materialism, fitness, and health labeled a "yuppie lifestyle." As the 1990s emerge, it is clear that 1970s and 1980s values are being rejected or molded into a different form. Time will tell what labels are applied to the 1990s generation. Generally speaking, middle-class values in the United States include individuality, material wealth, comfort, humanitarianism, physical beauty, democracy, newness, cleanliness, education, science and technology, the legal system, achievement, free enterprise, punctuality, rationality, independence, respectability, self-discipline, effort, and progress. The dominant U.S. value orientation was summarized as a *"moral orientation* with an emphasis on the *active instrumental mastery* of the world according to *set standards of performance"* by Williams in a classic 1970 study. His conclusions, valid for the dominant cultural group in U.S. society today, are shown in Table 1-4. Of course, a number of cultural groups in the United States do not subscribe to the dominant view.

Subcultures in the United States. According to the U.S. Census Bureau, in 1990, major subcultural groups in the United States included Hispanic (9 percent of the total U.S. population), black (12.1 percent), Native American (0.8 percent), and Asian/Pacific Islander (2.9 percent). Included in the 1990 census as distinct ethnic groups were blacks (African, Haitian, or Dominican Republic descent), persons of Spanish origin (Mexican, Puerto Rican, Cuban, and others), Asians and Pacific Islanders (Japanese, Chinese, Filipino, Korean, Vietnamese, Hawaiian, Guamian, Samoan, or Asian Indian descent, among others), and people of Native American ancestry (e.g., Alaska natives, Navajo, Sioux). Each of these groups has its own set of characteristics and values that can be visualized on a continuum anywhere from very similar to the dominant cultural group to distinctly different from that group.

By geographic region, Appalachia, the South, the West Coast (especially California), and New York can be singled out as unique subcultures. Age-related subcultures include the elderly and adolescents. By occupation, migrant farm workers, factory

Table 1-3. Comparison of major 20th-century value systems (1920–1980)

Generations	Traditional	In-Between	Rejection	Synthesis
Description	1920–1940s: see below	Late 1940–1950s (the "Searchers"): *pivotal group* with values tied to generations preceding and following it	1960s: see below	1970s–1980s: wait-and-see attitude, generally conservative, present orientation ("now is the good life")

Traditional Group	Rejection Group
Teamwork orientation	Individual expression
Spectator of life events	Participants in life
Authoritarian outlook; acceptance of institutional leadership	Democratic outlook; questioning of all leadership
Stability ("This is *the* way")	Experimental ("Try it, you may like it")
Problem oriented, systematic, specific	Process oriented (being a part of the process ("cause") even if no solutions)

Social order
  People in their place
  A time for everything
	Social status/equality: respect by ability to perform

Formal approach	Informal approach
Conformity	"Do your own thing"
Puritanical	Sensual

Materialistic
  Functional goods
  Value on wealth
	Materialistic
	  Enjoyment, excitement
	  Money taken for granted

Nuclear family
  Marriage sacred
  Duty to have children
	Lifestyle alterations
	  Marriage/divorce rites of society
	  Population control

Education
  Basic subjects
  Advanced degrees
	Education
	  Experiential methods (media, technology)

Work
  8–5 routine
  Goals of money, status
 	
  Company loyalty
	Work
	  Routine schedules dull; should be enjoyable, fun
	  Motivated by rewards other than money
	    (e.g., performance)
	  Loyalty to self, technology

Massey, M. (1977). What You Are Isn't Necessarily What You Will Be (Videotape No. 3123.03). Farmington, MI: Magnetic Video Corporation. By permission.

workers, professionals (e.g., doctors, nurses lawyers), and "celebrities" (such as actors and athletes) are examples of subcultural groups in the United States. Subcultures also can exist within subcultures. Families in a neighborhood, fraternities in a university, and nurses in a hospital are examples of this. All share interests, attitudes, and beliefs not shared by nonmembers.

Today, the idea of a "melting pot" culture in which new arrivals give up all their old traditions and values in order to become Americans is being questioned. American society is now more realistically seen as an intricate mosaic in which multiple ethnic, religious, geographic, and lifestyle factors play a part in the development of cultural variations. The emphasis today is on retaining one's unique ethnic and cultural values and traditions. Retaining ethnic traditions strengthens and enriches family life and provides security to younger family members, who realize that they are part of a continuing line of people with a past and a future.

Table 1-4. Common value orientations in the United States

Value Statement	Description
Active mastery, not passive acceptance.	Leads to low frustration tolerance, power emphasis, need for approval, ego assertion, and positive encouragement of desires.
Focus on the external world of things, not the inner experience of meanings and affects.	Stress is on palpable and immediate experiences; manipulation, not contemplation, is desired.
Open, not closed, world view.	Focus is on change, movement, progress, and the adaptive and accessible; outgoing and assimilative personality traits valued.
Rationalistic, not traditionalistic.	Past is deemphasized; orientation is toward future. Traditions are not accepted at face value.
Orderliness, not lack of organization.	Structure and form are important.
Universal, not particularistic, orientation.	Uniform laws and principles guide actions (such as the ideal of equal opportunities for all), although in reality some particularistic traits are evident (e.g., claims to special favors on the basis of friendship, kinship, or social status).
Emphasis on peer relationships, not superordinate-subordinate relationships.	Focus on all horizontal (e.g., "equality"), not vertical (hierarchical), relationships.
Individualistic, not group oriented.	Independence, autonomy, self-responsibility, and identity are important.

Williams, R. M. (1970). *American Society: A Sociological Interpretation*, 2d ed. rev. New York: Knopf. Reprinted by permission of the author.

It would be wrong, however, to discount entirely the melting pot metaphor. Through socialization and acculturation processes, a portion of the dominate culture "rubs off" on most members of American society. An Irish Catholic reared in the United States, for example, is not the same cultural being as a native of Ireland who is also Catholic, regardless of ethnic and religious ties. Although this Irish-Catholic American and her Lebanese Christian or Protestant black neighbors may have very different cultural traits, they all display common aspects of American culture that the native African, Lebanese, or Irish native would not share (e.g., love of hot dogs, watching the "soaps" on TV, discussing the latest baseball game, Republican versus Democratic politics).

Culture and Change

Cultures have both stabilizing and dynamic qualities that allow people to live together. From the time of our birth, subtle and constant forces pressure us to follow cultural patterns and norms. These norms tend to regulate life and make for predictable, stable social interactions. Concurrently, culture is a dynamic process that permits and incorporates change as a matter of course. Therefore, norms change to meet the needs of the group at any given time. Some cultural changes, usually involving deeply embedded values and taboos, are very slow, whereas others occur so rapidly that there is hardly time for new norms to develop around them. Such rapid change sometimes creates cultural confusion while norms and values "catch up" to behavioral changes. One example of such change is the increase in working mothers in the United States; although women have been entering the work force in increasing numbers since World

War II, the value that "a woman's place is in the home"—as reflected in people's attitudes toward such things as day care for children of working mothers—has been slower to change.

No aspect of life escapes cultural forces, including such biologically necessary activities as eating, elimination, and sex. All societies are faced with common basic problems regarding the persons's place and role in the universe. The different ways these problems are dealt with account for the almost infinite variety of human culture. Human expression and ingenuity are limitless. Cultures are seldom rooted only in necessity; although it is possible to survive without art, religion, humor, or music, no culture completely lacks such elements. Faced with the task of living, people express their solutions through a variety of cultural styles.

Cultural Belief Systems. Cultural meanings and beliefs develop from the shared experiences of a group in society and are expressed symbolically. The use of symbols to define, describe, and relate to the world around us is one of the basic characteristics of being human. One of the most common expressions of symbolism is *metaphorical*. In metaphor, one aspect of life is connected to another through a shared symbol; for example, the phrase "what a tangled web we weave" or "all the world's a stage" expresses metaphorically the relationship between two normally disparate concepts (such as human deception and a spider's web). People often use metaphors as a way of thinking about and explaining life's events.

Metaphorical thinking develops with the ability to symbolize. Sigerist (1967) proposed that our early human ancestors, having reached a certain level of civilization and faced with natural phenomena (e.g., lightning, floods, disease), used symbolism to come to the conclusion that supernatural forces or agents (the personification of nature) were at work. This connection among the natural, supernatural, and biologic represented the first development in metaphorical thinking. The various connections made between ideas and experiences over the course of time represent the historical metaphors of life as developed by various cultures of the world. The connections made are reflected (symbolically) in the technology, philosophy, religion, social organizations, economics, artistic expressions, literature, politics, and health/illness systems developed by any group of people. The use of metaphors is further discussed later in this chapter in the section "The Concept of Health."

Every group of people has found it necessary to explain the phenomena of nature. From the explanations developed emerges a common belief system. The explanations usually involve metaphorical imagery of magical, religious, natural/holistic, or biologic form. The range of explanations is limited only by the human imagination.

The set of metaphorical explanations used by a group of people to explain life's events and offer solutions to life's mysteries can be viewed as the group's *world view*. A world view also can be defined as a major paradigm. A *paradigm*, like any general perspective, is a way of viewing the world and the phenomena in it. Kuhn, who identified the concept of paradigm shifts, referred to a paradigm as the assumptions, premises, and glue that hold together a prevailing interpretation of reality. Paradigms are slow to change and do so only if and when their explanatory power is exhausted. Over the course of time, several major paradigms have emerged to define reality on Earth (see Box 1-1).

Box 1-1. World Views

World of harmony and unity: *Naturalistic* paradigm
World of goodness and rightness: *Moral* paradigm
World of beauty: *Aesthetic* paradigm
World of freedom, peace, and tranquility: *Social* paradigm
World of wonder and technology: *Magical* paradigm
World of wisdom, togetherness, and knowledge: *Cosmic* paradigm

---

The world view developed reflects the group's total configuration of beliefs and practices and permeates every aspect of life within the culture of that group. Members of a culture share a world view without necessarily recognizing it. Thinking itself is patterned on this world view, because the culture imparts a particular set of symbols to be used in thinking. Because these symbols are taken for granted, people do not normally question the cultural bias of their very thoughts. The use in the United States of the term *American* reflects such an unconscious cultural bias. This term is understood by citizens of the United States in the collective to refer only to the United States of America, although in reality it is a generic term referring to anyone on this continent, including Canadians, Mexicans, Colombians, and so on.

Another example of symbolism and world view can be seen in the way that nurses use such terms as *nursing care, health promotion*, and *illness* and *disease*. Nurses often take for granted that all their patients define and relate to these concepts in the same way that they do. This reflects an unconscious belief that the same cultural symbols are shared by all and therefore do not require reinterpretation in any given nurse-client context. Such an assumption accounts for many of the problems nurses face when they try to communicate with others who are not members of the "health profession" culture.

Dominant Cultural Paradigms. Although the range of symbolic expression may be infinite, three major world views dominate the explanations given for life events: the *magicoreligious, holistic*, and *scientific* paradigms. Aspects of all three can be found in most cultures, although one usually predominates. Understanding the ways in which each paradigm shapes the thought processes, values, beliefs, and practices of a given culture will help the nurse appreciate the ways in which people relate to the world around them. On paper, it is easy to separate the three paradigms into distinct categories; in reality, it is often more difficult to do so, especially on an individual level.

It is important to acknowledge all three paradigms in transcultural nursing. Most persons choose a blend of beliefs from the three major paradigms on which to base their own personal world views. These world views relate directly to the concept of "health" in the transcultural nursing framework because *all beliefs and values regarding health are derived from a persons's basic world view*. A particular client may believe primarily in the scientific paradigm but be influenced by aspects of a magicoreligious nature. In order to understand the individual client and respond appropriately, the nurse must be able to discern these world views. A more thorough discussion of each paradigm or world view is presented later in this chapter in the section "Health Belief Systems."

The Study of Culture. In order to understand culture and all its aspects, one must remember that culture develops in response to multiple forces. What seems at first strange or illogical to an outsider is often perfectly rational within a cultural context. From an outsider's vantage point, one can see the unique patterns that create a particular system, particularly if one has a command of the group's language and an awareness of the meanings of their customs, beliefs, and traditions. Learning to appreciate and understand another culture "from the inside out" is often difficult and time consuming, requiring motivation, openness, and energy, but the results can be very rewarding.

Since culture is a universal phenomenon, those traits which are common to all cultural groups can be studied. Cultural manifestations that are important to understand include language; diet and food habits; dress; ethics; social patterns of behavior; religious and other customs, rituals, and taboos; use of time and space; nonverbal communication; economic systems; attitudes toward change; and health/illness belief systems and practices. Included in social patterns of behavior are such things as male/female roles, authority and decision-making rules, work orientations, family orientations, and interpersonal relationships. Nurses are usually most interested in their clients' beliefs and practices regarding health matters. However, it is equally important to assess and understand the other components of culture. An outline for a thorough cultural assessment is presented in Table 1-5. A more complete discussion of cultural factors that are important in nursing assessment can be found in Chapter 2.

The Concept of Environment

The *environment* can be defined as all phenomena, tangible and symbolic, that impinge on and influence development, beliefs, and behavior. *Environment*, as used in this text, is divided into three parts: *physical, social,* and *symbolic.*

The *physical environment* includes such phenomena as climate, geography, housing, sanitation, and air quality. The physical environment is a factor in the development of any culture. For example, the climates of Alaska and Polynesia were decisive factors in the cultures that developed in both areas. The climate influenced such things as the type of housing built, the economies developed, and the clothing worn. The geographic area in which a society develops—whether rural or urban, near bodies of water or other natural structures—and the resources available in the land itself both play a part in determining a group's culture. The role of the physical environment can never be excluded in a discussion of culture.

The *social environment* includes all those structures associated with the socialization of a person into a group in society. This includes family, community, church, and state institutions, as well as the roles and functions of each. The family is the primary source of socialization and, by extension, of culture. Studying the dynamics of the family is a crucial part of learning the cultural background of any person. Religious orientation is a large part of a person's culture. Education, whether formal or informal, helps impart the cultural beliefs of the group. The economic and political systems of the group are social in nature and culture-specific. The health care delivery system is also an aspect of the social environment.

The *symbolic environment* refers to the music, art, history, language, and other symbols that provide a common means of communication and identification with a

Table 1-5. Guide for the assessment of cultural manifestations

I. Brief history of the origins of the cultural group, including location
II. Value orientations
   A. World view
   B. Code of ethics
   C. Norms and standards of behavior (authority, responsibility, dependability, competition)
   D. Attitudes toward:
      1. Time
      2. Work versus play/leisure
      3. Money
      4. Education
      5. Physical standards of beauty, strength
      6. Change
III. Interpersonal relationships
   A. Family
      1. Courtship and marriage patterns
      2. Kinship patterns
      3. Childrearing patterns
      4. Family function
         a. Organization
         b. Roles and activities (sex roles, division of labor)
         c. Special traditions, customs, ceremonies
         d. Authority and decision making
      5. Relationship to community
   B. Demeanor
      1. Respect and courtesy
      2. Politeness, kindness
      3. Caring
      4. Assertiveness versus submissiveness
      5. Independence versus dependence
   C. Roles and relationships
      1. Number and types
      2. Functions
IV. Communication
   A. Language patterns
      1. Verbal
      2. Nonverbal
      3. Use of time
      4. Use of space
      5. Special usage: titles and epithets, forms of courtesy in speech, formality of greetings, degree of volubility versus reticence, proper subjects of conversation, impolite speech
   B. Arts and music
   C. Literature
V. Religion and magic
   A. Type (modern versus traditional)
   B. Tenets and practices
   C. Rituals and taboos (e.g., fertility, birth, death)
VI. Social systems
   A. Economics
      1. Occupational status and esteem
      2. Measures of success
      3. Value and use of material goods
   B. Politics
      1. Type of system
      2. Degree of influence in daily lives of populace
      3. Level of individual/group participation
   C. Education
      1. Structure
      2. Subjects
      3. Policies

Table 1-5 (*continued*)

VII. Diet and food habits
    A. Values (symbolism) and beliefs about foods
    B. Rituals and practices
VIII. Health and illness belief systems
    A. Values, attitudes, and beliefs
    B. Use of health facilities (popular versus folk versus professional sectors)
    C. Effects of illness on the family
    D. Health/illness behaviors and decision making
    E. Relationships with health practitioners
    F. Biologic variations

group's values and norms. The symbolic environment provides shared meanings for the events that occur in the lives of people in a group and solidifies the group identity.

The Concept of Health

The second concept included in the theoretical foundation of transcultural nursing is *health*. Health is a central concept because all nurse-client interactions are focused on some aspect of health and nursing care. In this framework, the broad concept of health includes the concepts of wellness, disease, illness, and sickness. To appreciate clients' health orientations, it is important to understand their frame of reference regarding definitions and characteristics of health and illness, the cause and prevention of disease and the source of health, remedies and practices of healing, types of health care practitioners, and choice of health care systems.

Health has been defined variously as a state, a process, and a continuum ranging from death or disease to high-level wellness. The most common definition of health is the one proposed by the World Health Organization in 1947. It states that health is more than the absence of disease and includes the idea that health is a state of complete physical, mental, and social well-being. Other definitions focus on the wholeness or unity of the person and on the person's ability to function in activities of daily living. Many definitions of health include meeting one's needs for self-fulfillment or realizing one's potential. *Disease*, in contrast, is usually defined in terms of pathology or deviant behavior. In the case of deviant behavior, it is the group to which the individual belongs that defines what is "deviant" and what is not. Some definitions of disease are based on an underlying value system that equates disease with wrongdoing, evil, or punishment. The definitions of health and disease in any society are culturally determined.

"It is culture not nature that defines disease, although it is usually culture and nature which foster disease" (Hughes, 1978). Hughes observes that every society delineates what is normal and therefore healthy, yet what is normal is not universal. Health is rarely, if ever, a narrowly restricted concept dealing only with the well-being of the physical body. Even the early Greeks viewed health as a manifestation of harmony between human beings and the universe. Historically, health and disease have seldom been viewed in physical isolation or as distinct from misfortunes to crops, relationships between kin, or other complicated matters related to power and control.

From a sociological perspective, the concepts of disease, illness, and sickness can be distinguished. *Disease* relates to the biologic structure and functioning of the human body, as the body is composed of cells, tissues, organs, fluids, and various chemicals. *Illness* is a state of perception, a subjective feeling in which a person may describe symptoms of disease or discomfort. *Sickness* occurs when the personal state of illness becomes a social phenomenon through either visibility or communication. Each condition can occur in the absence of any of the others. During the process in which illness becomes social, role behaviors are modified.

What a person recognizes as illness or disease is culturally prescribed. A given biologic condition may or may not be considered an illness by the particular cultural group in which it occurs. In a classic 1966 study, Zola identified culture as a variable in symptom awareness and illness labeling. Zola's two major findings were (1) that illness is a more common phenomenon than acknowledged and (2) that what is treated seems unrelated to what would usually be thought of as the objective situation (seriousness of symptoms, degree of disability, and subjective discomfort). Zola hypothesized that some selective process operates to determine what is labeled as illness.

When an aberration is fairly prevalent or widespread, it is considered an everyday occurrence and therefore a normal state. Afflictions common enough in a group to be endemic, even clinical deformities, often may be accepted simply as part of the natural human condition.

In 1946, Ackerknecht described the African Thonga, who believe that intestinal worms, with which they are pervasively affected, are necessary for digestion. Among the Mano, also of Africa, primary and secondary yaws are so common that they are not considered a disease. North Amazonian Indians, among whom dyschronic spirochetosis is prevalent, accept the endemicity of this disorder to such an extent that its victims are thought to be normal, and persons who have not had the disfiguring disease are looked on as pathologic and consequently are unable to contract marriage (Hughes, 1978).

Congruence with society's major values is also important in the recognition of illness or disease. People who hear voices from spirits or are controlled by the "gods" are not seen as deviant in societies that believe in the presence of supernatural interventions in the affairs of people. Women who appear emaciated and "diseased" in one culture may be the model of health in a culture that places a value on thinness as a sign of physical beauty. Similarly, persons who are obese may be seen as "strong" and "healthy" in one culture and as "weak" and "unhealthy" in another. In this case, it is not the sign or symptom itself that is significant but the social context within which it occurs and within which it is perceived and understood.

Health Belief Systems

Generally, theories of health and disease/illness causation are based on the prevailing world view held by a group. Each of the three major world views, magicoreligious, holistic, and scientific, has its corresponding system of health beliefs. In two of these world views, disease is thought of an entity separate from self caused by an agent that is external to the body but that is capable of "getting in" and causing damage. This causative agent has been attributed to a variety of natural and supernatural phenomena.

Magicoreligious Health Paradigm.   In the magicoreligious paradigm, the world is an arena in which supernatural forces dominate. The fate of the world and those in it, including humans, depends on the actions of God, or the gods, or other supernatural forces for good or evil. In some cases, the human individual is at the mercy of such forces regardless of behavior. In others, humans are punished by the gods for their transgressions (Foster, 1976). Many Hispanic cultures are grounded in the magicoreligious paradigm. Magic involves the calling forth and control of supernatural forces for and against others. Some African and Caribbean cultures have aspects of magic in their belief systems. Even in Western culture there are examples of this paradigm, in which metaphysical reality interrelates with human society; for instance, Christian Scientists believe that physical healing can be effected through prayer alone (The graying of a church, 1987).

Ackerknecht (1971) states that "magic or religion seems to satisfy better than any other device a certain eternal psychic or 'metaphysical' need of mankind, sick and healthy, for integration and harmony." Magic and religion are logical in their own way, but not on the basis of empirical premises; that is, they defy the demands of the physical world and the use of one's senses, particularly observation. In the magicoreligious paradigm, disease is viewed as the action and result of supernatural forces causing the intrusion of a disease-producing foreign body or entrance of a health-damaging spirit.

Widespread throughout the world, according to Hughes (1978), are five categories of events that are believed to be responsible for illness in the magicoreligious paradigm. These categories, derived from the work of Clements (1932), are sorcery, breach of taboo, intrusion of a disease object, intrusion of a disease-causing spirit, and loss of soul. One or any combination of these belief categories may be offered to explain the origin of disease. Eskimos, for example, refer to soul loss and breach of taboo (breaking a social norm, such as committing adultery). West Indians and some African and American blacks believe the malevolence of sorcerers is the cause of many conditions. *Mal ojo*, or the "evil eye," common in Hispanic and other cultures, can be viewed as the intrusion of a disease-causing spirit.

In the magicoreligious paradigm, illness is initiated by a supernatural agent, with or without justification, or by another person who engages the services of a sorcerer or practices sorcery himself or herself. The cause-effect relationship is not an organic one; rather, the cause of health or illness is mystical. Health is seen as a *gift* or *reward* given as a sign of God's blessing and good will. Illness may be seen as a sign of God's special favor, insofar as it gives the affected person the opportunity to resign himself to God's will, or it may be seen as a sign of God's *possession* or as a *punishment*.

In addition, in this paradigm, health and illness are viewed as belonging first to the community and then to the individual. Therefore, one person's actions may directly or indirectly influence the health or illness of another person. This sense of community is virtually absent from the other paradigms.

In the United States and Canada, some members of many Hispanic and African-American communities subscribe to this system of health beliefs, which influence their approach to health care. Table 1-6 illustrates some of the beliefs and conditions commonly defined according to a magicoreligious paradigm in these two cultural groups.

Scientific or Biomedical Health Paradigm. The second paradigm, the scientific, is the newest and most removed from the interpersonal, human arena of life. According to this world view, life is controlled by a series of physical and biochemical processes that can be studied and manipulated by humans. The scientific paradigm is characterized by several specific forms of symbolic thought processes. The first is *determinism*, which states that a

Table 1-6. Health beliefs and conditions in a magico-religious paradigm

Culture/Folk Illness	Etiology	Signs/ Symptoms	Practitioner	Treatment
Hispanic				
Susto (fright)	An individual experiences a stressful event at some time prior to the onset of symptoms. The stressor may vary from death of a significant person, to a child's nightmare, to inability to adequately fulfill social role responsibility. Children are more susceptible to susto. It is believed that the soul or spirit leaves the body.	Restlessness during sleep Anorexia Depression Listlessness Disinterest in personal appearance	Curandero or Espiritualista (Espiritista)	A ceremony is performed using branches from a sweet pepper tree and a candle. Motions by the ill person and the curer are performed that form a cross. Three Ave Marias, or credos (Apostles' Creed), are said.
Empacho	Bolus of undigested food adheres to the stomach or wall of intestine. The cause may be the food itself, or due to eating when one is not hungry or when one is stressed.	Stomach pain Diarrhea Vomiting Anorexia	Family member Sabador Curandero	Massage of the stomach or back until a popping sound is heard. A laxative may be given.
Caida de la mollera (fallen fontanel)	Trauma—a fall or blow to the head or the rapid dislodging of a nipple from an infant's mouth causes the fontanel to be sucked into the palate.	Inability to suckle Irritability Vomiting Diarrhea Sunken fontanel	Family member Curandero	One or more of these: Insert a finger into the child's mouth and push the palate back into place. Hold the child by the ankles with the top of the head just touching a pan of tepid water for a moment or two. Apply a poultice of soap shavings to the fontanel. Administer herb tea.
Mal ojo (evil eye)	A disease of magical origin cast by a person who is jealous or envious of another person or something the person owns. The evil eye is cast by the envious person's vision upon the subject, thereby heating the blood and producing symptoms. Usually the victim is a beautiful child who is envied or admired but is not touched by the admirer. The admirer may inflict the evil eye without even being aware of it. If the child is admired and then touched by that person the evil eye is not inflicted.	Fever Diarrhea Vomiting Crying without apparent cause.	Curandero Brujo	Passing an unbroken egg over the body or rubbing the body with an egg to draw the heat (fever) from the body. Prayers such as the Our Father or Hail Mary may be said simultaneously with the passing of the egg. The egg is then broken in a bowl, placed under the head of the bed and left there all night. By morning if the egg is almost cooked by the heat from the body this is a sign that the sick person had mal ojo.
Mal puesto (evil)	Illness caused by a hex put on by a brujo (witch) or curandero, or by another person knowledgeable about witchcraft.	Vary considerably Strange behavior changes Labile emotions Convulsions	Curandero Brujo	Varies, depending on the hex.

Table 1-6 (*continued*)

Culture/Folk Illness	Etiology	Signs/ Symptoms	Practitioner	Treatment
Black				
High blood (too much blood)	Diet very high in red meat and rich food. Belief that high blood causes stroke.	Weakness Paralysis Vertigo or other signs/symptoms related to a stroke.	Family member, friend, spiritualist, or self. The latter does this after referring to a Zodiac almanac	Take internally lemon juice, vinegar, epsom salts, or other astringent food to sweat out the excess blood. Treatment varies depending on what is appropriate according to the Zodiac almanac.
Low blood (not enough blood—anemia is conceptualized)	Too many astringent foods, too harsh a treatment for high blood. Remaining on high blood pressure medication for too long.	Fatigue Weakness	Same as for high blood	Eat rich red meat, beets. Stop taking treatment for high blood. Consult the Zodiac almanac.
Thin blood (predisposition to illness)	Occurs in women, children, and old people. Blood is thin until puberty, and remains so until old age except in women.	Susceptibility to illness.	Individual	Individual should exercise caution in cold weather by wearing warm clothing or by staying indoors.
Rash appearing on a child after birth. No specific disease name—the concept is that of body defilement.	Impurities within the body coming out. The body is being defiled and will therefore produce skin rashes.	Rash anywhere on the body; may be accompanied by fever	Family member	Catnip tea as a laxative or other commercial laxative. The quantity and kind depend on the age of the individual.
Diseases of witchcraft, "hex," or conjuring	Envy and sexual conflict are the most frequent reasons for hexing another person.	Unusual behavior Sudden death Symptoms related to poisoning (e.g., foul taste, weight loss, nausea, vomiting) A crawling sensation on the skin or in the stomach Psychotic behavior	Voodoo Priest(ess) Spiritualist	*Conja* is the help given the conjured person. Treatment varies, depending on the spell cast.

Hautman, M. A. (1979). Folk health and illness beliefs. *The Nurse Practitioner*, 4(4), 27. By permission.

cause-and-effect relationship exists for all natural phenomena. The second, *mechanism*, relates life to the structure and function of machines; according to mechanism, it is possible to control life processes through mechanical and other engineered interventions. The third form is *reductionism*, according to which all life can be reduced or divided into smaller parts; study of the unique characteristics of these isolated parts is thought to reveal aspects or properties of the whole. One of the ideas of reductionism is *Cartesian dualism*, the idea that the mind and the body can be separated into two distinct entities. The final thought process is *objective materialism*, according to which what is real can be observed and measured. There is a further distinction between subjective and objective realities in this paradigm.

The scientific paradigm disavows the metaphysical. It usually ignores the holistic forces of the universe as well, unless explanations for such forces fit into the symbolic forms discussed above. Members of most Western cultures, including the dominant American cultural group, espouse this paradigm. When the scientific paradigm is applied to matters of health, it is often referred to as the *biomedical model*.

To study a mysterious object and to understand its many facets, it is usually necessary to take that object apart and examine its components. This is precisely what scientists and doctors, in part, have done to human beings. In their effort to comprehend human beings, they have taken them apart, torn them away from their natural environment, divorced their minds from their bodies, fragmented even their physical beings— dissecting system from system, organ from organ, and tissue from tissue.

In the final analysis, science has reduced human beings to a molecular, even atomic level so that they are no longer whole and living beings but rather mechanized, dehumanized abstractions. Moreover, scientists in the past not only have split humans into particles but have neglected to reunite them. Thus, until recently, human beings have been left in a sadly disjointed state, being appreciated as a group of parts rather than as a total entity.

This statement reflects many of the facets of the biomedical model of health and disease. Biomedical beliefs and concepts dominate medical thought in Western societies and must be understood to appreciate the practice of modern medicine. In the biomedical model, all aspects of human health can be understood in physical and chemical terms. This fosters the belief that psychological processes can be reduced to the study of biochemical exchanges. Only the organic is real and worthy of study. Effective treatment consists of physical and chemical interventions, regardless of human relationships.

In this model, disease is viewed, metaphorically, as the breakdown of the *human machine* as a result of wear and tear (stress), external trauma (injury, accident), external invasion (pathogens), or internal damages (fluid and chemical imbalances or structural changes). Disease is held to cause illness, to have a more or less specific cause, and to have a predictable time course and set of treatment requirements. This paradigm is similar to the magicoreligious belief in external agents, having replaced supernatural forces with germs.

Using the metaphor of the machine, Western medicine uses specialists to take care of the "parts"; "fixing" a part enables the machine to function. The *computer* is the analogy for the brain; *engineering* is a task for biomedical practitioners. The discovery of DNA has led to the field of "genetic engineering," an eloquent biomedical metaphor. The symbols used to discuss health and disease reflect the American cultural values of aggression and mastery: Microorganisms *attack* the body; *war* is raged against these *invaders*; money is donated for the *campaign* against cancer; and illness is a *struggle* in which the patient must *put up a good defense* (Andrews, Herberg, and Rigdon, 1983). The biomedical model defines health as the absence of disease or the signs and symptoms of disease. To be healthy, one must be free of all disease.

Holistic Health Paradigm. The holistic paradigm is similar to the magicoreligious world view. In the holistic paradigm, the forces of nature itself (or *herself*—she is generally personified) must be kept in "natural balance" or "harmony." Human life is only one aspect of nature and a part of the general order of the cosmos. Everything in the universe has a place and a role to perform according to natural laws that maintain order. Disturbing these laws creates imbalance, chaos, and disease. Native American and Asian cultures usually have a holistic world view. Although the holistic paradigm has existed for centuries in many parts of the world, it did not become popular in the United States until the late 1970s. Although it was once thought by many people that the choice of holistic health care was based on class and economic factors, that perception began to change. Part of the holistic paradigm's rising popularity was due to increasing dissatisfaction with the biomedical model as a cure-all for the ills associated with modern lifestyles and a growing perception that Western health professionals had failed to communicate effectively with their clients or fulfill client expectations.

In the biomedical model, the cause of tuberculosis is clearly defined as the invasion of the *Mycobacterium*. In the holistic paradigm, according to which disease is the result of multiple environment-host interactions, tuberculosis is caused by the interrelationship of poverty, malnutrition, overcrowding, and the *Mycobacterium*. The holistic world view is well illustrated in Silko's 1977 novel *Ceremony*, which is based on the experiences of a young Navajo man confronted with mental illness.

The holistic paradigm seeks to maintain a sense of balance or harmony between humans and the larger universe. Explanations for health and disease are based not so much on external agents as on imbalance or disharmony among the human, geophysical, and metaphysical forces of the universe.

The term *holistic*, coined in 1926 by Jan Christian Smuts, defines an attitude or mode of perception in which the whole person is viewed in the context of the total environment. Its Indoeuropean root word, *kailo*, means "whole, intact, or uninjured." From this root have come the words *hale, hail, hallow, holy, whole, heal*, and *health*. The essence of health and healing is the quality of wholeness we associate with healthy functioning and well-being (Sobel, 1979).

In this paradigm, health is viewed as a positive process that encompasses more than the absence of signs and symptoms of disease. It is not restricted to biologic or somatic wellness but rather involves broader environmental, sociocultural, and behavioral determinants. In this model, "diseases of civilization," such as unemployment, racial discrimination, ghettos, and suicide, are just as much illnesses as are biomedical diseases.

Metaphors used in this paradigm, such as *healing power of nature, health foods*, and *Mother Earth*, reflect the connection of humans to the cosmos and nature. Voltaire's statement that "the efficient physician is the man who successfully amuses his patient while nature effects a cure" stems from this belief system. The belief system of Florence Nightingale, who emphasized nursing's control of the environment so that patients could heal "naturally," also was holistic.

A strong metaphor in the holistic paradigm is exemplified by the Chinese concept of *yin and yang*, in which the forces of nature are balanced to produce harmony (Capra, 1982, pp. 109–110):

The yin force in the universe represents the female aspect of nature. It is characterized as the negative pole, encompassing darkness, cold, and emptiness. The yang, or male force,

Herbal remedies are sometimes used to maintain balance or harmony.

is characterized by fullness, light, and warmth. It represents the positive pole. An imbalance of forces creates illness.

Illness, then, is the outward expression of disharmony. This disharmony may be due to seasonal changes, emotional imbalances, or any other pattern of events. Illness is not perceived as an intruding agent, but a natural part of life's rhythmic course.

Going in and out of balance is seen as a natural process that happens constantly through the life cycle. Accordingly . . . no sharp line [is drawn] between health and illness. Both . . . are seen as natural and as being part of a continuum. They are aspects of the same process in which the individual organism changes continually in relation to the changing environment.

An example of yin and yang conditions assigned to body organs and health conditions is shown in Table 1-7.

In the holistic health paradigm, because illness is inevitable, perfect health is not the goal. Rather, achieving the best possible adaptation to the environment by living

Table 1-7. Examples of Yin and Yang conditions and organs

	Health Conditions	Organs
Yin	Cancer	Kidney
	Lactation	Liver
	Menstruation	Lungs
	Postpartum period	Spleen
	Pregnancy	
	Shivering	
	Wasting	
Yang	Constipation	Bladder
	Hangover	Gallbladder
	Hypertension	Intestines
	Infection	Stomach
	Sore throat	
	Toothache	
	Upset stomach	
	Venereal disease	

From Yin and Yang in the health-related food practices of three Chinese groups by E. K. Ludman and J. M. Newman, *Journal of Nutrition Education*, Vol. 16, 1984, © Society for Nutrition Education. Reprinted by permission.

according to society's rules and caring appropriately for one's body is the ultimate aim. This places a greater emphasis on preventive and maintenance measures than does Western medicine.

Another common metaphor for health and illness in this paradigm is the *hot/cold theory of disease*. This is founded on the ancient Greek concept of the four body humors: yellow bile, black bile, phlegm, and blood. These humors are balanced in the healthy individual. The treatment of disease becomes the process of restoring the body's humoral balance through the addition or subtraction of substances that affect each of these humors. Foods, beverages, herbs, and other drugs are all classified as hot or cold, depending on their effect, not on their actual physical state. Disease conditions are also classified as either hot (dysentery, sore throat) or cold (earache, rheumatism). The result of imbalance or disharmony is thought to lead to internal damage and altered physiologic functions. Medicine is directed at correcting the imbalance as well as restoring body functioning. Each cultural group defines what it believes to be hot and cold entities; little agreement exists across cultures, although the concept of hot and cold is itself widespread, being found in Asian, Hispanic, black, Arab, Muslim, and Caribbean societies.

The Art and Practice of Healing

The system of healing and the use of specific healers emerge directly from the prevalent world view of a culture. The idea that one person can heal another is ancient and widespread, perhaps even universal (Moerman, 1979). Healers decisively mediate between culture and nature, a form of "cultural physiology." Over the years, healing has been attributed to all sorts of rituals, including trephining, cupping, leeching, the laying on of hands, and the use of herbs and drugs. Each treatment method is based on the prevalent belief system operating at the time.

According to Dubos (1979), all peoples throughout history have simultaneously practiced two methods of healing: *organic*, in which drugs, surgery, and diet are used to treat traumatic injuries and certain pathologic conditions, and *nonorganic*, in which semimystical or religious practices are used to influence the mind of the patient and thereby cure certain specified physical and/or mental states. Examples of nonorganic healing practices include chants, prayers, pilgrimages, and the use of amulets.

Healers in most societies are prepared and equipped to deal with the spirit world as well as the natural world. The variety of healers in any society depends on the nature and number of competing and complementary health belief systems. Healers may be housewives, priests, gypsies, physicians, sorcerers, or medicine men (Table 1-8). Nontraditional and new forms of healing emerging in U.S. culture include biofeedback, yoga, therapeutic touch, acupressure, and reflexology. Ancient healing rituals that have been

Table 1-8. Healers and their scope of practice

Culture/Folk Practitioner	Preparation	Scope of Practice
Hispanic		
Family member	Possesses knowledge of folk medicine	Common illnesses of a mild nature that may or may not be recognized by modern medicine.
Curandero	May receive training in an apprenticeship. May receive a "gift from God" that enables her/him to cure. Knowledgeable in use of herbs, diet, massage, and rituals.	Treats almost all of the traditional illnesses. Some may not treat illness caused by witchcraft for fear of being accused of possessing evil powers. Usually admired by members of the community.
Espiritualista or Spiritualist	Born with the special gifts of being able to analyze dreams and foretell future events. May serve apprenticeship with an older practitioner.	Emphasis on prevention of illness or bewitchment through use of medals, prayers, amulets. May also be sought for cure of existing illness.
Yerbero	No formal training. Knowledgeable in growing and prescribing herbs.	Consulted for preventive and curative use of herbs for both traditional and Western illnesses.
Sabador (may refer to a chiropractor by this title)	Knowledgeable in massage and manipulation of bones and muscles.*	Treats many traditional illnesses, particularly those affecting the musculoskeletal system. May also treat nontraditional illnesses.
Black		
"Old Lady"	Usually an older woman who has successfully raised her own family. Knowledgeable in child care and folk remedies.	Consulted about common ailments and for advice on child care. Found in rural and urban communities.
Spiritualist	Called by God to help others. No formal training. Usually associated with a fundamentalist Christian church.	Assists with problems that are financial, personal, spiritual or physical. Predominantly found in urban communities.
Voodoo Priest(ess) or *Hougan*	May be trained by other priests(esses). In the U.S. the eldest son of a priest becomes a priest. A daughter of a priest(ess) becomes a priestess if she is born with a veil (amniotic sac) over her face.	Knowledgeable about properties of herbs; interpretation of signs and omens. Able to cure illness caused by voodoo. Uses communication techniques to establish a therapeutic milieu like a psychiatrist. Treats blacks, Mexican Americans, and Native Americans.
Chinese		
Herbalist	Knowledgeable in diagnosis of illness and herbal remedies.	Both diagnostic and therapeutic. Diagnostic techniques include interviewing, inspection, auscultation, and assessment of pulses.

*Preparation is for *Sabador*, not chiropractor.

Hautman, M. A. (1979). Folk health and illness beliefs. *The Nurse Practitioner*, 4(4), 31. By permission.

found effective over time such as offerings, sacrifices, magic ceremonies, preventive charms, and amulets are still used today. Many early rites (circumcision, baptism) also have survived the test of time and are practiced in attenuated form. The art of healing in any culture, including the United States, involves more than just the practice of Western biomedicine.

In any given culture, organic and nonorganic aspects of healing are integrated into a specific health care system. Cultures that predominately subscribe to a magicoreligious belief system acknowledge that some ailments are purely physical and can be treated with organic interventions (e.g., casting of a broken leg), and cultures that subscribe to biomedical principles still use some natural or metaphysical medicine. Healing methods are determined in part by local conditions and natural resources (climate, topography, available herbs, plants, and food stuffs) and in part by the way the culture views the relationship of humanity to the physical-social environment, the cosmos, and the deities (Dubos, 1979).

Types of Healing Systems. The healing, or health care, system can be defined as the total package of arts, sciences, and techniques used to restore and maintain health in a given cultural group or society. In complex societies in which several cultural traditions flourish, practitioners compete. No single homogeneous tradition guides the healing arts; there are at least as many different healing traditions and practitioners as there are people with diverse backgrounds.

Today diseases occur faster than they can be cured or prevented. Many people's first line of defense is the use of health foods, megavitamins, diets, herbal teas, and exercise regimens, as well as family home remedies such as hot lemonade, honey tea, chicken soup, and grandma's special poultice or recipe. Just about all of us practice fairly frequently some form of *private* or self-prescribed health care. Additionally, most Americans avail themselves of *professional* health care, based on Western scientific medical traditions.

There also exists a wide variety of other treatment modalities not explicitly derived from the traditional Western scientific base that is often called *folk medicine.* Unfortunately, there is a tendency in the United States to think of medical traditions outside the Western mode as "primitive," "whimsical," "exotic," and/or "outmoded." However, such connotations are not universal, and many Americans use folk, or *popular,* medicine as a supplement to or instead of Western modes of treatment. In most societies, all forms of healing systems peacefully coexist, and all have their own loyal proponents.

Health systems are often chosen according to the nature of the existing problem. Chronic nonincapacitating disorders are amenable to treatment by popular or private means, whereas more acute and critical disorders are treated by scientific medicine. Kleinman's (1980) three-part classification of healing systems is a well-accepted model.

Popular Sector. It is customarily believed that professionals organize health care for laypeople. On the contrary, laypeople typically activate their own health care by deciding when and whom to consult, whether or not to comply, when to switch treatments, whether care is effective, and whether they are satisfied with the quality of care. In this sense, the popular sector, which includes individual, family, social, and community networks, functions as the chief source and the most immediate determinant of health care.

In the United States, 70 to 90 percent of all illness episodes are managed by self-treatment in the popular sector. The popular sector also sets its own standards for health and health maintenance activities, one of its primary sources of information being lay literature such as *Ladies' Home Journal, Family Circle,* and *Good Housekeeping* magazines. Television also provides health information through a variety of advertisements, "health spots," and most pervasively, the portrayal of TV characters, who to much of the public represent normal, healthy individuals. Television portrays methods of coping with obesity, colds, headaches, nervous tension, and more dramatically, cancer, alcoholism, drug addiction, and unwanted pregnancy. Behaviors and attitudes toward health as shown on television are shaped by and in turn help shape popular beliefs and attitudes toward health.

Professional Sector. Any organized professional healing group is part of the professional sector. In the United States, the medical profession has held a legal/political monopoly in this area for most of this century; however, their position has been challenged recently by the comeback in popularity of more traditional practitioners, such as osteopaths, chiropractors, naturopaths, and homeopaths. Other health care professions, such as nursing and pharmacy, are also part of the professional sector. Traditional Chinese medical healers and the practitioners of Ayurvedic medicine in India are also professional healers.

Folk Sector. The folk sector is a mixture of many components, including all nonprofessional, nonbureaucratic specialties. Often classified according to secular and sacred categories, folk healers range from priests and shamans to fortune tellers, astrologers, and geomancers. Unlicensed practitioners such as lay midwives, bone setters, some dentists, and herbalists are part of the folk sector, as are religious practitioners such as spiritualists, Christian Science healers, and users of scientology.

The folk sector makes much use of such healing devices as meditation, charms, amulets, manipulation and massage, prophecy, and herbal medications. In the United States, a large quasi-legal folk sector has always been available to health care consumers. Usually forced to operate in the shadows of professional medicine, the folk sector has nevertheless thrived. Members of many ethnic and regional communities in the United States are accustomed to seeking advice or treatment from folk practitioners.

New arrivals to this country contribute to all sectors by establishing the same types of health care services found in their native communities (Pickwell, 1989; Aroian, 1990; Carbal et al., 1990; Kraut, 1990; DeSantis and Thomas, 1990; Lipson, 1991; 1992; Meleis, Lipson, and Paul, 1992; Awasum, 1992; Patel, 1992).

Choice of Healing Systems. Families vary greatly in the way they combine professional, folk, and popular health care beliefs and practices. Families "shop" for and assemble their own package of health services. Dominant use of one system over another varies from culture to culture; however, in most societies, the simultaneous use of several sectors is normal. Nurses must be aware of the popular and folk as well as professional health systems available in their communities in order to fully appreciate the range of services available to and used by their clients (Hobus, 1990).

Persons may choose popular systems over professional ones because of a lack of understanding of the severity of the illness, a lack of means to pay for scientific medicine, religious beliefs and practices, an inability to communicate owing to language barriers, a distrust of health professionals due to the impersonality of professional service and the long waits involved, pride and modesty, fear of unfamiliar practices, hospitalization, and medical personnel, a desire for a quick and easy cure with a minimum of pain and frustration, and a wealth of misinformation regarding care.

Kleinman (1980) portrays the professional sector in a negative light, presenting evidence that the professional sector requires that its form of clinical reality be accepted as the only legitimate reality. He asserts that health professionals usually are insensitive to the views of clinical reality held by other healers and to the expectations and beliefs of their patients. Sobel (1979) claims that Western health care makes several faulty assumptions: (1) that health equals medical care, (2) that medical care equals Western scientific medical care, and (3) that Western scientific health care equals the biomedical model. This is reflected in the behavior of health professionals, the expectations of the public, and the evaluation of health care. The equation of health with medical care suggests that the way to improve health is to provide more and "better" medical care; as faulty as this view may be, it seems to be the dominant American attitude toward health care.

Health Orientations in the United States

Matters of health in the United States are closely linked to duty and conscience. One "ought" to eat right, get enough sleep, exercise, watch one's weight, and do everything else that is considered "good" for one's health. One is responsible for one's body, and in return for living up to that responsibility, one "ought" to be free of pain, disease, or premature death. As long as the body is doing what it "should," it is considered healthy.

Health is viewed by many Americans as a necessity. Any interference with one's health is seen as something to be challenged and overcome. Since health is valued, it is "good" to be healthy and "bad" to be sick. It is one's duty to try to stay well or "get better" if one is sick. If one does not do one's best to live up to this responsibility, one is considered weak, irresponsible, and a failure. Such *value judgments*, which are ingrained early in life and are common to us all, can lead to *victim blaming*, in which persons are blamed for things that are due to socioeconomic, political, ecological, or other forces and therefore are clearly outside of their control (Ryan, 1971).

The dominant health paradigm in American society is the biomedical model, based on a scientific world view. The pattern of medical intervention in this model is characterized by physicians, nurses, hospitals, technology, clinical practices, and laboratory research. The biomedical model is reflected in the public's use of medical facilities and its willingness to believe that science can "cure" anything, given enough time, money, and faith.

However, there are also other systems of health beliefs and practices in our culture. Two of these are holistic health practices, as seen in the self-care/self-help "wellness" movement, and lay and nontraditional (as opposed to nonprofessional) medical practices, as carried out by heralists, homeopaths, lay midwives, and chiropractors. In addition, the services of various other practitioners, such as sorcerers, astrologers, spiritualists, medicine men, and priests, are commonly available to members of U.S. society.

The Concept of People

Environment
health
people
ns

The third concept forming the theoretical foundation of transcultural nursing is *people*. All societies are made up of collections of individuals who reflect to one degree or another the shared cultural heritage of the group. Just as important as an appreciation of cultural diversity is an acknowledgment of individual variation. Individuals share some part of the cultural heritage of their group but never all of it. The nature and extent of one's participation in the cultural traditions valued by society are influenced by personal forces, both internal and external, such as temperament, education, motivation, maturity, and past experience. Although culture is a blueprint for living, no individual fully masters all the knowledge and skills or is motivated by all the values of any culture. All learning is selective; individuals must learn what of the design to apply and what they can avoid. Individual variations within any cultural group are normal.

Social norms may be interpreted and applied in a variety of ways. In addition, because many norms conflict with one another, the rules of behavior are not always clear and therefore involve a certain amount of choice. For example, the Catholic nurse giving care to a patient who is contemplating an abortion may be asked to provide that patient with health information that conflicts with the nurse's personal religious beliefs and the values of her religious community. The nurse may ask to be assigned to another client or decide that the client's right to accurate information outweighs her own personal considerations; in either case, the nurse chooses between conflicting norms.

Norms also may be evaded, especially when the individual knows that they are weakly enforced; speed limits on the highway are a case in point. Finally, some norms are not learned by all members of the society. This is obvious in a pluralistic society, in which subcultures create their own norms and standards. The task facing the nurse is to answer the question, "Who is this person [family, group], my client?" To do this, the nurse must be able to assess roles individuals assign to others and the status given to the role players. Kasl and Cobb (1966) first defined the types of behaviors clients assume once they have recognized a symptom. *Health behavior* is any activity taken by a person who believes himself or herself to be healthy for the purpose of preventing disease or detecting disease in an asymptomatic stage. *Illness behavior* is any activity undertaken by a person who feels ill for the purpose of defining the state of his or her health and of discovering a suitable remedy. *Sick role behavior* is any activity undertaken by a person who considers himself or herself ill for the purpose of getting well.

Many classic studies exist that helped to identify the specifics of health/illness behaviors and the decision-making processes involved in seeking health care (Freidson, 1961; Suchman, 1965; Fabrega, 1973, 1979; Chrisman, 1977). The most widely known of these is the work done on the health belief model, begun in the 1950s by Rosenstock, Hochbaum, Kegeles, and Leventhal (Rosenstock, 1974a and b). This model is based on the premise that three sets of factors influence the course of behaviors and practices carried out to maintain health and prevent disease: one's beliefs about health and illness; personal factors, such as age, education, and knowledge or experience with a given disease condition; and cues to action, such as advertisements in the media, the illness of a relative, or the advice of friends.

The specific beliefs referred to include perceived susceptibility to disease, perceived severity of the illness, perceived threat of the disease condition, and perceived costs and benefits of care. Figure 1-3 shows how these perceptions influence help-seeking deci-

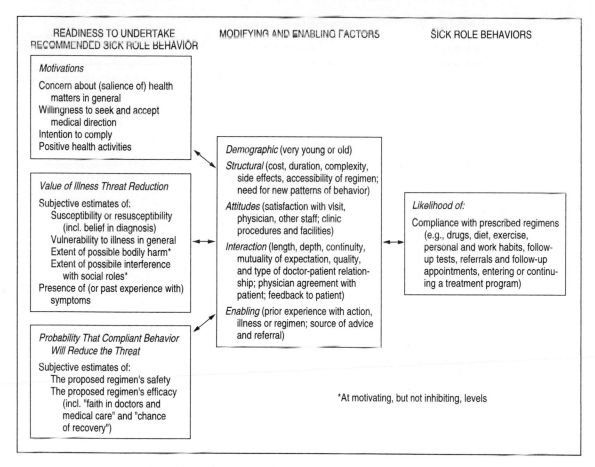

Figure 1-3. The health belief model, expanded to predict and explain sick role behavior. (Becker, M. (1974). The health belief model and sick role behavior. Health Education Monographs, 2 *(4), 409–419. Reprinted by permission of Human Sciences Press, Inc. 72 Fifth Avenue, New York, NY 10011.)*

sions and sick role behaviors, such as whether to comply with treatment. Several research studies in nursing support the health belief model and its application to nursing practice. Two notable studies are those by Mikhail (1981) and Champion (1984).

A useful model of illness behavior has been proposed by Mechanic (1978), who outlines 10 determinants of illness behavior that are important in the help-seeking process (Table 1-9). Knowledge of these factors can help the nurse appreciate the client's behaviors and decisions regarding seeking and complying with health care. Awareness of these motivational factors can help nurses offer the appropriate assistance to clients as they work through the illness process.

Every culture has some *taboos,* or forbidden topics, words, or actions. Breaking taboos carries a social stigma, frequently the penalty of harm and, in some cases, even death. *Rituals* are prescribed codes of behavior that are closely related to a culture's ideology. Ritualized behavior is symbolic, repetitive, stereotyped, formal, standardized, and patterned.

Table 1-9. Mechanic's determinants of illness behavior

Determinant	Description
Quality of symptom	The more frightening or visible the symptom, the greater is the likelihood that the individual will react or that others will intervene.
Seriousness of symptom	The perceived threat of the symptom must be serious for action to be taken. Often others will step in if the person's behavior is considered dangerous (e.g., suicidal behavior) but will be unaware of potential problems if the person's behavior seems natural ("he always acts that way").
Disruption of daily activities	Behaviors that are very disruptive in work or other social situations are likely to be labeled as illness much sooner than the same behaviors occurring in a family setting. An individual whose activities are disrupted by a symptom is likely to take that symptom seriously even if on another occasion he would consider the same symptom trivial (e.g., acne just before a date).
Rate and persistence of symptom	The frequency of a symptom is directly related to its importance; a symptom that persists is also likely to be taken seriously.
Tolerance of symptom	The extent to which others, especially family, tolerate the symptom before reacting varies; individuals also have different tolerance thresholds.
Sociocognitive status	A person's information about the symptom, knowledge base, and cultural values all influence his perception of illness.
Denial of symptom	Often, the individual or members of his family need to deny a symptom for personal or social reasons. The amount of fear and anxiety present can interfere with symptom perception.
Motivation	Competing needs may motivate a person to delay or enhance symptoms. A person who has no time or money to be sick will often not acknowledge the seriousness of his symptoms.
Assigning of meaning	Once perceived, the symptom must be interpreted. Often people explain symptoms within normal parameters ("I'm just tired").
Treatment accessibility	The greater the barriers to treatment—whether psychological, economic, physical, or social—the greater the likelihood that the symptom will not be interpreted as serious or that the person will seek an alternative form of care.

Reprinted with the permission of The Free Press, an imprint of Simon & Schuster, from *Medical Sociology*, Second Edition by David Mechanic. Copyright © 1978 by The Free Press.

In order to understand the social aspects of ritualization, we must know where and when rituals are most likely to occur. The anthropologist Arnold Van Gennep (1960) published his classic work on *rites of passage* in 1909. The lives of individuals in society, Van Gennep observed, are punctuated by passages from one status to another, from newborn, to social infant, to child, to initiated and married adult, to the mourned and remembered dead. Rituals mark the severance of an individual from an old status, entry into and temporary containment in a marginal state between old and new, and finally full assumption of the new. The three phases were called the rites of *separation, transition,* and *reintegration* or *incorporation.*

The Concept of Nursing

The fourth and central concept in our discussion is *nursing.* The concept encompasses the practitioner (the nurse), the process (nursing care), and the interaction between the nurse who delivers nursing care and clients.

The Professional Nurse

For the most part, nurses have the same value system, beliefs, and attitudes as the dominating middle class in American society. In addition, as members of the health team, nurses belong to a culture unto itself, with its own set of values, attitudes, and practices. Nursing is one of the largest health subcultures. The "typical American nurse" is white, middle class, Anglo-Saxon, Protestant, female, and socialized into a subculture termed *health care professional, subdivision nurse.* Nurses are immersed in a value system of rational, analytic, biomedical principles, which is reflected in their attitudes and behaviors. However, to care for other people, nurses must be able to accept a wide diversity of ideas, beliefs, and practices about health and illness that may bear little resemblance to their own.

According to Spector (1991), nurses enter the health care profession with their own unique concepts of health. During the socialization process into nursing, they are expected to shed their old values and thoughts, adapt new scientific concepts, learn new attitudes, and develop behavior patterns that are in line with their new "culture." Nurses are socialized to believe that "modern medicine" as taught and practiced in Western civilization is the answer to all of humanity's health needs.

When socialized nurse A meets otherwise socialized client* B, several factors are at play: the cultural background of each, the expectations and beliefs of each about health care, the cultural context of the encounter (home, clinic, hospital), and the degree of congruence between the two persons' sets of beliefs and values. Thus the stage is set, so to speak, for a cultural encounter.

Cultural Encounters

Whenever persons from two different cultures meet, learning is possible. *Acculturation* refers to the process by which a given cultural group adapts to or learns how to take on the behaviors of another group. Acculturation also has been defined as an unconscious fusion of attitudes, values, and beliefs. However, acculturation does not always occur automatically, and complete acculturation is difficult and not even desirable. Various degrees of acculturation to the dominant group exist in a pluralistic society. Change related to practical matters of daily living occurs more readily than change in basic values and beliefs. On an individual level, any encounter with another human being is a cultural encounter. In most instances, the two parties share enough common cultural ground to meet and communicate; this is not always the case, however.

Cultural Stumbling Blocks

Ineffective interethnic relations can lead to prejudice, discrimination, and racism. All three are due to a combination of factors, including the following:

1. Lack of understanding of ethnic groups other than one's own.

---

* Use of the term *client* is in itself a manifestation of cultural change based on a shift in values regarding the nature of the relationship between the nurse and the recipient of care. This term was adopted in response to middle-class desires to be in control of personal health care and identification of patients as "health care consumers."

2. Stereotyping of members of ethnic groups without consideration of individual differences within the group.
3. Judgment of other ethnic groups according to the standards and values of one's own
   group.
4. Assignment of negative attributes to the members of other ethnic groups.
5. View of the quality and experiences of other groups as inferior to those of one's own
   group.
   a. *Prejudice* is a hostile attitude toward individuals simply because they belong to a
      particular group presumed to have objectionable qualities.
   b. *Discrimination* is the differential treatment of individuals because they belong to a
      minority group.
   c. *Racism* is a mixed form of prejudice (attitude) and discrimination (behavior)
      directed at ethnic groups other than one's own.

Because culture influences people so strongly, including the way they feel, think,
act, and judge the world, it is not atypical for people to subconsciously restrict their view
of the world. Such restriction to the point of an inability to accept other cultures' ways of
organizing reality is called *ethnocentrism*. Every group considers its own way of life the
natural and best way. In ethnocentrism, which is an intense identification with the
familiar and devaluation of the foreign, beliefs and behaviors that are unfamiliar or
people who are different from one's own cultural group are treated with suspicion and
often hostility.

Any event must be interpreted against the social setting in which it occurs. The
context provides the meaning of the event, connects the event to others and to the values
of the society, and makes sense out of what would otherwise seem unreasonable. In an
ethnocentric orientation, all behavior is judged from a single frame of reference, pre-
cluding the possibility of a rounded interpretation. This often leads to a form of cultural
paternalism, or "I know what's best for you" attitude. Ethnocentrism refers to the
unconscious tendency to look at others through the lens of one's own cultural norms
and customs and to take for granted that one's own values are the only objective reality.
If that reality forms the standard against which all judgments regarding other people's
actions are made, it is an ethnocentric bias.

At a more complex level, the ethnocentrist regards others as inferior or immoral and
believes his or her own ideas are intrinsically good, right, necessary, and desirable while
remaining unaware of his or her own value judgments. Clearly, ethnocentrism can
prevent one from accepting others and can lead to a clash of values, shaky interpersonal
relationships, and poor communication.

Other cultural stumbling blocks also have been identified (Clark, 1984). The first is
cultural blindness, in which one ignores differences and proceeds as if these did not exist.
The American health care system is a prime example. It is based solely on the dominant
pattern of health beliefs and practices and usually ignores any deviations from the
established pattern. In the hospital setting, only "American" food is served. Nurses are
guilty of such blindness when they assume that all patients can read the printed health
teaching forms they use, when they advocate a diet high in milk proteins for an Asian or
black client without considering the possibility of lactose intolerance, or when they
impose blanket rules such as "no more than two visitors at a time" or "no visitors under

16 years of age." In cultural blindness, the perpetrator is unaware that anything is out of the ordinary; he or she simply has no awareness of another cultural perspective.

A second cultural stumbling block is *culture shock*, in which the individual is stunned by cultural differences and even immobilized until he or she is able to work through his or her feelings related to the vastly different nature of the alien culture. Culture shock is most likely to occur in response to behavior in a different culture that is disapproved of or forbidden in one's own. The stronger the taboos in one's own culture against a certain behavior, the greater is one's shock when confronted with that behavior. Culture shock also can occur in response to language and communication difficulties; one may become frustrated and disoriented when familiar words and gestures suddenly have new meanings or one is unable to express commonplace phrases in an intelligible form. Culture shock leads to feelings of helplessness and discomfort. Contact with another culture can make one angry and acutely uncomfortable.

Culture conflict is a third stumbling block. People often feel threatened when they become aware of cultural differences. They respond by ridiculing the beliefs and traditions of others in order to bolster their own security in their own values.

A fourth stumbling block is *cultural imposition*, or the expectation that everyone should conform to the majority, whatever their personal beliefs.

Stereotyping, the fifth block, is perhaps the most common. When people stereotype, they assume conformity to a major pattern. However, persons do not conform like robots; they are not carbon copies of others but individuals. Stereotyping is expecting people to act in a characteristic manner without regard to individual characteristics. It is generally derogatory and occurs because of lack of exposure to enough people in a particular cultural group on the basis of which to form realistic expectations. Stereotyping leads to a further lack of understanding and lack of appreciation of the wide range of differences among people.

One example of stereotyping is the health professional's view of "folk" medicine. Nurses often take a condescending view of folk health practices and practitioners (nonprofessionals, by their standards) and typically stereotype such activities as "quackery," "exoticness," "weirdness," or "uninformed superstition" before taking the time to learn anything about the practice or practitioner in question or making any attempt to view them in a cultural context.

Cultural Building Blocks

When cultural diversity is recognized and respected, *cultural sensitivity* occurs. It occurs in health care with an awareness on the part of caregivers that cultural factors are significant in health and illness. Cultural sensitivity is prerequisite for personal, comprehensive nursing care.

It is important that nurses be knowledgeable about the cultural groups represented by their clients. The task is to fit the environment of the health care system (with its own culture) as closely as possible to the client environment. The culturally sensitive nurse will try to modify her or his care to include folk practices and practitioners whenever possible and to act as an advocate for those from diverse cultural groups. An example of culturally sensitive care is illustrated by the nurses in an Idaho hospital who encourage Native American clients to wear amulets and feathers and to use other items related to special healing ceremonies. As a result, Native American clients have gained respect for their nursing care and nurses.

Cultural relativism is the attempt to understand other cultural systems in their own terms, not in terms of one's own culture. Behavior is always relative to the context in which it is learned. One key to cultural relativism is assessment of each person as an individual and not merely as a member of a group. However, most people are proud of their cultural characteristics, and these should not be ignored by health care providers.

Kumorek (1978) discusses three types of cross-cultural experiences that should be considered in any interpretation of cultural encounters. First are experiences that have the *same outward form but differ in meaning*. For example, a patient is told by the nurse to come to the clinic at 2:00 P.M. To the patient, the meaning of this statement is "come in the afternoon." To the nurse, the meaning is "be here at 1:45 P.M. so that we can get started at 2:00."

The second variation is an experience in which *meaning and form are similar, but time or place differs*. The nurse tells Mrs. Jones, "You are to take three pills a day, at mealtimes." What the nurse thinks she is communicating is that Mrs. Jones should take one pill at three separate times: breakfast, lunch, and dinner. In Mrs. Jones' family, however, only one major meal is eaten during the day, and Mrs. Jones is not oriented to thinking of three separate mealtimes; what she hears is, "Take three pills together once each day." Both the nurse and Mrs. Jones leave the interaction believing that they have understood each other.

The third variation comprises experiences in which *different forms exist for the same intended meaning*. Examples of this are numerous: patting a child's head, a sign of affection in American culture but a taboo in some Asian cultures; shaking one's head from side to side, which connotes "no" to an American but "yes" to an Indian; flexing one's fingers in rapid succession, a sign for "goodbye" to an American but of "come here" to an Afghan.

Culturally Competent Nursing Care

The usefulness of culture as a concept is the direction it provides to nurses in understanding their own health values and behaviors as well as those of their clients. Cultural norms and standards are deeply ingrained. It is easy to feel impatient with or intolerant of and to judge others who are different. The more nurses can recognize their own biases and blind spots, the better they can overcome them when dealing with others.

When we take behavior out of its context and try to explain it within our own familiar guidelines (our context), we risk misinterpretation as well as mismanagement. Labeling of patients as "difficult," "hostile," "neurotic," or "a problem" is often due to cultural insensitivity. In a typical nurse-client encounter, both parties act on their own basic assumptions of what is right and wrong, rational or irrational, and good or bad. Every individual has some degree of ethnocentrism and belief in the correctness or rightness of his or her own way of life. When one believes that one's own way is right and "best," it is easy to label those whose behavior is different as strange or unenlightened.

In a classic argument, Macgregor (1960) discussed two basic misconceptions that can arise from such ethnocentric thinking. The first misconception is the assumption that *all human nature is alike*. It should be clear by now that the cultural traditions of the society in which one is reared are as responsible for one's experiences, preferences, values, and behaviors as are biologic drives. One's own assumptions are often based on ideas and beliefs not held by others. The second misconception, which characterizes the dominant U.S. value system, is the belief that *reason is a controlling force in behavior*. Western societies, including American culture, are commonsense-oriented. Westerners are worshippers of rationality and reason, and what appears to them to be nonrational is considered irrational, stubborn, ignorant, or stupid. However, one cannot improve the health of others by simply extolling the virtues of scientific health knowledge and assuming that the recipients of health education will rationally change themselves and their ways to adopt advocated health procedures.

The way to avoid cultural conflict is to understand oneself and others. The nurse must find a way of caring for a client that matches the client's perception of the health problem and his or her treatment goals. As a rule, the more different the client is from the provider, the more difficult this task becomes. In our society, such differences are usually ethnic, socioeconomic, geographic, educational, or occupational. The nurse can be aware of and yet still have difficulty not making value judgments about the personal and social problems (such as poverty, unemployment, welfare, and drug and alcohol use) of other people. It is time for health care providers to critically examine the sociocultural context within which health and illness exist and health care is delivered. Individuals from different cultures perceive and classify their health problems in specific ways and have certain expectations about the way they should be helped (Adams, Briones, and Rentfro, 1992; D'Avanzo, 1992). These health orientations may or may not be complementary to the American or Canadian health care delivery systems.

In a classic work, Branch and Paxton (1976) have identified several objectives for nurses that minimize transcultural conflicts, including the following:

1. Delivery of holistic patient care that emphasizes the interrelationships among person, environment (culture), health, and nursing.
2. Facilitation of the nurse-client relationship through the development of special resources, such as bilingual nurses, translators, and bicultural nurses.
3. Establishment of norms allowing family involvement in healing processes.
4. Identification and knowledge about nontraditional community resources, such as local herbalists or specialty stores.
5. Referral to appropriate folk and popular healers for certain illnesses.
6. Use of in-service programs to further explain community-specific health practices.
7. Promotion of cultural pluralism as a concept in the education of nursing students.

Care and Caring Concepts in Nursing

In addition to a discussion of the concept of the nurse (practitioner) as a cultural being and the concept of nurse-client interactions (cultural encounters), an exploration of the concept of *care* (phenomenon) and *caring* (process) from a transcultural perspective is crucial to an understanding of the theoretical foundations of transcultural nursing. The concepts of *care* and *caring* are receiving increasing attention from theorists (Watson, 1985; Ray, 1989; Morse et al., 1990; Chinn, 1991; Cohen, 1991; Leininger, 1991) who see care as the cornerstone of nursing practice.

Caring, a concept central to nursing, has many cultural dimensions that need to be further elaborated and applied to practice. Does the meaning of caring for another person apply equally across cultures? How do caring practices differ? Are all caring situations similar? Are caring behaviors similar across situations? What determines which caring behaviors to use in a given situation? Are "caring about" and "caring for" a person two aspects of the same phenomenon, or are they separate issues? Can a person who does not "care about" another individual give that other person "nursing care"? These and other questions need to be addressed before we will fully understand caring as a cultural phenomenon and how it affects nursing care.

Leininger (1991) emphatically states that care is the essence of nursing and the distinct, dominant, central, and unifying focus of nursing practice. She further states that the theory of culture care was developed especially "to discover the meanings and ways to give care to people who have different values and lifeways. It is a theory designed ultimately to guide nurses to provide nursing care that fits or is congruent with the people being helped" (p. 7).

Leininger (1993) offers several useful definitions:

Care: Refers to phenomena that reflect assistive, enabling, supportive, or facilitative mode to help an individual or group with evident or anticipated needs to maintain, improve, or ease a human condition or lifeway.

Caring: Refers to action or decision-oriented behaviors of an individual or group that reflect signs or assistive, enabling, supportive, or facilitative ways to maintain, improve, or ease a human condition or lifeway.

Culture care: Refers to culturally derived assistive, supportive, or facilitative acts toward or for another individual or group with evident or anticipated needs in which decisions and actions are made by nurses that are beneficial and lead to well-being or a health state.

Transcultural nursing: Refers to a formal area of study (research and education) and practice focused on the cultural care (caring) values, beliefs, and practices of individuals or groups from a particular culture in order to provide culture-specific and/or cultural universal care that promotes culturally congruent well-being or health to individuals, families, and institutions.

In addition to identifying the central concept of caring, Leininger (1988a, 1991) has identified caring constructs such as comfort, support, compassion, helping, nurturing, and protection. Research on each of these and other transcultural caring concepts will contribute to the growing body of knowledge in transcultural nursing.

The Study of Transcultural Caring Concepts

The entire process of nursing care delivery from a transcultural perspective requires further scrutiny by nurse researchers. One logical starting place is with the concept of "nursing process" itself. The nursing process is an expression of nursing's value system and its use of logical, systematic thought processes in a deductive, analytic manner. The nursing process is a metaphor for the way in which nurses approach decision making and make judgments about potential solutions to client problems. Whether this metaphor does justice to the art and science of nursing practice is debatable. However, no one has seriously challenged the use of this metaphor in nursing, except in the area of nursing diagnoses (Kelley and Frisch, 1990; Geissler, 1991).

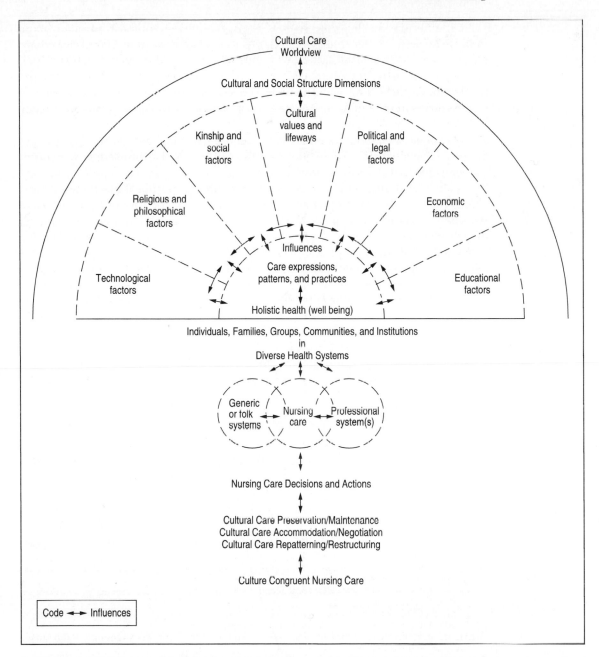

Figure 1-4. Leininger's sunrise model to depict theory of cultural care diversity and universality. (Leininger, M. M. (1991). Culture Care Diversity and Universality: A Theory of Nursing, p. 43. New York: National League for Nursing Press. Reprinted by permission.)

Certainly the nursing process does not represent the approach of other, more intuitive healers. Further study would clarify areas of agreement and conflict. Perhaps patient compliance and satisfaction with nursing care would increase if the approach used were more familiar to the patients receiving the care, or perhaps clients' participation in mutual goal setting would increase if nurses could better explain how the nursing process differs from (and relates to) traditional methods with which clients are already familiar.

Many questions about the nature of transcultural nursing care can be explored from the preceding discussion. These questions also can be posed as problem statements or questions for further study and research.

As shown, transcultural nurse researchers are addressing these questions and similar concerns. The papers presented at Transcultural Nursing Society conferences and workshops, as well as those published throughout the nursing literature, offer examples of such attempts. However, although the theoretical foundations of transcultural nursing can be identified and conceptual frameworks are available, such as the sunrise model of Leininger (Fig. 1-4), additional research, study, and thoughtful analysis can only increase the scope, complexity, and usefulness of the field of transcultural nursing.

Summary

The goal of this chapter was to provide an overview of the theoretical concepts that form the foundation for transcultural nursing. This should assist the reader to understand the discussions that follow on issues related to transcultural nursing in a variety of contexts and settings.

References

Ackerknecht, E. (1946). Natural diseases and rational treatment in primitive medicine. *Bulletin of the History of Medicine, 19*, 467–497.

Ackerknecht, E. (1971). *Medicine and Anthropology*. Baltimore: Johns Hopkins Press.

Adams, R., Briones, E., and Rentfro, A. (1992). Cultural consideration: Developing a nursing care delivery system for a Hispanic community. *Nursing Clinics of North America, 27*(1), 107–117.

American Nurses Association (1986). *Cultural Diversity in the Nursing Curriculum: A Guide for Implementation* (ANA No. G-171:1–11). Kansas City, MO: American Nurses Association.

Andrews, M. M. (1992). Cultural perspectives on nursing in the 21st century. *Journal of Professional Nursing, 8*(1), 1–9.

Andrews, M. M., Herberg, P., and Rigdon, I. (1983). A comparison of three health-illness paradigms. Unpublished manuscript.

Aroian, K. (1990). A model of psychological adaptation to migration and resettlement. *Nursing Research, 39*(1), 5–10.

Awasum, H. (1992). Health and nursing services in Cameroon: Challenges and demands for nurses in leadership positions. *Nursing Administration Quarterly, 16*(2), 8–13.

Bernal, H., and Froman, R. (1993). Influences on the cultural self-efficacy of community health nurses. *Journal of Transcultural Nursing, 4*(2), 24–31.

Blenner, J. (1991). Health care providers' treatment approaches to culturally diverse infertile clients. *Journal of Transcultural Nursing, 2*(2), 24–31.

Branch, M. F., and Paxton, P. P. (Eds.) (1976). *Providing Safe Nursing Care for Ethnic People of Color*. New York: Appleton-Century-Crofts.

Burkhardt, M. A. (1993). Characteristics of spirituality in the lives of women in a rural Appalachian city. *Journal of Transcultural Nursing, 4*(2), 12–18.

Calvillo, E., and Flaskerud, J. (1991). Review of literature on culture and pain of adults with focus on Mexican-Americans. *Journal of Transcultural Nursing, 2*(2), 16–23.

Campinha-Bacote, J. (1991). Community mental health services for the underserved: A culturally specific model. *Archives of Psychiatric Nursing, 5*(4), 229–235.

Campinha-Bacote, J., and Ferguson, S. (1991). Cultural considerations in childrearing practices: A transcultural perspective. *Journal of the National Black Nurses Association, 5*(1), 11–17.

Capra, F. (1982). *The Turning Point*. New York: Bantam Books.

Carbal, H., Fried, L. E., Levenson, S., et al. (1990). Foreign-born and US-born black women: Differences in health behaviors and birth outcomes. *American Journal of Public Health, 80*(1) 70–72.

Champion, V. (1984). Instrument development for health belief model constructs. *Advances in Nursing Science, 6*(3), 73–85.

Chinn, L. (Ed.). (1991). *Anthology of Caring*. New York: National League for Nursing.

Chrisman, N. J. (1977). The health seeking process: An approach to the natural history of illness. *Culture, Medicine and Psychiatry, 1*, 351–377.

Chrisman, N. J. (1990). Cultural shock in the operating room: Cultural analysis in transcultural nursing. *Journal of Transcultural Nursing, 1*(2), 33–39.

Clark, M. (1959). *Health in the Mexican American Culture*. Berkeley: University of California Press.

Clark, M. (1984). *Community Nursing: Health Care for Today and Tomorrow*. Reston, VA: Reston Publishing Co.

Clements, F. E. (1932). Primitive concepts of disease. *University of California Publications in Archeology and Ethnology, 32*(2), 185–252.

Cliff, J. (1992). Nursing and health services in Australia. *Nursing Administration Quarterly, 16*(2), 60–63.

Cohen, J. (1991). Two portraits of caring: A comparison of the artists. *Journal of Advanced Nursing, 16*, 1–4.

D'Avanzo, C. (1992). Bridging the cultural gap with Southeast Asians. *MCN: American Journal of Maternal Child Health Nursing, 17*(4), 204–208.

Davis, C. F. (1992). Culturally responsive nursing management in an international health care setting. *Nursing Administration Quarterly, 16*(2), 36–39.

DeSantis, L., and Thomas, J. (1990). The immigrant Haitian mother: Transcultural nursing perspective on preventive health care for children. *Journal of Transcultural Nursing, 2*, 2–15.

Dobson, S. (1991). *Transcultural Nursing*. London: Scutari.

Dougherty, M. C., and Tripp-Reimer, T. (1985). The interface of nursing and anthropology. *Annual Review of Anthropology, 14*, 219–241.

Dubos, R. (1979). Medicine evolving. In D. S. Sobel (Ed.), *Ways of Health*, pp. 21–44. New York: Harcourt Brace Jovanovich.

Eliason, J., and Macy, N. (1992). A classroom activity to introduce cultural diversity. *Nurse Educator, 17*(3), 32–36.

Fabrega, H., Jr. (1973). Towards a model of illness behavior. *Medical Care, 11*, 470–484.

Febrega, H., Jr. (1979). The ethnography of illness. *Social Science and Medicine, 13A*, 565–576.

Foster, G. M. (1976). Disease etiologies in non-Western medical systems. *American Anthropologist, 78*, 773–783.

Freidson, E. (1961). *Patients' View of Medical Practice*. New York: Russell Sage Foundation.

Frye, B. (1990). The Cambodian refugee patient: Providing culturally sensitive rehabilitation nursing care. *Rehabilitation Nursing, 15*(3), 156–158.

Gates, M. (1991). Transcultural comparison of hospitals and hospice as caring environments for dying patients. *Journal of Transcultural Nursing, 2*(2), 3–15.

Geissler, E. (1991). Nursing diagnoses of culturally diverse patients. *International Nursing Review, 38*(5), 150–152.

Giger, J. N., and Davidhizar, R. E. (1991). *Transcultural Nursing: Assessment and Intervention*. St. Louis: C. V. Mosby.

The graying of a church (1987). *Newsweek*, August 3, p. 60.

Hahn, R. A., and Kleinman, A. (1983). Belief as pathogen, belief as medicine: "Voodoo death" and the "placebo phenomenon" in anthropological perspective. *Medial Anthropology Quarterly, 14*(4), 3, 16–19.

Harnar, R., Amarsi, Y., Herberg, P., and Miller, G. (1992). Health and nursing services in Pakistan: Problems and challenges for nurse leaders. *Nursing Administration Quarterly, 16*(2), 52–59.

Hautman, M. A. (1979). Folk health and illness beliefs. *Nurse Practitioner, 4*(4), 23–24.

Hirschfeld, M., and Holleran, C. (1992). Challenges to nursing from the World Health Organization and the International Council of Nurses. *Nursing Administration Quarterly, 16*(2), 1–3.

Hobus, R. (1990). Living in two worlds: A Lakota transcultural nursing experience. *Journal of Transcultural Nursing, 2*, 33–36.

Hughes, C. (1978). Medical care: Ethnomedicine. In M. Logan and E. Hunt (Eds.). *Health and the Human Condition*, pp. 150–157. Belmont, CA: Wadsworth.

Kasl, S., and Cobb, S. (1966). Health behavior, illness behavior and sick role behavior. *Archives of Environmental Health, 12*, 246–266.

Kavanaugh, K., and Kennedy, P. (1992). *Promoting cultural diversity*. Newbury Park, NJ: Sage.

Kelley, J., and Frisch, N. (1990). Use of selected nursing diagnoses: A transcultural comparison between Mexican and American nurses. *Journal of Transcultural Nursing, 2*(1), 16–22.

Kirkpatrick, S., and Cobb, A. (1990). Health beliefs related to diarrhea in Haitian children: Building transcultural nursing knowledge. *Journal of Transcultural Nursing, 1*(2), 2–12.

Kleinman, A. (1980). *Patients and Healers in the Context of Culture.* Berkeley, CA: University of California Press.

Kluckhohn, F. (1979). Dominant and variant value orientations. In P. J. Brink (Ed.), *Transcultural Nursing: A Book of Readings,* pp. 63–81. Englewood Cliffs, NJ: Prentice-Hall.

Kraut, A. (1990). Healers and strangers: Immigrant attitudes toward the physician in America: A relationship in historical perspective. *Journal of the American Medical Association, 163*(12), 1807–1811.

Kroeber, A. L., and Kluckhohn, C. (1952). *Culture: A Critical Review of Concepts and Definitions.* New York: Vintage Books.

Kumorek, M. (1978). Afghanistan: A cross-cultural view. Unpublished manuscript.

Lane, S., and Meleis, A. (1991). Roles, work, health perceptions and health resources of women: A study in an Egyptian delta hamlet. *Social Sciences and Medicine, 33*(10), 1197–1208.

Lawson, L. V. (1990). Culturally sensitive support for grieving parents. *American Journal of Maternal Child Nursing, 15*(2), 76–79.

Leininger, M. (1967). The cultural concept and its relevance to nursing. *Journal of Nursing Education, 6,* 27.

Leininger, M. (1970). *Nursing and Anthropology: Two Worlds to Blend.* New York: John Wiley & Sons.

Leininger, M. (1978). *Transcultural Nursing: Concepts, Theories and Practices.* New York: John Wiley & Sons.

Leininger, M. (1988a). *Care: The Essence of Nursing and Health.* Detroit: Wayne State University Press.

Leininger, M. (1988b). Leininger's theory of nursing: Cultural care diversity and universality. *Nursing Science Quarterly, 1*(4), 152–160.

Leininger, M. (1989a). Editorial. *Journal of Transcultural Nursing, 1*(1), 1–2.

Leininger, M. (1989b). Transcultural nurse specialists and generalists: New practitioners in nursing. *Journal of Transcultural Nursing, 1*(1), 4–16.

Leininger, M. (1991). *Culture Care Diversity and Universality: A Theory of Nursing.* New York: National League for Nursing.

Leininger, M. (1993). Some transcultural nursing definitions of key concepts/constructs. Unpublished handout from the Educational Issues Conference of the Transcultural Nursing Society, Boston College School of Nursing, Boston, June 1993.

Lindquist, G. (1990). Integration of international and transcultural content in nursing curricula: A process for change. *Journal of Professional Nursing, 6,* 272–279.

Lipson, J. (1992). Integration of international and transcultural content in nursing curricula: A process for change. *Journal of Professional Nursing, 6,* 272–279.

Lipson, J. (1991). Afghan refugee health: Some findings and suggestions. *Qualitative Health Research, 1*(3), 349–369.

Lipson, J., and Bauwens, E. (1988). Uses of anthropology in nursing. *Practicing Anthropology, 10,* 4–5.

Lopez, J., and Hendrickson, S. (1991). Family visits and different cultures. *Axone, 12*(3), 59–62.

Ludman, E. K., and Newman, J. M. (1984). Yin and yang in the health-related food practices of three Chinese groups. *Journal of Nutrition Education, 16,* 4.

Macgregor, F. C. (1960). *Social Science in Nursing.* New York: John Wiley & Sons.

Macgregor, F. C. (1967). Uncooperative patients: Some cultural interpretations. *American Journal of Nursing, 67,* 88–91.

McKenna, M. (1984). Anthropology and nursing—The interaction between two fields of inquiry. *Western Journal of Nursing Research, 6*(4), 423–431.

Massey, M. (1977). What You Are Isn't Necessarily What You Will Be (Video Tape No. 3123.03). Farmington, MI: Magnetic Video Corporation.

Mechanic D. (1978). *Medical Sociology.* New York: The Free Press.

Meleis, A. (1991). Between two cultures: Identity, roles and health. *Health Care for Women International, 12,* 365–378.

Meleis, A. (1992). AAN expert panel report: Cultural competent health care. *Nursing Outlook, 40*(6), 277–283.

Meleis, A., Lipson, J., and Paul, S. (1992). Ethnicity and health among five Middle Eastern immigrant groups. *Nursing Research, 41*(2), 98–103.

Mikhail, B. (1981). The health belief model: A review and critical evaluation of the model, research, and practice. *Advances in Nursing Science, 4*(1), 65–82.

Millon-Underwood, S. (1992). Educating for sensitivity in cultural diversity. *Nurse Educator, 17*(3), 7.

Moerman, D. (1979). Anthropology of symbolic healing. *Current Anthropology, 20*(1), 59–80.

Morse, J. M. (1988). Transcultural nursing: Its substance and issues in research and knowledge. *Recent Advances in Nursing, 18,* 129–141.

Morse, J., Solberg, S., Neander, W., et al. (1990). Concepts of caring and caring as a concept. *Advances in Nursing Science, 13*(1), 1–14.

Muecke, M., and Srisuphan, W. (1990). From women in white to scholarship: The new nurse leaders in Thailand. *Journal of Transcultural Nursing, 1*(2), 21–32.

Orque, M., and Bloch, B. (1985). Culture, ethnicity and nursing. In P. Potter and A. Perry (Eds.), *Fundamentals of Nursing*, pp. 413–438. St. Louis: C. V. Mosby.

Orque, M. S., Bloch, B., and Monrroy, L. S. (1983). *Ethnic Nursing Care*. St. Louis: C. V. Mosby.

Osborne, O. (1969). Anthropology and nursing: Some common traditions and interests. *Nursing Research, 18*(3), 251–255.

Park, J. H. (1992). Nursing administration in Korea. *Nursing Administration Quarterly, 16*(2), 78–83.

Patel, N. (1992). Nursing in India. *Nursing Administration Quarterly, 16*(2), 72–77.

Phillips, S., and Lobar, S. (1990). Literature summary of some Navajo child health beliefs and rearing practices within a transcultural nursing framework. *Journal of Transcultural Nursing, 1*(2), 13–20.

Pickwell, S. (1989). The incorporation of family primary care for Southeast Asian refugees in a community-based mental health facility. *Archives of Psychiatric Nursing, 3*(3), 173–177.

Porter, C., and Villarruel, A. (1991). Socialization and caring for hospitalized African- and Mexican-American children. *Issues in Comprehensive Pediatric Nursing, 14*(1), 1–16.

Potter, P., and Perry, A. (1993). *Fundamentals of Nursing: Concepts, Process and Practice*, 3d ed. St. Louis: C. V. Mosby.

Ray, M. (1989). Transcultural caring: Political and economic visions. *Journal of Transcultural Nursing, 1*(1), 17–21.

Reeb, R. (1992). Granny midwives in Mississippi. *Journal of Transcultural Nursing, 3*(2), 18–27.

Rosenbaum, J. (1991). Widowhood grief: A cultural perspective. *Canadian Journal of Nursing Research, 23*(2), 61–76.

Rosenstock, I. (1974a). The health belief model and preventive health behavior. *Health Education Monographs, 2*(4), 354–385.

Rosenstock, I. (1974b). Historical origins of the health belief model. *Health Education Monographs, 2*(4), 328–335.

Rothenburger, R. (1990). Transcultural nursing: Overcoming obstacles to effective communication. *AORN Journal, 51*(5), 1357–1363.

Roessler, G. (1990). Transcultural nursing certification. *Journal of Transcultural Nursing, 1*, 59.

Ryan, W. M. (1971). *Blaming the Victim*. New York: Vintage Books.

Samovar, L., and Porter, R. (1991). *Intercultural communication*, 6th ed. Belmont, CA: Wadsworth.

Sigerist, H. E. (1967). *A History of Medicine. I: Primitive and Archaic Medicine*. New York: Oxford University Press.

Silko, L. M. (1977). *Ceremony*. New York: Viking Books.

Sobel, D. S. (Ed.) (1979). *Ways of Health*. New York: Harcourt Brace Jovanovich.

Spangler, Z. (1992). Transcultural care values and nursing practices of Philippine-American nurses. *Journal of Transcultural Nursing, 4*(2), 28–37.

Spector, R. (1991). *Cultural Diversity in Health and Illness*, 3d ed. Nowalk, CT: Appleton-Century-Crofts.

Spector, R. (1993). Culture, ethnicity and nursing. In P. Potter and A. Perry (Eds.), *Fundamentals of Nursing*, 3d ed., pp. 95–116. St. Louis: C. V. Mosby.

Stevens, P. E., Hall, J., and Meleis, A. (1992). Examining vulnerability of women clerical workers from five ethnic racial groups. *Western Journal of Nursing Research, 14*(6), 754–774.

Suchman, E. (1965). Stages of illness and medical care. *Journal of Health and Human Behavior, 6*, 114–128.

Tullman, D. (1992). Cultural diversity in nursing education: Does it affect racism in the nursing profession? *Journal of Nursing Education, 31*(7), 321–324.

Tylor, E. B. (1871). *Primitive Culture*, Vols. 1 and 2. London: Murray.

U.S. Bureau of the Census (1990). *General Population Characteristics*. Washington, D.C.: U.S. Government Printing Office.

Van Gennep, A. (1960). *The Rites of Passage* (trans. by M. B. Vizedom and G. L. Caffee). Chicago: University of Chicago Press (originally published 1909).

Villarruel, A., and Ortiz de Montellano, B. (1992). Culture and pain: A Mesoamerican perspective. *Advances in Nursing Science, 15*(1), 21–32.

Watson, J. (1985). *Nursing: Human Science and Human Care*. Norwalk, CT: Appleton-Century-Crofts.

Weller, B. (1991). Nursing in a multicultural world. *Nursing Standards, 5*(30), 31–32.

Wenger, A. (1992). Transcultural nursing and health care issues in urban and rural contexts. *Journal of Transcultural Nursing, 3*(2), 4–10.

Williams, R. M., Jr. (1970). *American Society: A Sociological Interpretation*, 3d ed. rev. New York: Knopf.

Wuest, J. (1991). Harmonizing: A North American Indian approach to management of middle ear disease with transcultural nursing implications. *Journal of Transcultural Nursing, 3*(1), 5–14.

Zola, I. (1966). Culture and symptoms: An analysis of patients presenting complaints. *American Sociological Review, 31*, 615–630.

2

Transcultural Nursing Care

Margaret M. Andrews
(With selected contributions by Joyceen S. Boyle)

Introduction

Chapter 1 introduced the theoretical foundations of transcultural nursing. Chapter 2 will discuss selected theories, concepts, principles, and research findings as they relate to transcultural nursing care of clients—individuals, families, groups, communities, and institutions—in diverse health care systems. It is our belief that all nursing care is transcultural because each person—nurse as well as client—is a cultural being.

This chapter will introduce the principles, concepts, theories, and research findings that enable nurses to provide excellent transcultural nursing care that is culturally relevant and contextually meaningful. After an introductory critique of the prevailing nursing paradigm, which embraces the use of nursing diagnoses and theories that may have relevance for some clients from diverse cultural backgrounds, the key concepts in transcultural nursing care will be examined. Concepts such as culture values, cross-cultural communication, culture and nutrition, traditional healers, spiritual healers, cultural meaning of symptoms, biocultural variations in health and illness, clinical decision making and nursing actions, as well as evaluation of care will be explored. Perspectives of care for clients who have various cultural backgrounds will be discussed.

We believe that experienced transcultural nurses synthesize culturally relevant data about clients and apply their knowledge and skills when caring for people from various cultures. For the purpose of clarity, the components that comprise transcultural nursing care will be introduced as if they existed separately from each other. Nurses are likely to find that in clinical nursing practice, the process may not follow the linear, sequential order presented in this chapter (Andrews, 1992).

The anticipated outcome is that nurses will have the knowledge and skills necessary to provide excellent transcultural nursing care for clients from many culturally diverse

Margaret M. Andrews and Joyceen S. Boyle: TRANSCULTURAL CONCEPTS IN NURSING CARE, SECOND EDITION. © 1995 J.B. Lippincott Company.

backgrounds. Although some textbooks focus on the federally defined minority groups or selected racial/ethnic cultures and subcultures, we believe that given the multicultural complexion of contemporary society, nurses should be prepared to care for clients from diverse cultural backgrounds. Sometimes cultural stereotyping may be perpetuated when a recipe-like approach to clients from specific cultural groups is used; i.e., there is a tendency by the nurse to view all members of a group homogeneously and to expect certain beliefs or practices because of preconceptions that may or may not apply to the client.

Critique of the Prevailing Nursing Paradigm

In this chapter, we will use the culturally based values, attitudes, beliefs, and practices of clients—individuals, families, groups, communities, and institutions—representing various cultural backgrounds to guide transcultural nursing care. Recognizing the so-called new curriculum revolution in nursing education, we approach transcultural nursing care from a perspective that may or may not match the organizing or theoretical frameworks used in some nursing programs or the problem-solving approach called "nursing process" that is frequently used to teach students about nursing care.

Often, the nursing care of clients from culturally diverse backgrounds fails to "fit" or be congruent with the prevailing nursing paradigms. Metaphors such as a spider's web or a multicolored woven rug can be used to demonstrate the intricate and complex interweaving of the threads that together comprise a person's culture. The process used by the spider or weaver bears little resemblance to the recipe-like nursing process in which the nurse sequentially assesses, diagnoses, plans, intervenes, and evaluates clients' care. For example, in considering the sociocultural dimensions of nursing care, nurses may find themselves evaluating the effectiveness of the interventions administered by a highly skilled folk healer before planning or implementing nursing interventions, which are usually biomedical and Western in nature. Thus evaluation precedes the other steps of the nursing process and necessitates that this be reordered. From an empirical and practical perspective, the nursing process often fails to match the clinical reality faced by the nurse.

As indicated by Leininger (1991a), the interconnections among the cultural and social structure dimensions—cultural values and lifeways, kinship, and social, religious, philosophical, technological, political, legal, economic, educational, historical, environmental, and language factors—are embedded and interwoven in such an intricate manner that it is often impossible to sort or separate them from one another. Similarly, all these factors are integral to transcultural nursing care—whether referring to the process by which information is gathered or its content.

Transcultural Perspectives on Nursing Diagnoses

The nursing diagnosis classification system in the United States and Canada was developed to define the phenomena of nursing and to identify those health care problems which are within the scope of nursing practice. Since 1973 when the first North American Nursing Diagnosis Association (NANDA) conference was held, the use of nursing diagnoses has grown rapidly. From 1977 to 1982, fourteen nurse-theorists worked to develop an organizing framework for the classification of nursing diagnoses.

The theorists proposed a model in which the phenomenon of concern to nursing is the "unitary man (person)," who is conceived as an open system in mutual interaction with the environment. Individual health and uniqueness are manifested in nine pattern characteristics: exchanging, communicating, relating, valuing, choosing, moving, receiving, knowing, and feeling. These pattern characteristics are now referred to as *human response patterns* (Feild, 1991; Fitzpatrick, 1991).

Many North American nursing texts use the NANDA taxonomy for application of the nursing process, and the use of nursing diagnoses as a step in the nursing process has spread to China, Japan, England, and Australia (Kelley and Frish, 1990). Currently, the American Nurses Association and NANDA are working to prepare the NANDA taxonomy for possible inclusion in the World Health Organization's *International Classification of Diseases* (ICD), after which the taxonomy would become a standard international classification for nursing (Fitzpatrick et al., 1989).

Such advances in the use of nursing diagnoses could be helpful in developing standard terms for nursing phenomena that would allow compilation of health statistics based on nursing problems or conditions. There are, however, substantive objections to the use of NANDA diagnostic categories and defining characteristics in international or transcultural contexts. The following summarizes some of the major concerns raised by transcultural nursing experts.

First, the nursing diagnosis taxonomy is based, to large extent, on Anglo-American Western cultural values, norms, and standards, which have questionable relevance and usefulness with many non-Anglocized cultures and subcultures. The diagnoses are built into a classification system based on labeling that is unintentionally culturally insensitive and may even stereotype clients (Geissler, 1991, 1992; Leininger, 1990). Second, there are obvious language problems in exporting the NANDA system, since there are limited linguistic taxons or language terms that might enable nurses from non-Anglo backgrounds to identify their local or specific cultural conditions, and some terms cannot be translated to communicate accurate meanings and uses (Geissler, 1991, 1992; Leininger, 1990). Third, selection from the current list of nursing diagnoses may result in cultural imposition by the nurse; i.e., the nurse may impose culturally inaccurate and inappropriate labels on clients from culturally diverse backgrounds by choosing from a predetermined list of options. Furthermore, the taxonomy lacks culture-specific conditions or illnesses, e.g., culture-bound syndromes (Geissler, 1991, 1992; Leininger, 1990; McFarland and McFarlane, 1989). Fourth, questions must be raised concerning the consistency with which diagnostic labels are used by nurses either within one culture or across cultures. In a study by Kelley and Frish (1990), the use of selected nursing diagnoses by Mexican and American nurses was compared. Findings indicate that nurses did not demonstrate consistency with each other in the use of diagnoses either within each group or between groups. The researchers concluded that further study and documentation of how diagnoses are understood and used by nurses are needed before widespread international or transcultural use is encouraged. Fifth, none of the NANDA diagnoses focus on cultural care nursing phenomena, and there are no transcultural nursing or anthropologic taxons found within the different categories. Rather, the more pathologic and medically oriented negative conditions are emphasized. Positive health descriptors, caring modalities, and assets or strengths of cultures in dealing with human conditions, values, and lifeways need to be added (Leininger, 1990). Sixth, the rules or norms for categorizing physical and emotional states fail to accommodate or provide for transcultural variations of Western and non-Western conditions (Geissler, 1991, 1992; Leininger, 1990). Seventh, there are a number of ethical and moral issues related to the NANDA taxonomy being used worldwide that need to be examined (Leininger, 1990).

In summary, the nursing diagnoses are focused primarily on biophysical and psychological "disturbances," "alterations," "impairments," "distresses," or some deficit or disruptive states that have been developed by North American nurses. The NANDA taxonomic patterns reveal a bias for psychophysical illnesses with very few patterns that are cultural care, health conditions, or well-being expressions. In following the NANDA system, the nurse is guided to assess clients with disturbed, impaired, or dysfunctional psychological or biophysical diseases. From a transcultural nursing perspective, this taxonomic bias limits the nurse's ability to obtain an accurate and holistic perspective about clients who are well and want to maintain wellness. The NANDA diagnostic classification system needs to be reevaluated, reconsidered, and refocused into transculturally relevant, meaningful, and useful transcultural nursing perspectives. Perhaps it would be more appropriate to discuss the nurse's "knowledge deficits" of the client's culture. Does the nurse have basic knowledge sufficient to know and understand the client's culture? If the client is misjudged, misinterpreted, or mistreated due to the nurse's cultural ignorance, what are the ethical, legal, or cultural consequences? The nurse's cultural knowledge deficits should be addressed before the nurse assesses and uses the nursing diagnostic categories (Leininger, 1991) (see Research Box 2-1).

Transcultural Perspectives on Nursing Theories

A number of nurse-scholars have developed theories of nursing, and some have suggested that nursing science would be enhanced by the development of a metatheory. Although we intend to communicate no value judgments on the nursing theories developed to date, it seems that Leininger's (1991) theory of culture care diversity and universality gives precedence to understanding the cultural dimensions of human care and caring.

As discussed in Chapter 1, Leininger's theory focuses on describing, explaining, and predicting nursing similarities and differences focused primarily on human care and caring in human cultures. Leininger uses world view, social structure, language, ethnohistory, environmental context, and the generic (folk) and professional systems to provide a comprehensive and holistic view of influences in culture care and well-being. The three modes of nursing decisions and actions—culture care preservation and/or maintenance, culture care accommodation and/or negotiation, and culture care repatterning and/or restructuring—are presented to demonstrate ways to provide culturally congruent nursing care. Among the strengths of Leininger's theory is its flexibility for use with individuals, families, groups, communities, and institutions in diverse health systems. Leininger's sunrise model depicts the theory of cultural care diversity and universality and provides a visual schematic representation of the key components of the theory and the interrelationships among the theory's components. As the world of nursing and health care has become increasingly multicultural, the theory's relevance has increased as well.

Although it is beyond the scope of this chapter to review all the recognized nursing theories from a transcultural perspective, the reader is encouraged to critically evaluate

Research Box 2-1. Cultural Relevance of Nursing Diagnoses

E. M. Geissler (1992). Nursing diagnoses: A study of cultural relevance. *Journal of Professional Nursing, 8*(5), 301–307.

This study examines the adequacy/inadequacy of three nursing diagnoses with cultural etiologies: (1) impaired verbal communication related to cultural differences, (2) impaired social interaction related to sociocultural dissonance, and (3) noncompliance related to patient value system. A five-point rating scale to validate the defining characteristics of the NANDA nursing diagnoses was administered to the membership of the American Nurses Association Council on Cultural Diversity and the International Transcultural Nursing Society, with a response rate of 42 percent (*n* = 245). The research tool listed the NANDA defining characteristics and cultural etiology for each diagnosis. The subjects also wrote and ranked other defining characteristics they used to make the diagnosis in clinical practice. Percentage distribution results indicate that no defining characteristic meets the NANDA criteria for a major or minor defining characteristic. By collapsing categories, seven were acceptable only as minor defining characteristics. Respondents' 113 suggestions for additional characteristics were content analyzed. Based on respondents' suggestions, the definitions for each diagnosis were reworked and new culture-related factors were added. Additional suggestions from transcultural nursing experts form a data base for future research to expand the use of the currently limited components of NANDA diagnoses with culturally diverse patients.

the cultural relevance of a theory before using it with clients from culturally diverse backgrounds. It is especially important to analyze the assumptions of the theory from a transcultural vantage point. For example, let us consider Orem's (1980) self-care theory. As defined by Orem, *self-care* is "the practice of activities that individuals initiate and perform on their own behalf in maintaining life, health, and well-being" (Orem, 1980, p. 35). The concept of self-care with a central focus on the individual, self-control, and autonomy may be counter to the cultural beliefs, values, and norms found in some cultures, especially in non-Western cultures. As evident in Anglo-American and European cultures, the dominant Western values of individualism, autonomy, independence, self-reliance, self-control, self-regulation, and self-management may be the source of cultural conflict with non-Western cultures that have almost the opposite values. In many non-Western cultures, individuals promote and maintain the caring role of others reflecting values such as interdependence, interconnectedness, understanding, presence (being with), and responsibility for others. In contrast, the idea of self-care "deficits" or mobilizing clients to become self-sufficient, independent, or self-reliant is often an enigma because their world view and cultural values are so different, especially if they are not acculturated to Western norms. Furthermore, the consequences of promoting self-care among people who value group interdependence, cooperation, and responsibility for others need to be examined critically. What are the short- and long-term consequences of mobilizing people to be self-carers when their culture values "other-care" norms? (Leininger, 1992).

Cultural Competence, Cultural Competencies, and Excellence in Transcultural Nursing Care

Although some nurses use the term *cultural competence* as a collective noun to refer to the "complex integration of knowledge, attitudes, and skills which enhance cross-cultural communication and appropriate/effective interactions with others" (American Academy of Nursing, 1993), we believe that there are cultural competenc*ies* that represent learning in the cognitive, affective, and psychomotor domains and assume the nurse's skill in critical thinking.

In the context of our discussion of transcultural nursing care, we will identify the traits that we believe characterize excellence in transcultural nursing as well as the minimal competencies that are important for the learner to master. We will examine culture values, cultural self-assessment, and specific areas in which knowledge about one's own and others' cultural values, beliefs, attitudes, and practices affect health, illness, and health-seeking behaviors of individuals, families, groups, and communities in diverse health care systems. Some of the cultural competencies may be useful when nurses practice, teach, research, or administer in multicultural work or other institutional settings. When appropriate, the psychomotor skills (e.g., assessing darkly pigmented clients for cyanosis, jaundice, or anemia; caring for the hair and skin of African-American clients) necessary to provide culturally competent care will be presented.

Nurses must communicate effectively not only with clients from diverse cultures but also with nurses whose cultural backgrounds may differ from their own.

Cultural Assessment

Cultural or *culturological nursing assessment* refers to a "systematic appraisal or examination of individuals, groups, and communities as to their cultural beliefs, values, and practices to determine explicit nursing needs and intervention practices within the cultural context of the people being evaluated" (Leininger, 1978, pp. 85–86). Because they deal with cultural values, belief systems, and lifeways, cultural assessments tend to be broad and comprehensive, although it is possible to focus on a smaller segment. Cultural assessment consists of both *process* and *content*. The process aspect concerns the nurse's approach to the client, consideration of verbal and nonverbal communication, and the sequence/order in which data are gathered. The content of the cultural assessment consists of the actual data categories in which information about clients is gathered.

There are several cultural assessment instruments or tools available, and the reader may want to review them. The first has been developed by us and is found in Appendix A. The second is Leininger's "Acculturation Health Care Assessment Tool for Cultural Patterns in Traditional and Non-Traditional Lifeways" (Leininger, 1991). This tool provides a general qualitative profile or assessment of traditional or nontraditional orientation of informants of their patterned lifeways. Health care influencers are assessed with respect to world view, language, cultural values, kinship, religion, politics, technology, education, environment, and related areas.

The third is Bloch's "Assessment Guide for Ethnic/Cultural Variation" (Orque, Bloch, and Monrroy, 1983), which is especially useful from a clinical practice perspective. Bloch identifies *cultural data categories* such as ethnic origin, race, place of birth, relocations, habits, customs, values and beliefs, behaviors valued by culture, cultural sanctions and restrictions, language and communication processes, healing beliefs and practices, and nutritional variables or factors; *sociological data categories* such as economic status, educational status, social network, family as supportive group, supportive institutions in the ethnic/cultural community, and institutional racism; *psychological data categories* such as self-concept, mental and behavioral processes, religious influences, and psychological and cultural responses to the stress and discomfort of illness; and *biologic/physiologic data categories* such as racial-anatomic characteristics, growth and development patterns, variations in body systems, skin and hair physiology, diseases more prevalent among ethnic/cultural groups, and diseases to which the ethnic/cultural group has increased resistance. Each data category has accompanying guideline questions/instructions.

With increasing frequency, health care agencies are developing cultural assessment tools or modifying existing assessment instruments to include the cultural dimensions of care. Readers are encouraged to examine the previously cited instruments and compare them with the assessment tools used in clinical facilities with which they are familiar.

Culture Values

In order to provide culturally congruent and excellent nursing care that is meaningful in its cultural context, nurses must examine culture values. As indicated in Chapter 1, *culture values* refer to the powerful, persistent, and directive forces that give meaning, order, and direction to the individual's, group's, family's, or community's actions, decisions, and lifeways, usually over a span of time (Leininger, 1978). Throughout this chapter the reader will be encouraged to examine culture values and to apply knowledge from the liberal arts as well as from nursing and other health sciences in providing transcultural nursing care.

Between cultures and even within one culture, values vary along a continuum. Many Asian, Islamic, and tribal societies make loyalty to the group their highest value. In these cultural groups, individual values are subservient to whatever is best for the group. In most parts of North America, however, individuality is emphasized, representing the opposite end of the continuum. Individual rights are protected, sometimes even to the detriment of others or of the whole group. This stimulates individual creativity but weakens social stability.

Some cultures, such as German and Swiss societies, place a high value on orderliness; e.g., schedules are worked out carefully and are respected. In other cultures, such as Mexican-American and many Native American tribes, time is of little importance, and schedules are very flexible. Many North American cultures value cleanliness highly, whereas others (e.g., sub-Saharan African nations), especially where water is scarce, do not place a high value on cleanliness. Different cultures define cleanliness in different ways. For example, cleanliness of clothing is accomplished in many Western societies with commercial detergents and automatic washing machines, whereas members of other societies (parts of India and Africa) wash clothing by hand in rivers using rocks and natural cleansing agents. One of the authors recalls when a Nigerian friend who was studying in the United States remarked that his clothes "always looked dirty" when washed in the automatic washing machine, whereas they had been "so clean and fresh" when washed by hand in the river. This anecdote illustrates not only the different ways in which cleanliness is expressed but also the universal nature of the stage of culture shock in which the host country is perceived as being dirty.

The Anglo-American obsession for bodily cleanliness and the compulsion to eliminate body odors is reflected in a multimillion dollar business for the manufacturer of deodorants, perfumes, aftershave lotions, and similar products. In other cultures, the natural odor of the body is valued, and little effort is made to disguise it. Ironically, some colognes and perfumes such as those with musk oil are marketed to U.S. and Canadian people for their more natural odor, which is alleged to give its wearer more sex appeal.

All cultures emphasize the importance of telling the truth and view deception as wrong. They differ widely, however, in their definitions of the terms *truth* and *deception*. One culture believes that truth is what corresponds most closely with reality regardless of the consequences. Another culture may hold a pragmatic view of truth as being that which brings the greatest benefit to the person or the group. Deception is that which loses advantage, prestige, or favor. Consider the implications of truth as a culture value when deciding whether to inform a client about his or her impending death.

Most cultures believe that stealing is wrong but define *stealing* differently. For one culture, stealing is taking something that belongs to another person or for which one has no culturally accepted claim. In another culture, stealing occurs only when one takes something belonging to another member of the loyalty group. It is quite permissible, and even encouraged, to take what belongs to someone outside the group, especially if that person is more affluent. One of the authors recently consulted with nurses at a large midwestern urban hospital who complained that gypsies were stealing supplies and equipment from the outpatient department. While recognizing that the culture value concerning stealing was operational, the nursing intervention focused on ways to protect the hospital's property and discourage the behavior.

Culture values are frequently contained in the folklore and literature of people as well as in their proverbs. Table 2-1 summarizes the core metaphors and themes found in

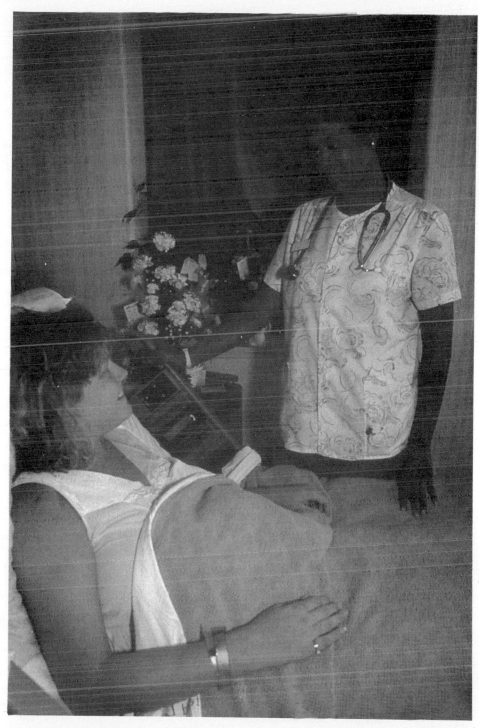

Because they deal with cultural values, beliefs, and practices, cultural assessments are the foundation on which nursing care is based.

Table 2-1. Culture values in folklore and literature

Group	Core Metaphors and Themes
African	Interdependence, flexible kinship, courage in overcoming natural forces and adversity, reliance on spiritual forces
Anglo-American	Rugged individualism, self-reliance, self-determination
Arab	Muslim belief in the Koran, *In Sha'a Allah* (if Allah wills) tradition, admonitions that things take time in life
Chinese	Confucian belief in filial piety, hierarchical affiliation
English	Self-contained, class-determined individualism
German	Correctness, orderliness, discipline
Greek	Honor
Hindu	Purification, immersion, submission, fusion
Irish	Roman Catholic belief in morality, respectability
Japanese	Group harmony, interdependence, politeness, honor
Jewish	Courage in facing adversity and religious persecution, relationship with God, spiritual/religious themes, the Torah
Native American	Harmony with nature, coping with natural and human obstacles encountered in life's journey
Portuguese	Family, voyage of exploration and discovery
Puerto Rican	Respect and personalism
Russian	Hardships, open and closed society, political themes

Table 2-2. Proverbs and Anglo-American values

Proverb	Value
Cleanliness is next to godliness.	Cleanliness
A penny saved is a penny earned.	Thriftiness
Time is money.	Time thriftiness
Don't cry over spilt milk.	Practicality
Waste not, want not.	Frugality
Early to bed, early to rise, makes a man healthy, wealthy, and wise.	Diligence, work ethic
God helps those who help themselves.	Initiative
It's not whether you win or lose, but how you play the game.	Good sportsmanship
A man's home is his castle.	Privacy, value of personal property
No rest for the wicked.	Guilt, work ethic
You've made your bed, now sleep in it.	Responsibility, retaliation
Don't count your chickens until they've hatched.	Practicality
A bird in the hand is worth two in the bush.	Practicality
The squeaky wheel gets the grease.	Aggressiveness
Might makes right.	Superiority of physical power
There's more than one way to skin a cat.	Originality, determination
A stitch in time saves nine.	Timeliness of action
All that glitters is not gold.	Wariness
Clothes make the man.	Concern for physical appearance
If at first you don't succeed, try, try again.	Persistence, work ethic
Take care of today, and tomorrow will take care of itself.	Preparation for future
Laugh and the world laughs with you; weep and you weep alone.	Pleasant outward appearance

From L. R. Kohls (1984). *Survival Kit for Overseas Living*, pp. 28–29. Yarmouth, Maine: Intercultural Press.

the cultural stories of selected groups. Table 2-2 summarizes some common proverbs that reflect 20 basic values of Anglo-Americans. It is evidently much more effective in teaching to say, "Don't cry over spilt milk" than "You'd better learn to be practical." By examining the proverbs of other cultures, it is possible to infer basic values embraced by the majority of the population.

In interacting with clients from various cultural backgrounds, it is important to be aware of one's own cultural values, attitudes, beliefs, and practices. For example, nurses must know how they relate to various groups of people in the society. In Box 2-1, the reader is invited to explore his or her level of response to 30 types of individuals who represent 5 general categories: ethnic/racial, social issues/problems, religious, physically/mentally handicapped, and political.

Similarly, the nurse's comfort level and knowledge of clients from various cultural groups are important factors in transcultural nursing care. Noting that community health nurses were being asked to care for clients from culturally diverse backgrounds about whose culture the nurses have little knowledge or experience, Bernal and Froman (1987, 1993) studied the confidence levels of community health nurses when caring for people from three culturally distinct groups: blacks, Puerto Ricans, and Southeast Asians. Based on data collected from 190 community health nurses, the researchers concluded that they could not report a single item for which, on average, nurses perceived even a moderate degree of confidence in providing care to clients from the three groups. In examining the demographic variables, the researchers concluded that

Text continues on p. 62

Box 2-1. How Do You Relate to Various Groups of People in the Society?

Described below are different levels of response you might have toward a person.

Levels of Response
1. *Greet:* I feel I can *greet* this person warmly and welcome him or her sincerely.
2. *Accept:* I feel I can honestly *accept* this person as he or she is and be comfortable enough to listen to his or her problems.
3. *Help:* I feel I would genuinely try to *help* this person with his or her problems as they might relate to or arise from the label-stereotype given to him or her.
4. *Background:* I feel I have the *background* of knowledge and/or experience to be able to help this person.
5. *Advocate:* I feel I could honestly be an *advocate* for this person.

The following is a list of individuals. Read down the list and place a checkmark next to anyone you would *not* "greet" or would hesitate to "greet." Then move to response level 2, "accept," and follow the same procedure. Try to respond honestly, not as you think might be socially or professionally desirable. Your answers are only for your personal use in clarifying your initial reactions to different people.

(continued)

Box 2-1 (continued)

	Level of Response				
	1	2	3	4	5
Individual	Greet	Accept	Help	Background	Advocate
1. Haitian	☐	☐	☐	☐	☐
2. Child abuser	☐	☑	☐	☐	☐
3. Jew	☐	☐	☐	☐	☐
4. Person with hemophilia	☐	☐	☐	☐	☐
5. Neo-Nazi	☐	☐	☐	☐	☐
6. Mexican American	☐	☐	☐	☐	☐
7. IV drug user	☐	☐	☐	☐	☐
8. Catholic	☐	☐	☐	☐	☐
9. Senile, elderly person	☐	☐	☐	☐	☐
10. Teamster Union member	☐	☐	☐	☐	☐
11. Native American	☐	☐	☐	☐	☐
12. Prostitute	☐	☐	☐	☐	☐
13. Jehovah's Witness	☐	☐	☐	☐	☐
14. Cerebral palsied person	☐	☐	☐	☐	☐
15. ERA proponent	☐	☐	☐	☐	☐
16. Vietnamese American	☐	☐	☐	☐	☐
17. Gay/lesbian	☐	☐	☐	☐	☐
18. Atheist	☐	☐	☐	☐	☐
19. Person with AIDS	☐	☐	☐	☐	☐
20. Communist	☐	☐	☐	☐	☐
21. Black American	☐	☐	☐	☐	☐
22. Unmarried expectant teenager	☐	☐	☐	☐	☐
23. Protestant	☐	☐	☐	☐	☐
24. Amputee	☐	☐	☐	☐	☐
25. Ku Klux Klansman	☐	☐	☐	☐	☐
26. White Anglo-Saxon	☐	☐	☐	☐	☐
27. Alcoholic	☐	☐	☐	☐	☐
28. Amish person	☐	☐	☐	☐	☐
29. Person with cancer	☐	☐	☐	☐	☐
30. Nuclear armament proponent	☐	☐	☐	☐	☐

Scoring Guide: The previous activity may help you anticipate difficulty in working with some clients at various levels. The 30 types of individuals can be grouped into 5 categories: ethnic/racial, social issues/problems, religious, physically/mentally handicapped, and political. Transfer your checkmarks to the following form. If you have a concentration of checks within a specific category of individuals or at specific levels, this may indicate a conflict that could hinder you from rendering effective professional help.

Box 2-1 (continued)

Individual	1 Greet	2 Accept	3 Help	4 Background	5 Advocate
Ethnic/racial					
1. Haitian American	☐	☐	☐	☐	☐
6. Mexican American	☐	☐	☐	☐	☐
11. Native American	☐	☐	☐	☐	☐
16. Vietnamese American	☐	☐	☐	☐	☐
21. Black American	☐	☐	☐	☐	☐
26. White Anglo-Saxon	☐	☐	☐	☐	☐
Social issues/problems					
2. Child abuser	☐	☐	☐	☐	☐
7. IV drug user	☐	☐	☐	☐	☐
12. Prostitute	☐	☐	☐	☐	☐
17. Gay/lesbian	☐	☐	☐	☐	☐
22. Unmarried expectant teenager	☐	☐	☐	☐	☐
27. Alcoholic	☐	☐	☐	☐	☐
Religious					
3. Jew	☐	☐	☐	☐	☐
8. Catholic	☐	☐	☐	☐	☐
13. Jehovah's Witness	☐	☐	☐	☐	☐
18. Atheist	☐	☐	☐	☐	☐
23. Protestant	☐	☐	☐	☐	☐
28. Amish person	☐	☐	☐	☐	☐
Physically/mentally handicapped					
4. Person with hemophilia	☐	☐	☐	☐	☐
9. Senile elderly person	☐	☐	☐	☐	☐
14. Cerebral palsied person	☐	☐	☐	☐	☐
19. Person with AIDS	☐	☐	☐	☐	☐
24. Amputee	☐	☐	☐	☐	☐
29. Person with cancer	☐	☐	☐	☐	☐
Political					
5. Neo-Nazi	☐	☐	☐	☐	☐
10. Teamster Union member	☐	☐	☐	☐	☐
15. ERA proponent	☐	☐	☐	☐	☐
20. Communist	☐	☐	☐	☐	☐
25. Ku Klux Klansman	☐	☐	☐	☐	☐
30. Nuclear armament proponent	☐	☐	☐	☐	☐

there is no clear profile distinguishing the transculturally efficacious nurse from less confident colleagues. Finally, the data revealed that nurses did not believe they had any more knowledge or expertise about any one of the cultural groups than about others. The results of this study indicate that nurses are not being provided with experiences that prepare them to care for clients from culturally diverse backgrounds and that they lack confidence when delivering care to clients from these populations.

Culture Values and Culture Care Meanings

Among the greatest challenges for the nurse is to provide care from the client's values and care meanings using what may be relevant or helpful from professional knowledge. The nurse should be aware of the great diversity of constructs and should realize that care has different expressions, meanings, and referents, with no ethical or moral judgment implied. Table 2-3 summarizes the human care expressions and patterns of cultures for selected groups that have been studied by transcultural nurse researchers.

Cross-Cultural Communication

Inherent in any nurse-client interaction is communication. To begin the discussion on cross-cultural communication, it is necessary to examine the ways in which people from various cultural backgrounds communicate with each other. Needless to say, communication between individuals having the same cultural background may be fraught with pitfalls. When nurses communicate with others from cultural backgrounds unlike their own and with those for whom English is a second language, the probability of miscommunication increases significantly.

According to Meharabian (1972), communication is transmitted primarily by body cues (55 percent) and paralinguistic cues such as voice (38 percent); only 7 percent of communication is transmitted by words. Cultural differences have been noted in many social customs. Matsumoto and Kudoh (1987) report that for the Japanese, interpretation of body postures is influenced by issues concerning status and power, whereas for Anglo-Americans, interpretation of body postures is influenced by interpersonal judgments of "likes" and "dislikes."

Communication with Family Members and Significant Others

Although the nurse naturally will want to communicate directly with the client, assuming that the individual's health condition permits, there are likely to be other significant persons in the client's life with whom the nurse will interact. When caring for clients from culturally diverse backgrounds, it is necessary to identify those significant others whom the client perceives to be important in his or her care and who may be responsible for decision making that affects his or her health care. For example, for many clients, *familism*—which emphasizes interdependence over independence, affiliation over confrontation, and cooperation over competition—may dictate that important decisions affecting the client be made by the family, not the individual alone.

Despite local and national divorce statistics, the family remains the basic social unit in which children are raised and learn culturally based values, beliefs, and practices about health and illnesses—indeed about life itself. Children are socialized by parents, grandparents, aunts and uncles, and others in their family at young ages; later, during

Table 2-3. Cultural values and culture care meanings and action modes for selected groups

Cultural Values Are:	Culture Care Meanings and Action Modes Are:

Anglo-American Culture (Mainly U.S. Middle and Upper Classes)

1. Individualism—focus on a self-reliant person	1. Stress alleviation by
2. Independence and freedom	-Physical means
3. Competition and achievement	-Emotional means
4. Materialism (things and money)	2. Personalized acts
5. Technology dependent	-Doing special things
6. Instant time and actions	-Giving individual attention
7. Youth and beauty	3. Self-reliance (individualism) by
8. Equal sex rights	-Reliance on self
9. Leisure time highly valued possible	-Reliance on self (self-care)
10. Reliance on scientific facts and numbers	-Becoming as independent as
11. Less respect for authority and the elderly	-Reliance on technology
12. Generosity in time of crisis	4. Health instruction
	-Teach us how "to do" this care for self
	-Give us the "medical" facts

Mexican-American Culture*

1. Extended family valued	1. Succorance (direct family aid)
2. Interdependence with kin and social activities	2. Involvement with extended family
3. Patriarchal (machismo)	("other care")
4. Exact time less valued	3. Filial love/loving
5. High respect for authority and the elderly	4. Respect for authority
6. Religion valued (many Roman Catholics)	5. Mother as care decision maker
7. Native foods for well-being	6. Protective (external) male care
8. Traditional folk-care healers for folk illnesses	7. Acceptance of God's will
9. Belief in hot-cold theory	8. Use of folk-care practices
	9. Healing with foods
	10. Touching

Haitian-American Culture**

1. Extended family as support system	1. Involve family for support (other care)
2. Religion—God's will must prevail	2. Respect
3. Reliance on folk foods and treatments	3. Trust
4. Belief in hot-cold theory	4. Succorance
5. Male decision maker and direct caregivers	5. Touching (body closeness)
6. Reliance on native language	6. Reassurance
	7. Spiritual healing
	8. Use of folk food, care rituals
	9. Avoid evil eye and witches
	10. Speak the language

African-American Culture†

1. Extended family networks	1. Concern for my "brothers and sisters"
2. Religion valued (many are Baptists)	2. Being involved with
3. Interdependence with "blacks"	3. Giving presence (physical)
4. Daily survival	4. Family support and "get togethers"
5. Technology valued, e.g., radio, car, etc.	5. Touching appropriately
6. Folk (soul) foods	6. Reliance on folk home remedies
7. Folk healing modes	7. Rely on "Jesus to save us" with prayers and
8. Music and physical activities	songs

(continued)

Table 2-3 (*continued*)

Cultural Values Are:	Culture Care Meanings and Action Modes Are:
North-American Indian Culture‡	
1. Harmony between land, people, and environment	1. Establishing harmony between people and environment with reciprocity
2. Reciprocity with "Mother Earth"	2. Actively listening
3. Spiritual inspiration (spirit guidance)	3. Using periods of silence ("Great Spirit" guidance)
4. Folk healers (shamans) (the circle and four directions)	4. Rhythmic timing (nature, land and people) in harmony
5. Practice culture rituals and taboos	5. Respect for native folk healers, carers, and curers (use of circle)
6. Rhythmicity of life with nature	6. Maintaining reciprocity (replenish what is taken from Mother Earth)
7. Authority of tribal elders	7. Preserving cultural rituals and taboos
8. Pride in cultural heritage and "nations"	8. Respect for elders and children
9. Respect and value for children	

* These findings were from the author's transcultural nurse studies (1970, 1984) and other transcultural nurse studies in the United States during the past two decades.
** These data were from Haitians living in the United States during the past decade (1981–1991).
† These findings were from the author's study of two southern U.S. villages (1980–1981) and from a study of one large northern urban city (1982–1991) along with other studies by transcultural nurses.
‡ These findings were collected by the author and other contributors in the United States and Canada during the past three decades. Cultural variations among all nations exist, and so these data are some general commonalities about values, care meanings, and actions.
From M. M. Leininger (1991). *Culture Care Diversity and Universality: A Theory of Nursing*, pp. 355–357. New York: National League for Nursing Press. Reprinted by permission.

childhood and adolescence, by teachers, clergy, peers, and others. The essence of *family* consists of living together as a unit. Relationships that may seem apparent sometimes warrant further exploration when the nurse interacts with clients from culturally diverse backgrounds. For example, most Anglo-Americans define siblings as two persons with either the same mother, the same father, the same mother and father, or the same adoptive parents. In some Asian cultures, a sibling relationship is defined as any infants breast fed by the same woman. In other cultures, certain kinship patterns, such as maternal first cousins, are defined as sibling relationships. In some African cultures, anyone from the same village or town may be called "brother" or "sister."

Certain ethnoreligious subcultures, such as members of the Roman Catholic religion (who may be further subdivided by ethnicity, such as Italians, Polish, Spanish, Mexican, and so forth), recognize relationships such as "godmother" or "godfather" in which an individual who is not the biological parent promises to assist with the moral/ spiritual development of an infant and agrees to care for the child in the event of parental death. The godparent makes these promises during the religious ceremony of baptism.

When communicating with the parent or parent surrogate of infants and children, it is important to identify the primary provider of care and the key decision maker who acts on behalf of the child—this/these individual(s) may or may not be the biological parents. Among some Hispanic groups, for example, female members of the nuclear or extended family such as sisters and aunts are primary providers of care for infants and children. In some African-American families, the grandmother may be the decision maker and primary caretaker of children. Talking with the right person(s) is paramount for effective communication to occur. The same principles operate when the client is an adult. In many Asian cultures, it is the obligation and duty of the eldest son to assume primary responsibility for his aging parents and to make health care decisions for them.

When making health-related decisions, members of selected culturally diverse backgrounds in which lineal relationships predominate may seek assistance from other members of the family and allow a relative (e.g., parent, grandparent, or elder brother) to make decisions about important health-related matters. If collateral relationships are valued, decisions about the client may be interrelated with the impact of illness on the entire family or group. For example, among the Amish, the entire community is affected by the illness of a member because the community pays for health care from a common fund, members join together to meet the needs of both the sick person and his or her family throughout the illness, and the roles of dozens of people in the community are likely to be affected by the illness of a single member. The individual values orientation concerning relationships is predominant among the dominant cultural majority in America. Although members of the nuclear family may participate to varying degrees, decision making about health and illness is often an individual matter.

Introductions

Because initial impressions are so important in all human relationships, cross-cultural considerations concerning introductions warrant a few brief remarks. In order to ensure that a mutually respectful relationship is established, nurses should introduce themselves and indicate to the client how they prefer to be called, i.e., by first name, last name, or title. They should elicit the same information from the client because this enables nurses to address the person in a manner that is culturally appropriate and could actually spare considerable embarrassment. For example, it is the custom among some Asian and European cultures to write the last name first; thus the nurse will be sure to have the client's name correct.

Space, Distance, and Intimacy

Both the client's and nurse's senses of spatial distance are significant in cross-cultural communication, with the perception of appropriate distance zones varying widely among cultural groups. Although there are individual variations in spatial requirements, people of the same culture tend to act similarly. For example, Anglo nurses may find themselves backing away from clients of Hispanic, East Indian, or Middle Eastern origins who seemingly invade the nurse's personal space with regularity in an attempt to bring the nurse closer into the space that is comfortable to them. While nurses may be uncomfortable with the close physical proximity of these clients, the clients are perplexed by the nurse's distancing behaviors and may perceive the nurse as aloof and unfriendly.

Because individuals are not usually consciously aware of their personal space requirements, they frequently have difficulty understanding a different cultural pattern. For example, sitting close may be perceived by one client as an expression of warmth and friendliness but by another as a threatening invasion of personal space. According to Watson (1980), Americans, Canadians, and British require the most personal space, whereas Latin American, Japanese, and Arabs need the least.

Summarized in Table 2-4 are the four distance zones identified for the functional use of space that are embraced by most Anglo-American nurses.

Table 2-4. Functional use of space by Anglo-American nurses

Zone	Remarks
Intimate zone (0 to 1½ ft)	Visual distortion occurs Best for assessing breath and other body odors
Personal distance (1½ to 4 ft)	Perceived as an extension of the self similar to a "bubble" Voice is moderate Body odors inapparent No visual distortion Much of the physical assessment will occur at this distance
Social distance (4 to 12 ft)	Used for impersonal business transactions Perceptual information much less detailed Much of the interview will occur at this distance
Public distance (12+ ft)	Interaction with others impersonal Speaker's voice must be projected Subtle facial expressions imperceptible

Data from E. Hall (1963). Proxemics: The study of man's spatial relations. In I. Gladston (Ed.), *Man's Image in Medicine and Anthropology*, pp. 109–120. New York: International University Press.

Interactions between nurse and client are influenced by the degree of intimacy desired—which may range from very formal interactions to close personal relationships. For example, some Southeast Asian clients expect nurses and other health care providers to be authoritarian, directive, and detached. In seeking health care, some clients of Chinese decent may expect the health care provider to intuitively know what is wrong with them, and nurses may actually lose some credibility by asking a fairly standard interview question such as, "What brings you here?" The Asian parent may be thinking, "Don't you know why I'm here? You're supposed to be the one with all the answers."

The emphasis on social harmony among Asian and Native American clients may prevent the full expression of concerns or feelings. Such reserved behavior may leave the nurse with the impression that the client agrees with or understands the nurse's explanation. Nodding or smiling by Asians may merely reflect their cultural value for interpersonal harmony, not agreement with what has been said by the nurse. Nurses may distinguish between socially compliant client responses aimed at maintaining harmony and genuine concurrence by obtaining validation of assumptions. This may be accomplished by inviting the client to respond frankly to suggestions or by giving the client "permission" to disagree.

In contrast, Appalachian clients traditionally have close family interaction patterns that often lead them to expect close personal relationships with health care providers. The Appalachian client may evaluate the nurse's effectiveness on the basis of interpersonal skills rather than professional competencies. Some Appalachian clients may be uncomfortable with the impersonal, bureaucratic orientation of most health care institutions.

In cultures in which the kiss is used as a form of greeting, it is important to note how and where (one cheek or both, mouth) one kisses. Kissing in traditional Asian cultures is considered to be an intimate sexual act, not permissible in public, whereas kissing in most Western cultures has the meaning of friendship and is considered a form of social greeting (Lapierre and Padgett, 1991).

Those of Latin American or Mediterranean origins often expect a high degree of intimacy and may attempt to involve nurses in their family system by expecting the nurse to participate in personal activities and social functions. These individuals may come to expect personal favors that extend beyond the scope of what most nurses believe to be professional practice and may feel it is their privilege to contact nurses at home during any time of the day or night for care (Lipson and Meleis, 1983; Meleis, Lipson, and Paul, 1992).

Overcoming Communication Barriers

In general, health care providers expect behavior to consist of undemanding compliance, an attitude of respect for the health care provider, and cooperation with requested behavior, especially while in the hospital, clinic, or other health care facility. Although clients may ask a few questions for the purpose of clarification, slight deference to recognized authority figures, i.e., nurses and other health care providers, is often expected. Clients from culturally diverse backgrounds, however, may have significantly different perceptions about the appropriate role of the individual and his or her family when seeking health care. If nurses find themselves becoming annoyed that a client is asking too many questions, assuming a defensive posture, or otherwise feeling uncomfortable, it might be appropriate to pause for a moment to examine the source of the conflict from a transcultural perspective.

During illness, culturally acceptable *sick role behavior* may range from aggressive, demanding behavior to silent passivity. Researchers have found that complaining, demanding behavior during illness is often rewarded with attention among American Jewish and Italian groups, whereas Asian and Native American patients are likely to be quiet and compliant during illness. Children are socialized into these sick role behaviors at early ages.

Many Asian clients may provide the nurse with the answers they think are expected, behavior consistent with the dominant cultural value for harmonious relationships with others. Thus the nurse should attempt to phrase questions or statements in a neutral manner that avoids foreshadowing an expected response. Appalachian clients may reject a nurse whom they perceive as "prying" or "nosey" because of a cultural ethic of neutrality that mandates minding one's own business and avoiding assertive or argumentative behavior.

Nonverbal Communication

Basically, there are five types of nonverbal behaviors that convey information about the client: vocal cues, such as pitch, tone, and quality of voice, including moaning and groaning; action cues, such as posture, facial expression, and gestures; object cues, such as clothes, jewelry, and hair styles; use of personal and territorial space in interpersonal transactions and care of belongings; and touch, which involves the use of personal space and action (Lapierre and Padgett, 1991).

According to Eckman et al. (1987), there is evidence that facial expressions of emotions are universal. Matsumoto (1989) examined the contribution of the eyes to judgment of anger and fear using both American and Japanese faces. In nearly every case, the judgments of anger (raised eyebrows) expressed by Japanese subjects were the same as those expressed by American subjects. Eckman et al. (1987) found high agreement on facial expressions of emotion across 10 different cultures.

Unless nurses make an effort to understand the client's nonverbal behavior, they may overlook important information such as that which is conveyed by facial expressions, silence, eye contact, touch, and other body language. Communication patterns vary widely transculturally even for such conventional social behaviors as smiling and handshaking. Among many Hispanic clients, for example, smiling and handshaking are considered an integral part of sincere interactions and essential to establishing trust, whereas a Russian client might perceive the same behavior by the nurse as insolent and frivolous (Tripp-Reimer and Lauer, 1987).

Wide cultural variation exists when interpreting *silence*. Some individuals find silence extremely uncomfortable and make every effort to fill conversational lags with words. Conversely, many Native Americans consider silence essential to understanding and respecting the other person. A pause following the nurse's question signifies that what has been asked is important enough to be given thoughtful consideration. In traditional Chinese and Japanese cultures, silence may mean that the speaker wishes the listener to consider the content of what has been said before continuing. Other cultural meanings of silence may be found. The English and Arabs may use silence out of respect for another's privacy, whereas the French, Spanish, and Russians may interpret it as a sign of agreement. Asian cultures often use silence to demonstrate respect for elders. Among some African-Americans, silence is used in response to what they perceive is a ridiculous question (Dandy, 1990; Tripp-Reimer and Lauer, 1987).

Eye contact is perhaps among the most culturally variable nonverbal behaviors. Although most nurses have been taught to maintain eye contact when speaking with clients, individuals from culturally diverse backgrounds may attribute other culturally based meanings to this behavior. Asian, Native American, Indochinese, Arab, and Appalachian clients may consider direct eye contact impolite or aggressive, and they may avert their own eyes when talking with the nurse. Native Americans often stare at the floor during conversations, a culturally appropriate behavior indicating that the listener is paying close attention to the speaker. Some African Americans use oculistics (eye rolling) in response to what is perceived to be a ridiculous question. Among Hispanic clients, respect dictates appropriate deferential behavior in the form of downcast eyes toward others on the basis of age, sex, social position, economic status, and position of authority. Elders expect respect from younger individuals, adults from children, men from women, teachers from students, and employers from employees. By virtue of their authority status as health care providers, in the nurse-client relationship with Hispanic clients, eye contact is expected by the nurse but will not necessarily be reciprocated by the client (Dandy, 1990; Lapierre and Padgett, 1991).

In some cultures, including Arab, Hispanic, and African American groups, *modesty for both women and men* is interrelated with eye contact. For Muslim-Arab women, modesty is, in part, achieved by avoiding eye contact with males (except for one's husband) and keeping the eyes downcast when encountering members of the opposite sex in public situations. In many cultures, the only woman who smiles and establishes eye contact with men in public is a prostitute. Hasidic Jewish males also have culturally based norms concerning eye contact with females. Nurses may observe the male avoiding direct eye contact and turning his head in the opposite direction when walking past or speaking to a woman. The preceding examples are intended to be illustrative, not exhaustive.

Nurses are urged to give careful consideration to issues concerning *touch*. While recognizing the benefits reported by many in establishing rapport with clients through touch, including the promotion of healing through therapeutic touch, physical contact with clients conveys various meanings cross-culturally. In many cultures, such as Arab and Hispanic societies, male health care providers may be prohibited from touching or examining either all or certain parts of the female body. Adolescent girls may prefer female health care providers or may actually refuse to be examined by a male. The nurse should be aware that the client's significant others also may exert pressure on nurses by enforcing these culturally meaningful norms in the health care setting.

Touching children also may have associated meaning transculturally. For example, approximately 80 percent of the world's people believe in *mal ojo*, which literally translated means "evil of the eye." In this culture-bound syndrome, the child becomes ill as a result of excessive admiration by another person. Many Asians believe that one's strength resides in the head and that touching the head is a sign of disrespect. Thus nurses need to be aware that patting a child on the head or examining the fontanelles of a Southeast Asian infant should be avoided or done only with parental permission. Whenever possible, nurses should explore alternative ways to express affection or to obtain information necessary for assessment of the client's condition (e.g., hold the child on the lap, observe for other manifestations of increased intracranial pressure or signs of premature fontanelle closure, or place one's hand over the mother's while asking for a description of what she feels).

Sex/Gender Considerations

Violating norms related to appropriate male-female relationships among various cultures may jeopardize the nurse's therapeutic relationship with clients and their families. Among Arab Americans, nurses may find that adult males avoid being alone with members of the opposite sex (except for their wives) and are generally accompanied by one or more male companions when interacting with females. The presence of the companion(s) conveys that the purpose of the interaction is honorable and that no sexual impropriety will occur. Some women of Middle Eastern origin do not shake hands with men, nor do men and women touch each other outside the marital relationship. Given that clients who have recently immigrated are in various stages of assimilation, traditional customs such as these may or may not be practiced. If in doubt, the nurse should ask the client or observe the client's behaviors.

Nonverbal behaviors are culturally very significant, and failure to adhere to the *cultural code* (set of rules or norms of behavior used by a cultural group to guide their behavior and to interpret situations) is viewed as a serious transgression. The best way to ensure that cultural variables have been considered is to ask the client about culturally relevant aspects of male-female relationships, preferably at the time of admission or early in the relationship.

In concluding this section, a brief comment about same-sex relationships will be made. In some cultures, it is considered an acceptable expression of friendship and affection to openly and publicly hold hands with or embrace members of the same sex without any sexual connotation being associated with the behavior. For example, the nurse may note that although a Nigerian American woman may not demonstrate overt affection for her husband or other male family members, she will hold hands with female relatives and friends while walking or talking with them. Nurses may find that clients display similar behaviors toward them and should feel free to discuss cultural differences and similarities openly with the client. The discussion should include how each person feels about the cultural practice and exploration of mutually acceptable— and unacceptable—avenues for communicating.

Language

One of the greatest challenges in cross-cultural communication occurs when the nurse and client speak different languages. When assessing non-English-speaking clients, nurses may find themselves in one of two situations—either struggling to communicate effectively through an interpreter or communicating effectively when there is no interpreter.

Non-English-Speaking Clients. Interviewing the non-English-speaking person requires a bilingual interpreter for full communication. Even the person from another culture or country who has a basic command of English (those for whom English is a second language) may need an interpreter when faced with the anxiety-provoking situation of entering a hospital, encountering a strange symptom, or discussing a sensitive topic such as birth control or gynecologic or urologic concerns. Ideally, a trained medical interpreter should be used. This person knows interpreting techniques, has a health care background, and understands patients' rights. The trained interpreter also is knowledgeable about cultural beliefs and health practices. This person can help the nurse to bridge the cultural gap and can give advice concerning the cultural appropriateness of the nurse's recommendations.

Although the nurse will be in charge of the focus and flow of the interview, the interpreter should be viewed as an important member of the health care team. It is

Nurses must identify the primary decision maker when helping patients to choose among treatment options. In some cultures, the biological parent, especially if young in age, may consult with other family members before making health care decisions affecting children.

tempting to ask a relative, friend, or even another client to interpret because this person is readily available and likely is anxious to help. This violates confidentiality for the client, however, who may not want personal information shared. Furthermore, the friend or relative, though fluent in ordinary language usage, is likely to be unfamiliar with medical terminology, hospital or clinic procedures, and medical ethics.

Whenever possible, work with a bilingual member of the health care team. Ideally, the nurse should ask the interpreter to meet the client before hospitalization to establish rapport and to obtain basic descriptive information about the client such as age, occupation, educational level, and attitude toward health care. This eases the interpreter into the relationship and allows the client to talk about aspects of his or her life that are relatively nonthreatening.

When using an interpreter, the nurse should expect that the interaction with the client will require more time than when caring for English-speaking clients. It will be necessary to organize nursing care so that the most important interactions or procedures are accomplished first, before any of the parties (including the nurse) become fatigued.

There are two styles of interpreting, line-by-line and summarizing. Translating line-by-line ensures accuracy, but it takes more time. Both the nurse and the client should speak only a sentence or two and then allow the interpreter time. The nurse should use simple language, not medical jargon that the interpreter must simplify before it can be translated. Summary translation goes faster and is useful for teaching relatively simple health techniques with which the interpreter is already familiar. Be alert for nonverbal cues as the client talks. This can give valuable data. A skilled interpreter also will note nonverbal messages and pass them on to the nurse.

Summarized in Box 2-2 are suggestions for the selection and use of an interpreter. Although use of an interpreter is the ideal, nurses may find themselves in situations with a non-English-speaking client when no interpreter is available. Box 2-2 also presents some suggestions for overcoming language barriers when there is no interpreter.

Box 2-2. Overcoming Language Barriers

Use of an Interpreter
- Before locating an interpreter, be sure that the language the client speaks at home is known, since it may be different from the language spoken publicly (e.g., French is sometimes spoken by well-educated and upper-class members of certain Asian or Middle Eastern cultures).
- Avoid interpreters from a rival tribe, state, region, or nation (e.g., a Palestinian who knows Hebrew may not be the best interpreter for a Jewish client).
- Be aware of sex/gender differences between interpreter and client. In general, same sex/gender is preferred.
- Be aware of age differences between interpreter and client. In general, an older, more mature interpreter is preferred to a younger, less experienced one.
- Be aware of socioeconomic differences between interpreter and client.
- Ask the interpreter to translate as closely to verbatim as possible.
- An interpreter who is a nonrelative may seek compensation for services rendered.

(continued)

Box 2-2 *(continued)*

Recommendations for Institutions
- Maintain a computerized list of interpreters who may be contacted as needed.
- Network with area hospitals, colleges, universities, and other organizations that may serve as resources.
- Utilize the translation services provided by telephone companies (e.g., American Telephone and Telegraph Company).

What to Do When There Is No Interpreter
- Be polite and formal.
- Greet the person using the last or complete name. Gesture to yourself and say your name. Offer a handshake or nod. Smile.
- Proceed in an unhurried manner. Pay attention to any effort by the patient or family to communicate.
- Speak in a low, moderate voice. Avoid talking loudly. Remember that there is a tendency to raise the volume and pitch of your voice when the listener appears not to understand. The listener may perceive that the nurse is shouting and/or angry.
- Use any words known in the patient's language. This indicates that the nurse is aware of and respects the client's culture.
- Use simple words, such as *pain* instead of *discomfort*. Avoid medical jargon, idioms, and slang. Avoid using contractions. Use nouns repeatedly instead of pronouns. Example: Do *not* say, "He has been taking his medicine, hasn't he?" Do say, "Does Juan take medicine?"
- Pantomime words and simple actions while verbalizing them.
- Give instructions in the proper sequence. Example: Do *not* say, "Before you rinse the bottle, sterilize it." Do say, "First, wash the bottle. Second, rinse the bottle."
- Discuss one topic at a time. Avoid using conjunctions. Example: Do *not* say, "Are you cold and in pain?" Do say, "Are you cold [while pantomiming]?" Are you in pain?"
- Validate if the client understands by having him or her repeat instructions, demonstrate the procedure, or act out the meaning.
- Write out several short sentences in English, and determine the person's ability to read them.
- Try a third language. Many Indo-Chinese speak French. Europeans often know three or four languages. Try Latin words or phrases, if the nurse is familiar with the language.
- Ask who among the client's family and friends could serve as an interpreter.
- Obtain phrase books from a library or bookstore, make or purchase flash cards, contact hospitals for a list of interpreters, and use both formal and informal networking to locate a suitable interpreter.

Adapted from M. Andrews (1992). Transcultural considerations: Crosscultural communication. In C. Jarvis, *Physical Examination and Health Assessment*, p. 75. Philadelphia: W.B. Saunders. Reprinted by permission.

Culture and Nutrition

Perhaps one of the most important factors in promoting, maintaining, and restoring a client's health is the nurse's ability to encourage the intake of the right types and quantities of foods. The degree to which the nurse is successful may make the difference between a rapid return to health and a slow, prolonged recovery or none at all. For centuries, diet has been used by many cultures in the treatment of specific disease conditions, the promotion of health during pregnancy, the fostering of growth and development for infants and children, and even instilling magical hope that the ingestion of certain foods could lead to the prolongation of one's earthly life. Recent research has linked nutritional components to many diseases (heart attack, stroke, ulcers, certain types of cancer), and diet is frequently considered in the prevention and treatment of many physical and emotional disorders.

Dietary Self-Assessment

Before nurses can understand the dietary beliefs and practices of another culture, they must become familiar with their own. One example of dietary cultural bias involves classifying foods according to which are considered edible and which are not. Each person classifies foods into five groups according to whether the food is considered inedible, edible by animals (but not humans), edible by humans (but not my kind), edible by humans (but not by me), and edible by me.

Culture and Food

Culture is a primary influence on how an individual decides which food belongs in which category. For example, clay is sold for consumption in parts of Africa but not in other parts of the world. In France, corn is considered animal feed not fit for human consumption, whereas in the United States, corn is a popular vegetable. Due to religious beliefs, some Jewish, Muslim, and Seventh-Day Adventist clients consider pork inedible, whereas members of many other religions would eat it without hesitation. Eating dog or horse meat is unacceptable to most Anglo-Americans, yet these meats are enjoyed by some people having Asian or African heritage. Foods such as beef and chicken may be enjoyed by the majority of Americans but not by those who follow a vegetarian diet (Kittler and Sucher, 1990).

Stereotypically, members of the Anglo-American culture eat bacon and eggs for breakfast in the morning, sandwiches for lunch (usually between 11:00 A.M. and 1:00 P.M.), and meat and potatoes or rice for supper, some time in the evening. Some cultures make few distinctions between what is served at different meals, and others vary in what foods are considered appropriate. For example, soup is commonly eaten at every meal by Vietnamese, and beans are enjoyed at breakfast, lunch, and supper by many Mexicans. Cheese and olives are popular breakfast foods in the Middle East, and peanut butter is added to many dinner dishes in West Africa (Kittler and Sucher, 1990).

The nurse needs to be aware that the culturally based dietary preferences of clients may necessitate access to specialty food stores. Although many grocery stores in large urban areas carry a variety of ethnic food items that are enjoyed by the population at large, some specialty foods are difficult or impossible for large grocery chains to stock.

Types of food eaten, meal patterns, food preparation, and methods of eating are culturally determined behaviors taught to children by adults.

Often located in ethnic neighborhoods, specialty grocery stores frequently carry products not available elsewhere and serve as a meeting place where members of a particular cultural group can gather—to speak their native language, reminisce about their homeland, and talk about their shared cultural heritage.

Nurses need to be aware that culture determines meal patterns. Asking a client what was eaten at breakfast, lunch, and supper reflects the nurse's ethnocentric bias that three meals are the norm. Among many Native American and Latin American groups, two meals a day are usually eaten. In Spain, four meals a day plus frequent snacks are customary. In some nomadic African tribes, one meal is consumed every other day. Futhermore, what foods constitute a meal may be a factor in diet analysis. For example, in India, a meal is only a meal if rice or another traditional grain food (such as flat bread) is served. Although other foods are eaten in large quantities, they may be considered snacks if no rice or bread is consumed.

Among some African-American groups, particularly in rural southern areas, large quantities of rich foods may be consumed on weekends, while the typical weekday diet is considerably lighter. Many groups tend to feast, often in the company of family and friends, on selected holidays. For example, many Christians eat large dinners on Christmas and Easter and consume other traditional high-calorie, high-fat foods such as seasonal cookies, pastries, and candies. It should be noted that holy days may be celebrated at various times depending on the religious calendar followed. Many Jewish families celebrate selected religious holy days with rich ethnic foods, often eaten in quantities that exceed consumption during the nonholiday period. Nurses need to be familiar with the religious and ethnic calendars of clients from various groups in order to be aware of the influence of religion and culture on diet. This information is especially significant for clients with diabetes, hypertension, and other conditions in which diet plays a key role.

Cultural Meanings of Food

People often use food in building and maintaining human relationships. Food brings people together, promotes common interests, and stimulates the formation of bonds with other people and society. Sharing a meal frequently is a sign of affection and friendship, whereas refusal to eat with someone is reflects anger, hostility, rejection, punishment, or mistrust. It is rare for enemies to share a meal. Box 2-3 presents some examples of the cultural meanings of food.

Body Image, Food, and Culture

Definitions of the ideal body size and shape vary from one culture to another and change with time. Cultural images of ideal body size and methods used to achieve it have been the topic of lively discussion for many years, and the multi-million-dollar diet industry illustrates that much time, energy, and money is spent on people's efforts at achieving the culturally appropriate body build.

Food may be used in the celebration of life events such as birthdays or to promote familial alliances, solidify social ties, express caring, show appreciation, and foster interpersonal closeness among family and friends. Celebration of this teenager's birthday includes the traditional lighting of candles, one for each year of life.

Box 2-3. Selected Examples of Cultural Meanings of Food

Critical life force for survival

Relief of hunger

Peaceful coexistence

Promotion of health and healing

Prevention of disease or illness

Expression of caring for another

Interpersonal closeness or distance

Promotion of kinship and familial alliances

Solidification of social ties

Celebration of life events (e.g., birthday, marriage)

Expression of gratitude or appreciation

Recognition of achievement or accomplishment

Business negotiations

Information exchange

Validation of social, cultural, or religious ceremonial functions

Way to generate income

Expression of affluence, wealth, or social status

In addition to recognizing a group's definitions of ideal weight or size, nurses can benefit from an appreciation of the significance associated with thinness and fatness. Concern with ideal body size and shape begins in infancy. Research indicates that when asked to identify the ideal body size, most Puerto Ricans and Cubans selected a plumper body, whereas the majority of Anglos chose a thinner figure as ideal for infants.

Research has demonstrated that both excessively thin and excessively obese people have increased morbidity and mortality. Obesity, for example, has been shown to increase the risk of heart attack, stroke, hypertension, diabetes, musculoskeletal problems, and others. The hazards facing underweight people are not as well documented but include greater risks from infectious diseases, including tuberculosis.

Religion, Cultural Theories, and Food

As discussed in Chapter 12, cultural food practices are often intertwined with religious dietary restrictions. Many religions use foods as symbols in celebrations and rituals. Knowing the client's religious practices related to food enables the nurse to suggest improvements or modifications that will not conflict with dietary laws. Similarly, cultural dietary beliefs may be interconnected with yin/yang and hot/cold theories, especially during pregnancy and illness.

Buddhist woman remembers deceased relatives on Chinese New Year with fresh fruit and oil, symbolic of the nourishment needed for the spirit journey, and by lighting incense, which rises to the heavens with her prayers.

The nurse should recognize that food itself is only one part of eating. In some cultures, social contacts during meals are restricted to members of the immediate or extended family. The nurse should be aware of the individual's preference, particularly in situations fostering group dining, such as psychiatric/mental health institutions, extended-care facilities, and nursing homes, which sometimes encourage clients to eat in small groups. Traditional group nutrition education also may be inappropriate when it conflicts with cultural restrictions. In some Middle Eastern cultures, men and women eat meals separately, or women may be permitted to eat with their husbands but not with other males. Although certain practices may seem very unusual to the American nurse, it is important that cultural diversity be respected.

Promoting Dietary Change

The nurse should be aware that the degree to which clients from culturally diverse backgrounds adhere to advice concerning dietary change may be less than expected. If a client's values are inconsistent with the underlying rationale for recommended change, the probability of adherence is low. Clients may agree verbally to do something out of courtesy or fear but fail to act on the nurse's recommendations. Limited understanding of a health-related disorder may act as a disincentive for dietary change, particularly when there are no signs or symptoms to relieve. For example, clients with hypertension may perceive no need for a low-sodium diet because the clinical manifestations of disease are absent. The nurse should explain the concept of blood pressure in a culturally meaningful manner and provide a rationale for the recommended dietary modification. Be aware that if the dietary suggestions seem to imply increased cost (e.g., suggesting an increased protein intake), clients from low-income groups may perceive the recommendation as unrealistic, and the nurse may need to teach clients how to achieve the desired goal in a manner that is financially reasonable.

Having realistic expectations will give the nurse a sense of accomplishment and avoid feelings of frustration. Knowledge that an eating practice is harmful does not necessarily promote change in that behavior, as is commonly seen in persons who are obese or who smoke. This is true regardless of the client's cultural background, educational level, socioeconomic status, or religious affiliation. The nurse must balance the clients' rights to determine their own future against the nurse's need to promote change. The goal should be to provide advice and recommendations in a positive and culturally appropriate manner, which encourages learning and promotes behavioral change. The decision to comply with the nurse's advice is up to the client.

Traditional Healers

As discussed in Chapter 1, most cultures have traditional (sometimes referred to as folk or generic) healers, most of whom speak the native tongue of the client, make house calls, and cost significantly less than healers practicing in the biomedical/scientific health care system. In addition, many cultures have lay midwives (e.g., parteras for Hispanic women), doulas (support women for new mothers and babies), or other health care providers available for meeting the needs of pregnant women and newborns.

Traditional healers should be an integral part of the health care team and should be included in as many aspects of the client's care as possible. For example, the nurse might include the traditional healer in obtaining a health history and in determining what treatments already have been used in an effort to bring about healing. When discussing traditional remedies, it is important to be respectful and to listen attentively to women and others who effectively combine spiritual and herbal remedies for a wide variety of illnesses, both physical and psychological in origin. Chapter 12 provides detailed information about the religious beliefs and spiritual healers for major religious groups.

Culture and Symptoms

All symptoms are believed to have cultural meanings. The tendency to interpret symptoms only as manifestations of a biologic reality should be questioned. According to Wenger (1993), nurses should not assume that the perceived symptoms or complaints of clients are equivalent to the names of recognized diseases or syndromes familiar to nurses, physicians, and other professional healers. *Symptoms* are defined as phenomena experienced by individuals that signify a departure from normal function, sensation, or appearance and/or physical aberrations. As individuals experience symptoms, they interpret them and react in ways that are congruent with their cultural norms. Symptoms cannot be attributed to another person; rather, individuals experience symptoms from their knowledge of bodily function and sociocultural interactions. When people experience symptoms, they are perceived, recognized, labeled, reacted to, ritualized, and articulated in ways that make sense within the cultural world view of the person experiencing the symptoms (Good and Good, 1980; Wenger, 1993).

Experientially, symptoms are defined according to the perception of the meaning attributed to the event that is perceived in relation to other sociocultural factors and biologic knowledge. People develop culturally based explanatory models to explain how their illnesses work and what their symptoms mean (Kleinman, Eisenberg, and Good, 1978).

The search for cultural meaning in understanding symptoms involves a translation process that includes the world views of both nurse and client. Nurses need to assess the symptoms within the sociocultural and ethnohistorical context of the client. The nurse should learn the terms clients use for symptoms and the meanings attributed to the specific symptoms. Simultaneously, the nurse must translate the scientific meaning generally attributed to physiologic and psychological data and therapeutic intervention. Through negotiation and analysis, the cultural meanings of the symptoms are restructured in a manner that is congruent with the nurse's professional knowledge so that, ultimately, decisions can be made about culture-congruent nursing care (Wenger, 1993).

Culture-Bound Syndromes

Although all illness may be culturally defined, ethnopsychiatrists and psychological anthropologists have used the term *culture-bound syndromes* when referring to disorders restricted to a particular culture or group of cultures because of certain psychosocial characteristics of those cultures. For example, anorexia nervosa is believed to be a Western culture-bound syndrome because the condition is largely confined to Western cultures or those non-Western cultures undergoing the process of Westernization, such as Japan. Culture-bound syndromes are thought to be illnesses created by personal, social, and cultural reactions to malfunctioning biologic or psychological processes and can only be understood within defined contexts of meaning and social relationships (Kleinman, 1980). Table 2-5 summarizes selected culture-bound syndromes found in specific ethnic/cultural groups.

Biocultural Variations in Health and Illness

The purpose of this discussion is to identify selected biocultural variations that sometimes are found in clients from various cultural backgrounds. Accurate assessment and evaluation of clients require knowledge of normal biocultural variations that are found

Table 2-5. Selected culture-bound syndromes

Group	Disorder	Remarks
Whites	Anorexia nervosa	Excessive preoccupation with thinness; self-imposed starvation
	Bulimia	Gross overeating and then vomiting or fasting
African Americans/Haitians	Blackout	Collapse, dizziness, inability to move
	Low blood	Not enough blood or weakness of the blood that is often treated with diet
	High blood	Blood that is too rich in certain things due to ingestion of too much red meat or rich foods
	Thin blood	Occurs in women, children, and old people; renders the individual more susceptible to illness in general
	Diseases of hex, witchcraft, or conjuring	Sense of being doomed by spell; gastrointestinal symptoms, e.g., vomiting; hallucinations; part of voodoo beliefs
Chinese/S. E. Asian	Koro	Intense anxiety that penis is retracting into body
Greeks	Hysteria	Bizarre complaints and behavior because the uterus leaves the pelvis for another part of the body
Hispanics	Empacho	Food forms into a ball and clings to the stomach or intestines causing pain and cramping
	Fatigue	Asthma-like symptoms
	Mal ojo, "evil eye"	Fitful sleep, crying, diarrhea in children caused by a stranger's attention; sudden onset
	Pasmo	Paralysis-like symptoms of face or limbs; prevented or relieved by massage
	Susto	Anxiety, trembling, phobias from sudden fright
Native Americans	Ghost	Terror, hallucinations, sense of danger
North India Indians	Ghost	Death from fever and illness in children; convulsions, delirious speech (or incessant crying in infants); choking, difficulty breathing; based on Hindu religious beliefs and curing practices
Japanese	Wagamama	Apathetic childish behavior with emotional outbursts
Korean	Hwa-byung	Multiple somatic and psychological symptoms; "pushing up" sensation of chest; palpitations, flushing, headache, "epigastric mass," dysphoria, anxiety, irritability, and difficulty concentrating; mostly afflicts married women

among healthy members of selected populations and assessment skills that enable the nurse to recognize variations that occur in illness. The following remarks are intended to be illustrative, not exhaustive. As more research on biocultural variations is conducted, undoubtedly there will be additions and perhaps some modifications.

General Appearance

The assessment of general appearance consists of a survey of the whole person covering general health state and any obvious physical characteristics such as the skin color and other overt, readily apparent biocultural variations. In assessing the client's general appearance, the nurse should consider four areas: physical appearance, body structure, mobility, and behavior. The *physical appearance* includes age, sex, level of consciousness, facial features, and skin color (evenness of color tone, pigmentation, intactness, presence of lesions or other abnormalities). *Body structure* includes stature, nutrition, symmetry, posture, position, and body build/contour. *Assessment of mobility* includes gait and range of motion. *Behavior* includes facial expression, mood and affect, speech, fluency of speech, ability to communicate ideas, appropriateness of word choice, and dress. With respect to dress, it should be noted that some members of selected ethnoreligious groups wear characteristic clothing that may suggest to the nurse that further assessment of cultural beliefs and practices is warranted. The nurse will readily recognize the outward appearance of ethnic and/or religious affiliation by the client's dress for the following groups: Amish wear characteristic clothing similar to that worn during the 19th century; some women from India wear saris; some Muslim-Arab men wear kafias (headdress) and long robes (*Note:* the same individual may wear Western-style clothing on other occasions); and members of the Church of Jesus Christ of Latter-Day Saints (Mormons) may wear special underwear called temple garments. Although dress or clothing suggests a particular ethnic and/or religious affiliation, the nurse should avoid stereotyping individual clients and explore the meaning of the dress, along with other ethnoreligious beliefs and practices, with the client and/or significant others.

Body Proportions, Height, and Weight

Biocultural variations are found in the body proportions of individuals, largely due to differences in bone length. In general, white males are 1.27 cm (0.5 in) taller than African-American males, whereas White and African-American women are, on average, the same height. Sitting/standing height ratios reveal that African Americans of both sexes have longer legs and shorter trunks than whites. Because proportionately most of the weight is in the trunk, white men appear more obese than African-American men. This characteristic is reversed for women. Clients of Asian heritage are markedly shorter, weight less, and have smaller body frames. Despite their longer legs, African-American women are consistently heavier than white women at every age, with African-American women carrying an average of 9.1 kg (20 lb) more than white women between the ages of 35 to 64 years (Overfield, 1985).

Bone length, as revealed by stature, shows definite biocultural differences, with African Americans having longer legs and arms than whites. Asians and Native Americans have, on average, longer trunks and shorter limbs than whites. African Americans tend to be wide-shouldered and narrow-hipped, whereas Asians tend to be wide-hipped and narrow-shouldered. Shoulder width is largely produced by the clavicle. Because the clavicle is a long bone, this explains why taller patients have wide shoulders, whereas shorter clients have narrower shoulders.

It is well known that children of migrants to this country are taller than counterparts in their country of origin. For example, Japanese Americans residing in Hawaii are taller than those Japanese living in Japan. Although the sitting/standing height ratio is the same, Italians in California are 3.8 cm (1.5 in) taller than those of the same age living in Italy (Hulse, 1968; Overfield, 1985). This indicates that the increase in height occurs in both the long bones and the spine.

The height increase in migrants is theorized to be the result of two factors: (1) better nutrition in the United States and (2) decreased interference with growth from infectious diseases during the formative years. Furthermore, the overall height of Americans increased 1.8 cm (0.7 in) for men and 1.3 cm (0.5 in) for women during a 10-year period.

There are also biocultural differences in the amount of body fat and the distribution of fat throughout the body. In general, individuals from the lower class are more obese than those from the middle class, who are more obese than members of the upper class. In addition to socioeconomic considerations, African Americans tend to have smaller (1 mm) skinfold thicknesses in their arms than whites, but the distribution of fat on the trunk is similar.

Skin

An accurate and comprehensive examination of the skin of clients from culturally diverse backgrounds requires that the nurse possess knowledge of biocultural variations and skill in recognizing color changes, some of which may be very subtle. Awareness of normal biocultural differences and the ability to recognize the unique clinical manifestations of disease are especially important for darkly pigmented clients.

The assessment of a client's skin is subjective and highly dependent on the nurse's observational skill, ability to recognize subtle color changes, and repeated exposure to individuals having various gradations of skin color. *Melanin* is responsible for the various colors and tones of skin observed among people from culturally diverse backgrounds. Melanin protects the skin against harmful ultraviolet rays, a genetic advantage accounting for the lower incidence of skin cancer among darkly pigmented African-American and Native American clients.

Normal skin color ranges widely, and there are health care practitioners who have made attempts to describe the variations seen by labeling observations with some of the following adjectives—*copper, olive, tan,* and various shades of *brown* (*light, medium,* and *dark*). In observing pallor in clients, the term *ashen* is sometimes used. Of most clinical significance, particularly for clients whose health condition may be linked to changes in the skin color, is the nurse's ability to note a baseline color and to recognize variations that occur in the same individual.

Mongolian spots, irregular areas of deep-blue pigmentation, are usually located in the sacral and gluteal areas but sometimes occur on the abdomen, thighs, shoulders, or arms. During embryonic development, the melanocytes originate in the neural crest (near to the embryonic nervous system) and migrate into the fetal epidermis. Mongolian spots resemble neurons with dendritic appendages that insert themselves well up into the epidermal cells. Embryonic pigment leftovers, Mongolian spots are located at an epidermal depth greater than ordinary and give the skin a bluish coloration.

Mongolian spots are a normal variation in children of African, Asian, or Latin descent. By adulthood, these spots become lighter but are frequently still visible. Mongolian spots are present in 90 percent of African Americans, 80 percent of Asian and Native Americans, and 9 percent of whites. If the nurse is unfamiliar with Mongolian spots, it is important to exercise caution so that they are not confused with bruises. Recognition of this normal variation is particularly important when dealing with children who might be erroneously identified as victims of child abuse.

Vitiligo, a condition in which the melanocytes become nonfunctional in some areas of the skin, is characterized by unpigmented skin patches. Vitiligo affects more than 2 million Americans, primarily dark-skinned individuals. Clients with vitiligo also have a statistically higher than normal chance of developing pernicious anemia, diabetes mellitus, and hyperthyroidism. These factors are believed to reflect an underlying genetic abnormality.

Other areas of the skin affected by hormones and, in some cases, differing for culturally diverse clients are the sexual skin areas, such as the nipples, areola, scrotum, and labia majora. In general, these areas are darker than other parts of the skin in both adults and children, especially among African-American and Asian clients. When assessing these skin surfaces on dark-skinned clients, the nurse must observe carefully for erythema, rashes, and other abnormalities because the darker color may mask their presence.

Cyanosis is the most difficult clinical sign to observe in darkly pigmented persons. Because peripheral vasoconstriction can prevent cyanosis, the nurse needs to be attentive to environmental conditions such as air conditioning, mist tents, and other factors that may lower the room temperature and thus cause vasoconstriction. In order for the client to manifest clinical evidence of cyanosis, the blood must contain 5 g of reduced hemoglobin in 1.5 g of methemoglobin per 100 ml of blood.

Given that most conditions causing cyanosis also cause decreased oxygenation of the brain, other clinical symptoms, such as changes in the level of consciousness, will be evident. Cyanosis usually is accompanied by increased respiratory rate, use of accessory muscles of respiration, nasal flaring, and other manifestations of respiratory distress. The nurse must exercise caution when assessing persons of Mediterranean descent for cyanosis because their circumoral region is normally dark blue.

Jaundice

In both light- and dark-skinned clients, *jaundice* is best observed in the sclera. When examining culturally diverse individuals, caution must be exercised to avoid confusing other forms of pigmentation with jaundice. Many darkly pigmented people, e.g., African Americans, Filipino Americans, and others, have heavy deposits of subconjunctival fat that contains high levels of carotene in sufficient quantities to mimic jaundice. The fatty deposits become more dense as the distance from the cornea increases. The portion of the sclera that is revealed naturally by the palpebral fissure is the best place to accurately assess color. If the palate does not have heavy melanin pigmentation, jaundice can be detected there in the early stages (i.e., when the serum bilirubin level is 2–4 mg/100 ml). The absence of a yellowish tint of the palate when the sclerae are yellow indicates carotene pigmentation of the sclerae rather than jaundice. Light- or clay-colored stools and dark golden urine often accompany jaundice in both light- and dark-skinned clients. If the nurse is to distinguish between carotenemia and jaundice, it will be necessary to inspect the posterior portion of the hard palate using bright daylight or good artificial lighting.

Pallor

When assessing for *pallor* in darkly pigmented clients, the nurse may experience difficulty because the underlying red tones that give brown or black skin its luster are absent. The brown-skinned individual will manifest pallor with a more yellowish brown color, and the black-skinned person will appear ashen or gray. Generalized pallor can be observed in the mucous membranes, lips, and nail beds. The palpebrae, conjunctivae, and nail beds are preferred sites for assessing the pallor of anemia. When inspecting the conjunctiva, the nurse should lower the lid sufficiently to visualize the conjunctiva near the outer canthus as well as the inner canthus. The coloration is often lighter near the inner canthus.

In addition to skin assessment, the pallor of impending shock is accompanied by other clinical manifestations, such as increasing pulse rate, oliguria, apprehension, and restlessness. Anemias, particularly chronic iron-deficiency anemia, may be manifest by the characteristic "spoon" nails, which have a concave shape. A lemon-yellow tint of the face and slightly yellow sclerae accompany pernicious anemia, which is also manifested by neurologic deficits and a red, painful tongue. The nurse also will note the following symptoms in the presence of most severe anemias: fatigue, exertional dyspnea, rapid pulse, dizziness, and impaired mental function.

Erythema

The nurse may find that it is difficult to assess *erythema* (redness) in darkly pigmented clients. Erythema is frequently associated with localized inflammation and is characterized by increased skin temperature. The degree of redness is determined by the quantity of blood present in the subpapillary plexus, whereas the warmth of the skin is related to the rate of blood flow through the blood vessels. When assessing inflammation in dark-skinned clients, it is often necessary to palpate the skin for increased warmth, tautness or tightly pulled surfaces that may be indicative of edema, and hardening of deep tissues or blood vessels. The nurse will find that the dorsal surfaces of the fingers will be the most sensitive to temperature sensations. The erythema associated with rashes is not always accompanied by noticeable increases in skin temperature. Macular, papular, and vesicular skin lesions are identified by a combination of palpation and inspection, combined with the client's description of symptoms. For example, persons with macular rashes usually will complain of itching, and evidence of scratching will be apparent. When the skin is only moderately pigmented, a macular rash may become recognizable if the skin is gently stretched. Stretching the skin decreases the normal red tone, thus providing more contrast and making the macules appear brighter. In some skin disorders with generalized rash, the nurse will observe that the hard and soft palates are the locations where the rash is most readily visible.

The increased redness that accompanies carbon monoxide poisoning and the blood disorders collectively known as the *polycythemias* can be observed in the lips of dark-skinned clients. Because lipstick masks the actual color of the lips, the nurse should ask the client to remove it prior to inspection.

Petechiae

In dark-skinned clients, *petechiae* are best visualized in the areas of lighter melanization, such as the abdomen, buttocks, and volar surface of the forearm. When the skin is black or very dark brown, petechiae cannot be seen in the skin. Most of the diseases that cause bleeding and microembolism formation, such as thrombocytopenia, subacute bacterial endocarditis, and other septicemias, are characterized by the presence of petechiae in the mucous membranes as well as the skin. The nurse will find that petechiae are most easily visualized in the mouth, particularly the buccal mucosa, and in the conjunctiva of the eye.

In assessing *ecchymotic lesions* caused by systemic disorders, the nurse will note that they are found in the same locations as petechiae, although their larger size makes them more apparent on dark-skinned individuals. When differentiating petechiae and ecchymoses from erythema in the mucous membrane, pressure on the tissue will momentarily blanch erythema but not petechiae or ecchymoses.

Musculoskeletal System

The nurse will note that many normal biocultural variations are found in clients' musculoskeletal systems. The long bones of African Americans are significantly longer, narrower, and denser than those of whites (Farrally and Moore, 1975). Bone density by race and sex reveal that African-American males have the densest bones, thus accounting for the relatively low incidence of osteoporosis in this population. Bone density in the Chinese, Japanese, and Eskimos is below that of white Americans (Garn, 1964).

Curvature of the body's long bones varies widely among culturally diverse groups. Native Americans have anteriorly convex femurs, whereas African Americans have markedly straight femurs, and whites are intermediate. This characteristic is related to both genetics and body weight. Thin African Americans and whites have less curvature than average, whereas obese African Americans and whites display increased curvatures. It is possible that the heavier density of the bones of African Americans helps to protect them from increased curvature due to obesity. Table 2-6 summarizes reported biocultural variations occurring in the musculoskeletal system.

Thorax

Biocultural differences in the size of the thoracic cavity significantly influence pulmonary functioning, as determined by vital capacity and forced expiratory volume (Oscherwitz, 1972; Lapp, 1974). In descending order, the largest chest volumes are found in whites, African Americans, Asians, and Native Americans. Even when the shorter height of Asians is considered, their chest volume remains significantly lower than that of whites and African Americans.

Table 2-6. Biocultural variations in the musculoskeletal system

Component	Remarks
Bone	
Frontal	Thicker in African-American males than in white males
Parietal occiput	Thicker in white males than in African-American males
Palate	Tori (protuberances) along the suture line of the hard palate
	Problematic for denture wearers
	Incidence:
	African Americans 20%
	Whites 24%
	Asians Up to 50%
	Native Americans Up to 50%
Mandible	Tori (protuberances) on the lingual surface of the mandible near the canine and premolar teeth
	Problematic for denture wearers
	Most common in Asians and Native Americans; exceeds 50% in some Eskimo groups
Humerus	Torsion or rotation of proximal end with muscle pull
	Whites > African Americans
	Torsion in African Americans is symmetrical; torsion in whites tends to be greater on right than left side
Radius	Length at the wrist variable
Ulna	Ulna or radius may be longer
	Equal length
	Swedes 61%
	Chinese 16%
	Ulna longer than radius
	Swedes 16%
	Chinese 48%
	Radius longer than ulna
	Swedes 23%
	Chinese 10%
Vertebrae	Twenty-four vertebrae are found in 85 to 93% of all people; racial and sex differences reveal 23 or 25 vertebrae in select groups
	Vertebrae Population
	23 11% of African-American females
	25 12% of Eskimo and Native American males
	Related to lower back pain and lordosis
Pelvis	Hip width is 1.6 cm (0.6 in) smaller in African-American women than in white women; Asian women have significantly smaller pelvises
Femur	Convex anterior Native American
	Straight African American
	Intermediate White
Second tarsal	Second toe longer than the great toe
	Incidence:
	Whites 8–34%
	African Americans 8–12%
	Vietnamese 31%
	Melanesians 21–57%
	Clinical significance for joggers and athletes
Height	White males are 1.27 cm (0.5 in) taller than African-American males and 7.6 cm (2.9 in) taller than Asian males
	White females = African-American females
	Asian females are 4.14 cm (1.6 in) shorter than white or African-American females
Composition of long bones	Longer, narrower, and denser in African Americans than in whites; bone density in whites > Chinese, Japanese, and Eskimos
	Osteoporosis lowest in African-American males; highest in white females

Table 2-6 (*continued*)

Component	Remarks
Muscle	
Peroneus tertius	Responsible for dorsiflexion of foot
	Muscle absent:
	Asians, Native Americans, and whites — 3–10%
	African Americans — 10–15%
	Berbers (Sahara desert) — 24%
	No clinical significance because the tibialis anterior also dorsiflexes the foot
Palmaris longus	Responsible for wrist flexion
	Muscle absent:
	Whites — 12–20%
	Native Americans — 2–12%
	African Americans — 5%
	Asians — 3%
	No clinical significance because three other muscles are also responsible for flexion

Based on data reported by T. Overfield (1985). *Biologic Variation in Health and Illness: Race, Age, and Sex Differences.* Menlo Park, CA: Addison-Wesley.

Hair

Perhaps one of the most obvious and widely variable cultural differences occurs with assessment of the hair. African Americans' hair varies widely in texture. It is very fragile and ranges from long and straight to short, spiraled, thick, and kinky. The hair and scalp have a natural tendency to be dry and require daily combing, gentle brushing, and the application of oil. By comparison, clients of Asian backgrounds generally have straight, silky hair.

Obtaining a baseline hair assessment is significant in diagnosing and treating certain disease states. For example, hair texture is known to become dry, brittle, and lusterless with inadequate nutrition. The hair of African-American children with severe malnutrition, as in the case of marasmus, frequently changes not only in texture but also in color. The child's hair often becomes straighter and turns a reddish copper color. Certain endocrine disorders are also known to affect the texture of hair.

Eyes

Biocultural differences in both the structure and color of the eyes are readily apparent among clients from various cultural backgrounds. Racial differences are evident when examining the palpebral fissures. Persons of Asian background are often identified by their characteristic epicanthal eye folds, whereas the presence of narrowed palpebral fissures in non-Asian individuals may be diagnostic of a serious congenital anomaly known as *Down's syndrome* or *trisomy 21*.

There is culturally based variability in the color of the iris and in retinal pigmentation, with darker irises having darker retinas behind them. Individuals with light retinas generally have better night vision but can suffer pain in an environment that is too light. The majority of African Americans and Asians have brown eyes, whereas many individuals of Scandinavian descent have blue eyes. The nurse needs to be sensitive to the illumination of rooms and to the discomfort that bright lights might cause (Overfield, 1985).

Ears

Ears come in a variety of sizes and shapes. Earlobes can be free-standing or attached to the face. Ceruminous glands are located in the external ear canal and are functional at birth. Cerumen is genetically determined and comes in two major types: (1) dry cerumen, which is gray, flaky, and frequently forms a thin mass in the ear canal, and (2) wet cerumen, which is dark brown and moist. Asians and Native Americans (including Eskimos) have an 84 percent frequency of dry cerumen, whereas African Americans have a 99 percent and whites have a 97 percent frequency of wet cerumen (Overfield, 1985). The clinical significance of this occurs when examining or irrigating the ears. The nurse should be aware that the presence and composition of cerumen are not related to poor hygiene, and caution should be exercised to avoid mistaking the flaky, dry cerumen for the dry lesions of eczema.

Mouth

Cleft uvula, a condition in which the uvula is split either completely or partially, occurs in 18 percent of some Native American groups and 10 percent of Asians. The occurrence in whites and African Americans is rare. *Cleft lip* and *cleft palate* are most common in Asians and Native Americans and least common in African Americans (Emanuel, 1971; Overfield, 1985).

Leukoedema, a grayish white benign lesion occurring on the buccal mucosa, is present in 68 to 90 percent of blacks but only 43 percent of whites (Martin and Crump, 1972). Care should be taken to avoid mistaking leukoedema for oral thrush or related infections that require treatment with medication.

Oral hyperpigmentation also shows variation by race. Usually absent at birth, hyperpigmentation increases with age. By age 50 years, 10 percent of whites and 50 to 90 percent of African Americans will show oral hyperpigmentation, a condition that is believed to be caused by a lifetime of accumulation of postinflammatory oral changes (Overfield, 1985; Wasserman, 1974).

Teeth

Because teeth are often used as indicators of developmental, hygienic, and nutritional adequacy, the nurse should be aware of biocultural differences. While it is rare for a white baby to be born with teeth (1 in 3000), the incidence rises to 1 in 11 among Tlingit Indians and to 1 or 2 in 100 among Canadian Eskimo infants (Jarvis and Gorlin, 1972). Although congenital teeth are usually not problematic, extraction is necessary for some breast-fed infants.

The size of teeth varies widely, with the teeth of whites being the smallest, followed by blacks and then Asians and Native Americans. The largest teeth are found among Eskimos and Australian Aborigines (Overfield, 1985). Larger teeth cause some groups to have prognathic, or protruding, jaws, a condition that is seen more frequently in

African and Asian Americans. The condition is normal and does not reflect an ortho-dontic problem.

Agenesis (absence) of teeth varies by race, with absence of the third molar occurring in 18 to 35 percent of Asians, 9 to 25 percent of whites, and 1 to 11 percent of African Americans (Brothwell, Carbonell, and Goose, 1963). Throughout life, whites have more tooth decay than African Americans, which may be related to socioeconomic status as much as to biocultural variation. Complete tooth loss occurs more often in whites than in African Americans despite the higher incidence of periodontal disease in African Americans. Approximately one-third of whites 45 years or older have lost all their teeth, compared with 25 percent of African Americans in the same age group (Kelly, VanKirk, and Garst, 1967).

The differences in tooth decay between African Americans and whites can be explained by the fact that African Americans have harder and denser tooth enamel, which makes their teeth less susceptible to the organisms that cause caries. The increase in periodontal disease among African Americans is believed to be caused by poor oral hygiene. When obvious signs of periodontal disease are present, such as bleeding and edematous gums, a dental referral should be initiated.

Mammary Venous Plexus

Regardless of gender, the superficial veins of the chest form a network over the entire chest that flows in either a transverse or a longitudinal pattern. In the transverse pattern, the veins radiate laterally and toward the axillae. In the longitudinal pattern, the veins radiate downward and laterally like a fan. These two patterns occur with different frequencies in the two populations that have been studied. White women have the recessive longitudinal pattern 6 to 10 percent of the time, whereas this pattern occurs 30 percent of the time in Navajos. The only known alteration of either pattern is produced by breast tumor (Spuhler, 1950). Although this variation has no clinical significance, it is mentioned so that if nurses note its presence during physical assessment, they will recognize it as a nonsignificant finding.

Secretions

The *apocrine* and *eccrine sweat glands* are important for fluid balance and for thermo-regulation. Approximately 2 to 3 million glands open onto the skin surface through pores and are responsible for the presence of sweat. When contaminated by normal skin flora, odor results. Most Asians and Native Americans have a mild to absent body odor, whereas whites and African Americans tend to have strong body odor.

Eskimos have made an interesting environmental adaptation whereby they sweat less than whites on their trunks and extremities but more on their faces. This adaptation allows for temperature regulation without causing perspiration and dampness of their clothes, which would decrease their ability to insulate against severe weather and would pose a serious threat to their survival.

The amount of chloride excreted by sweat glands varies widely, and African Americans have lower salt concentrations in their sweat than do whites. A study of Ashkenazi Jews (European descent) and Sephardic Jews (North African and Middle Eastern descent) revealed that those of European origin had a lower percentage of sweat chlorides (Levin, 1966). This variation may be significant when caring for clients with renal or cardiac conditions or with children having cystic fibrosis.

Laboratory Tests

The nurse should be aware that biocultural variations occur with some laboratory tests, such as measurement of *hemoglobin/hematocrit, serum cholesterol, serum transferrin*, and *two amniotic fluid constituents*. The normal *hemoglobin level* for African Americans is 1 g lower than for other groups, a factor that should be considered in the treatment of anemia. Data indicate that Native Americans, Hispanics, Asian Americans, and whites do not differ.

The difference between African Americans and whites with respect to *serum cholesterol* is quite interesting. At birth, African Americans and whites have similar serum cholesterol levels, but during childhood, African Americans have higher serum cholesterol levels than whites (5 mg/100 ml). These differences reverse during adulthood, when African-American adults have lower serum cholesterol levels than white adults. The Pima Indians have considerably lower serum cholesterol levels than whites both during childhood (20 to 30 mg/100 ml lower) and adulthood (50 to 60 mg/100 ml lower).

In a study of children 1 to 3¹/₂ years of age, *serum transferrin* levels were found to differ between white and African-American children. The mean values for serum transferrin ranged from 200 to 400 mg/100 ml, with white children having a mean value of 319.7 and African-American children a mean of 341.4. The higher serum transferrin levels in African-American children may be due to their lowered hemoglobin/hematocrit levels (Ritchie, 1979). Transferrin levels increase in the presence of anemia. If the hemoglobin/hematocrit levels are normally lower in African Americans, then higher transferrin levels should be considered normal (Overfield, 1985).

The *lecithin/sphingomyelin ratio* is a laboratory measurement of the amniotic fluid that indicates fetal pulmonary maturation. The ratio is used to calculate the risk of respiratory distress syndrome in premature infants. This ratio differs between blacks and whites, as does the pulmonary maturity it predicts (Olowe and Akinkugbe, 1978). African Americans have higher ratios than whites from 23 to 42 weeks of gestation. Lung maturity, measured by a lecithin/sphingomyelin ratio of 2.0, is reached 1 week earlier in African Americans than in whites, i.e., at 34 versus 35 weeks. The risk of respiratory distress syndrome is 40 to 50 percent for a ratio score between 1.5 and 1.9 for premature white infants but not for premature African-American infants. Premature infants of African-American heritage have a much lower risk of respiratory distress syndrome at the same low ratio scores. When the lecithin/sphingomyelin ratio is determined before induction of labor or elective cesarean section, the racial difference should be considered in making the decision (Overfield, 1985).

Ethnopharmacology

Ethnic differences in drug response and metabolism have been identified by numerous researchers. The majority of studies providing evidence for transcultural differences in pharmacokinetic and pharmacodynamic properties of various drugs have compared individuals of Asian, African-American (Lin, 1986: Wood and Zhou, 1991), Hispanic, and Native American descent (Mendoza, et al., 1991) with whites.

Differences in pharmacokinetics may be genetic or may be due to environmental influences. Among African-American and white individuals, only about 9 percent are considered to be slow metabolizers, whereas 32 percent of Asians are. There also is evidence of variability in protein binding based on ethnicity. Finally, habits such as smoking and drinking alcohol are known to speed drug metabolism, while a low-protein, high-carbohydrate diet is known to slow metabolism. The fact that whites and African Americans drink significantly more alcohol than Asians and eat differently may provide an environmental explanation for the greater drug impact experienced by Asian clients.

According to Lefley (1990), African-American clients are significantly misdiagnosed as psychotic, viewed as more violent by staff, and spend more time in seclusion than whites, Hispanics, or Asians. Thus the actual dose of medication prescribed for African-American clients may be more a function of staff perception than a decision based on serum levels or clinical observations (Keltner and Folks, 1992).

According to Lin (1986), Asians in general and Chinese clients in particular require significantly smaller doses of neuroleptics, tricyclic antidepressants (TCAs), and lithium than do whites, sometimes one-half the dose. Similar differences have been reported between Indian or Pakistani clients and white clients.

Perception of Side Effects

Research indicates that Asian clients are more sensitive to neuroleptics than are whites. In one study, Asian clients began experiencing extrapyramidal effects at dosages approximately one-half that administered to whites. At equivalent doses, 95 percent of Asians experienced extrapyramidal effects, whereas only 67 percent of whites and African Americans experienced those side effects. Hispanic clients taking TCAs experienced side effects at half the dosage observed in whites. African Americans are more susceptible to TCA delirium than Whites (Keltner and Folks, 1992).

Culture and Level of "Compliance"

Comparing three subgroups from Southeast Asia (Hmong, Cambodian, and Laotian), the client's failure to take the medication as prescribed accounted for changes in plasma levels in approximately one-half the subjects in a study by Kroll et al. (1990). Thus cultural influences were concluded to account for a significant degree of "noncompliance." Members of some ethnic groups may perceive that medication should have a short-term effect and are not culturally conditioned to continue medication that does not produce an immediate response (Keltner and Folks, 1992; Kroll et al., 1990).

A less empirical but real consideration is the issue of the client's confidence and trust in the health care provider. Based on a combination of historical fact and myth, some Hispanic clients do not have confidence nor trust in white health care providers. Other cultural considerations, such as traditional beliefs and practices, undoubtedly influence "compliance" (Keltner and Folks, 1992; Mendoza et al., 1991).

Culture and Disease Prevalence

According to the U.S. Department of Health and Human Services' *Healthy People 2000* report (USDHHS, 1992), for the past generation, the United States as a whole has enjoyed improvement in the health status of its people. Despite this fact, there continues to be disparity in deaths and illnesses experienced by members of the federally defined racial/ethnic minority populations. It is well known that diseases are not distributed equally among all segments of the population but rather tend to cluster around certain racial and ethnic subgroups. Knowledge of abnormal biocultural variations occurring with increased incidence among members of various cultural groups or subgroups is important because nurses are able to focus their assessment according to the increased statistical probability that a particular condition may occur. For example, if the nurse is examining an African-American child with gastrointestinal symptoms of flatulence and diarrhea, he or she may focus more on the possibility of lactose intolerance or sickle cell anemia, while considering cystic fibrosis, known primarily among white children, a much less likely source of the problem. Thus, in conducting a systematic health assessment of the client, nurses will want to be certain that they have gathered the appropriate biocultural data.

The distribution of selected genetic traits and disorders prevalent among children from selected cultural groups is discussed in Chapter 4. Table 2-7 provides an alphabetical listing of selected diseases and their increased or decreased incidence among members of certain cultural groups.

Clinical Decision Making and Nursing Actions

After comprehensive cultural assessment and physical examination have been completed, the nurse is ready for clinical decision making and nursing actions. Leininger (1991a) suggests three major modalities to guide nursing judgments, decisions, and actions for the purpose of providing culturally congruent care that is beneficial, satisfying, and meaningful to the people nurses serve. The three modes are *cultural preservation and/or maintenance, cultural care accommodation and/or negotiation*, and *cultural care repatterning and/or restructuring*.

Cultural preservation and/or maintenance refers to "those assistive, supporting, facilitative, or enabling professional actions and decisions that help people of a particular

Table 2-7. Biocultural aspects of disease

Disease	Remarks
Alcoholism	Indians have double the rate of whites; lower tolerance to alcohol among Chinese and Japanese Americans
Anemia	High incidence among Vietnamese due to presence of infestations among immigrants and low iron diets; low hemoglobin and malnutrition found among 18.2% of Native Americans, 32.7% of blacks, 14.6% of Hispanics, and 10.4% of white children under 5 years of age
Arthritis	Increased incidence among Native Americans Blackfoot 1.4% Pima 1.8% Chippewa 6.8%
Asthma	Six times greater for Native American infants <1 year; same as general population for Native Americans, ages 1–44 years

Table 2-7 (continued)

Disease	Remarks
Bronchitis	Six times greater for Native American infants <1 year; same as general population for Native Americans, ages 1–44 years

Cancer	Nasopharyngeal: High among Chinese Americans and Native Americans
	Esophageal: No. 2 cause of death for black males aged 35–54 years
	Incidence:
	   White males 3.5/100,000
	   Black males 13.3/100,000
	Liver: Highest among all ethnic groups are Filipino Hawaiians
	Stomach: Black males twice as likely as white males; low among Filipinos
	Cervical: 120% higher in black females than in white females
	Uterine: 53% lower in black females than white females
	Most prevalent cancer among Native Americans: biliary, nasopharyngeal, testicular, cervical, renal, and thyroid (females) cancer
	Lung cancer among Navajo uranium miners 85 times higher than among white miners
	Most prevalent cancer among Japanese Americans: esophageal, stomach, liver, and biliary cancer
	Among Chinese Americans, there is a higher incidence of nasopharyngeal and liver cancer than among the general population

Cholecystitis	*Incidence:*
	   Whites 0.3%
	   Puerto Ricans 2.1%
	   Native Americans 2.2%
	   Chinese 2.6%

Colitis	High incidence among Japanese Americans
Diabetes mellitus	Three times as prevalent among Filipino Americans as whites; higher among Hispanics than blacks or whites Death rate is 3–4 times as high among Native Americans aged 25–34 years, especially those in the West such as Utes, Pimas, and Papagos *Complications* Amputations: Twice as high among Native Americans vs. General U.S. population Renal failure: 20 times as high as general U.S. population, with tribal variation, e.g., Utes have 43 times higher incidence
G6PD	Present among 30% of black males
Hepatitis	12% of Vietnames refugees are hepatitis-B surface antigen carriers
Influenza	Increased death rate among Native Americans ages 45+
Ischemic heart disease	Responsible for 32% of heart-related causes of death among Native Americans
Lactose intolerance	Present among 66% of Hispanic women; increased incidence among blacks and Chinese
Myocardial infarction	Leading cause of heart disease in Native Americans, accounting for 43% of death from heart disease; low incidence among Japanese Americans
Otitis media	7.9% incidence among school-aged Navajo children vs. 0.5% in whites Up to 1/3 of Eskimo children <2 yrs have chronic otitis media Increased incidence among bottle-fed Native Americans and Eskimo infants
Pneumonia	Increased death rate among Native Americans ages 45+
Psoriasis	Affects 2–5% of whites, but <1% of blacks; high among Japanese Americans
Renal disease	Lower incidence among Japanese Americans
Sickle cell anemia	Increased incidence among blacks
Trachoma	Increased incidence among Native Americans and Eskimo children (3 to 8 times greater than general population)
Tuberculosis	Increased incidence among Native Americans Apache 2.0% Sioux 3.2% Navajo 4.6%
Ulcers	Decreased incidence among Japanese Americans

Based on data reported in G. Henderson and M. Primeaux (1981). *Transcultural Health Care*. Menlo Park, CA: Addison-Wesley; M. S. Orque, B. Bloch, and L. S. Monrroy (1983). *Ethnic Nursing Care: A Multicultural Approach*. St. Louis: C. V. Mosby; T. Overfield (1985). *Biologic Variation in Health and Illness: Race, Age, and Sex Differences*. Menlo Park, CA: Addison-Wesley.

culture to retain and/or preserve relevant care values so that they can maintain their well-being, recover from illness, or face handicaps and/or death'' (Leininger, 1991a, p. 48; see also Jackson, 1993).

Cultural care accommodation and/or negotiation refers to ''those assistive, supporting, facilitative, or enabling creative professional actions and decisions that help people of a designated culture to adapt to, or to negotiate with, others for beneficial or satisfying health outcome with professional careproviders'' (Leininger, 1991a, p. 48). Cultural negotiation is sometimes referred to as *culture brokering* (Jackson, 1993; Jezewski, 1990, 1993).

Cultural care repatterning and/or restructuring refers to ''those assistive, supporting, facilitative, or enabling professional actions and decisions that help a client(s) reorder, change, or greatly modify their lifeways for new, different, and beneficial health care pattern while respecting the client(s) cultural values and beliefs and still providing a beneficial or healthier lifeway than before the changes were coestablished with the client(s)'' (Leininger, 1991a, p. 49).

These models are care-centered and are based on use of the client's care knowledge. Negotiation increases understanding between the client and the nurse and promotes culturally congruent nursing care.

The nurse also may find that it is useful to access professional nursing organizations or other resources when caring for clients from culturally diverse backgrounds and when working in a multicultural work environment (Andrews, 1992). Appendix D provides names and addresses of selected professional organizations that may be helpful to nurses in work settings that are characterized by a multicultural staff.

Evaluation

Evaluation of the effectiveness of clinical decisions and nursing actions should occur in collaboration with the client and his or her significant others—which may include members of the extended family, traditional healers, those with culturally determined, nonsanguine relationships, and friends. A careful evaluation of each component of the transcultural nursing interaction should be undertaken in collaboration with the client. It may be necessary to gather further data, reinterpret existing findings, redefine mutual nurse-client goals, or renegotiate roles and responsibilities of the nurse and/or the client and his or her support system.

Summary

In this chapter the components that comprise excellence in transcultural nursing care have been examined. All nursing care is transcultural because each person—nurse as well as client—is a cultural being. Principles, concepts, theories, and research findings that affect transcultural nursing care have been presented. A brief critique of the prevailing nursing paradigm, which embraces the use of nursing diagnoses, was presented. Theories that may have questionable relevance for some clients from diverse cultural backgrounds were reviewed, and problems of application for some cultural groups were discussed. Culture values, cross-cultural communication, cultural assessment, traditional healers, cultural perceptions of symptoms, biocultural variations in health and illness, clinical decision making and nursing actions, and evaluation of care were explored.

References

American Academy of Nursing (1993). Promoting cultural competence in and through nursing education. Draft, Subpanel on Cultural Competence in Nursing Education, American Academy of Nursing, New York.

Andrews, M. M. (1992). Cultural perspectives on nursing in the 21st century. *Journal of Professional Nursing, 8*(1), 7–15.

Bernal, H., and Froman, R. (1993). Influences on the cultural self-efficacy of community health nurses. *Journal of Transcultural Nursing, 4*(2), 24–31.

Bernal, H., and Froman, R. (1987). The confidence of community health nurses in caring for ethnically diverse populations. *Image: The Journal of Nursing Scholarship, 19*(4), 201–203.

Brothwell, D. R., Carbonell, V. M., and Goose, D. H. (1963). Congenital absence of teeth in human populations. In Brothwell, D. R. (Ed.), *Dental Anthropology*. New York: Pergamon Press, 179–189.

Dandy, E. (1990). Sensitizing teachers to cultural differences: An African-American perspective. National Dropout Prevention Conference, Nashville, Tenn.

Eckman, P., Friesan, W., O'Sullivan, M., Diacoyanni-Tarlatzis, I., Krause, R., and Pitcairn, T. (1987). Universal and cultural differences in the judgments of facial expressions of emotion. *Journal of Personality and Social Psychology, 53,* 712–717.

Emanuel, I. (1972). The incidence of congenital malformations in a Chinese population: The Taipei Collaborative Study. *Teratology, 5* (2), 159–170.

Farrally, M. R. and Moore, W. J. (1975). Anatomical differences in the femur and tibia between Negroes and Caucasians and their effect on locomotion. *American Journal of Physical Anthropology, 43*(1), 63–69.

Feild, I. (1991). Response of Feild to Leininger's nursing diagnosis article. *Journal of Transcultural Nursing, 3*(1), 25–20.

Fitzpatrick, J. J. (1991). Taxonomy II: Definitions and development. In R. A. Carroll-Johnson (Ed.), *Classification of Nursing Diagnoses: Proceedings of the Ninth Conference* (pp. 78–97). St. Louis: North American Nursing Diagnosis Association.

Fitzpatrick, J. J., Kerr, M. E., Saba, V. K., et al. (1989). Translating nursing diagnosis into ICD code. *American Journal of Nursing, 89*(4), 493–495.

Garn, S. M. (1964). Compact bone in Chinese and Japanese. *Science, 143*(3613), 1439–1441.

Geissler, E. M. (1992). Nursing diagnoses: A study of cultural relevance. *Journal of Professional Nursing, 8*(5), 301–307.

Geissler, E. M. (1991). Transcultural nursing and nursing diagnoses. *Nursing and Health Care, 12*(4), 190–192.

Good, B. J., and Good, M. J. D. (1980). The meaning of symptoms: A cultural hermeneutic model for clinical practice. In L. Eisenberg and A. Kleinman (Eds.), *The Relevance of Social Science for Medicine*. Boston: D. Reidel.

Jackson, L. E. (1993). Understanding, eliciting and negotiating clients' multicultural beliefs. *Nurse Practitioner, 18*(4), 30–43.

Jarvis, A., and Gorlin, R. J. (1972). Minor orofacial abnormalities in Eskimo population. *Oral Surgery, 33,* 417–427.

Jarvis, C. (1992). *Physical Examination and Health Assessment*. Philadelphia: W. B. Saunders.

Jezewski, M. A. (1993). Culture brokering as a model for advocacy. *Nursing and Health Care, 14*(2), 78–85.

Jezewski, M. A. (1990). Culture brokering in migrant farmworker health care. *Western Journal of Nursing Research, 12*(4), 497–513.

Kelley, J., and Frish, N. C. (1990). Use of selected nursing diagnoses: A transcultural comparison between Mexican and American nurses. *Journal of Transcultural Nursing, 2*(1), 16–22.

Kelly, J., VanKirk, L., and Garst, C. (1967). Total teeth loss in adults. *Vital Health Statistics, 11*(27), 1–23.

Keltner, N. L., and Folks, D. G. (1992). Psychopharmacology update: Culture as a variable in drug therapy. *Perspectives in Psychiatric Care, 28*(1), 33–36.

Kittler, P. G., and Sucher, K. P. (1990). Diet counseling in a multicultural society. *The Diabetes Educator, 16*(2), 127–134.

Kleinman, A. (1980). *Patients and Healers in the Context of Culture*. Berkeley, CA: University of California Press.

Kleinman, A., Eisenberg, L., and Good, B. (1978). Culture, illness and care: Clinical lessons from anthropologic and cross-cultural research. *Annals of Internal Medicine, 88,* 251–258.

Kroll, J., Linde, P., Habenict, M., et al. (1990). Medication compliance, antidepressant blood levels, and side effects in Southeast Asian patients. *Journal of Clinical Pharmacology, 10*(4), 27–29.

Lapierre, E. D., and Padgett, J. (1991). How can we become more aware of culturally specific body language and use this awareness therapeutically? *Journal of Psychosocial Nursing, 29*(11), 38–41.

Lapp, N. L. (1974). Lung volumes and flow rates in Black and White subjects. *Thorax, 29,* 185–188.

Lefley, H. (1990). Culture and chronic mental illness. *Hospital and Community Psychiatry, 41,* 277–286.

Leininger, M. M. (1992). Self-care ideology and cultural incongruities: Some critical issues. *Journal of Transcultural Nursing, 4*(1), 2–4.

Leininger, M. M. (1991). *Culture Care Diversity and Universality: A Theory of Nursing.* New York: National League for Nursing Press.

Leininger, M. M. (1990). Issues, questions, and concerns related to the nursing diagnosis cultural movement from a transcultural nursing perspective. *Journal of Transcultural Nursing, 2*(1), 23–32.

Leininger, M. M. (1978). *Transcultural Nursing: Concepts, Theories, and Practices.* New York: John Wiley & Sons.

Levin, S. (1966). Effect of age, ethnic background and disease on sweat chloride. *Israeli Journal of Medical Science, 2*(3), 333–337.

Lin, T. (1986). Multiculturalism and Canadian psychiatry: Opportunities and challenges. *Canadian Journal of Psychiatry, 31*(7), 681–690.

Lipson, J. G., and Meleis, A. I. (1983). Issues in health care of Middle Eastern patients. *Western Journal of Medicine, 139,* 854–861.

Martin, J. L., and Crump, E. P. (1972). Leukoedema of the buccal mucosa in Negro children and youth. *Oral Surgery, 34*(1), 49–58.

Matsumoto, D. (1989). Face, culture, and judgments of anger and fear: Do the eyes have it? *Journal of Nonverbal Behavior, 13,* 171–188.

Matsumoto, D., and Kudoh, T. (1987). Cultural similarities and differences in the semantic dimensions of body postures. *Journal of Nonverbal Behavior, 11,* 171–188.

McFarland, G., and McFarlane, E. (1989). *Nursing Diagnosis and Intervention: Planning for Patient Care.* St. Louis: C. V. Mosby.

Meharabian, A. (1972). *Nonverbal Communication.* Chicago: Aldine Publishing Company.

Meleis, A. L., Lipson, J. G., and Paul, S. M. (1992). Ethnicity and health among five Middle Eastern immigrant groups. *Nursing Research, 41*(2), 98–103.

Mendoza, R., Smith, M. W., Poland, R. E., et al. (1991). Ethnic psychopharmacology: The Hispanic and Native American perspective. *Psychopharmacology Bulletin, 27*(4), 449–461.

Olowe, S. A. and Akinkugbe, A. (1978). Amniotic fluid lecithin/sphingomyelin ratio: Comparison between an African and a North American community. *Pediatrics, 62*(1), 38–41.

Orem, D. E. (1980). *Nursing: Concepts of Practice,* 2d Ed. New York: McGraw-Hill Book Company.

Orque, M. S., Bloch, B., and Monrroy, L. A. (1983). *Ethnic Nursing Care.* St. Louis: C. V. Mosby.

Oscherwitz, R. (1972). Differences in pulmonary functions in various racial groups. *American Journal of Epidemiology, 96*(5), 319–27.

Overfield, T. (1985). *Biologic Variation in Health and Illness.* Menlo Park, CA: Addison-Wesley.

Ritchie, R. F. (1979). Specific proteins. In J. B. Henry (Ed.), *Clinical Diagnosis and Management by Laboratory Methods.* Philadelphia: W. B. Saunders, 228–258.

Spuhler, J. N. (1950). Genetics of three normal morphological variations: Patterns of superficial veins of the anterior thorax, peroneus tertius muscle, and number of vallate papillae. *Cold Spring Harbor Symposium on Quantitative Biology, 15,* 175–189.

Tripp-Reimer, T., and Lauer, G. M. (1987). Ethnicity in families with chronic illness. In L. M. Wright and M. Leahy (Eds.), *Families and Chronic Illness* pp. (77–99). Springhouse, PA: Springhouse.

United States Department of Health and Human Services, Public Health Service. (1992). *Health People 2000.* Boston: Jones and Bartlett Publishers.

Wasserman, H. P. (1974). *Ethnic Pigmentation: Historical, Physiological, and Chemical Aspects.* New York: American Elsevier.

Watson, O. M. (1980). *Proxemic behavior: A Cross Cultural Study.* The Hague, Netherlands: Mouton Press.

Wenger, A. F. (1993). Cultural meaning of symptoms. *Holistic Nursing Practice, 7*(2), 22–35.

Wood, A. J., and Zhou, H. H. (1991). Ethnic differences in drug disposition and responsiveness. *Clinical Pharmacokinetics, 20,* 1–24.

II

A Developmental Approach to Transcultural Nursing

3

Transcultural Nursing Care of the Childbearing Family

Jana Lauderdale
Deborah L. Greener

Introduction

Because pregnancy and childbirth are social, cultural, and physiologic experiences, any approach to culturally competent nursing care of childbearing women and their families must focus on the interaction between cultural meaning and biologic functions (Kitzinger, 1982). Childbirth is a time of transition and social celebration of central importance in any society, signaling a realignment of existing cultural roles and responsibilities, psychological and biologic states, and social relationships. Raphael (1976) describes these rites of passage as *matrescence* (mother-becoming) and *patrescence* (father-becoming). The different ways in which a particular society views this transitional period and manages childbirth are dependent on the culture's consensus about such things as health, medical care, reproduction, and the role and status of women (Oakley, 1977). The dominant cultural view of pregnancy and childbirth in the United States is that of pregnancy as a disease or incipient disease state (Johnston, 1980). Health care focuses on the pregnant woman and fetus, while the father and other family members or significant others, if they are included at all, are relegated to observer rather than participant status. Dominant cultural practices or rituals in the United States include formal prenatal care (including childbirth classes), ultrasound to view the fetus, and hospital delivery. Monitoring fetal status, inducing labor, providing anesthesia for labor and delivery, and placing the woman in the lithotomy position during the birth are all part of routine hospital care provided in the United States today. A highly specialized group of nurses, obstetricians, perinatologists, and pediatricians actively monitors the mother's physiologic status, delivers the infant, and provides newborn care. However, because there is not total cultural agreement in this country about the value of these practices, some health care providers elect to offer their pregnant clients alternative

Margaret M. Andrews and Joyceen S. Boyle: TRANSCULTURAL CONCEPTS IN NURSING CARE, SECOND EDITION. © 1995 J.B. Lippincott Company.

health care services. These alternatives include in-hospital and free-standing birth centers and care by nurse-practitioners and nurse-midwives, who promote family-centered care and emphasize pregnancy as a normal process requiring minimal technologic intervention.

Additionally, there are subcultural groups within the United States that have very different practices, values, and beliefs about childbirth and the roles of women, men, social support networks, and health practitioners. These include proponents of the "back to nature" movement, who are often vegetarian, use lay midwives for home deliveries, and practice herbal or naturopathic medicine. Other subcultures (the concept of subculture was described in Chap. 1) include African Americans, Native Americans, Hispanics, Middle Easterners, and Asians. Additionally, religious background, regional variation, age, urban or rural background, sexual preferences, and other individual characteristics may all contribute to cultural differences in the experience of childbirth.

Great variations exist in the social class, ethnic origin, family structure, and social support networks of women, men, and families in the United States. Despite these differences, many health care providers assume that the changes in status and rites of passage associated with pregnancy, birth, parenting, and fertility control are experienced similarly by all people. In addition, the individual or cultural experiences of mother-becoming or father-becoming are frequently disrupted by the emphasis of Western medicine on obstetric technology (Haire, 1972; Milinalre, 1974; Arms, 1975; Wertz and Wertz, 1977; McBride, 1982). Many of the traditional cultural beliefs, values, and practices related to childbirth are viewed by professional nurses as "old-fashioned" or "old wive's tales." Although these customs are changing rapidly, many women and families are attempting to preserve their own valued patterns of experiencing childbirth. Nurses and other health professionals must begin to incorporate individual beliefs and cultural practices into health care in order to reduce some of the cultural conflict and begin to humanize American obstetrics (McClain, 1982).

The purpose of this chapter is to explore the cultural patterns, rituals, and beliefs that may influence the experience of childbirth and childbearing. The experience of the woman as well as of her significant others during pregnancy, birth, and the postpartum period is described; infant care and fertility control are also discussed. Specific suggestions for nurses who provide care to childbearing women and their families are presented for each of the areas discussed.

Pregnancy

All cultures recognize pregnancy as a special transition period, and many have particular customs and beliefs that dictate activity and behavior during pregnancy. Ford (1964), Mead and Newton (1967), Newton and Newton (1972), and Oakley (1980) have reviewed childbirth from a cross-cultural perspective, surveying literature from traditional non-Western societies as well as from Western cultural groups. Recent literature on childbirth customs in the United States has focused on accounts of differing beliefs and practices relative to pregnancy among varying ethnic groups. This section describes some of the biologic and cultural variations that may influence the provision of nursing care during pregnancy.

Biologic Variations

Knowledge of certain biologic variations resulting from genetic and environmental backgrounds is important for nurses caring for childbearing families. For example, pregnant women who have sickle cell trait and are heterozygous for the sickle cell gene are at increased risk for asymptomatic bacteriuria and urinary tract infections such as pyelonephritis. This places them at greater than normal risk for premature labor as well (Pritchard, MacDonald, and Gant, 1984). Although heterozygotes are found most commonly among African Americans (8–14 percent), individuals living in the United States who are of Mediterranean ancestry, as well as of Germanic and Native American descent, may occasionally carry the trait (Overfield, 1985; Thompson and Thompson, 1983). If both parents are heterozygous, there is a 1 in 4 probability that the infant will be born with sickle cell disease. Presently, statistics indicate that of the children born with sickle cell disease, 50 percent live to adulthood. Of those surviving the disease, many experience chronic complications throughout their lives (Bullock and Jilly, 1975).

Another important biologic variation relative to pregnancy is diabetes mellitus. The incidence of both non-insulin-dependent and gestational diabetes has been found to be much higher that normal among some Native American groups, a problem that increases maternal and infant morbidity. Illnesses that are common among European-American clients may manifest themselves differently in Native American clients. For example, a Native American woman may have a high blood sugar level but be asymptomatic for diabetes mellitus, yet the mortality rate for diabetes in pregnant Native American women is high. Diabetes during pregnancy, particularly with uncontrolled hyperglycemia, is associated with an increased risk of congenital anomalies, stillbirth, macrosomia, birth injury, cesarean section, neonatal hypoglycemia, and other problems. The incidence of gestational diabetes is 10 to 40 times greater among the Pima and Papago Indians of Arizona than in the general U.S. population (Pettit et al., 1980). Early detection and blood glucose screening are mandatory among high-risk populations to reduce complications during pregnancy and childbirth.

Other cultural groups whose members may have health conditions that place women or their fetuses at risk are recent refugees from Southeast Asia. Significant numbers of Thais and Cambodians have abnormal hemoglobins (A_2 and E), and it is not uncommon to observe a hemoglobinopathic microcytic anemia coexisting with a dietary or folic acid deficiency anemia. Pregnancies in Southeast Asian women also may be complicated by parasites (45–75 percent), a reactive venereal disease research laboratory (VDRL) test (signifying treponemal syphilis or yaws), tuberculosis (62 percent of recent Southeast Asian refugees aged 19 years or older have a positive TB skin test), and symptomatic or asymptomatic hepatitis B. Because of the frequency of these health problems, pregnant Southeast Asian refugees should be screened with a complete blood count and a stool hepatitis screen (HBsAg) to rule out active disease or carrier status. Treatment for these conditions may or may not be undertaken during pregnancy; some of the indicated pharmacologic agents may be embryotoxic (Erickson and Hoang, 1980; Nelson and Hewitt, 1983; Pickwell, 1983; Boehme, 1985).

Cultural Variations

Despite recent cultural changes that have made it more acceptable for women to have careers and pursue alternative lifestyles, the dominant cultural expectation for American women is motherhood within the context of the nuclear family. Changing cultural expectations have influenced many middle-class American women and couples to delay childbearing until their late twenties or early thirties and to have small families. Single women in their thirties are making choices about childbearing that may not involve a marital relationship. Some lesbian couples are choosing to bear children. This particular group of women faces special psychosocial dilemmas related to their lifestyle and social stigma. The most common fear reported is the fear of unsafe and inadequate care from the practitioner once their sexual orientation is revealed (Logan and Dawkins, 1986). There are many similarities in lesbian and heterosexual pregnancies, and the parallels should not be overlooked by health care providers. Issues of sexual activity, psychosocial changes related to attaining the maternal tasks of pregnancy, as described by Rubin (1984), and birth education need to be addressed with lesbian couples. Special needs of the lesbian couple requiring assessment include social discrimination, family and social support networks, obstacles in becoming pregnant (i.e., coitus versus artificial insemination), lesbian maternal role development, legal issues of adoption by the partner, and coparenting role management (Tash and Kenney, 1993). In order to meet their special needs and provide sensitive and appropriate care, caregivers must come to understand the lifestyle of the lesbian couple and work with them in addressing not only their physical but also their psychosocial concerns.

Emphasis is being placed increasingly on the quality of pregnancy and childbirth, and many childbearing women rely on nontraditional support systems. Although involvement of the father in prenatal classes and prenatal visits is becoming accepted, few health care providers and institutions incorporate extended family and/or social networks into plans of care. For couples who are married, white, middle-class, and infrequent users of their extended family for advice and support in childbirth-related matters, this may not be critical. However, for other cultural groups, including African Americans, Hispanics, Asians, and Native Americans, the family and social network (especially the grandmother and other maternal relatives) are of primary importance in advising and supporting the pregnant woman (Rose, 1978; Bryant, 1982).

An interesting example of cultural differences in the perception and utilization of kin and social support during pregnancy has been provided by Horn (1983). This study described cultural differences among young pregnant white, black, and Native American women in two U.S. cities. The Native American teens expressed a strong belief that either family or their "people" would take care of them, although this was not always reflected in actual practice. They related that their culture placed a high value on validating the feminine role through early pregnancy. African-American teenagers stated that their families would, and actually did, help them meet all their needs during pregnancy. They explained that although the accepted norm in their culture was completion of an education prior to marriage and a family, no negative sanctions were placed on them for not meeting these expectations. The white adolescent mothers believed that early motherhood indicated failure and was not valued or accepted by society. This group of teens perceived, and actually received, little or no familial or social support except from boyfriends and worried about meeting such basic needs as food and shelter.

Another area in which cultural variation has important implications is in women's perception of the need for formalized assistance from health care providers during the antepartum period. Western medicine is generally perceived as having a curative rather than a preventive focus. Indeed, many health care providers view pregnancy as a disaster waiting to happen, a physiologic state that at any moment will become pathologic. Because many American subcultural groups perceive pregnancy as a normal physiologic process, not seeing themselves as ill or in need of the curative services of a doctor, they often delay seeking or even neglect to seek prenatal care. Many women say, "I was feeling just fine, no problems, but last time the doctor really yelled at me when I didn't come in, so I thought I'd better come to clinic. But I'm just fine." Other factors, such as a lack of transportation or financial resources, language barriers, and misunderstanding of routine procedures may all affect compliance with formal prenatal care.

An example of how women's perceptions for the need of antepartum care vary is described in a study by Campanella, Korbin, and Acheson (1993). Fifteen Amish women from Ohio described their perinatal beliefs and how they used the available health care system during a total of 76 pregnancies. Prior to the study, local health care providers commonly believed that Amish women underutilized available prenatal and birth care resources.

The findings from this study indicated that Amish women utilize perinatal care based on their beliefs about pregnancy and childbirth and in relation to cost, transportation, and child care. Amish women reported initiating prenatal care earlier for first pregnancies and progressively later with increasing parity and with the increasing knowledge that pregnancy was indeed a "nonproblematic" condition. However, all the women reported seeking immediate medical attention if a serious problem arose, i.e., bleeding, etc. During pregnancy, vitamins and herbal teas were commonly used in preparation for childbirth and usually were recommended by Amish family members/or a midwife. Usual daily routines were encouraged to continue throughout pregnancy. A normal pregnancy course for an Amish woman consisted of following recommendations on vitamin and herb use from family and friends, going to a physician for prenatal care, and finally being delivered out of the hospital (either at home or at the Amish birthing center) by a midwife. Hospitals were spoken of positively in terms of "safety" and "getting additional rest." Negative statements involved "the lack of privacy" and "high cost."

Findings from this study indicated that Amish women are not opposed to the technologic aspects of childbirth but that they select modern technology to meet their individual and cultural needs. For example, the use of fetal monitoring is viewed as helpful in situations where there may be a problem, i.e., cord compression. This study emphasized the need to look beyond conformity and homogencity when providing health care to the culturally different childbearing woman.

Among many subcultural groups, women perceive little personal control over the outcome of pregnancy except through the avoidance of activities and foods that are considered taboo. The evolvement of food taboos in the pregnant Korean woman's diet is thought to stem from the danger and uncertainty associated with pregnancy and childbirth (Bauwens, 1978). Taboos include chicken, duck, rabbit, goat, crab, sparrow, pork, and blemished fruit. These foods are not eaten in an attempt to guard the child from unwanted physical characteristics; for example, eating chicken may cause bumpy skin or blemished fruit an unpleasant face (Kim and Mo, 1977). In a Hindu woman's life, pregnancy is considered a hot period. Hot foods (i.e., animal products, chillies, spices, and ginger) and gas-producing foods are avoided because they are believed to cause overexcitement, inflammatory reactions, sweating, and fatigue. If eaten too early in pregnancy, hot foods are believed to cause miscarriage and fetal abnormality (Turrell, 1985). Conversely, cold foods (i.e., milk products, milk, yogart, cream, and butter), most vegetables, and foods that are sour in taste are thought to strengthen and calm the pregnant woman.

Many women do not understand the emphasis placed on urinalysis, blood pressure readings, and abdominal measurements that occur regularly in Western prenatal care. For traditional women, the vaginal examination may be so intrusive and embarrassing that they may avoid attending clinic or request a female physician or midwife (Bash, 1980; Meleis and Sorrell, 1981; Nelson and Hewitt, 1983). Common discomforts of pregnancy may be managed through folk, herbal, home, or over-the-counter remedies on the advice of a relative (generally the maternal grandmother) and friends (Snow, Johnson, and Mayhew, 1978). Health care providers must make efforts to meet the needs of women from traditional cultures by explaining health regimens so that they have meaning within the cultural belief system. However, such explanations are only an initial step. Visits can be made to the home, or group prenatal visits based on self-care models can be instituted by nurses in local community centers. Additionally, nurses can incorporate significant others into the plan of care. Nurses can provide information during prenatal visits on normal fetal growth and development, as well as discuss how the health and behavior of the mother and those around her can influence fetal outcome.

The use of an interpreter can be invaluable when interacting with non-English-speaking clients and families. However, the use of an interpreter in a clinic, classroom, or home setting requires skill and judgment. Many women who do not speak English are uncomfortable unless the interpreter is female and even then may be embarrassed when discussing personal matters in front of an additional stranger. The attitudes of the interpreter also may affect communication. For example, if a woman describes a belief in magical forces, the interpreter may assume that the nurse has no interest in such a belief and intentionally omit it from the translation. Another source of miscommunication is the difficulty of translating some Westernized expressions, especially medical terms and jargon, into other languages. The nurse should speak clearly to the woman herself rather that to the interpreter using minimal technical and scientific language. The nurse also should ask the interpreter to convey the woman's words as accurately as possible.

Regular formal prenatal classes that emphasize preparation for labor and delivery are primarily attended by married, middle-class, educationally advantaged couples. Some attempts have been made to provide outreach to other groups, but many women learn about labor and delivery from their families and social support networks. In addition to recognizing these valid forms of childbirth preparation, nurses can develop innovative programs that allow for cultural variation, including classes during clinic hours in busy urban settings, teen-only classes, single-mother classes, group classes combined with prenatal checkups at home, classes on rural reservations, and presentations that incorporate the older, "wise" women of the community. In addition, nurses can organize prenatal classes in languages other than English. Some barriers that may be encountered in prenatal education are embarrassment on the part of women about performing exercises in front of men other than their husbands and language differences that are insurmountable without skilled female interpreters.

Another cultural variation involves beliefs about activities during pregnancy. A *belief* is something held to be actual or true on the basis of a specific rationale or explanatory model. *Prescriptive beliefs*, which are phrased positively, describe expectancies of behavior; the more common *restrictive beliefs*, which are phrased negatively, limit choices and behaviors. Many people believe that the activity of the mother, and to a lesser extent of the father, is influential on newborn outcome. Box 3-1 describes some prescriptive and restrictive beliefs and taboos that provide cultural boundaries for parental activity during pregnancy. These beliefs are attempts to increase a sense of control over the outcome of pregnancy.

Positive or prescriptive beliefs may involve wearing special articles of clothing, such as the *muneco* worn by some traditional Hispanic women to ensure a safe delivery and prevent morning sickness. Other beliefs and practices involve certain ceremonies, such as the White Shell Woman Way among traditional Navajos, and recommendations about physical and sexual activity. Negative or restrictive beliefs are widespread and numerous and include activity, work, and sexual, emotional, and environmental proscriptions. *Taboos*, or restrictions with serious supernatural consequences, include the Orthodox Jewish avoidance of baby showers and divulgence of the infant's name before the infant's official naming ceremony (Bash, 1980). A Hispanic taboo involves the traditional belief that an early baby shower will invite bad luck or *mal ojo*, the evil eye (Kay, 1978).

Many folk beliefs surround the prediction of the infant's sex. Health care professionals are sometimes heard saying, "A slow heartbeat means a boy; a faster heartbeat means a girl." There is even an over-the-counter urine-testing kit that purports 90 percent accuracy in predicting the newborn's sex. Hispanic women may say, "A girl is carried on the right side of the abdomen"; African-American women may note, "Boys are carried high and pointy, and girls are carried low"; and Appalachian women may say, "If you tie your wedding ring on a string and hold it over your wrist, the baby will be a boy if it swings back and forth and a girl if it turns in a circle" (Frankel, 1977; Kay, 1978; Day, 1983). Many of these types of beliefs, which are often contradictory even within one cultural group, are described in the professional literature.

Another area of cultural significance that requires nursing assessment surrounds beliefs regarding gender prediction based on the parents' attitudes, values, and beliefs. The meaning parents attach to having a son, a daughter, or a multiple pregnancy varies from culture to culture. Traditionally, the male gender is highly regarded, which places females in a position of "less than favorable." Twin births also carry a significance that varies from culture to culture. Twins are viewed as a special blessing by the Yoruba tribe and as a curse by the Ibo tribe in the same West African nation of Nigeria.

Nurses sometimes say, "Oh, that's just superstition" or "That's an old wive's tale," when a client mentions a belief or practice that seems to the nurses unusual or foreign. It is important to remember that many current or recent practices in American obstetrical care, such as routine episiotomy or perineal shaving, have minimal scientific validation and may seem just as unusual or foreign to others. Nurses must be able to differentiate among beliefs and practices that are harmful, benign, and health promoting. Very few cultural customs related to pregnancy are truly dangerous; although they may cause a woman to limit her activity and her exposure to some aspects of life, they are rarely harmful to her or her fetus.

One situation in which a prescriptive belief may cause harm occurs when there is a poor neonatal outcome and the mother blames herself. For example, the mother whose fetus has died from a cord accident and who believes that hanging laundry caused the

Box 3-1. Cultural Beliefs about Activity and Pregnancy

Prescriptive Beliefs
- Remain active during pregnancy to aid the baby's circulation (Crow Indian).
- Remain happy to bring the baby joy and good fortune (Pueblo and Navajo Indians, Mexican, Japanese).
- Sleep flat on your back to protect the baby (Mexican)
- Keep active during pregnancy to ensure a small baby and an easy delivery (Mexican).
- Continue sexual intercourse to lubricate the birth canal and prevent dry labor (Haitian, Mexican).
- Continue daily baths and frequent shampoos during pregnancy to produce a clean baby (Filipino).

Restrictive Beliefs
- Avoid cold air during pregnancy (Mexican, Haitian, Asian).
- Do not reach over your head or the cord will wrap around the baby's neck (black, Hispanic, white, Asian).
- Avoid weddings and funerals or you will bring bad fortune to the baby (Vietnamese).
- Do not continue sexual intercourse or harm will come to you and the baby (Vietnamese, Filipino, Samoan).
- Do not tie knots or braid or allow the baby's father to do so because it will cause difficult labor (Navajo Indian).
- Do not sew (Pueblo Indian, Asian).

Taboos
- Avoid lunar eclipses and moonlight or the baby may be born with a deformity (Mexican).
- Don't walk on the streets at noon or five o'clock because this may make the spirits angry (Vietnamese).
- Don't join in traditional ceremonies like Yei or Squaw dances or spirits will harm the baby (Navajo Indian).
- Don't get involved with persons who cast spells or the baby will be eaten in the womb (Haitian).
- Don't say the baby's name before the naming ceremony or harm might come to the baby (Orthodox Jewish).
- Don't have your picture taken because it might cause stillbirth (black).

cord to encircle the baby's neck or body may suffer severe guilt. The nurse who is sensitive to her pain might say, "Many people say that if you reach over your head during pregnancy, it will cause the cord to wrap around the baby's neck. Have you heard this belief?" Once the woman responds, the nurse can explore her feelings about the practice. Do others in her family or social support network share her beliefs? The nurse may share her own views by saying, "I have not read in any medical or nursing books that this practice was related to a cord problem, although I know that many people share your belief." The discussion can then continue, focusing on the feelings and perceptions of the event as it is experienced by the woman and her family.

Other important topics for nurses caring for pregnant women are cultural beliefs about food and dietary intake during pregnancy. Many variations in dietary patterns and preferences exist among childbearing women in the United States.

Birth

Beliefs and customs surrounding the experience of labor and delivery are influenced by the fact that the physiologic process is basically the same for all cultures. Factors such as cultural attitudes toward the achievement of birth, methods of dealing with the pain of labor, recommended positions during delivery, the preferred location for the birth, the role of the father and the family or social support network, and expectations of the health care practitioner may vary according to degree of acculturation to Westernized child-birth customs, geographic location, religious beliefs, and individual preference.

The concept of achievement versus atonement in birth refers to the way in which a culture defines the birth process as a praised achievement worthy of celebration or a defilement or state of pollution necessitating ritual purification (Newton and Newton, 1972). In the American culture, birth is often viewed as an achievement, unfortunately, not for the mother but rather for the medical staff. The obstetrician "manages" the labor and "delivers" the infant; for this active role, the doctor is often profusely thanked even before the mother is praised or congratulated. Gifts and celebrations are centered around the newborn rather than the mother. The recent consumer movement in childbirth and the upsurge of feminism have caused some redefinition of this cultural focus and encouraged women and their partners to assume active roles in the management of their own health and birth experiences. Unfortunately, some women who have prepared themselves for a totally "natural" childbirth may feel a sense of personal trauma and failure if they receive an analgesic or require a cesarean section delivery (Hott, 1980; Mercer and Stainton, 1984). Nurses must identify how much personal control and involvement are desired by a woman and her family during the birth experience. If expectations and plans made before labor are altered during labor and birth, the nurse should involve the woman and her significant others in all significant changes and allow the woman to verbalize her feelings following the birth.

All cultures have an approach to birth rooted in a tradition in which childbirth occurs at home, within the province of women. For many generations, traditions among the poor included use of "granny" midwives by rural Appalachian whites and blacks and "parteras" by Mexican Americans (Frankel, 1977; Kay, 1978). A dependence on self-management, a belief in the normality of labor and birth, and a tradition of delivery at home may cause many women to arrive at the hospital only in advanced labor (Frankel, 1977; Nelson and Hewitt, 1983). The need to travel a long distance to the

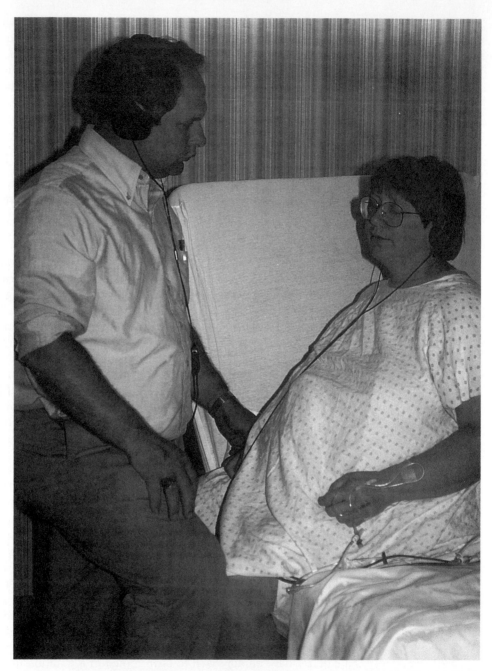

This couple is using music therapy to promote relaxation and to control the pain of labor. Active throughout the pregnancy, labor, and delivery, this husband provides comfort and emotional support and coaches his wife throughout the entire labor and delivery.

closest hospital also may be a factor contributing to arrival in late labor or to out-of-hospital delivery for many Native American women living on rural, isolated reservations.

Despite the traditional emphasis on female support and guidance during labor, the recent inclusion of husbands or male partners in American labor and birth rooms has been seen as positive by women of many cultures. Women from such diverse cultures as Mexican American, Cambodian, and Native American report a desire to have their husbands or partners present during labor and birth. Unfortunately, many American hospitals still maintain rules that limit the support person to the spouse or prevent a husband from attending the birth unless he has attended a formal childbirth education program with his wife. Another source of conflict is the desire of many women to have their mother or some other female relative or friend present during labor and birth. Because many hospitals have rules limiting the number of persons who may be present, the expectant mother may be forced to make a difficult choice among the people close to her.

Some women and families, particularly those from Orthodox Jewish, Islamic, Chinese, and Asian Indian backgrounds, may follow strict religious and cultural prohibitions against the viewing of the woman's body by either the husband or any other man, or they may practice separation of the husband and wife once the "bloody show" or cervical dilation has occurred (Bash, 1980; Meleis and Sorrell, 1981; Flint, 1982; Pillsbury, 1982). In cultures in which the husband's presence is not believed to be appropriate, nurses may mistakenly assume a lack of involvement or interest on the part of the man.

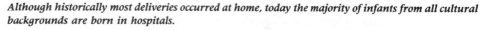

Although historically most deliveries occurred at home, today the majority of infants from all cultural backgrounds are born in hospitals.

Women from many cultural groups report fear and anxiety about the pain of labor (Affonso, 1978; Kay, 1982; Dempsey and Gesse, 1983). In the past it was commonly believed that women from Asian and Native American cultures are very stoic and do not feel pain in labor (Stanton, 1979); such views are ethnocentric and should be avoided. Many factors interact to influence labor and the perception of pain in labor; these include cultural attitude toward the normalcy and conduct of birth, expectations of how a woman should act in labor, the role of significant others, and the physiologic processes involved. For example, when Filipino women were asked how they would act in labor, many said it was best to lie quietly (Affonso, 1978). By contrast, Middle Eastern women are verbally expressive during labor, sometimes crying and screaming loudly while refusing pain medication (Meleis and Sorrell, 1981). Samoan women may believe that no verbal expressions of pain are permissible, with only "spoiled" Caucasian women needing any analgesia (Clark and Howland, 1978). According to Kay (1978), Hispanic women are traditionally instructed by their *parteras* to endure pain with patience and close the mouth, for opening it to cry out would cause the uterus to rise. Japanese, Chinese, Vietnamese, Laotian, and other women of Asian descent maintain that screaming or crying out during labor or birth is shameful; birth is believed to be painful but something to be endured (Okamoto, 1978; Rose, 1978; Stringfellow, 1978; Nelson and Hewitt, 1983). Although many of the women from these cultures are deemed unprepared by some health professionals because they do not use formal breathing and relaxation techniques, they often employ culturally appropriate ways of preparing for labor and delivery. These culturally approved methods of childbirth preparation may include assisting with or participating in births from the time of adolescence, listening to birth and baby stories told by respected elderly women of the community, or following special dietary and activity prescriptions in the antepartal period.

Positions for labor and birth have traditionally favored the upright posture (walking, kneeling, squatting, sitting, or standing) rather than the supine position, which until recently was the norm in American obstetrics (Naroll, Naroll, and Howard, 1961). The dominant American cultural preference for the supine position in labor and the lithotomy position in birth have been shown to be unphysiologic and even dangerous practices (Haire, 1972; Caldeyro-Barcia, 1979; Roberts, 1980). Many women of all cultures prefer an upright posture, desire to move about in labor, and want to give birth without being restrained in a position that holds their legs apart in the air with metal stirrups. Numerous anecdotal reports in the literature describe "typical" birth positions for women of diverse cultures, from the seated position in a birth chair favored by Mexican-American women to the squatting position frequently chosen by Laotian Hmong women. The nurse who cares for laboring women should realize, however, that the choice of labor and birth positions is influenced by many factors other than culture and that the socialization that takes place on arrival to a labor and delivery unit may prevent women from stating their preferences.

The recent increase in home births among American women can be attributed to a desire for more personal control over birth and a fear of medical intervention in an essentially normal process (Bauwens and Anderson, 1978). Many women who are naturopathic or holistic health proponents choose home birth with a lay midwife, but the desire for an uncomplicated birth among one's own family and social support network, without medical interference, crosses cultural and socioeconomic lines. Personal communications from women of Hispanic, Native American, and Asian backgrounds reveal that many would like to have the opportunity to have a midwife- or physician-attended home birth but are not aware of the available alternatives.

Economically disadvantaged women from culturally diverse backgrounds have few birth options; most labor and give birth in large public hospitals. Routinized patterns of care and decreased individualization are common in these institutions. These and other problems, such as language barriers, make the provision of culturally sensitive care during the birth process a challenge for nurses.

Postpartum

While Western medicine considers pregnancy and birth the most dangerous and vulnerable time period for the childbearing woman, many other cultures place much more emphasis on the postpartal period. These cultural differences, particularly as they relate to restrictive dietary customs, activity levels, and certain taboos and rituals associated with purification and seclusion, may seem incomprehensible to the nurse. Routine nursing care usually includes the promotion of a varied diet, adequate fluid intake, and self-care and personal hygiene practices such as showering, tub or sitz bathing, ambulation, and exercise. However, these prescriptive beliefs and practices, common in American obstetric care, may seem foreign and dangerous to the members of some cultural groups.

For many cultures, the concept of postpartum vulnerability is based on one or more beliefs related to imbalance or pollution. *Imbalance* is perceived to be due to disharmony caused by the processes of pregnancy and birth, and *pollution* is seen to be caused by the "unclean" bleeding associated with birth and the postpartum period (Horn, 1981). Restitution of physical balance and purification may occur through many mechanisms, including dietary prescriptions and restrictions, ritual baths, seclusion, restriction of activity, and other ceremonial events.

The core concepts related to the perceived imbalance in the mother's physical state are the humoral hot/cold theory, a meaning system for many Hispanics and blacks, and the yin (cold) and yang (hot) theory practiced by the Chinese and some other Asians (see Chap. 1 for a discussion of these concepts). Pregnancy is considered a "hot" physical state. Because a great deal of the heat of pregnancy is thought to be lost during the birth process, postpartum practices focus on restoring the balance between cold and hot or yin and yang.

The period of postpartum vulnerability and seclusion in most non-Western cultures varies between 7 and 40 days. Hispanic women, especially primagravidas, may follow a set of postpartum dietary and activity regulations called *la dieta* (Kay, 1978, Horn, 1981) or *la cuarentena* (Gaviria, Stern, and Schensul, 1982; Zapeda, 1982). The Hispanic *partera*, or midwife, will stay at the home of the mother for several hours following the delivery, with a follow-up visit the next day. Philpott's (1979) study of traditional Hispanic postpartum practices described how the *partera* disposed of the placenta through burial so that animals would not eat it, since it was believed that if a dog eats the placenta, the mother will be unable to bear subsequent children. It also was believed that to bury the placenta would prevent the mother from having pain. If the baby was female, the placenta was buried close to home so that the daughter would not go far away.

Some Chinese-American women also follow similar postpartum rules, as do some South African Americans, Southeast Asians, Filipinos, and Haitian women. Although the rules themselves are highly variable, common components focus on the avoidance of cold, whether in the form of air or food. In some cultures, water and air are considered cold at all times and must be avoided by the postpartum woman lest serious harm occur. An example of a belief concerning immediate harm from cold is the Haitian belief that exposure to air may cause a uterine cold; such entrance of air into the vagina is thought to be prevented through the use of a sanitary pad (Dempsey and Gesse, 1983). Another example of a belief concerning extended harm attributable to exposure to cold in the postpartum period is the Asian belief that arthritis, asthma, and other chronic health problems can result from contact with cold water (Horn, 1981).

This very real fear of the harmful effects of cold air and water in the postpartum period can result in significant cultural conflict when the woman and baby are hospitalized during the postpartum period. Attitudes and beliefs about bathing, showering, shampooing, ambulation, and other self-care practices should be assessed by the nurse in a nonjudgmental manner. Many women will pretend to follow the activities suggested by nurses, even to the extent of going into the shower, running the water, and pretending to follow instructions, while avoiding all contact with the dangerous substance (Horn, 1981). Exposure to air conditioners and fans, even in warm weather, is also considered very dangerous by some women. Thoughtful postpartum nurses can help women wear appropriate clothing and provide extra blankets. The common use of perineal ice packs and sitz baths to promote healing in the immediate postpartum period can be replaced with the use of heat lamps, heat packs, and anesthetic or astringent topical agents for women who prefer to avoid cold influences. The routine distribution of pitchers of icewater to all postpartum women can be replaced by a practice of giving women a choice of water at room temperature, warm tea or coffee, broth, or other beverages. Another common hospital custom that may need to be modified for some postpartum women is the offer of orange juice (a cold, acidic beverage) right after delivery.

Dietary prescriptions and restrictions are common in the postpartum period. Women of different cultures learn what foods are considered appropriate to eat during the postpartal period; Hispanic women may want a corn gruel called *atole;* Navajo women are encouraged to drink a hot herbal tea; and Chinese women believe that eating chicken every day is beneficial to their health. Most dietary patterns are based on a humoral (hot/cold) theory and represent ways in which it is believed that heat can be restored and the influence of cold diminished. Hispanic women believe that it is important to avoid acidic foods, which are considered cold, such as vegetables, citrus fruits, pork, chili, and tomatoes (Kay, 1978). Haitian women avoid eggplant, okra, tomatoes, black pepper, cold drinks, milk, rice, bananas, and fish (Dempsey and Gesse, 1983). Chinese and other Asian women may restrict their consumption of such cold foods as green vegetables, fruits, meats (except chicken), and fish (Pillsbury, 1982), and southern black women may avoid hog chitterlings, liver, and onions (Carrington, 1978). Postpartum nurses may note that mothers eat little of the food provided by the hospital and rely on foods brought in either overtly or covertly by their families.

Activity is also often regulated in the postpartum period. Cultural rationale for restriction of activities may be related to the concept of vulnerability through either imbalance or pollution. Activity regulation related to the concept of disharmony or imbalance includes the avoidance of air, cold, and spirits. Hispanic women, particularly primiparas, are encouraged by their mothers and grandmothers to remain indoors and avoid strenuous work. They may wear a *faja*, a heavy cotton abdominal binder or girdle, which is believed to prevent cold air from entering the uterus. It is believed that the head, shoulders, and feet should be covered or blindness, mastitis, frigidity, or sterility may result (Kay, 1978). Asian women also may adhere to such activity restrictions. Pillsbury (1982) describes the Chinese custom of "doing the month," which includes prohibitions against going outside into the sunshine, coming into contact with drafts, walking about, reading, or crying. Thai women may fear *lom phit dyan*, an illness caused by air or wind and characterized by postpartum weakness, nausea, and hypersensitivity to odors; to prevent this condition, many Thai women tie a string around their wrist to prevent soul loss and follow certain food and activity taboos (Kunstadter, 1978). Many African-American women view themselves as "sick" during the period of postpartal lochial flow, just as they do during menstruation. Activity restrictions during this time may include the avoidance of bathing, showering, and washing the hair, as well as heavy work (Carrington, 1978). Jimenez and Newton (1979) reviewed postpartum activity and work among 195 societies and found that about half the cultural groups advocated a return to full duties by 2 weeks postpartum. Another quarter of the groups believed that it was appropriate to return to full activity by 5 or 6 weeks postpartum.

In some cultures, women are considered to be in a state of impurity or pollution during the postpartum period. Consequently, ritual seclusion and activity elimination may be practiced to reduce the risk of increasing personal vulnerability to spirit influence or of spreading evil and misfortune. In many cultures this time coincides with the period of lochial flow or postpartum bleeding. Common proscriptions or taboos include seclusion and avoidance of contact with others, avoidance of contact with food or objects, and avoidance of sexual relations. A ritual bath may mark the end of the state of pollution; for Navajo women, this may occur on the fourth postpartum day; for Hispanic women, at 2 weeks postpartum; and for Orthodox Jewish women, on the seventh day after cessation of the lochial flow (Bash, 1980; Kay, 1982). American feminists have considered many menstrual and postpartum taboos as indications of misogyny and the suppression of the basic rights of women in traditional patriarchal cultures, yet many of the postpartum restrictions related to activity serve useful and health-promoting functions. First, seclusion of mother and baby reduces the risk of infection to both. Second, the avoidance of regular duties and customs related to hospitality, such as food preparation, effectively promotes rest for a woman who requires it for healing and lactation. Third, the proscription against resumption of sexual relations, which in some cultures is extended through lactation, serves to protect the mother against another pregnancy too soon. Finally, the enforced closeness of mother and baby fosters successful breast feeding and the early initiation of mother-infant attachment. Many women in both economically advantaged and disadvantaged households are unable to reduce their activity for extended periods postpartum. Most American women return to work, either within or outside the home, by 2 to 4 weeks postpartum.

Infant Care

The dominant American attitudes about infants and approaches to infant care have undergone some recent changes. With the increase in women in the work force, fathers are becoming more involved in infant care, and nonrelatives are frequently used as babysitters or day-care providers. Although children are valued and bearing and raising children within the nuclear family remain important, increasing numbers of American women are focusing on careers, delaying childbirth, limiting family size, or bearing and raising children outside a nuclear family structure. Members of some cultures or religions may view childbearing differently. The birth of a child is crucial for many Hispanic, Navajo, African-American, Middle Eastern, and Mormon women, whose social role and status are attained through reproduction within the marital relationship (Carrington, 1978; Kay, 1980; Meleis and Sorrell, 1981; Stark, 1982: Wright, 1982). Preference for a male child exists among families of many cultures, particularly Middle Eastern and Asian. Lesbian mothers may prefer to raise a female infant (Wolf, 1982). Nurses may have difficulty accepting the mother's or family's initial display of disappointment if the infant is not of the culturally desired sex.

Approaches to specific newborn care practices, such as feeding, circumcision, and cord care, also may vary among cultural groups. In American culture, the proportion of women choosing to breast feed has steadily increased in recent years, although low-income women continue to choose bottle feeding more frequently than do economically advantaged women. Many factors may act as important barriers to successful breast feeding. These include cultural beliefs about the roles of women, female sexuality, and mothering; the attitudes and past experiences of the doctors and nurses the mother sees; the support, or lack of it, of the family; and economic and cultural institutions that support the "American way" of bottle feeding (Raphael, 1973; Lawrence, 1980; Arango, 1984). Bryant (1982) has shown that among Anglo families in Florida, the husband has significant input into the decision about infant feeding, while other

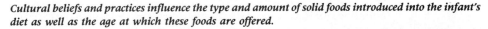

Cultural beliefs and practices influence the type and amount of solid foods introduced into the infant's diet as well as the age at which these foods are offered.

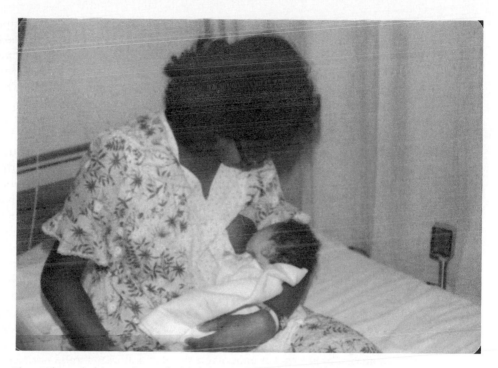

The mother's decision to breast feed is interrelated with cultural beliefs about the roles of women, female sexuality, and mothering.

members of the family and social support network have little influence on the decision. Puerto Rican and Cuban women in Bryant's Florida sample relied heavily on the opinion of the maternal grandmother and other female relatives and friends. According to Nelson and Hewitt (1983), most Laotian Hmong women choose to bottle feed, perhaps because bottle feeding is viewed as the modern or American way. Nurses who counsel mothers about breast feeding and other infant feeding practices must be aware of the multiplicity of factors influencing feeding choice and encourage parents to make choices based on personal beliefs and professional advice.

Circumcision (removal of the foreskin of the penis) continues to be widely practiced in the United States, despite a lack of agreement about the medical advantages of this operation. The religious practice of circumcision is followed by Jews all over the world; considered a sacred ritual, it is performed by a trained *mohel* (circumcisor) on the eighth day of life (Bash, 1980). For nonreligious reasons, circumcision is also commonly practiced among white and black Americans, but it is rarely practiced among Native American, Asian, and Hispanic families. In a study of the variables affecting parents' decisions about circumcision, Harris (1986) reported that none of the major factors that seem to influence the decision are based on logical reasoning or fact but arise out of value systems and cultural beliefs. Parents in Harris's study decided in favor of circumcision largely on the basis of a desire for the male child to be anatomically similar to his father, siblings, and peers; the assumption that circumcision is always done in American culture; the false belief that infants do not feel the pain of the procedure; the possibility of future sexual problems; and hygienic or cosmetic reasons. Participants in Harris's study also were influenced by Biblical guidance for the procedure, the feeling that the operation should be performed "just in case," and medical advice. Even the pediatricians in Harris's study who stated that they were against circumcision all had sons who had been circumcised. Emotional attachment to doing things in the patterns of one's own culture is very strong. Nurses who counsel parents about circumcision must be aware of their own cultural values and biases about the procedure so that they can provide parents with the appropriate medical facts.

Care of the infant's umbilical cord varies within and between cultures. Perry (1982) reviewed transcultural customs surrounding cord care and found many diverse rituals, customs, and beliefs. The current American cultural customs surrounding cord care include cord clamping and sterile severance at delivery and air drying of the stump. No dressings or bindings are used, and the application of an alcohol or dye preparation several times daily is believed to speed drying. Once the cord stump dries and falls off, it is discarded. In contrast, Hispanic, Filipino, and black women may use an abdominal binder or belly band to protect the umbilical area against dirt, injury, or hernia, and some Hispanic and Filipino women may apply oils to the cord stump (Affonso, 1978; Carrington, 1978; Kay, 1978). Hospital, clinic, or office nurses may never see this binder because it is often removed before a visit to the health care provider, but a community health nurse may see such practices on home visits. When asked about cord care practices, women often report that they are following the recommendations of the maternal or paternal grandmother. In general, nurses should not recommend binding and the application of oil to the cord stump because of the risk of infection. Women who use binders despite the recommendations of health professionals should be taught to keep the cord area as dry and clean as possible and to recognize signs of infection.

In the dominant American culture, an infant is frequently wrapped warmly in blankets, placed in an infant seat or stroller, and put to sleep in a crib in a nursery. Mothers of other cultures may choose to carry or wrap their infants differently; women from some cultures carry their babies with them at all times, pick them up immediately when they cry, and sleep with them (Affonso, 1978; Clark and Howland, 1978; Stringfellow, 1978; Berenstein and Kidd, 1982). Southeast Asian babies may be carried in a hip sling or a blanket carrier; American Indian infants, particularly Navajo, are often carried in cradleboards. A cradleboard is a traditional wooden frame into which an infant is bundled and tied. The Navajo believe that the cradleboard was given to the people by the White Shell Woman, and each part has particular significance; the wooden arch in front of the baby's face signifies the rainbow, the loops of lacing depict the rays of the sun, the lacing itself represents lightning, and the footrest is the image of a small rainbow (Morgan, 1982). The cradleboard is properly blessed before use and can be carried, attached to the mother's back, hung from a tree, or propped up to keep the baby comfortable, safe, and secure (Farris, 1978).

Fertility Control

The literature provides only limited information about cultural beliefs and practices related to the control of fertility. The biologic, or "natural," fertility of a woman varies depending on a number of factors. These factors include her monthly probability of conceiving, the probability of intrauterine mortality, the duration of the postpartum

Culturally acceptable methods used by parents to carry infants include strapping the baby closely to the mother's body with cloth, a practice prevalent in traditional Chinese culture.

period during which she is unlikely to ovulate or conceive, and the likelihood of sterility (MacCormack, 1982). These biologic variables are further modified by cultural and social variables, including marriage and residence patterns, diet, religion, availability of abortion, incidence of venereal disease, and the regulation of birth intervals by cultural or artificial means. The focus of this section is the cultural and artificial regulation of birth intervals.

Commonly used methods of contraception in the United States include hormonal contraception (i.e., "the pill"), intrauterine devices (IUDs), permanent sterilization, and to a lesser degree, barrier and "natural" methods. Natural methods of family planning are based on the recognition of fertility through signs and symptoms and abstinence during fertile periods. The religious beliefs of some American cultural groups may affect their use of fertility controls such as abortion or artificial regulation of conception; for example, Catholics may follow church edicts against artificial conception control, and Mormon families may follow their church's teaching about the spiritual responsibility to have large families and promote church growth (Stark, 1982).

The ability to control fertility successfully also requires an understanding of the menstrual cycle and the times and conditions under which pregnancy is more or less likely to occur. According to Scott (1978), each woman holds culturally defined and learned sets of beliefs about her bodily functions. When these functions change, the woman may perceive the changes as abnormal or unhealthy. Because the use of artificial methods of fertility control may alter the body's usual cycles, women who use them may become anxious, consider themselves ill, and discontinue the method. Scott's (1978) study revealed that Bahamian, Cuban, Haitian, and Puerto Rican women in Florida were dissatisfied with hormonal and intrauterine contraception because of the alteration these methods caused in their menstrual cycles. Native American women also monitor their monthly bleeding cycles closely and believe in the importance of monthly menstruation for maintaining harmony and physical well-being. Contraceptives such as the IUD are generally better accepted than hormonal methods because of the normal or increased flow associated with the IUD. Because the mechanism of action of an IUD may include the expulsion of a fertilized ovum, some women oppose use of the IUD on religious grounds.

In a recent study by Yusu, Siedlecky, and Byrnes (1993), 980 Turkish, Lebanese, and Vietnamese immigrant women living in Sydney, Australia, were surveyed regarding family planning. Both the Lebanese and Turkish women were better informed about modern forms of contraception (i.e., the pill, condoms, and IUDs) than were Vietnamese women. Currently, use of the pill and traditional methods of birth control (abstinence, prolonged breast feeding, rhythm, and withdrawal) were the most common forms of birth control regardless of ethnicity. However, Turkish women continued to rely on abortion as a means for contraception as well. Condom use was low among Lebanese husbands but high among the young Turkish and Vietnamese groups. IUDs were employed more often among Turkish women, with sterilization being the contraceptive method of choice for both Lebanese and Turkish women over age 40. Only two Vietnamese women reported husbands having had vasectomies, probably indicating a low cultural acceptance of this form of contraception. Lucas (1984) also described a similar nonacceptance of vasectomy among immigrants living in the United States.

Religious belief systems also can influence birth control choices. For example, the Hindu religion teaches that the right hand is clean and the left one is dirty. The right hand is for holding religious books and eating utensils, with the left hand being used for holding dirty things, such as genitals. This belief becomes problematic for some forms of contraceptives that require the use of both hands, such as a diaphragm (Bromwich and Parson, 1990). Buddhism values a celibate life and natural things. Modern contraceptives are not considered by the Buddhist religion to be natural, making contraceptive use unacceptable (Bromwich and Parson, 1990). Guatemalan women believe strongly in privacy; therefore, skirts are kept on during intercourse and childbirth. Some Guatemalan women also believe it is improper to touch or expose their genitals, making traditional birth control methods such as abstinence or the rhythm method much more acceptable (Cosminsky, 1982). Birth spacing in the African culture traditionally has been to employ a taboo on postpartum sexual activity, with some women leaving their home for up to 2 years in order to avoid pregnancy (Miller, 1992).

According to Shain (1982), who reviewed abortion practices and attitudes from a cross-cultural perspective, abortion has been one of the most universally prevalent methods of fertility control throughout recorded history. Women may perform their own abortions or seek help from others, and the techniques they have used are extremely varied. However, few cultural groups give abortion unqualified social approval. In the United States, religious affiliation is the variable most closely associated with attitudes toward abortion.

Nurses who provide family planning services also can provide culturally sensitive fertility counseling. Most important, nurses can help women define their own sense of gynecologic well-being and their own attitudes and beliefs about fertility, conception, and birth. Then clients can decide whether they wish to select a culturally and personally appropriate method. Some members of diverse cultural groups in the United States believe that pressure to select a family planning method is placed on minorities because of a classist and racist desire to limit the growth of minority groups. Nurses must be careful to ask women and families about their desire for contraception or fertility regulation in a nonjudgmental way. "Are you interested in discussing ways to space children or prevent pregnancy?" or "How do you feel about having children at this time?" may be a culturally sensitive way to initiate a discussion about fertility.

Summary

Cultural beliefs and practices are continuously evolving and changing, and data do not exist on the cultural experience of childbearing among all the different cultures in the world. Nurses must therefore acknowledge the range of different cultural beliefs and value systems and individually explore the meaning of health and childbirth with all the families they meet. Nurses also must work actively to reduce the experience of cultural shock for childbearing families, remembering that American medical beliefs and practices may seem strange, irrational, and superstitious to others. Cultural shock can be related to a conflict between the nurse's attitudes and beliefs and the values, beliefs, and practices of the women and families for whom the nurse cares. Nurses must evaluate their own attitudes, beliefs, and values and attempt to discover why they carry out certain rituals, procedures, or patterns of nursing care.

Of course, not all nurses are expected to agree with or subscribe to all the different cultural variations in belief or practice related to pregnancy, childbirth, and fertility control. But it is important for the nurse to remember that all behavior must be evaluated from within the context of the individual and her or his cultural background and experience. The particular behaviors themselves are not as significant as the relationship of those behaviors to the personal values held by the woman and her family (Okamoto, 1978). Nurses who strive to foster health-promoting attitudes and behaviors must begin at the most basic level: empathic concern and respect for the individual. By incorporating the assessment of cultural beliefs and practices into the clients' plans of care, nurses demonstrate respect, reduce stress due to feelings of isolation and alienation, and take a beginning step toward developing culturally appropriate patterns of caring for childbearing women and their families.

References

Affonso, D. D. (1978). The Filipino American. In A. L. Clark (Ed.), *Culture, Childbearing and Health Professionals.* Philadelphia: F. A. Davis.

Arango, J. O. (1984). Promoting breast feeding: A national perspective. *Public Health Report, 99*(6), 559–565.

Arms, S. (1975). *Immaculate Deception: A New Look at Women and Childbirth in America.* Boston: Houghton Mifflin.

Bash, D. M. (1980). Jewish religious practices related to childbearing. *Journal of Nurse-Midwifery, 25*(5), 39–42.

Bauwens, E. E. (1978). *The Anthropology of Health.* St. Louis: C.V. Mosby.

Bauwens, E., and Anderson, S. (1978). Home births: A reaction to hospital environmental pressure. In E. Bauwens (Ed.), *Anthropology of Human Birth.* St. Louis: C.V. Mosby.

Berenstein, J. L., and Kidd, Y. A. (1982). Childbearing in Japan. In M. A. Kay (Ed.), *Anthropology of Human Birth.* Philadelphia: F. A. Davis.

Boehme, T. (1985). Hepatitis B: The nurse-midwife's role in management and prevention. *Journal of Nurse-Midwifery, 30*(2), 79–87.

Bromwich, P., and Parsons, T. (1990). *Contraception: The Facts,* 2d ed. Oxford: Oxford University Press.

Bryant, C. A. (1982). The impact of kin, friend, and neighbor networks on infant feeding practices. *Social Science Medicine, 16,* 1757–1765.

Bullock, W. H., and Jilly, P. N. (1975). Hematology. In R. A. Williams (Ed.), *Black Related Diseases* (pp. 234–272). New York: McGraw-Hill.

Campanella, K., Korbin, J., and Acheson, L. (1993). Pregnancy and childbirth among the Amish. *Social Science Medicine, 36*(3), 333–342.

Caldeyro-Barcia, R. (1979). The influence of maternal position on time of spontaneous rupture of the membranes, progress of labor, and fetal head compression. *Birth and Family Journal, 6,* 7–16.

Carrington, B. W. (1978). The Afro-American. In A. L. Clark (Ed.), *Culture, Childbearing and Health Professionals.* Philadelphia: F. A. Davis.

Clark, A. L., and Howland, R. I. (1978). The American Somoan. In A. L. Clark (Ed.), *Culture, Childbearing and Health Professionals.* Philadelphia: F. A. Davis.

Cosminsky, S. (1982). Childbirth and change: A Guatemalan study. In C. P. MacCormack (Ed.), *Etiology of Fertility and Birth.* New York: Academic Press.

Day. A. Y. (1983). Childbearing practices in the Appalachian culture. *Frontier Nursing Service Quarterly Bulletin, 59*(1), 1–7.

Dempsey, P. A., and Gesse, T. (1983). The childbearing Haitian refugee—Cultural applications to clinical nursing. *Public Health Report, 98*(3), 261–267.

Erickson, R. V., and Hoang, G. N. (1980). Health problems among Indochinese refugees. *American Journal of Public Health, 70*(9), 1003–1005.

Farris, L. (1978). The American Indian. In A. L. Clark (Ed.), *Culture, Childbearing and Health Professionals.* Philadelphia: F. A. Davis.

Flint, M. (1982). Lockmi: An Indian midwife. In M. A. Kay (Ed.), *Anthropology of Human Birth.* Philadelphia: F. A. Davis.

Ford, C. S. (1964). *A Comparative Study of Human Reproduction.* New Haven: Human Relations Area Files Press.

Frankel, B. (1977). *Childbirth in the Ghetto: Folk Beliefs of Negro Women in a North Philadelphia Hospital Ward.* San Francisco: R & E Research Associates.

Gaviria, M., Stern, G., and Schensul, S. L. (1982). Sociocultural factors and perinatal health in a Mexican-American community. *Journal of the National Medical Association, 74*(10), 983–989.

Haire, D. (1972). *The Cultural Warping of Childbirth.* Minneapolis: International Childbirth Education Association.

Harris, C. C. (1986). Cultural values and the decision to circumcise. *Image: Journal of Nursing Scholarship, 18*(3), 98–104.

Horn, B. M. (1981). Cultural concepts and postpartal care. *Nursing and Health Care, 2*(9), 516–517, 526–527.

Horn, B. M. (1983). Cultural beliefs and teenage pregnancy. *Nurse Practitioner, 8*(8), 35–39.

Hott, J. R. (1980). Best laid plans. *Nursing Research, 29,* 20–27.

Jimenez, M. H., and Newton, N. (1979). Activity and work during pregnancy and the postpartum period: A cross-cultural study of 202 societies. *American Journal of Obstetrics and Gynecology, 15*(2), 171–176.

Johnston, M. (1980). Cultural variations in professional and parenting patterns. *JOGN Nursing, 9*(1), 9–13.

Kay, M. A. (1978). The Mexican American, In A. L. Clark (Ed.), *Culture, Childbearing and Health Professionals.* Philadelphia: F. A. Davis.

Kay, M. A. (1980). Mexican, Mexican-American, and Chicana childbirth. In M. B. Melville (Ed.), *Twice a Minority: Mexican-American Women.* St. Louis: C.V. Mosby.

Kay, M. A. (1982). Writing an ethnography of birth. In M. A. Kay (Ed.), *Anthropology of Human Birth.* Philadelphia: F. A. Davis.

Kim, K., and Mo, S. (1977). A study of food taboos on the Jeju island: Focused on pregnancy. *Korean Journal of Nutrition, 10,* 49–57.

Kitzinger, S. (1982). The social context of birth: Some comparisons between childbirth in Jamaica and Britain. In C. P. MacCormack (Ed.), *Ethnography of Fertility and Birth.* New York: Academic Press.

Kunstadter, P. (1978). Do cultural differences make any difference? Choice points in medical systems available in northwestern Thailand. In A. Kleinman. P. Kindstadter, E. R. Alexander, and J. L. Gate (Eds.), *Culture and Healing in Asian Societies: Anthropological, Psychiatric, and Public Health Studies.* Cambridge, MA: Schenkman Publishing Company.

Lawrence, R. A. (1980). *Breastfeeding: A Guide for the Medical Profession.* St. Louis: C. V. Mosby.

Logan, B. B., and Dawkins, C. E. (1986). *Family Centered Nursing in the Community.* Menlo Park, CA: Addison-Wesley.

Lucas, D. (1984). Sterilization in Canberra. *Journal of Biosocial Science, 16,* 335–342.

McBride, A. B. (1982). The American way of birth. In M. A. Kay (Ed.), *Anthropology of Human Birth.* Philadelphia: F. A. Davis.

McClain, C. (1982). Toward a comparative framework for the study of childbirth: A review of the literature. In M. A. Kay (Ed.), *Anthropology of Human Birth*. Philadelphia: F. A. Davis.

MacCormack, C. P. (1982). Biological, cultural, and social adaptation in human fertility and birth: A synthesis. In C. P. MacCormack (Ed.), *Ethnography of Fertility and Birth*. New York: Academic Press.

Mead, M., and Newton, N. (1967). Cultural patterning of perinatal behavior. In S. A. Richardson and A. F. Guttmacher (Eds.), *Childbearing: Its Social and Psychological Aspects*. Baltimore: Williams & Wilkins.

Meleis, A. I., and Sorrell, L. (1981). Bridging cultures: Arab American women and their birth experiences. *Maternal Child Nursing, 6,* 171–176.

Mercer, R. T., and Stainton, M. C. (1984). Perceptions of the birth experience: A cross-cultural comparison. *Health Care for Women International, 5,* 29–47.

Milinaire, C. (1974). *Birth*. New York: Crown Publishers.

Miller, M. A. (1992). Contraception outside North America: Options and popular choices. *NAACOG's Clinical Issues, 3*(2), 253–265.

Morgan, R. (1982). Personal communication.

Naroll, F., Naroll, R., and Howard, F. H. (1961). Position of women in childbirth. *American Journal of Obstetrics and Gynecology, 82,* 943–954.

Nelson, C. C., and Hewitt, M. A. (1983). An Indochinese refugee population in a nurse-midwifery service. *Journal of Nurse-Midwifery, 28*(5), 9–14.

Newton, N., and Newton, M. (1972). Childbirth in cross-cultural perspective. In J. G. Howells (Ed.), *Modern Perspectives in Psycho-Obstetrics*. New York: Brunner/Mazel.

Oakley, A. (1977). Cross-cultural practices. In T. Chard and M. Richards (Eds.), *Benefits and Hazards of the New Obstetrics*. Philadelphia: J.B. Lippincott.

Oakley, A. (1980). *Women Confined: Towards a Sociology of Childbirth*. New York: Schocken Books.

Okamoto, N. I. (1978). The Japanese American. In A. L. Clark (Ed.), *Culture, Childbearing and Health Professionals*. Philadelphia: F. A. Davis.

Overfield, T. (1985). *Biologic Variation in Health and Illness*. Menlo Park, CA: Addison-Wesley.

Perry, D. (1982). The umbilical cord: Transcultural care and customs. *Journal of Nurse-Midwifery, 27*(4), 25–30.

Pettit, D. J., Knowler, W. C., Baird, H. R., and Bennet, P. H. (1980). Gestational diabetes: Infant and maternal complications of pregnancy in relation to third-trimester glucose tolerance in Pima Indians. *Diabetes Care, 3*(3), 458–464.

Philpott, L. L. (1979). A Descriptive Study of Birth Practices and Midwifery in the Lower Rio Grande Valley of Texas. Ph.D. dissertation, University of Texas Health Science Center, Houston School of Public Health.

Pickwell, S. (1983). Health screening for Indochinese refugees. *Nurse Practitioner, 8*(4), 20–21, 25.

Pillsbury, B. (1982). "Doing the month": Confinement and convalescence of Chinese women after childbirth. In M. A. Kay (Ed.), *Anthropology of Human Birth*. Philadelphia: F. A. Davis.

Pritchard, I. A., MacDonald, P. C., and Gant, N. F. (1984). *William's Obstetrics*, 17th Ed. Norwalk, CT: Appleton-Century-Crofts.

Raphael, D. (1973). *The Tender Gift: Breastfeeding*. New York: Schocken Books.

Raphael, D. (1976). Matrescence, becoming a mother, a new/old rite de passage. In F. X. Grollig and H. B. Haley (Eds.), *Medical Anthropology*. Paris: Mouton Publishers.

Roberts, J. (1980). Alternative positions for childbirth: II. Second stage of labor. *Journal of Nurse-Midwifery, 25*(5), 13–19.

Rose, P. A. (1978). The Chinese American. In A. L. Clark (Ed.), *Culture, Childbearing and Health Professionals*. Philadelphia: F. A. Davis.

Rubin, R. (1984). *Maternal Identity and the Maternal Experience*. New York: Springer Publishing Company.

Shain, N. S. (1982). Abortion practices in cross-cultural perspective. *American Journal of Obstetrics and Gynecology, 142*(3), 245–251.

Snow, L., Johnson, S. M., and Mayhew, H. E. (1978). The behavioral implications of some old wive's tales. *Obstetrics and Gynecology, 51*(6), 727–732.

Stanton, M. E. (1979). The "myth" of natural childbirth. *Journal of Nurse Midwifery, 24*(2), 25–28.

Stark, S. (1982). Mormon childbearing. In M. A. Kay (Ed.), *Anthropology of Human Birth*. Philadelphia: F.A. Davis.

Stringfellow, L. (1978). The Vietnamese. In A. L. Clark (Ed.), *Culture, Childbearing and Health Professionals*. Philadelphia: F.A. Davis.

Tash, D., and Kenney, J. (1993). The lesbian childbearing couple: A case report. *Birth, 20*(1), 36–40.

Thompson, J., and Thompson, M. (1983). *Genetics in Medicine*, 3d Ed. Philadelphia: W.B. Saunders.

Turrell, S. (1985). Asians expectations: Customs surrounding pregnancy and childbirth. *Nursing Times, 81*(18), 44–46.

Wertz, R. W., and Wertz, D. C. (1977). *Lying In: A History of Childbirth in America*. New York: Macmillan.

Wolf, D. G. (1982). Lesbian childbirth and artificial insemination: A wave or the future. In M. A. Kay (Ed.), *Anthropology of Human Birth*. Philadelphia: F.A. Davis.

Wright, A. (1982). Attitudes toward childbearing and menstruation among the Navajo. In M. A. Kay (Ed.), *Anthropology of Human Birth*. Philadelphia: F.A. Davis.

Yusu, F., Siedlecky, S., and Byrnes, M. (1993). Family planning practices among Lebanese, Turkish and Vietnamese women in Sydney. *Australian New Zealand Journal of Obstetrics and Gynecology, 33*(1), 8–16.

Zapeda, M. (1982). Selected maternal-infant care practices of Spanish-speaking women. *JOGN Nursing, 11*(6), 371–374.

4

Transcultural Perspectives in the Nursing Care of Children and Adolescents

Margaret M. Andrews

When the teacher asked a class of Amish children to write down what they had learned about the human body, one boy gave the following response:

"Our body is divided into three parts, the branium, the borax, and the abominable cavity. The branium contains the brain, if any. The borax contains the lungs, the lights and the heart. The abominable cavity contains the five bowels—A, E, I, O and U."

Byler, E. (1992). Plain and Happy Living: Amish Recipes and Remedics. (p. 80). Cleveland, OH: Goose Acres Press.

Introduction

By the year 2000, children aged 18 years and younger from culturally diverse groups are expected to comprise one-third of the U.S. and Canadian populations. Society depends on its children for its future and provides its offspring with care, nurturance, and socialization. Cultural survival depends on transmission of values and customs from one generation to the next, a process that relies on children and adolescents for its success.

The purpose of this chapter is to examine the ways in which culture affects the nursing care of children and adolescents. Children and adolescents may find themselves living in families in which there is racial, ethnic, and/or religious diversity. For this reason, the chapter begins with a discussion of family and culture and then examines normal growth and development, nutrition, sleep, elimination, parent-child relationships, sex roles, child-rearing practices, health, and illness from a transcultural nursing perspective.

Family and Culture

For centuries, the family has been implicitly and explicitly recognized as a critical social unit mediating cultural beliefs and practices, including those concerning health and illness, from one generation to the next. Culture, like language, is acquired early in life, and cultural understanding is typically established by age 5. Every interaction, sound, touch, odor, and experience has a cultural component that is absorbed by the child even when it is not directly taught. Lessons learned at such early ages become an integral part of thinking and behavior. Table manners, the proper behavior when interacting with adults, and the rules of acceptable emotional response are anchored in culture.

Margaret M. Andrews and Joyceen S. Boyle: TRANSCULTURAL CONCEPTS IN NURSING CARE, SECOND EDITION. © 1995 J.B. Lippincott Company.

There are many beliefs and behaviors learned at an early age that persist into adulthood. For example, children learn rules about how to dress in different settings and discover that one's attire in a place of worship varies from that in a school. Children from various cultural backgrounds learn that eating may involve using a knife, fork, and spoon; chopsticks; or one's right hand. There are many rules about speaking to adults. Depending on the culture, children may be permitted to initiate conversation with an adult; required to use titles of respect; taught to look at the adult while speaking; or expected to look down at the floor when interacting with an adult as a sign of respect.

Unfortunately, there is a dearth of research linking cultural factors to the ways in which families respond to and cope with illnesses and disabilities during childhood and adolescence. The following discussion provides a summary of current research and theory development on this important topic.

Over time, culture has influenced family functioning in a great variety of ways, including marriage forms, choice of mates, postmarital residence, family kinship system, rules governing inheritance, household and family structure, family obligations, family-community dynamics, and alternative family formations. Historically, the family has been the conduit for cultural transmission, providing a natural environment in which traditions are passed from generation to generation, as well as updated throughout the ages to keep culture and ethnic heritages alive. In turn, the traditions themselves have given families a sense of stability and support from which members draw comfort, guidance, and a means of coping with the problems of daily life (Burgio, 1991; Tseng and Hsu, 1991; McCubbin et al., 1993).

Children and adolescents live in a variety of family constellations. Although there are various ways to categorize families, the following are commonly recognized types of families in which children and adolescents may be members: *nuclear* [husband, wife, and child(ren)], *extended* (nuclear plus blood relatives), *blended* [husband, wife, and child(ren) from previous relationships], *single-parent* [one parent and child(ren)], *communal* (group of men, women, and children), *cohabitation* [unmarried man and woman sharing a household with child(ren)], and *gay* [same-gender couples and child(ren)].

Each family modifies the culture of the larger group in ways that are uniquely its own. Some beliefs, practices, and customs are maintained, whereas others are altered or abandoned. Although it is helpful for nurses to have a basic knowledge of their clients' cultural backgrounds, it is also necessary to view each family on an individual basis. Assumptions or biased expectations cannot be allowed to replace accurate assessment of children, adolescents, and their families. As discussed in Chapter 1, it is essential for the nurse to remember that not all members of a cultural group fit the textbook description of that cultural stereotypical behavior. For example, although many Chinese-American children behave in the stereotypical manner, showing respect for authority, polite social behavior, and moderate-to-soft voice, there are some who are disrespectful, impolite, and boisterous. Individual differences, changing norms over time, degree of acculturation, length of time the family has lived in a country, and other factors account for variation in the stereotype.

The behavior of children and adolescents is influenced by child-rearing practices, parental beliefs about involvement with children, and type and frequency of disciplinary measures. Although both parents exert an influence on the child's orientation to health, research indicates that a wide cultural variability exists, with the mother being the most influential parent in the majority of cultural groups (Gutierrez and Sameroff,

Nurses should avoid gender-related cultural stereotypes about single heads of household. Men, as well as women, may find themselves as heads of household, often as a result of spousal death, divorce, or separation.

1990; Johnston, 1977; Tolson and Wilson, 1990). Thus identifying the attitudes, values, and beliefs about health and illness held by the parents and other primary providers of care is an important part of the cultural assessment of the family.

According to Richman, Miller, and LeVine (1992), mothers' attitudes toward health and illnesses are related to their educational level because the "school experience provides women with verbal skills and models of adult-child verbal instruction that they would not acquire without schooling and that are carried forward into the way they care for their infants as parents" (p. 620). Furthermore, mothers with little formal education tend to be more fatalistic about illness and less concerned with detecting clinical manifestations of disease in their children than well-educated mothers. The former also are less likely to follow up on precautionary measures suggested by health care providers. A mother who believes that people have no control over whether they become sick is not apt to have an approach to health in which there is anticipatory guidance or accident prevention and may not comply with recommended immunization schedules. Nursing interventions with a mother who believes that there is much a person can do to keep from becoming ill will be different with regard to the nature of health education and counseling provided by the nurse.

With a knowledge of the belief system(s) of the family, the nurse has data from which to choose approaches and priorities. For a mother who is not oriented to prevention of illness or maintenance of health, focusing energies on teaching might not be very productive; it might be more useful to spend time designing family follow-up or establishing an interpersonal relationship that invites the parent to follow recommended immunization schedules, well-child care, and other aspects of health promotion. The nurse also should be prepared to understand why the mother who is less educated and embraces a fatalistic philosophy may fail to show up for scheduled well-child appointments while arriving for an appointment when she believes her child is sick.

Extended Family

In the dominant Euro-American society, the nuclear family is frequently considered the norm, and it is the unit upon which most health care programs are designed. Cross-nationally, however, the nuclear family is a rarity. In only 6 percent of the world's societies are families as isolated and nuclear as in the United States (Groce and Zola, 1993). The extended family is far more universally the norm. Kin residence sharing has long been acknowledged as characteristic of many African-American, Mexican-American, Amish, and other groups. Sharing a residence with a relative may represent a viable alternative in efficiently managing scarce resources necessary for successful child rearing and an adaptation for survival and protection (Garcia Coll, 1990).

In societies where the extended family is the norm, parents, particularly young parents, may be considered too inexperienced to make major decisions on behalf of their child, and key decisions are frequently made in consultation with more mature relatives such as grandparents, uncles, aunts, cousins, or other kin. Sometimes non-blood-related persons are considered to be part of the extended family. Among many Mexican, Puerto Rican, Filipino, French, Italian, Polish, and other people who belong to the Roman Catholic religion, godparents may be involved in key decisions concerning the child and may be expected to participate in some aspects of the child's upbringing.

Godparents are often seen as important role models for the children and valuable sources of support for the children.

In some African nations, anyone residing in the same village is referred to as a "brother" or "sister," thus extending the family orientation beyond biologic relationships. Among the Amish, the extended family may consist of members of an entire community, and a young couple may turn to that community for assistance with decision making, finances, and emotional and spiritual support.

While U.S./Canadian laws and customs will undoubtedly ensure that parents retain the right to make decisions on behalf of their child, it would behoove nurses to include members of the extended family in the plan of care. Often, in an attempt to empower the parents, nurses and other members of the health care team have failed to include or involve grandparents, cousins, and others who have accompanied the parents. Nurses need to challenge the sometimes unstated belief that participation by "outsiders" is disruptive, since this assumption may not be valid. Indeed, parents may be unable to come to a final decision until others have been consulted, and parental requests for others to be included on such occasions should be respected (Groce and Zola, 1993). Nurses should ask the parents if anyone besides themselves will be participating in the decision making that affects their child.

Cultural groups may differ not only in the central role played by families but also in the way they are structured hierarchically. In many parts of the world, distinct lines are drawn between members of society based on family connections, education, and wealth, and all members of the society are keenly aware of where they fit within this hierarchy. For example, in nations such as India, the existence of a caste system has been an integral component of the social order for many centuries. It should be noted that nurses and other members of the health care team also are assigned a hierarchical position. Confusion may result when health care professionals who are viewed as holding a position at the upper end of the hierarchy and whose opinion is highly valued ask the parent whether a certain health-related intervention is acceptable. In many cultures, health care professionals are presumed to know the answers, and asking for feedback indicates a lack of knowledge or training in the professional.

The impact of the extended family or of the social support network on the child's development becomes particularly important when considering the number of single-parent households in some culturally diverse groups. More than one-half (55.3 percent) of all African-American children are born to a single mother, and three of every five (59.9 percent) African-American children under the age of 3 are not living with both parents. Among Puerto Ricans living in the United States, 44 percent of families are headed by single women (Garcia Coll, 1990; U.S. Census Bureau, 1990).

Each family modifies the culture of the larger group in ways that are uniquely its own. Some practices, beliefs, and customs are maintained; others are altered or abandoned. Although it is helpful for nurses to have a basic knowledge of their clients' cultural backgrounds, it is also necessary for them to view each family they encounter on an individual basis. Assumptions or biased expectations cannot be allowed to replace accurate assessments of children and their families. As discussed in Chapter 1, it is essential for the nurse to remember that not all members of a cultural group fit the textbook description of that culture's stereotypical behavior. Cultural stereotyping can hinder the nurse-family relationship and result in care that is culturally irrelevant and inappropriate. As Montagu (1977) states:

No single individual ever gains a knowledge of the whole of his culture. As a member of his culture, the individual is equipped to participate in it, not to become a mere repository of it.

Normal Growth and Development

Growth and development of infants and children is similar in all cultures, but important racial, ethnic, and sex differences can be identified. From the moment of conception, the developmental processes of the human life cycle take place in the context of culture. Throughout life, culture exerts an all-pervasive influence on the developing infant, child, and adolescent. When assessing children, the nurse must understand the relationship between the biologic and cultural aspects of development.

In assessing the growth and development of a child, it is important to determine the child's correct age. Stated age may vary according to culture. For example, the Vietnamese consider that infants are 1 year old at birth and that they become another year old at the next *Tet*, or New Year. Furthermore, some Vietnamese learned when immigrating that it was necessary to give inaccurate information about their children's ages in order to meet legal requirements for entrance into the United States. Thus an apparently simple question about a child's age is a potential source of miscommunication. Moreover, an apparently straightforward question about a child's age is more complex than the nurse might expect, and it may adversely affect the nurse-parent relationship, particularly if the parent misperceives the reason underlying the question. Unfortunately, many immigrants from Southeast Asian nations have had politically motivated, negative experiences at the hands of health care providers in their country of origin. As a result of these experiences, many parents project these same negative qualities onto health care providers in the United States or Canada, especially when "suspicious" questions are asked.

Birth weights differ between Western and non-Western neonates, a fact that is ignored by "standard growth grids." Western infants are slightly heavier at birth than are non-Western infants, and the size of a typical 1-year-old Western infant is greater in mean body weight, length, and head and chest circumference than that of a non-Western infant (Achar and Yankauer, 1962; Meredith, 1969). Western infants generally score lower than non-Western infants on tests of psychomotor development, including examinations at birth. Tooth eruption occurs earlier in Asian and black infants than in Caucasian infants. In some cultures, the standard Western developmental pattern of sitting-creeping-crawling-standing-walking-squatting is not followed. For example, the Balinese infant goes from sitting to squatting to standing (Mead and Macgregor, 1951). Hopi children begin walking about a month and a half later than Anglo children (Dennis and Dennis, 1940), which is paradoxical, given the advanced motor development that generally characterizes members of traditional societies (Geber, 1956).

During the second year of life, children in traditional societies begin to lose their advantage on tests of motor development. By age 2, their mean scores have fallen below those of Western children. The differences in physical growth continue, so school-aged children of Euro-American background are taller and heavier than their traditional counterparts (Meredith, 1969). Typical 8-year-olds from different ethnic groups, for example, may differ by as much as 4 inches in height and 15 pounds in weight.

Certain growth patterns can be identified across cultural boundaries: There is a pattern regardless of culture of general-to-specific abilities, from the center of the body to the extremities (proximal-distal development) and from the head to the toes (cephalocaudal development). Adult head size is reached by the age of 5 years; the remainder of the body continues to grow through adolescence. Physiologic maturation of organ systems, such as the renal, circulatory, and respiratory systems, occurs early, whereas maturation of the central nervous system continues throughout and beyond childhood.

The growth spurt of adolescence involves the skeletal and muscular systems, leading to significant changes in size and strength in both sexes, but particularly in males. North American Caucasian youths aged 12 to 18 years are 22 to 33 lb heavier and 6 in taller than Filipino youths the same age (Overfield, 1985). Black teenagers are somewhat taller and heavier than white teens up to age 15 years (Overfield, 1985). Japanese adolescents born in the United States or Canada are larger and taller than Japanese born and raised in Japan owing to differences in diet, climate, and social milieu. Adolescence also involves changes in the physiologic functioning of body systems, including the reproductive system. The emotional changes experienced by adolescents are related to both physical and cultural factors.

Preparation for adulthood is culturally determined. In some traditional cultures, socialization into adult roles is gradual, beginning in early childhood. For example, agricultural societies encourage children to assume gender-related roles that slowly develop and evolve until adult status is achieved. Boys are taught by their fathers and older brothers how to milk the cows, plant and sow the fields, mend fences, and so forth. Girls stay with their mothers, who teach them how to cook, sew, and care for younger siblings in the home. By the time adulthood is reached, both sexes are well equipped to function in the roles demanded of mature members of the culture. In other cultures, the transition to adulthood is abrupt, occurring in the late teen years or early twenties. Many middle- and upper-class parents allow, and even encourage, a prolonged adolescence, particularly when it involves the acquisition of additional education.

Cross-Cultural Research on Children's Growth and Development

Research in a variety of cultures has provided evidence of impressive regularities across cultures in developmental phenomena. For example, there is similarity cross-culturally in the sequence and timing of developmental milestones in infant development, smiling, and separation distress and in the order of stages in language acquisition. Developmental researchers who have worked in other cultures have become convinced that human functioning cannot be separated from the cultural and more immediate context in which children develop.

Not all developmental theories formulated on the basis of observations with Western children have cross-cultural generalizability. Investigations of the universality of the stages of development proposed by Piaget, the family role relations emphasized by Freud, and patterns of mother-infant interaction taken to index security of attachment have resulted in modifications to the assumptions of generality as a result of cross-cultural data. For example, findings that the highest stage of Piaget's theory of formal operations seldom can be seen in non-Western cultures prompted Piaget to modify his theory in 1972 to suggest that the formal operational stage may not be universal but rather a product of an individual's expertise in a specific domain (Rogoff and Morelli, 1989).

Several researchers have compared white, African-American, and Mexican-American families in reports of child-rearing attitudes and behaviors. Mexican-American parents of low socioeconomic status reported being less authoritarian, less achievement-oriented, more protective, and emphasizing less individual responsibility than African-American and white parents of the same socioeconomic group. African-American and Mexican-American parents expect children to overcome the dependency of infancy as soon as possible, e.g., early development of control over body functions (walking, weaning, toileting) and feelings (Garcia Coll, 1990).

When maternal perceptions of cries of Anglo, African-American, and Cuban-American mothers were compared, Anglo-American mothers found infant cries more distressing, urgent, arousing, and "sick sounding" than did African Americans, while Cuban Americans shared similarities with both groups. Cultural variation also occurred in the caregiving responses to the cries, with Anglo-American mothers waiting longer to give a pacifier than African-American mothers. White mothers also chose to pick up and cuddle the infants more than their African-American counterparts. Conversely, African-American mothers generally chose to cuddle infants the least, and Cubans chose to cuddle and give a pacifier more often than the other two groups. Thus not only did the groups perceive the infants' cries differently, but they also reported giving different caregiving responses. These results suggest cultural differences in mothers' developmental goals for their infants and in the way they perceive, react, and behave in response to their infants' cues, behaviors, and demands (Garcia Coll, 1990).

Summarized in Research Box 4-1 are findings from studies conducted on various aspects of child growth and development among culturally diverse groups.

 Research Box 4-1. Child Growth and Development Among Culturally Diverse Groups

Aponte, R., French, R., and Sherrill, C. (1990). Motor development of Puerto Rican children: Cross-cultural perspectives. *Perceptual and Motor Skills, 71*, 1200–1202.

Test of gross motor development administered to 300 Puerto Rican children, ages 5 to 7, revealed test-manual norms for U.S. children were applicable for all except 7-year-old girls.

Garcia Coll, C. T. (1990). Developmental outcome of minority infants: A process-oriented look into our beginnings. *Child Development, 60*, 270–289.

Review article on the development of minority children from birth to 3 years of age indicates that five factors influence developmental outcome of minority infants: (1) cultural beliefs and caregiving practices, (2) health status and health care practices, (3) family structure and characteristics, (4) socioeconomic factors, and (5) biologic factors.

Research Box 4-1 (*continued*)

Malina, R. M. (1988). Racial/ethnic variation in the motor development and performance of American children. *Canadian Journal of Spt Science, 13*(2), 136–143.

Black infants are advanced in motor development during first 2 years. School-aged black boys run faster, perform better vertical jumps than white or Mexican-American peers.

Rotheram-Borus, M. J., and Phinney, J. S. (1990). Patterns of social expectations among black and Mexican-American children. *Child Development, 61*, 542–556.

Patterns of social expectations among 213 black and Mexican-American children (third and sixth grades) were studied using responses to videotaped scenes of everyday social encounters with same-ethnic, unfamiliar peers at school. Mexican-American children reported expectations for sharing and relying on authority figures more often and apologizing, getting angry, and initiating action less often than their black peers. Emotional responses decreased and socially desirable responses increased with grade for both groups. Ethnic differences were greater at the sixth grade than at the third grade for both groups. Girls apologized and sought help from teachers more often than boys. High self-esteem was significantly correlated with being similar to one's own group.

Smith, J. D., and Caplan, J. (1988). Cultural differences in cognitive style development. *Developmental Psychology, 24*(1), 46–52.

Children in several cultures develop a similar cognitive style on the Matching Familiar Figures Test (MFFT). At first, children become more reflective (slow-accurate), then more fast-accurate. Japanese children outperformed others.

Widmayer, S. M., Peterson, L. M., Larner, M., et al. (1990). Predictors of Haitian-American infant development at twelve months. *Child Development, 61*, 410–415.

Perinatal and early childhood influences on development of 66 Haitian-American children were assessed using birth weight, household crowding, parental contributions to the child-rearing environment (the home), and developmental progress at 12 months on the Bayley Scales of Infant Development. Environmental differences influence infant development in subtle but significant ways among Haitians from the lower socioeconomic class.

Nutrition

As discussed in Chapter 2, health status is, in part, dependent on nutritional intake, so nutritional status and health are integrally linked. Although the United States is the world's greatest food-producing nation, nutritional status has not been a priority for many people in this country. An estimated 1 million U.S. children suffer from malnutrition serious enough to interfere with brain development. Many Southeast Asian refugees, for example, were in a prolonged state of malnutrition before emigrating, and illegal aliens, migrants, poor African Americans in rural and inner-city areas, Appalachians, and others living at the poverty level may be unable to provide their children with an adequate food intake.

Malnutrition is not found exclusively among children from the lower socioeconomic class. Many middle- and upper-class children, including some obese children, are also malnourished. Obesity frequently begins during infancy, when mothers succumb to pressures to overfeed. For example, all Vietnamese parents surveyed by Stringfellow and associates (1981) indicated that babies should be fat. Many other cultural groups also equate being fat with being healthy.

The popularity of fast-food restaurants and "junk" foods has resulted in a high-calorie, high-fat, high-cholesterol, and high-carbohydrate diet for many children. Parents are frequently involved in numerous activities outside of the house and have little time for traditional tasks such as cooking meals. The prevailing attitude among many couples with children is that cooking and housekeeping chores are a choice rather than a necessity. This view toward domestic chores is often held by parents from both affluent and disadvantaged populations. Because fast foods have intrinsic nutritional value, their benefit needs to be evaluated on the basis of age-specific requirements. For example, the total caloric needs of children of specific ages should be calculated and then compared with total caloric intakes during a typical day.

As discussed in Chapter 2, the extent to which families have retained their ethnic practices at mealtime varies widely. Because a hospitalized child's recovery may be enhanced by familiar foods, the nurse needs to assess the influence of culture on pediatric clients' eating habits. By close collaboration with a dietitian, the nurse can lead a hospitalized child to eat. For example, the nurse can foster an environment at mealtime that closely simulates the home. Family members can be encouraged to visit during meals or to join the child for meals, if this is appropriate. For example, the majority of Vietnamese parents believe that children should be fed separately from adults and that they should acquire "good table manners" by age 5 years. Depending on dietary restrictions necessitated by the child's medical condition, parents should be encouraged to prepare familiar foods at home and bring them to the hospital. The child should be encouraged to eat in the manner that is customary at home. For example, the Asian child who eats with chopsticks at home should be encouraged to do so in the hospital (Story and Harris, 1989; Stringfellow, Liem, and Liem, 1981).

Sleep

Although the amount of sleep required at various ages is similar across cultures, differences emerge. To promote rest, the nurse needs to identify the child's usual pattern by asking the parents about the normal bedtime routine at home. The child may have a favorite toy or story. Depending on the family's religious persuasion, parents may encourage the child to say a prayer at bedtime. The nurse should allow the child's familiar routine to be continued in the hospital as much as possible. For example, Vietnamese infants are not allowed to sleep alone. Small siblings usually sleep in the same bed, often in the parents' room. This practice occurs regardless of the size of the house. American Samoan mothers sleep with their newborns for the first 2 to 3 months of life.

Culture determines the type of foods eaten and the manner in which they are consumed. Many Chinese-American children enjoy traditional Chinese cuisine as well as American foods. They are frequently skillful users of both chopsticks and American eating utensils (knife, fork, and spoon).

The type of bed familiar to the child also may vary considerably. In a traditional American Samoan home, infants sleep on a pandanus mat covered with a blanket, and sometimes a pillow is used. A cradleboard is used by a number of American Indian tribes. Constructed by a family member, a cradleboard is made of cedar, pine, or pinon wood; it may be decorated in various ways, depending on the affluence of the family and on tribal customs. After completion, the cradleboard is blessed in a traditional manner. The cradleboard helps the infant feel secure and can be moved around with ease while the family engages in work, travel, or other activities (Phillips and Lobar, 1990).

In the United States and Canada, the common developmental milestone of sleeping for 8 uninterrupted hours by age 4 to 5 months is regarded as a sign of neurologic maturity. In many other cultures, however, the infant sleeps with the mother and is allowed to breast feed on demand with minimal disturbance of adult sleep. In such an

 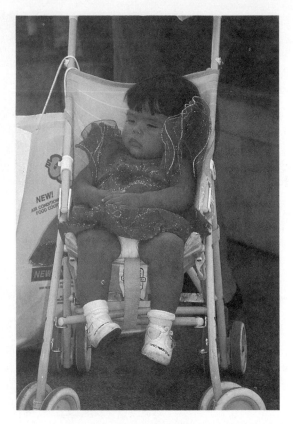

*In most cultures, parents and other care providers use devices that enable the child to sleep while being transported from place to place with relative ease. **(Left)** Use of cradleboards, created many centuries before the infant seat to promote infant mobility and safety, is still prevalent among many Native American tribes. **(Right)** Mexican-American child in a stroller.*

arrangement, there is less parental motivation to enforce "sleeping through the night," and infants continue to wake up every 4 hours during the night to feed, which is approximately the frequency of feeding during the day. Thus it appears that this developmental milestone, in addition to its biologic basis, is a function of the context in which it develops (Rogoff and Morelli, 1989; Super, 1981).

Elimination

Elimination refers to ridding the body of wastes. The gastrointestinal, genitourinary, respiratory, and integumentary systems are responsible for this function. Bowel and bladder elimination are of primary concern to many parents. Toilet training is a major developmental milestone, perhaps more for the parents than for the child. Toilet training is taught through a variety of cultural patterns.

Most children achieve dryness by 2¹/₂ to 3 years of age. Bowel training is more easily accomplished than bladder training. Daytime, or diurnal, wetting is less frequent than nighttime, or nocturnal, wetting. Some cultures start toilet training a child before the end of the first year and consider the child a "failure" if dryness is not achieved by 18 months. In other cultures, children are not expected to be dry until 5 years of age. Boys have a more difficult time achieving bladder control than girls.

A child's constipation is a persistent concern among parents who expect a ritualistic daily pattern. In some cultures, infants are purged when they are a few months of age to remove evil spirits from the body.

The role of the nurse is to acknowledge that toilet training can be taught through a variety of cultural patterns but that physical and psychosocial health are promoted by accepting, flexible approaches. A previously toilet-trained child may become incontinent as a result of the stress of hospitalization but will regain control quickly when returned to his or her familiar home environment. The nurse should reassure parents that regression in hospitalized children is normal and expected.

Menstruation

Attitudes toward menstruation are often culturally based, and the adolescent girl may be taught many folk beliefs at the time of puberty. Among Mexican Americans, menstruation is often considered an unpleasant but natural condition requiring circumspect behavior. For example, menstruating females are not permitted to walk barefooted, wash their hair, or take showers or baths. In encouraging hygienic practices, the nurse should respect cultural directives by encouraging sponge bathing, frequent changing of sanitary pads or tampons, and other interventions that promote cleanliness without violating cultural mandates.

Some Mexican Americans believe that sour or iced foods cause menstrual blood to coagulate, and some Puerto Rican teenagers have been taught that drinking lemon or pineapple juice will increase menstrual cramping (Sanovitis and Murillo-Rodhe, 1979). The nurse should be aware of these beliefs and should respect personal preferences concerning beverages. The teenager has probably been taught the folk practices by her mother or by an older female in her family, who may be watchful during the girl's menstrual periods. If menstruation coincides with hospitalization, the nurse needs to respect the teenager's preferences and may need to reassure the mother or significant other that their cultural practices will be respected.

Some Mexican Americans believe that delayed menses are caused by the stoppage of blood flow, a condition treated by the administration of certain herbs. Among other cultural groups, menstrual cramping may be treated with home remedies. The nurse should ask the adolescent girl whether she takes anything special during menstruation or in the absence of menstrual flow. It may be necessary to verify the amount and type of home remedy and to determine its interactive effect with prescription medicines.

Adolescent girls of Islamic religious persuasion, such as those of Palestinian, Lebanese, Jordanian, Saudi Arabian, and other Near or Middle Eastern nations and some African nations, have cultural/religious prohibitions and duties during and after menstruation. In Islam, blood, according to the *shari'ah* (Islamic law), is *najis*, or unclean. The blood of menstruation, as well as blood lost during childbirth, renders the female impure or potentially polluting. In Islamic legal language, the term used to refer to menstruation is *hayz*, and the menstruating female is referred to as *ha'iz*.

Because one must be in a pure state in order to pray, the *ha'iz* are forbidden to perform certain acts of worship such as touching the *Qur'an* (Koran), entering a mosque, praying, and participating in the feast of Ramadan. During the menstrual period, sexual intercourse is forbidden for both males and females. When the menstrual flow stops, the girl or woman performs *ghusl*, a special washing to purify herself (Luna, 1989; Rizvi, 1984).

In Islam, sexual pollution applies equally to males and females. For males, sexual intercourse and the discharge of semen is an act that renders them impure. A *junub* is a man or woman who has become impure, or *najis*, because of sexual intercourse. They must perform the ritual *ghusl* before being able to perform the prayer (Luna, 1989).

Parent-Child Relationship

Separation anxiety, the crying and behavior upset that occurs when the child is separated from the primary provider of care, has been studied across cultures. Ainsworth (1967) has shown that East African children develop separation anxiety at about age 6 months, 4 months earlier than North American infants. Indications of both separation anxiety and stranger anxiety, the distress displayed by an infant when confronted with an unfamiliar human face, appear somewhat earlier in Guatemalan Indian infants than in North American infants (Lester, 1974). The significance of these findings is that cultural differences do occur and that common environmental factors may be responsible for these differences. Less frequent separations from the mother and other people, closer living quarters, and larger numbers of siblings are all characteristic of the non-American groups studied.

The effect on the child of having multiple caretakers, as opposed to the mother alone, also has been studied (Mead, 1928; Ainsworth, 1967; Pearson et al., 1990; Campinna-Bacote and Ferguson, 1991), especially in terms of attachment to the mother and affective responses later in life. In a study of American infants, 1-year-olds were found to be more emotionally dependent on their mothers and were involved in more emotional interactions with them. These behaviors occurred when the infants had been reared exclusively by their mothers rather than by other females as well as their mothers. Rabin (1965) reported that children reared in the communal nurseries of Israeli *kibbutzim* subsequently form ties to their parents that are in some ways weaker than their peer attachments. However, both Western and non-Western infants have been shown to form initial attachments with more than one person and then to rapidly supplement these with further attachments.

Schaffer (1971) points out that initial attachments must be followed by a process of detachment, the letting go of the object of attachment, at least physically. Perhaps detachment is accompanied by an internal response in which the child learns to experience and express affect to selected others. The long-term effects of the number, intensity, and duration of early attachments on affective development require additional investigation in diverse cultural settings (Ogbu, 1981).

Children's relationships with their mothers and fathers are culturally determined. Some cultures encourage children to participate in family decision making and to discuss or even argue points with their parents. Some African-American families, for example, encourage children to express opinions verbally and to take an active role in all family activities. Many Asian parents value respectful, deferential behavior toward adults, who are considered experienced and wise. The Asian-American child is not expected to make decisions independently. The witty, fast reply that is viewed in some Western cultures as a sign of intelligence and cleverness might be punished in some non-

Western circles as a sign of rudeness and disrespect. Certain American Indian groups value a silent pause between a question and an answer. Such a pause is an indication that the question is worthy of the time necessary for a pondered answer. Physical punishment of American Indian children is rare. Instead of using loud scoldings and reprimands, Indian parents generally discipline with a quiet voice, telling the child what is expected. During breast feeding and toilet training Indian children are permitted to set their own pace. Parents are permissive and nondemanding.

Many African-American parents place an emphasis on having their children "behave" and "be good." Crying excessively is viewed as behaving in a "bad way," although the mother's tone of voice is often soft, especially with infants. Holding children closely and playing with them for extended periods of time may be viewed as "spoiling" by the parents. Spoiling does not prepare children for the adversity and uncertainty of everyday life in the real world. The parents' purpose in not spoiling their children is to have them realize from infancy on that life has frustrations and to learn to cope with them early. Caring is expressed during feeding, bathing, and diapering, but some parents exercise restraint when the child is crying. African-American parents may nickname a child, often during infancy, as suggested by the baby's actions, personality, appearance, or some incident involving the baby (Greathouse and Miller, 1981; McLoyd, 1990; Tolson and Wilson, 1990).

From the moment of birth, the Vietnamese mother has her infant with her almost constantly. A mother carries the child around with one arm, the child's leg straddling her hip, even during naps. If the mother is not holding the child and the child begins to cry, the mother picks up the infant instantly. The Filipino-American mother also responds quickly to the physical needs of the infant when crying begins. "Bad mothers" are those who fail to attend to their babies' crying immediately. In a Vietnamese family, the newborn is the responsibility of the mother, who is assisted and advised by the grandmother and older aunts. In some cultures, both parents assume responsibility for the care of children; in other cultures, the relationship with the mother is primary, with the father remaining somewhat distant.

Relationship with Other Family Members

Early in the nurse-parent relationship, the nurse needs to identify the significant others in the child's family. Child rearing and decision making frequently lie with members of the family other than the biological parents. Grandparents, aunts, and uncles may have significant roles in some cultures. For example, these adult relatives are given honored positions and are sources of advice and counsel in some Chinese American families. Mexican-American children often have many women to mother them. A teenage sister may be entirely responsible for the child care of a younger sibling. Other relatives may be named coparent to the Mexican-American mother. Sometimes a female relative asks the mother whether she may baptize the baby, meaning that she will sponsor the child in baptism, arrange a party, and agree to raise the child in case the natural parents die. It is not uncommon for a grandmother or sister to "adopt" one of a Mexican-American mother's children. Among the Vietnamese who have recently arrived in the United States, the grandmother frequently is the primary provider of care, since the mother often works. The mother or grandmother cares for children during the first year of life, after which time older siblings are permitted to assist in child care. Relationships with various family members are culturally based and dependent on the preferences of the parents.

Sex Roles

In all known human societies, adult males differ from adult females in both primary and secondary sex characteristics. On average, males have higher oxygen-carrying capacity in the blood (Tanner, 1961), a higher muscle-fat ratio, more body hair, a larger skeleton, and greater height (D'Andrade, 1966). Behaviorally, there are also differences between the two sexes, especially in the division of labor. Ultimate political and military authority always resides with males. Occasionally, a female occupies the single highest political position, such as a presidency or prime ministership, but males constitute the larger power base.

For children, sex differences can be identified cross-culturally in six classes of behavior: nurturance, responsibility, obedience, self-reliance, achievement, and independence (Barry, Bacon, and Child, 1967). Differences between males and females appear early in life and form the basis for adult roles within a culture. Male neonates are larger and more vigorously active and have more muscle development, a higher basal metabolic rate, and a higher pain threshold (Rosenberg and Sutton-Smith, 1972). Female neonates react more positively to comforting than do males (Moss, 1967). By 14 weeks of age, girls may be conditioned through the use of auditory reinforcers, and boys may be conditioned through the use of visual reinforcers, but not vice versa (Watson, 1969). By the age of 4 months, girls focus longer than boys on facelike masks, indicating that girls are more interested in faces or facelike configurations (Kagan, 1970).

Numerous behaviors are largely associated with one gender, with infrequent reversals across cultures occurring for the most part. In the division of labor, cooking is carried out by females in more than 90 percent of societies. Sexual initiative is largely reserved for men, and sexual modesty is primarily a female trait. Fantasy productions, such as drawing and designs, and projective preferences suggest that males typically are represented by and make projecting angular designs, whereas females are represented by and make more open, rounded designs (Kohlberg, 1966); this difference is often interpreted to be the result of body imagery. Research supports the observation that boys engage in physical aggression more frequently than girls.

Variability in sex-role behavior is a common occurrence. The majority of people in a society adopt most of the behavior defined as appropriate to their biologic sex, but there are many exceptions. Sex roles are themselves highly variable, by age and by social class, among other ways. The stringency of expectations also varies so that females in the United States and Canada can violate sex-role norms with fewer explicit sanctions than can males. Across cultures, even the number of sex roles is subject to variations.

Child-Rearing Practices

In an effort to understand how people from various cultures construe their private and social worlds, social scientists have identified various ways to describe the mode that people find comfortable and socially acceptable. For example, there are some subcultures in which a predominantly *cognitive* mode prevails, whereas others are characterized by an *emotional* one. For many Anglo-Americans, the attributes of cognitive behavior such as their emphasis on logic, rationality, and control are dominant, whereas members of many North American subcultural groups emphasize feeling states, with emotional encounters being of more importance. These different constructions of the world are not accidental cultural developments but rather reflect different philosophical legacies. Also, these constructions occur on a continuum and are not intended to be dichotomous categories.

Among white middle- and upper-class Anglo-Americans, for example, children are socialized from a very early age to learn to control their feelings and emotions, especially in public places. On the other hand, they are trained to become independent, self-determining, achievement-oriented, and *work-* and *activity-centered*. In a work- and activity-centered society, relationships are formed on the basis of shared commonalities. One is expected to "work" at a relationship—in a marriage, in a family situation, with colleagues at work, and with friends at a social level.

In a *relationship-oriented* society, feelings and emotions are not repressed, and their expression is generally encouraged. Crying, dependence on others, and high levels of emotionality are socially acceptable. No agenda of shared commonalities is necessary for the cultivation of a relationship. Examples of subcultures that are relationship-oriented include Italian, Hispanic, and East Indian.

Anglo-American culture is predominantly characterized by *free will* or *free agency*, whereas *determinism* is found in certain subcultural groups. The expression, "Live free or die," and the freedoms guaranteed by the U.S. Constitution reflect the strong value placed on free will by the dominant Anglo-American cultural group. Children are raised to make choices and to exercise their free will. Members of other subcultures, however, may hold beliefs that support determinism. For example, in India, the law of *karma*, which involves determinism and fatalism, has shaped people's view of life for centuries.

The law of *karma* states that every happiness or sorrow in a person's life is the predetermined effect of actions committed some time in the present life or in one of numerous past lives. Things do not happen because we make them happen. Things happen because they are destined to happen. Does this mean that Indian children whose families believe in the law of *karma* are raised to believe that they have no free will? Does this render prevention and other primary prevention measures useless? Paradoxically, determinism and the Indian concept of *karma* are balanced with belief in prayer, religious observances, and amulets, which are referred to as *taveez*. By employing potential mediators of cosmic intervention, unpleasant, untoward happenings may be prevented. Thus primary prevention measures are accepted. It is important to remember that the majority of parents cross-culturally want their children to be healthy and will engage in child-rearing practices that they believe will promote health and prevent illness (Laungani, 1989).

The nurse needs to be sensitive to a wide variety of child-rearing practices when caring for children from different cultural backgrounds. A few examples are presented to illustrate types of child-rearing practices likely to be encountered by the nurse. Of course, in addition to being aware of generalized cultural practices, the nurse should observe parent-child interactions and discuss child-rearing practices with the parents.

In general, Vietnamese parents demonstrate permissiveness with respect to feeding, toileting, and sex play. A mother may masturbate her male child during this first 5 years to ensure his ability to perform sexually as an adult. Genital fondling of girls may be practiced during infancy as a means of quieting a fussy baby.

Culture influences the design of children's toys. The Amish belief that prohibits the fashioning of graven images is reflected in these faceless dolls.

Strict child-rearing practices tend to prevail among American Samoans. Children are not permitted to challenge their parents' or elders' authority, and physical punishment is common and swiftly executed. Children learn at an early age to stay out of the way of adults. Physical punishment is viewed as a means of gaining respect and showing concern for the child. American Samoa's first law against child abuse was not passed until 1977 owing to strong convictions that punishment belongs within the family (Oneha and Magyary, 1992).

Health and Health Promotion

As discussed in Chapter 1, the concept of *health* varies widely across cultures. Regardless of culture, most parents desire health for their children and engage in activities that they *believe* to be health-promoting. Because health-related beliefs and practices are such an integral part of culture, parents may persist with culturally based beliefs and practices even when scientific evidence refutes them, or they may modify them to be more congruent with contemporary knowledge of health and illness.

Summarized in Research Box 4-2 are selected studies pertaining to health promotion, identification of risk factors, and disease prevention among Native American children. Summarized in Research Box 4-3 are findings of a study on a community-based health education program for Haitian mothers in which preventive health care for infants and preschool children was the focus.

Research Box 4-2. Health Promotion and Disease Prevention Among Native American Children

Botash, A. S., Kavey, R. W., Emm, N., and Jones, D. (1992). Cardiovascular risk factors in Native American children. *New York State Journal of Medicine, 92*(9), 378–381.

In a screening program at the Onondaga Nation School involving 95 school children, 55 representing 39 interrelated families, six cardiovascular risk factors were evaluated. Family histories were positive for diabetes mellitus in 72 percent, for cardiovascular disease in 54 percent, and for passive inhalation of smoke in 90 percent of families. Physical examination of children revealed obesity in 42 percent, hypertension in 22 percent, and fingerstick cholesterol levels greater than 170 mg/dl in 25 percent. Overall, 85 percent of participants had three or more risk factors for cardiovascular disease.

Broderick, E., Mabry, J., Robertson, D., and Thompson, J. (1989). Baby bottle tooth decay in Native American children in Head Start centers. *Public Health Reports, 104*(1), 50–54.

Dentists who treat Native American children have noted that this population suffers from a high prevalence of baby bottle tooth decay. In a survey of Navajo and Cherokee Head Start students ages 4 to 5 years, with an overall prevalence of 70 percent (*n* = 97), the condition was revealed to be significantly higher than in other populations.

Bulterys, M. (1990). High incidence of sudden infant death syndrome among northern Indians and Alaska natives compared with southwestern Indians: Possible role of smoking. *Journal of Community Health, 15*(3), 185–194.

This study shows that there is a significant difference in the incidence of sudden infant death syndrome (SIDS) between the northern Indians (4.6 per 1000 live births) and the southwestern Indians (1.4 per 1000 live births). The prevalence of maternal cigarette smoking during pregnancy is exceptionally high among northern Indians and Alaska natives, while it is low among southwestern Indians. The difference in smoking habits may explain the excess risk of SIDS among Indians in the northern region.

Gilbert, T. J., Percy, C. A., Sugarman, J. R., et al. (1992). Obesity among Navajo adolescents: Relationship to dietary intake and blood pressure. *American Journal of Diseases of Children, 146*, 289–295.

Blood pressures, dietary intakes, and self-perceived body image of 352 Navajo Indian adolescents were measured. Thirty-three percent of girls and 25 percent of boys were obese according to body mass index criteria. The high prevalence of obese adolescents and the apparent effect of the increased weight on blood pressure in this population indicate the need for interventions aimed at improving dietary habits and fitness levels.

Research Box 4-3. A Community-Based Health Education Program

DeSantis, L., and Thomas, J. T. (1992). Health education and the immigrant Haitian mother: Cultural insights for community health nurses. *Home Health Nursing.* 9(2), 87–96.

In a descriptive survey of 30 Haitian mothers in southeast Florida, informants were interviewed about the value of health education received while seeking preventive health care for infants and preschool children in community health settings, their access to health education, and their perceptions of what community health care providers could do to assist them in improving child health. Nurses were considered the best persons to do health teaching; radio and clinic lectures were preferred to the media. Teaching was valuable if it was understandable and practical, reinforced parenting abilities, and allowed time for questions.

Illness

The family is the primary health care provider for children and adolescents. It is the family that determines when a child is ill and decides to seek help in managing an illness. The acceptability of illness and sick-role behaviors for children and adolescents is determined by the family. Societal trends in illness orientation and economic stress both influence the cultural beliefs that are passed from generation to generation. As discussed in Chapter 1, health, illness, and treatment (cure/healing) are part of every child's cultural heritage. In every society there is an organized response to defined health problems. Certain people are designated as being responsible for deciding who is sick, what kind of sickness the person has, and what kind of treatment is required to restore the person to health.

Among many cultural groups, traditional health beliefs coexist with Western medical beliefs. Members of a cultural group choose those components of traditional or folk beliefs which seem appropriate to them. A Mexican-American family, for example, may take a child to both a physician and a *curandera*, a traditional healer. After visiting the physician and the *curandera*, the mother may consult with her own mother and then give her sick child the antibiotics prescribed by the physician and the herbal tea prescribed by the traditional healer. If the problem is viral in origin, the child will recover because of innate immunologic defenses, independent of either treatment. Thus both the herbal tea of the *curandera* and the penicillin prescribed by the physician may be viewed as folk remedies; neither intervention is responsible for the child's recovery.

Belief systems about specific symptoms are culturally unique. In Hispanic culture, *susto* (see Chap. 2 for a discussion of culture-bound syndromes) is caused by a frightening experience and is recognized by the symptoms of nervousness, loss of appetite, and loss of sleep. Mexican-American babies must be protected from various illnesses. *Pujos* (grunting) is an illness manifested by grunting sounds and protrusion of the umbilicus. It is believed to be caused by contact with a woman who is menstruating or by the infant's own mother if she menstruated before 40 days after delivery. This affliction is believed to be cured by tying a piece of fabric from the woman's clothing around the baby's waist for 3 days or by intervention from the traditional healer.

The evil eye, *mal ojo,* is an affliction feared throughout much of the world. The condition is said to be caused by an individual who voluntarily or involuntarily injures a child by looking at or admiring him or her. The individual has a desire to hold the child, but the wish is frustrated, either by the parent of the infant or by the reserve of the individual. Several hours later, the child may cry and develop symptoms of fever, vomiting, diarrhea, and loss of appetite. The child's eyes may roll back in the head, and he or she will become listless.

Mal ojo usually is prevented by touching or patting a child when admiring him or her. The treatment of this illness requires a *curandera,* who prays and massages the child with oil. Some *curanderas* pass an unbroken raw egg over the child's body. The egg is then cracked and placed in a bowl of water under the crib. This process draws the fever from the child and poaches the egg.

The parents of this hospitalized infant are from the South Pacific island of Tonga. They are visiting their infant and have brought a pre-school-aged sibling (not pictured) to see her brother in the hospital.

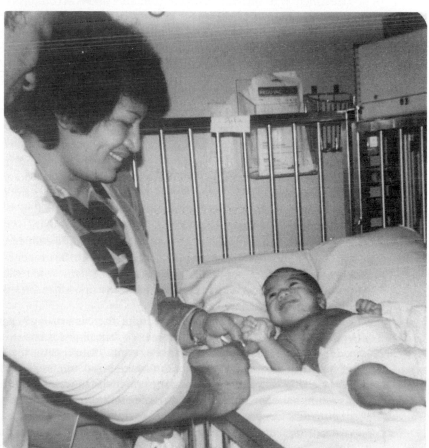

Because the most serious threat to the infant with *mal ojo* is dehydration, the nurse encountering this problem in the community health setting needs to assess the severity of the dehydration and initiate a plan for fluid and electrolyte replacement. The nurse should emphasize the potential seriousness of dehydration to the parents and should teach them the warning signs that will alert them to impending danger in the future. A simple explanation of the causes and treatment of dehydration is warranted. If the parents adhere strongly to traditional beliefs, the nurse should respect their desire for the *curandera* to participate in the care. Parents or grandparents may wish to place an amulet, talisman, or religious object such as a crucifix or rosary on the child or near the bed.

Caida de la mollera, or fallen fontanel, has a variety of causes for the Mexican American, such as failure of the midwife to press preventively on the palate after delivery. Falling on the head, abrupt removal of the nipple from the infant's mouth, and failure to place a cap on the infant's head also have been identified as causes of *caida de la mollera*. Symptoms of this condition include crying, fever, vomiting, and diarrhea. Given that health care providers frequently note the correspondence of these symptoms with those of dehydration, many parents see *deshidratacion* (dehydration) or *carencia de agua* (lack of water) as synonymous with *caida de la mollera*.

Treatment is directed at raising the fontanel and is accomplished either by holding the baby upside down over a pan of water and lowering the baby's body until the fontanel is immersed three times or by pressing very hard on the palate with the thumb. The infant's fontanel is then sucked up and "held up" by mixtures of egg white, rue, and other herbs.

Empacho, a digestive condition recognized by Mexicans, is caused by the adherence of undigested food to some part of the gastrointestinal tract. This condition causes an internal fever, which cannot be observed but which betrays its presence by excessive thirst and abdominal swelling caused by drinking water to quench the thirst. Children, who are prone to swallowing chewing gum, are most likely to suffer from *empacho*, but it may affect persons of any age.

Among the Vietnamese, traditional practices are employed before or in conjunction with Western medical treatment. For an upper respiratory tract infection, small, heated glass bottles may be applied to the back, where suction is created to take out the "bad" air and blood. To decrease a fever, a basil leaf is tied to the wrist with a piece of cheesecloth. For colic, a silver coin is dipped in wine and rubbed or scratched on the back. It is believed that this practice makes hairs grow in the proper direction and rids the child of "bad wind." Since nudity is thought by Vietnamese to make one vulnerable to bad winds, children should be exposed as little as possible during examinations and treatments.

Among some Hindus from northern India, there is a strong belief in *ghost illness* and *ghost possession*, culture-bound syndromes or folk illnesses based on the belief that a ghost enters its victim and tries to seize its soul. If successful, the ghost causes death. After conducting extensive field work in India, Freed and Freed (1991) concluded that there is a relationship between infant and childhood illnesses and death caused by ghost illness. Illness and the supernatural world are linked by the concepts of ghosts and fever, a supernatural being in the *Mahabharata* and the *Puranas*.

One of the symptoms of ghost illness is a voice speaking through a delirious victim, a symptom that may be found in children and adults but not in infants unable to speak.

The voice is identified as the ghost that is trying to take its victim's soul. Other symptoms are convulsions and body movements, indicating pain and discomfort, and choking or difficulty breathing, which are interpreted as a death rattle because a ghost is trying to take the victim's soul through its throat and mouth. In the case of an infant, incessant crying is a symptom (Freed and Freed, 1991). Infants who cannot speak can be diagnosed as having ghost illness but not ghost possession. The psychological state of the parents is often involved in the diagnosis, and some believe that ghosts may be cultural scapegoats for the illness and death of children. A mother or father may be relieved of psychic tension from feelings of personal guilt when their infant or small child becomes ill and dies by transferring the blame for the death to a ghost.

In *ghost possession*, the victims go through alternate states of consciousness such as falling into a semiconscious or unconscious state with a voice or voices speaking from them. During these episodes, the victim may attempt suicide, whereas afterwards, amnesia usually occurs. According to *the Diagnostic and Statistical Manual of Mental Disorders III*, ghost possession, which was formerly classified as hysterical neurosis, is a dissociative disorder, or if a biologic factor is involved, it is a somatoform conversion disorder. Curing for ghost illness and ghost possession includes practices from the *Atharva-Veda* (the most ancient Sanskritic literature), Ayurvedic medicine, Unani prophetic medicine, and Western biomedicine.

Distinguishing Child Abuse from Folk Healing

Child abuse and neglect have been documented throughout human history and are known across cultures. In the early 1960s, child maltreatment in the United States became prominent as pediatricians documented radiologic evidence and other symptoms of abuse and neglect in well-publicized reports (Kempe et al., 1962). International attention to child maltreatment emerged in the late 1970s, and the International Society for the Prevention of Child Abuse and Neglect (ISPPCAN) has held international congresses and regional meetings to explore physical abuse and neglect, sexual molestation, child prostitution, nutritional deprivation, emotional maltreatment, and institutional abuse from a cross-national perspective (Doek, 1991; Korbin, 1990).

Cross-cultural variability in child-rearing beliefs and practices have created a dilemma that makes establishment of a universal standard for optimal child care, as well as definitions of child abuse and neglect, extremely difficult. The following widely accepted definition of child abuse and neglect in the United States pertains to any person under the age of 18 years: "The injury, sexual abuse, sexual exploitation, or negligent treatment or maltreatment of a child by any person under circumstances which indicate that the child's health, welfare, and safety is harmed thereby. . . . this subsection shall not be construed to authorize interference with child-raising practices, including reasonable parental discipline, which are not proved to be injurious to the child's health, welfare, and safety" (*West's Revised Code of Washington Annotated*, 1990, p. 121).

Korbin (1991) has identified three levels in formulating culturally appropriate definitions of child maltreatment: (1) cultural differences in child-rearing practices and beliefs, (2) idiosyncratic departure from one's cultural continuum of acceptable behavior, and (3) societal harm to children.

The *first level* encompasses practices that are viewed as acceptable in the culture in which they occur but as abusive or neglectful by outsiders. For example, in Turkey and many Middle Eastern cultures, despite warm temperatures, infants are covered with multiple layers of clothing and may be observed to sweat profusely because parents believe that young children become chilled very easily and die from exposure to the cold. Many African nations continue to practice rites of initiation for boys and girls, usually at the time of puberty. In some cases, ritual circumcision—of both boys and girls—is performed without anesthetic, and the ability to endure the associated pain is considered to be a manifestation of the maturity expected of an adult. In the United States and Canada, the African-American family's focus on physical forms of discipline may present controversial and ethical issues for the nurse (Campinha-Bacote and Ferguson, 1991).

The *second level*, idiosyncratic abuse or neglect, signals a departure from the continuum of culturally acceptable behavior. Some societies (Turkish, Mexican, and others), for example, permit fondling of the genitals of infants and young children to soothe them or encourage sleep. However, such fondling of older children or for the sexual gratification of adults would fall outside of the acceptable cultural continuum (Korbin, 1991).

At the *third level*, societal conditions such as poverty, inadequate housing, poor maternal and child health care, and lack of nutritional resources either contribute powerfully to child maltreatment or are considered maltreatment in and of themselves. African-American children are three times as likely as white children to die of child abuse, but considerable disagreement exists about whether race differences exist in the prevalence of child abuse independent of socioeconomic factors such as income and employment status (Children's Defense Fund, 1985; McLoyd, 1990). Nurses need to become knowledgeable about folk beliefs, child-rearing practices, and cultural variability in defining child maltreatment.

In analyzing child maltreatment from the perspective of two island nations in the Pacific Basin, American Samoa and the Federated States of Micronesia, Oneha and Magyvary (1992) identify four nursing implications. First, nurses need *knowledge of the beliefs and practices of diverse cultural groups*, such as kinship structure, parenting patterns, and cultural values and norms. Second, *legal accountability* requires nurses to report reasonable cause or suspicion of child abuse to appropriate authorities without fear of recrimination. Third, nurses are expected to make *culturally relevant interventions derived from transcultural nursing assessments*. Unless substantial transcultural nursing knowledge guides the assessment and intervention, maltreatment of children may be misunderstood or incorrectly assessed. Caution needs to be exercised when using standard nursing diagnoses such as "altered parenting" because this fails to provide for cultural variations and is based on a Western perception of wellness (Leininger, 1990). Fourth, nurses need to advocate for *culturally diverse health care approaches*. The importance of culturally diverse practices needs to be reflected in the membership of professional organizations, child abuse teams, and child protective services. Nurses need to promote family participation and involvement in decisions about policy and services, especially in communities in which the background of health care providers does not reflect the culture of those being served.

Selected research studies on child abuse and neglect are summarized in Research Box 4-4. Summarized in Table 4-1 are four Southeast Asian folk healing practices that produce physical marks on the child's body. Although child abuse laws vary from state to state, child abuse generally encompasses any physical injury caused by other than accidental means. The nurse has both a legal and a moral obligation to report to the

Research Box 4-4. Cross-Cultural Studies on Child Maltreatment

Hong, G. K., and Hong, L. K. (1991). Comparative perspectives on child abuse and neglect: Chinese versus Hispanics and whites. *Child Welfare League of America, 70*(4), 463–475.

In a sample of 150 individuals, equally divided among Chinese, Hispanics, and whites, it was found that the Chinese were more tolerant of parental conduct than the Hispanics and whites and were less likely to ask for investigation by protective agencies in potential cases of child abuse and neglect.

Rao, K., DiClemente, R. J., and Ponton, L. E. (1992). Child sexual abuse of Asians compared with other populations. *Journal of the American Academy of Child and Adolescent Psychiatry, 31*(5), 880–886.

In a retrospective chart review of a child sexual abuse clinic, substantiated sexual abuse cases of Asian victims were compared with random samples of black, white, and Hispanic victims. Asian victims showed a distinct demographic profile, suffered less physically invasive forms of abuse, were more likely to become suicidal, were less likely to display anger and sexual acting out, and had less supportive primary caretakers than non-Asians.

proper authorities coining, burning, and any other healing practices that result in bruising or other types of injury to the child's skin.

Although the nurse should make every effort to incorporate cultural practices into nursing care, practices that result in bodily harm to children cannot be allowed. This raises some poignant and controversial ethical issues for the nurse. The following guidelines are suggested for handling cases in which folk healing practices result in bodily harm to the child.

First, the nurse should discuss the folk healing practice with the parents and encourage voluntary discontinuation. If the parents refuse to stop, the nurse should check with the local children's protective services organization to clarify the legal aspects of the practice. It is important for the nurse and the local children's protective services staff to agree that a specific case of suspected abuse is reportable, and the nurse should err on the side of ensuring the child's safety whenever there is any doubt.

If the nurse is unsure about a coining or burning case, an ethnic caseworker or cultural representative should be asked to assess the child. Contacting the police should be avoided, except in the case of a life-threatening emergency, because many Southeast Asians have a great fear of police. Parents should be advised that coining and burning are illegal in this country and that a children's protective services worker will investigate the

Table 4-1. Southeast Asian folk healing practices

<table>
<tr><td colspan="2" align="center">Coining (Cao gio)</td></tr>
<tr><td>Appearance:</td><td>Superficial ecchymotic, nonpainful areas with petechiae usually appearing between the rib bones on the front and back of the body and resembling strap marks. Coining may also be done along the trachea or on either side of the trachea, vertically along the inner aspect of both upper arms, or along both sides of the spine.</td></tr>
<tr><td>Conditions treated:</td><td>Pain, colds, heat exhaustion, vomiting, headache</td></tr>
<tr><td>Procedure:</td><td>A special menthol oil or ointment is applied to the painful or symptomatic area. Then the edge of a coin is rubbed over the area with firm downward strokes. The procedure is mildly uncomfortable.</td></tr>
<tr><td>Belief:</td><td>The "coining" exudes the "bad wind." Appearance of a deep reddish-purple skin color is confirmation that the person indeed had "bad wind" in the body and that coining was the appropriate treatment. If only redness appears, the client must consult a healer or doctor for another treatment.</td></tr>
<tr><td>Age of patient:</td><td>Infants a few months old through seniors</td></tr>
<tr><td>Practiced by:</td><td>Mien, Vietnamese, Cambodian (rare), Lao (rare), Ethnic Chinese</td></tr>
<tr><td>Who applies the treatment:</td><td>Any adult</td></tr>
<tr><td colspan="2" align="center">Burning (Poua)</td></tr>
<tr><td>Appearance:</td><td>Asymmetrical, superficial, painful burns 1/4 in diameter appearing either as a single burn in the center of the forehead or as two nearly symmetrical vertical rows down the front or back of the body, often including the neck.</td></tr>
<tr><td>Conditions treated:</td><td>Any kind of pain—including pain from a cough or diarrhea—as well as serious conditions such as failure to thrive</td></tr>
<tr><td>Procedure:</td><td>A tall, weedlike grass is peeled and allowed to dry. The end is dipped in heated, melted pork lard and the tip is then ignited and applied to the skin in the area requiring treatment (e.g., joints are burned for failure to thrive). The treatment is painful and always the treatment of last resort.</td></tr>
<tr><td>Belief:</td><td>The burning exudes the noxious element causing the pain or illness.</td></tr>
<tr><td>Age of patient:</td><td>Infants a few months old through seniors</td></tr>
<tr><td>Practiced by:</td><td>Mien, Cambodian (rare)</td></tr>
<tr><td>Who applies the treatment:</td><td>In Mien culture the treatment is performed only by a skilled healer. In Cambodian culture any experienced adult may do it.</td></tr>
<tr><td colspan="2" align="center">Cupping (Ventouse)</td></tr>
<tr><td>Appearance:</td><td>Circular, nonraised, ecchymotic, painful burn marks 2 in in diameter, usually appearing in symmetrical, vertical rows of two to four cups on the left and right sides of the chest, abdomen, and back, or singly as one cup on the forehead. Cupping is rarely practiced in the United States.</td></tr>
<tr><td>Conditions treated:</td><td>Pain, bodyache, headache</td></tr>
<tr><td>Procedure:</td><td>Though borrowed from the French, the specific procedure in Southeast Asia varies among ethnic groups. The principle is to create a vacuum inside a special cup by igniting alcohol-soaked cotton inside the cup. When the flame extinguishes, the cup is immediately applied to the skin of the painful site. Suction is created, and the skin is pulled up inside the mouth of the cup. The cup remains in place 15 to 20 minutes or until the suction can be easily released. The procedure is painful.</td></tr>
<tr><td>Belief:</td><td>The suction exudes the noxious element. The greater the "bruise," the greater the seriousness of the illness.</td></tr>
<tr><td>Age of patient:</td><td>Adults, occasionally teens</td></tr>
<tr><td>Practiced by:</td><td>H'mong, Mien, Lao (rare), Cambodian (rare), Vietnamese, Ethnic Chinese</td></tr>
<tr><td>Who applies the treatment:</td><td>Any adult, except in Vietnamese culture, in which only a skilled nurse or healer may do it.</td></tr>
</table>

Table 4-1 (continued)

Pinching (*Bat gio*)	
Appearance:	Intensely ecchymotic, isolated, nonsymmetrical areas. May be present anywhere on the body, including on the forehead between the eyes, vertically along the trachea, in a "necklace" pattern around the base of the neck, on both sides of the upper chest, on the upper arms (left and right), along the spine, or to either side of the spine.
Conditions treated:	Localized pain and a variety of minor and more serious conditions, including lack of appetite, heat exhaustion, dizziness, fainting, blurred vision, any minor illness, cough, fever. Pinching is a *very common* practice.
Procedure:	Index and middle finger of one hand are flexed and firmly applied to the skin in a quick, pinching motion. Tiger balm, a penetrating, mentholated ointment may be massaged into the area before pinching. The H'mong may pinch first, then prick the area with a sharp needle to draw blood and thus "draw out" the noxious elements.
Belief:	Pinching exudes the bad wind or noxious element.
Age of patient:	Children over 10 years old in most cultures; adults only in H'mong culture
Practiced by:	H'mong, Mien, Laotian, Vietnamese, and Cambodian
Who applies the treatment:	Any adult

From Schreiner, D., Multnomah County Health Services Division (1981). S.E. Asian folk healing practices/child abuse? Indochinese Health Care Conference, Eugene, Oregon. September 18, 1981, pp. 2–5. Reprinted by permission.

situation and pursue legal action against the parents to protect the child from further harm.

The nurse needs to remember that to the parents these healing traditions are often essential and meaningful approaches to helping the child recover from an illness. Whereas a U.S. or Canadian parent may treat a child's cold with fluids, rest, and aspirin, the Southeast Asian parent may use coining. Although neither approach cures the cold, the latter interferes with medical intervention that might provide symptomatic relief for the child and even results in physical harm to the child.

If the injury caused by coining and burning results in disruption of skin integrity, infection may result, causing further harm to the child. Although the nurse is encouraged to foster individual personal rights and to respect cultural differences, protecting children from physical injury caused by folk healing practices is of primary importance.

Biocultural Influences on Childhood Disorders

Children are born with a genetic constitution that has been inherited from their parents, who in turn have inherited their own genetic composition. The child's genetic makeup affects his or her likelihood of both contracting and inheriting specific conditions. Table 4-2 summarizes the distribution of selected genetic traits and disorders by population or ethnic group. The table is intended to be illustrative, not exhaustive.

In both children and adults, genetic composition has been demonstrated to affect the individual's susceptibility to specific diseases and disorders. It is often difficult to separate genetic influences from socioeconomic factors such as poverty, lack of proper nutrition, poor hygiene, and such environmental conditions as lack of ventilation, inadequate sanitary facilities, lack of heating during cold weather, and insufficient clothing to provide protection during winter months. Other factors responsible for differing susceptibilities to specific conditions are variations in natural and acquired

Table 4-2. Distribution of selected genetic traits and disorders by population or ethnic group

Ethnic or Population Group	Genetic or Multifactorial Disorder Present in Relatively High Frequency
Aland Islanders	Ocular albinism (Forsius-Erikkson type)
Amish	Limb girdle muscular dystrophy (IN—Adams, Allen counties)
	Ellis-van Creveld (PA—Lancaster county)
	Pyruvate kinase deficiency (OH—Mifflin county)
	Hemophilia B (PA—Holmes county)
Armenians	Familial Mediterranean fever
	Familial paroxysmal polyserositis
Blacks (African)	Sickle cell disease
	Hemoglobin C disease
	Hereditary persistence of hemoglobin F
	G6PD deficiency African type
	Lactase deficiency, adult
	β-Thalassemia
Burmese	Hemoglobin E disease
Chinese	Alpha thalassemia
	G6PD deficiency, Chinese type
	Lactase deficiency, adult
Costa Ricans	Malignant osteopetrosis
Druze	Alkaptonuria
English	Cystic fibrosis
	Hereditary amyloidosis, type III
Eskimos	Congenital adrenal hyperplasia
	Pseudocholinesterase deficiency
	Methemoglobinemia
French Canadians (Quebec)	Tyrosinemia
	Morquio syndrome
Finns	Congenital nephrosis
	Generalized amyloidosis syndrome, V
	Polycystic liver disease
	Retinoschisis
	Aspartylglycoasaminuria
	Diastrophic dwarfism
Gypsies (Czech)	Congenital glaucoma
Hopi Indians	Tyrosinase positive albinism
Icelanders	Phenylketonuria
Irish	Phenylketonuria
	Neural tube defects
Japanese	Acatalasemia
	Cleft lip/palate
	Oguchi disease
Jews	
Ashkenazi	Tay-Sachs disease (infantile)
	Niemann-Pick disease (infantile)
	Gaucher disease (adult type)
	Familial dysautonomia (Riley-Day syndrome)
	Bloom syndrome
	Torsion dystonia
	Factor XI (PTA) deficiency
Sephardi	Familial Mediterranean fever
	Ataxia-telangiectasia (Morocco)
	Cystinuria (Libya)
	Glycogen storage disease III (Morocco)

Table 4-2 (continued)

Ethnic or Population Group	Genetic or Multifactorial Disorder Present in Relatively High Frequency
Orientals	Dubin-Johnson syndrome (Iran)
	Ichthyosis vulgaris (Iraq, India)
	Werdnig-Hoffman disease (Karaite Jews)
	G6PD deficiency, Mediterranean type
	Phenylketonuria (Yemen)
	Metachromatic leukodystrophy (Habbanite Jews, Saudi Arabia)
Lapps	Congenital dislocation of hip
Lebanese	Dyggve-Melchoir-Clausen syndrome
Mediterranean people (Italians, Greeks)	G6PD deficiency, Mediterranean type
	βThalassemia
	Familial Mediterranean fever
Navaho Indians	Ear anomalies
Polynesians	Clubfoot
Poles	Phenylketonuria
Portuguese	Joseph disease
Nova Scotia Acadians	Niemann-Pick disease, type D
Scandinavians (Norwegians, Swedes, Danes)	Cholestasis-lymphedema (Norwegians)
	Sjögren-Larsson syndrome (Swedes)
	Krabbe disease
	Phenylketonuria
Scots	Phenylketonuria
	Cystic fibrosis
	Hereditary amyloidosis, type III
Thai	Lactase deficiency, adult
	Hemoglobin E disease
Zuni Indians	Tyrosinase positive albinism

From Cohen, F. L. (1984). *Clinical Genetics in Nursing Practice*, pp. 23–24. Philadelphia: J.B. Lippincott Company. Reprinted by permission.

immunity, intermarriage, geographic/climatic conditions, ethnic background, race, and religious practices. Some studies have attempted to explain differences in susceptibility solely on the basis of the cultural heritage, but they have not succeeded in doing so. This section examines some common conditions in which genetic constitution seems to be a factor.

Immunity. Perhaps one of the most frequently cited examples of the connection between immunity and race is that of malaria and the sickle cell trait in Africans. Black Africans possessing the sickle cell trait are known to have increased immunity to malaria, a serious endemic disease of the tropics. Thus blacks with the sickle cell trait survived malarial attacks and reproduced offspring who also possessed the sickle cell trait; as dictated by Mendelian probability, eventually they developed the disease sickle cell anemia.

Intermarriage. Intermarriage among certain cultural groups has led to a wide variety of childhood disorders; for example, there is an increased incidence of ventricular septal defects among the Amish and of mental retardation in a number of other groups. In the extreme, intermarriage among groups having few members can lead to total extinction; the number of Samaritans in Israel, for example, has dwindled to a handful of surviving, aging members.

Geography/Climate. Geographic/climatic factors may be illustrated by the classic example of a common communicable disease of childhood, rubeola (measles). Owing either to mutation of the rubeola virus or to increased individual resistance to the virus, measles became a virtually universal benign childhood disease in many parts of the world during the 19th century. Although the majority of children experienced few ill effects from measles, certain populations, such as children in the Hawaiian Islands, were severely or even mortally affected when explorers and missionaries brought the virus to their lands.

Ethnicity. Although the role of socioeconomic factors in tuberculosis—such as overcrowding and poor nutrition—cannot be disregarded, ethnicity also appears to be a factor in this disease. Group with a relatively high incidence of tuberculosis are American Indians living in the Southwest, Vietnamese refugees, and Mexican Americans. Ethnicity is also linked to several noncommunicable conditions. For example, Tay-Sachs disease, a neurologic condition affecting Ashkenasic (but not Sephardic) Jews of northeastern European descent, and phenylketonuria (PKU), a metabolic disorder primarily affecting Scandinavians, are congenital abnormalities known to be most prevalent among specific ethnic groups (Overfield, 1981, 1985).

Race. Race has been linked to the incidence of a variety of disorders of childhood. For example, the endocrine disorder cystic fibrosis primarily affects white children, whereas sickle cell anemia has its primary influence among African Americans and those of Mediterranean descent. African-American children are known to be at risk for inherited blood disorders, such as thalassemia, G6PD deficiency, and hemoglobin C disease, and an estimated 70 to 90 percent of African-American children have an enzyme deficiency that results in difficulty with the digestion and metabolism of milk.

Hereditary Predisposition to Disease. The predisposition to certain diseases also has been linked to cultural influences. For example, the incidences of pneumonia and diabetes are especially high among African Americans, and those of dysentery, alcoholism, and suicide are high among Native American children and adolescents. Mexican-American children are known to succumb to pneumonia more frequently than Anglos of similar socioeconomic status.

Chronic Illness and Disability in Children

Chronic illnesses and disabilities have become the dominant health care problem in North America and are the leading causes of morbidity and mortality. According to Groce and Zola (1993), the following three issues seem to be almost universal, appearing prominently and consistently in cross-cultural studies:

1. The culturally perceived cause of a chronic illness or disability is significant in all cultures studied to date. The reason why an illness or disability is believed to have

occurred In a particular individual and/or family will play a significant role in determining family and community attitudes toward the child.

2. The expectations for survival for the infant or child with a chronic illness or disability will affect both the immediate care the child receives and the amount of effort expended in planning for future care and education.
3. The social roles that society believes to be appropriate for disabled or chronically ill children and adults (often based on a consensus about their productive potential and beliefs about transmission of the disorder) will help determine the amount of resources a family and community invest in an individual. This includes issues of education and training, participation in family and community social life, the latitude permitted for individual autonomy, and the long-range planning done by or undertaken for the individual over the course of a lifetime.

Culturally Perceived Causes of Chronic Illness and Disability

As indicated in Chapter 1, illness is viewed by many cultures as a form of punishment. The child and/or family with a chronic illness or disability may be perceived to be cursed by a supreme being(s), to have sinned, or to have violated a taboo. In some cultural groups, the affected child is seen as tangible evidence of divine displeasure, and its arrival is accompanied throughout the community by prolonged private and public discussions about what wrongs the family may have committed.

In a number of African, Caribbean, and Pacific Basin societies, as well as among many Native American tribes, witchcraft is strongly linked to ill health and disability. An individual who has been bewitched is presumed to be a victim, but not necessarily seen as innocent. Friends may fear close association with such a person, believing that a spell may be cast on them.

Inherited disorders and illnesses are frequently envisioned as being caused by a family curse that is passed along from one generation to the next through blood. Within such families, the nurse's desire to determine who is the carrier for a particular gene might be interpreted as an attempt to discover who is at fault and may be met with family resistance.

Folk beliefs mingled with eugenics, particularly throughout western and southern Europe, have resulted in the idea that many chronic conditions, particularly mental retardation, are the products of intermarriage among close relatives. The belief that a chronically ill or disabled child may be the product of an incestuous relation may further complicate attempts to encourage parents to seek assistance.

In societies in which belief in reincarnation is strong, such as among Southeast Asian groups or in Indian society, a disability is frequently seen as direct evidence of a transgression in a previous life, on the part of either the parents or the child. Those who are disabled are frequently avoided or discounted because of their past lives and are encouraged to lead particularly virtuous lives this time around. Answerable to both the past and the future, too little time and energy are often devoted to improving life in the present.

Among those who believe that chronic illness and disability are caused by an imbalance of hot/cold or yin/yang, the burden of responsibility lies with the affected individual. For many individuals from Latino or Southeast Asian cultures, the cause and potential cure lie within the individual. He or she must try to reestablish equilibrium through regaining balance. Unfortunately for those with permanent disabilities who cannot be fully healed within this conceptual system, society may perceive them as living in a continually impure or diseased state.

Traditional beliefs are tenacious and tend to remain even after genetic inheritance or physiologic patterns of chronic disease progression are explained to the family. Often new information is quickly integrated into the traditional system of folk beliefs, as evidenced by the addition of currently prescribed medications to the hot/cold classification system embraced by many Hispanic families. An explanation of the genetic transmission of disease may be given to a family, but this does not guarantee that the older belief in a curse or bad blood will disappear.

When disability is seen either as a divine punishment, an inherited evil, or the result of a personal state of impurity, the very presence of a child or adult with a disability may be something about which the family is deeply ashamed or with which they are unable to cope. In addition to public disgrace, among some families, especially immigrant groups from eastern Europe and Southeast Asia, parents may fear that disabled children will be taken away and institutionalized against their will.

Finally, it must be emphasized that some cultural explanations of the cause of chronic disease or disability are quite positive. A recent study of Mexican-American parents of chronically ill children found that the informants believed that a certain number of ill and disabled children would always be born into the world (Madiros, 1989). Many Mexican-American parents who embrace Roman Catholicism believe that they have been singled out by God for the role because of the past kindnesses to a relative or neighbor who was disabled. They often stated that they welcome the birth of the disabled infant as God's will (Groce and Zola, 1993).

Expectations for Survival

Regardless of ethnicity or race, parents of disabled and chronically ill children express concern with prognosis. Although sophisticated technology in North America can now ensure the physical survival of many children with congenital anomalies, the parents may be influenced by cultural attitudes and practices that developed during the pre-technologic era. Such attitudes may compromise attempts to encourage parents to plan realistically for their child's future. Either neglecting or overprotecting an ill or disabled child can have adverse implications for healthy psychological development.

In the past, a child with a disability often was denied the chance for education and intellectual stimulation. Among some Chinese groups, children with physical defects often were considered a punishment for the parents' or ancestors' sins and were frequently abandoned or sold into slavery. Prior to World War II, the handicapped in China received little attention from educational or social agencies, and as recently as the 1980s, many physically handicapped children were being abandoned by their families. According to traditional Shinto beliefs practiced in Japan, illness was a state that was considered polluting, calling for temporary separation and even ostracization from the group (Cheng, 1990).

Cultural expectations are not easily categorized or compartmentalized into groups in which long-term survival is expected and groups where it is not. How one is believed to be restored to health is also at times an important issue and has implications for long-term planning. For example, in some African-American households, particularly those which are strongly affiliated with Christian churches, hope for even the most critically ill child is frequently encouraged, with families praying for miracles in the face of somber medical prognostications.

Studies of Asian-American children with disabilities indicate that parents tend to be more pessimistic about their child's outcome than peers from other cultural groups whose children have equivalent disabling conditions (Elfert, Anderson, and Lai, 1991; Mary, 1990). In Chinese culture, for example, the family rather than the individual is the major unit of society. This view of the family incorporates specific hierarchical roles and formalized rules of behavior and conduct, with one of the greatest ascribed obligations being that of a child's obligation to his or her parents. While infants are treated very indulgently, there are strict demands on school-aged Chinese children to behave and to help with household chores; thus they serve a useful purpose in the family unit. Siblings of disabled and chronically ill children are frequently admonished that it is their obligation to look after the affected child's education and future. Similarly, as an adult member of society, it is expected that one will look after aging parents. The birth of a disabled child may cause Chinese parents to worry about their own future well-being.

For many Chinese-American parents, once the immediate crisis of survival has passed, the child's illness is interpreted in terms of how it will affect the child's future. Parents may be dissatisfied with treatment that they see as only treating the symptoms but not getting at the root of the problem, e.g., asthma, epilepsy. Chinese-American parents may not encourage the use of a prosthesis, such as an artificial arm or hearing aid, because they believe it does not really change anything for the child. If the prosthesis is unable to make the child well, why bother with it? Parents may gradually discontinue visits to health care providers when they perceive that "nothing is happening" (i.e., the child is not being restored to "normal"). Nurses should be cautioned against labeling this behavior as noncompliant or neglectful; rather, the cultural context of the parent's behavior needs to be examined carefully.

Social Roles

Culture affects the social roles that the chronically ill and disabled children will be able to assume throughout life. Where society dictates limited occupational roles and few social roles for individuals with a chronic illness or disability, the time, energy, and expense invested in educating a child with a disability may be regarded by family members and their support system as unnecessary.

In many societies, the roles given to disabled individuals outside the home may be severely restricted—often with a hierarchy of "more acceptable" to "less acceptable" based on the nature of the illness or disability. For example, among the dominant Euro-American group, social acceptance for children whose conditions require them to use wheelchairs or crutches is greater than for those with epilepsy or mental retardation. Children with visual or hearing impairments are generally more favorably regarded than those with mental or emotional illnesses. There are significant cross-cultural variations in this hierarchy.

Certain cultural practices and value systems within ethnic or racial groups must be understood, even if the practices and values are not those with which the nurse feels comfortable. For example, gender bias in favor of male children is found in many cultures. A Chinese or Indian family may be willing to go to great lengths to obtain expert health care or arrange for special education for a disabled son. On the other hand, daughters, especially disabled ones, may be considered poor financial risks and may be given fewer family resources and paid less attention by the parents. This does not mean, however, that the girls are unloved; rather, males are perceived culturally to be of more value.

Groce and Zola (1993) relate the case of a 22-year-old mentally retarded woman whose family had recently emigrated from southern Italy. The parents reacted strongly (and negatively) to the suggestion that their daughter move into a nearby group home. No amount of discussion of the advantages and independence their daughter would enjoy could persuade them. In further discussions with the parents, the health care providers learned that, traditionally, no proper Italian woman in their social circles lived alone until she was married. The parents applied the same rules to two older, college-educated daughters as they did to the mentally retarded daughter.

Summarized in Research Box 4-5 are studies of parents' perceptions of children with various disabilities and chronic illnesses from a transcultural perspective.

Research Box 4-5. Parental Perceptions of Disabled and Chronically Ill Children from a Transcultural Perspective

---

Debout, L., and Bradford, A. (1992). Cross-cultural attitudes toward speech disorders. *Journal of Speech and Hearing Research, 35*, 45–52.

This study used a questionnaire to look at attitudes toward four disorders, cleft palate, dysfluency, hearing impairment, and misarticulations, among 166 university students representing English-speaking North American culture and several other cultures (Chinese, Southeast Asian, and Hispanic). Results revealed significant group differences on items involving the subjects' beliefs about the emotional health of persons with speech disorders and about the potential ability of speech-disordered persons to change their own speech. Many Asian cultures consider only physical disabilities in children worthy of professional treatment, and the Japanese informants indicated that the child's problems in school were all due to "not trying hard enough."

Cheng, L. L. (1990). Asian-American cultural perspectives on birth defects: Focus on cleft palate. *Cleft Palate Journal, 27*(3), 294–300.

The treatment of birth defects and other disabilities is influenced by cultural beliefs of the individual, family, and society. The recent influx of Asian/Pacific immigrants and refugees has challenged health care professionals to provide appropriate services to individuals with cleft palate and their families from these populations. The issues of folk and religious beliefs are complex, and the variations among them are often intertwined. Their comprehension is important because studies have reported a higher incidence of cleft lip and/or palate among Asian/Pacific populations. Successful communication with Asian individuals requires recognition and consideration of cultural diversity and differing interactional styles.

Research Box 4-5 (*continued*)

Elfert, H., Anderson, J. M., and Lai, M. (1991). Parents' perceptions of children with chronic illness: A study of immigrant Chinese families. *Journal of Pediatric Nursing, 6*(2), 114–120.

The perceptions of parents of children with long-term health problems in 16 Chinese immigrant families and 15 Euro-Canadian families were studied. Results indicate that the Euro-Canadian parents see the illness or disability as affecting only particular aspects of the child's life, while the child as a whole is seen as normal. The Chinese parents more frequently describe the illness as having global effects on many aspects of the child's present and future life. The researchers suggest that how a parent perceives a child's illness affects how a parent cares for the child and interacts with health care providers.

Mary, N. L. (1990). Reactions of black, Hispanic, and white mothers to having a child with handicaps. *Mental Retardation, 28*(1), 1–5.

Sixty black, Hispanic, and white mothers of young children with disabilities were interviewed to explore their feelings and reactions to their child. Findings reveal that Hispanic mothers reported an attitude of self-sacrifice toward the child and greater spousal denial of the disability more often than did the other mothers. Stages of reaction from strong negative feelings to later periods of adjustment were more often reported by both Hispanic and white subjects. Although severity of retardation was not predictive of parental reporting of stages, parents of children who received a diagnosis within a month of birth were more likely to report subsequent adjustment stages.

Toliver-Weddington, G. (1990). Cultural considerations in the treatment of craniofacial malformations in African-Americans. *Cleft Palate Journal, 27*(3), 289–293.

African Americans represent the second largest ethnic group in the United States. Because of their African heritage and cultural practices in the United States, acceptance of the diagnosis and treatment of craniofacial anomalies are different from those of other groups. Positive aspects of the culture that augment the treatment of disorders include the strength of the family and a strong religious belief system. Factors that may impede the effectiveness of clinical intervention are economics and accessibility to health care.

Culture and Adolescent Development

Havighurst (1972) suggests eight subtasks that adolescents must complete before entering adulthood: (1) develop new and more relationships with peers, (2) accept a sex role, (3) accept one's physical appearance, (4) become emotionally independent from parents, (5) prepare for marriage and family life, (6) prepare for economic independence, (7) acquire an ideology and value system, and (8) achieve and accept socially responsible behavior. Each task is believed to be important in accomplishing the central task of adolescence, achieving an identity.

Havighurst indicates that the tasks are both historically and culturally relative and acknowledges that variation exists in the type and timing of the tasks faced by adolescents raised in different cultural or subcultural settings. In a cultural-ecologic model, Ogbu (1981) theorizes that development occurs along multiple pathways and suggests that successful development is defined by the culture's "implicit theory of success." This theory is important because it defines for members of the culture the range of available cultural tasks or social positions, their relative value or importance, the competencies essential for attainment or performance, the strategies for attaining the positions or obtaining the tasks, and the expected penalties and rewards for failure and successes. In order to achieve culturally defined success, individuals must demonstrate competency at the series of tasks that confront them across the life course. Because the demands and opportunities differ in various cultures or subcultures, however, the competencies required for mastery of cultural tasks also may differ.

From a cultural-developmental task perspective, competent development occurs with successful completion of the tasks that confront the individual at different points in the life course and concomitant development of the social and cognitive skills required by the task and permitted by the culture. Adolescents from a wide range of cultural backgrounds are believed to face different tasks at different points in their lives. For example, consider the Amish. For many Amish young adults, marriage occurs in the late teens (versus early to middle twenties among many Anglo-Americans). Among some Old Order Amish groups, there is a tradition in which the eldest son brings his bride to live in the house of his parents and continues to engage in farming, blacksmithing,

Male and female role differences are taught to children early in life and form the basis for adult roles within a culture. This Amish boy is learning to plough a field, a skill that will later enable him to assume adult responsibilities within a culture whose members reside primarily in rural areas.

carpentry, or other occupation that he has learned from his father. As the son's family grows in size, an in-law suite is added to the main house, and the parents reside there for the remainder of their lives. For many years into adulthood, the son continues to have economic interdependence with his parents as well as prolonged emotional dependence on them—when compared with counterparts in the dominant Anglo-American culture. Conversely, achievement of the task related to accepting socially responsible behavior for the Amish male and female is likely to occur at a much younger age due to the Amish concept of community and their cultural/religious value system.

Klaczynski (1990) has examined the role of cultural developmental tasks in the development and modification of the adolescent's social-cognitive functioning and the roles of both individual and contextual/environmental factors in the production of competencies. Future research is necessary to assess cultural-developmental tasks for individuals and groups representing various cultures and subcultures. The reader is referred to Chapter 5 for a discussion of culture and development during adulthood.

Special Health Care Needs of Adolescents

There are approximately 22 million adolescents in the United States and Canada. Teenagers are in a process of evolving from childhood to adulthood, and they belong not only to the cultural groups that have formed the basis for their values, attitudes, and beliefs but also to the subculture of adolescents. This subculture links the adolescent with other adolescents through a system of socially transmitted behaviors and belongings, such as clothing, music, and status symbols, including motorcycles, automobiles, videocassettes, compact discs, and stereos. The adolescent subculture has its own set of values, beliefs, and practices that may or may not be in harmony with those of the cultural group that previously guided the teenagers' behaviors.

The society of adolescents is a subculture that is vaguely structured, without formal written laws or codes, in which conformity with the peer group is emphasized. One of the most outstanding characteristics of the adolescent subculture is preoccupation with clothing, hairstyles, and grooming. Clothing mirrors the personal feelings of the adolescent and ensures identity with the peer group (Klaczynski, 1990).

In the hospital setting, gowns may stifle the individual's sense of identity, so the adolescent should be permitted to wear familiar clothing whenever the style does not interfere with safety, comfort, or hygiene. For females, there is no harm in allowing a small amount of makeup, jewelry, or other items of apparel that might be important. Males also may wear jewelry, such as bracelets and earrings.

Regardless of whether nurses personally approve of the adolescent's taste in apparel, they should ask the following questions: Does the preferred clothing or accessories promote the teenager's cleanliness and hygiene? The nurse has the right and responsibility to prohibit the wearing of soiled clothing or to request that clothing be laundered before it is worn. Does the clothing or accessory item permit adequate blood circulation? If clothing is tight or constricting, it may interfere with healing or safety. In order to gain the cooperation of the adolescent, the nurse should explain the rationale underlying any concerns about clothing. The adolescent's need to conform to peer norms is important. Rejection by members of the peer reference group may be a fate worse than the illness for which the adolescent is hospitalized.

The nurse may notice that female refugees or recent immigrants prefer to dress in traditional clothing. Some males also may elect to wear traditional clothing, but Western-style attire is likely to be more acceptable for men than for women. It is important for the nurse to determine what the adolescent finds most comfortable to wear during hospitalization.

Because of the relationship between some diseases and socioeconomic status, many low-income adolescents from African-American, Puerto Rican, Mexican-American, and Native American/Canadian subgroups have a higher than normal incidence of infectious diseases, orthopedic and visual impairments, mental illness, and untreated dental caries. This group of teenagers from low-income, culturally diverse backgrounds is more vulnerable than normal to illness and is more likely to live in an area in which health care is inadequate or absent. Consequently, low-income teenagers have a wide range of diagnosed and undiagnosed diseases. As these adolescents change from dependent children into independent adults, these disorders may interfere with their development of a positive body image, sexual and personal identity, and value system, with their preparation for citizenship, and with their independence from their parents.

Adolescents from culturally diverse groups in the United States and Canada may face greater difficulty in identity formation than adolescents from the dominant culture. Owing as much to socioeconomic factors as to ethnicity, some teenagers from culturally diverse groups, albeit not all, are exposed to only limited or inadequate adult role models and may therefore lack some of the advantages of teenagers from the Caucasian majority.

Although some adolescent behaviors are believed to be culturally universal—such as the physiologic changes associated with puberty, rebellion, and testing of independence and autonomy—the expression of these changes may vary with the individual and may be related to the individual's cultural heritage; in other words, the cultural expression of the conflicts resulting from the changes of adolescence varies. For example, playing loud music may be an acceptable expression of asserting autonomy for an African-American youth but not for a Southeast Asian teen.

Communicating with Adolescents

Without minimizing the importance of nonverbal communication, this section focuses primarily on verbal communication. For adolescents from many cultural groups, English is a second language. In the case of adolescent members of refugee families, English may not be spoken, written, or understood at all. For example, because of a 1984 agreement between the governments of Vietnam and the United States, more than 500 Vietnamese children of American service personnel have emigrated to this country and are now in foster homes throughout the 50 states. Although the majority of Vietnamese teenagers are fluent in English, it is sometimes necessary to use an interpreter, especially during severe illness. It has long been recognized that all people regress under the stress of illness, and this may manifest itself as a return of the adolescent to his or her primary language.

As discussed in Chapter 2, the nurse should be aware of gender- and age-related customs before selecting an interpreter. For example, an adolescent girl may be uncomfortable with an older male interpreter, and an older male may find a young interpreter of either sex unacceptable. The nurse must be careful to identify correctly the national origin of the client before seeking an interpreter. Vietnamese, Cambodians, and Laotians, for example, are all Southeast Asians, but there are vast differences in their languages, as well as in their health-related attitudes, values, and beliefs.

Even when English is the client's primary language, the nurse should not take for granted that communication is occurring. People from culturally diverse groups may have their own unique vocabulary that can be misinterpreted by the nurse. For example, the African-American adolescent may use the expression "tripping out" to mean intentionally acting silly or foolish. If the nurse misconstrues this to refer to substance abuse, the results of the miscommunication may be problematic for both parties. "Black English" is highly functional in some circles of the African-American community and is widely spoken and understood.

Nurses should avoid adopting expressions used by teenagers unless they are certain of the meaning of these expressions. A nurse who attempts to use but instead misuses teenage jargon will appear foolish. The nurse may find that teenagers voluntarily abandon jargon when interacting with them. The use of certain vocabulary gives the user a sense of insider status, a feeling of pride and self-worth through group identification. Thus it is frequently more important for the nurse to translate ethnic expressions, slang, black English, or other special language than to use it. It is the nurse's responsibility to assess the level of comprehension when providing care for teenagers and to communicate effectively.

Teenagers from non-English-speaking families often have mastered the art of being bicultural (or sometimes tricultural). At home they speak, dress, and behave in a manner that will gain them acceptance by their ethnic group, while in school or the work world they speak English, dress in keeping with the fashions of the dominant culture, and behave in a manner similar to that of the group from which they seek acceptance.

The nurse should realize that adolescents from different groups may express themselves in different ways. For example, Filipino teenagers often avoid direct expression. Japanese adolescents may find the open expression of feelings and confrontational behavior to be in direct conflict with cultural values. Some Chinese adolescents are discouraged from showing emotions, especially anger, because this is in conflict with a very deeply rooted belief that harmonious relationships with others are more important than individual feelings.

The nurse must be aware of nonverbal communication when caring for adolescents, especially the significance of touch. Even though many adolescent males exchange hugs with other males as they celebrate athletic victories, some males may perceive this and other types of physical contact as a threat to their masculinity. When touching adolescents, handshakes and gentle taps on the shoulder are usually acceptable. Public expression of any emotion may be prohibited for some Japanese, Chinese, and Filipino-Americans. When caring for teenagers from cultural groups in which expression of emotions is encouraged, the nurse may misperceive the intensity of degree of feeling that is being expressed.

For most cultural groups, nudity is unacceptable. The need to undress for a physical examination should be explained, and modesty should be protected. The Hispanic or Latino female may refuse to be examined by a male physician or nurse. Every effort must be made to have the adolescent and the nurse be of the same gender. If the physician or nurse performing a physical assessment or procedure is of the opposite sex, there should be a health care provider of the same sex present throughout.

Adolescent Health Care

Cultural Identification

When a group of adolescents with a separate and distinct culture exists in an environment that is strongly influenced by a majority culture, the nurse may predict that the situation provides fertile territory for potential problems. There might be conflicting attitudes, beliefs, and values as well as differences in language, dress, behaviors, and traditions. Because of these potential cultural conflicts, it is often assumed that adolescents from culturally diverse backgrounds will have a particularly difficult time, being caught between parents and older relatives who have deep identification with a certain ethnic/racial group and teachers and peers who reflect the majority culture. However, does cultural identification result in problems for adolescents, or does it enable them to avoid problems? According to Oetting and Beauvais (1991), bicultural youths are as strong as those with a high identification with a single culture. It is not mixed cultural identification but weak cultural identification that creates problems.

It should be noted that Native American, Hispanic, Caucasian-American, African-American, and Asian-American cultures are already pluralistic. These terms are, in fact, only collective nouns that represent combinations of people from many different subcultures and subgroups. These broad cultural groups already represent people with the need to constantly adapt to and deal with dissonant cognitive constructs. In fact, resolving these kinds of internal conflicts can be an essential element to personal/emotional growth and development (Oetting and Beauvais, 1991).

Selected Adolescent Health Problems

A period of growing independence and experimentation, adolescence is a time of changing health hazards. Adolescents are in the process of establishing patterns of behavior that will continue throughout adulthood. Attitudes and behaviors related to diet, physical activity, use of alcohol, tobacco, and other potentially harmful substances, safety, and sexual behavior frequently persist throughout adulthood. Many of the most important risk factors for chronic disease in later years have their roots in youthful behavior. The earlier cigarette smoking begins, for example, the less likely the smoker is to quit. Three-fourths of high school seniors who smoke report that they smoked their first cigarette by grade 9 (USDHHS, 1991).

Irrespective of race or ethnicity, the three leading causes of death during adolescence and young adulthood are *unintentional injuries, homicide*, and *suicide*. Teenagers are also facing health-related problems such as *substance abuse, sexually transmitted diseases*, including AIDS, and *pregnancy*.

Unintentional Injuries. Accidents or unintentional injuries account for approximately one-half of all deaths among people aged 15 through 24 years, and three-fourths of these deaths involve motor vehicles. More than half of all fatal motor vehicle accidents among people in this age group involve alcohol. Nearly 60 percent of 8th and 10th graders reported not using safety belts on their most recent ride.

Among Native Americans, death from unintentional injuries is $2^1/_2$ times more common than for the general U.S. population, with motor vehicle accidents accounting for most of these deaths. One study of the Hopi Indians revealed that other accidental causes of death include falls from pickup trucks, mesas, and pueblo roofs, suicide attempts in jails, and assaults (USDHHS, 1991). Efforts to reduce motor vehicle accidents have included raising the minimum drinking age in many states, lowering the speed limit on highways, and requiring safety belt use.

Homicide. Homicide is the second leading cause of death among all adolescents and young adults, and it is the number one cause of death among African-American youths. In recent years, the homicide rate for young African-American males has increased by 40 percent to nearly 86 per 100,000, more than 7 times the rate for white males. Since 1914, when U.S. national mortality data were tabulated for the first time by cause of death and race, death rates from homicide among nonwhite males have exceed those for white males by factors as 12 to 1 (USDHHS, 1991).

Homicide rates for nonwhite females have consistently exceeded those for both white males and females. Similarly, data show a consistent annual trend of proportionally decreasing nonwhite victimization. African Americans continue to be greatly overrepresented as homicide victims. Most homicides are committed by persons who are of the same race and ethnicity as their victims. Among African Americans and Native Americans, homicides tend to involve acquaintances more often than family members or strangers and usually involve persons in their twenties. Acquaintance homicides most often occur within a private residence; one-third occur in the street. Among Hispanics, the homicide rate is $2^1/_2$ times greater than the rate for whites. The risk of a Hispanic male being a homicide victim is 5 to 10 times greater than for a Hispanic female, depending on age (USDHHS, 1991).

Ethnicity and race, however, appear not to be as important a risk factor for violent death as socioeconomic status. Differences in homicide rates among racial and ethnic groups are significantly reduced when socioeconomic factors are taken into account.

As with motor vehicle accidents, about half of all homicides are associated with alcohol use. Nationwide, 10 percent are drug-related, but in many urban areas, the rate is substantially higher. More than half of all homicide victims are relatives or acquaintances of the perpetrators. Most are killed with firearms (USDHHS, 1991).

Suicide. Whereas suicide is the second leading cause of death among young white males aged 15 to 24 years, the rate among African-American adolescents and young adults is half that of whites. Both white and African-American young women have relatively lower suicide rates (4.7 and 2.3 respectively) than young men. Reviews of suicide patterns among Native American youths reveal wide variations among tribes, variations that are believed to be related to physical environment, the process of imitation, social environment (group integration, cohesion, regulation), poverty, economic change, and rational choice. One study of Crow Indians revealed that as a group, Crow children tended to experience traumatic losses of family members and friends with much greater frequency than children in the population at large, and they responded with characteristic interpersonal distancing/isolation and sadness (loneliness, withdrawal) without anger. There is an almost complete absence of research focusing on depression experienced by Native American adolescents and children, let alone the relationship of depression to suicide in these groups. As is the case with homicides, 60 percent of suicides among adolescents and young adults are committed with firearms (McShane, 1988; USDHHS, 1991).

Substance Use and Abuse. Conceptualizations of substance abuse and addiction have changed during the past 25 years, with the terms *substance use* and *substance abuse* coming into common usage in the 1970s. Earlier conceptualizations focused on either alcoholism or drug addition as singular addictive disorders. Contemporary trends in theories about the use of substances and associated problems is the identification of core commonalities occurring in a variety of substance use or compulsive behavior syndromes.

The operational definitions of substance use and abuse have been debated widely along with the substances that various experts believe should be included. Traditionally, alcohol and illicit "street drugs" have been recognized as substance abuse. More recently, however, misuse of prescription medications such as tranquilizers or analgesics and eating disorders such as bulimia and compulsive overeating have been included. As a parenthetical note, I would like to remark that some anthropologists have identified bulimia as a culture-bound syndrome characteristic of the dominant Euro-American white culture as part of its obsession with thinness and youthfulness.

For the purpose of this discussion on selected issues in adolescent health care, abuse of alcohol and illicit drugs will be explored briefly from a transcultural perspective.

Alcoholism. Given that alcohol is associated with 50 percent of deaths caused by motor vehicle accidents, fires, and drownings in U.S. adolescents, the health implications are evident. In a study of American high school seniors by Bachman, Wallace, O'Malley, et al. (1991), alcohol use among white and Native American males was found to be relatively high, while use by blacks and Asian Americans was lower, with one-half of the males and one-third of the females reporting use of alcohol during the past month. Heavy drinking is less prevalent among Puerto Rican and other Latin American males, and even lower among black males and Asian American males. The reasons cited for drinking varied cross-culturally. The most common reason given for drinking by Caucasian, black, and Hispanic adolescents was to relax; in contrast, Indochinese youth tended to drink to forget.

Most teenagers have their first alcoholic drink between the ages of 12 and 15 years. The median age for the first social drink for white males is 11 years. Alcohol among African-American teens sometimes serves as an informal rite of passage from childhood to adulthood, with black males reporting more adverse effects from alcohol than their female counterparts.

Alcohol use and abuse in the adolescent has implications for school performance, suicide, accidents, and many other problems. The nurse should determine the reasons for drinking, the amount consumed and frequency of consumption, and the effects of the drinking on growth and development, particularly on nutritional intake. Positive activities such as sports, social organizations, and other acceptable outlets for adolescent energy are sometimes helpful for adolescents struggling with the early stages of alcohol abuse. For those individuals whom the nurse identifies as alcoholics, professional counseling and assistance from groups such as Alcoholics Anonymous should be encouraged.

Drug Abuse. Although adolescents from a variety of cultural backgrounds may be tempted to experiment with drugs, a particularly high degree of addiction among Puerto Rican youths has been reported. As a result of drug abuse, the Puerto Rican community faces many complex problems. Among the reasons cited for the tendency to abuse drugs are lack of marketable skills, low educational level, and depression, characteristics common among low-income youths of other cultural backgrounds as well.

Hispanic/Latino youths have been identified as indiscriminate users of drugs, with marijuana being the most frequently abused drug. Like many substance abusers, these youths tended to abuse many types of drugs and to combine drug abuse with alcohol abuse.

The nursing intervention for adolescent drug abuse is beyond the scope of this text, but the reader is referred to other references on this topic at the end of this chapter.

Teenage Pregnancy. One of the major concerns for parents and adolescents during the teen years is pregnancy. Unwed parents are found in all societies. For many years, researchers have studied the problem of teenage pregnancy, which is reportedly at epidemic proportions today. In a study of cultural beliefs of teenagers who became pregnant, Horn (1990) determined that 20 percent of teenagers are sexually active by age 14 years and that 50 percent are active by age 19 years. Thirty-five percent of sexually active female teenagers become pregnant.

In one Midwestern U.S. city, a family service called the Teen Father Program has reported reaching, recruiting, and registering hundreds of young fathers from culturally diverse backgrounds. The young fathers who participated in the program tended to feel alienated from the mainstream of society and faced social and economic problems related to the fulfillment of appropriate masculine roles. In addition, these problems tend to interfere with their fathering role and responsibilities.

No practical means of preventing early sexual activity has been found. Advertising, television, permissive parents, lack of morality, and other factors promote early sexual experimentation. Freeman and associates (1984) found that the more sexual topics were discussed between teenagers and their mothers, the less likely the adolescents would be to have a sexual experience.

In researching the Puerto Rican experience, Cordasco and Bucchioni (1973) found that very little is taught in the household regarding sexuality. This area is considered taboo. Most teenagers are also very shy about discussing this topic in the classroom. This attitude might be due to the adolescents' families' view of the subject or to their ignorance of the subject matter. Hale (1982) reports that sexual competence is generally taught by the peer group. According to Hale, most black males begin sexual exploration between the ages of 10 and 13 years. They tend to be judged by peers on the basis of their success in seduction.

Because most teenagers look to other teenagers for sexual information, the nurse can assist by properly preparing peer counselors, who may effect teen compliance with contraceptive use. These peer counselors might be available on telephone hotlines or in mobile medical vans, since some adolescents may lack money for transportation to reach a clinic. Some experts believe that the optimal setting for the prevention of adolescent pregnancy would be a special teenage clinic that would be open after normal business hours and would allow teenagers to come with a friend. The nurse may have to promote flexible hours to accommodate youngsters. In addition, it is important for the nurse to listen, show interest, and be nonjudgmental when providing information about sex and pregnancy. It is equally important for the nurse to avoid showering the teenager with a lot of advice and information that cannot be absorbed at one time.

In the Native American culture, pregnancy is considered normal; however, the unmarried mother may be ostracized. In a comparison study of attitudes of Caucasians, African Americans, and Native Americans, Horn (1990) found that Caucasian subjects approved of the prevention of pregnancy, while Native American teenage girls tended to value pregnancy, believing it validated their feminine role. This value of pregnancy seems to correlate with the findings of Lewis (Staples, 1984), who reported that children are considered sexual beings in African-American culture. Interestingly, the African-American male child's sexual identity is more easily tied to his definition of himself as a sexual being than to behavior that has been defined arbitrarily as masculine. Staples (1984) observes that traits such as independence and assertiveness do not vary between males and females in African-American society. A boy understands that he is a male on the basis of his sexuality, and a girl realizes that she is female on the basis of her sexuality and her ability to bear children. In other words, some African-American females think of childbearing as a validation of their femaleness. Consequently, African Americans may have a positive attitude toward childbearing regardless of the circumstances, which may help explain the disproportionate numbers of births among unwed African-American teenagers. According to Horn (1990), becoming a mother at a young age, although not highly desirable, has a fairly high level of acceptance among African-American teenagers. This orientation to motherhood may account in part for the selection of pregnancy over abortion by most pregnant African-American teenagers.

Horn (1990) further reports that beliefs about contraceptives and their availability vary among cultures. For example, African-American adolescents tend to believe that contraceptives are appropriate. However, birth control pills and IUDs were not considered acceptable because they are believed to promote illness by altering the menstrual cycle. In addition, some African-American adolescents believe that the pill and the IUD dry the mucous membranes, and still others believe that refraining from intercourse for 5 days after menses is an effective method of contraception.

Finally, many Native American teenagers do not believe that contraception should be used until after the first baby is born. The findings of Horn (1990) reveal that pregnancy within Native American culture requires both modern medicine and the medicine man; thus, whenever possible, the nurse should blend folk beliefs with Western biomedicine.

Many adolescents have insufficient knowledge about effective contraceptive use. This illustrates the need for earlier education on contraceptives as well as access to contraceptive services. The nurse can help teenagers from culturally diverse backgrounds understand that there are options and provide support for decisions made with respect to those options. Nurses who work with adolescents on a continuing basis are in a good position to counsel adolescents through the chain of sexual decision making (Brindis, 1992; Kulig, 1988; Raines, 1991).

Transcultural Nursing Care of Children and Adolescents

A few principles of care for specific cultural groups have been provided to illustrate the practical ways in which culturally competent nursing care should be provided. The examples are intended to be illustrative, not exhaustive.

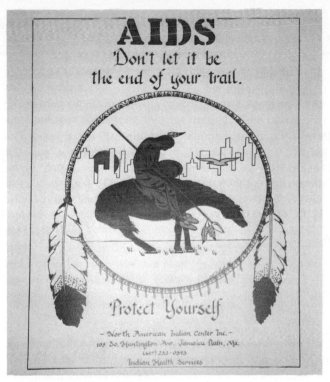

This poster warning about the dangers of AIDS is displayed in many health care facilities serving Native American teenagers.

Hair Care

Despite its importance, hair care is sometimes omitted for African-American children because white nurses are unfamiliar with proper care. The hair of African-American children varies widely in texture and is usually fragile. Hair may be long and straight, or it may be short, thick, and kinky. The hair and scalp have a natural tendency to be dry and require daily combing, gentle brushing, and application to the scalp of a light oil, such as Vaseline or mineral oil. For females (and some adolescent males), the hair may be rolled on curlers, braided, or left loose according to personal preference. Bobby pins or combs may be used to keep the hair in place. If an individual has corn-rowed braids, the scalp may be massaged, oiled, and shampooed without unbraiding the hair. Some African Americans prefer straightened hair, which may be obtained chemically or thermally. Hair that has been straightened with a pressing comb will return to its naturally kinky state when exposed to moisture or humidity or when hair growth occurs. Box 4-1 provides a regimen for shampooing the hair of African-American children and adolescents.

Children of Asian descent tend to have straight hair that does not require the same amount of care as the hair of most African Americans or whites. Principles related to personal hygiene apply to children of all racial and ethnic backgrounds, but the specific manner in which care is given may vary widely. When in doubt, the nurse should ask the child's parent or extended family member how hair care is carried out at home.

Box 4-1. Shampooing the Hair of Black Children

---

1. Select a mild shampoo. Dandruff is best controlled by shampoos containing zinc pyrithione.
2. Wet hair and apply shampoo directly to scalp. Lather and rinse with warm water.
3. If additional luster and body are desired, add protein conditioner. Allow conditioner to remain in contact with skin for at least 1 full minute, or as directed.
4. Rinse with warm water.
5. Remove excess water with towel using squeezing motion.
6. Apply small amount of light oil to scalp using fingertips. Vaseline or mineral oil may be used unless client has a preference for a commercial formula.*

*Note: Chemical relaxers should be applied only by licensed beauticians.

Children may feel more secure if a parent or close family member actually provides the care. If the nurse determines that the child would benefit from care by a familiar caregiver from home, the rationale for requesting family intervention should be explained. Comments that the nursing staff is too busy or uninterested in providing hair care should be avoided; rather, the benefit to the child's security and sense of well-being should be emphasized.

Facial Hair Care

Textural variations are found in the facial hair of culturally diverse males during adolescence and adulthood. Many Asian teenage males have light facial hair and require infrequent shaving, whereas African-American males tend to have a heavy growth of facial hair requiring regular attention.

Some African-American teenage males have tightly curled facial hair, which when shaved curls back on itself and penetrates the skin. This results in a local foreign-body reaction on the face which may lead to the formation of papules, pustules, and multiple small keloids. Some African-American males may prefer to grow beards rather than shave, particularly when they are ill.

Before shaving a client, the nurse should determine the client's usual method of facial grooming and should attempt to shave or apply depilatories (agents that remove hair) in a similar manner. When using depilatories, the nurse should protect the skin from irritation by keeping the chemical from contacting the client's nose, mouth, eyes, and ears. Straight and safety razors are contraindicated when depilatories are used because they may cause local irritation to the skin.

Skin Care

When bathing a client, the nurse should remember that some parts of the outermost skin layer are removed by the washcloth. Such sloughed skin, which will be evident on the washcloth and in the bathwater, will vary in color depending on the ethnic group of the person being bathed. The sloughed skin of a black child, for example, will be a brownish black color. This does not mean that the child was dirty; the normal sloughing of skin is simply more evident in African Americans than in whites. The more melanin present, the darker the skin color will be. Because dryness is more evident on darkly pigmented skin, Vaseline, baby oil, lanolin cream, and lotions can be applied after the bath to give the skin a shiny, healthy appearance.

Touch

The significance of touch as a healing gesture by nurses is well known. However, several cultural considerations should be remembered when touching children. Because some Vietnamese believe that touching the head may take away the spirit, the nurse should touch the Vietnamese child's shoulder or back instead of the head. Similarly, some Hispanic parents may hold cultural beliefs concerning the touching of the child by unknown nonfamily members. When in doubt, the nurse should ask the child's parents what is culturally appropriate concerning touch by a stranger.

Evaluation of the Nursing Care Plan

To evaluate the cultural components of the nursing care plan, the nurse should first ask a few probing questions to determine whether the plan was successful in achieving the mutual goals established with the child's parents. Second, if the goals were not met, the nurse should ask a few probing questions to determine the reasons for failure. Were the child's parents included in the planning and implementation of the nursing care? Were extended family members included in the plan? Did the true decision maker in the family participate in the care plan? For example, it may be that the grandmother, grandfather, uncle, aunt, or other extended family member—not the biological mother or father—may be the family decision maker. Third, if the goals were met, the reasons for their success should be evaluated and communicated to other nurses for future reference. Other members of the health care team should be involved in the evaluation, including traditional healers or folk practitioners.

Application of Cultural Concepts to Nursing Care

Two case studies follow in which cultural principles are applied to nursing care. The first concerns a new graduate's efforts at providing culturally sensitive care for an Amish infant having surgical repair of a ventricular septal defect. The second deals with a 3½-year-old child with end-stage renal disease whose mother is a Jehovah's Witness.

Case Study 4-1

Maria Gonzalez, an enthusiastic new graduate, argues heatedly with her nursing supervisor, certain that her persuasive, rational approach will win her case, if not the pure "rightness" of her cause. Located approximately 50 miles from a sophisticated urban university medical center is a rural Amish community. With frequent intermarriage has come some serious, but surgically correctable, cardiac defects among the offspring of the Amish. Members of the Amish community have become a familiar nursing "problem" for the staff of this large children's hospital. Arriving in "unreasonably large groups," several adults, adolescent girls, and younger children often come to visit Jeremiah, a 6-month-old with ventricular septal defect. The problem of overnight accommodation for the extended "family," which includes members of the biological family as well as of the extended Amish community, has become a topic of lively debate among the nursing staff. Sensitive to the cultural practices and beliefs of the Amish child and his family, the new graduate begins her argument on behalf of the family's right to adhere to Amish cultural practices.

The supervisor listens impatiently as Maria argues her case for cultural sensitivity and quickly interrupts with her decision. "These people are such a nuisance. They don't even know how to flush the toilets when they visit the hospital. This isn't a hotel. They can just go back to their horses and buggies, outhouses, and old-fashioned ways. The answer is *No!* The natural, biological mother or father may spend the night. Everyone else is to go home. And that's final."

The use of the Amish in this case is illustrative of many cultural groups characterized by an extended family network and by cultural beliefs and practices that differ from those of the health care providers of the dominant health care delivery system. The case example warrants attention for the many issues it raises. The cultural concepts relevant to nursing practice in this situation are illustrated in Box 4-2. As shown, the nature of the nursing problem is complex and multifaceted. The interconnectedness of the various components of the child's situation with the larger system is often minimized or disregarded. The values and beliefs of both the nurses within the health care delivery system and the Amish extended social network must be considered. For the purpose of analysis, some fundamental conflicts in values and beliefs have been identified. Similarities and differences also have been indicated in the nursing plan of care (Box 4-2).

Having conducted a cultural assessment, identified mutual goals, and compared underlying attitudes, values, and beliefs among the Amish parents and the health care

The use of horse and buggy exemplifies the traditional values of the Amish.

Box 4-2. Nursing Plan of Care: Hospitalization

Goal: Child's recovery and ultimate discharge from the hospital (return to parents) in an optimal state of health.

This is a mutual goal of the Amish child's parents and of the health care providers within the health care system.

In order to plan care for this child, the nurse needs to examine the underlying attitudes, values, and beliefs of the two groups that are in conflict. Points on which there is agreement must be identified as well.

Amish	**Health Care Providers**
Family	
Large families; agricultural lifestyle; extended sociocultural-religious network of Amish community members who can be counted on to assist the natural parents.	Small family units; urban lifestyle; nuclear family
Cooperation and support among extended family, especially in stressful "crisis" times such as hospitalization of a child	Individual responsibility by nuclear family; mother and father primarily responsible
Amish community members show interest and concern by visiting.	Visiting by grandparents and siblings accepted only under specified conditions (i.e., at times and places convenient for the nurses)
Concept of family includes non-blood relatives.	Concept of family includes only biologically related persons.
Parental Obligations	
Children are a part of a larger cultural group; adult members of the larger community have various relationships and obligations to the children and parents even though they are not biologically related.	Mother and father are responsible for children; *one* adult may stay with patient overnight, preferably natural mother or father Hospital facilities do not allow for a larger number of visitors, who clutter rooms, violate fire safety rules, and hinder work. A request for information from every visitor is time-consuming and perceived as an interruption to the nurse's work.
Economic Considerations	
Communal sharing of resources; hospital bill is paid from a common fund; entire bill is paid in cash upon discharge.	Health insurance; bureaucratic, moderately "slow" in processing claims after discharge Sense of anonymity and impersonal large amounts of cash are available for claims; decreasing with diagnostic related groups (DRGs) and government regulation of health care but still viewed as large, rich, source of money

(continued)

Box 4-2 *(continued)*

Traditional and Religious Values

Religious values permeate all aspects of daily living; time set aside daily for prayer and reading of scripture.

Religion is important, in some families often in proportion to the degree of illness; usually worship is limited to a single day of the week, such as Saturday or Sunday.

Illness afflicts both the just and the less righteous and is to be endured with patience and faith.

Illness is part of a cause-effect relationship; science and technology will one day conquer illness.

Protestant work ethic (in an agricultural, rural sense)

Protestant work ethic (in an urban sense)

Dress is according to 19th century traditions; specific colors and styles indicate marital status.

Fashions occur in trends; wide range of "acceptable" dress

Married men wear beards; single men are clean-shaven.

Whether a man shaves is a matter of personal preference.

Simple, rural lifestyle; family-oriented living. For religious reasons, avoid "modern" conveniences such as electricity; use candle/kerosene lights, outdoor sanitary facilities.

Use electricity/nuclear energy; indoor plumbing is the norm; view flush toilets as "ordinary."

providers, the nurse is ready to engage in activities that will promote health or identify nursing care problems (sometimes referred to as nursing diagnoses). Having done this, the nurse examines potential nursing interventions from a transcultural perspective. When making nursing care decisions or actions, Leininger's cultural care preservation/maintenance, cultural care accommodation/negotiation, and cultural care repatterning/restructuring will be useful in providing culture-congruent care. Finally, the nurse, in collaboration with the parents and significant others who may be members of the extended family, should evaluate the effectiveness of the nursing care from a transcultural nursing perspective.

The key to successful nursing care is conducting a comprehensive cultural assessment during which appropriate and relevant cultural information is gathered. In addition, nurses need to compare these data with what they know about the health care system within their institution or agency. How does change occur? What parts of the system need to be manipulated to bring about the desired change? Who are key persons to involve in effecting change? In this case involving the Amish child, the nurse is clearly pushing for a policy change, for which she has no support from her immediate nursing supervisor. Is a compromise possible? How legitimate are the arguments against having the extended family room in with the child? Are there legal implications? What ramifications does the proposed change have for the welfare of other patients? Can fire safety regulations be met without necessitating expensive changes in the hospital building? What are the adverse effects on the child if the extended family cannot spend the night? Are the natural parents able to understand the rules of the hospital and to adapt to the situation?

There are no definitive solutions or answers to these questions. The purpose of this case study has been to demonstrate the complexity of the problem and to emphasize the necessity for thoughtful analysis of various facets of the problem. The ability to apply knowledge from the liberal arts—psychology, anthropology, religion/theology, history, economics, sociology, and others—to the nursing care of children from culturally diverse backgrounds is invaluable.

As discussed in Chapter 2, if nurses want to provide excellent transcultural nursing care, cultural assessment is the foundation upon which it is based. With practice and repeated experiences assessing children and adolescents from various cultural backgrounds, the nurse will gain the knowledge and skill needed to conduct comprehensive, meaningful cultural assessments. In reflecting on the practical aspects of conducting cultural assessments, some nurses comment on the busy and rapid pace of a typical pediatric unit and argue that there is insufficient time to conduct cultural assessments on their patients. The few minutes needed to take a cursory admission history may be the only time a professional nurse spends assessing those aspects of the individual patient and family which have cultural significance. Cultural assessment should be an integral part of the admission routine for all children and adolescents, not an additional data category that is perceived to be optional. Cultural information that the nurse fails to obtain during the cultural assessment is frequently overlooked by other members of the health team as well. The missing cultural data may result in an unnecessarily prolonged period of recovery or in care that is culturally inappropriate.

The next case study is presented to illustrate the depth of understanding that can be gained when cultural stereotyping is avoided and sufficient data are gathered.

Case Study 4-2

Billy X is a 3½-year-old with end-stage renal disease. A renal transplant is indicated for Billy upon admission, but his mother indicated Jehovah's Witnesses as her religious preference for her son, and Jehovah's Witnesses are opposed to organ transplants. Billy has been admitted 12 times for peritonitis secondary to continuous peritoneal dialysis, upon which his life depends.

Dr. P. remarks to Mrs. X that it's "too bad your religion doesn't allow organ transplantation." When the nurse enters the room, Mrs. X says, "You know that I'm Jehovah's Witness, but Billy's father isn't. Maybe you could get permission from him for the transplant."

The court has frequently intervened in cases involving a child with a life-threatening illness that could be averted by low- to minimal-risk interventions when the parents refuse "orthodox" treatment for religious, personal, or cultural reasons. This is a drastic measure that can sometimes be avoided.

Billy's case has been presented to illustrate several principles. Initially, the situation appears fairly straightforward: Mrs. X is Jehovah's Witness. All Jehovah's Witnesses are religiously opposed to organ transplantation and blood transfusions. Therefore, Billy X's mother will not agree to the renal transplant. In analyzing the case, however, the nurse rapidly realizes that there is an underlying complexity. This case is intended to highlight the need for the nurse to allow for individuality, change, conflicts of norms, and ongoing data gathering, concepts that will be discussed in the next section.

Allowing for Individuality

The anthropologist van Velsen (1967) argues that no culture can be understood without allowing for the range of individual manifestations such as norms or general rules of conduct which are translated and manipulated by individuals. The problem of individual variation is often handled by labeling observed behavior as exceptional or accidental. Variations do occur within and are part of the same social order in which the traditional stereotypical case exists. Mrs. X needs to be viewed as an individual, not just as a typical member of a particular religious group. This case is intended to highlight the very human, personal, unique dimension that needs to be considered, not to identify the lack of adherence to tenets of a particular religion by its members. By avoiding the pitfall of cultural stereotyping, the health care providers might have discovered earlier that Mrs. X's individuality allowed for a solution to the problem.

Allowing for Change

Allowing for change is an important principle to consider when dealing with persons from different cultural backgrounds. False assumptions underlie many observations and interpretations. Homogeneity and the relative stability of a cultural group are often forcibly imposed on individual members, with those who fail to adhere to such norms being viewed as exceptions. Although change occurs gradually within most large groups, evolution and development occur wherever there is life. Societal values and beliefs change slowly among subgroups of society as well as in society as a whole. For example, shifts in societal attitudes toward divorce, abortion, and roles for women have all evolved during the past few decades. Considerable changes have occurred within nursing as well. For instance, the taking of blood pressure was formerly within the practice of medicine, but today nurses, and even patients, are seen as being able to perform this skill with accuracy.

Conflicts of Norms

Conflicts of norms and the resulting choice of action open to individuals must be accounted for by the nurse. Ideal norms of conduct and actual behavior are not necessarily closely interconnected. The reality is a complex interaction that is not always easy to disentangle or to explain.

Mrs. X has demonstrated that she is dealing with conflicting norms. Although her religious background as a Jehovah's Witness prohibits organ transplantation, she refers the nurse to her husband, who will permit the surgical procedure to be done. This decision enables Mrs. X to "save face" among her church-related social network yet achieves her desired goal of her son's health and perhaps even his life. A word of caution is in order. Remaining nonjudgmental is imperative for the nurse; in social processes there are no right or wrong views but rather differing views representing different personalities, values, and beliefs.

Ongoing Cultural Assessment and Data Gathering

Ongoing cultural assessment (sometimes referred to as *data gathering*) should be an integral part of the child's nursing care. For example, Mrs. X had repeatedly stated her religious affiliation with each of the 12 hospital admissions, but during the most recent one she revealed her willingness to allow the decision about transplantation to be made by Billy's father, who had no religious objections to the procedure. As additional information became known through ongoing cultural assessment, the nurse and other members of the health care team had the opportunity to modify the child's care. In this case, the nurse went from the care of a child with repeated peritonitis to the care of a child having a renal transplant.

Finally, the nurse should note that cross-national perspectives on various pediatric illnesses are sometimes helpful in the transcultural nursing care of children and adolescents. For a discussion of prevalent health problems of children and adolescents worldwide, the reader is referred to Chapter 14. Summarized in Research Box 4-6 is a research study on Japanese mothers' responses to the diagnosis of childhood diabetes. The nurse is encouraged to examine the research in terms of its implications for the nursing care of children with diabetes in both Japan and North America.

Summary

Culture exerts an all-pervasive influence on children and adolescents and determines the nursing care appropriate for the individual child, parents, and extended family members. Knowledge of the cultural background of the child and family is necessary for the provision of excellent transcultural nursing care. The nurse's cross-cultural communication must convey genuine interest and allow for expression of expectations, concerns, and questions.

Culture influences the child's physical and psychosocial growth and development. Basic physiologic needs such as nutrition, sleep, and elimination have aspects that are culturally determined. Parent-child relationships vary significantly among families of different cultural and ethnic backgrounds, and individual differences among those with the same background add to the complexity. Cultural beliefs and values related to health and illness influence health-seeking behaviors by parents and determine the nature of caring and curing expected.

There is a dearth of information specifically about adolescents from different cultures. Therefore, health professionals need to learn about, study, and document findings about teenagers. Regardless of the cultural background of an adolescent, the transition has to be made from childhood to adulthood. This may be complicated when the adolescent's values, beliefs, and practices conflict with traditional cultural values or with those of the dominant U.S. or Canadian culture in which the teenager lives. The blending of an old and a new culture by an adolescent presents problems for the family as well as for the individual.

Learning Activities

1. Arrange for an observational experience in a classsroom at a school known to have children from various cultures. Compare and contrast the behaviors observed. Does the student-teacher interaction vary according to cultural background? What culturally based attitudes, values, and beliefs are reflected in the children's behaviors? If possible, ask the students how they believe they should relate to teachers, nurses, and other adults. Ask the teacher(s) to discuss cultural similarities and differences in the classroom.

Research Box 4-6. Cross-National Perspectives: Japanese Mothers' Responses to the Diagnosis of Childhood Diabetes

Koizumi, S. (1992). Japanese mothers' responses to the diagnosis of childhood diabetes. *Journal of Pediatric Nursing, 17*(2), 154–160.

Type I insulin-dependent diabetes mellitus (IDDM), or juvenile-onset diabetes mellitus, presents a challenge to children and adolescents, their parents, siblings, and health care providers. In order to survive this serious disease, the children and their families must maintain a balance between daily insulin requirements, exercise, and diet. In Japan, as in many countries, responsibility for maintaining control of the child's diabetes usually rests with the mother.

The sample consisted of 28 Japanese mothers, ages 20 to 50 years (mean age 37.5). The mean age of their diabetic children was 8 years (range 1–15 years). Thirteen of the children were boys and 15 were girls. Using a semistructured interview, researchers met with the mothers for approximately 1½ hours on six occasions (immediately after diagnosis, after 3 months, after 6 months, after 12 months, after 18 months, and after 24 months). The interview topics included family factors, the mother's adaptation to living with a diabetic child, regulation of the diabetes, the child's adaptation and knowledge about IDDM, and self-regulation of diabetes. The State Trait Anxiety Inventory in Japanese also was administered during the same time to determine the mothers' anxiety level.

The findings revealed that Japanese mothers who had newly diagnosed diabetic children responded with shock, defensive retreat, and increased anxiety. Although many mothers had a strong reaction and suffered depression, weight loss, pain, and feelings of exhaustion, they adapted to the diagnosis by the end of the first year. Although anxious about the diagnosis, fathers had little knowledge about the disease and limited participation in the daily management of the child's care.

Compared with an American study, some of the mothers' coping patterns were similar; others were related specifically to accepted Japanese cultural practices. For example, during the "honeymoon" period, mothers reported seeking Chinese medicine and health food. Three mothers (10.7 percent) sought physicians who would diagnose their children as not having diabetes. Two mothers (7.1 percent) also sought religious treatment for the illness. Japanese mothers used several characteristic coping strategies, such as resignation, holding out, and believing in religion. Nurses need to be aware that mothers of all cultural backgrounds face a variety of psychological stressors after their children are diagnosed with IDDM. Although there are predictable patterns of response among parents of all cultural groups, there also are culture-specific responses.

2. When caring for a child from a cultural background different from your own, spend time talking with the child's parents or primary provider of care about child-rearing beliefs and practices (e.g., discipline, toilet training, diet, and related topics). Who is the primary provider of care? Compare and contrast the parental responses with your own beliefs and practices.

3. When assigned to the Pediatric Unit, observe the number and relationship of visitors for children from various cultures. Who visits the child? If non-related visitors come, what is their relationship to the child? How do various visitors interact with the child? With the parent(s)?

4. When caring for a child from a cultural background different from your own, ask the parent(s) or primary provider(s) of care to tell you what they believe causes the child to be healthy and unhealthy. To what cause(s) do they attribute the current illness/hospitalization? What interventions do they believe will help the child to recover? Are there any healers outside of the professional health care system (e.g., folk, indigenous, or traditional healers) whom they believe could help the child return to health?

5. If your hospital has a play room, observe the types of toys and books available. For which group(s) are the majority of these items intended? Do books and toys represent various cultures? What is the role of nurses in determining culturally appropriate books and toys? Are there any items you believe should be added to (or removed from) the play room to better meet the cultural needs of hospitalized children?

References

Achar, S. T., and Yankauer, A. (1962). Studies on the birth weight of South Indian infants. *Indian Journal of Child Health, 11*, 157–167.

Ainsworth, M. D. S. (1967). *Infancy in Uganda*. Baltimore: Johns Hopkins University Press.

Andrews, M., and Owens, P. T. (1973). *Black Language*. Los Angeles: Seymour and Smith.

Bachman, J. G., Wallace, J. M., O'Malley, P. M., et al. (1991). Racial/ethnic differences in smoking, drinking, and illicit drug use among American high school seniors, 1976–1989. *American Journal of Public Health, 81*(3), 372–377.

Barry, H., Bacon, M. K., and Child, I. L. (1967). Definitions, ratings, and bibliographic sources of child-training practices of 110 cultures. In C. S. Ford (Ed.), *Cross-Cultural Approaches* (pp. 293–331). New Haven: HRAF Press.

Brindis, C. (1992). Adolescent pregnancy prevention for Hispanic youth: The role of schools. *Journal of School Health, 62*(7), 345–351.

Burgio, G. R. (1991). The child between nature and culture. *Klinische Padiatrie, 203*(3), 67–71.

Campinha-Bacote, J., and Ferguson, S. (1991). Cultural considerations in child-rearing practices: A transcultural perspective. *Journal of the National Black Nurses Association, 5*(1), 11–16.

Cheng, L. L. (1990). Asian-American cultural perspectives on birth defects: Focus on cleft palate. *Cleft Palate Journal, 27*(3), 294–300.

Children's Defense Fund (1985). *Black and White Children in America: Key Facts*. Washington, D.C.: CDF.

Cintas, H. M. (1989). Cross-cultural variation in infant motor development. *Physical and Occupational Therapy in Pediatrics, 8*(4), 1–20.

Cordasco, F., and Bucchioni, E. (1973). *The Puerto Rican Experience*. New York: Littlefield, Adam & Co.

D'Andrade, R. G. (1966). Sex differences and cultural institutions. In E. E. Maccoby (Ed.), *The Development of Sex Differences* (pp. 174–204). Stanford: Stanford University Press.

Dennis, W., and Dennis, M. G. (1940). The effect of cradling practices upon the onset of walking in Hopi children. *Journal of Genetic Psychology, 56*, 77–86.

Doek, J. E. (1991). Management of child abuse and neglect at the international level: Trends and perspectives. *Child Abuse and Neglect, 15* (Suppl. 1), 51–56.

Elfert, H., Anderson, J. M., and Lai, M. (1991). Parents' perceptions of children with chronic illness: A study of immigrant Chinese families. *Journal of Pediatric Nursing, 6*(2), 114–120.

Freed, R. S., and Freed, S. A. (1991). Ghost illness of children in North India. *Medical Anthropology, 12*, 401–417.

Freeman, E. W., et al. (1984). Urban Black adolescents who obtain contraceptive services before and after their first pregnancy. *Journal of Adolescent Health Care, 5* (3):183–190.

Garcia Coll, C. T. (1990). Developmental outcome of minority infants: A process-oriented look into our beginnings. *Child Development, 60,* 270–289.

Geber, M. (1956). Developpements psychomoteur de l'enfant africain {Psychomotor development of the African infant}. *Courrier, 6,* 17–28.

Greathouse, B., and Miller, V. G. (1981). The black American. In A. L. Clark (Ed.), *Culture and Childrearing* (pp. 68–95). Philadelphia: F.A. Davis.

Groce, N. E., and Zola, I. K. (1993). Multiculturalism, chronic illness and disability. *Pediatrics, 91*(5), 1048–1055.

Gutierrez, J., and Sameroff, A. (1990). Determinants of complexity in Mexican-American and Anglo-American mothers' conceptions of child development. *Child Development, 61,* 384–394.

Hale, J. E. (1982). *Black Children: Their Roots, Culture and Learning Styles.* Provo, UT: Brigham Young University Press.

Havighurst, R. J. (1972). *Developmental Tasks and Education.* New York: McKay.

Holder, B. (1992). Ethnicity and family factors in adolescent substance abuse. *Addiction Nursing Network, 4*(2), 53–58.

Horn, B. M. (1990). Cultural concepts and postpartal care. *Journal of Transcultural Nursing, 2*(1), 48–51.

Horn, B. M. (1983). Cultural beliefs and teenage pregnancy. *Nurse Practitioner, 8*(9) September, 35–39.

Horn, B. M. (1981). Cultural concepts and post partal care. *Nursing and Health Care, 2*(3), 516–517, 526–527.

Johnston, M. (1977). Folk beliefs and ethnic cultural behavior in pediatrics: Medicine or magic. *Nursing Clinics of North America, 12*(1), 77–84.

Kagan, J. (1970). The many faces of response. In P. Kramer (Ed.), *Readings in Developmental Psychology Today* (pp. 9–15). Del Mar, CA: CRM Books.

Kempe, C. H., Silverman, F. N., Steele, B. F., et al. (1962). Child abuse. *Journal of the American Medical Association, 181,* 17–24.

Klaczynski, P. A. (1990). Cultural-developmental tasks and adolescent development: Theoretical and methodological considerations. *Adolescence, 25*(100), 811–823.

Kohlberg, L. (1966). Cognitive-developmental analysis of children's sex-role concepts & attitudes. In E. E. Maccoby (Ed.), *The Development of Sex Differences* (pp. 82–173). Stanford: Stanford University Press.

Korbin, J. E. (1991). Cross-cultural perspectives and research directions for the 21st century. *Child Abuse and Neglect, 15* (Suppl. 1), 67–77.

Kulig, J. C. (1988). Conception and birth control use: Cambodian refugee women's beliefs and practices. *Journal of Community Health Nursing, 5*(4), 235–246.

Laungani, P. (1989). Accidents in children—An Asian perspective. *Public Health, 103,* 171–176.

Leininger, M. M. (1990). Issues, questions, and concerns related to the nursing diagnosis cultural movement from a transcultural nursing perspective. *Journal of Transcultural Nursing, 2*(1), 23–32.

Lester, B. M. (1974). Separation protest in Guatemalan infants: Cross-cultural and cognitive findings. *Developmental Psychology, 10,* 79–85.

Luna, L. J. (1989). Care and Cultural Context of Lebanese Muslims in an Urban U.S. Community: An Ethnographic and Ethnonursing Study Conceptualized within Leininger's Theory. Doctoral dissertation, Wayne State University, Detroit, Michigan.

Madiros, M. (1989). Conception of childhood disability among Mexican-American parents. *Medical Anthropology, 12,* 55–68.

McCubbin, H. I., Thompson, E. A., Thompson, A. I., et al. (1993). Culture, ethnicity, and the family: Critical factors in childhood chronic illnesses and disabilities. *Pediatrics, 91*(5), 1063–1070.

McLoyd, V. C. (1990). The impact of economic hardship on black families and children: Psychological distress, parenting, and socioemotional development. *Child Development, 61,* 311–346.

McShane, D. (1988). An analysis of mental health research with American Indian youth. *Journal of Adolescence, 11,* 87–116.

Mead, M. (1928). *Coming of Age in Samoa.* New York: William Morrow.

Mead, M., and Macgregor, F. C. (1951). *Growth and Culture.* New York: G. P. Putnam's Sons.

Meredith, H. V. (1969). Body size of contemporary groups of eight-year-old children studied in different parts of the world. *Monographs of the Society for Research in Child Development, 34*(1), 350–356.

Montagu, A. (Ed.) (1977). *Culture and Development.* Englewood Cliffs, NJ: Prentice Hall.

Moss, H. A. (1967). Sex, age, and state as determinants of mother-infant interaction. *Merrill-Palmer Quarterly, 12,* 19–36.

Oetting, E. R., and Beauvais, F. (1991). Orthogonal cultural identification theory: The cultural identification of youth. *International Journal of the Addictions, 25*(5A & 6A), 655–685.

Ogbu, J. (1981). Origins of human competence: A cultural-ecological perspective. *Child Development, 52,* 413–429.

Oneha, M. F., and Magyary, D. L. (1992). Transcultural nursing considerations of child abuse/maltreatment in American Samoa and the Federated States of Micronesia. *Journal of Transcultural Nursing, 4*(2), 11–17.

Overfield, T. (1985). *Biologic Variation in Health and Illness: Race, Age and Sex Differences.* Menlo Park, CA: Addison-Wesley.

Overfield, T. (1981). Biological variation: Concepts from physical anthropology. In G. Henderson and M. Primeaux (Eds.), *Transcultural Health Care.* Menlo Park, CA: Addison-Wesley.

Pearson, J. L., Hunter, A. G., Ensminger, M. E., and Kellam, S. G. (1990). Black grandmothers in multigenerational households: Diversity in family structure and parenting involvement in the Woodlawn Community. *Child Development, 61,* 434–442.

Phillips, S., and Lobar, S. (1990). Literature summary of some Navajo child health beliefs and rearing practices. *Journal of Transcultural Nursing, 1*(2), 13–20.

Rabin, A. I. (1965). *Growing Up in the Kibbutz.* New York: Springer-Verlag.

Raines, T. G. (1991). Family-focused primary prevention of adolescent pregnancy. *Birth Defects, 27*(1), 87–103.

Richman, A. L., Miller, P. M., and LeVine, R. A. (1992). Cultural and educational variations in maternal responsiveness. *Developmental Psychology, 28,* 614–621.

Rivzi, S. (1984). *Taharat and Najasat: The Book of Cleanliness.* Canada: Sexsmith.

Rogoff, B., and Morelli, G. (1989). Perspectives on children's development from cultural psychology. *American Psychologist, 44*(2), 343–348.

Rosenberg, B. G., and Sutton-Smith, B. (1972). *Sex and Identity.* New York: Holt, Rinehart and Winston.

Sanovitis, A., and Murillo-Rodhe, J. (1979). The Puerto Rican. In A. L. Clark (Ed.), *Culture, Childbearing and Health Professionals* (pp. 110–126). Philadelphia: F.A. Davis.

Schaffer, H. R. (1971). *The Growth of Sociability.* Baltimore: Penguin Books.

Staples, R. (1984). The mother-son relationship in the black family. *Ebony, 84* October, 74–78.

Story, M., and Harris, L. J. (1989). Food habits and dietary change of Southeast Asian refugee families living in the United States. *Journal of the American Dietetic Association, 89*(6), 800–803.

Stringfellow, L., Liem, N. D., and Liem, L. D. (1981). The Vietnamese in America. In A. L. Clark (Ed.), *Culture and Childrearing* (pp. 228–241). Philadelphia: F.A. Davis.

Super, C. M. (1981). Behavioral development in infancy. In R. H. Munroe, L. L. Munroe, and B. B. Whiting (Eds.), *Handbook of Cross-Cultural Development* (pp. 181–270). New York: Garland.

Tanner, J. M. (1961). *Education and Physical Growth.* New York: International Universities Press.

Tolson, T. F. J., and Wilson, M. N. (1990). The impact of two and three-generational black family structure on perceived family climate. *Child Development, 61,* 416–428.

Tseng, W. S., and Hsu, J. (1991). *Culture and Family: Problems and therapy.* New York: Haworth Press.

U.S. Bureau of the Census (1990). A comparison of child-rearing practices among Chinese, immigrant Chinese, and Caucasian American parents. *Child Development, 61,* 429–433.

U.S. Department of Health and Human Services, Public Health Service. (1991). *Healthy People 2000: National Health Promotion and Disease Prevention Objectives.* Washington, DC: U.S. Government Printing Office, DHHS Publication No. (PHS) 91-50212.

van Velsen, J. (1967). The extended case method and situational analysis. In A. L. Epstein (Ed.), *The Craft of Social Anthropology* (pp. 129–153). London: Travistock.

Watson, J. S. (1969). Operant conditioning of visual fixation in infants under visual and auditory reinforcement. *Developmental Psychology, 1,* 508–516.

West's Revised Code of Washington Annotated (1990). St. Paul, MN: West Publishing Company.

5

Transcultural Perspectives in the Nursing Care of Middle-Aged Adults

Joyceen S. Boyle

Introduction

This chapter discusses transcultural aspects of health and nursing care associated with developmental events in middle age and the adult years. The first section presents an overview of cultural influences on adulthood, followed by a discussion of the stages of psychosocial development and cultural variations. The second section gives examples of problems faced by middle-aged adults of different cultures who are experiencing health problems and developmental transitions. How culture influences responses to health problems and developmental transitions will be described.

Until recently, little interest, attention, or research has been directed toward developmental processes and health concerns in adulthood. In addition, developmental differences among adults have not been examined cross-culturally. The lack of specific descriptive terms for such a significant portion of the life span is in itself an interesting cultural phenomenon.

Cultural Influences on Adulthood

Development in adulthood has been termed "the empty middle" by Bronfenbrenner (1977), another indication of Western culture's lack of interest in the adult years. Traditionally, these years have been viewed as one long plateau that separates childhood from old age. Berger (1983) has suggested that for earlier generations of a more traditional society, adulthood may have been a time of stability. Decisions affecting marriage and career were made in the late teens, and drastic changes seldom occurred afterward. However, over the past two or three decades, the pattern of a stable adulthood in American society has changed dramatically. Sociocultural factors have precipitated

Margaret M. Andrews and Joyceen S. Boyle: TRANSCULTURAL CONCEPTS IN NURSING CARE,
SECOND EDITION. © 1995 J.B. Lippincott Company.

tremendous changes, producing crises and other unpredictable events in adult lives. Divorce, career change, increased mobility, the sexual revolution, and the women's movement have had a profound impact on the adult years.

Myerhoff (1978) noted that although there are no universal criteria for any of the identified life stages, and although the associated milestones and attributed experiences may differ considerably, all known societies have an age known as "adulthood." Neugarten (1968) observed that each culture has quite specific chronologic standards for appropriate adult behavior; these cultural standards prescribe the ideal ages at which to leave the protection of one's parents, to choose a vocation, to marry, to have children, and so on. As a result of each culture's sense of social time, individuals tend to measure their accomplishments and adjust their behavior according to a kind of social clock. Awareness of the social timetable is frequently reinforced by the judgments and urgings of friends and family, who say, "It's time for you to . . . " or "You are getting too old to . . . " or "Act your age." Social time varies even by subculture in the United States.

Thus culture exerts important influences on human development in that it provides a means for recognizing stages in the continuum of individual development throughout the life span. It is culture that defines "social age," or what is judged appropriate behavior for each stage of development during the phases of the life cycle. In some societies, adult role expectations are placed on young people when they reach a certain age. A number of cultures have clear rites of passage that mark the line between youth and adulthood. In modern American society, however, there are no definitive boundaries, although legal sanctions confer some rights and responsibilities at ages 18 and 21 years. In our culture there is no single criterion for the determination of when young adulthood begins, since individuals experience and cope with growth and development differently and at different chronologic ages (Hill and Humphrey, 1982).

Adulthood as such is usually divided into young adulthood and middle adulthood. Starck (1988) suggested that "in essence, the young adult struggles to achieve intimacy with persons outside the nuclear family while establishing a career, whereas the middle adult concentrates on making a contribution to society through work and/or family" (p. 4). Exactly how individuals pursue these developmental tasks and how they cope with and manage the challenges of adulthood are influenced by their cultural values, traditions, and background.

Many personality theorists, such as Freud, Erikson, and Fromm, cite maturity as the major criterion of adulthood. Jung recognized young adulthood as a time of coping with the demands of emotional involvements in family, work, and community (Hill and Humphrey, 1982). According to Erikson (1963), the developmental task at middle adulthood is the attainment of generativity versus stagnation. Generativity is accomplished through parenting, working in one's career, participating in community activities, or working cooperatively with peers, spouse, family members, and others to reach mutually determined goals. According to Hill and Humphrey (1982), the mature adult has a well-developed philosophy of life that serves as a basis for leadership, stability, and objectivity. Individuals in adulthood assume numerous social roles, such as spouse, parent, child of aging parent, worker, friend, organization member, and citizen. Each of these social roles involves expected behaviors established by the values and norms of society. Through the process of socialization, the individual is expected to learn the behaviors appropriate to the new role. In the United States, young adults are usually able to establish goals that are relatively specific and definitive; however, life experiences obviously play a major part in determining whether an individual can establish and maintain these goals. In many ways, Erikson's and other theorists' views of what occurs in middle adulthood are the biases of middle-class "Anglo" values and experiences. In Chapter 1, this constellation of characteristics was attributed to predominantly white, Anglo-Saxon, Protestant (WASP) views and behaviors. For many cultural groups in this country, mastery of "mainstream" developmental tasks is not easily managed, and in some cases, it may even be undesirable. For some groups, developmental tasks may be accomplished through culturally defined patterns that are different from or outside the norm of what is expected in the dominant culture. Furthermore, there are now some authors who suggest that developmental stages and the associated developmental tasks of adulthood have been derived primarily from studies of men, and thus women may experience adult development somewhat differently (Gilligan, 1982a, 1982b). Some of these differences are described in the next section.

Psychosocial Development During Adulthood

Throughout life, each individual is confronted with developmental tasks—responses to life situations encountered by all persons experiencing physiologic, psychological, and sociologic changes. Although the developmental tasks of childhood are widely known and have long been studied, those critical experiences of adulthood are less familiar to most nurses.

Havighurst (1974) identified seven developmental tasks or stages of middle adulthood. The first task is reaching and maintaining satisfactory performance in one's career. Success in a career seems based on behaviors and attitudes that arise in a traditional white, middle-class value system that values the male working role. A successful career is enhanced for a middle-aged male if his wife has assumed primary responsibility for management of the household and supervision of their children. For men and women without "spouses" (or an equivalent person to manage domestic tasks and child rearing), success in a career may seem less important or may be more difficult because of division of time and energy. Lipson (1991), in her work with Afghan refugees, found that while family life is the core of Afghan culture, role conflict sometimes occurred from the husband's unwillingness or inability to obtain employment. When the wife was able to find menial employment (e.g., hotel maid), this threatened her husband's traditional patriarchal role and altered the power structure between them.

At the present time in the United States, to expect members of certain groups, such as ethnic minorities, newly arrived refugees, or the homeless, to achieve satisfaction from jobs that interest them or from status derived from succeeding in a career is unrealistic and indicates a lack of sensitivity to the problems faced by these groups. In addition, plant closings, "downscaling" in workplaces, decreased production, and high unemployment have posed problems for many workers. Thus, although the work role is valued in American society, the attainment of a successful career may not be realistic for some minority groups or even certain individuals within the majority culture, many of whom are returning to school in preparation for a "second career."

Havighurst (1974) defines the second major task of adulthood as achieving social and civic responsibility. Social and civic responsibilities are in part culturally defined. Whereas members of the dominant American culture may value achieving an elected office in the local PTA or Rotary Club, other cultures may emphasize different goals. For example, religious obligations may be given priority over civic responsibilities. Becoming an elder or a lay pastor may be highly valued by some African Americans. Among religious groups such as the Latter-Day Saints (Mormons) or the Amish, being appointed a lay bishop may be more valued than career success. Usually, traditional religious groups have not encouraged the emergence of women in leadership roles within the church structure or the wider society. Thus broadly defined developmental tasks that include recognition and acknowledgment outside the family group may conflict with the traditionally defined role for women. Some religious and ethnic or cultural groups believe that a woman's place is in the home, and women who attempt to succeed in a career or in activities outside the home or group are frowned on by other members of the group. Civic responsibilities that relate to children or domestic matters may be viewed as appropriate for women to assume, whereas others may be viewed as more within the province of men. Middle Eastern and Southeast Asian cultures emphasize responsibilities and contributions to the extended family or clan rather than to the wider society. Family ties are of great importance to many traditional cultural groups residing in the United States.

The third developmental task of adulthood is to accept and adjust to the physiologic changes of middle age. Age-related physical changes begin in middle adulthood and ultimately necessitate adjustments in activities of daily living, lifestyle, and attitude. The rapid acceptance of cosmetic surgery and the interest in procedures such as suction lipectomies tell much about the way some members of American culture resist or attempt to delay the physiologic changes associated with late adulthood. On the other hand, the effects of aging may be more easily accepted by members of such cultural groups as Asian Americans, whose traditional values include respect for and deference to the elderly.

The fourth developmental task of middle-aged adults is to help teenage children become responsible adults. The age at which young persons marry and become independent varies by custom or cultural norm as well as by socioeconomic status. Generally speaking, adults of lower socioeconomic status leave school, begin work, marry, and become parents and grandparents at earlier ages than middle- or upper-class adults do. It is relatively common in American society for an 18-year-old, for example, to move away from home to pursue higher education or to find employment. Indeed, early independence, or "leaving home," is encouraged by many American families, although this trend has decreased as the American economy has declined. Other cultural groups, such as those from the Middle East and Latin America, place more emphasis on the extended family; even after marriage, a son and his new wife may choose to live very close to both families and to visit relatives several times each day. Families from some cultural groups such as Hispanics may be reluctant to allow their young daughters to leave home until they marry.

Havighurst's fifth developmental task of adulthood involves a change in the roles and relationships of individuals with their parents. Adjusting to aging parents and responsibilities toward them, as well as finding appropriate solutions to problems created by aging parents, is faced by many adult Americans as they approach middle age. Placing an aged mother or father in a nursing home may be a decision made with reluctance and only when all other alternatives have been exhausted. Such actions may be totally unacceptable to some members of other cultural groups, in which family and community structures would facilitate the complex care required by an aged ill person and would exert a great deal of social pressure on an adult son or especially a daughter who failed in this obligation.

The sixth and seventh developmental tasks defined by Havighurst place emphasis on the role of wife or husband and establishment of strong friendships along with increasing enjoyment of leisure activities. The relationship of wife and husband is often enhanced in middle adulthood, although divorce at this time is becoming a more frequent occurrence in the United States. The frequent need for both spouses to work may conflict with traditional roles and cause feelings of guilt and shame on the part of the husband. Some women continue to assume all responsibility for domestic chores while working outside the home and experience considerable stress and fatigue as a result of multiple role demands. An emphasis on an emotionally close interpersonal relationship between a husband and wife may be a culturally defined value. Studies have suggested that in some groups, such as Hispanic cultures, women develop more intense relationships or affective bonds with their children or relatives than with their husbands. Latin men, in turn, may form close bonds with siblings or friends, ties that meet the needs for companionship, emotional support, and caring that might otherwise be expected from their wives (O'Kelly, 1980).

Gender roles and how men and women go about establishing personal ties with either sex are heavily influenced by culture. Berger (1983) observed that in American society, women are more likely to have intimate, self-disclosing friendships with other women than men have with other men. A man's male friends are likely to be working, drinking, or playing "buddies." In southern Europe and the Middle East, men are allowed to express their friendship with each other with words and embraces. Such expressions of affection between men are uncommon in American culture and might be attributed to homosexuality.

Thus affiliation and friendship needs in adulthood and the satisfaction of these needs are facilitated or hindered by culture. Social support, family ties, and friendship needs can be met through the extended family and kinship system or through other culturally prescribed groups such as churches, singles bars, work, and civic associations. An individual's health may be affected by such ties, since persons who have a reliable set of close friends and an extensive network of acquaintances are usually healthier—both emotionally and physically—than those without friends. Lifestyle, a powerful influence on health status, involves the practice of health habits and a guiding philosophy of life to promote a positive outlook. Individual and family lifestyles vary according to resources and cultural values and traditions. Changing American lifestyles are creating realignment of the division of labor, roles, and values of the family. In turn, adult growth and development in middle age are undergoing profound changes.

Health-Related Situational Crises

The preceding section described cultural influences, developmental tasks, and selected cultural variations in adulthood. This section contains two case studies of adults from different cultural groups who experience health problems that are compounded by cultural factors as well as by situational or developmental crises.

The Onset of Chronic Illness in Native American Culture

In addition to the developmental or maturational changes discussed in the preceding section, all manner of situational crises may impinge on individuals in middle age. A few affect only the individual, but many others occur in the family system and affect children, spouse, aging parents, or other close relatives. A chronic disease, for example, affects not only the individual with the disorder but also the entire family system. Danielson, Hamel-Bissell, and Winstead-Fry (1993) indicated that health professionals need a better understanding of how families influence the health-related behavior of their members because definitions of health and illness and reactions to them form during childhood within the family context. When the illness has cultural connotations, the issues become more complex; medical treatment and nursing care must take into account the cultural history, values, beliefs, and practices that influence the client and family's ability to cope with the illness as well as assessing whether the interventions are congruent with their culture.

Type II Diabetes and Native Americans. Non-insulin-dependent diabetes (NIDDM), or type II diabetes, is commonly seen among Native Americans; indeed, the high incidence of this disorder in certain tribes has been a concern to health officials for a number of years (Sugarman et al., 1990). Type II diabetes can be a serious disease, with numerous complications that have profound consequences. The incidence of end-stage renal disease among Native Americans has risen dramatically and is now a major public health problem (Newman et al., 1990). No cases of end-stage renal disease had been diagnosed among Ute Indians living on a Utah reservation before 1978. However, only 5 years later, 11 patients were receiving treatment for end-stage renal disease, and an additional 38 diabetics had constant proteinuria or renal impairment (Tom-Orme, 1984).

In recent years, the incidence of diabetes among some Native American tribes has increased markedly (Wiedman, 1989). Blainey (1991) observed that the incidence of NIDDM "markedly increases when a community moves from a traditional to a modernized lifestyle, changing the diet from low-calorie, high-fiber foods to high-calorie, refined foods, and the lifestyle from a physically active to a more sedentary form" (p. 1364). A study of the Ute Indian tribe in Utah found that the prevalence of diabetes was 4 times the statewide rate, and the rate of diabetic nephropathy was 43 times the rate for the diabetic population in Utah generally. Thirty percent of the outpatient visits in some Public Health Service facilities were for diabetes-related problems (U.S. Department of Health and Human Services, 1982). In some tribes, the rate of newly diagnosed diabetes was as high as 25 percent. Tom-Orme (1984) stated that diabetes was rare among Native Americans before 1940, but at the present time, it is one of the most devastating health problems among adult members of that cultural group. The highest prevalence rates are found among the Pima Indians of Arizona, with 50 percent of the population over age 35 years affected (Knowler et al., 1981). Rates are also high in the Seneca of Oklahoma and the Cherokee of North Carolina. Lower rates of diabetes are found in the Navajo, Hopi, and Apache tribes (Tom-Orme, 1984), although there are indications that the incidence of diabetes is increasing in these populations also (Sugarman et al., 1990).

The reasons for this epidemic of diabetes mellitus are believed to be related to a rapid change from subsistence agriculture to an industrial economy. Some years ago, Neel

(1962) hypothesized that some Native Americans have an underlying genetic propensity for the disease that is triggered by changes in dietary practices and increasing obesity. A "thrifty gene" hypothesis also has been proposed. According to this theory, during the centuries when Native Americans lived a migrating, hunting-and-gathering existence marked with periods of feast and famine, a "thrifty gene" developed as a result of natural selection. This gene might have affected carbohydrate metabolism and storage during times when food was plentiful so that carbohydrates could be stored in the body to provide energy during periods of scarcity. Furthermore, changes from high levels of physical activity to a sedentary lifestyle are hypothesized to influence carbohydrate metabolism. According to this theory, Native Americans continue to store carbohydrates in excess even though periods of food scarcity or famine no longer occur. The result is obesity, and for many Native Americans, ultimately type II diabetes occurs. West (1978) has shown that NIDDM rates do tend to be higher in tribes in which obesity is prevalent and uncommon in tribes in which the majority have lean physiques. Many illnesses that are familiar among white patients may have different manifestations in Native Americans. White (1977) reported that Native American may have a high blood sugar level but be asymptomatic for diabetes mellitus. Although the specific role of genetic factors is not yet clear, there is a biocultural variation among Native Americans with diabetes that must be taken into account when planning for nursing care; at the same time, other social and cultural factors also must be considered.

Native American Cultural Views of Diabetes. Because of the high incidence of diabetes on reservations, public health professionals have instigated a number of special programs related to diabetes (Tom-Orme and Hughes, 1985; Leonard, Leonard, and Wilson, 1986). Many reservations have intervention programs that include diabetes clinics, nutrition classes, and outreach programs, all of which emphasize patient and family education. A great deal of attention has been directed toward encouraging early screening, health learning, and more participation in health care activities. Culturally related problems that are directly associated with the high incidence of diabetes on the reservation have been identified. For example, some Native Americans living in reservation communities tend to view diabetes as a "white man's disease," a condition that Native Americans did not experience before the coming of white people and the acculturation process. As a result, health services and the "white" health professionals are sometimes viewed by Native Americans with suspicion and distrust. Ironically, Tom-Orme (1984) reported that when health professionals on a Ute reservation attempted to introduce a risk-reduction and health-promotion curriculum to public school classrooms attended by Ute children, some non-Native Americans objected to their children's exposure to a diabetes-related curriculum because they believed that diabetes was a "Native American problem." These parents did not understand that similar risk factors exist for both diabetes and various cardiovascular diseases and that non-Native Americans are at risk for developing these chronic conditions too.

Case Study 5-1

Harry Cloud is a 53-year-old Ute living on a reservation in a rural area of a western state. Mr. Cloud was recently diagnosed as having type II diabetes. He is married and has four children, 12 to 17 years of age.

Like other Ute people living on the reservation, Harry Cloud grew up exposed to the conflict between Native Americans and the dominant culture. This has not contributed to a trusting and helpful nurse-client relationship. Mr. Cloud has seen some of his friends and neighbors develop diabetes, succumb to numerous complications, and eventually die. The widespread attention that has been given to diabetes has caused some Native Americans to feel stigmatized. They resent being labeled as "diabetics," and at some hospitals, the term *diabetic clinic* has been replaced with *medical clinic*. In addition to being a serious chronic disease with physiologic complications, diabetes can be a source of considerable psychological stress. For example, the possibility of impotency is a cause of uncertainty and worry among many male diabetics.

Health-Promotion Strategies and Nursing Interventions. Most nurses believe that priorities of nursing management for Mr. Cloud are that he lose weight and incorporate changes in eating habits and regular exercise into his lifestyle. However, these health goals may be compromised by social and cultural factors. According to current medical standards, Mr. Cloud has been overweight since he was a teenager. Assuming that he understands the seriousness of his condition and genuinely desires to lose weight, there still may be cultural factors that conflict with these goals. Nurses can become more culturally sensitive to cultural norms and values of clients such as Mr. Cloud by listening carefully, being empathetic, recognizing the client's self-interest and needs, being flexible, having a sense of timing, using the client's and family's resources, and giving relevant information at the appropriate time.

Like many other adults, Mr. Cloud has fairly definite preferences about food and the way it is prepared and served. At most family meals, meat is usually fried, and potatoes are boiled and served with gravy. In lieu of potatoes, biscuits with gravy are a favorite dish. Fresh fruits and vegetables are expensive and are in limited supply at stores near the reservation. Canned vegetables are served on occasion; corn is a favorite. What is known as "junk food" appears frequently with meals—soda pop, potato chips, and prepackaged pastries and desserts. It is a diet high in simple carbohydrates and fats and low in fiber, protein, vitamins, minerals, and calories with nutritional benefits. Clearly, a great deal of symbolism is attached to food in every culture. Clark (1992) suggested that "food can function as a focus of emotional association [and as] a channel for interpersonal relationships" (p. 307). Traditionally, the Ute people came together in the early fall— a time of increased food supply—to share food and friendship. According to Conetah (1982), a tribal leader and historian, the social interaction at such gatherings was of primary importance. As bearers of this tradition, Mr. Cloud and other Ute people on the reservation enjoy their communal meals and wonder why health professionals "blame food for all our health problems."

As a tribal government official, Mr. Cloud leads a pronounced sedentary life. He enjoys driving a new four-wheel-drive pickup truck. Almost no one on the reservation walks anywhere. Jogging is something that crazy white men do. Aerobic dancing is a subject for jokes and derogatory comments. Weight gain is viewed as a normal accompaniment of adulthood; thinness is a cause for worry. Two factors in Mr. Cloud's favor are that he does not smoke and is not addicted to alcohol, although he drinks heavily on occasion.

From this vignette, the nurse can examine nursing priorities. A major area of concern involves the differences in cultural beliefs and values, particularly those about weight loss and exercise in a cultural group that values frequent eating or feasting with friends and relatives. In addition, the cultural view of body size or shape is important to consider. The Utes, as well as some other Native Americans, prefer a physique that most health care professionals would call obese. If Mr. Cloud were to lose 15 or 20 pounds, his aunt might say, "You are wasting away!" or his friends might tell him, "You look sick."

The nurse must constantly discriminate between the standards of the dominant white culture and those of the client's cultural group. Tom-Orme (1984) suggested that although an ideal body-weight chart may be used, desirable weight can instead be computed on the basis of a large body frame. Positive reinforcement should be given for weight loss, but primary emphasis should be on a balanced diet and regular physical activities such as walking. In addition, Mr. Cloud can be encouraged to change the types of food that he eats, decreasing simple carbohydrates and fats while increasing complex carbohydrates and high-fiber foods such as whole grains, legumes, and potatoes. The nurse can help him plan the appropriate food exchanges in his daily diet.

Nurses providing care to clients such as Mr. Cloud also will need to consider other cultural factors that ultimately influence the nursing goals. The Ute people frequently do not exhibit inner-directed behavior and are uncomfortable measuring individual performance against others. The concepts of self-care and control are seemingly in conflict with values and norms of the Ute culture (Tom-Orme, 1984). Health professionals determine "control" in diabetic clients by such physiologic indicators as blood pressure, blood glucose, and body weight, all of which are evaluated by a fixed norm. For a Ute, a more culturally acceptable approach is evaluation of these measures in relation to his or her own individual progress.

Sometimes nurses assume that increased skills or knowledge will increase the ability of clients to manage their own care. However, such information should be evaluated carefully as well as the manner of communication. For example, some Ute people are very uneasy about discussions of personal body functions. Before the widespread use of blood glucose monitoring, Mr. Cloud would have been extremely uncomfortable if instructed to test his urine, particularly if the instructions were given in a group setting or a similar "public" atmosphere. Tom-Orme and Hughes (1985) observed that some Utes perceive illness as an "unpleasant topic to discuss with anyone." Such individuals may perceive their illness as a confidential and private matter. They may wonder, "Why do you want to know about that?" or, "It's my problem; why are you interested in it?" (Research Box 5-1 presents a study describing the development of diabetes educational material for Native Americans.)

To help Mr. Cloud with his adjustment to his diabetes, the nurse may want to get the assistance of a community health representative (CHR), auxiliary health workers who have been used successfully by the Public Health Service. A CHR is a member of the local community and as such understands the attitudes, values, and lifestyles of residents. CHRs receive additional training on health problems that are of special concern in the community. Their purpose is to bridge the gap between Native Americans and white health professionals.

An important aspect of culturally sensitive nursing care is understanding and accepting cultural differences that cannot always be bridged in the course of client-nurse interactions. To become comfortable working with culturally diverse clients, nurses must understand their own strengths and limitations, both personally and professionally. Choosing to use a CHR to help reach nursing goals more quickly and more tactfully is an appropriate nursing judgment. Only when Mr. Cloud is convinced that it is to his advantage to make changes in his daily living patterns can the plan of care have a reasonable chance of success. The nurse is ultimately responsible for planning, implementing, and evaluating nursing care, but for health promotion to be successful, it must first be acceptable to the client.

Research Box 5-1. Diabetes Education for Native Americans

Hosey, G. M., Freeman, W. L., Stracqualursi, F., and Gohdes, D. (1993). Designing and evaluating diabetes education material for American Indians. *The Diabetes Educator, 16*(5):407–414.

This study described the development and evaluation of diabetes education material for Native Americans and Alaska natives living in Washington, Oregon, and Idaho. Fifty-five percent of the sample read at fifth-grade level or higher. Diabetes educational material was found to be about tenth-grade level. The project members developed diabetes education material that was targeted to a fifth- to seventh-grade level. Evaluation showed that 62 percent of the target audience understood the educational material. This article indicated that there is frequently a serious mismatch between available educational material and client reading skill. The sample also indicated that inclusion of culturally appropriate factors, such as Native American motifs and references to Native American lifestyles, promoted understanding of the educational material.

Creativity and innovation are necessary if suggestions for modifications in lifestyle are to be implemented by clients and their families. For example, the nurse should not expect that sweeping changes in Mr. Cloud's eating habits will occur overnight, and it is important that Mr. Cloud and his wife make the choices themselves. The family support system is especially important with Native Americans. Mrs. Cloud does the grocery shopping, meal planning, and food preparation; her strong support will be crucial if her husband is to change his eating patterns. Instead of stressing that losing weight is the goal, the nurse should highlight the positive aspects of a healthy, natural diet over artificially sweetened, high-fat, "junk" food. Rather than requiring regular monitoring of weight, which some clients find demeaning, it might be more acceptable to ask Mr. Cloud to keep track of changes by the notches on his belt. Although blood glucose monitoring could provide precise feedback on the effects of certain foods and exercise, it would probably be more culturally acceptable to emphasize healthy foods and regular physical activity. An important factor to discuss with this family is that changes in Mr. Cloud's eating habits will benefit his wife and children also. The nursing plan should increase the entire family's understanding about proper food and exercise as well as the resources within the family and community. The nurse is in a position to refer, teach, and counsel Mr. Cloud and his wife and can facilitate their use of available resources.

Nursing prescriptions of physical activity also may be a problem for Mr. Cloud, given his cultural background and geographic setting. Certainly, the value of health should be stressed rather than weight reduction and exercise. Encouragement of participation in sports such as baseball or basketball might be appropriate. Aerobic exercise has been demonstrated to have a positive effect on increased glucose metabolism not only during activity but also for several hours afterward. The nurse might suggest that Mr. Cloud spend some time with his sons and "get out in the mountains" (as opposed to "hiking"). Fishing and hunting could be encouraged; the Ute people have traditionally participated in these activities, and many Ute men enjoy them. Any physical activity will be more acceptable if it is congruent with overall lifestyle and cultural context.

Participation in Native American dances, such as the Bear Dance, also could be encouraged. A few successful fitness programs are congruent with Native American cultural traditions and heightened community identification have been reported. Fitness programs have been developed to help Zuni diabetics learn healthy lifestyles and in the process control their blood glucose levels and lose weight (Fitness program restores Zuni tradition of running, 1986: Leonard, Leonard, and Wilson, 1986). Tennis, swimming, or racquetball would be inappropriate for Mr. Cloud because the reservation does not have the proper facilities for these sports and cultural traditions do not encourage these activities. Walking and other aerobic activities such as swimming, stationary biking, and aerobic exercise classes are becoming more culturally acceptable for Native Americans. Gradually, as tribes cope with a high incidence of type II diabetes, the influence of positive peer support will have an important impact on supporting healthy behavioral changes.

Most important is that the nurse should emphasize positive factors such as health and a healthy lifestyle rather than negative factors such as control of diabetes, complications, weight reduction, and exercise. The nurse's choice of words and the emphasis are important. Mr. Cloud and his family should be encouraged to pursue *health* and *wellness* rather than thinness. *Nutrition* rather than *diet, supplementation* rather than *deprivation*, as in the *substitution* of fruit for candy bars, whole grains for doughnuts, and vegetables for sugared snacks. A focus on disease, special diets, special exercise, special treatments, and special medications takes away from normal activities of daily life, including family life, work, and leisure.

Psychosocial Development and Nursing Interventions. The first priority of nursing care for Mr. Cloud and his family is to help them understand and adjust to the impact of diabetes. The diagnosis of this condition precipitated a situational crisis for the family that can best be resolved by the provision of culturally relevant health-promotion and risk-reduction strategies. When Mr. and Mrs. Cloud are comfortable with the management of the diabetes, the nurse can introduce other long-term nursing goals. The diabetic health teaching and nursing interventions provided to the Cloud family should focus on wellness and health promotion. The nurse can continue this emphasis by helping the family successfully manage developmental tasks common to adulthood.

Mr. Cloud and his wife may face problems in the completion of the developmental tasks discussed earlier. Havighurst suggests that an important developmental task for middle-aged adults is career success. Having a job is important to Mr. Cloud and his family, but Native American culture does not place the kind of emphasis on work and career that the wider American society does. What is important for the nurse to assess and acknowledge is that Mr. Cloud is working and able to provide for his family's basic needs. Career success is not valued for traditional Native American women, but Mrs. Cloud can be encouraged in her role of providing help and care to family members and in promoting the health of her husband and children.

The second task of adulthood defined by Havighurst involves relationships with others and the community. Social and civic responsibilities among Native Americans are met almost entirely at the level of the extended family and tribe. These ties and associations are very strong, are often complex, and are not readily understood by outsiders. Given that the Cloud family lives on a reservation and participates in its cultural activities, it can be assumed that this aspect of their life is satisfactory.

The third developmental task of adulthood proposed by Havighurst is acceptance and adjustment to the physiologic changes of middle age. Because diabetes has become so common on the Ute reservation in the last few years, many Utes view middle age as the time when diabetes will develop. The health-promotion strategies and nursing interventions described earlier will help Mr. Cloud and his family come to terms with diabetes and adjust to other health-related changes.

Havighurst's fourth developmental task is that of helping teenagers become responsible adults. It is important that Mr. and Mrs. Cloud include their children in health education activities and solicit their participation in lifestyle changes. Hughes (1984) stated that many young Utes believe that diabetes is an "old person's disease" and do not see the value of changing their health behavior. They are fatalistic about developing diabetes if a member of their family has been so diagnosed. Hughes (1984) described a highly permissive parent-child relationship among the Ute people that allows young persons to make their own decisions without overt directions from their parents. This may create obstacles in familial compliance with a diabetic regimen. Obtaining the cooperation of the Cloud children in such changes as diet and physical activity may be the most challenging problem a nurse faces.

Havighurst's other developmental tasks pertinent to this case study involve relationships with spouse and friends. The nurse must understand the importance of cultural ties with kin and other members of the tribe so as to also understand that family support is crucial when an illness develops and is a necessary factor for successful health promotion and maintenance in diabetic care.

The last task suggested by Havighurst involves increased enjoyment of leisure activities. Mr. Cloud and members of his family can be encouraged to develop leisure activities that are congruent with cultural practices and will enhance the health status of all members of the family. Some of these activities were described in the preceding section.

The Refugee Experience: Haitian-American Culture

During the last 25 years, the United States has experienced the influx of considerable numbers of individuals (both legally and illegally) from such diverse areas of the world as Southeast Asia, Central America, Eastern Europe, the Middle East, Cuba, and Haiti. For some refugees and immigrants, traumatic life events have been followed by the stress of coping with a new culture and a different environment. These experiences may predispose individuals to problems in adult development, as well as to certain health problems. The following case study illustrates how a situational crises created by the refugee experience has hindered the psychosocial development of one individual (the mother of the family) by disrupting developmental tasks related to family and work patterns. Nursing interventions that are based on cultural implications and a development framework are discussed.

Haitian Refugees: Background and Context. To provide appropriate care to Haitian Americans, nurses must have some knowledge about the social and political events that have occurred in Haiti and must understand the issues that have influenced Haitian migration to the United States. Haiti has experienced a very troubled social and political history that has produced crippling poverty, economic insecurity, revolutions, and political turmoil. Many Haitians, seeing little opportunity for improvement in miserable living conditions and the overall economic situation, have fled their country in search of freedom and opportunity elsewhere (U.S. Committee for Refugees, 1986).

During recent times of political unrest, poor Haitians have given all their money to private entrepreneurs and boarded unseaworthy boats for a chance to escape to a better life. Although Haitians have been migrating to the United States for many years, most of them who came prior to 1980 were upper-class individuals who were able to obtain permanent residence and citizenship with little difficulty and usually assimilated rather quickly into the dominant culture. This changed in 1980 as a result of a change in U.S. immigration policies.

From April to October of 1980, the Mariel boat lift from Cuba took place. In order not to be discriminatory, the State Department created a special status called "Cuban-Haitian entrant, status pending." The "entrant" category described a temporary status and was used rather than political asylum. However, the "entrant" status created its own problems, since Haitian immigrants were placed in a bureaucratic limbo because they could not apply for resident status or citizenship (U.S. Committee for Refugees, 1986). In October of 1980, the immigration policies were changed again to prevent further migration of Haitian refugees, and a maritime interdiction program was later initiated to turn back Haitian refugees at sea. However, during the period 1980–1982, over 36,000 Haitians arrived in southeast Florida, some of them through legal channels, but the majority of them entered this country illegally (Frankenhoff, 1985).

At the present time, many adult Haitian women leave their children with relatives in Haiti and come to the United States by themselves. Leaving children behind is a common practice because Haitian mothers fear interdiction and detention in the United States and do not want their children placed with strangers. Their intent is to send for their children once they get settled in the United States; however, to date, immigration policies of the U.S. government have not permitted this. As a result, many Haitian women have entered new consensual unions and have had additional children after settling in this country (DeSantis, 1986). Restrictive as well as changing immigration policies have created many difficulties for Haitian refugees. Haitians who have managed to make it to the United States face a very real risk of being arrested, detained, and deported by immigration officials. In addition to these fears, the federal government's refusal to grant political asylum to Haitians deprived the refugees of benefits under the new 1980 Refugee Act. DeSantis (1990) noted that Haitian refugees placed additional demands on community resources already under pressure from the needs of the area. Local taxpayers have often resented the additional demands when the federal government was reluctant or refused to reimburse local and state governments for monies expended on the care and resettlement of Haitian refugees. These policies helped to create and reinforce hostility and resentment toward the newly arrived Haitians.

In addition, Haitians have been subjected to prejudice and discrimination because they are black; they are also very poor and lack the educational skills necessary to do well in U.S. society. Furthermore, they have been stigmatized by their early classification as an at-risk group for acquired immune deficiency syndrome (AIDS) and human immune virus (HIV) disease (Nachman and Dreyfuss, 1986; Cosgray, 1991). DeSantis (1990) reported that health care professionals experienced considerable frustration and difficulty in meeting the health care needs of Haitian refugees in part because the large numbers of Haitians overwhelmed the health care system. Furthermore, most health professionals did not understand their language, culture, or health beliefs and practices.

Many Haitian entrants do not qualify for most federal assistance programs, cannot bring older children to the United States, and live in fear that they may be deported. The fear of deportation or arrest has made many Haitians refugees extremely reluctant to use the health care system unless they are very ill and in a crises situation. DeSantis (1990) stated that the Immigration Reform Act of 1986 should have assisted in alleviating the concerns that many Haitians had about their entrant classification, since many Haitians entering before and during 1982 were given amnesty and allowed to apply for citizenship. Instead, the tedious and expensive application process and the requirement that all entrants being processed for residency had to be tested for AIDS had a very negative impact.

Case Study 5-2

Monique St. Clair is the 35-year-old mother of two young girls, ages 2 and 4 years. The family lives with relatives in a large apartment complex in Miami, Florida. Mrs. St. Clair was born in Haiti and grew up in a poor family who lived on the outskirts of Port Au Prince, the capital city. Mrs. St. Clair left her oldest child, a boy now 17 years old, in the care of family members and came to the United States with a maternal aunt and a cousin. Together the three of them have comprised an extended family that has grown by the addition of the cousin's married spouse, their children, and Mrs. St. Clair's conjugal mate and their two children. The term *conjugal mate* is used by DeSantis (1990) to refer to unmarried adult males who live in a conjugal relationship with women in the household. Such a common-law marriage is common in Haitian families living in the United States and Haiti and is predominant among the poor (Cosgray, 1991). This kind of arrangement imposes much of the responsibility for caring for and meeting the needs of the family on the mother. Child rearing is shared by older children and extended family members, but by and large, it is the mother who bears much of the burden and responsibility for the children.

Like other poor Haitian women, Mrs. St. Clair and her aunt work as maids in a motel in a poor section of the city. Mrs. St. Clair has a low-paying, low-status job that has no benefits such as sick leave or health insurance. Studies of Haitian families in southeast Florida determined that the median household income was only $8500 yearly despite the fact that two or more persons from the household were employed (DeSantis, 1990). Obviously, this limited income is way below the poverty level set by the U.S. government for families of similar size.

Few licensed day-care centers are available in the Miami Haitian community. When her cousin is not employed, she will babysit Mrs. St. Clair's two little girls, but when her cousin is working, Mrs. St. Clair pays one of her neighbors to watch the children. Family resources for child care that might have been available in Haiti are unavailable to mothers in the United States, so Mrs. St. Clair feels fortunate that she has female kin that are intermittently available to help her with the children.

Traditional Haitian Health Beliefs. Many of the illnesses affecting the Haitian-American community are potentially preventable or controllable through self-care measures. DeSantis and Halberstein (1992) and DeSantis (1985, 1988) have described many of the health problems in the Haitian population. They include a high prevalence of general malnutrition, hypertension, pediatric and adult HIV/AIDS, infant diarrhea and nursing bottle caries, measles and other childhood communicable diseases, suicide, and depression, as well as tuberculosis. Like other cultural groups, many Haitian Americans rely on traditional health beliefs and practices, and this has major implications for nursing practice not only for illness care but also for health promotion and wellness. The practice of voodoo, the African-Haitian religious belief system, is not uncommon. Cosgray (1991) described voodoo as a religious system practice that dates back to the preslavery days of Africa; it was brought by slaves to Haiti in the 17th and 18th centuries. Voodoo practitioners are *houngans* (male) or *mambos* (female) and are further divided into other classifications that are not as well defined. The voodoo practitioners of Haiti are powerful figures with magical powers; they claim to be able to change themselves into animals, to pass through locked doors, and to perform other supernatural acts. Because of its association with black magic, voodoo is perceived as superstition by health care providers, and many Haitian Americans will not readily admit that they practice voodoo for fear of ridicule. The importance of voodoo in daily life and as a therapeutic system is pervasive and cannot be overemphasized.

Generally speaking, Haitian folk diseases or traditional illnesses can be divided into illnesses that result from natural causes and those which result from supernatural causes. Since the causes are attributed to different sources, treatment is sought from different caregivers. Probably the most frequently used traditional practitioner is the herbalist who prescribes various herbs and home remedies to treat natural illnesses. Diseases of supernatural origin are believed to have been bought about because the individual had a breach with his or her "spirit protector." Haitians brought the belief from Africa that an individual is surrounded or enveloped by a variety of powerful, dominate spirits (Cosgray, 1991). When this protection is disturbed, the individual or a close family member becomes ill. Magical powers may be employed for the purposes of destroying one's enemies or healing the sick. Haitian Americans frequently hold a holistic conceptualization of man's relationship to God and to the external environment. In traditional Haitian belief systems, supernatural entities are a part of the external world. Thus reliance on God and prayer to affect everyday life—i.e., money, a job, health, sickness—is a central element in the Haitian world view. DeSantis (1993) noted that Haitians in her study stressed the social, behavioral, and feeling dimensions of health. A core theme in the Haitian health belief system is the status of one's blood as an indicator of illness (DeSantis, 1993; Laguerre, 1981; Farmer, 1988; Scott, 1975). DeSantis (1993) stated that

> the amount [of blood] (too much or too little), color viscosity (thick or thin), turbulence (quiet or rushing) of flow, degree of impurities (good/bad or clean/dirty), and rise and fall of blood in the body are diagnostic of health and illness in traditional Haitian ethnomedicine. (p. 15)

These beliefs about blood and body fluids extend to menstruation, whereby the monthly menstrual flow is believed to cleanse the body of impurities and restore a woman to a healthy "clean" state. DeSantis and Tappen (1990) stated that Haitian women believe that they need to be extra careful during menstruation because they are more vulnerable to illness at this time. Likewise, the diagnosis of HIV/AIDS is frequently termed "bad blood" (DeSantis, 1993).

Illnesses that result from natural causes such as colds or cuts are expected to occur frequently and to last only a short period of time. Many Haitian Americans believe in the hot and cold theory of disease found in many Latin American countries. This theory classifies food, medications, illness, and other body conditions as either "hot" or "cold."

The assignment to hot or cold categories has nothing to do with the temperature of the object but rather its essence or essential qualities. The basic idea is an attempt to achieve balance between the hot and cold forces. For example, if a person had a "hot" disease, it would be appropriate to treat it with a "cold" medication or food. The postpartum period is considered one of the hottest states possible, and the patient is restricted from eating hot foods, which would make the condition unhealthy (Kirkpatrick and Cobb, 1990). Examples of "cold" foods that would be encouraged by those who believe in traditional health practices during the postpartum period would include avocado, cashew nuts, mango, pineapple, banana, and grapefruit and orange juice (Wiese, 1976).

In a study of infant feeding practices among Haitian mothers, DeSantis (1986) described another belief related to breast milk that has implications for the health and nutrition of breast-fed babies. It is believed that mothers may suffer from a condition that causes their milk to "spoil," and when this happens, it is believed that the breast milk turns into a poisonous substance, making the baby very ill. The obvious cure is to wean the baby from the breast immediately.

These traditional beliefs influence Mrs. St. Clair's child-rearing practices, and she is careful that her children do not become too hot or too cold and that they take care to avoid drafts of cold air. When they were babies, Mrs. St. Clair kept them heavily clothed to prevent cold air from entering the body through the umbilical cord while it was healing or through the sutures of the fontanel line. She also used numerous magico-religious measures such as a multicolored bead necklace to ward off harm or spells of bad luck as well as curses from evil people. In addition, Mrs. St. Clair frequently prayed to God to protect her children, to grant them good health, and to prevent evil or harm from befalling them.

Mrs. St. Clair uses the professional health care system on occasion, usually only for the children rather than for herself. The cost of an office visit to a physician has been a tremendous barrier, so she has tended to use public health facilities. She has taken the children to the health department for their immunizations, but this has been sporadic because of her work schedule. As a result, the children's immunizations are not complete, and they have lacked continuous well-child care. When they are ill, Mrs. St. Clair treats them with home remedies such as poultices, herbal baths, and home-brewed teas. She is extra cautious during their illnesses about the effects of hot and cold foods and other factors on their health status. Sometimes when she can afford them, she will purchase over-the-counter medications such as cough syrup or laxatives. Purgatives or laxatives are often administered on a routine basis because periodic purging is central to Haitian health culture and is seen as a method of ridding the blood and body of impurities (DeSantis, 1988, 1990).

Developmental Assessment and Nursing Interventions. The following discussion focuses on Mrs. St. Clair's role and psychosocial development in relation to the social and cultural expectations that are placed on Haitian mothers. The preceding example used Havighurst's list of developmental tasks to assess the psychosocial adult needs of a Native American adult; this discussion uses Erikson's (1963) view of middle adult development.

According to Erikson, the developmental task of middle adulthood is the attainment of generativity rather than stagnation. *Generativity*, in Erikson's terms, is a concern for oneself, as well as for the growth and development of one's children, peers, the community, and society. According to Berger (1983), all of Erikson's stages share one general characteristic: They are centered on each person's relationship to the social environment. Generativity is accomplished through parenting, success in one's career, participation in community activities, and working cooperatively with peers, spouse, family members, and others to reach mutually determined goals.

Haitian-American women often are the major providers for their families in terms of financial contributions as well as emotional and social support. The strength of the family structure develops from a sense of obligation of its members to the family unit. This sense of obligation can be easily identified in Haitian mothers, but Haitian fathers, even though they may be absent from the family a great deal, also feel deep pride and a sense of obligation to their families. As described earlier, the social, political, and economic situation of Haitian refugees is such that women often have what could be described as two families. The first family consists of the children left behind in Haiti with relatives, and the second family consists of children born in the United States in consensual unions. Often the children's father is unable to assume economic responsibility for his family, primarily because of the migratory nature of his work or the lack of steady employment. Many Haitian-American mothers, however, try to send a small amount of money back to Haiti each month to help their family's meager financial resources or to support children left behind with family, friends, or distant kin.

Because of the refugee experience, Mrs. St. Clair is stressed in a variety of ways and is unable to successfully complete adult development tasks. However, nurses must realize that notions about adult development and what adults should do are influenced by our own cultural views of what is proper or normal for men, women, and families. Our values suggest that men are the providers, support their families, and are heads of households. "Proper" women marry, bear and raise children, manage the household, depend on men for economic support, and accept a subordinate position in the home. Although poverty, racism, and discriminatory immigration policies have kept Haitian women from complying with the family ethic, they are nevertheless judged by its terms. The nurse might wonder why Mrs. St. Clair does not insist on marriage or why she continues to allow her conjugal mate to live with her family when he appears to contribute little financial assistance. For that matter, how could a "good" mother ever leave her child behind in Haiti for relatives to care for? In addition, our values in the United States are oriented toward individualism—an emphasis on individual worth, individual attainment, and individual growth and development. Other cultures, such as Haitian culture, emphasize families and kinship more than individuals, and the Haitian is taught to be subordinate to family, church, and government authorities. They are more comfortable when cooperating with others rather than taking the initiative in any activity. An individual's self-worth as such is directly related to his or her position within the family unit. One way for the nurse to promote Mrs. St. Clair's growth and development is to emphasize her success as a parent and her positive relationship with her mate, her immediate family members, and neighbors. In addition, Mrs. St. Clair is fulfilling her obligations to her family in Haiti. Haitian parents never really abandon their children emotionally or financially.

New Ways of Coping. Numerous authors (DeSantis, 1990, 1993; Laguerre, 1984) have pointed out that Haitian Americans lost the emotional and social support of extended kin when they left Haiti. They have endured poverty in the United States and have experienced discrimination here because they are black and have been stigmatized because of their early association with AIDS and/or HIV disease. With such high-risk and culturally diverse groups, nursing interventions to support growth and development and promote health must be directed at both individuals and families as well as at the community level. The refugee experience has mandated that Mrs. St. Clair learn to manage on her own in a new culture. In some ways, the refugee experience has empowered Haitian women like Mrs. St. Clair. They have learned new ways of coping and have developed new skills that have enabled them to manage in a new environment. On the other hand, the refugee experience has not been as beneficial for the Haitian men. Some of them may resent the growing financial, social, and independent role of women and the changing concepts of gender roles. Traditionally, Haitian men were heads of households, made decisions about their families, and handled the family finances. This situation changed with the refugee experience, and often men now find themselves peripheral to family life. Although many Haitian men do help with child care and household chores, these are new roles for them. It is especially important not to condemn the Haitian refugee woman for allowing the male to remain in the household and to make many decisions about the family. These new kind of relationships are often fragile, and frequently there is a potential for domestic violence, a phenomenon of concern in the Haitian community.

There are a number of things that Mrs. St. Clair can do to enhance her coping skills and thus enable her to better provide for herself and her family. DeSantis (1990) has pointed out that much of the stress affecting the Haitian community, such as poverty and an undefined residency status, are external to and beyond the direct control of health care professionals. However, these are the very factors that contribute to illness and raise significant barriers to preventive care. Nurturing cultural networks that exist in the Haitian community and the sense of interdependence that exists will strengthen the community and the individuals who live there. Helping the community mobilize its efforts to develop day-care facilities and other needed resources is an important nursing intervention. Members of the Haitian community share a common bond arising from the refugee experience, and they want to help themselves as a community. Health care professionals who wish to effect change for the Haitian community must work in the sociopolitical arena to bring about those needed changes.

Helping Mrs. St. Clair find health care for her children, including well-child care, that is available and affordable is important, but it is equally important that Mrs. St. Clair be encouraged to take actions that will promote her own health. Often a way for the nurse to win a Haitian mother's trust is to show interest and concern about her children. Once a trusting relationship is established, then Mrs. St. Clair will be able to focus on her own needs and concerns. Enhancing her coping skills will decrease psychological and emotional stress, but Mrs. St. Clair needs to be concerned with her physical health also. A sensitive nurse can help Mrs. St. Clair to understand that rest, exercise, and an adequate diet will help her manage her family and work more expeditiously. Teaching her how to do breast self-examination and encouraging an annual pap smear are appropriate interventions that should be followed by helping Mrs. St. Clair find appropriate care that is low in cost and convenient. Numerous factors contribute to the decision as to whether or not to use family planning methods, and a holistic, culturally sensitive approach that considers her traditional health beliefs is needed to assist Mrs. St. Clair in choosing a method that she believes will be safe and comfortable. It is important to take into account that traditional Haitian beliefs suggest that the number of children a family has depends on God, not on the use of contraceptive practices. Since Mrs. St. Clair may become pregnant again, given her age, the importance of seeking early prenatal care to ensure both maternal and infant health must be incorporated in health teaching.

In addition to increasing resources and services, Jones and Meleis (1993) have suggested that something more is needed. They stated, ''If individuals are not active participants in creating and using these resources, gaps between the resources and the individual's health will continue to grow'' (p. 7). Thus empowerment of individuals may be that necessary link. Empowerment includes helping Mrs. St. Clair develop a critical awareness of her situation and enables her to master her environment to achieve and maintain health for herself and her family. The most culturally appropriate way to empower Mrs. St. Clair is to help her make certain that her children are healthy and can take advantage of the resources available in the community for them. Enhancing generativity for Mrs. St. Clair means recognizing, promoting, and enhancing her abilities to meet her own and her family's needs, solve their own problems, and mobilize necessary resources to take control of their own lives.

Summary

All individuals are confronted with developmental tasks, those culturally defined ways of responding to life situations. The example of a middle-aged Native American with diabetes was presented, and culturally appropriate ways that the nurse might implement nursing care were suggested. Emphasizing wellness and health through transcultural nursing strategies rather than stressing compliance with a diabetic regimen is more acceptable to this Native American group. Use of traditional family and community support systems and resources should be encouraged, since these ties are of particular significance in Native American culture.

The second transcultural case study concerned a Haitian-American family living in the United States. The major nursing role with this family was promoting successful completion of adult developmental tasks by enhancing the mother's ability to cope with her many responsibilities and tasks. Although these developmentally specific interventions will not solve all the problems facing this family, such nursing guidance will help family members plan ahead, realistically anticipate outcomes, and cope with them in a manner that decreases stress and pressure, particularly on the mother. In this example, the mother was experiencing difficulties related to the adult stage of development, such as rearing children and adequately providing for the financial support of her family. These difficulties were embodied in the multiple crises confronted by the family in the last few years as well as the diminished support system outside of the immediate kin group.

Learning Activities

1. Interview a colleague or a person from another cultural group. Ask about family roles and how they are depicted. Are these role descriptions typical of how traditional roles are described in the literature? If not, what are some of the reasons why they have changed?

2. Interview a middle-aged client from another cultural group. Ask about the client's experiences within the health care system? What were the differences the client noted in health beliefs and practices? Ask the client about his or her health needs during middle age.

3. Using the cultural assessment guidelines provided in Chapter 2, conduct a cultural assessment of a middle-aged client of another cultural group. How might the assessment data differ if the client were older? Or younger?

4. Review the literature on Mexican-American culture. Describe the traditional Mexican-American family.

References

Berger, K. S. (1983). *The Developing Person Through the Life Span*. New York: Worth.

Blainey, C. A. (1991). Diabetes mellitus. In M. L. Patrick, S. L. Woods, R. F. Craven, et al. (Eds.), *Medical-Surgical Nursing: Pathophysiological Concepts*, 2d Ed. (pp. 1362–1393). Philadelphia: J. B. Lippincott.

Bronfenbrenner, U. (1977). Toward an experimental econology of human development. *American Psychologist, 32*: 513–531.

Clark, M. J. (1992). *Nursing in the Community*. East Norwalk, CN: Appleton & Lange.

Conetah, F. A. (1982). *A History of the Northern Ute People*. K. L. MacKay and F. A. O'Neil (Eds.), Salt Lake City: University of Utah Printing Service.

Cosgray, R. E. (1991). Haitian Americans. In J. N. Giger and R. E. Davidhizer (Eds.), *Transcultural Nursing: Assessment and Intervention*. St. Louis: C. V. Mosby.

Danielson, C. B., Hamel-Bissell, B., and Winstead-Fry, P. (1993). *Families, Health and Illness: Perspectives on Coping and Intervention*. St. Louis: C. V. Mosby.

DeSantis, L. (1985). Childrearing beliefs and practices of Cuban and Haitian parents: Implications for nurses. In M. A. Carter (Ed.), *Proceedings of the Tenth Annual Transcultural Nursing Conference*, (pp. 54–79). Salt Lake City, UT: The Transcultural Nursing Society.

DeSantis, L. (1986). Infant feeding practices of Haitian mothers in South Florida: Cultural beliefs and acculturation. *Maternal Child Nursing Journal, 15*: 77–89.

DeSantis, L. (1988). Cultural factors affecting newborn and infant diarrhea. *Journal of Pediatric Nursing, 3*(6): 391–398.

DeSantis, L. (1990). The immigrant Haitian mother: Transcultural nursing perspective on preventive health care for children. *Journal of Transcultural Nursing, 2*(1): 2–15.

DeSantis, L., and Tappen, R. M. (1990). Preventive health practices of Haitian immigrants. In J. F. Wang, P. S. Simoni, and C. L. Nath (Eds.), *Proceedings of the West Virginia Nurses' Association Research Symposium. Vision of Excellence: The Decade of the Nineties* (pp. 7–15). Charleston, WV: West Virginia Nurses' Association Research Conference Group.

DeSantis, L., and Halberstein, R. (1992). The effects of immigration on the health care system of South Florida. *Human Organization, 51*(3): 223–234.

DeSantis, L. (1993). Haitian immigrant concepts of health. *Health Values. 17*(6): 3–16.

Erikson, E. (1963). *Childhood and Society*, 2d Ed. New York: Norton.

Farmer, P. (1988). Bad blood, spoiled milk: Bodily fluids as moral barometers in rural Haiti. *American Ethnologist, 15*(1): 62–83.

Fitness program restores Zuni tradition of running. *Health Links: The Nation's Education for Health Newsmagazine*, March 1986.

Frankenhoff, C. A. (1985). Cuban, Haitian refugees in Miami: Public policy needs for growth from welfare to mainstream. *Migration Today, 13*(3): 7–13.

Gilligan, C. (1982a). Adult development and women's development: Arrangement for a marriage. In J. Z. Giele (Ed.), *Women in the Middle Years* (pp. 89–114). New York: John Wiley & Sons.

Gilligan, C. (1982b). *In a Different Voice: Psychological Theory and Women's Development*. Cambridge, MA: Harvard University Press.

Havighurst, R. J. (1974). *Developmental Tasks and Education*. New York: David McKay.

Hill, P. M., and Humphrey, P. (1982). *Human Growth and Development Throughout Life: A Nursing Perspective*. New York: John Wiley & Sons.

Hughes, C. C. (1984). Report on Ute Indian Health Beliefs. Unpublished paper, Utah Diabetes Control Program, Utah State Health Department.

Jones, P. S., and Meleis, A. I. (1993). Health is empowerment. *Advances in Nursing Science, 15*(3): 1–14.

Kirkpatrick, S., and Cobb, A. (1990). Health beliefs related to diarrhea in Haitian children: Building transcultural nursing knowledge. *Journal of Transcultural Nursing, 1*(2): 2–12.

Knowler, W. C., Pettitt, D. J., Savage, P. J., and Bennett, P. H. (1981). Diabetes incidence in Pima Indians: Contributions of obesity and parental diabetes. *American Journal of Epidemiology, 113*: 144–156.

Laguerre, M. S. (1981). Haitian Americans. In A. Harwood (Ed.), *Ethnicity and Medical Care* (pp. 172–210). Cambridge, MA: Harvard University Press.

Leonard, B., Leonard, C., and Wilson, R. (1986). Zuni diabetes project. *Public Health Reports, 101*(3): 282–288.

Lipson, J. G. (1991). Afghan refugee health: Some findings and suggestions. *Qualitative Health Research, 1*(3): 349–369.

Myerhoff, B. (1978). Aging and the aged in other cultures: An anthropological perspective. In E. Bauwen (Ed.), *The Anthropology of Health*. St. Louis: C. V. Mosby.

Nachman, S. R., and Dreyfuss, G. (1986). Haitians and AIDS in South Florida. *Medical Anthropology Quarterly, 17*(2): 32–33.

Neel, J. V. (1962). Diabetes mellitus: A "thrifty" genotype rendered detrimental by progress. *American Journal of Human Genetics, 14*: 353–362.

Neugarten, B. (1968). *Middle Age and Aging: A Reader in Social Psychology*. Chicago: University of Chicago Press.

Newman, J. M., Marfin, A. A., Eggers, P. W., and Helgerson, S. D. (1990). End-stage renal disease among Native Americans, 1983–86. *American Journal of Public Health, 80*(3): 318–319.

O'Kelly, C. G. (1980). *Women and Men in Society*. New York: VanNostrand.

Scott, C. S. (1975). The relationship between beliefs about the menstrual cycle and choice of fertility regulation methods within five ethnic groups. *International Journal of Gynaecology and Obstetrics, 13*: 105–109.

Starck, P. (1988). Young and middle adults. In M. Stanhope and J. Lancaster (Eds.), *Community Health Nursing: Process and Practice for Promoting Health*, 2d Ed. (pp. 475–498). St. Louis: C. V. Mosby.

Sugarman, J. R., Hickey, M., Hall, T., and Gohdes, D. (1990). The changing epidemiology of diabetes mellitus among Navajo Indians. *Western Journal of Medicine, 153*: 140–145.

Tom-Orme, L. (1984). Diabetes intervention on the Uintah-Ouray reservation. In M. Carter (Ed.), *Proceedings of the Ninth Annual Transcultural Nursing Conference*. Salt Lake City: Transcultural Nursing Society.

Tom-Orme, L., and Hughes, C. C. (1985). Health beliefs about diabetes mellitus in an American Indian tribe: A preliminary formulation. In M. Carter (Ed.), *Proceedings of the Tenth Annual Transcultural Nursing Conference*. Salt Lake City: Transcultural Nursing Society.

U.S. Committee for Refugees (December, 1986). *Despite a Generous Spirit: Denying Asylum in the United States*. Washington: American Council for Nationalities Service.

U.S. Department of Health and Human Services, Public Health Service, National Institutes of Health (1982). *Diabetes in the 80's*. Report of the National Diabetes Advisory Board. Washington: U.S. Government Printing Office.

West, K. (1978). *Diabetes in American Indians: Advances in Metabolic Disorders*. New York: Academic Press.

Wiedman, D. W. (1989). Adiposity or longevity: Which factor accounts for the increase in type II diabetes mellitus when populations acculturate to an industrial technology? *Medical Anthropology, 2*: 237–253.

Wiese, J. (1976). Maternal nutrition and traditional food behavior in Haiti. *Human Organization, 35*(2): 193–200.

White (1977). Giving health care to minority patients. *Nursing Clinics of North America, 12*(1): 27–40.

6

Transcultural Perspectives in the Nursing Care of the Elderly

Margaret A. McKenna

Introduction

Nursing has long recognized that the experience of aging may be seen as a developmental experience rather than as a period of decline. Two underlying developmental tasks are (1) reflecting on one's life experiences while integrating these in a meaningful way and (2) showing a concern for establishing guidelines for the next generation. In various practice settings, nurses implement this positive view of aging by interpreting behaviors and health needs of aging adults in light of potential development of the client and the client's personal strengths and resources.

In the future, more older individuals will require nursing interventions in community and clinical settings as the elderly experience what has been termed *population frailty* (Verbrugge, 1989). There are several projections that highlight why the future aging population will have increasing disability as well as increasing life expectancy (Rice and LaPlante, 1988). These projections are (1) *tertiary prevention*—costly medical interventions will have successfully resuscitated and prolonged life for individuals who would otherwise have died; (2) *secondary prevention*—chronic illnesses that might prove to be fatal are treated successfully, resulting in more elderly people with diseases for a longer duration; and (3) *primary prevention*—lifestyle changes diminish comorbidity and the chances of acquiring disease (Verbrugge, 1989). The latter is evident in centers for health promotion for senior citizens and in increased media attention on exercise regimens that contribute to sectors of the aging population living longer and being active and healthy.

The older population therefore challenges nurses to (1) meet mixed levels of intensive personal health services depending on the presence of chronic conditions, (2) provide health maintenance, preventive, and restorative activities for persons resid-

Margaret M. Andrews and Joyceen S. Boyle: TRANSCULTURAL CONCEPTS IN NURSING CARE, SECOND EDITION. © 1995 J.B. Lippincott Company.

ing in facilities and independently, (3) coordinate social and ancillary health services for persons residing in various community settings, including shared housing and long-term care facilities, and (4) provide culturally appropriate communication and intervention based on the background of the older person.

The number of individuals aged 65 years and over will be increasing in the next decades, as indicated in Table 6-1. The technological developments mentioned above and the existence of social services will provide for the basic physical well-being of the elderly but will fail to address the losses of prestige and social integration often encountered by the aging population (Keith, Fry, and Ikels, 1990). Nursing, as a caring profession, will be addressing the social, psychological, emotional, and cultural needs of the aging population in facility- and community-based sites.

Nurses can assess how alterations and strengths in elderly patients' physiologic and psychological status affect their abilities to perform daily activities, and nurses can use this knowledge to plan and implement care. Variations exist in the ways some aged people manage chronic illness episodes and cope with disruptions in social roles and the loss of occupational positions. Various factors, including cultural heritage, spiritual outlook, social status, economic status, and social support networks, influence the ways that older people behave, adapt, and interact with others (Keller, Leventhal, and Larson, 1989; Sanchez-Ayendez, 1989; Leininger, 1991).

This chapter emphasizes how culture shapes the way persons view aging and affects how persons manage interpersonal crises and alterations in health that often accompany aging. Culture partially explains variability between aged groups of persons in the manner in which they function, carry out daily activities, and adjust to the numerous changes associated with aging. Culture is not the only determinant of behavior, but it is a critical component in understanding interactions, including the patient-nurse relationship. The purposes of this chapter are the following:

1. *To identify how culture shapes the phenomenon of aging.* The first section describes how culture influences the way aging is defined and viewed by participants, citing American culture as an example.
2. *To identify how culture explains some of the variations observed in health and illness experiences among older persons.* Culture determines, at least in part, how aging persons decide they are ill and how they seek care. Selected cross-cultural material relevant to the illness experience in the elderly is given in the section entitled, "Growing Old and Becoming Sick."
3. *To describe some features of aging that are common across cultures.* The section discusses how nurses can assess needs and problems common to aged persons yet consider

Table 6-1. Projected growth of the U.S. older population

Year	Percent of Population			
	65 to 74 Years	75 to 84 Years	85 and Over	65 and Over
2000	6.6	4.6	1.8	13.0
2050	9.7	6.9	5.2	21.8

United States Senate (1987). *Developments in Aging: A Report to the Special Committee on Aging*, p. 11. Washington: U.S. Government Printing Office.

cultural differences in helping clients achieve need satisfaction. Some evidence from nursing studies conducted with members of different cultural groups are presented in the section entitled, "Cultural Dimensions of Developmental Aspects of Aging."

4. *To provide guidelines for nursing interventions with older clients that will be perceived as culturally appropriate and acceptable.* An example of the health care needs for an elderly immigrant Nicaraguan woman is presented. Interventions that are appropriate for that family and for other elderly persons are identified in the final sections of this chapter, including the identification of strategies for minimizing barriers to receiving nursing and health care.

The American View of Aging

Nurses and nursing ⌐   th the assessment phase of the nursing process ⌐   ents, nurses first need to assess their own aging individuals. The nurse's attitudes that is common in society, the theories definitions of aging, and the nurse's

society perspective of aging, "Old hat compares and contrasts with the erican emphasis on independence, itude that the aged, who no longer esteem and thus can be ignored. as unpaid volunteers producing s of the older family member to der community are overlooked. erican attitude reflects different e persons in our society show members similar to family patterns in Ch   traditional European cultures.

aware of several theories that explain the activities of the aging indi   Three theoretical positions that are relevant in planning nursing care for older persons are the disengagement theory, the activity theory, and the continuity theory. The characteristics of these positions are summarized in Box 6-1.

These different theoretical positions are relevant when we recognize that aging members of varied cultural backgrounds will be influenced by the cultural values and theory of aging that are appropriate to their group. The prevalent theory about aging will influence how older people respond to changes associated with aging. In American culture, many older persons experience society withdrawing from them, or the older person is disengaging from society through change in role function in retirement, loss of role with death of a spouse, and reduction in social interaction with disruption of home life and occupation. The result is an older person with a damaged self-concept who is disengaging from social interaction. Nurses also recognize that some older persons continue many of the activities learned in middle age, tend to work against societal limitations on their social world, and are more capable of achieving self-actualization (Havighurst, 1968).

Box 6-1. Theories Relevant to Planning Nursing Care for Older Individuals

---

Disengagement theory: Older people and society mutually fall into a natural pattern of withdrawal, which is usually desired by the older person (Havighurst, 1968).

Activity theory: Aged person substitutes activities in light of society withdrawing participation from the older person (Havighurst, 1968).

Continuity theory: Majority of older people lead active lives and maintain the relationships and strategies that have been central in earlier years. Retired people continue perceptions of themselves and their lives that fit with their own histories. (Atchley, 1989)

The conclusions of a study of elderly Japanese showed that the most satisfied and most healthy persons were the most active, which is consistent with the concepts of activity theory (Palmore and Maeda, 1985). A study of Puerto Rican elderly women living in Boston indicated that the women maintained family relationships and roles as they aged, supporting the concepts of continuity theory (Sanchez-Ayandez, 1989).

Old age has been variously defined in chronologic and functional terms. In this chapter, the terms *aging, elderly*, and *aged person* are used interchangeably and refer to persons aged 65 and older, with due recognition that this is a term of convenience and merely a chronologic category that is relevant in mainstream American society. Nurses working with elderly persons in inpatient settings or outpatient settings in adult day care or home health care are familiar with definitions of aging. These notions influence how older persons view themselves and how health care providers interact with aged patients.

Functional Age

A comparative view of many societies indicates that old age is most commonly defined in functional terms: (1) a shift in occupational role, including relinquishing employment, (2) changing one's social role as head of household, or (3) altering one's tasks within the family. Retirement is the most frequent functional alteration of old age. Successful retirement is usually accompanied by a viable income and good health status, but not all individuals ease into retirement. It can be a very stressful time for elderly individuals who are widowed or divorced and who do not have social contacts as a source of support and communication. Retirement may be especially stressful for individuals with chronic or acute illness episodes and for those clients who have not had opportunities to develop any interests or activities. Elderly individuals who have not had regular employment and who may lack retirement benefits and other financial resources find that when retirement is imposed, they face more stress and uncertainty (Kelly and Westcott, 1991).

Older immigrants are most disillusioned with immigration when they experience cultural disequilibrium that affects their occupational role. For example, older Russian

Japanese nursing home resident in an **ikebana** *(flower arranging) activity class in a Japanese-American extended-care facility. (Courtesy of Seattle Keiro Nikkei Concerns.)*

Jewish emigrés who may have had professional positions in the former Soviet Union are often unable to find any means of employment in the United States. They often must resign themselves to forced retirement and a much poorer existence than anticipated (Brod and Huertin-Roberts, 1992).

For many elderly persons, the decision to have physical and social security includes selling a home so that they have personal resources available to enter a congregate-care or extended-care facility. The inevitability of the loss of one's home and the associated perception of loss of control contribute to negative self-perceptions, loss of morale, and diminished self-esteem among the elderly. The necessity of many elderly residents relocating to congregate-care facilities also indicates that the aged as a group are not accorded the position of making decisions about the allocation of community resources that would allow them to remain self-sufficient in the community.

Nurses will note clients expressing different attitudes ranging from resignation to acceptance of changes in residence. A nurse can recognize that the clients' attitudes will affect their behavior, self-esteem, and physical and social activity in the facility. A further implication is that the nurse understands that the attitudes of the aged individual have been influenced by social and peer groups that are significant. Older persons may regard peers as "being old enough to go to a nursing home" or "still young enough to live alone." The nurse's awareness that residents of nursing home facilities have socially influenced attitudes and expectations helps the nurse to be more understanding of client adjustment to residential placement and enables the nurse to help clients in a sensitive manner.

A class in ceramics at an activity center for urban elderly Japanese Americans. (Courtesy of Seattle Keiro Nikkei Concerns.)

Nurses providing care to older clients and families from different cultural backgrounds will notice that functional abilities required for family and social participation vary by cultural context. For example, the availability of certain physical and personal supports helps elderly persons with various impairments maintain independence in different types of living situations.

Does the family modify the environment and assist in home care so an aged member can remain at home? Are adult children expected to provide meals to aging parents? Is a grandchild expected to do errands and accompany a grandparent so that the grandparent can live alone? Some older persons of different cultural backgrounds, including Native Americans and Mexican Americans, who have given material and social support to their children and grandchildren may expect reciprocal help in their advancing years. On the other hand, older persons who pride themselves on being independent may not want to accept any help from their children or grandchildren. The older relatives struggle to be independent in financial, personal care, and social matters until a sudden illness or incapacitation forces a dramatically dependent relationship (Keith, Fry, and Ikels, 1989).

One component of cross-cultural functional definitions of aging is to compare the activity of the older person in their family. Native American communities refer to social role functioning, including being a grandparent, to define who is an elder (Weibel-Orlando, 1989). A persistent intergenerational family pattern is the presence of the grandmother in black families. In black families, the grandmother often takes a direct role in child rearing, whereas white grandparents may be more geographically isolated and offer primarily affection to their grandchildren (Denham and Smith, 1989). The black grandmother is depicted in biographic accounts as a hard-working woman of courage, hope, and dignity. The grandmother tells stories to teach the children how to survive—she is a source of the literary tradition and a transmitter of spirituality (Braxton, 1989). More than twice as many young blacks live in households headed by elderly family members compared with whites (Mutran, 1985; Hilker, 1991).

Older immigrants and members of Hispanic cultural groups may assist their families in several ways. For example, a national sample of older Hispanics found that 30 percent reported providing child care to younger family members, 50 percent reported assisting in family decisions, and 12 percent provided financial assistance to family members (Westat, 1989). This compares with a national average of 19 percent of older Americans providing child care regularly and 15 percent occasionally caring for their grand-children. More grandparents in Japan and France (31 percent) more frequently provide regular care than do grandparents in Great Britain (19 percent) (Palmore and Maeda, 1985).

In assessing the functional status of older clients, nurses know to assess self-reliance or dependence in activities of daily living. Nurses also should expand their assessment to include identification of the activities the older adult performs in the family. Any illness incurred by the grandparent may interfere with the performance of personal activities of daily living as well as the ability to care for younger family members. As part of the nursing assessment, the nurse notes if elderly patients are primary-care providers for grandchildren or other family members. Today, many grandparents are caring for grandchildren while parents work or when the parents are incapacitated or otherwise unable to care for their children.

Chronologic Age

American society defines people as old at the chronologic age of 65 years and imposes retirement in most professions. Forced retirement has serious repercussions on the self-concept and dignity of the retiree, including a loss of belonging, separation from peers, loss of instrumental role, and, of course, a decreased income. Nurses and health policymakers recognize that there is often incongruity between chronologic age and functional age, for many persons are more productive at age 65 than retirement rules indicate. Public health nurses who work in clinics for the elderly and visit them in their homes recognize a wide range of functional abilities in persons over the age of 65 years. Research in gerontology has indicated that 50 percent of individuals who are 70 years old consider themselves to be middle-aged (Keller, Leventhal, and Larson, 1989).

Changes in retirement rules indicate a move in our society's desire to achieve congruity between chronologic and functional definitions of old age.

The relevance of chronologic definitions of old age to nurses and health care professionals is the recognition that stress resulting from retirement affects the health and well-being of the elderly. Reaction to retirement may range from mild depression to physical illness, which should be considered in planning care for the elderly. Nurses may provide preventive care and/or anticipatory guidance in referring clients to do pre-retirement planning.

A comparison between older working individuals in the United States and Japan indicates that 55 percent of workers aged 65 to 69 years and 39 percent of workers aged 70 to 74 years continue to work in Japan contrasted with 26 and 18 percent, respectively, in the United States (Palmore and Maeda, 1985).

The American older person's primary source of social identity is changed at retirement age, when, for example, a 65-year-old person is no longer a sales manager or a school principal. A person who has expressed control over aspects of achieved identity, such as receiving an education or advancing in an occupation, is likely to feel displaced into a category of "being old" because age, which is an ascribed feature, dominates any accomplishments of achieved identity.

This concept of achieved and ascribed characteristics is useful in understanding the identity of the aged in cultural and ethnic groups. Nurses who work with elderly individuals and their families often become aware that families and groups either primarily define identity in achieved criteria, such as occupation, or ascribed criteria, such as age. An example illustrates that some persons, including black Americans or members of other ethnic groups, such as Japanese Americans who were forced into internment camps during World War II, have lifelong experiences with an ascriptive identity because of their race. Aging members of the dominant American culture perceive their accomplishments in education and occupation as forming their achieved identity. Older Hispanic women may be accorded *respeto* (respect) contingent on their ascribed status as old adults and old parents and not on their achieved status or power.

Conclusion of American Views of Aging

The definitions of aging in functional and chronologic terms or categories indicate that there are no arbitrary or widely accepted markers for old age. In practice in different clinical settings, nurses may provide care to aged clients who are defined chronologically as old but who, in functional terms, are active and productive. Nurses can assess the social and functional abilities of their elderly clients when providing care, support, or advice. Nurses frequently work in an interdisciplinary setting to provide care to elderly clients and should be familiar with the definitions and concepts related to aging that are used by various professionals.

Growing Old and Becoming Sick: Cross-Cultural Variations in Illness Among the Elderly

A theme of this chapter is that culture explains variability in individual responses to aging so that behavior and interactions of members of certain groups, such as elderly Russian emigrés or Southeast Asian refugees, will vary from those of older members of the dominant American culture (Brod and Heurtin-Roberts, 1992; Tran, 1991). Nurses caring for chronically ill elderly persons recognize that not only do clients suffer physiologic disturbances labeled as disease, but they also have an illness, which is a personal and social experience largely determined by one's culture.

This section emphasizes cross-cultural variations in the experience of disease and illness among the elderly. The following paragraphs indicate that socioeconomic status affects varying rates of disease cross-culturally. The next two sections include adherence to folk health systems and the ways that social support systems influence illness-related behavior of elderly clients. This section also suggests how nurses can appropriately intervene with elderly clients based on an awareness of culturally determined differences in illness.

Socioeconomic Status

National health data indicate that socioeconomic status and health status vary among elderly whites, African Americans, Native Americans, and Hispanic Americans (Wray, 1992). The work histories of members of cultural groups, including long careers in agricultural labor, have precluded coverage within the Social Security or Medicare systems. Thus many elderly persons, and especially elderly members of ethnic groups of color, face out-of-pocket health care expenses on limited incomes. Pacific/Asian, black, Hispanic, and Native American elderly persons generally have lower incomes than majority populations; 80 percent of older black women and 50 percent of older Hispanic women live in poverty. More than one out of five Pacific/Asian elders have incomes below the poverty level, which is a 33 percent higher proportion than the national average (Kim, 1983). Nearly 51 percent of Native Americans over the age of 65 receive incomes below the poverty level (U.S. Bureau of the Census, 1991).

Most elderly persons, including the ethnic elders, have two major socioeconomic problems: obtaining sufficient income and paying health care costs. Nurses assessing health care costs of the elderly and working with aged clients in their homes often find that ethnic elderly clients cannot afford personal health care costs. In 1988, 83 percent of elderly Hispanics had Medicare coverage compared with 96 percent of all elders. Only 21 percent of older Hispanics purchased a supplemental Medicare insurance compared with 65 percent of all elders (Commonwealth Fund Commission, 1989). Family members may be paying health care expenses of the aged member.

There are several implications for health care and nursing intervention that are related to the disproportionate percentage of elderly ethnic clients in low socioeconomic levels. Lower socioeconomic status is correlated with a higher prevalence of disease and a higher age-specific death rate (Sullivan and Lewin, 1988). There is another correlation between low economic status and the experience of more bed-disability days and restricted activity with higher rates of illness. Hispanics and Native Americans have higher mortality rates from diabetes and infectious and parasitic diseases compared with non-Hispanic whites and African Americans (U.S. Public Health Service, 1990). Two of the leading causes of death among African-American, Hispanic, and Native American elders are diabetes and hypertension. When data are adjusted for age, Hispanics in the Southwest have lower death rates from heart disease and malignant neoplasms than do white non-Hispanics (U.S. Public Health Service, 1990).

Thus these findings explain why nurses caring for elderly clients from diverse cultures must consider the effects of such factors as lower socioeconomic status on the incapacitating illnesses of their clients. The socioeconomic status of the client affects his or her predisposition to disease, as well as rate of recovery, maintenance of health, and/or successful management of chronic disease.

Sources of Care

Culture influences how elderly clients will determine if they are ill and how they will seek care for their symptoms. Significant numbers of foreign-born elderly persons possess characteristics that will predispose them to the use of traditional sources of care. Elderly immigrants may speak their native language, be suspicious of English-speaking health care workers or social service agency personnel, have limited incomes, and experience transportation and financial barriers in access to available sources of care.

The stressful life experiences of some older adults also will make them reluctant to seek services and distrustful of care provided by health care professionals who are culturally different from themselves. To illustrate, older Russian immigrants coming to North America from the former Soviet Union have experienced two world wars, civil wars, and political revolution. In surviving a stressful environment that depleted their coping mechanisms and personal energy, they are often distressed and experience problems in adjustment later in life.

Research has shown that some Native American elders may be distrustful of non-Native American health care providers, may not expect to be treated fairly, and may expect adverse consequences from the health care experience (Kramer, 1992). Many Native American elders are put off by the overly firm handshake of many health care providers and prefer the formality of a light touch (Rhoades, 1990). Similarly, some Native American elders feel that excessive eye contact and the invasiveness of some procedures are an affront to one's privacy and dignity (Rhoades, 1990).

The desire for treatment by professionals who are culturally like themselves is shared across cultural boundaries. For example, Mormons express a desire to have care provided by Mormons, elderly Jewish clients prefer to have care provided by Jewish care providers, and elderly Chinese prefer other Chinese to care for them. In a survey of European Americans, Latvian, Lithuanian, and Greek elderly persons preferred care provided by members of their own cultural groups (Kalish, 1986).

Some aged persons rely on their families and on the use of traditional folk medicines that may be obtained from the older person's native land. The use of traditional folk sources of care concurrently with or in place of the basic health care system is not limited to members of easily recognizable cultural or ethnic groups but is common to nearly all persons. Since clients may make a dual use of a folk system and the health care system familiar to the nurse, it is important that nurses obtain data on where clients go for care and who treats them.

For example, a 70-year-old man with degenerative joint disease, raised in West Virginia, recalled his mother rubbing liniment and kerosene on her aching joints. The patient said his people were all farmers, and he could remember seeing the red glass bottles of rubbing liniment out in the barn. He now resided in an urban area in the Northwest and was cared for by a nurse-practitioner. He took ibuprofen as prescribed for relief of his joint pain, but he also occasionally rubbed kerosene and sheep liniment on the affected joints. He explained to a visiting nurse that his joints felt like they were not lubricated enough, and an oil-based rubbing compound seemed to penetrate the joints and relieve discomfort. The nurse's role was to ascertain that occasional use of the rubbing compound did not make the patient's degenerative joint disease any worse. The client's belief that the rubbing compound improved his condition allowed him to comply with a prescribed program of exercise. The nurse diagnosed that he had some impairment of joint mobility that was relieved by pain medication and local applications. The nurse's future plan was to assess for any skin breakdown as a result of the rubbing compound, but its use was not discouraged at this time.

Elderly clients also may make use of traditional folk practices to prevent illness. Elderly members of several culture groups maintain ideas about what practices keep them well and what infractions of behavior may lead to illness. Preventive measures may combine a magical or religious element such as burning a candle, wearing an amulet, or reciting a prayer. Preventive measures for an elderly Pueblo Indians may include wearing an arrowhead, offering cornmeal to the spirits, and maintaining good relations with the spirits to help ensure good health. The nurse can recognize preventive actions such as amulets and prayers are adequate health promotion as far as the patient is concerned, so the nurse can only try to provide illness-prevention and health-maintenance acts that reinforce the patient's preventive actions.

Social Support Systems

The amount and type of support that members of a cultural group provide to its elders affect how the elders cope with illness episodes. Strong social support networks are of value in crisis situations when persons need a sense of security, identity, and worthiness (Preston and Grimes, 1987). An adequate social support system may serve as a buffer against social and traumatic losses, such as retirement and widowhood, and prolonged crisis situations, such as chronic illnesses (Preston and Grimes, 1987).

Immediate family members are the primary sources of social support for older individuals in cases of illness. Among the elders who continue to reside in the community, 75 percent receive some assistance or care from a family member (Malonebeach and Zarit, 1991). Family caregivers for dependent elders have been the subject of many research studies in the last decade (Barusch and Spaid, 1989; Rosenthal, Matthews, and Marshall, 1989). Usually, studies have looked at the primary caregiver, with less attention paid to supportive activities of siblings who assist the elderly relative. There are culturally influenced differences in the patterns of caregiving among members of different cultural groups. Historically, a higher proportion of elderly persons from diverse cultures have been cared for in home environments than have elders who are white (Wray, 1992). White elderly persons comprise 23 percent of the nursing home residents aged 85 and older in the United States (Wray, 1992). Hispanic and Asian/Pacific Islander elderly persons each compromise 10 percent of the nursing home population aged 85 years or older (Wray, 1992). In a study of southwestern Native American elders and Hispanics, the respondents felt closer to their families, enjoyed being with family members more, and argued less with family members (Harris, Begay, and Page, 1989).

Research has indicated that family care of the elderly in other cultures may be supported for several reasons: as a substitute for formal services, as a more affordable alternative, as a caring option that is consistent with cultural values and preferences, and as a result of language barriers (Chapleski, 1989; Krause, 1990; Kravitz, Pelaez, and

Rothman, 1990). In large extended families, there may be more siblings providing partial services and care to an elderly family member. Differences in patterns of caregiving would be expected given the uniqueness of families and family histories (Malonebeach and Zarit, 1991).

Family histories will be influenced by the challenging situations that older generations have endured, the social and economic crises that may have been weathered, and the personal triumphs of family members. The shared history of incidents will influence the behavior of older and younger family members. For example, Chinese Americans and Japanese Americans have been singled out as scapegoats in periods of economic depression and have been regarded as enemies in times of international conflict. Japanese-American elderly developed various means of coping with these life stresses, including maintenance of cultural values of family unity and harmony.

The importance of family support is compounded for older refugees. In instances of forced migration, the traditional family structure may have been destroyed in the country of origin, and relationships with family members may have been altered. When older refugees arrive in the new host country, they may be isolated for several social and cultural reasons. Older refugees may not speak English and also may have lost their social position, their country, and their home. The psychological stress related to cultural change is more intense for older refugees (Moon and Pearl, 1991). The older refugee may rely exclusively on younger family members for economic and social support because he or she has few financial resources and lacks immediate access to health and housing services.

There are two theoretical perspectives that offer an explanation for the situation of the older member of an ethnic group. *Age-stratification theory* asserts that members of an entire ethnic group may be in a subordinate position; thus aging members have a further reduction in their status. In contrast, according to what is termed *modernization theory*, the stress of acculturation may reduce the status of the elderly (Filinson, 1992).

In a study of 258 elderly Indochinese refugees, including Ethnic Vietnamese, Chinese Vietnamese, and Laotians, those refugees who resided with immediate family members had a higher sense of social adjustment (Tran, 1991). However, elderly individuals who shared a living space with many extended family members and nonkin had a lower sense of social adjustment. The older refugee usually has left behind in his or her country of origin, a career, and social status associated with that career. The younger refugee may adjust more readily and begin a new occupation. The older refugee has a greater loss of status and status inconsistency that supports an inverse relationship between age and social adjustment (Tran, 1991).

The adjustment problems of a group will depend on the cultural background as well as other factors, including age and education levels. The disruption of their personal, social, and family roles wrought by migration shapes individual adjustment behavior that may lead to some commonalties that transcend cultural boundaries. The length of residence in the relocated country, as well as education and household structure, influences the older individual's adjustment. For example, Korean elderly who are recent immigrants will have traditional Confucian values, emphasizing the family and authority, in contrast to the dominant society emphasis on the individual (Moon and Pearl, 1991). As children and grandchildren adopt American values and associated independence, the elders perceive a loss of respect and authority. Elderly Polish, Cuban, and Puerto Rican immigrants may similarly feel a diminishing sense of respect and authority. Older immigrants from the former Soviet Union have sometimes been reluctant refugees, leaving their country with their children primarily to keep the family unit intact. The policy was that the unit of emigration was the family rather than the individual (Brod and Heurtin-Roberts, 1992).

Nurses also recognize that in the absence of support systems, the ethnic elder may be unable to cope with a complex system of health care. Nurses may assist elderly clients to evaluate the unique nature of their social networks, seek caretakers, activate social contacts for support, and develop a safe plan of care. In planning intervention, nurses assess support systems and care providers as well as disparities that may exist between the elderly person's expectations for family care and the reality of what family members and community support can actually provide.

Elderly individuals who have made major adjustments in their lifestyles from their homelands to the United States and from a rural sector to urban living may not be aware of health care alternatives, preventive programs, health care benefits, and screening programs for which they are eligible. Nurses act as brokers, introducing community services to elderly clients and their families that can sustain family members providing some in-home care to the elderly and help to maintain elderly persons in the community. Nurses providing care in hospital settings or in the community often ask several questions as part of the nursing assessment:

Is the elderly person isolated from culturally relevant supportive persons or enmeshed in a caring network of relatives and friends?

Has a culturally appropriate network replaced family members in performing some caring functions for an elderly person?

Does the elderly person expect family members to provide care, including nurturance and other humanistic aspects of care that the family members are unable to provide?

Does language create a barrier in an elderly person's receipt of care from available community resources?

The nurse interested in providing culturally sensitive care to the elderly accepts the challenge of assessing many areas for possible intervention and prevention with the patient. The outcome of assessment and planning with the patient and family is a mutually agreed on plan of care that improves quality of care for the aged.

For example, an 80-year-old Filipino man previously treated for prostate cancer was admitted to a hospital and found to have pancreatic cancer. His nursing diagnoses included total self-care deficit, alteration in bowel and bladder elimination, and impairment of skin integrity. His two daughters were exhausted from caring for their mother, who had died of breast cancer in the past year. The nurse who was coordinator of patient services talked with the daughters and learned that they could not undertake terminal care for their father at this time, since both had young families they believed they had neglected in providing terminal care at home to their mother.

The nurse asked the daughters to tell their father that arrangements could be made for him to go to a nursing home. The nurse was frustrated to learn that over a week had gone by and the daughters had not told their father of impending nursing home placement. A nurse colleague who understood Filipino culture explained that family duty was a serious social obligation. By not caring for their father, the daughters experienced "loss of face" and brought shame on themselves. The daughters believed that members of the Filipino community would criticize them for placing their father in a nursing home. The daughters asked the physician to tell their father that the hospital staff wanted him to go to a nursing home. This action would lessen the burden of decision making from the family and allow the daughters to maintain their pride and save face in the community. As a result, the father did not become angry with his daughters, and they could continue to meet his emotional and psychological needs.

Conclusion of Cross-Cultural Variations in Illness Among the Elderly

Nurses interacting with aged persons representing diverse cultural traditions become sensitive to how cultural factors determine individuals' responses to growing old and often to becoming ill, that is, how persons react to aging and to illness. Culture determines why aging cultural and ethnic group members vary in some of the diseases they incur and in the ways they respond to illness. They may incorporate magical and religious aspects to try to maintain health and may feel very vulnerable to illness. Taking preventive actions and trying to fight off disease are culturally specific approaches to maintaining health in the dominant society America.

Elderly patients will make use of folk systems of care if they seem specific to their illness. Nurses can provide culturally appropriate interventions to elderly minority clients that support the clients' use of traditional medicine at the same time the client also complies with health care provided by the nurse. The presence of social support systems buffers patients from the impact of chronic lingering illnesses occurring frequently in the elderly. In planning care, the nurse assesses availability of family caregivers and presence of an extended social support system, as well as agency personnel who can be included in community-based care of the elderly. The nurse includes data on support systems and involves client, family, and significant others in mutually agreed on goal setting.

Cultural Dimensions of the Developmental Aspects of Aging

Throughout the life span, persons face various developmental tasks that have been more widely studied for children and young adults than for the aging population. To some extent, what comprises satisfying these tasks, such as what makes one older person feel secure or what gives a person a feeling of self-fulfillment, is determined by one's cultural background. Each patient is also influenced by heredity and environmental, socioeconomic, and occupational factors that affect feelings of personal worth and fulfillment.

Development in older adulthood is not all progressive; some changes in older adulthood replace youthful characteristics. Stability and reluctance to accept change that occurs in the elderly replaces flexibility. Stability is developmentally appropriate, for it allows the elderly person to be viewed as a stabilizing force in society, against which younger persons may exercise flexibility in taking risks and meeting new challenges. However, an alternative position is that most older people also have a good capacity for change because they have had a lifetime of dealing with new events and they accept change as a normal part of growing old. The implication for nursing care is to recognize that some elderly clients adapt readily to changes in their lifestyles, probably due to a lifetime of change, while other elderly clients require specific intervention to lessen the impact of a change of residence, change in income level, and change in social role.

Several developmental aspects of aging are relevant to the nursing care of elderly clients. These developmental tasks are referred to in the following subsections as satisfaction of basic needs, fulfillment of other needs, and achievement of integrity.

Satisfaction of Basic Needs

The basic needs that older persons strive to satisfy are (1) safety, (2) security, and (3) dignity, which follow in Maslow's conceptualization of needs after an individual has met biologic needs. The desire of an older person to satisfy basic needs is not unique, but the older person's approach to satisfy these needs is more limited than that of younger adults (Boettcher, 1985). An aged person desires personal security as well as financial security. Elderly Americans rank fears about loneliness secondary only to fears of crime, poor health, and inadequate income.

For a sector of the older population, a hotel room or apartment is their only security. Lack of physical stamina and intimidation by crowds and the unfamiliar outside world sometimes discourage aged persons from leaving their apartments. Many poor elderly clients who have been residents of single-room inner-city apartments are being forced from those buildings in light of urban renewal. The security of finding affordable housing on an income from Social Security is becoming more challenging in large metropolitan areas, which makes the satisfaction of basic needs much more difficult and makes the achievement of higher-order needs even more unobtainable.

Fulfillment of Other Needs

The aged also want to satisfy their needs for self-determination and self-actualization. Self-actualization is a complex process of striving to make actual all the potential facets of selfhood that are unique to each individual. In striving toward self-actualization, the aged adult desires to find meaning and usefulness in his or her life and to maintain self-esteem. Some elderly residents in extended-care facilities find that crafts, hobbies, or volunteering to help other residents provides meaning to life and can be a source of self-esteem. Elderly community residents may participate in group activities (e.g., painting classes, dancing lessons, cooking demonstrations) at a senior center or pursue their hobbies independently.

Many elderly persons cannot direct their energies to self-actualization when they are overwhelmed by damage to their self-esteem. Self-determination and self-actualization needs are not readily met if family members and others are overly protective and controlling (Boettcher, 1985). Nurses can be flexible and encourage patients to exert some control over the planning and scheduling of some aspects of their care. Nurses also recognize that older persons have a need for autonomy that can be expressed as their deciding what intrusions will be allowed in their space and on their time.

An example that demonstrates cross-cultural variations in achieving autonomy and self-determination is found in the contrast of an aging "Yankee" American and an elderly Soviet Jewish patient. A visiting nurse, assuming that an elderly retired American merchant marine captain wanted to exert his autonomy, encouraged him to set up a

An active elderly resident at a street fair.

schedule of exercises and pain medications for his healing hip fracture. The patient was very cooperative in his plan of care and steadily improved in his mobility.

The same visiting nurse encountered a different attitude working with a 78-year-old Russian woman who had a colostomy and required teaching and follow-up at home. The young nurse in street clothes asked the patient about wound discharge, dressing changes, use of medications, and when the patient thought it would be most appropriate to change ostomy appliances. The nurse was initially baffled by the Russian patient's reluctance to talk and her insistence that the doctor should come to see her. By asking the patient, "What do you expect the doctor to do? and "What do you expect me to do?" the nurse realized that this patient was not used to determining a schedule for her own treatments. The patient expressed her autonomy in her displeasure with the nurse's intrusion into her life when she perceived that the nurse did not seem to be an authority in helping the patient to recover. The nurse recognized that the patient was accustomed to a more paternal relationship with a physician and expected to be told what to do. The nurse realized that she looked young and uninformed in the patient's eyes, especially when the nurse asked the patient how her healing stoma looked. On later visits to the patient, the nurse shifted her approach and told the patient what to expect, giving the patient more information while teaching her what to do.

The nurse recognized that most elderly Americans value self-determination of one's schedule and plan of care, but encouraging self-determination for the Russian patient was not perceived as acceptable. The nurse found that the more structured plan of care was more appropriate in helping this elderly Russian client to feel secure and cared for in a patient-nurse relationship.

Achieving Integrity

Erikson (1955) defined the need to find meaning in one's late adult years as a task of achieving integrity versus despair. The developmental steps toward achieving integrity are conservation of personal energy, directing energy inward, finding meaning in one's life through sharing traditions and values, and finally working on closure of life and preparing for death. Elderly persons tend to use their energies selectively, generally thinking about an overall problem and delegating details to others. Nurses working in community settings often find that elderly clients turn over details of their finances, health insurance, and utility payments to their children or supportive others. Turning over tedious tasks such as paying bills allows older people time to direct their energy inward. They have energy to review their lives and to develop an inner awareness.

The older adult then tries to find meaning in life and to recognize how one's life had a purpose. Older persons may be reflective on the successes and failures of their lives, which often includes transforming conflict situations into meaningful experiences. There are many potential sources of conflict for older family members with their adult children and grandchildren.

Nurses may assess that elderly clients differ from their adult children in their views of the importance of several dimensions indicated in Box 6-2 (Bond and Harvey, 1991; Treas and Bengston, 1987). The greater are the disparities between the adult children's views and the elderly clients' views, the more conflict becomes apparent in the intergenerational family. When caring and supportive relationships between generations become more strained, it is less likely that the older person will move toward integrating his or her life experiences.

In a Canadian study of rural family groups including Mennonites and non-Mennonites, Bond and Harvey (1991) found that older parents, in contrast to their adult children, reported more time together, less conflict, greater affection, and more adherence to family norms between the generations. This finding exemplifies the desire of the older generation to integrate life experiences and to derive feelings of self-worth from

---

Box 6-2. Dimensions of Solidarity Among Generations of Family Members

Associational solidarity: How much the generations contact one another and do things together.

Functional solidarity: What the generations do for one another.

Consensus solidarity: The extent of agreement and openness between the generations.

Normative solidarity: The similarity of ideas and values between generations of family members.

Affectional solidarity: Feelings of closeness and warmth between family members of different generations.

Bond, J. B., and Harvey, C. D. (1991). Ethnicity and intergenerational perceptions of family solidarity. *International Journal of Aging and Human Development*, 33(1): 36. © 1991, Baywood Publishing Co., Inc. Reprinted by permission.

interactions and relationships. Japanese immigrants have been described as continuing their traditional values of harmony and suppression of conflict that place family unity and autonomy above the needs of the individual for personal self-determination (Lock, 1983).

These findings support the conclusion that the older generation tries to minimize intergenerational differences. This tendency confirms what Erikson termed the development task of "integrity versus despair" when an older individual reflects on the value and perceived worth of one's life. One minimizes conflicts, including intergenerational conflicts, in an effort to have a stronger sense of belonging that makes one feel worthwhile. In achieving integrity, elderly persons have a need to bring closure of life and acceptance of their eventual death. A nurse may interpret this need to a patient's family and be a sensitive listener when the client works through this step toward achieving integrity rather than despair. Older people need to be given uninterrupted time and privacy for a purposive life review, which can be considered in planning care.

Achieving Developmental Tasks

Cultural factors including culture group history, life experiences including immigration, and coping patterns that cultural groups develop all interact to determine an individual's actions related to achieving security, autonomy, and integrity. The age at which individuals immigrated and whether they immigrated alone or as a family unit will influence the formation of personal characteristics that will affect their achievement of basic needs and higher-order needs, including self-actualization and integrity.

Individuals from different cultural backgrounds have migrated at different stages in their lives. European Americans in their seventies may have been adolescents fleeing Poland or Czechoslovakia before World War II. Southeast Asians leaving Cambodia, Laos, and Vietnam in the 1970s and 1980s may have had careers in their homeland and immigrated as adults. Many emigrés from the former Soviet Union or Central American nations have been over the age of 65 at the time of migration, having decided to accompany adult children. Individuals will have been at different developmental stages at the time of their immigration that will later affect their behavior, including health- and illness-related behavior.

There are numerous examples from transcultural nursing studies that assist nurses in assessing the social and historical conditions influencing the older client. Nurses can gain an appreciation of the struggle of older individuals for self-actualization and their intention to transmit cultural values to a younger generation in light of the collective experiences of cultural group members.

Cross-Cultural Nursing Studies. Most transcultural nursing studies on the elderly have included some accounts of the social and historical events influencing cultural group practices, as well as descriptions of dimensions of caring. Selected studies that were published in the period 1980–1990 were reviewed to describe some of the common contexts and experiences of the older populations that are relevant for developing guidelines for practice. The work done in transcultural nursing with the elderly often emphasized a culturally influenced characteristic of the study population: The aging Appalachians valued individualism (Lewis, Messner, and McDowell, 1985); the older Zuni patients guarded their native healing system and prided themselves in belonging to housing, kinship, and clan groups (Dicharry, 1986); older Asians valued the social hierarchy (Chae, 1987); and Samonans emphasized service and cooperation with an acknowledged leader (Shiamoto and Ishida, 1988).

Several dimensions that the researchers described for the selected cultural groups are summarized in Table 6-2. The table also highlights features of the historical situation, social situation, and current context that exert some influence on the health- and illness-related practices of the elderly clients.

In looking at the components that transcend the studies, there are significant similarities across cultural groups: demographic trends such as migration, changing social structures such as demands for equal rights, structural forces such as discrimination, and historical events such as political conflict. These changing historical and social circumstances characterize the developmental experiences and behavior of each cultural

Table 6-2. Summary of transcultural nursing studies of elderly groups, 1980–1990

Study (Author, Publication Date)	Population	Current Status	Historical Factors	Social Factors
Clavon, 1986	African Americans	Fragmentation of families, experienced assimilation	Slavery, forced migration	Matrifocal family
Shomaker, 1981	Elderly Navajo nursing home residents	Adjusting to new routines; use of water and electricity in indoor environs	Recent availability of nursing homes	Positive grandparent-grandchild relationships
Lewis et al., 1985	Community residents in Appalachia, KY, GA, VA, NC, SC	Selection of isolated residence	Limited contact with health care; descendants of Celts who stress life in harmony with nature	Intense interpersonal relations; elderly are respected as providers
Dicharry, 1986	Zuni-Pueblo (western New Mexico)	Living on reservation; 84% speak Native American language; 68% at poverty level	Adherence to religious rituals	Multigenerational families; younger members migrate from their families of origin
Shiamoto and Ishida, 1988	Samoans in Western and American Samoa	Modernization disrupts dietary and family living patterns, lessens elders' control over family subsistence activities	Adaptation of Samoans to cities on mainland is successful due to family support but with much psychological stress	Reciprocal support extends to *aiga* (family) members, younger serving the elderly
Chae, 1987	Older Asians not differentiated by national origin	Loss of familiar; language barrier; shifting traditions; changing cultural roles	Immigration that disrupts Confucian norms and ideals; racial discrimination	Social isolation; disorganization for some elderly; reduced intergenerational conflict between old and young
Saunders, 1984	Armenians living in the U.S., primarily CA	Persecution by Turks 1915, by Moslems	United by common school, churches	Value collective goals; maintain extended family structure
McKenna, 1989	Mexican Americans	Socioeconomic conditions have necessitated rural-urban migration	Variations by rural and urban residence	Value extended family collectivism

group and age cohort. The hardships endured by the elderly client may increase striving for autonomy in later years. The desire to remain autonomous diminishes the readiness of the client to receive health restorative and health maintenance care from a nurse and increases the likelihood that the patient will want to be self-reliant.

The historical and social circumstances of each group also influence the nature of health care interactions. For example, members of some cultural groups will find it very difficult to accept care from a nurse of a dominant mainstream cultural group if the elderly client recalls discriminatory practices in previous health care interactions.

The contexts of each group may vary, but they place similar demands on members of cultural groups to retain their cultural patterns or to modify their culturally influenced patterns of behavior in light of the values, attitudes, and orientations in their new locales. For example, Navajo clients may face changes in their lifelong activities of daily living when they relocate to a nursing home, as do Samoans who enter a congregate-care facility. The finding that the groups of elderly clients who were studied all retained their traditional values while modifying their behavior indicates that the preservation of lifelong values provided the feelings of belonging and connectedness that gave meaning to one's life experiences. If nurses develop an awareness of the life experiences and traditional values of the elderly client, then they will be able to develop culturally appropriate care.

The example of Americans in Appalachia can be used to demonstrate that coping patterns and behavior developed by cultural group members in response to life experiences and historical conditions influence elderly clients' responses in seeking health care and in meeting developmental tasks. Though representing diverse cultural heritages, many elderly Appalachian clients are generally independent; self-determination is a high priority for many (Burkhardt, 1993). Historically, Appalachians experienced isolation as a way of life, since the original settlers in that region built their farmsteads away from neighbors. The mountainous terrain further contributed to limited transportation. Because nurses had to walk or travel on horseback to see patients, many elderly Appalachians had limited contact with health care providers. Thus some elderly Appalachians have had limited contact with nurses owing to historical factors, limited transportation, and rugged terrain; as a result, they may be skeptical of modern health care. An Appalachian client's long-standing practice of consulting with a "granny" woman, or folk healer, may continue even if the client accepts the health-maintenance acts provided by the nurse. Some elderly clients likely grew up with an awareness of folk healers and herb doctors, who provided various herbs, including foxglove and yellow root, for common ailments such as malaise, chest discomfort, weak heart, and upper respiratory infections.

Because the Appalachian client is accustomed to being autonomous, the nurse should explain the purpose of the recommended nursing actions and let the patient make his or her own decision. The nurse should recognize that the elderly client needs time to consider options for care, including acceptance of help from a health care agency. As part of the life review, the elderly clients need time to consider alternative plans of care in relation to their living situation and to past experiences with health care providers.

The nurse should treat each patient with regard for personal dignity. Many Appalachian residents are person-oriented, in contrast to the more object-oriented members of the dominant society. Elderly Appalachian clients will have recollections of visiting with each other and maintaining intense relationships with persons of similar circumstances. The family is cohesive, and several generations often live close to each other, proving mutual support. Maintenance of family ties is basic to the dignity of elderly clients, many of whom care for grandchildren and offer material support to family members. Illness disrupts the usual roles of the elderly client, so care includes recognition of the need for the client to regain a position in the family and a sense of fulfillment.

The nurse may observe that elderly clients have a fatalistic attitude as they recollect the past and bring closure to life as a means of achieving personal integrity. The elderly Appalachian client may be fatalistic about the many losses in life; this can be understood as a coping response, a way of protecting oneself against the disappointments of an often harsh life (Lewis, Messner, and McDowell, 1985). Many Appalachians have a belief in a divine existence rather than attending a particular church, which indicates that they maintain an individualistic approach in their religious beliefs (Burkhardt, 1993).

In sum, a culturally sensitive approach directs the nurse to assess each elderly client's life experiences, coping patterns, and cultural group's historical situations for their impact on the client's adjustment to the challenges of aging. These challenges to maintain security, dignity, autonomy, and self-determination will be variously met by elderly clients acting in ways that are culturally appropriate for them.

A Transcultural Example: Assessment and Intervention with a Recently Migrated Family

The case of Norma and her family is representative of the situation of elderly Nicaraguans who immigrate to the United States. The case of elderly Latin American immigrants is selected because almost one-quarter of Latino persons who have arrived in the United States are 55 years of age or older (Westat, 1989). In a study of Nicaraguans in the San Francisco Bay Area, two-thirds of the older residents were female and one-third of the women lived with extended family (Wallace, 1992).

The situation of multigeneration families is also becoming more common as more women return to the labor market with child care entrusted to a grandmother. Some elderly family members are also caring for grandchildren in light of the parents' death or incapacitation due to illness associated with AIDS or other diseases, including those related to alcohol and substance abuse.

Case Study 6-1

Adella was 35 years old and initially came to the San Francisco Bay Area to locate near her brother. Many Central Americans are more likely to move as a family unit than are Mexicans (Wallace, 1992). Adella worked as a housekeeper and arranged to bring her three children, who were living in Nicaragua—Tomas, 8 years old; Alicia, 10 years old; and Gabriella, 12 years old—to live with her. Adella grew increasingly concerned with the moral upbringing of her children, so she arranged for her mother, Norma, to also come to the Bay Area.

Norma is 68 years old and has been a widow for 19 years. She was living with a daughter, Florencia, and her family of two teenaged boys in Managua, Nicaragua. Norma, of course, spoke Spanish and she continued to speak Spanish to Adella's three children when she arrived in the United States. Adella decided that the children would learn English in school and that the grandmother, Norma, should continue to speak to them in Spanish at home. Research has supported that the persistence of Spanish is the most common indicator of Latino culture and identity (Mainous, 1989).

Norma also could visit with her other daughter, Maria, who would take her to mass at the Catholic Church attended by other Nicaraguan immigrants. Norma was asked to help plan a meal for the Nicaraguan community after a special mass for the feast of Santo Domingo (the patron saint of Managua).

Norma's patterns of activity are illustrative of the successful personal development and social adjustment of the elderly immigrant. This development depends on several factors: (1) involvement in the socialization of grandchildren and transmission of language to grandchildren, (2) preservation of one's ethnic heritage, and (3) involvement in social events in local community.

Leininger (1985) uses the concept of "cultural care preservation" to refer to the assistive, facilitative, or enabling acts that preserve cultural values and lifeways viewed as beneficial to the care recipients. Nurses can support Norma's practices that retain her cultural pride and heritage and foster her sense of well-being and positive mental health.

The preservation of ethnic heritage is inclusive of three aspects of ethnicity. One is a desire to retain *cultural ethnicity*, that is, the values that are passed from one generation to another. The second is *religious ethnicity*, which refers to continuing specific practices (e.g., feast days of a selected saint) that are unique to a cultural group. The third aspect of ethnicity is *national ethnicity*, which refers to the feelings of sharing a common background with others in the country of origin.

Norma lived in the same apartment with Adella and Tomas, Alicia, and Gabriella. Norma remained alone in the apartment for much of the day during the school year. She prepared breakfast for the children before they left for school and she prepared the evening meal, because the children's mother, Adella, worked at two housekeeping jobs. Her time with the children provided her with the opportunity to pass her attitudes and values to the grandchildren (cultural ethnicity). When she could attend church and informal get-togethers with other Nicaraguans at the church, she fulfilled religious and national ethnicity.

Norma's patterns of activity continued until she experienced severe abdominal pains and diarrhea. Adella gave her mother some pills she bought at the drugstore to stop the diarrhea. Norma did not take the pills, although she told Adella that she did. She asked Adella to go to a *botanica* and get her some tea to drink. Adella was able to locate a *botanica* in the neighborhood where she lived and brought home a small bundle of herbs for tea. Norma drank the tea for 2 days. She felt better but the symptoms persisted.

Adella persuaded Norma to attend the *Clinica* where the nurses and physicians spoke Spanish. While waiting, Norma commented that the nurses were not Nicaraguan, which she could easily detect in their speech. This illustrates that Spanish-speaking populations are heterogeneous. In metropolitan areas, there are many Spanish-speaking groups located in close proximity to each other. The similarities in language do not indicate similar cultural traditions, since Mexicans, Mexican Americans, Salvadorans, and Nicaraguans may reside in neighborhoods in West Coast cities and Dominicans, Puerto Ricans, Cubans, and Mexican Americans may reside in neighborhoods in East Coast cities.

Norma was given medication by the doctor in the clinic, and she agreed to take it, but she continued to take the herbal tea with the medicine. When her symptoms resolved, she attributed her improved status to the tea and not to the medicine.

This pattern of attributing health to lay remedies is characteristic of the help-seeking patterns of many people from different cultural groups. The use of lay medicine and over-the-counter remedies is common in some other cultural groups. The majority of illness episodes are actually resolved outside the biomedical setting as individuals consult with their significant others and social networks, often deciding to try an available medication that is suggested by a relative, friend, or contact.

Older individuals will have culturally influenced attitudes and values regarding health and illness. Many immigrants will retain beliefs about the causes of illness, nature of symptoms, and associated treatments that are the practices of their countries of origin. The nurse may use a nonjudgmental attitude and ask the elderly client his or her preferences for self-care. The nurse may ask the older patient:

"Have you eaten any foods to make your problem better?"
"Have you used some of the herbs that you can get in your neighborhood?"
"Did you talk to someone else and follow their advice about your health?"
"What do you expect your treatment to be?"
"Is there something else you wish us to do for you?"

Asking the older client questions similar to these may reveal the patient's use of traditional remedies and also may indicate their beliefs that are influenced by their cultural heritage.

Norma supervised the children until one day when she fell on the stairs and fractured her hip. She was taken to the hospital by an emergency aide crew. At the hospital, a nurse in the emergency room was able to speak to her in Spanish and call Adella. Norma initially feared the forced hospitalization because she thought she would have to pay for it, and only after several reassuring conversations with her daughter and her nurse did she realize that she had state Medicaid coverage.

As her discharge approached, the physician prepared to send Norma home, assuming that Adella would care for her. While Adella was interested in caring for her mother, she had been working outside the home for 10 hours a day, 6 days a week, and she feared the loss of her jobs. Besides, she had already taken leave when Norma was in the hospital. The nurse suggested that Norma needed a referral for visiting nurse services, including a home health aide. Attention to the cultural background of the client should not assume that relatives will provide home care that precludes referrals for home health services. Norma did receive in-home services, and the home health aide was Mexican American. There are well-developed in-home service networks employing bilingual, multicultural personnel in many urban areas. In rural areas, the lack of availability of services is a barrier to in-home services for many Spanish-speaking elderly persons.

Multidimensional Nursing Analysis

The nurse working with Norma and her family used a comprehensive approach, to assess the interrelated needs of the elderly client, including physical health, mental status, functional abilities, mobility, personal care, maintenance tasks such as cooking and housecleaning, and social and economic needs. The nurse noted how the encompassing context of the family, that is, their kinship and social and cultural patterns that influenced Norma's perceived health, mental status, and functional abilities, should be incorporated into a care plan.

The nurse provided dimensions that are relevant in the care of the elderly client: awareness of changing social structures and sociohistorical events that influence the client's responses to health care. The nurse assessed that Norma was not familiar with the setting of American hospitals and home health care agencies. This was Norma's introduction to a system of multidisciplinary health care providers who performed tasks family members might have done for a hospitalized relative in her homeland. Norma also was reluctant to receive care because she associated health care with excessive costs. The nurse could also assess that Norma, like many other Central American immigrants, had relocated under rather adverse conditions.

There are several aspects of nursing care for Norma and her family that can be highlighted:

Spiritual Needs. The nurse gathered that Norma's attendance at the Spanish services at the nearby Catholic Church were an indication of the importance of religion in her life. Interest in religion may increase with age as the older person begins closure on life experiences, or persons may attach more importance to religion as they age when religion has been meaningful throughout their lives. From a developmental perspective, the nurse noted that religious beliefs provided a sense of meaning in the later years as well as a sense of closure of life. Finding meaning in life and developing a feeling that life has been worthwhile are important developmental tasks of the elderly.

Kinship Factors Affecting Health and Illness. The interdependence of generations in this family illustrates a growing trend in families of different cultural backgrounds. The nurse may use intergenerational resources to augment health care services. In many traditional Hispanic families, there is a great deal of mutual support, sustenance, and interaction among family members. The interaction in this family with the reliance on Norma as a primary caregiver illustrates an emerging pattern of family practices.

Data collected by the nurse in interviews confirm the idea that the family continues to be supportive of its elders. While Hispanic families generally are supportive of elders, there are differences in the patterns of Central American, Caribbean, and Mexican-American Hispanics. Generally, these are age-integrated communities where the elderly have been afforded more status than in dominant mainstream American culture.

The family remains a flexible structure that helps the elderly client deal with the environment and the emotional and psychological aspects of adjustment to aging and to relocation. The reliance on extended family members continues for emotional support and material support.

Feelings of familism are quite strong, so family members are frequently primary providers of support, succorance, and stress alleviation (Leininger, 1991). Nurses need to assess the presence of family members as nurturant caregivers and as a source of morale to older family members and plan with the family how each member can assist and support the client. Nurses may develop plans for home care that provide relief, respite care to family caregivers, or supplement nurturing aspects of care for elderly Latin Americans with appropriate community resources. The family can provide many personal nursing acts that a health care agency cannot provide, and similarly, a visiting nurse agency can provide health instruction, medication monitoring, hygiene, and rehabilitation that family members cannot easily provide. The nurse coordinates family care with agency care in a comprehensive plan of care.

However, nurses are cognizant of sociology research that expresses differing views on the social and functional importance and nature of immigrant families. Nurses need to assess the extent that urban migration, increased education of younger generations, and varying degrees of acculturation affect family support. The nurse can recognize that family does not automatically mean a multigenerational family in a single residence and so assess support available from family members. Maldonado (1988) maintains that Mexican-American elderly persons may be more likely to live independently while remaining in close contact with their kin, a residence pattern that has been described commonly in dominant society American culture.

A nurse can identify that a small circle of intimate contacts may well be more helpful than a large, scattered network of casual contacts in countering the losses and demoralizing effects of aging (McFarlane et al., 1983). Nurses can identify that supportive and assistive functions may be carried out by family members or may be assumed by personal networks or group alliances that bolster the functions of the family. A large extended family is not common to all immigrant families, and for many persons, their social networks assume duties that might have once been performed by family members. Making certain that the support system is adequate and as such buffers some of the traumatic losses incurred in late adulthood is an important nursing function.

Psychological Factors Influencing Health and Illness. Several psychological factors, including potential alienation and the potential to develop depression, influence perceptions and behavior related to health and illness. Most elderly immigrants have experienced discontinuities in moving from their homeland and sometimes an additional move to an urban area. Breaks with tradition and homeland contribute to depression, decreased morale, and low self-esteem. Disruptions that many elderly persons have experienced in their lives cause shifts in values that are also stressful and demoralizing, further causing them to be depressed and alienated.

Appropriate intervention in working with elderly clients may be at an individual or group level to encourage participation in social groups, culturally oriented groups, or retiree clubs. The nurse can try to counteract the elderly client's declining morale by sensitizing the family to their elder member's needs or by working at a health program planning level to develop aged mental health programs, including recollection and life review therapy sessions. Nursing intervention that is sensitive to cultural discontinuities experienced by clients should try to promote self-esteem, morale, and feelings of good mental health.

To assess clients' sense of social well-being, try to assess if clients believe that their social interactions are satisfying. Elderly persons who have experienced high morale, in the absence of strong interactions with kin, may have substituted social interactions with peers.

Nurses who coordinate social and mental health services for elderly populations should do so with increased sensitivity to cultural group differences and needs. Providers also need to be aware of recruiting minority elderly people to such programs and building satisfying relationships with all elderly clients.

When traditional patterns and family lifestyles are disrupted, the lives of the elderly are likely to be more stressful. Older persons may experience the severest amount of alienation from societal values and from their adult offspring who are adopting new cultural values.

Cultural Values Relevant to Health and Illness. When the nurse recognizes that values of health and illness, such as a focus on present conditions and a lack of anticipation of future discomforts and symptoms, are consistent with a cultural group's encompassing view of the world, the nurse can plan care based on the client's perspective. These notions of health and illness are maintained by members of a sociocultural group and are not easily relinquished, while patients also may make use of the dominant society health care system. Some Hispanic clients consider illness as a punishment from God. Members of Hispanic cultures who attribute illness to the imbalance between God and themselves and the environment will likely seek spiritual treatment through an *espiritualista* (spiritualist).

The nurse's role is to respect the fact that the elderly client has had a long exposure to folk and spiritual healing in which the client places strong faith and trust. The nurse often acts as a broker for the client and explains to the health care team the client's need for spiritual care or folk healing. The nurse facilitates the client's receipt of traditional spiritual or folk care when it can be incorporated with other nursing actions and does not jeopardize the patient's health or safety.

Summary of Nursing Care. Nurses who identify how kinship, psychological, and cultural factors interact in the lives of aging persons also note that socioeconomic status affects physical health, mental status, and functional status. Intervention is then based on lessening the negative impact of such factors as loss of social roles and income and increasing the influence of such positive factors as presence of supportive others. The nurse does not impose culturally influenced values on clients and/or families; instead, clients are encouraged to pursue culturally specific behavior, including social and church activities and the use of folk therapies that promote and sustain physical health, as well as mental and functional status.

Summary

Culture defines who is old, establishes rituals for identifying the elderly, sets socially acceptable roles and expectations for behavior of the elderly, and influences attitudes toward the aged. Culturally influenced attitudes and behavior related to the elderly were presented in this chapter. Culturally determined responses to aging that are common in American society were described along with information about other cultural groups. A cultural approach to understanding aging recognizes that individuals may be trying to satisfy needs that are fairly common across cultural backgrounds, but variations noted in the attitudes and behavior of individuals are to a large extent culturally determined. Culture serves as a guide to elderly persons on the ways they fulfill their needs, for it determines what actions and kinds of behavior are considered acceptable.

In American society, various attitudes ranging from acceptance to denial and respect to disrespect are exhibited in and toward a heterogeneous elderly population. Elderly persons have been described as disengaging from society or remaining active in society by shifting their outlooks and activities. Practitioners explain away old age and use old age to explain ailments that cannot be attributed to other causes. Generalizations to older persons across different social and group contexts, economic and educational status, familial and institutional settings are limited.

Within cultural group contexts, individual variation is quite evident in response to the physiologic signs and psychosocial demands of increasing age. The examples of the Appalachian context and an immigrant family were presented as evidence of how persons develop responses to health and illness that differ from the views of the nurse. Different attitudes, practices, and behavior among elderly persons are the result of their heritage, experiences, education, occupation, and socioeconomic status. Evidence of cultural variation makes nurses aware of their own cultural backgrounds and traditions and of the values underlying nursing practices. A guide to nursing practice may be to "assess and not to assume" the influence of culture in shaping the meaning of health and illness to individuals and in determining health- and illness-related behavior. Nursing strategies that are set to stereotyped images of all elderly persons are not acceptable; instead, care should be based on individual differences in education, income, residence, and level of acculturation, all of which affect elderly client attitudes and behavior.

Cultural Perspective

In adopting a cultural perspective in working with older persons of different cultural orientations, the nurse should understand that the main task of elderly individuals is to achieve a sense of integrity in accepting responsibility for their own lives and in having a sense of accomplishment. Individuals who achieve integrity see aging as a positive experience, make adjustments in their personal space and social relations, maintain a sense of usefulness, and begin closure and life review.

Elderly persons initially have to meet their physiologic needs, and many have to cope with chronic illness. All persons develop explanatory models of their illness episodes that may diverge from professional health care concepts. Elderly persons who have used folk medicine and recollect other experiences in their lives may develop notions of illness quite different from the views of the nurse. Elderly individuals who are working through the task of finding meaning in their lives may try to find meaning in each illness episode. Nurses can recognize that elderly persons are trying to understand the impact of illness on their lives and can provide information to clients on the purposes and consequences of treatments, procedures, and medications. As a result, clients often come to see their views of illness as important, and they seek the opinions of health care providers to compare with their existing knowledge.

In providing care to elderly clients, the nurse adjusts the usual nurse-patient interaction of explaining procedures and teaching about medications, diet, and exercise. Nurses who express the "why" of a procedure to a client rather than details of "how" something works will be better received by the elderly client. It may be more helpful to clients if the nurse helps them to find the personal meaning of a stressful event or the purpose of a procedure than to deliver particulars of therapy.

Older persons also find meaning in their lives by sharing their traditions and values with others. Nurses can facilitate an older client's participation in a cultural heritage group or in a congregate nutrition program where elders exchange their ideas with peers and younger contacts. Nurses can recognize the positive aspects of an elderly person developing a relationship with a younger person to whom the aged person can tell stories or teach a skill such as cooking or painting.

It is especially important for nurses to consider the elderly patient's perspective in at least three general areas: how the person perceives health and illness, what expectations the person has of care, and how nursing can support culturally determined patterns of dealing with health and coping with illness.

Patient's Perspective on Illness

Elderly persons may have adapted to varying degrees of incapacitation and will tend to report only severe illnesses. Identify what the patient defines as a health problem and what significance this problem has for the patient. Ask the elderly patient, "What is good health? How is your health?" Try to identify how the older person defines health in general, for some persons identify themselves as "being in good shape for an old man or woman."

Culture-Specific Caring Behaviors

Older persons have varying reactions to receiving health care. They have developed expectations for care based on their past experiences and on their knowledge of their friends' encounters with health care providers. Ask the elderly client, "What would you expect or like a nurse to do for you?" The elderly person's expectations for care also will be determined by his or her cultural background, which may influence the person to use traditional folk medicine in varying combinations with the basic medical system. A hospitalized elderly Greek-American woman was drinking herbal tea that her daughter had prepared for her. She felt that the tea settled her stomach and would help her sleep, and she did not want to take a PRN sleeping medication. The nursing student caring for this patient included the use of herbal tea in the patient's plan of care because it was effective in preparing the patient for an evening's sleep.

Nurses caring for elderly persons in many clinical settings should assess if elderly persons perceive nursing care as culturally appropriate. Patients may more readily accept personal care, and there may be caring practices specific to the patient's culture that are preferred by the patient. Aamodt (1984) described the importance of being available to just sit with an ill person and of preparing coffee as culturally determined caring rituals for elderly Norwegian-American women. Nurses should support the elderly patient's culturally defined caring rituals because these activities promote and maintain health.

The Older Americans Act (OAA) mandated that services should be provided to the elderly in America with special attention to the low-income minority aged with greatest economic need. Whether older individuals will use services depends on several factors, including the culturally influenced factors that have been stressed in this chapter.

There are numerous barriers explaining the decreased use of services by elderly clients, especially elderly persons of culturally diverse backgrounds, as indicated in Box 6-3. There are also various strategies suggested to overcome barriers and encourage elderly clients' service use.

Even when services are available, elderly clients may not use them because they do not find the services attractive and appropriate. The perceived differences between the clients and the providers will make the services seem less appropriate. Many elderly clients who come in contact with health care providers who appear different from themselves and do not speak the same language will be less likely to seek care from these health professionals.

The hesitancy on the part of elderly clients, especially clients from cultural groups and ethnic groups of color, is understandable given the context of the individuals. Persons who are now 70 in 1994 were 40 when the Public Accommodations Act was

---

**Box 6-3. Barriers That May Impede Communication
and Service Delivery to the Older Person**

Internal barriers
Lack of knowledge of perceived need for service
Lack of knowledge of existing services
Lack of knowledge needed to enroll in a service
Perception that one is not entitled to services
Desire to remain self-sufficient
Perception that providers are rude, address older clients in overly familiar
terms, and interrupt the elderly

Contextual barriers
Space: lack of private space for most interactions that occur in clinical
settings
Position: embarrassing position of the client in relation to the health care
provider
Technology overload: presence of signs, contact with many personnel
Sensory overload: printed instructions, verbal messages, visual cues, video-
tapes

Service barriers
Lack of access
Affordability of care
Availability of services

---

passed by Congress in 1964 and the Voting Rights Act was passed in 1965 (Yeatts, Crow, and Folts, 1992). Because many of these ethnic elderly experienced acts of discrimination throughout most of their adult lives, they are more suspicious of services provided in culturally diverse settings. The stressful life experiences of some older adults also will make them reluctant to seek services and to be distrustful of care provided by health care professionals who are ethnically different from themselves.

Strategies to reduce these differences are to encourage nurses and health care providers to speak the language of the population being served. Other strategies include

Encouraging health care professionals to be sensitive to the background and previous
health care experiences of the target groups
Listening attentively to the elderly patient's complaints
Listening to related conversation to assess for underlying signs of depression
Eliciting information about the elderly patient's preferences for diet and include them in
the plan of care
Inquiring about significant others and available support
Listening for indications of recent loss, including home, loved one, significant source of
support

Elderly persons may develop their own means of coping with illness through self-care, family support, and social group support systems. Other cultures have developed attitudes and specific caring behaviors for the elderly that may include humanistic care and identification of family members as care providers. Nurses in outpatient settings or in home health care agencies should identify persons who are available as care providers and assist these individuals. In addition, it is increasingly important that nurses also recognize the expanded care provider role taken by the elderly client who is raising a grandchild or is caring for another family member. Nurses caring for the elderly client should include attention to the client's familial and social roles and develop care plans to maintain and or restore the individual to his or her usual roles and patterns of activity.

Learning Activities

1. Identify the categories of homemaker services, home health aides, visiting nurse services, elder day-care centers, and respite care, as well as the availability of these services that support older individuals in their desire to remain in their own homes.
2. Arrange to visit a life-care community (a congregate-care facility, extended-care facility) in your community to assess the philosophy of care in that facility. Consider the approach of the facility you visit in light of dominant American society values. Does the facility reflect the concepts of continuity, disengagement, or activity theory?
3. Interview an attendee at a senior center nutrition program or a community activity that is focused on seniors. Include in your interview what the older person perceives as significant events in his or her life, his or her perception of cultural group identity, feelings of discrimination as a member of this cultural group or as an older person, attitude toward health care services, and early life experiences of the older person. Have any of these factors influenced the older person's perceptions of their health and illness?
4. Attend a support group for persons with a chronic illness that is taught in your community (e.g., arthritis self-help course). Observe who attends the class, and listen to their reasons for attending. Can you relate their perceptions of illness to the broader experience of having an illness in our society?
5. Get permission to attend a gathering of elders identified by their cultural heritage Native American elders salmon bake, Norwegian Americans independence celebration, interned Japanese Americans gathering). Assess, if you can, the shared experiences and recollections that give the group a sense of identity.

References

Aamodt, A. (1984) Care, culture and human response: Emerging nursing theory for practice. In J. Uhl (ed.), *Proceedings of the Ninth Annual Transcultural Nursing Society Conference.* Salt Lake City: Transcultural Nursing Society.

Atchley, R. C. (1989) A continuity theory of normal aging. *The Gerontologist, 29*: 183–189.

Barusch, A. S., and Spaid, W. M. (1989). Gender differences in caregiving: Why do widows report greater burden? *The Gerontologist, 29*(5): 667–676.

Boettcher, E. G. (1985). Linking the aged to support systems. *Journal of Gerontological Nursing, 11*(3): 27–33.

Bond, J. B., and Harvey, C. D. (1991). Ethnicity and intergenerational perceptions of family solidarity. *International Journal of Aging and Human Development, 33*(1): 33–44.

Braxton, J. (1989). *Black Women Writing Autobiography: A Tradition within a Tradition.* Philadelphia: Temple University Press.

Brod, M., and Heurtin-Roberts, S. (1992). Older russian emigrés and medical care. *Western Journal of Medicine, 157*: 333–336.

Burkhardt, M. A. (1993). Characteristics of spirituality in the lives of women in a rural Appalachian community. *The Journal of Transcultural Nursing, 4*(2): 12–18.

Chae, M. (1987). Older Asians. *Journal of Gerontological Nursing, 13*(11): 11–17.

Chapleski, E. E. (1989). Determinants of knowledge of services to the elderly: Are strong ties enabling or inhibiting? *The Gerontologist, 29*: 539–545.

Clavon, A. M. (1986). Black elderly. *Journal of Gerontological Nursing, 12*(5): 6–12.

Denham, T. E., and Smith, C. W. (1989) The influence of grandparents on grandchildren: The review of the literature and the sources. *Family Relations, 38*: 345–350.

Diehauy, E. K. (1986). Delivering home health care to the elderly in Zuni Pueblo. *Journal of Gerontological Nursing, 12*(7): 25–29.

Erikson, E. H. (1955). Growth and crises of the healthy personality. In C. Kluckhorn, H. A. Murray, and D. M. Schneider (Eds.), *Personality in Nature, Society and Culture.* New York: Knopf.

Filinson, R. (1992). Ethnic aging in Canada and the United States: A comparison of social policy. *Journal of Aging Studies, 6*(3): 273–287.

Harris, M. B., Begay, C., and Page, P. (1989). Activities, family relationships and feelings about aging in a multicultural elderly sample. *International Journal of Aging and Human Development, 29*(2): 103–117.

Havighurst, R. (1968). Disengagement and patterns of aging. In B. Neugarten (Ed.), *Middle Age and Aging.* Chicago: University of Chicago Press.

Hilker, M. A. (1991). Generational viewpoints in culturally diverse literature: Commentary. *International Journal of Aging and Human Development, 33*(3): 211–215.

Kalish, R. A. (1986). The meanings of ethnicity. In C. L. Hayes, R. A. Kalish, and D. Guttman (Eds.), *European American Elderly: A Guide for Practice.* New York: Springer.

Keith, J., Fry, C., and Ikels, C. (1990). Successful aging in cultural context. In J. Sokolovsky (Ed.), *Growing Old in Other Societies,* 2d Ed. South Hadley, MA: Bergin & Garvey.

Keller, M. L. Leventhal, E. A., and Larson, B. (1989). Aging: The lived experience. *International Journal of Aging and Human Development, 29*(1): 67–82.

Kelly, J., and Westcott, G. (1991). Ordinary retirement: Commonalties and continuity. *International Journal of Aging and Human Development, 32*(2): 81–89.

Kim, P. (1983). Demography of the Asian-Pacific elderly: Selected problems and implications. In R. McNeely and J. Cohen (Eds.), *Aging in Minority Groups.* Beverly Hills: Sage Publications.

Kramer, B. J. (1992). Health and aging of urban American Indians. *Western Journal of Medicine, 157*: 281–285.

Krause, N. (1990). Illness behavior in later life. In R. H. Binstock, and L. K. George (Eds.), *Handbook of Aging and the Social Sciences.* New York: Academic Press.

Kravitz, S. L., Palacz, M. B., and Rothman, M. B. (1990). Delivering services to elders: Responsiveness to populations in need. In S. A. Bass, E. A. Kutza, and F. M. Torres-Gil (Eds.), *Diversity in Aging* (pp. 47–72). Glenview, Ill: Scott-Foresman.

Leininger, M. (1991). *Culture Care Diversity and Universality: A Theory of Nursing.* New York: National League for Nursing.

Leininger, M. (1985). Transcultural care diversity and universality. A theory of nursing. *Nursing and Health Care, 6*: 208–212.

Lewis, S., Messner, R., and McDowell, W. A. (1985). An unchanging culture. *Journal of Gerontological Nursing, 11*(8): 21–26.

Lock, M. (1983). Japanese responses to social changes: Making the strange familiar. *The Western Journal of Medicine. 139*(6): 25–30.

Mainous, A. G. (1989). Self-concept as an indicator of acculturation in Mexican Americans. *Hispanic Journal of Behavioral Sciences, 11*(2): 178–189.

Maldonado, R. (1988). El barrio: Perceptions and utilization of the Hispanic neighborhood. In. S. R. Applewhite (Ed.), *Hispanic Elderly in Transition.* New York: Greenwood Press.

Malonebeach, E. E. and Zarit, S. H. (1991). Current research issues in caregiving to the elderly. *International Journal of Aging and Human Development 33*(2): 103–114.

McFarlane, A. H., Norman, G. R., Streiner, D. L., and Roy, R. G. (1983). The process of social stress: Stable, reciprocal, and mediating relationships. *Journal of Health and Social Behavior,* (24): 160–173.

McKenna, M. (1989). Twice in need of care: A transcultural nursing analysis of elderly Mexican Americans. *Journal of Transcultural Nursing, 1*(1): 46–52.

Moon, J., and Pearl, J. H. (1991). Alienation of elderly Korean-American immigrants as related to place of residence, gender, age, years of education, time in the U.S., living with or without children and living with a spouse. *International Journal of Aging and Human Development, 32*(2): 115–124.

Mutran, E. (1985). Intergenerational family support among blacks and whites: Response to culture or to socioeconomic differences. *Journal of Gerontology, 40*: 382–389.

Palmore, E. and Maeda, D. (1985). *The Honorable Elders Revisited.* Durham: Duke University.

Preston, D. and Grimes, J. (1987). A study of differences in social support. *Journal of Gerontological Nursing, 13*(2): 36–40.

Rhoades, E. E.. (1990). Profile of American Indians and Alaska Natives. In *Minority Aging—Essential Curricula Content for Selected Health and Allied Health Professions*. Washington: U.S. DHSHS publication HRS-P-DV 90-4.

Rice, D. P., and LaPlante, M. P. (1988). Chronic illness, disability and increasing longevity. In S. Sullivan and M. E. Lewin (Eds.), *The Economics of Long Term Care and Disability* (pp. 9–55). Washington: American Enterprise Institute for Public Policy Research.

Rosenthal, C. J., Mathews, S. H., and Marshall, V. W. (1989). Is parent care normative? The experience of a sample of middle aged women. *Research on Aging, 11*(2): 244–260.

Sanchez-Ayendez, M. (1989). Puerto Rican elderly women: The cultural dimension of social support networks. *Women and Health, 14*: 239–252.

Saunders, V. (1984). Profiles of elderly Armenians. *Journal of Gerontological Nursing, 10*(11): 26–29.

Shiamoto, Y., and Ishida, D. (1988). The elderly Samoan. *Public Health Nursing, 5*(4): 219–221.

Shomaker, D. M. (1981). Navajo nursing homes: Conflict of philosophies. *Journal of Gerontological Nursing, 7*: 531–536.

Sullivan, S., and Lewin, M. E. (Eds.) (1988). *The Economics of Long Term Care and Disability*. Washington: American Enterprise Institute for Public Policy Research.

Tran, T. V. (1991) Family living arrangement and social adjustment among three ethnic groups of elderly Indochinese refugees. *International Journal of Aging and Human Development, 32*(2): 91–102.

Treas, J., and Bengston, V. L. (1987). The family in later years. In M. B. Sussman and S. K. Steinmetz (Eds.), *Handbook of Marriage and the Family*. New York: Plenum Press.

United States Bureau of the Census (1991). Press releases on 1990 census data. Washington: U.S. States Department of Commerce, Economics and Statistics Administration.

United States Public Health Service (1990). *Health United States, 1989*. Hyattsville, MD: National Center for Health Statistics.

Verbrugge, L. M. (1989) Recent, present, and future health of American adults. In J. E. Breslow and J. E. Fielding (Eds.), In *Annual Review of Public Health* (pp. 333–362). Palo Alto, CA: Annual Review.

Wallace, S. P. (1992). Community formation as an activity of daily living: The case of Nicaraguan immigrant elderly. *Journal of Aging Studies, 6*(4): 365–383.

Weibel-Orlando, J. (1989). Elders and elderlies: Well-being in old age. *American Indian Cultural Research, 13*: 75–84.

Westat, R. (1989). *A Survey of Elderly Hispanics: Final Report*. Baltimore, MD: Commonwealth Fund Commission on Elderly People Living Alone.

Wray, L. A. (1992). Health policy and ethnic diversity in older Americans: Dissonance or harmony? *Western Journal of Medicine Special Edition, 157*: 357–361.

Yeatts, D. E., Crow, T., and Folts, E. (1992). Service use among low-income minority elderly: Strategies for overcoming barriers. *The Gerontologist, 32*(1): 24–32.

III

*Clinical Topics and Issues
in Transcultural Nursing*

7

Alterations in Lifestyle: Transcultural Concepts in Chronic Illness

Joyceen S. Boyle

Introduction

This chapter discusses transcultural concepts that can be used in the care of clients who are experiencing alterations in lifestyle due to chronic diseases. Although changes in daily routines may be necessitated by many factors, clients with a chronic disease frequently require culturally sensitive nursing interventions. Helping clients and families from diverse cultures change long-standing patterns in their daily activities presents challenges for nurses.

This chapter provides culturally relevant background information related to one chronic disease—hypertension—and discusses nursing problems that frequently are presented by clients who must alter their lifestyles to maintain or promote their health. Nursing interventions based on cultural knowledge help clients adjust more easily and help nurses work effectively and comfortably with all clients, especially those from different cultural backgrounds.

Nursing problems related to alterations in living may be identified in clients who have chronic diseases or other long-term health problems that require changes in patterns of daily living. In this chapter, hypertension is used as a prototype; however, much of the information discussed here can be generalized to the nursing care of any client making lifestyle changes. The first section of this chapter focuses on cultural considerations in the care of clients who have hypertension, risk factors in hypertension, and nursing problems arising from common lifestyle changes in chronic illness. The second part of the chapter discusses social and cultural factors to be considered in the care of clients who have a chronic illness. The factors that are discussed include family support systems, coping behaviors, beliefs, health practices, and the role of traditional healers. This section provides background information that is helpful in understanding

Margaret M. Andrews and Joyceen S. Boyle: TRANSCULTURAL CONCEPTS IN NURSING CARE, SECOND EDITION. © 1995 J.B. Lippincott Company.

how clients adjust to and manage chronic illness. This knowledge is important when planning and implementing successful nursing strategies.

The Nursing Management of Clients with Hypertension

Like other chronic diseases, hypertension is a serious health problem not only because it causes significant mortality and morbidity but also because its treatment poses complex nursing and medical problems. These problems relate primarily to the difficulty clients experience in complying with long-term drug regimens and lifestyle changes that require major behavioral adaptations. Often these behavioral changes are related to cultural patterns and traditions, such as dietary habits, daily activities, and lifestyles. As individuals live longer, there is an increased likelihood that they will develop a chronic disease such as hypertension. Because such large numbers of persons are at risk for developing hypertension, health professionals must increasing direct their efforts toward prevention, helping clients to implement lifestyle changes that will decrease their risk for developing hypertension.

Fortunately, as in other chronic diseases, the early detection and treatment of hypertension have received increased attention in the past few years. With this focus on disease prevention and health promotion, the nursing role has expanded, and nurses have assumed broad responsibilities in the prevention of disease and the promotion and maintenance of health. Comprehensive management of hypertension must include community-based programs for detection, referral, evaluation, and treatment of hypertension. Nurses are playing a major role in the planning and implementation of such programs. In addition, nurses are frequently responsible for the identification, assessment, referral, and follow-up care for clients with hypertension. Nurses who are managing the care of hypertensive clients over long periods of time provide aspects of counseling, education, and guidance directed toward helping individuals adjust to their condition on a daily and long-term basis.

Although clients might be culturally different from nurses who work in community hypertension programs, it is important that nurses know something about the clients they serve and not assume that because they come from a different cultural group they lack information about hypertension or any other condition. For example, Ailinger (1982) studied hypertension knowledge in a Hispanic community and found that 64 percent of the subjects had adequate knowledge of the definition, etiology, diagnosis, risk factors, treatment, prognosis, and sequelae of hypertension. Admittedly, knowledge of hypertension does not guarantee careful compliance with a treatment regimen, but it is an indication of where to start when planning an intervention program for either individuals or communities.

Many clients will do fairly well initially in complying with their physicians' instructions, but motivation to comply with a prescribed regimen often lessens over time and becomes problematic for long-term care. Often, clients do not feel any better when they take prescribed medications; indeed, sometimes they feel worse because of the side effects of the drug therapy. Other aspects of treatment for hypertension involve considerable changes in patterns of daily life that are difficult to implement and even more challenging to maintain. The lifestyle changes that contribute to control of blood pressure are sodium restriction, weight reduction, cessation of smoking, development of effective methods for coping with stress, regular exercise, and lifelong drug therapy. As could be predicted, many clients fail to comply for various reasons. A major focus of this chapter is the cultural implications of these lifestyle changes.

African Americans and the Increased Risk for Hypertension

Historically and continuing to the present time, there is a troubling disparity in the health status of African Americans when compared with that of white Americans. Overall, 38 percent of African Americans have high blood pressure compared with 29 percent in the white population (National Heart, Lung, and Blood Institute, 1985). Although surveys indicate that most adults with high blood pressure are aware of their condition, only about one-quarter to a third of them have their blood pressure under control. This remains a problem despite the fact that many persons could reduce their blood pressure to normal through programs of physical activity and weight loss, reduced sodium and alcohol intake, stress management, and medications when necessary (U.S. Department of Health and Human Services, 1990). More than two decades ago, Boyle (1970) found that hypertension is not only more frequent among African Americans but also develops earlier in life, is often more severe, and causes more premature deaths than in whites. In addition, African Americans are more susceptible to the malignant form of essential hypertension. The relationship of sex and age to hypertension follows different patterns in African Americans than in whites. Furthermore, there is no clear correlation between obesity and hypertension in African Americans, but there is such a correlation in whites. Spector (1991) noted that available data indicate that most African Americans with hypertension do not receive adequate treatment often because they lack access to services. According to Heckler (1985), proportionately twice as many African Americans as whites lack basic medical insurance.

Although African Americans are at higher risk for developing hypertension, other cultural groups in the United States are also affected by hypertension, a common cardiovascular disorder. Nursing problems arise because clients encounter difficulties in following medical and nursing advice. These problems are further compounded if nurses fail to understand the nature of the problems experienced by clients and to take these problems into account when planning and implementing care. Nursing care for the client with hypertension involves human experiences with personal, familial, and sociocultural implications. As Charmaz (1991) pointed out, living with a chronic illness takes time and effort. There are "good" days and "bad" days (p. 5). Providing care requires an understanding of cultural components, such as values, health beliefs, and practices, as well as an appreciation of the client's daily life experiences.

Lifestyle Changes in Chronic Illness

Societal changes in the 20th century, along with improved sanitation and technological innovations, have brought major improvements in living for large numbers of people and have made it possible for chronic diseases to increase both in terms of numbers and diversity of form. Nevertheless, recognition of the relationship between lifestyle and health status or of the impact of disease on individuals has been slow to emerge. The disease-centered orientation of the biomedical model has had a powerful influence on the way in which nurses have managed care of clients with long-term nursing problems. However, the impact of disease on human beings is more than biologic, and the nursing management of hypertension, or any other chronic disease, must draw on conceptual frameworks that include cultural, social, and behavioral concepts relevant to the multidimensional and social character of chronic diseases.

In order to assist culturally different clients in the management of chronic illness, nurses must be aware of the multiple dimensions of the condition and how the family system influences the course of illness. The family is the major context in which the challenges of coping with illness are resolved (Leahey and Wright, 1987). Balancing the need for help and support from family and friends with the need for personal control and independence has less to do with the disorder itself than with the management of symptoms and social relationships. The most challenging task of nurses is helping clients make lasting changes in dietary patterns and exercise habits as well as adherence to a medication regimen, all of which are discussed in this section. The cultural implications discussed here are fairly general and should be considered for all clients, regardless of cultural background.

Adherence to a Long-Term Medication Regimen

Certainly an important nursing priority in providing care to a client with hypertension is that of maintaining blood pressure at an acceptable level and helping the client learn about the condition and treatment modalities. Nursing assessments should focus on determining the client's compliance potential and understanding the client's lifestyle. *Client compliance* can be defined as adherence to a prescribed therapeutic regimen; compliance with medication regimens is especially important if high blood pressure is to be controlled successfully. Educational efforts need to be directed toward compliance with lifelong therapy. Clients' concerns with health, their perceptions of the severity of their hypertension and their own vulnerability, as well as their confidence in modern health care and health care providers will all affect the likelihood of compliance with the prescribed pharmaceutical regimen.

Roberson (1992) studied the meaning of compliance in a sample of rural African Americans. She found that sample members and health professionals defined compliance differently and that each group had different goals for treatment. Her informants assumed that they were in compliance with their medical regimen if they "felt good" or when their physician told them they were "doing fine." Most of them sought treatment approaches from physicians that were manageable, livable, and, from their perspective, effective. Most of them saw themselves as managing quite well, even though a health professional might label them "noncompliant." A few of them consulted traditional healers such as root doctors for their hypertension.

Before providing information or teaching a hypertensive client about hypertension, the nurse should understand that it is extremely difficult for many persons, regardless of their culture, to understand how they can have a serious illness such as hypertension in the absence of any symptoms. For some clients, a logical response to the lack of symptoms would be to decrease their medications or perhaps even discontinue taking them. The "silent" nature of hypertension needs to be addressed repeatedly. Clients must have confidence in the accuracy of the diagnosis of hypertension. This means that each client needs a thorough explanation of the condition in a manner that is compatible with that individual's health beliefs. Only if the nurse understands the clients' health beliefs and is willing to spend time listening and learning about their perception of the disease can this be accomplished.

Each time the client's blood pressure is measured, precise explanations should be provided to the client and family. It is usually advisable for clients to have an individualized record for their own use where blood pressure measurements can be recorded. Clients should be encouraged to participate in decision making about their care. This may be difficult for members of certain cultural groups or ethnic minorities because of previous adverse experiences with both health care providers and the health care system.

The quality of the client–health care provider relationship influences the nature of compliance. Nurses, especially those working in community hypertension clinics, should organize their activities in such a manner that clients can see the same nurse each visit and there is adequate time and privacy to discuss individual concerns. Anderson and Bauwens (1981) noted that the complexity of the therapeutic regimen for hypertension is an important factor in noncompliance. They suggested that efforts should be made to make the prescribed therapy as simple and inexpensive as possible, since the more changes or alterations that individuals must make in their lifestyles, the more difficult it is for them to comply. Certainly, clients need to be reassured that their participation in the management of hypertension is essential. The nurse should actively encourage them to discuss any problems or concerns and should be sensitive to client concerns. Clients should be assured that such information is genuinely desired by the health professional.

Coping with the side effects of medications poses problems for many clients. With some drugs, side effects can be alleviated by a change in medication schedule. The medication schedule should be discussed with the client, and active participation in planning and meeting nursing goals should be encouraged. The long-term costs of medications may be a genuine burden for some clients, and they may find this subject difficult to discuss with health professionals.

Some antihypertensive medications, including guanethidine, methyldopa, and reserpine, may cause sexual dysfunction. Using anticipatory guidance, the nurse should discuss the possibility of such side effects with clients and spouses, since drugs and dosages can be changed to alleviate this side effect. Clients and spouses should be encouraged by the nurse to discuss any problems they might have with sexual dysfunction. The nurse can take the lead in these discussions, attempting to put spouses and clients at ease and to establish an atmosphere that is open and not embarrassing. Male clients from Latino cultures or other cultures that emphasize male superiority may find such side effects of medication intolerable. Only sensitive awareness on the part of the nurse may indicate that changes in drugs or dosages are necessary.

Adherence to pharmaceutical regimens over a long period of time requires that clients understand precisely why the medication is necessary and that clients believe the medication is helpful in alleviating health problems or symptoms. Consideration of cultural factors that might influence the nurse-client relationship will help the nurse understand the nature of the problems faced by a client who is attempting to comply with long-term drug therapy.

Diet and Exercise Patterns

The major emphasis in the dietary management of hypertension consists of sodium restriction; calorie restriction is included if the client is overweight, since weight gain is associated with an increased frequency of hypertension. One of the single most important factors in the prevention or elimination of high blood pressure is weight loss; sometimes the loss of just 10 or 15 pounds can bring blood pressure back to normal.

As with any other area of nursing care, the first step in assisting the client with dietary management is to begin with a detailed assessment of the client's eating preferences and dietary habits. Are there particular foods that clients believe they should eat to control or influence hypertension? Do clients or family members believe that the client should avoid any particular foods? For example, Snow (1974, 1983) indicated that some black clients confuse hypertension with a folk illness known as "high blood," for which they believe that it is important to eat astringent foods such as vinegar, lemon juice, and pickles and to avoid salts, fat, meats, and sweets. Roberson (1992) found that altering eating habits was viewed by some individuals as being far more difficult than following medication regimens. Some individuals in Roberson's study thought that because medication would control their blood pressure, they were free to eat anything they wanted. Most persons, however, tried consciously to reduce foods such as salt because they believed it was not good for them. A few added a home remedy to food such as sprinkling vinegar over a porkchop, a practice that they believed would neutralize the "bad effects" of pork. Often such folk beliefs and practices coexist along with biomedical practices, such as taking antihypertensive medications. Whenever clients must change their eating habits, the client's cultural background must be considered by nurses who are trying to help them.

Alcohol consumption needs to be assessed in clients with hypertension. Although the exact relationship is unknown, the consumption of alcohol appears to raise blood pressure. A study by Kaiser-Permanente found that three or more drinks per day is a definite risk factor in hypertension (Klatsy, 1977). Native Americans are at high risk for hypertension because of their high rate of alcohol consumption (U.S. Department of Health, Education and Welfare, 1978). Clients should be advised of this risk factor.

Because there is a strong correlation between hypertension and physical inactivity, as well as obesity, it is usually important in a weight-loss program for clients to increase their activity level as well as changing their diets. Advising the client about an exercise program calls for a careful evaluation of social and cultural factors that could influence nursing advice. Expecting clients to jog or walk in the evenings when they live in a high-crime area is inappropriate. Recommendations to join a spa or a fitness center or to enroll in a diet program are based on white middle- and upper-class value systems and behaviors. Such strategies need careful evaluation, together with the client's assets and goals, before nursing interventions can be formulated that are realistic and congruent with the client's goals, lifestyle, and cultural values.

Cultural and Behavioral Factors: Influences on Lifestyle

As discussed in Chapter 1, the range of cultural influences on the health of individuals is considerable. The remaining portion of this chapter focuses on three major components of cultural systems that shape individuals' reactions to chronic illness and help determine just how well individuals are able to make healthful changes in lifestyle. A description of family systems, coping styles, and health beliefs and practices is used to illustrate the significance of cultural influences on responses to chronic illness. Understanding something about these cultural factors will enable the nurse to anticipate client behavior and to plan care that is as congruent as possible with already established habits and lifestyles.

Family Support Systems: A Basis for Alterations in Lifestyle

Because the family is usually the individual's most important social unit, it provides the social context within which illness occurs and is resolved and within which health promotion and maintenance as well as treatment are defined and carried out. Being immersed in a chronic illness for a long period of time can isolate people as they lose common interests and can no longer share pursuits or hobbies with friends or family members (Charmaz, 1991). How the family as a unit or how individual members react to the client's illness may influence compliance with the treatment regimen. Thus a major consideration in nursing goals for clients who require alterations in lifestyle is the degree of congruence between the goals of the nurse and the goals of the family. The family is crucial in defining health and illness, in deciding whether to seek care, and in deciding how to use health care services (Wright and Leahey, 1987). Chapter 1 discussed cultural influences on health behavior and provided background information about how health decisions are made.

The nurse can recognize and use the family's role in altering the health status of a member, supporting lifestyle changes, and promoting and maintaining health. This requires an appreciation of the role of the family in diverse cultures. As a general rule, many cultural or ethnic groups in this country have variations of strong extended families. In the seven ethnic minority groups discussed by Orque, Bloch, and Monrroy (1983), the family was shown to be a principal source of support during illness. In the absence of family members, clients from other cultural groups may use alternative support groups such as religious or social organizations.

Some African-American families may demonstrate interchangeable roles for male and female as well as extended ties and networking among significant others. McAdoo (1981) described the African-American extended family as one in which there are strong generational ties among family members. Such families may be headed by the oldest female in the household. When members of African-American families are separated geographically from one another, they often remain in close contact with each other. This extension across geographic boundaries connects family units and individuals to a strong extended family network. Such families have a built-in mutual aid system for maintaining and helping individual members. LaFargue (1980), who has studied survival strategies in black families, states that "nurses are often unaware that black families have the social resources to immerse themselves in a domestic circle of kinfolk who will help them." When planning care that involves lifestyle changes for an African-American client, it is important to include key family members. It is especially important to enlist their support and encouragement in those nursing goals which significantly affect activities of daily living and/or affect the roles of other family members.

Latino families also have a strong sense of obligation to family members, and often the needs of the family are considered more important than those of the individual. In many Latino families, sex roles are clearly differentiated. Often the cultural values reinforce the view that the father is the head of the household, the provider, and the decision maker; his culturally defined role may be threatened if he is told that he has a chronic illness that will require long-term adaptations. Because of the strong family orientation of Latino families, the family plays a significant role in all aspects of the ill member's life, including either rejection or reinforcement of healthy lifestyle changes. It is therefore crucial that the family be involved in the plan of care from the beginning. Other cultural groups, such as Asian Americans, certain groups of European descent, and some religious groups, are also known for their strong family ties. Native Americans living in urban environments have strong ties to extended family members who have remained on the reservations and return frequently to visit even over considerable distances. For many American families, family solidarity and closeness have their basis in elements of traditional culture.

In addition to having strong family traditions, many cultural groups have a pronounced sense of "community," often as a result of discrimination or acculturation problems. In the past, immigrants to the United States often responded to initial rejection and hostility by bonding together and forming their own social organizations and services. These communities still offer their members social contacts, self-expression, leadership opportunities, and a sense of security and solidarity. Although it is not always possible to generalize, ethnic cultures as a rule tend to emphasize collective loyalties, especially to the family but also to the community.

Community bonds should be given careful consideration by nurses who are planning community-based nursing services. Many members of ethnic communities feel uncomfortable if they must leave familiar sites and places to seek health care. Screening and educational facilities can be established in local community schools, work settings, markets, community centers, or other places that are integral parts of the natural pathways of the community. It is always best to plan sites for health care that are located within the context of the community.

Coping Behaviors in Health and Illness

Although the term *coping ability* has broad usage, it is used here to indicate those behaviors which clients may use in the management of their long-term illness. Cultural groups have distinct prescriptions or guidelines for what they view as appropriate behavior in certain circumstances. Asian clients may use a certain coping style that at first may appear baffling or perplexing to health professionals. For example, with an emphasis on keeping interpersonal harmony, the Chinese are particularly conscious of a need to be agreeable to others. An Asian client may therefore nod her head in affirmation to everything the nurse says about her medication regimen regardless of whether she understands the instructions or has any intention of complying with the medication regimen. Her learned way of interacting with someone who is in authority denotes respect, and outward compliance dictates her reaction, at least up to a certain point. Such respectful behavior may make it difficult for the nurse to accurately evaluate or interpret the client's behavior in relation to nursing care needs. Orque (1983) suggested that Vietnamese clients may hesitate to ask the nurse questions in a group setting, since questioning of any authority figure may be interpreted as a sign of disrespect. In this situation, the group context in which health education is provided influences the manner in which clients cope with illness. Obviously, in such cultural groups, a one-on-one educational setting might be more appropriate.

Cultural beliefs about prescribed gender roles also may influence how persons cope with illness. Hautman and Bomar (1992) found that gender was important in how hypertension was conceptualized and described by African Americans. Females tended to believe that hypertension and stress were related. They discussed the need to talk and not keep things bottled up. On the other hand, male responders thought stress should be dealt with through action not talk. Other studies (Staples, 1982) have shown that African-American men hesitate to express their feelings or seek support because they see it as a sign of weakness. Such culturally defined feelings may influence how clients cope with stress and, ultimately, could affect their physical health as well.

Martinez (1978) observed that a Mexican-American client may find himself in difficulty if he is expected to disagree with an Anglo point of view. Direct argument with or contradiction of another person, especially a health professional, may be seen as rude and disrespectful. Latino culture's emphasis on good manners dictates that in any teaching program or dialogue the person be agreeable and not reveal his or her genuine opinion unless he or she knows the other person well or can take the time to differ tactfully. In such a situation, the nurse may assume that the client is in complete agreement with the treatment goals; such an error in judgment may later lead to disappointment and frustration.

In contrast, dominant American values include an emphasis on assertiveness, on questioning what one does not understand, and on open expression of feelings. Understanding how clients from different cultures use coping styles or strategies, the nurse can develop greater sensitivity in the care of clients from varied backgrounds and can plan care with clients and families that takes cultural factors into account.

Another cultural factor that influences clients' coping behaviors when they attempt to make changes in lifestyle is the culturally defined notion of what is appropriate to discuss with others, including health professionals. Murillo-Rohde (1981) says that among the cultural values of Latino Americans is the firm belief that one does not reveal personal or family information to strangers or even friends if this information has no relevance for them. Nurses should be culturally sensitive to such beliefs and help clients understand why such information is necessary and how it can help in planning and implementing care. Clients may even be reluctant to share details about health status and medical regimens with their families if they believe that such information will only cause them worry and anxiety. Therefore, the nurse who wishes to incorporate the assistance of the family or persons in other support systems into the care of the client should determine from the client whether this is appropriate and what information can be shared. Persons of Anglo-American cultural heritage are usually willing to discuss private and family matters relatively freely. Murillo-Rohde (1981) suggested that a Hispanic who is reluctant to disclose information to his or her family is also unlikely to disclose personal information to nurses involved in the management and provision of his or her nursing care. Only by being aware of such cultural factors and by establishing a nurse-client relationship that is based on cultural sensitivity can nurses obtain the kind of information that will enable them to provide care that is culturally acceptable to their clients.

Much has been written of the influence of fatalism in Latino cultures. Martinez (1978), for example, suggested that fatalism often can lead to a defeatist attitude, suggesting that there is little, if anything, that one can do about the course of life events. It follows that the best way to make life endurable is submission and acceptance. Obviously, such a world view presents a challenge to the nurse who is interested in assisting clients to make changes in their lifestyles and to become active participants in the management of chronic illness. Persons with such a conception of life may be highly resistant to the nurse's attempts to initiate lifestyle changes. Many clients may wish to improve their health status but do not try to do so because they have no expectations of success. If the nurse takes the time to explain what the nursing goals are, how the client can plan and initiate changes, how these changes fit into the client's lifestyle and goals, and what variations and alternatives are possible, it is more likely that the nurse and client can arrive at mutually agreed on goals and that the client will benefit from participation in the plan of care.

Health Beliefs

The client's attitudes and beliefs regarding health and illness should be ascertained. Chapter 1 described how clients may make a distinction between disease and illness. For many individuals, illness represents personal, interpersonal, and cultural reactions to discomfort. This may be especially evident in the client who is struggling to cope with the limitations posed by a chronic disease and who may relate primarily to limitations in daily activities. Illness, or the manner in which one perceives, experiences, and copes with a chronic disease, is culturally shaped. How clients talk about and describe health problems, the manner in which they exhibit or show symptoms, when and to whom they go for treatment, and whether they accept or reject prescribed treatments are all affected by cultural beliefs. Kleinman, Eisenberg, and Good (1978) suggest that the difficulties in living that result from a sickness are usually a source of worry for clients. Nurses should address those areas which are of concern to clients and family members. It is these concerns that are problematic in the care of clients with chronic diseases.

An understanding of the client's health beliefs and practices can be obtained from the data collected during the nursing assessment. The questions that might be asked by the nurse are shown in Box 7-1. What the client believes about hypertension and its causes, symptoms, and treatment may be thought of as the client's explanatory model of

---

Box 7-1. Questions for a Client Who Has Hypertension

What do you think caused your high blood pressure?

Why do you think it happened when it did?

What effect will having high blood pressure have on you?

What kind of treatment do you think you should receive?

Do you believe high blood pressure can be serious? Why?

Do you think your high blood pressure will last over a long period of time?

What are some of the problems that your illness has caused?

Some persons forget to take daily medications; does this happen to you?

What have you done to help you remember to take your pills?

What are the things about high blood pressure that frighten or worry you?

illness (Kleinman, Eisenberg, and Good, 1978). The term *explanatory model* is preferable to the term *folk health beliefs,* which derogatorily implies something "folksy," primitive, and nonscientific. The information obtained in the nursing assessment will enable the nurse to understand similarities and differences between the client's beliefs and attitudes regarding the illness and the nurse's own beliefs and attitudes. It takes a conscious and sustained effort on the part of the nurse to develop an understanding of cultural factors that influence a client's behavior. Some of the most important factors are those which relate to what the client experiences as illness or what causes problems for the client in everyday situations. Allowing clients to describe the difficulties they encounter on a personal and daily basis provides clues about basic values and attitudes regarding the impact of illness on activities in daily living. (See Research Box 7-1.)

A classic study (Snow, 1974) about health beliefs of low-income African Americans residing in Tucson, Arizona, can be used to illustrate how health beliefs influence the many ways that clients use to deal with a chronic disease such as hypertension. Snow (1974) described black cultural beliefs as a composite of the classic medicine of an earlier day, European folklore regarding the natural world, rare African traits, and selected beliefs derived from modern scientific medicine. Three major themes emerged from the data that Snow collected from black informants: (1) that the world is a dangerous and hostile place, (2) that the individual is liable to attack from either a punitive God or his malicious fellow humans, and (3) that the individual is helpless and has no internal resources with which to combat such an attack but must depend on outside aid. Snow's

Research Box 7-1. Alterations in Lifestyle: Transcultural Concepts in Chronic Illness

Barbee, E. L. (1994). Healing time: The blues and African-American women. *Health Care for Women International,* 15(1): 53–60.

Barbee explored dysphoric mood states experienced by 15 African-American women. The women identified three categories of depressed moods: feeling down/low, the blues, and depression. They described the blues as being on a continuum from mild to severe. Coping strategies for mild blues included self-comforting, solitary behaviors, whereas strategies for dealing with severe blues were spiritual, interpersonal, and solitary. Barbee suggested that the blues is an African-American cultural construct that differs qualitatively from the conception of feeling blue as determined by psychology or psychiatry. This construct symbolizes a transformative and regenerative experience that facilitates introspection and spiritual renewal for African-American women: a metaphor for healing time. While this study should not be generalized widely, the results are indicative that some cultural groups view dysphoria differently than do health professionals.

informants also classified phenomena causing illness as natural or unnatural or in terms of oppositions, expressed by proverbs stating that for every birth there is a death, that every illness has its cure, that every poison has an antidote, and so on. Snow suggests that this belief is largely responsible for the lack of acceptance of the chronicity of diseases; her informants believed that most illnesses were curable. She states, "If every illness has its cure, then what one must do is to find it; a new medicine, another treatment, a different doctor, faith healing perhaps—and the search is on" (p. 84).

Snow also described beliefs held by her informants regarding body physiology. Blood was described as being high or low, thick or thin, good or bad, clean or defiled. The blood system was believed to be in a constant state of change or flux and to respond directly to a number of internal and external stimuli. Snow suggests that this belief may preclude acceptance of the idea that certain conditions are chronic. If individuals believe that all they have to do to change the state of blood (and improve their health) is to wait for different weather conditions or to make a minor dietary change, it makes little sense to them to be told that a condition will last a lifetime. Another belief described in Snow's study is that the amount of blood in the body is not static but can increase or decrease, the level being affected primarily by diet. Extremes are viewed as dangerous. "High blood" is often terminologically confused with high blood pressure; strokes are believed to be caused by excess blood backing up into the brain. Certain foods are thought to have the property of bringing "high blood" down to more acceptable levels.

Another study of health beliefs among southern African Americans was conducted by Roberson (1983). She also found that a commonly described health problem was "high blood." This term was frequently confused with hypertension by both clients and local health professionals. Roberson found that informants conceptualized "high blood" in terms of blood volume, thickness, or even elevations of the blood in the body (e.g., "blood rushes to your head"). Thus they attributed causation primarily to factors they believed would "run blood up," such as salt, fat, meats, and sweets. Other causal factors in "high blood" were mental or emotional state, the nature of the person, the person's relationship with God or the devil, fate, or eternal forces, such as enemies putting a "conjure" on a person.

Some members of Latino cultures and other groups believe that an illness is sent by God as punishment for sin. Appalachian whites may explain sickness as "the wrath of God." Such cultural beliefs may present some difficulties for the nurse trying to help clients understand their illness; on the other hand, religious beliefs and practices also may help clients cope with their illness. Clients who view disease as a punishment from God may turn to culturally prescribed ways to deal with such an illness, such as praying, visiting a shrine, offering candles to a patron saint, or performing other healing rituals. Such activities should be supported by the nurse, since they do not preclude participation in other treatment options. Many Americans place a considerable emphasis on religion in their daily lives, and religion serves to explain many everyday happenings. This generalization applies to fervent believers as well as to nominal Catholics, Protestants, and members of other religious groups. Religious beliefs help us cope with many ordinary occurrences, including illness, and expressions of religious beliefs should be assessed and incorporated in the plan of care.

General beliefs about health and illness can be related to the care of clients who are attempting to change their behavior in response to a chronic disease. Henderson and Primeaux (1981) listed a number of characteristics that apply in general terms to traditional Native Americans. One of these characteristics is present orientation, or the tendency to live in the present without concern for the long-term future. Such a view on the part of a client poses a challenge to the nurse who is helping the client adjust to a chronic illness and the many changes that are necessary over a long period of time in daily life activities.

The concept of balance or harmony is an important health belief in many cultural groups. Often, everyday health beliefs and practices emphasize moderation to avoid excesses that bring on illness. Chinese Americans and members of Southeast Asian cultural groups may adhere to the yin/yang theory, according to which imbalances in either yin or yang may bring about illness or disease. Persons of Latino descent also may include concepts of balance or harmony among their health beliefs, including concepts of hot/cold and strong/weak. Hot and cold qualities are common notions in cultural explanations of health and illness states. The qualities of hot and cold have no relation ship to actual temperature but are ascribed states of various objects, persons, diseases, and treatment practices, including medications. Just how these particular health beliefs influence clients with hypertension or other chronic diseases is not well understood. However, failure to consider how these cultural concepts might apply to the care of culturally diverse clients may lead to inappropriate nursing actions.

Use of Traditional Healers and Other Health Practices

For many cultural groups, traditional practices involve consultation with different types of practitioners rather than professional medical doctors or nurses. Henderson and Primeaux (1981) stated that "the Indian medicine man is a vivid reminder that long before physicians, nurses, social workers and counselors intruded into their lives, Native Americans had folk cures for physical and mental illnesses." According to Wilson (1983), many Native Americans seek health care in a clinic or hospital only after going to a native healer. Often clients simultaneously seek care from both traditional healers and physicians, leading to a practice known as "dual use" of care providers.

The use of traditional practitioners has been well documented among Native Americans. Wilson (1983) suggested that many tribal practitioners use their knowledge in prevention, health maintenance, and treatment regimens. Unlike the tendency in Western culture to separate theology and medicine, religious beliefs and healing practices are interwoven in Native American culture. Total healing of the mind, body, and soul of a Native American patient is not complete if one who still believes and practices traditional ways is prevented from practicing them.

Similarly, clients of Hispanic descent may seek the services of a *curandero*, or traditional healer. Other cultural groups also may seek out persons who are culturally defined caregivers. For example, the black church acts as a cultural caretaker for many black persons, and the black minister may be the appropriate person to reinforce health beliefs and practices in traditional cultural systems. Jordan (1979) observed that other cultural healers that may be used in the black American cultural system are older women who have herbal knowledge, the spiritualist who has received the gift of healing from God, the voodoo priest or priestess, and the root doctor. Bailey (1991) suggested that African Americans tend to consult alternative health practitioners because of the limitations of their personal resources and the sociocultural environment. In addition, many older African Americans may believe that alternative practitioners may have some influence over life's general misfortunes and injustices.

Only a few studies have examined the use of traditional practices in the treatment of hypertension. One study (Payne, 1980) examined black clients' use of root teas, herbal teas, and food extracts such as garlic tablets to treat hypertension. The findings of this study were unclear as to the effects of home remedies on blood pressure readings and body weight. However, the study revealed that clients routinely use a wide variety of substances to treat hypertension, including yellow root, vinegar, cream of tartar, garlic water, vinegar and honey, water with lemon juice, and Epsom salts.

Many religious groups in the dominant American culture also incorporate religious leaders into healing practices. Almost all individuals have some form of belief system that guides their life decisions and to which they turn in times of stress. A person's religious beliefs frequently give meaning to illness. Usually the client is the best source of information in planning for involvement of cultural healers or members of the clergy.

Certainly it cannot be assumed that all members of a particular culture will seek alternative treatment outside the professional system, but many clients from all cultures do. The decision to seek alternative care is an individual one and must be elicited carefully during the nursing history. Persons who suffer from chronic illnesses seem particularly prone to seek alternative care in part because health professionals cannot offer a "cure." Knowledge of what a client believes and does about an illness is helpful in planning for nursing interventions that require the client's active participation.

Summary

Health professionals should develop a respect for the cultural beliefs and practices of clients even when they run counter to scientific medical systems. These beliefs and practices have survived for generations and may be quite effective in helping clients. Attempting to change deeply held health beliefs through ridicule and skepticism not only may fail but also may alienate clients.

Cultural concepts can help the nurse improve care to culturally diverse clients. Such knowledge will help nurses fully appreciate the impact of culture on themselves and clients and enable them to provide nursing care on a personal basis. The cultural dimensions of an individual client are as important to assess as are the physiologic and psychological states. Incorporation of cultural knowledge into the nursing process is especially important in the care of clients with chronic disease. Nursing care can help clients cope successfully with illness by encouraging alterations in lifestyle that enable clients to minimize symptoms and improve health status. Cultural knowledge forms the basis of understanding needs and planning care, especially when substantial daily alterations in living must be made. Ongoing daily life situations are strongly influenced by cultural context, and alterations in daily living will be successful only when the nursing process includes consideration of the client's cultural setting, social relations, and daily environment. Understanding how cultural factors relate to health and illness is essential knowledge on which to base decisions about the care of the clients.

Learning Activities

1. Interview a culturally different client who has hypertension (or substitute another chronic illness). Ask the client the questions shown in Box 7-1.

2. Locate a traditional healer or an "alternative" practitioner such as a chiropractor in your community. Make an appointment to discuss health beliefs about disease causation and treatment. Ask about training and/or preparation for the healing role.

3. Analyze the major causes of excess morbidity in a subcultural group in your geographic area. Propose culturally appropriate solutions to the chronic health problems faced by that group.

4. Provide examples of negative responses by nurses or other health professionals to clients from other cultures. How might the health care professionals have engaged in culturally appropriate care?

References

Ailinger, R. L. (1982). Hypertension knowledge in a Hispanic community. *Nursing Research, 31*(4): 207–210.

Anderson, S. V., and Bauwens, E. (1981). *Chronic Health Problems: Concepts and Application*. St. Louis: C. V. Mosby.

Bailey, E. J. (1991). *Urban African American Health Care*. Lanham, MD: University Press of America, Inc.

Boyle, E., Jr. (1970). Biological pattern in hypertension by race, sex, body weight, and skin color. *Journal of the American Medical Association, 213*: 1637–1643.

Charmaz, K. (1993). *Good Days and Bad Days: The Self in Chronic Illness*. Newark, NJ: Rutgers University Press.

Hautman, M. A., and Bomar, P. (1992). Gender differences in knowing about hypertension: The black experience. *Health Care for Women International, 13*(1): 57–65.

Heckler, M. M. (1985). *Report of the Secretary's Task Force on Black and Minority Health*. Washington: U.S. Government Printing Office.

Henderson, G., and Primeaux, M. (1981). *Transcultural Health Care*. Menlo Park, CA: Addison-Wesley.

Jordan, W. C. (1979). The roots and practices of voodoo medicine in America. *Urban Health, 8*: 38–41.

Klatsky, A. K. (1977). Alcohol consumption and blood pressure: Kaiser-Permanente multiphasic health examination data. *New England Journal of Medicine, 296*: 1194.

Kleinman, A., Eisenberg, L., and Good, B. (1978). Culture, illness and care: Clinical lessons. Anthropologic and cross-cultural research. *Annals of Internal Medicine, 88*: 251–258.

LaFargue, J. P. (1980). A survival strategy: Kinship networks. *American Journal of Nursing, 80*: 1636–1640.

Leahey, M., and Wright, L. M. (1987). Families and chronic illness: Assumptions, assessment and intervention. In L. M. Wright and M. Leahey (Eds.), *Families and Chronic Illness* (pp. 55–76). Springhouse, PA: Springhouse.

Martinez, R. A. (1978). *Hispanic Culture and Health Care*. St. Louis: C. V. Mosby.

McAdoo, H. D. (1991). *Black Families*, Part II. Beverly Hills: Sage Publications.

Murillo-Rohde, I. (1981). Hispanic American patient care. In G. Henderson and M. Primeaux (Eds.), *Transcultural Health Care*. Menlo Park, CA: Addison-Wesley.

National Heart, Lung, and Blood Institute (1985). Hypertension prevalence and the status of awareness, treatment, and control in the United States. Final report of the subcommittee on definition and prevalence of the 1984 joint national committee. *Hypertension 7*(3): 457–468.

Orque, M. S. (1983). Nursing care of South Vietnamese patients. In M. S. Orque, B. Bloch, and L. S. Monrroy (Eds.), *Ethnic Nursing Care: A Multicultural Approach* (pp. 245–269). St. Louis: C. V. Mosby.

Orque, M. S., Bloch, B., and Monrroy, L. S. (1983). *Ethnic Nursing Care: A Multicultural Approach*. St. Louis: C. V. Mosby.

Payne, Z. A. (1980). Diet and folk remedies: The influence of cultural patterns on medical management. *Urban Health, 9*: 24–28.

Roberson, M. H. B. (1983). Folk Health Beliefs and Practices of Rural Black Virginians (Doctoral dissertation, University of Utah, 1983). *Dissertation Abstracts International, 44*: 2113B.

Roberson, M. H. B. (1992). The meaning of compliance: Patient perspectives. *Qualitative Health Research, 2*(1): 7–26.

Snow, L. F. (1974). Folk medical beliefs and their implications for the care of patients: A review based on studies among black Americans. *Annals of Internal Medicine, 81*: 82–96.

Snow, L. F. (1983). Traditional health beliefs and practice among lower-class black Americans. *Western Journal of Medicine, 139*(6): 820–828.

Spector, R. (1991). *Cultural Diversity in Health and Illness*, 3d Ed. Norwalk, CN: Appleton & Lange.

Staples, R. (1982). *Black Masculinity*. San Francisco: Black Scholar Press.

U.S. Department of Health, Education, and Welfare (1978). *The Service*. Rockville, MD: Health Services Administration Pub. No. (HSA) 78-1003.

U.S. Department of Health and Human Services (1990). *Healthy People 2000: National Health Promotion and Disease Prevention Objectives*. Washington: U.S. Government Printing Office, Publication No. (PHS) 91-50213.

Wilson, U. M. (1983). Nursing care of American Indian patients. In M. S. Orque, B. Bloch, and L. S. Monrroy (Eds.), *Ethnic Nursing Care: A Multicultural Approach* (pp. 271–295). St. Louis: C. V. Mosby.

Wright, L. M., and Leahey, M. (1987). *Families and Chronic Illness*. Springhouse, PA: Springhouse Corporation.

8

Transcultural Perspectives in Mental Health

Kathryn Hopkins Kavanagh

Introduction

There was a time when mental illness did not exist in Western society. People had problems and some were psychotic, but whether tolerated, pitied, shunned, or punished and whether they lived out their years or died, the "mad" were more likely to be viewed as fools or possessed than ill. With the social conscience of the 18th century, the mentally ill were given refuge in asylums, where, isolated and in large part gratefully forgotten by society, they received little more than shelter (Conrad and Schneider, 1992). Today's mentally ill are for the most part in the community, where they often confront severe social and economic strains while mental health care and needs continue to change (Billings, 1993).

The "browning of America" refers to changes in the U.S. population and to projections that by the middle of the 21st century the average resident, as defined by Census statistics, will trace his or her ancestry to Africa, Asia, the Pacific Islands, or the Hispanic or Arab worlds rather than to European roots (Henry, 1990). By 2050, for example, one out of every five Americans will be Hispanic (U.S. Census Bureau, as cited by U.S. Department of Health and Human Services, 1991). However, human diversity is not limited to culture or ethnicity. It exists everywhere that there are differences, which include age, sex, experience, socioeconomic status, social views, gender preferences, race, and so on. It is important to keep in mind that transcultural nursing is limited to neither health care nor culture in the sense of ethnicity; it involves all human diversity.

The United States may be the most diverse society that has ever existed, yet the nation is only now breaking away from stereotyped "one size fits all" expectations of medical treatment and nursing care. New themes related to diversity in mental health care are developing: advocacy and empowerment (Dunst, Trivette, and Deal, 1988),

Margaret M. Andrews and Joyceen S. Boyle: TRANSCULTURAL CONCEPTS IN NURSING CARE, SECOND EDITION. © 1995 J.B. Lippincott Company.

participatory decision making, diversity (Kavanagh and Kennedy, 1992), pluralism, and multiculturalism (Locke, 1992). In short, clients are increasingly committed to recognition of rights for their reference groups, as well as involvement in their health care. This means that they expect care that matches their cultural standards.

This chapter discusses transcultural nursing as it relates specifically to psychiatric and mental health nursing. The goal is to present a practical and flexible framework that includes a balance of sensitivity, knowledge, and skills (Kavanagh and Kennedy, 1992). The framework presented is premised on the value of respectful, open, mutual communication and collaborative relationships with clients. Conversely, the medium for both collaborative treatment and diversity management is mutual communication. This approach portrays the client as someone more expert about his or her situation than the health care provider is and from whom the nurse (or other provider) can learn to understand the situation as the client does. The transcultural nurse is conceptualized as someone with the ability to manage diversity effectively, when management of diversity is defined as helping each person to reach his or her full potential (Thomas, 1991).

A balance of sensitivity, knowledge, and skills allows nurses to link awareness and sensitivity with knowledge of typical, expectable group patterns. Sensitivity and knowledge, in combination with cultural assessment, communication, and other mental health nursing skills, can produce respectful, culturally acceptable, and effective nursing interventions for diverse peoples in specific, individual situations. However, limiting attention to sensitivity leaves the sensitive nurse powerless, since he or she still lacks the knowledge and skills required to act knowingly on the issue. Knowledge of expectable cultural patterns provides starting places against which the reality of a given situation can be tested. Such knowledge differs from stereotypes, which lock out real evidence through acknowledgment of only that which was expected. Lack of sensitivity, knowledge, and skill may be involved when people are labeled "noncompliant," "problem patients," or too resistant or defensive to benefit from treatment or to recognize the value of the care being offered. Might it be that the client's ideas about care and caring (and their expression) simply differ from those of the nurse?

Mental Illness and Mental Disease

In many ways, health and illness are more central to transcultural psychiatric/mental health nursing than are mental diseases. Much of the counseling, therapy, and other care given by mental health professionals focuses on illness prevention and making everyday life better. The distinction between illness and disease is important. Illness emphasizes subjective behavioral, psychological, sociocultural, and experiential dimensions of disorders. Disease, in contrast, pertains to chemical, physiologic, and other organic and objective phenomena related to sickness (Helman, 1990). Biologic disorders of memory, perception, and feeling surely exist, as do compensatory processes of rationalization and action that are strongly influenced by social and cultural factors. Rates of mental illness and of mental diseases do not seem to vary much among groups when social and economic factors are controlled. There is no conclusive evidence that mental illness rates vary with race or other intrinsic human characteristics, although they are clearly associated with low socioeconomic status, low educational level, separation, and loss.

Four-fifths of the global population lives in non-Western countries, while most psychiatric resources are in Western societies. The schizophrenias, manic-depressive disorders, major depressions, and anxiety disorders are thought to occur throughout the world. Depression anxieties and somatiform disorders (that is, the expression of problems in physical rather than psychological signs and symptoms) are probably more prevalent in the non-Western world than are infectious diseases (Kleinman, 1991). However, despite international epidemiologic and research efforts, there are at present no international polices or centers focused on mental health treatment programs comparable with, for example, the World Health Organization. The global emphasis has been on physical health (Kleinman, 1991).

Every society has systems of beliefs and practices related to health care and specific persons trained as healers. There are many places where biomedicine is not widely available and most people depend on traditional healers, although they also exist (and are depended on) in modern, Westernized societies. Whereas shamans and traditional healers are often not very effective with chronic mental disorders, the outcome for some conditions tends to be more positive in those societies where clients are not negatively stigmatized and are not alone with their problems. In Western societies, persons with psychiatric disorders tend to be devalued, which can demoralize, isolate, dehumanize, and curtail the development of potential support systems (Beiser et al., 1987). American individualism and self-reliance further reinforce a tendency toward social isolation and alienation. Additionally, many individuals cross cultures, which requires special psychosocial resilience and adaptation (Kim and Gudykunst, 1988; McCubbin and McCubbin, 1988; Ory et al., 1991).

There is probably more variation among etiologic beliefs of mental health care professionals than is commonly acknowledged, but belief in relatively impersonal, natural causation generally prevails. For a variety of reasons or simply by chance, parts, systems, families, or individuals take on characteristics that are assessed as dysfunctional. In contrast, members of many cultural groups believe that illness is caused by a supernatural being (a deity or god), a nonhuman being (such as an ancestor, a ghost, or an evil spirit), or another human being (a witch or sorcerer). The sick person in such a case is viewed as a victim not responsible for his or her condition or its resolution. Some peoples have no concept of accident, so every phenomenon is accounted for as the result of intent by an outside force.

Diagnosis: Problems with Normality and Abnormality

The division of illnesses into physical and mental categories is Western, although every society labels some behaviors as abnormal. The cultural assumption that mind and body are somehow separate, which is now increasingly challenged in terms of relationships between healing and the mind (Moyers, 1993; Goleman and Gurin, 1993), has for several centuries strongly swayed Western ideas about normality and abnormality. What is considered "normal" and what is "abnormal" are based on cultural perspective. Culture influences expression, presentation, recognition, labeling, explanations for, and distribution of illness.

Interpretations of health and of even overt signs of physical disease vary widely. Mental health and mental illnesses are more difficult than physical disorders to delineate because of the lack of readily observable, discrete, and organic phenomena. The symptoms of mental illness, dependent as they are on behavioral expression, vary because they depend on social definitions rather than physical measures. Assessment is based on the appropriateness of behaviors (e.g., dress, posture, smell, gestures, speech, and facial expression) that lack fixed standards and depend on context and social relationships to differentiate what is normal from what is abnormal. Although psychiatry is part of Western biomedicine, it deals with ambiguous areas such as self and symbolic behavior, deviance and marginality, power and control (Fabrega, 1989). Diagnoses involve social competence, which, to be evaluated sensitively, must be assessed against culture-specific criteria. Many cultures do not dichotomize normality and abnormality as rigidly as Western societies often tend to or even distinguish health from illness. These may be viewed as we are now beginning to—as multidimensional, continual, and perhaps overlapping (Helman, 1990), with ideas about mental health and mental illness mixed with those about medicine. To members of such societies, concepts such as mental health have little meaning. The distinction between illness and health may be based on the ability to perform one's normal roles in society. A physician's diagnosis, prognosis, and treatment, based on imprecise and unobservable phenomena, may seem ludicrous.

The pattern used by a client to express concern or disorder is referred to as a *language of distress* (Helman, 1990). Close examination of how people express themselves and interact is essential in understanding relationships between psychiatric and social factors. The same phenomena (for example, visions and dream states, trance states, hallucinations, delusions, belief in spirits, speaking in "tongues," drug or alcohol intoxication, or suicide) may be judged normal or abnormal according to the settings and circumstances in which they occur (Conrad and Schneider, 1992). At times, cultural groups encourage altered states of consciousness that may be viewed as mental disturbances to others. However, because addictive substances (such as alcohol, tobacco, and opiates) in most societies were traditionally reserved for use during special times or rituals, widespread related health problems were seldom problematic. Today, on the other hand, Western redefinition of deviant alcohol and drug use as disease (rather than as a social, moral, or legal issue) has made this a primary mental health concern (Conrad and Schneider, 1992).

How symptoms are expressed and how they are perceived and treated by others vary widely. Although psychotic disorders occur in every society and the primary symptoms (that is, social and emotional withdrawal, auditory hallucinations, general delusions, flat affect, mood changes, and insomnia) occur across cultures, the secondary features of these disorders are highly influenced by culture (Tripp-Reimer, 1984). For example, in some groups, guilt and suicide ideation do not accompany depression; in others, they frequently do. In various Melanesian societies, suicide is an acceptable escape from problems ranging from marital dissension, illness, sorcery, and spinsterhood to criticism from others (Romannucci-Ross, 1983). Analogously, in some groups, somatic (physical) rather than psychological symptoms are prominent among depressed individuals; in others, such as middle-class European Americans, psychological "blues" prevail. Somatization pertains to a preoccupation with physical symptoms that are thought to have a psychological rather than physical cause. Somatic symptoms that express psychological distress occur at high rates, for example, among clients who are Hispanic (Escobar, 1987) or Chinese (Kleinman, 1988). It would not be unusual for nurses to encounter clients who deny being depressed but complain of headaches, backaches, stomach aches, and other physical phenomena prompted (and sometimes consciously associated) with sorrow and suffering.

The content of delusions and hallucinations also reflects cultural patterns. For instance, the content may be primarily psychological, religious or spiritual, moral or social, naturalistic or supernatural, or physical or medical. In western Ireland, psychiatric patients tend to have delusions of a religious nature (Scheper-Hughes, 1978), while American schizophrenics more often have persecution delusions involving electromagnetic or other secular phenomena (Oltmanns and Maher, 1988; Helman, 1990), believing perhaps that their toasters talk to them or current from electrical outlets is altering their thinking. Likewise, some groups may associate sex with guilt, while others do not (Sanday and Goodenough, 1990; Bohannan, 1992). For example, middle-class European-American criticism of sex and pregnancy outside of marriage among African Americans does not take into account the social history that made many black women vulnerable to unwanted sexual activity and which, over time, helped many to redefine extramarital sex and pregnancy as events apart from moral apprehension.

Some conditions, such as posttraumatic stress disorder, can occur in various forms anywhere. Others, known as *culture-bound syndromes*, exist within specific cultural groups. Some conditions may represent labeling differences, as in China, where the term *neurasthenia* is widely used for symptoms produced by social stressors and may correspond to what Western medicine refers to as *depression*. Some conditions fall into categories of folk illnesses that defy Western psychiatric identification, although they are very real to the persons experiencing them. Examples of folk illnesses include fright or soul loss (*susto*), which is often associated by Hispanics with a sudden start or sneeze. Various conditions thought to result from the evil eye (*mal ojo*) are believed to occur unintentionally when, for instance, a nurse fails to touch a child he or she has noticed or examined. Herbal remedies, rubbing, massage, and other physical manipulations by *curanderos* (*curanderas*, if they are women) are typical treatments. These might be used with home remedies (such as teas) or prayers and trips to religious shrines or charismatic folk healers to alleviate distress.

The United States has numerous folk illnesses, such as "nervous breakdown," which occur throughout the society. There are also culture-bound syndromes. Anorexia nervosa, for example, occurs only where food is abundant. Other culture-bound syndromes are seen more often in traditional, nonindustrialized societies and in immigrants from those. Despite the exotic nature of many of the classic culture-bound syndromes, it is useful to know of the existence of these ethnic or "reactive" psychoses (Yap, 1977). Several culture-bound syndromes are described in Box 8-1.

Misdiagnosis [for example, with overdiagnosis of antisocial disorders and psychoses and underdiagnosis of depressions (Brown, 1990)] is a major problem among members of groups that differ from the European-American, middle-class, Christian, and male orientation that dominates American culture (Collins et al., 1990; Secundy, 1992). An example of a commonly misdiagnosed folk illness is "falling out," a stress-relieving pattern of shaking and falling that typically occurs when sympathetic others are present and is seen among African Americans, Haitians, Anglos, and other southern ethnic groups (Weidman, 1979; Gaines, 1992). Adding to the complexity of psychiatric diagnoses is the fact that despite the influence of culture on patterned psychological and physical conditions, there are also individual or idiosyncratic explanations and expressions of behavior.

Box 8-1. Culture-Bound Syndromes

Amok: An acute reaction resulting from morbid hostility (Yap, 1977). Our vernacular term "running amok" comes from the frenzied lashing out associated with this syndrome.

Malignant anxiety: Acute anxiety states with panic and varying degrees of egodisorganization (Yap, 1977) that have been associated with criminality and loss of stable culture due to colonialism.

Pibloktog: "Arctic hysteria" among Polar Eskimos. Accounts are of bizarre, overdramatized behavior, such as running naked through the snow (Parker, 1977).

Susto: A traumatic, anxiety-depressive state with psychophysiologic changes; "fright sickness" that results from such stimuli as a fall, a thunderclap, meeting some threat, or other frightening experiences. Susto causes anxiety, insomnia, listlessness, loss of appetite, and social withdrawal. This folk illness occurs throughout Latin America (Rubel, 1977; Uzzell, 1977).

Trance dissociation: Possession syndromes occurring in various parts of the world with varying degrees of social sanction (Yap, 1977). This differs from primary schizophrenic reactions and is believed to be caused by disease, the loss of one's soul, or the invasion of a benign or evil spirit. In some circumstances, it is viewed as a mystical state. Some Native American vision quests resulted in altered states of consciousness similar to this.

Voodoo death: "Magical" or sociocultural death that has been explained as the result of "flight or fight" response, belief in the power of threat and suggestion, and the acceptance of hopelessness (Lex, 1977).

There is a "new cross-cultural psychiatry" (Kleinman, 1988) that extends the thinking of many psychiatrists to allow for culturally based explanatory models of client behavior. However, at the same time, the widely used series of American Psychiatric Association's *Diagnostic and Statistical Manuals of Mental Disorders* (e.g., DSM-III and DSM-III-R) requires surrender of many cultural insights (Conrad and Schneider, 1992; Eisenbruch, 1992). These frameworks organize symbolic and instrumental evidence of those forms of deviance which are considered medical concerns (Conrad and Schneider, 1992), providing the medical community with administratively useful classifications for diagnosis and record keeping. However, despite varying cultural expressions of psychiatric problems, in less affluent countries than the United States, where library funds are particularly limited, the *Diagnostic and Statistical Manual of Mental Disorders* standards tend to be used as the ultimate text on psychiatric diagnoses and categories (Littlewood, 1991; Eisenbruch, 1992). This seems contradictory to the evidence that although medical involvement in madness has been recorded for at least 2000 years, those aspects of treatment and care which foster transcultural understanding emerge more as humanitarian reform than biomedical accomplishment (Conrad and Schneider, 1992).

Mental Health Needs, Beliefs, and Practices

Realizing that perspectives are shaped by specific values and beliefs rooted in specific cultures, classes, and time periods allows objective assessment of diverse practices that people employ to promote health and cope with illness. Whether or not they are understood, people have reasons for their behavior. They may, for example, refuse to have blood drawn due to a belief that it could be used for sorcery or, as was traditionally believed in Japan, that blood contains the personality. It does not make sense to risk personality loss with blood donation or confusion with some else's as a consequence of transfusion. On the other hand, it does make sense for clients to alter their medication dosages when they believe that the "large" American physicians who prescribe medicines are likely to order too large a dose for someone of smaller statute (Goode, 1993). Appreciating that what is to one individual a "superstition" may be to someone else a firmly held explanation or belief allows the sensitive and knowledgeable nurse to objectively consider the behavior associated with that belief for its own merit, neutrality, or harm. Automatic discrediting of ideas or practices because they are unfamiliar, "old fashioned," or not scientific risks alienation of clients, as well as loss of potentially useful resources.

Mental health care is not a "one size fits all" proposition. Even mental health is not the same for everyone. Parenting is only one of myriad areas of concern to transcultural nurses, but it provides a useful example of the diversity inherent in fulfilling a universal need. Understanding parenting patterns requires discerning parents' ideas and expectations about their children, child-rearing traditions, and knowledge and beliefs about child development (Steinhausen et al., 1988), as well as assessment of the child and actual situation. Not everyone parents the same way; some, for example, may view "good parenting" as keeping a child safe, fed, and clean without including activities that stimulate cognitive, affective, and physical development. Parents, and particularly single adults, are more alone with child-rearing responsibilities in industrialized societies than is the case in societies in which extended families are more common and socialization responsibilities are shared with other adults. Growth and development are additionally influenced by cultural patterns that encourage protecting children from some facts of life while exposing them very early to others. In the United States, for example, children typically learn little about economically productive roles when they are young. However, although they may not observe their parents working, they are likely to be exposed at a tender age to adult sexual roles and to violence via the media.

Social and environmental conditions often lead to mental health problems. Substantial proportions of children and adolescents live in poverty, with severe mental health ramifications (Scheper-Hughes, 1987). Children and adolescents or every social class and ethnic background are vulnerable to sexual and physical abuse (Levinson, 1989). High rates of depression are associated with problems in areas of family and personal relationships, finances, and general living conditions. Crime, drug use, and suicide are prevalent problems that may be associated with limited perceived hope (Jackson, 1990; Poussaint, 1990). Although disorganized and dysfunctional families are not specific to the poor, the poor often have higher mortality and morbidity rates (Levinson, 1989). Painful separation, torture, loss, bereavement, and uncertainty have made posttraumatic stress syndrome a popular DSM-III diagnosis for persons of any age and any traumatic background (Eisenbruch, 1992).

Demographic shifts have implications for mental health. Lower levels of fertility mean that future elders will have fewer adult children and kin as potential caregivers. Increased geographic mobility and separate living styles result in loose social networks and increased social alienation. Immigration can lead to conflict between traditional and modern roles. Correspondingly, increased divorce rates often disrupt the flow of personal support. Today, many members of groups that were traditionally cohesive find themselves isolated from culturally relevant support persons (Bond and Harvey, 1991). Rapid increases in the populations of older adults have led to ethnogerontology, the study of relationships between culture and age and their impact on physical and mental well-being as contexts, roles, prestige, and social interaction patterns change (Sokolovsky, 1990; Fry, 1990; Burnside, 1988; Dewit, Wister, and Burch, 1988; Michelson et al., 1991).

The Challenge of Categories

Understanding social classification systems and interactive processes that facilitate communication and sensitivity, as well as those which perpetuate social distance and inequality, is important because these patterns strongly influence people's experiences. Everyone handles huge amounts of information every day. It is reasonable that categories are used to organize related items so that information does not become totally overwhelming. The problem with these groupings is that they may be based on stereotypes.

Stereotypes are simple links in memory between a person and a particular trait (Brislin, 1993). They create broad categories. Stereotypic ideas often capture characteristics that are real and common in the group (Seelye, 1993). However, stereotypes also may be out of date and dangerously limited. People tend to see what they expect to see, and stereotypes narrow vision by ignoring variations that occur naturally within groups. If one stereotypes all psychiatric patients as dangerous, for example, the generalization does not accurately represent the high percentage of patients who are not. When seen through stereotypic lenses, various realities are oversimplified. Aspects of individuality get left out that may be important to understanding and to providing care.

There is an important difference between stereotypes and generalizations. Stereotypes are like images frozen in time and cause one to see what one expects to see, even when reality differs from that. Descriptive generalizations, in contrast, serve only as changeable starting places. There are group patterns that are valuable to know. Nurses must be flexible enough to know those general patterns *and* to recognize variations when they occur. For instance, being aware that in many traditional societies women are expected (and expect) to follow the lead of the men in their families (whether father, husband, brother, or son) is helpful when caring for a female patient who defers to her male relatives for answers to questions even about herself. The same behavior among members of Westernized, modern societies may have different implications. One would have to explore the situation further to avoid risking intervening on the basis of stereotypes that may not fit the individuals involved. The ways that these interactive processes relate to each other are condensed in Figure 8-1.

Stereotypes are particularly dangerous when they involve negative beliefs about a group. These lead to *prejudgment* (or *prejudice*) that ignores actual evidence. Prejudice involves negative feelings about groups different from one's own, regardless of how they are different. These attitudes are based on limited knowledge, limited contact, and

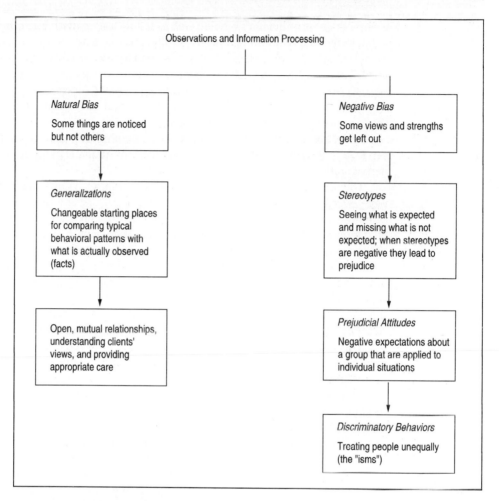

Figure 8-1. Social classification and interactive processes influence how we relate to others. How these processes relate to each other is shown above.

emotional responses rather than on careful observation and thought. They are beliefs, opinions, or points of view that are formed before the facts are known. Facts that contradict a prejudice may be left unexplored or be ignored (Kluegel and Smith, 1986). For example, a nursing student expected a Chinese patient to like rice, drink tea, and use chopsticks to eat. When he grabbed a fork off someone else's tray, it was interpreted as aggressive behavior due to a combination of the student's fixed cultural expectations and negative stereotypes about both psychiatric patients and people who are ethnically and racially different than she is. The frustrated patient was angry about being expected to "act Chinese."

Stereotypes can be favorable as well as unfavorable, although both types disregard real facts for preconceived notions. Take, for example, a situation in which an individual of Asian or Asian-American background is expected to excel in school or mathematics due to stereotypes that associate Asians with scholarly accomplishments. Since every group has some individuals who do well in school and in math and others who do not, Asian individuals who struggle academically must contend with a sense of group as well as individual failure. The same process is seen in many forms: a child may be expected to do well because his or her older siblings did, people with glasses may be expected to read a lot of books, or all blacks may be expected to be great dancers or athletes. These are not negative stereotypes, but they are potentially harmful because they impose expectations that are unrealistic, just as negative stereotypes do.

There are several types of prejudice that are commonly observed in health care and can lead to discriminatory behavior there. Discrimination is prejudice that is expressed behaviorally.

The time when African Americans and other blacks, Asians, and Native Americans were overtly discriminated against and prevented from entering the U.S. social and economic mainstream is officially over. However, the stereotypes and prejudices associated with racial status may have mellowed, but they remain despite formal integration. For instance, negative stereotypes associating African Americans with poverty, drugs, and violence do not do justice to the fact that most African Americans are not poor and have nothing to do with either drugs or violence. Assuming that a patient is on welfare because he or she is black or that addiction is an issue or physical aggression a likelihood may lead to treatment that is different from that given clients who are not African American. Similarly, other negative stereotypes and prejudices result in unequal treatment.

These discriminatory interaction patterns have acquired the label "isms" because of their common word endings. Each "ism" involves a tendency to judge others according to similarity with or dissimilarity from a standard considered ideal or normal. Whatever the issue or level (personal or group), an "ism" is centered on one's own or a group's judgment (Brislin, 1993). Centered on oneself, for example, one is *egocentric*. When an entire society puts forth one way of doing or thinking as best, it is *sociocentric*, as in Eurocentric or Afrocentric education. Ethnic groups are groups that share historical and sociocultural backgrounds while existing within a larger society (Essed, 1991). We frequently hear about ethnocentric views. Nearly every ethnic group sees itself as "best." However, in a society composed of multiple groups, care must be taken to counteract such biases, or discrimination and social injustices occur. (See Box 8-2.)

Ethnicity

In the early part of this century, the goal was to Americanize the many peoples who came from all over the world to make their homes in the United States. They had to learn English and become as much a part of the dominant culture as they could, often compromising or even giving up their original cultures. Times have changed. As the century closes, people from diverse ethnic and other backgrounds expect, demand, and are viewed as deserving opportunities to preserve their various lifestyles, beliefs, and practices. Some people find the trend toward increased diversity (particularly recognition of ethnic, racial, and gender-oriented groups) threatening. Others view it as an opportunity to make America live up to its democratic ideals (Wali, 1992). In any event, this transition is occurring. And nurses must be prepared to care for this diverse population.

Many differences in mental health care needs are attributable to ethnic variation (Comas-Diaz and Griffith, 1988), although it must be remembered that there is signifi-

Box 8-2. The "Isms"

Egocentrism: The assumption that oneself is superior to others. An example of this involves someone who has never been diagnosed as mentally ill (a staff member, for instance) who thinks he or she is better than those who are diagnosed as ill.

Ethnocentrism: The assumption that one's own cultural or ethnic group is superior to that of others. *Ethnicity* refers to cultural differences and should not be confused with race. Ethnocentrism occurs, for example, when everyone is expected to speak English and to know the rules (many of which are implicit) for living in this society.

Sociocentrism: The assumption that one society's way of knowing or doing is superior to others. It may be assumed, for instance, that biomedicine is effective and folk medicines are not. Actually, there is much evidence that this is not always the case. Many traditional societies have highly effective, community-oriented ways of treating those patients that modern Western medicine calls "psychiatric."

Racism: The assumption that members of one race are superior to those of another (*Race* refers to presumed biologic differences.)

Sexism: The assumption that members of one sex are superior to those of the other. For example, women have historically been viewed as less rational and more emotional and subject to mental illness than men.

Heterosexism: The assumption that everyone is or should be heterosexual and that heterosexuality is superior and expectable. It is relatively recently that homosexuality was redefined as a lifestyle rather than a disease.

Agism: The assumption that members of one age group are superior to those of others. Young patients and staff may not be taken as seriously as those who are older.

Adultism: The assumption that adults are superior to youths and can or should control, direct, reprimand, reward, or deprive them of respect. Children in American society are, for example, often interrupted or ignored by adults. They may not be given choices that allow them to learn how to cope with specific situations.

Sizism: The assumption that people of one body size are superior to or better than those of other shapes and sizes. Positions involving interaction with the public, for example, may be denied individuals who are very heavy or who otherwise fail to meet the standards of ideal appearance.

Classism/elitism: The assumption that certain people are superior because of their social and economic status or position in a group or organization. This often assumes that those with more money or education are superior. A poorly dressed high school drop-out, for example, may not be given the same treatment options offered to a well-dressed college graduate.

"Ableism": The assumption that the able-bodied and sound of mind are physically or developmentally superior to those who are disabled, retarded, or otherwise different. An example of "ableism" is not offering a chronically ill patient choices due to the assumption that he or she does not want to or cannot make decisions.

cant diversity within each group, as well as between groups, and that many people cross groups, identifying with and belonging to several. Another important factor is that some peoples are very traditional in their views, while others are more acculturated and modern, although again there can be great variation within groups and even families. Despite the limitations imposed because ethnic categories are not mutually exclusive in a diverse society such as the United States, it is useful for transcultural nurses to be aware of the generalized patterns associated with those aggregates who represent increasingly large proportions of the total population.

African Americans

Distinguished from others who come to the United States from the Caribbean Islands or from Africa, African Americans today are very diverse. Long-term discrimination in a predominately "white" culture has perpetuated a focus on differences and leaves "blacks" and "whites" artificially divided. The mental health movement has drawn attention to African-American resilience and strengths and away from association of difference with psychopathology (Ruiz, 1990). Contemporary African Americans often remain enthusiastic about religion and spirituality, are characterized as adaptable and bicultural (that is, able to function in two worlds, one black and one white, which requires considerable effort and energy), and typically value work and education despite a history of limited opportunity to acquire or utilize them. Strong networks tend to extend beyond households to multiple collateral relationships. Expectations for culturally congruent care among African Americans generally include general concern for one another (the "brothers and sisters") (Leininger, 1984). In a society in which dark skin rendered people socially invisible for centuries, genuine respect and acknowledgment are essential to acceptable care.

African-American folk medicine, traditionally not separated into mental and physical components, contains elements of various origins. In the early 19th century, Haitian slaves rebelling against French masters brought with them a form of voodoo (a blend of European Catholicism and African tribal religions with modified aspects of humoral pathology). This spread through the Protestant-American South and assimilated practices from 17th and 18th century European occultism, probably due to the insistence on using English rather than African languages. Reflecting its multiple origins, black folk medicine today provides widely varied terms and methods, including, for example, *root medicine, rootwork, mojo, conjuring, voodoo,* and *hoodoo.* There remains a tendency to bring to the health care situation a mixture of somatic, psychological, and spiritual problems (Capers, 1985).

In African-American folk systems, diseases may be from natural causes or spiritual in nature (e.g., punishment for sins or violation of sacred beliefs) (Wood, 1989). Etiologies may be viewed as natural (such as failure to protect the body against inclement weather) or unnatural (such as divine punishment for sin) and tend to represent a perspective that holds the world to be a dangerous and hostile place. The individual is traditionally viewed as vulnerable to outside attack and as dependent on outside help (Snow, 1977). This perspective was reinforced by nearly three centuries of slavery and then one of struggle for full rights.

Native Americans

There are more than 500 different Native American, including American Indian and Alaska native, tribes and nations. Some are recognized by the federal government and others at only the state or local level. Most Native American populations shared a traditional orientation to being in the present (rather than to doing and to the future, which is more typical of European Americans), to cooperation rather than competition, to giving rather than keeping, and to respect for age rather than youth (Attneave, 1982). The Native American life cycle emphasizes rhythmic, natural phenomena. The "real Native American" is in balance as a living being and works toward achieving Native American goals; self-development is never completed. Noninterference is valued, and behaviors that imply manipulation or control may be offensive. The astute clinician makes sure that the Native American client is aware of the consequences of behavior but then leaves it to the individual to decide how to proceed. Silence and conservative show of interest (including, for example, minimizing eye contact) are respectful, caring behaviors.

The potential for personal confusion is obvious in a situation where mainstream society devalues most of the concepts integral to traditional Native American philosophies and ideologies. Native American ideas about health and illness place less emphasis on dysfunction of the body than is typical of biomedicine and more on relationships within society. For many Native Americans, health typically denotes a special, balanced relationship between humankind and its physical, relational, and supernatural environment; illness implies having fallen out of balance with the world.

Traditional self-care prevention measures may include religious or magical elements (for example, burning candles, wearing amulets, reciting prayers, wearing or carrying an arrowhead, or making offerings) (McKenna, 1989). Although the prevalence of alcohol and drug use varies by tribe and by age within tribes, Native Americans tend to have higher rates of alcoholism than those presented by other groups. Associated phenomena include high suicide rates among the young, domestic (spouse and child abuse) violence (Myers, 1990), and homicide (Bell, 1990). Stress-producing socioeconomic situations accompanied by psychological, cultural, and spiritual stressors lead to perceptions of loss and depression. Those who are least acculturated to white society and who have strong tribal identity tend to have the fewest problems. Group therapies with an emphasis on society have been found especially useful for treatment. Often these are family-network therapy and traditional Native American group talking and purification therapies (Manson, Walker, and Kivlahan, 1987).

Hispanic Americans

The terms *Latino* and *Hispanic* generally refer to Spanish ethnicity, language skills, and ancestry but also imply significant cultural variation. Some common themes among Hispanic Americans include Catholicism (although increasing numbers of Hispanics are turning to Protestant religions and Pentecostal sects), orientation toward extended family systems [which may include godparents (*compadres*) and other nonbiological kin], distinctly different roles for men and women, a high value of respect for self and others, the priority of spiritual and humanistic over commercial values, clear hierarchy and patriarchy, and fairly common reliance on folk systems of medicine. Since Hispanic Americans tend to value being listened to and having time spent with them, task-oriented hurrying about is viewed as noncaring. Involvement, loving, and empathy are valued caring behaviors (Leininger, 1984). There is wide variability in levels of acculturation (that is, integration into the mainstream American system). While the average Mexican American was born in the United States and many members of other Hispanic groups are American by birth, numerous others are immigrants.

Spanish-American folk medicine, despite some variation with place and group, clearly reflects its humoral antecedents, as well as Catholic ritual and beliefs about supernatural influences. Many illnesses are "hot" or "cold," so sufferers are treated with medicines and foods of opposite characteristics. These qualities do not refer to temperature but to symbolic properties. Care and treatment regimens can be negotiated with patients within this framework.

Asian Americans

Americans of Asian ancestry represent diverse cultures from Japan, China, Korea, India, the Philippines and other Pacific islands, and Southeast Asia. Education and hard work have paid off for many Asian immigrants, although the "Asian success story" fails to take into account that there are many poor Asian Americans (despite low rates of dependence on public assistance and welfare), and a notable discrepancy between education level and income persists (Sue, 1981).

Strong Asian values generally involve harmonious interpersonal relationships, webs of obligation, and fear of shame (which is a social concept, in contrast to the Westernized notion of guilt, which is more individualized) (Shon and Ja, 1982). The family is of great importance, and family sharing is a major construct in care. Respect, especially for family, elders, and those in authority, is seen as vital. Respect is expressed through recognition of family members and in listening to and valuing their input (Leininger, 1984). Reciprocity and generosity are highly valued. Disruptive and conflict situations are viewed as noncaring (Leininger, 1984).

Traditional Asian health care practices include such varied preventative strategies as worshipping gods and ancestors and striving for balance in all aspects of life (Burnside, 1988). The goal of balance also permeates all culturally congruent treatments. Asian societies share a tradition of Chinese medicine (which is more general than Western medicine because it has a single unifying theoretical basis), as well as of shamanism. There is a strong reliance on Chinese medicine for specific problems and for prevention. Traditional healers draw on biologic, psychological, social, and ecologic evidence to diagnose conditions arising from disruptions in the client's life; his or her brain and body may be out of balance, for example, and his or her relationships with past lives, ancestors, and destiny may be disturbed in some way (Kuo and Kavanagh, in press). Inappropriate behavior may leave the patient vulnerable to brain collapse, ancestral vengeance, and interference from evil spirits and people. Communication is viewed as fundamental to the healer-patient relationship.

The Chinese have characteristic ways of dealing with mental illness in the family, starting with a protracted period of intrafamilial coping with even serious psychiatric illness, followed by recourse to friends, elders, and neighbors in the community, consultation with traditional specialists, religious healers, or general physicians, and finally, treatment from Western specialists. Although it may conflict with Western practices of multiple dosage in tablet or capsule form, many Asians prefer to use over-the-counter drugs that come in liquid form, as well as in single doses, as was typical of liquid preparations in Chinese folk practices (Rempusheski, 1989). Others believe that only injections will be effective.

For many Asian Americans, the forces of tradition are entangled with those of modernization. Traditionally providing most care within families despite the shame associated with mental illness, the strains and changes of recent urbanization and industrialization have led to increasingly diverse lifestyles and a need to discard stereotypes of well-satisfied, well-cared-for, and respected ill and elders (Hirayama, 1985–86; Lee, 1985–86; Moon and Pearl, 1991).

Middle Eastern Groups

In recent decades, the United States has experienced an influx of peoples from Middle Eastern and Northern African cultures. This has increased the traditionally Judeo-Christian American awareness of the complex cultural beliefs, values, and lifeways of members of predominately Islamic societies. Despite considerable cultural diversity among Middle Eastern peoples (Meleis, Lipson, and Paul, 1992), generally shared value orientations include Moslem (Muslim or Islamic) submission and obedience to God and prescribed rituals of prayer and washing. Strict concepts of what is allowed and forbidden (that is, clean and unclean, good and bad) impose important dietary and other rules that should be verified and accommodated as much as possible in health care situations. Class, status, education, modesty, and emotional expression are generally valued. Patriarchy and the centrality of religion typify Middle Eastern social and familial organizations. Elders are honored, gain in status, and interestingly, tend not to experience the senility common to more youth-oriented cultures (Luna, 1989).

Oriented traditionally to the present, making plans may not be valued by some Middle Easterners because the future is seen as neither uncertain nor preordained but as something that one accepts with fatalistic grace (Jalali, 1982). Nursing research indicates that Egyptian, Yemeni, Iranian, Armenian, and Arab immigrants to the United States who are more traditional in social integration, cultural attitudes, and family orientation tend to have less positive morale that those who are more acculturated (Meleis, Lipson, and Paul, 1992).

The Appeal of Alternative Systems

Folk and popular systems of health care continue to serve, to a greater extent than is often recognized by mental health personnel, to smooth harsh cultural gaps between traditional societies and the predominant American system. They are available in every American city, do not require going to unfamiliar places or being seen by people who are strangers, and are readily understandable to someone socialized to the group. Folk systems are also simply organized, relative to scientific systems, and relatively devoid of intimidating testing, technology, lengthy history taking (which often seems irrelevant to patients and families), and invasive diagnostic procedures. Interpersonal, social, and kinship relationships are emphasized, rather than the isolated individual. Traditionally, a focus on groups minimized the discomfort associated with unaccustomed attention to individuals outside the context of the family.

Experienced as more humanistic than scientific, traditional systems of knowing and healing are usually less mechanized, less urbanized, and less intellectualized than biomedicine, which is often focused on fixing dysfunctional parts or systems, limited in access, and dependent on rationality to the extent that emotional needs may be overlooked. Use of psychiatric resources is discouraged by professionals' intolerance for magical and religious orientations and practices, which is common when science and systems of symbolic beliefs and faith compete.

Communication

The crux of transcultural psychiatric/mental health nursing is communication, the style of which varies greatly with culture. Some of these differences are quickly evident, such as when mental health practitioners expect a degree of openness, verbosity, self-disclosure, emotional expression, and insight that reflects the dominant American culture (Young, 1988) rather than the client's orientation. Groups also vary widely in their ideas about appropriate stance, gestures, language, listening styles, and eye contact. Traditional Asian Americans, African Americans, and Native Americans (Wood, 1989) typically consider direct eye contact inappropriate and disrespectful.

Language differences can cause treatment to take much longer than treatment for English-speaking patients (Sherer, 1993), and it is often tempting to use the most available person to facilitate this process. However, dependence on family members to translate may complicate the situation; clients sometimes fabricate new problems to avoid stating the real ones in front of the individual who was solicited to translate. Although linguistic assistance is vital, some translators may actually interpret rather than translate what the client says. The nurse unfamiliar with the language may not realize whose views are being expressed.

As complex as they may be, crossing communication barriers and mutual identification of the problem or offending agent are only parts of the process. Transcultural care requires cultural negotiation and compromise (Goode, 1993). This may involve understanding how the client views and explains the problem and may extend, for example, to advocating the use of folk healers and herbal remedies along with prescribed treatments and medications or helping clients arrange traditional ceremonies associated with grieving and loss. In addition to accepting that communication is possible but that mistakes will at times occur, effective intervention requires sensitivity to the communication process, knowledge of expectable client-specific patterns of communication and care, and a set of practiced skills.

There are four primary transcultural communication skill areas (Kavanagh and Kennedy, 1992). The first is the ability to understand and state an issue or problem as it is perceived from the client's perspective. Nursing's advocacy role frequently involves articulation of problems or issues from clients' points of view to decrease the risk of misunderstanding and the imposition of values and norms that are not those of the client. Knowing a client's explanation for his or her problems allows the nurse to work with the client to resolve them (Kavanagh and Kennedy, 1992). Otherwise, the ideas that the client has about his or her problems may not articulate with the priorities, goals, and interventions posed by the nurse, who may become frustrated with the client's lack of "compliance."

The second and third skill areas involve recognizing and reducing resistance and defensiveness, which directly impede development of productive relationships between nurses and clients and further contribute to the basis for negative attitudes and labels such as "noncompliant." Accusations made by clients about practitioners' incompetence often stem directly from clients' perceptions that those providers are pursuing their own goals and do not acknowledge the clients' goals as important. Providers may be defensive about this; after all, they are doing what they have been instructed to do, just as clients expect to have their needs met and not the providers'.

Developing skills to decrease resistance or defensiveness includes learning to recognize specific ways in which such interactive processes are displayed. Sensitivity to only generalized forms of these phenomena does not facilitate effective intervention. Consider the difference between "He is always so nasty to me!" and "I feel defensive when he tells me I am too young to help him." The specific behavioral information contained in the latter version allows work to begin on problem resolution.

The fourth transcultural communication skill area involves recognition that everyone makes interactive mistakes from time to time. Although taking the risk of making an error is preferable to playing it so safe that communication is inhibited, venturing into unknown territory may go against the way nurses were socialized to behave. Communication recovery skills involving, for example, apology, humor, and redirection are reclamation techniques to use after a blunder. They reinforce confidence as well as competence because when it is known that there is something to fall back on, one is less likely to avoid interactions that may prove difficult. Being able to admit that one does not know everything is a powerful skill. Why should nurses expect themselves to know everything? There are more than 3000 cultures and untold numbers of cultural variations and interpretations. Using a learning stance, that is, letting clients know that they are experts about their cultures and that we wish to learn from them, allows space for real learning, as well as respectful communication and recovery from honest mistakes.

Humor can help bridge communicative gaps in transcultural settings even when direct communication is viewed as impertinent or otherwise offensive (Durant and Miller, 1988). For example, chiding the self for one's own silly ineptness can humanize situations that are otherwise intimidating and distancing. Nurses who can chide themselves with a chuckle when realizing that they just wished a Jewish client a "Merry Christmas" are unlikely to be considered insensitive. However, it must be remembered that respect is the essential ingredient to mutual communication. Awareness of the meaning of any experience from others' points of view is crucial. Humor related to some topics (for instance, race, sex, or ethnicity) is often considered socially unacceptable.

Communicating across cultures requires testing stereotypes against reality. When cognition and affect are impaired by mental illness, communication can be especially time consuming and complex, although it is no less important. Assumptions must be avoided. Unusual language use may, for example, represent cultural differences rather than thinking or hearing impairments, although those explanations also might be valid. The skilled communicator learns how to identify and bridge differences.

Transcultural nurses elicit clients' explanatory models through open-ended questions in lay terms (Kleinman, 1982). Explanatory models consist of clients' ideas about the cause of the illness; the reason for its onset at a given time; its pathophysiology and expected course and prognosis; such concepts as stress, coping, ethnicity, and spirituality; past experiences with health care workers and treatment modalities, illness behavior, and patterns of help seeking; and the treatment that they believe should be administered. A patient who believes, for example, that his or her illness is the result of having broken the rules (perhaps by committing a sin or breaking a taboo) may not believe that medication is going to resolve the problem. Some cathartic or purification ritual may be needed. Often such a remedy works best in conjunction with the biomedical approach.

Learning clients' perspectives reduces risk of conflict between and imposition of nurses' and other care providers' values and enables assessment of cultural orientation and related needs. Clinicians must express genuine interest in clients' views before most will share their ideas about their circumstances and beliefs, yet once sharing is established, many cultural and psychosocial themes in clients' lives can be explored effectively with even moderately disturbed individuals. Understanding specific explanatory models also allows access to conflicts, support, and communication patterns that may be key elements in the client's situation (Kleinman, 1982).

In mental health care, the goal of mutual communication as effective and appropriate intervention implies that it must be acceptable to the client as well as to health care professionals. It takes skill to examine communication patterns and their potential for creating either communicative barriers or mutually respectful interactions. Although, traditionally, nurse-client communication was often one-way, participatory health care requires this to change.

Sometimes clients are expected to follow different interactive rules than those used by nonclients, which prohibits mutual communication. A double set of standards is especially noticeable when clients who are seriously ill, mentally ill, or of different national origin or social class than the provider are not expected to respect basic rules of common decency (Kavanagh, 1988, 1991). Differences in social status and hierarchy and the fact that mental health personnel who are members of majority groups may never have experienced or critically examined the meaning of clients' minority status (which may involve any combination of gender, race, ethnicity, economic and social status, and diagnosis or health status) all have a tremendous impact on relationships, perceptions of problems, and perceptions of alternative interventions. Although members of ethnic and racial minority groups compose 22 percent of the U.S. population, only 8 percent of practicing physicians and 14.2 percent of people who enroll in registered nursing programs come from these minority backgrounds (Sabatino, 1993). It is important that sincere (not patronizing) interest be taken in clients' views and experiences and that they be taken seriously.

In short, mutual communication involves awareness and knowledge of social process and sensitivity to and recognition of barriers to acceptance and sharing. Most important is the ability to empathize, that is, to understand others' beliefs, assumptions, perspectives, and feelings. The effective communicator learns to acquire and understand, to the greatest extent possible, multiple perspectives. Tolerance and acceptance of others' attitudes, beliefs, and behaviors and the willingness to expose oneself as interested but still learning sensitivity, knowledge, and skills are important strategies.

Nurse, Know Thyself

Culture is learned and shared. It is learned both formally, as in class, and informally, by observation and experience. Cultural values and social norms may be stressors as well as media for expression. Culture is constantly changing yet not easily changed. It strongly influences, but does not determine, ideas and behavior. It does not involve race or biologic characteristics but only those values, beliefs, and ideals which people share. We all have culture, not only others who are "different." Culture is not always neat and orderly; various cultures and subcultures overlap. Values, attitudes, ideas, and patterns of behavior are shared in this time of instant and visual communication when many people are exposed to multiple cultures. We give little thought to eating Chinese food one day and Mexican food the next.

Caring behaviors exist in every culture, so nursing is sometimes misconstrued as essentially culture-free. However, specific nursing behaviors, as well as nurses themselves, reflect the cultural contexts in which they occur (Leininger, 1988). The dominant values of the United States shape its professional orientations. For example, Americans emphasize individualism and self-reliance, and these are reflected in the goals generally set forth for mental health clients. However, independence is not valued universally, and dependence in nonindustrial societies has different meanings. Where households are not so differentiated, there is a more obvious norm of generalized reciprocity, and life is more cohesive and collective. In much of the world, interdependence is valued, and independence is viewed with ambivalence or as pathologic.

Learning to understand the cultures of clients requires learning about your own cultural orientation and about yourself. "The one who would change others must himself be changed" (Milio, 1970, p. xi). The culture of the nurse interacts with the cultures of her or his clients. It is important to realize that culture includes the values and norms learned in the process of becoming a nurse (or a member of any other group) as well as those associated with ethnicity, age, class, or gender background. Understanding who we are requires close examination of one's own orientation to recognize where one's own sense of personal and social identity comes from and how it was formed. Ask yourself what kind of person you were socialized to be and how your social identity has changed and is changing. They are never static.

Such self-knowledge is critical to realizing which cultures or groups one tends to favor or avoid and which groups one negatively or unrealistically positively stereotypes. Such blind spots (that is, biases) can keep one from considering, for example, that a "nice middle-class grandmother" also might be a much conflicted lesbian who is addicted to cocaine. Each of us has attitudinal limitations that obscure facts from our consideration and vision. With whom do you feel strange and uncomfortable, and why? How do your concerns and biases affect who gets care and what type of care you give? It is well known than there are cultural preferences among mental health providers for clients who are young, attractive, verbal, intelligent, and successful (also known as YAVIS) (Wilson and Kneisl, 1983), while those who are considered quiet, unattractive, old, indigent, different, and stupid (that is, the QUOIDS) often get less attention.

Commitment to transcultural nursing assumes the recognition and value of human dignity, cultural relativism (that is, the idea that all perspectives have worth) as an acceptable and preferred philosophy, willingness to alter personal behavior in response to the transcultural interactive process, and willingness to monitor personal resistance and defensiveness. Consider how you feel about these criteria.

People may avoid professional mental health care because of incompatible values and beliefs, poverty, social stresses that occur among special populations but are not well understood by professionals, language barriers, lack of education, social isolation, stigma, bureaucratic barriers, and the maldistribution of services. It is crucial that the nursing process be examined from the cultural perspectives of health care providers *and* consumers to maximize appropriate utilization and quality care. Care can then be provided by informed practitioners in ways that are perceived as both acceptable and appropriate.

Culture and Psychiatric/Mental Health Nursing

Transcultural nurses utilize multiple ways of understanding to move beyond the rigidity of trying to fit diverse experiences, interpretations, and expectations into a few ready-made (but culture-bound) categories. All cultural groups share time-honored systems of health beliefs and practices; it is often nurses who can interpret expectations between groups. Sensitive culturologic interviews (Leininger, 1984) are required to know who clients are. Nursing, to provide culturally congruent care, attends to relationship between the self and others; between mental illness and such phenomena as poverty, suffering, violence, chronic illness, and aging; between the cultures of nursing and psychiatry and those of our clientele; and between nursing ethnics and the provision of appropriate care. When nurses and clients come from different cultural backgrounds, accurate diagnosis, treatment, and care depend on time-consuming special knowledge and skills.

Transcultural nursing may involve collecting information about specific cultures; acquiring a culturally acceptable ally or advocate for the client and/or a cultural consultant for the nurse; work with a translator; learning clients' behavioral, attitudinal, and cognitive norms; or ensuring that only culturally fair psychometric tests are used (Geller, 1988). Standardized tests are appropriate only when they are properly modified to fit cultural heritage and experiences. Some transcultural nurses view culture brokering as part of their role, bridging, linking, or mediating between groups that differ in background or orientation (LaFargue, 1985; Jezewski, 1990, 1993). Ideally, this is done with information from the client's perspective, for which the nurse serves merely to facilitate the opportunity to be heard. Other transcultural nurses define their responsibility more in terms of expediting situations in which clients can do their own negotiating.

Since mental illness occurs at roughly the same rate in every society (World Health Organization, 1973; Hughes, 1990), it stands to reason that a transcultural perspective is essential to appropriate mental health and psychiatric nursing care. The value of psychiatry is questionable if it is limited to middle-class Europeans and European Americans (Kleinman, 1988). In its current thinking, ethnopsychiatry, which involves culture-specific constructions of psychiatric systems attempts to move beyond the assumption that Western ways of understanding and treating are universally applicable. Mental health and mental illness are instead understood within the cultural contexts in which they develop (Gaines, 1992). The same challenge faces nursing; ethnonursing methods foster understanding of care-related phenomena from the perspectives of those people who experience the phenomena (Leininger, 1991).

It is essential for clients to feel accepted if they are to share with providers what they believe and practice outside the biomedical system. This will not happen if clients are left to assume that their beliefs and activities are not of interest to health care providers or will be rejected by them. It may be important, however, to know what the patient or client believes and does to minimize the possibility of harm from treatments or medicines that interact disadvantageously with those of the alternative systems. Although it is dangerous to assume that all indigenous approaches are innocuous, most practices are harmless, whether or not they are effective cures. Often such treatments provide valuable psychological support and, because of this contribution, should not discouraged.

Time harangues nurses and nursing. Routinization and efficiency are valued by the dominate culture; time is equated with money, and caring with time. Assumptions that coping patterns of clients and patients are or should be similar to those of nurses (and others socialized to the health care system) simplify care. Differences may be overlooked in efforts to avoid time-consuming complications. The risk involved in such behavior is that clients and providers may work with different strategies or toward dissimilar goals. The nurse, for example, may hurry to include all items relevant to health promotion for high-risk clients when it is the presence and time spent with them that the clients value, not the information.

The two largest consumer groups of mental health care today are the chronically, seriously mentally ill and the aged. The field of geropsychiatric nursing will require more and more skilled psychiatric nurses in the future for work with both the elderly and their caregivers. Nurses also are increasingly involved in rehabilitative training, resocialization programs, partial hospitalization centers, and support groups rather than the traditional one-to-one relationship. Hospital admissions have become increasingly brief, despite increased acuity and the management problems that presents. Even clients diagnosed with schizophrenia and the affective disorders, the major psychiatric illnesses, are maintained on psychotropic drugs in community and ambulatory settings (Franks and Faux, 1990). Psychiatric/mental health nurses are liaisons among clients, health care facilities, and families (Baldwin, 1993). As such, they can facilitate effective integration of multiple belief systems, or they can impose present expectations that lead to interventions oriented toward the practitioner's and health care system's values and goals rather than the client's.

Nurses question how they can learn all the relevant characteristics of the clients they care for (they cannot and should not try) and why they should know about group patterns when it is individuals with whom they work. The important thing is to ascertain a client's culture and what it means to him or her (or them, since many nurses work with families or other groups). It is not a matter of matching clients to their reference groups but of learning about and understanding the relationship involved. For example, is it more useful and accurate to ask "How is this client Norwegian or Lutheran?" than it is to ask "How Norwegian or Lutheran is this client?" The former question allows comparison of the answer against the exceptable patterns (that is, generalizations about Norwegians and Lutherans), whereas the latter question seeks a match between the client and stereotypic standards for his or her reference groups. Always to be avoided are the easy stereotypes: Chinese do this, and Latinos do that. Stereotypes do not work. While every group has discernible patterns that help distinguish it from other groups, most individuals also express beliefs or traits that do not match the group norm. One may be very traditional in one aspect and quite modern in others. Sometimes when people are ill they become more traditional in their expectations and thinking. There is also significant variation within as well as between groups. Knowledge of the group is valuable in as much as it provides a set of realistic expectations. However, only by learning about the individual or family at hand can the clinician understand in what ways the group patterns are meaningful.

Before 1950, psychiatric services in the United States were provided primarily at state hospitals (Mollica, 1983). Today, 60 percent of patients hospitalized in the United States with a primary psychiatric diagnosis are treated in general hospitals, and many of these occupy beds scattered throughout various areas rather than on designated psychiatric units (Summergrad, 1991). This means that many nurses who do not identify with care of the mentally ill are exposed to that population. Another reason that it is important for nurses to be culturally sensitive, knowledgeable, and skillful is that they are instrumental in the export of mental health concepts to other societies (Stanley, 1993). Nurses educated in the United States work throughout the world, as well as with people who come here from everywhere else. We must be aware of our potential as communicators of more than we intend.

Culture-Specific Care

It may be tempting to avoid close examination of basic values and beliefs because they seem amorphous, complex, or too intimate. However, a grasp of the concepts of normality, abnormality, ethnocentrism, relativism, pluralism, stereotyping, prejudice, and discrimination provides a basis for understanding how society handles differences in attitude and behavior. Social ranking (that is, social stratification) and its consequence, social inequality, affect human experience, opportunities, and availability, acceptability, and utilization of mental health care resources.

It is a myth that treating people differently because of racial, religious, ethnic, cultural, gender, or other characteristics implies prejudice and discrimination. That is an overused excuse to avoid dealing with issues that are part of societal processes. The problem with not acknowledging diversity is that it denies meaningful variations in real-life experience. It is not necessarily irrational for the individual who has been discriminated against because of his or her dark skin or the woman who has been raped to be paranoid. On the other hand, having one's experience discredited or made to seem unimportant is painful, and situations do not go away simply because they are ignored or avoided. Aspects of them may eventually surface.

In trying to satisfy the basic needs of his or her client, the transcultural nurse asks: "What do you expect [or want] the nurse to do for you?" (McKenna, 1989). Culturally congruent nursing care decisions and actions have the potential to intervene in three ways: cultural care preservation, accommodation, or repatterning (Leininger, 1988).

The need for cultural maintenance or preservation was demonstrated, for example, when a student from New Zealand came to a university mental health clinic with complaints of chronic headaches, sleeplessness, and inability to focus on his school work. He explained that the onset of these symptoms coincided with his father's death, about which he did not learn until it was too late to return for the burial rites. Because of his failure to be there when his mother especially needed his support, a relative "pointed a bone" at him, and that action, he believed, resulted in his present problems. A thorough assessment failed to produce additional reasons for the young man's somatic complaints, decreased academic achievement, and social discomfort. Fortunately, a clinician was located who previously worked in New Zealand and made herself available to work with both the clinic staff and the disturbed student. Together they delineated the problem, worked to understand what it would take to alleviate it, and participated in an adapted ceremony that allowed the client to believe that the effect of the "bone point-ing" had been neutralized. The student was at peace with the knowledge that it was through no fault of his that he had missed his father's funeral. He knew that further amends for the social transgression could wait until after successful completion of his studies, which would allow him to serve his reference group more effectively than would his premature return as an academic failure.

The second mode of nursing intervention involves assisting clients to negotiate or adapt new cultural ways (Leininger, 1988). As nurses become sensitive to the complex factors that influence clients' responses to care, they learn to negotiate. This mode of intervention is illustrated by the example of a 15-year-old Mexican-American girl who was referred to the mental health clinic after a suicide attempt. Her school attendance was sporadic, her grades were poor, and she was depressed. Both parents worked outside the home, and her older brothers had moved out, leaving her as primary caretaker for several young siblings. Although she had been dating a boy for several months, her parents planned to send her to Mexico to marry a man they knew there. When she argued with them about her household chores and her future, her boy friend ended their relationship, and the school threatened to suspend her for nonattendance, she cut her wrists. Maria verbalized anger, identity and role confusion, her guilt over rejection of her family, and her resentment of her parents' expectations and of her limited choices. Individual and family therapy with mental health clinical nurse special-ists helped negotiate a realistic and acceptable plan that would keep Maria in school (thus increasing her life choices later) while helping her bridge the gap between traditional and more modern ways. In a group with other young women, Maria was empowered by sharing and learning that there were aspects of her culture and her circumstances that she could accept, reject, ignore, and change.

A third approach to intervention involves culturally acceptable and appropriate care that enables change to new or different behavioral patterns that are meaningful, satisfying, and beneficial (Leininger, 1988). Changing the view that a person has of events requires altering the meaning the situation has (Pesut, 1991). However, the need for such restructuring is less common than that for cultural preservation and negotiation and involves only partial behavioral repatterning. Those cultural attributes which are useful are preserved, as was observed in an urban program designed to strengthen family processes. Families were encouraged to spend social time in the program's community center. When parents were confronted in writing (as well as with repri-mand) with the program's expectation that there would be no hitting on the premises, several families stopped coming. It was not until the staff realized the parents' need to learn alternative ways to set limits for children that those families began to feel comfort-able at the center. For many program participants, physical recourse was the only mode of discipline with which they were familiar; the no-hitting policy had been interpreted as meaning no discipline. Parents had to learn alternative ways of dealing with disciplin-ary issues and with stress, and children eventually learned that their parents would be consistent in their nonphysical limit setting, that punishments would correlate with the transgression, and that the expression of caring was not limited to physical evidence. With repatterning over time, meaningful verbal and other nonphysical ways of disci-plining were modeled, learned, and implemented.

Ideologic Conflict in Psychiatric/Mental Health Nursing

A growing awareness of the changing and complex nature of illness, the influence of social context, and the importance of holistic perspectives leaves nurses in a quandary when the dominant model in psychiatry focuses on organic and genetic factors as underlying causes of mental illness (Lutzen, 1990). For more than 40 years, nursing has been concerned with the therapeutic relationship; now there is concern that increased technology erects new barriers in that relationship. For many, "the decade of the brain," with its high-tech brain scans and powerful new drugs, threatens to forget the patient as a person (Goode, 1988). This may lead nurses who are trained as specialists but are surrounded by others who think differently to question their ability and worth (Arena and Page, 1992) or to resent what they consider the "dirty work" of social control (Brown, 1989; Morrison, 1990).

Ideologic conflict is surely not new in psychiatric/mental health care and continues to shadow nurse-physician and nurse-client relationships (Kavanagh, 1988, 1991). Continued frustration with a plethora of phenomena, many of them—such as poverty and discrimination—beyond the scope of medical treatment, confronts public psychiatric/mental health systems. Despite the medicalization of mental illness, nurses often feel that they must balance structural requirements (which may conflict) with operationalizing knowledge of care and therapy (which may be ambiguous), all the while communicating with persons who may communicate abnormally in a society that is ambivalent toward individuals who exhibit unpopular differences. Nursing must continue to explore diverse models of caring (Jecker and Self, 1991). Involvement of clients in a collaborative process, for instance, can enhance cultural care, as is described in the following example of transcultural nursing in a practice setting (Kavanagh et al., 1992).

An Example of Transcultural Mental Health Nursing in the African-American Community: An HIV/AIDS Prevention Program

With AIDS spreading at an alarming rate, effective AIDS prevention strategies for high-risk populations are essential. This involves sensitivity, knowledge, and skill related to personal and community dimensions, culture, and drug-related and sexual behaviors. The project described here was designed to assist methadone-dependent African-American women to take control of their lives, which is a major aspect of positive mental health among vulnerable populations (Franklin and Jackson, 1990; Kaplan, 1991; Thompson and Spacapan, 1991). A peer counseling format was used in groups of six to eight women with two nurse facilitators. These groups met for a maximum of 24 hours over 16 weeks to discuss ways in which the women could take control of their lives, make their own decisions about reproductive options and risks, and communicate effectively with others in their personal networks. Since education alone is not enough to change behavior, innovative prevention strategies congruent with values of the women's gender, ethnic, and drug subcultures are needed.

Based on the premise that positive feedback leads to the experience of reward for health-promoting behaviors (Jones, 1985), a negotiation or collaborative model rewards positive change while maximizing strengths and potential for empowerment. When the women's view conflicted with risk-reducing behaviors, group process focused on understanding and negotiating the differences. Occasionally, portions of the women's models of explanation or understanding indicated a need for restructuring (for example, when shoplifting, shooting drugs, or engaging in other risky and/or illegal behaviors), but that also was discussed openly, with an emphasis on culturally acceptable behavioral alternatives. The collaboration process involved ongoing sharing and respectful critique of perspectives. Attitudinally, the sessions focused on acceptance of the participants and fostering of their strengths. Emphasis on strengths (such as personal caring relationships and skills) allows culturally congruent interventions to be substituted for unrealistic goals, such as those focused on drug-free social networks when most personal contacts are both intensive and involved with drugs; complete ownership of responsibility for personal or community circumstances, which is unrealistic when some support is still needed; and perception of AIDS as a leading concern when everyday survival is much more pressing than a disease that may or may not occur and that, in any case, is oriented to the seemingly uncontrollable future. Particular attention was paid to relationships with others, trust, competence, confidence, positive thinking, personal direction, and self-identity (Dunston, 1990), of which cultural identity is one part (Collier and Thomas, 1988).

Persons who experience significant social stress often express a need for connection with others like themselves to retain meaningful and positive personal and ethnic identities in a predominantly European-American, middle-class society (Boyd-Franklin, 1987; Schneiderman, Furman, and Weber, 1989). Negotiated collaboration provides a useful intervention model and grassroots support for drug-using populations and members of ethnic minority and economically disadvantaged groups who historically have not often experienced culturally relevant professional intervention. It was recognized that the women who participated in the focus groups understood well their own and their community's problems.

AIDS was generally characterized by the participants as an important threat but as a concern secondary to drugs. The women tended to project negative self-concepts, often using themselves as negative examples during role plays and discussions. It was generally a laborious process for them to conceptualize and acknowledge their strengths (such as care given to children, concern for others, attempts to improve appearance or social and communication skills, and their perseverance in the methadone program). Open discussion emphasized the need for any effective intervention to be congruent with the perceptions and interpretations of the women who have the ability, experience, and opportunity to make positive changes in their community by promoting accurate knowledge and positive attitudes about practices that reduce the risk for AIDS. The need to rely on the other group members was reinforced by the fact that only one of the four doctorally prepared nurses who designed and ran the program was African American and none shared the participants' subcultural backgrounds of poverty and drug use.

The importance of learning from the women about their lives, values and norms, experiences, and communities was repeated often, and the women were encouraged to define and articulate their own perspectives, needs, and concerns. The nurses also shared their experiences and backgrounds, offering consultation in skill areas that could prove useful to the women in their efforts toward change, such as (1) increasing knowledge of AIDS, its transmission, and risk-reducing practices, (2) promoting use of negotiation in communication, use of condoms, and if using IV drugs, use of clean tools, (3) the importance and reinforcement of positive self-esteem (Mecca, Smelser, and Vasconcellos, 1989), and (4) mentoring the participants as peer counselors and neighborhood/community leaders. The women stated that a sense of control over their lives is essential to feeling capable of making responsible, assertive decisions. The need for control, including that realized as input into their treatment, was a recurrent theme and reinforced the appropriateness of negotiated collaboration as the framework for intervention.

Sharing exercises were utilized in most sessions. These included sentence-completion activities, role plays, role reversals (such as clients modeling how they would like to be counseled), and the writing and acting out of informal plays depicting real-life situations. Communication skills were modeled, made explicit, and critiqued. The role plays allowed practice of assertive behaviors, assessment of support resources, and structured problem solving. The nurses and the other participants assumed and interchanged roles. Having practiced and role played numerous scenarios in the group, the women became more skillful and confident about initiating discussions and relaying information outside the clinic. They also reported feeling more personally responsible for assertive and efficacious self care. Given a cast of five hypothetical characters (a woman who previously used IV drugs, her mother, her child, her boyfriend/husband, and a friend who lived next door), the women wrote plays based on observations and experiences in their communities and involving some aspect of AIDS. They readily immersed themselves in this group activity, through which they expressed strong feelings of frustration about their current situations and the hazards that both drugs and AIDS exert on their lives. Over time many of the women became more responsible for themselves and less dependent on drugs; they also were more sensitive to, knowledgeable about, and skillful at reducing those behaviors which put them and others at risk for HIV/AIDS.

Summary

As a practical science of caring (Bottorff, 1991), nursing strives to use strategies that lead to positive outcomes. How does the nurse incorporate cultural beliefs and practices into daily practice? Key points for the transcultural psychiatric/mental health nurse are summarized here.

Promote a Feeling of Acceptance. The nurse's role is to suggest illness-prevention and health-maintenance practices, as well as treatment strategies that fit with and reinforce clients' cultural beliefs and practices. Understand the clients' desire to please and their motivations to comply or not to comply. Often "noncompliance" occurs because clients are trying to preserve their own priorities (Morrison, 1990). Understand relationships between clients and authority, health care institutions, and bureaucracies. Whenever possible and appropriate, involve significant others and leaders of relevant local groups. Confidentiality is important, but ethnic and other leaders know the problems and often can suggest acceptable interventions. Try to make the setting comfortable. Consider colors, sound, atmosphere, scheduling expectations, seating arrangements, pace, tone, and other environmental variables. Be prepared for the fact that children go everywhere with members of some cultural groups, as well as with families who do not have options due to economic limitations; include them.

Establish Open Communication. Present yourself with confidence. Shake hands if it is appropriate. Ask how clients prefer to be addressed. Allow them to choose seating for comfortable personal space and culturally appropriate eye contact. Avoid assumptions about where people come from; let them tell you. Most people are pleased when others show sincere interest in them. Strive to gain the other's trust, but do not resent it if you do not get it. Avoid body language that may be offensive or misunderstood. Determine level of fluency in English and arrange for an interpreter if needed. Speak directly to the client, even if an interpreter is present. Choose a speech rate and style that promote understanding and demonstrate respect for the client. Avoid jargon, slang, and complex sentences. Do not expect clients to share your medical orientation. Use open-ended questions or questions phrased in several ways to obtain information, but be aware that some groups do not consider direct questions to be polite. Invite individuals to tell you stories about their problems and themselves. Determine reading ability before using any written materials.

Anticipate Diversity. Avoid stereotypes by sex, age, race, ethnicity, socioeconomic status, and other characteristics. Remember that cultural generalizations may not differ much from stereotypes, leading to prejudice if they are not open to being revised, that some people do not like having ethnic labels attached to them and wish to "be treated like everyone else," that culture is not restricted to people of color, that differences within groups may be greater than differences between groups, and that our own attitudes and blind spots may be more important than those of clients in terms of outcome. Understand your own cultural values and biases. Emphasize positive points and strengths of health beliefs and practices. Be respectful of values, beliefs, rights, and practices. Express interest in and understanding of other cultures without being judgmental. Some ideas may conflict with your own or with your determination to make changes, but every group and individual wants respect above all else. Show respect, especially for males, even if it is females or children you are particularly interested in. Males are often decision makers about health care.

Ask How You Can Affirm Diversity. Filling in an enlarged version of Table 8-1, called *ASK MAC* [for awareness, skills, and knowledge at the individual (me), agency, and community levels], is useful to help conceptualize and articulate what individual nurses can do.

Another useful learning exercise involves making lists of the groups of which you consider yourself an "insider" and of one or more groups in which you are an outsider.

Table 8-1. Regarding diversity, what can/will I help happen in each category and at each level?

	Diversity	A Awareness (Sensitivity to Issues)	S Skills (Actions to Take)	K Knowledge (Information about Issues)
M	Me	Goal: Behavior:	Goal: Behavior:	Goal: Behavior:
A	Agency	Goal: Behavior:	Goal: Behavior:	Goal: Behavior:
C	Community	Goal: Behavior:	Goal: Behavior:	Goal: Behavior:

As honestly and comprehensively as you can, compare the strengths and weaknesses of both groups. If possible, get an insider's perspective of the group(s) to which you do not belong. It is probable that the two groups will be found to have similar strengths and vulnerabilities, as well as a wide range of perspectives within each.

An excellent exercise to help pull together the sensitivity, knowledge, and skills needed for effective transcultural nursing involves interviewing someone from a culture (or subculture) significantly different from your own. Practice your communication skills to ask about ideas and practices related to health and illness. Then delve into the literature about that person's reference group(s). Whether your informant is from Tibet, gay, or a century old, it is likely that only a portion of what you read about the category that best represents that individual will apply. The third part of this exercise involves taking a look at yourself. How did who you are and how you communicate affect the interview?

Learn What Care Means to the Client. Understand what members of the cultural or subcultural group consider "caring," both attitudinally and behaviorally. Ask what they would like and expect to have happen. Acquire basic knowledge about cultural values, health beliefs, nutritional practices, and traditional health-related practices common to the group you are working with. Learn about expectations for personal hygiene (rituals for body, mouth, and hair care), ideas about health and illness (care and symbolism associated with body fluids and excretions, body temperature, activities of tending one's body, substances used in rituals, seasonal taboos, kinds of activities, time of day/year, gender rules, and other beliefs), and eating (kinds of foods, rituals, scheduling, amounts, environment for eating, implements/utensils, and taboos) (Rempusheski, 1989). Language and food are important symbols; respect and use them. Also know the folk illnesses and remedies common to the cultural group with which you are working. Inquire about over-the-counter and folk remedies being used; research indicates that up to 80 percent of treatments used by clients are not reported because professionals do not ask about them (Wood, 1989). Build on cultural practices, reinforcing those which are positive; do not discredit any beliefs or practices unless you know for sure that specific practices are harmful.

Understand Clients' Goals and Expectations. Negotiate goals that are explicit and realistic. Check for client understanding and acceptance of recommendations. Be patient; do not expect rapid change. Be sensitive when describing or writing about groups. Present a generally comprehensive perspective that emphasizes the positive over the negative. Relate social organization, structure, and process to each group's unique history. Do not confine descriptions of minority groups to problems or deviance. Acknowledge the diversity that occurs within as well as between and among groups. Integrate discussion of minority groups with that of majority groups to make it clear that issues, concerns, and relationships are shared. Beware of literature that uses deviant models rather than unbiased and fair information about groups. There is much of value to be found in both classic and modern literature, but it must be used critically due to the propensity for bias.

Learn to appreciate the richness of diversity as an asset rather than viewing it as a hindrance to communication and effective intervention. Honor the uniqueness of clients and their dignity and worth. Attempt to establish caring relationships that can overcome any cultural misstep, and strive to help clients obtain their self-determined goals, to learn clients' explanatory models, and to get to know yourself as an effective trans-cultural nurse.

Learning Activities

1. Interview a person from a Hispanic or another cultural group to learn more about cultural-bound syndromes or "folk" diseases. Ask specifically what persons from that cultural group believe about *mal ojo*, or the "evil eye." How can a mother protect a baby from the influences of the evil eye?
2. Interview clients, neighbors, or friends about "nerves" or "nervous breakdowns." What are the causes of such conditions? What are the appropriate treatments?
3. Examine the over-the-counter medications at your local pharmacy. Read the labels to determine which medications might be used for mental health conditions.
4. Identify factors in our society that negatively impinge on the mental health status of various cultural groups.

References

Arena, D. M., and Page, N. E. (1992). The impostor phenomenon in the clinical nurse specialist role. *Image, 24*(2): 121–125.

Attneave, C. (1982). American Indians and Alaskan Native families: Emigrants in their own homeland. In M. McGoldrick, J. K. Pearce, and J. Giordano (Eds.), *Ethnicity and Family Therapy* (pp. 55–83). New York: Guilford Press.

Baldwin, A. (1993). Psychiatric liaison nursing: A ready help in organizational change. *American Nurse* (February): 14.

Beiser, M., Waxler-Morrison, N., Iacono, W. G., et al. (1987). A measure of the "sick" label in psychiatric disorder and physical illness. *Social Science and Medicine, 25*(3): 251–261.

Bell, C. C. (1990). Black-black homicide: The implications for black community mental health. In D. S. Ruiz (Ed.), *Handbook of Mental Health and Mental Disorders Among Black Americans* (pp. 192–207). New York: Greenwood Press.

Billings, C. (1993). The "possible" dream of mental health reform. *American Nurse* (February): 5, 9.

Bohannan, P. (1992). *We, the Alien: An Introduction to Cultural Anthropology.* Prospect Heights, IL: Waveland.

Bond, J. B., and Harvey, C. D. H. (1991). Ethnicity and intergenerational perceptions of family solidarity. *International Journal of Aging and Human Development, 33*(1): 33–44.

Bottorff, J. L. (1991). Nursing: A practical science of caring. *Advances in Nursing Science, 14*(1): 26–39.

Boyd-Franklin, N. (1987). Group therapy for black women. *American Journal of Orthopsychiatry, 57*(3): 394–401.

Brislin, R. (1993). *Understanding Culture's Influence on Behavior.* Fort Worth: Harcourt Brace.

Brown, D. R. (1990). Depression among blacks: An epidemiologic perspective. In D. S. Ruiz (Ed.), *Handbook of Mental Health and Mental Disorders Among Black Americans* (pp. 71–93). New York: Greenwood Press.

Brown, P. (1989). Psychiatric dirty work revisited: Conflicts in servicing nonpsychiatric agencies. *Journal of Contemporary Ethnography, 18*(2): 182–201.

Burnside, I. M. (1988). *Nursing and the Aged.* New York: McGraw-Hill.

Capers, C. F. (1985). Nursing and the Afro-American client. *Topics in Clinical Nursing, 7*(3): 11–17.

Collier, M. J., and Thomas, M. (1988). Cultural identity: An interpretive perspective. In Y. Y. Kim and W. B. Gudykunst, (Eds.), *Theories in Intercultural Communication* (pp. 99–120). Newbury Park, CA: Sage Publications.

Collins, J. L., Sorel, E., Brent, J., and Mathura, C. B. (1990). Ethnic and cultural factors in psychiatric diagnosis and treatment. In D. S. Ruiz (Ed.), *Handbook of Mental Health and Mental Disorders Among Black Americans* (pp. 151–165). New York: Greenwood Press.

Comas-Diaz, L., and Griffith, E. E. H. (Eds.) (1988). *Clinical Guidelines in Cross-Cultural Mental Health.* New York: John Wiley and Sons.

Conrad, P., and Schneider, J. W. (1992). *Deviance and Medicalization: From Badness to Sickness.* Philadelphia: Temple University Press.

Dewit, D. J., Wister, A. V., and Burch, T. K. (1988). Physical distance and social contact between elders and their adult children. *Research on Aging, 10*(1): 56–79.

Dunst, C.; Trivette, C., and Deal, A. (1988). *Enabling and Empowering Families.* Cambridge, MA: Brookline Books.

Dunston, P. J. (1990). Stress, coping, and social support: their effects on black women. In D. S. Ruiz and J. P. Comer (Eds.), *Handbook of Mental Health and Mental Disorders Among Black Americans* (pp. 133–147). New York: Greenwood Press.

Durant, J., and Miller, J. (1988). *Laughing Matters: A Serious Look at Humor.* New York: John Wiley and Sons.

Eisenbruch, M. (1992). Toward a culturally sensitive DSM: Bereavement in Cambodian refugees and the traditional healer as taxonomist. *Journal of Nervous and Mental Disease, 180*(1): 8–10.

Escobar, J. I. (1987). Cross-cultural aspects of the somatization trait. *Hospital and Community Psychiatry, 38*(2): 174–180.

Essed, P. (1991). *Understanding Everyday Racism: An Interdisciplinary Theory.* Newbury Park, CA: Sage Publications.

Fabrega, H. (1989). An ethnomedical perspective of Anglo American psychiatry. *American Journal of Psychiatry, 146:* 588–596.

Franklin, A. J., and Jackson, J. S. (1990). Factors contributing to positive mental health among black Americans. In D. S. Ruiz and J. P. Comer (Eds.), *Handbook of Mental Health and Mental Disorders Among Black Americans* (pp. 292–307). New York: Greenwood Press.

Franks, F., and Faux, S. A. (1990). Depression, stress, mastery, and social resources in four ethnocultural women's groups. *Research in Nursing and Health, 13:* 283–292.

Fry, C. L. (1990). Cross-cultural comparison of aging. In K. F. Ferraro (Ed.), *Gerontology: Perspectives and Issues.* New York: Springer.

Gaines, A. D. (1992). *Ethnopsychiatry: The Cultural Construction of Professional and Folk Psychiatries.* Albany: State University of New York Press.

Geller, J. D. (1988). Racial bias in the evaluation of patients for psychotherapy. In L. Comas-Diaz and E. E. H. Griffith (Eds.), *Clinical Guidelines in Cross-Cultural Mental Health* (pp. 112–134). New York: John Wiley and Sons.

Goleman, D., and Gurin, J. (1993). *Mind Body Medicine.* Yonkers, NY: Consumer Reports.

Goode, E. E. (1988). How psychiatry forgets the mind. *U.S. News and World Report* (March 21): 56–58.

Goode, E. E. (1993). The cultures of illness. *U.S. News and World Report* (Feb. 15): 74–76.

Helman, C. G. (1990). *Culture, Health and Illness.* London: Wright.

Henry, W. A. (1990). Beyond the melting pot. *TIME* (April 9): 28–29.

Hirayama, H. (1985–86). Public policies and services for the aged in Japan. *Journal of Gerontological Social Work, 9:* 39–52.

Hughes, C. (1990). Ethnopsychiatry. In T. M. Johnson and C. F. Sargent (Eds.), *Medical Anthropology: A Handbook of Theory and Method* (pp. 133–148). New York: Greenwood Press.

Jackson, J. J. (1990). Suicide trends of blacks and whites by sex and age. In D. S. Ruiz (Ed.), *Handbook of Mental Health and Mental Disorders Among Black Americans* (pp. 95–109). New York: Greenwood Press.

Jalali, B. (1982). Iranian families. In M. McGoldrick, J. K. Pearce, and J. Giordano (Eds.), *Ethnicity and Family Therapy* (pp. 289–309). New York: Guilford Press.

Jecker, N. S., and Self, D. J. (1991). Separating care and cure: An analysis of historical and contemporary images of nursing and medicine. *Journal of Medicine and Philosophy, 16:* 285–306.

Jezewski, M. A. (1990). Culture brokering in migrant farm worker health care. *Western Journal of Nursing Research, 12:* 497–513.

Jezewski, M. A. (1993). Culture brokering as a model for advocacy. *Nursing and Health Care, 14*(2): 78–85.

Jones, E. E. (1985). Psychotherapy and counseling with black clients. In P. Pedersen, (Ed.), *Handbook of Cross-Cultural Counseling and Therapy.* Westport, CT: Greenwood Press.

Kaplan, R. M. (1991). Health-related quality of life in patient decision making. *Journal of Social Issues, 47*(4): 69–90.

Kavanagh, K. H. (1988). The cost of caring: Nursing on a psychiatric intensive care unit. *Human Organization, 47*(3): 242–251.

Kavanagh, K. H. (1991). Invisibility and selective avoidance: Gender and ethnicity in psychiatry and psychiatric nursing staff interaction. *Culture, Medicine and Psychiatry, 15:* 245–274.

Kavanagh, K. H., Harris, R. M., Hetherington, S. E., and Scott, D. E. (1992). Collaboration as a strategy for acquired immunodeficiency syndrome prevention. *Archives of Psychiatric Nursing, 6*(6): 331–339.

Kavanagh, K. H., and Kennedy, P. H. (1992). *Promoting Cultural Diversity: Strategies for Health Care Professionals.* Newbury Park, CA: Sage Publications.

Kim, Y. Y., and Gudykunst, W. B. (1988). *Cross-Cultural Adaptation: Current Approaches.* Newbury Park, CA: Sage Publications.

Kleinman, A. (1982). The teaching of clinically applied anthropology on a psychiatric consultation liaison service. In N. J. Chrisman and T. W. Maretzki, (Eds.), *Clinically Applied Anthropology* (pp. 83–115). Dordrecht, Holland: Reidel.

Kleinman, A. (1988). *Rethinking Psychiatry: From Cultural Category or Personal Experience.* New York: Free Press.

Kleinman, A. (1991). The Future Psychiatry. Special Department of Psychiatry Grand Rounds, University of Maryland Medical System, Baltimore, MD.

Kluegel, J. R., and Smith, E. R. (1986). *Beliefs about Inequality: Americans' Views of What Is and What Ought to Be.* New York: Aldine de Gruyter.

Kuo, C.-L., and Kavanagh, K. H. (in press). Culture and mental health: The Chinese perspective. *Issues in Mental Health Nursing.*

LaFargue, J. (1985). Mediating between two views of illness. *Transcultural Nursing,* 7: 70–77.

Lee, J.-J. (1985–86). Asian American elderly: A neglected minority group. *Journal of Gerontological Social Work,* 9: 103–116.

Leininger, M. (1984). Transcultural interviewing and health assessment. In P. B. Pedersen, N. Sartorius, and A. J. Marsella (Eds.), *Mental Health Services: The Cross-Cultural Context* (pp. 109–133). Beverly Hills, CA: Sage Publications.

Leininger, M. M. (1988). Leininger's theory of nursing: Cultural care diversity and universality. *Nursing Science Quarterly,* 1(4): 152–160.

Leininger, M. M. (1991). Ethnonursing: A research method with enablers to study the theory of culture care. In M. M. Leininger (Ed.), *Culture Care Diversity and Universality: A Theory of Nursing* (pp. 73–117). New York: National League for Nursing Press (Pub. No. 15-2402).

Levinson, D. (1989). *Family Violence in Cross-Cultural Perspective.* Newbury Park, CA: Sage Publications.

Lex, B. (1977). Voodoo death: New thoughts on an old explanation. In D. Landy (Ed.), *Culture, Disease and Healing: Studies in Medical Anthropology* (pp. 327–332). New York: Macmillan.

Littlewood, R. (1991). DSM-IV and culture: Is the classification valid? Paper presented at the NIMH/American Psychiatric Association meeting, Pittsburgh, PA.

Locke, D. C. (1992). *Increasing Multicultural Understanding: A Comprehensive Model.* Newbury Park, CA: Sage Publications.

Luna, L. J. (1989). Transcultural nursing care of Arab Muslims. *Journal of Transcultural Nursing,* 1(1): 22–26.

Lutzen, K. (1990). Moral sensing and ideological conflict. *Scandinavian Journal of the Caring Sciences,* 4(2): 69–76.

Manson, S. P., Walker, R. D., and Kivlahan, D. R. (1987). Psychiatric assessment and treatment of American Indians and Alaskan Natives. *Hospital and Community Psychiatry,* 38(2): 165–173.

McCubbin, H. I., and McCubbin, M. A. (1988). Typologies of resilient families: Emerging roles of social class and ethnicity. *Family Relations,* 37: 247–254.

McKenna, M. A. (1989). Transcultural perspectives in the nursing care of the elderly. In J. S. Boyle and M. M. Andrews (Eds.), *Transcultural Concepts in Nursing Care.* Glenview, IL: Scott, Foresman.

Mecca, A. M., Smelser, N. J., and Vasconcellos, J. (Eds.) (1989). *The Social Importance of Self-Esteem.* Berkeley: University of California Press.

Meleis, A. I., Lipson, J. G., and Paul, S. M. (1992). Ethnicity and health among five Middle Eastern immigrant groups. *Nursing Research,* 41(2): 98–103.

Michelson, C., Mulvihill, M., Hsu, M.-A., and Olson, E. (1991). Eliciting medical care preferences from nursing home residents. *Gerontologist,* 31(3): 358–363.

Milio, N. (1970). *9226 Kercheval: The Storefront that Did Not Burn.* Ann Arbor: University of Michigan Press.

Mollica, R. F. (1983). From asylum to community. *New England Journal of Medicine,* 308(7): 367–373.

Moon, J.-H., and Pearl, J. H. (1991). Alienation of elderly Korean American immigrants as related to place of residence, gender, age, years of education, time in the U.S., living with or without children, and living with or without a spouse. *International Journal of Aging and Human Development,* 32(2): 115–124.

Morrison, E. F. (1990). The tradition of toughness: A study of nonprofessional nursing care in psychiatric settings. *Image,* 22(1): 32–38.

Moyers, B. (1993). *Healing and the Mind.* New York: Doubleday.

Myers, L. J. (1990). Understanding family violence: An Afrocentric analysis based on optimal theory. In D. S. Ruiz (Ed.), *Handbook of Mental Health and Mental Disorders Among Black Americans* (pp. 183–189). New York: Greenwood Press.

Oltmanns, T. F., and Maher, B. A. (1988). *Delusional Beliefs.* New York: John Wiley and Sons.

Ory, F. G., Simons, M., Verhulst, F. C., et al. (1991). Children who cross cultures. *Social Science and Medicine,* 32(1): 29–34.

Parker, S. (1977). Eskimo psychopathology in the context of Eskimo personality and culture. In D. Landy (Ed.), *Culture, Disease and Healing: Studies in Medical Anthropology* (pp. 349–358). New York: Macmillan.

Pesut, D. J. (1991). The art, science, and techniques of reframing in psychiatric mental health nursing. *Issues in Mental Health Nursing, 12*(9): 9–18.

Poussaint, A. F. (1990). The mental health status of black Americans, 1983. In D. S. Ruiz (Ed.), *Handbook of Mental Health and Mental Disorders Among Black Americans* (pp. 17–52). New York: Greenwood Press.

Rempusheski, V. F. (1989). The role of ethnicity in elder care. *Nursing Clinics of North America, 24*(3): 717–724.

Romanucci-Ross, L. (1983). On madness, deviance, and culture. In L. Romanucci-Ross, D. A. Moerman, and L. R. Tancredi (Eds.), *The Anthropology of Medicine: From Culture to Method* (pp. 267–283). South Hadley, MA: J. F. Bergin.

Rubel, A. J. (1977). The epidemiology of a folk illness. In D. Landy (Ed.), *Culture, Disease and Healing: Studies in Medical Anthropology* (pp. 119–129). New York: Macmillan.

Ruiz, D. S. (Ed.) (1990). *Handbook of Mental Health and Mental Disorders Among Black Americans*. New York: Greenwood Press.

Sabatino, F. (1993). Culture shock: Are U.S. hospitals ready? Hospitals (May 20): 23–28.

Sanday, P. R., and Goodenough, R. G. (Eds.) (1990). *Beyond the Second Sex: New Directions in the Anthropology of Gender*. Philadelphia: University of Pennsylvania Press.

Scheper-Hughes, N. (1978). Saints, scholars, and schizophrenics: Madness and badness in western Ireland. *Medical Anthropology, 2*: 59–93.

Schneiderman, L., Furman, W. A., and Weber, J. (1989). Self-esteem and chronic welfare dependency. In A. M. Mecca, N. J. Smelser, and J. Vasconcellos (Eds.), *The Social Importance of Self-Esteem*, Berkeley: University of California Press.

Secundy, M. G. (1992). *Trials, Tribulations, and Celebrations: African-American Perspectives on Health, Illness, Aging and Loss*. Yarmouth, ME: Intercultural Press.

Seelye, H. N. (1993). *Teaching Culture: Strategies for Intercultural Communication*. Lincolnwood, IL: National Textbook Company.

Sherer, J. L. (1993). Crossing cultures: Hospitals begin breaking down the barriers to care. *Hospitals* (May 20): 29–31.

Shon, S. P., and Ja, D. Y. (1982). Asian families. In M. McGoldrick, J. K. Pearce, and J. Giordano (Eds.), *Ethnicity and Family Therapy* (pp. 208–228). New York: Guilford Press.

Snow, L. F. (1977). Popular medicine in a black neighborhood. In E. H. Spicer (Ed.), *Ethnic Medicine in the Southwest* (pp. 19–95). Tucson, AZ: University of Arizona Press.

Sokolovsky, J., (Ed.) (1990). *The Cultural Context of Aging: Worldwide Perspectives*. New York: Bergin and Garvey.

Stanley, S. (1993). Bringing mental health care to Russia. *American Nurse* (February): 12, 14.

Steinhausen, H.-C., Offer, D., Ostrov, E., and Howard, K. I. (1988). Transcultural comparisons of self-image in German and United States adolescents. *Journal of Youth and Adolescence, 17*(6): 515–520.

Sue, D. W. (1981). *Counseling the Culturally Different: Theory and Practice*. New York: John Wiley and Sons.

Summergrad, P. (1991). General hospital impatient psychiatry in the 1990s: Problems and possibilities. *General Hospital Psychiatry, 13*: 79–82.

Thomas, R. R. (1991). *Beyond Race and Gender: Unleashing the Power of Your Total Work Force by Managing Diversity*. New York: American Management Association.

Thompson, S. C., and Spacapan, S. (1991). Perceptions of control in vulnerable populations. *Journal of Social Issues, 47*(4): 1–21.

Tripp-Reimer, T. (1984). Cultural diversity in therapy. In C. M. Beck, R. P. Rawlins, and S. R. Williams (Eds.), *Mental Health-Psychiatric Nursing: A Holistic Life-Cycle Approach* (pp. 381–398). St. Louis: C. V. Mosby.

United States Department of Health and Human Services (1991). *Health People 2000*. Arlington, VA: CACI Marketing Systems.

Uzzell, D. (1977). Susto revisited: Illness as strategic role. In D. Landy (Ed.), *Culture, Disease and Healing: Studies in Medical Anthropology* (pp. 402–408). New York: Macmillan.

Wali, A. (1992). Multiculturalism: An anthropological perspective. *Report from the Institute for Philosophy and Public Policy* (University of Maryland College Park) *12*(1): 6–8.

Weidman, H. (1979). Falling out: A diagnostic and treatment problem viewed from a transcultural perspective. *Social Science and Medicine, B13*(2): 95–112.

Wilson, H. S., and Kneisl, C. R. (1983). *Psychiatric Nursing*. Reading, MA: Addison-Wesley.

Wood, J. B. (1989). Communicating with older adults in health care settings: cultural and ethnic considerations. *Educational Gerontology, 15*: 351–362.

World Health Organization (1973). *The International Pilot Study in Schizophrenia*. Geneva, Switzerland: WHO.

Yap, P. M. (1977). The culture-bound reactive syndromes. In D. Landy (Ed.), *Culture, Disease and Healing: Studies in Medical Anthropology* (pp. 340–349). New York: Macmillan.

Young, J. C. (1988). Rationale for clinician self-disclosure and research agenda. *Image, 20*(4): 196–199.

Suggested Readings

Aroian, K. (1993). Mental health risks and problems encountered by illegal immigrants. *Issues in Mental Health Nursing, 14*: 379–397.

Eisenbruch, M. (1991). From post-traumatic stress disorder to cultural bereavement: Diagnosis of Southeast Asian refugees, *Social Science and Medicine, 33*(6): 673–680.

Franks, F., and Faux, S. A. (1990). Depression, stress, mastery, and social resources in four ethnocultural women's groups, *Research in Nursing and Health, 13*: 283–292.

Jezewski, M. A. (1993). Culture brokering as a model for advocacy. *Nursing and Health Care, 14*(2): 78–85.

Lipson, J. G. (1993). Afghan refugees in California: Mental health issues. *Issues in Mental Health Nursing, 14*: 411–423.

Sluka, J. A. (1989). Living on their nerves: Nervous debility in Northern Ireland. *Health Care for Women International, 10*(2–3): 219–243.

9

Transcultural Concepts in Critical-Care Nursing

Patti Ludwig-Beymer

Introduction

Technology in the intensive-care unit is increasing at a rapid rate, bringing obvious advantages, such as ease and accuracy of monitoring physical conditions and faster treatment of critically ill patients. However, a major challenge accompanies this use of technology: nonphysiologic needs may not be identified and met as necessary. In addition, family members or other relatives may be subjected to high levels of stress when they visit these technological environments, which may affect the demands they make on nursing staff (Clifford, 1986).

Transcultural concepts have been largely ignored as an aspect of providing nursing care in critical-care settings. Many critical-care textbooks make no mention of culture when discussing the care of critically ill patients (Ahrens, 1991; Alspach, 1991; Kinney et al., 1991; Kinney, Packa, and Dunbar, 1988; Kitt and Kaiser, 1990; McLaughlin, 1990; Mims, 1990).

On the other hand, it is heartening to note that several textbooks are addressing culture when describing critical-care practice. For example, Donney, Guzzetta, and Kenner (1992) include a short section on cultural orientation and cultural practices as part of the nursing assessment conducted in the critical-care setting. Puntillo's textbook, *Pain in the Critically Ill* (1991), includes an important chapter on cultural aspects of pain. Last, Malloy and Hartshorn (1989) include an excellent chapter on culture and the meaning of illness in their textbook. However, the book is intended primarily for nurses providing acute care in the home. Thus the chapter has had little impact on practice in institutional settings.

The lack of integration between critical-care nursing and transcultural nursing may be explained in part by the relatively recent development of both areas. The formation of

Margaret M. Andrews and Joyceen S. Boyle: TRANSCULTURAL CONCEPTS IN NURSING CARE, SECOND EDITION. © 1995 J.B. Lippincott Company.

large intensive-care units with sophisticated and specialized equipment occurred in the early 1960s (Stanton, 1991). The field of transcultural nursing, although conceptualized in the mid-1950s, did not emerge until the later part of the 1960s (Leininger, 1978, 1991).

In addition, critical-care nursing historically has placed much emphasis on technical skills, procedures, and knowledge of the physical sciences. When patients and their families experience the crisis of hospitalization in a critical-care area, the nurse spends much energy providing curative interventions and physical care, often with little time available to help the family deal with the crisis (Caine, 1991). Adherence to the scientific or biomedical health paradigm (as described in Chap. 1) is strong in critical-care nursing. However, although scientific knowledge and technical skills are essential for critical-care nurses, alone they fail to provide sufficient background for the practice of professional nursing. Health and nursing services cannot be adequate, effective, or comprehensive in any setting unless cultural aspects of health and illness are considered (Leininger, 1978, 1991).

The purpose of this chapter is to describe the use of transcultural nursing knowledge in critical-care settings. This chapter discusses patient vulnerability, family issues, and the formulation of culturally relevant care for patients in critical-care units.

Patient Vulnerability

The delivery of culturally sensitive and congruent care (as described in Chap. 1) is imperative for nurses in all settings. This concept is particularly important in the critical-care setting, where the patient is especially vulnerable due to separation from family and significant others, separation from familiar references, and situational stress.

Separation from Family and Significant Others

When hospitalized in a critical-care unit, the patient is separated from family and significant others for long periods of time. While many critical-care units have relaxed their rigid family visiting policies, family members are still absent from the unit more than they are present. In addition, by defining a family member in white American kinship terms (generally nuclear), the critical-care unit may be isolating clients from important support offered by extended family members and friends.

Despite the high activity level, it is easy for patients and their family members to feel alone in a critical-care unit. Patients who come from traditional extended families are accustomed to interacting with a variety of family members. They may find the isolation to be particularly distressing. This forced separation from their family increases patients' vulnerability.

Even when family members are present, they are often prevented from delivering care because of the complexity and technical nature of care required (Reizian and Meleis, 1986) or because they feel uncomfortable in such a place. Families may even fear touching the patient because of the many tubes and machines attached to their loved one. The inability to touch is particularly alienating for cultural groups who express caring with overt gestures such as touching and where members expect care to be delivered by family members.

Separation from Familiar References

A second cause of vulnerability in critically ill patients involves separation from familiar references. Concepts such as time may have a different meaning for critical-care nurses and critically ill patients. The nurse may attempt to be reassuring by saying, "I'll check back with you in a little while." However, the patient's sense of time may be distorted by the hospitalization experience, resulting in anxiety and concern. In addition to the time distortion that occurs in a critical-care setting, there are also cultural differences in time expectation. For example, the client may wonder, "What is a 'little while?' " or "What if something happens to me before that time is up?" These distortions and differences should be clarified with patients on a routine basis. Nurses also should consider expectations surrounding the concept of time when working with family members of patients from diverse cultures, since not all cultures are as precise and "clock-oriented" as are critical-care settings.

Another cause of separation from familiar references is restriction of familiar objects. To reduce the amount of clutter in the area and prevent safety hazards, most critical-care units permit very few personal items. Instead, patients may be surrounded by items that have no meaning to them, yet often a few items that have cultural meaning, such as photographs, mementos, or familiar clothing, would be of comfort to patients.

A third familiar reference that may be restricted is sleep. Critical-care units are typically noisy, active places both day and night. Lights may shine continuously; the sounds of technical equipment, particularly shrill alarms, also make it difficult to sleep or rest. In addition, patients may be unaccustomed to sleeping alone or in Western-style beds. Instead, patients of diverse cultural groups may be more comfortable sleeping with others in the same room or bed or resting on mats on the floor. Conversely, the patient may be used to sleeping alone or in a separate room and may find it disconcerting to share a large unit with multiple patients of mixed genders.

Stress

A third cause of vulnerability affecting both critically ill patients and their families is stress. Literature in critical care addresses the nature and degree of stress experienced by patients and family members. However, cultural differences are not addressed. Pain, fear of death, isolation, loss, grief, sensory overload, sensory deprivation, and many other factors contribute to the stress experienced in a critical-care setting, and they are expressed by culturally diverse patients and families in a variety of ways. Common practices in critical-care units may be disturbing to many patients, especially to those from cultures other than the dominant Anglo-American culture. For example, given that many critical-care units lack a certain degree of privacy, patients who are side by side with members of the opposite sex may experience discomfort and embarrassment. Their situation is worsened by isolation from family.

Perhaps the most significant factor in the development of stress is the unknown. Exposure to the critical-care environment, where the patient observes strange procedures and hears unfamiliar words and noises, may result in culture shock. Certainly, the usual stress may be intensified by cultural differences. This is especially evident when the language of the patient is different from the language spoken by the health care providers, with communication in this situation quite difficult. Increased stress may even result in regression to a language spoken during childhood, a more safe and secure period. Patients who have not spoken their native language for years have reverted to that language while hospitalized for an acute illness or injury. To complicate matters further, support for both patients and family members is often fragmented in critical-care settings (Halm, 1990). Families must interact with a myriad of providers from many disciplines, with each person involved in only one aspect of the overall care. Concerned family members often lack one contact person to help them work through this fragmentation.

Nurses are challenged to demonstrate cultural sensitivity and plan and deliver culturally congruent care to vulnerable critically ill patients and their families.

Family Issues

Hospitalization for a critical illness is typically viewed as a crisis situation. Admission to the critical-care unit causes distress for both patients and families. Most of the staff's energy is devoted to providing patient care, with little time left to help the family deal with the crisis. Yet the family has a tremendous influence on the sick member's immediate and long-term recovery. Considering the patient as a member of a family unit is essential when attempting to provide comprehensive care. Critical-care nurses must identify the specific needs of family members and intervene appropriately to meet those needs (Wooley, 1990). By providing support and care for the family, the family can be healthier, leading to better care for the critically ill patient.

Establishing relationships with families in critical care is an essential part of high-quality care. Critical-care nurse-family relationships are important to the patient and the family and also benefit the nurse. These relationships require negotiation and must take into account the needs of family and nurse. Possible barriers include limited time, perception that families are stressors, dysfunctional response styles, and premature judgment. Essential skills are trust, empathy, respect, warmth, sensitivity, and touching. The nurse needs both verbal and nonverbal skills (Artinian, 1991).

Family Needs and Expectations

Numerous independent studies suggest that families of critically ill hospitalized patients have primary needs for assurance, proximity, and information (Hickey, 1990; Koller, 1991; Leske, 1991). Many of these studies have used the Critical Care Family Needs Inventory (CCFNI). The tool has established reliability and validity (Leske, 1988) and inventories five need areas: support, comfort, information, proximity, and assurance.

An early attempt to identify the needs of critical-care family members was made by Molter (1979). In this research, the need for hope was the most important universal need identified by critical-care family members. Other important needs included receiving adequate and honest information and feeling that the hospital staff members were concerned about the patient. These needs were most often met by nurses, followed by physicians and other sources of support. The relatives perceived the role of the health professional to be patient-focused only.

These findings have been corroborated by other researchers (Engli and Kirsivali-Farmer, 1993; Leske, 1986; Norris and Grove, 1986). Additional research (Price et al., 1991) suggested that critical-care family members need honest, intelligible, and timely information and need to feel assured that their loved one is being cared for by competent and caring people. In this study, however, the need to feel there was hope had lesser importance. When examining the immediate needs of families of neurologic/neurosurgical patients during the critical-care period, Bernstein (1990) found that the most important needs were communication, honesty, and reassurance.

In a phenomenological study, Titler, Cohen, and Craft (1991) identified six ways in which hospitalization in a critical-care unit affected the family unit, including lack of communication among family members, protecting children from anxiety-provoking information, overriding threat (exemplified by feelings of vulnerability, uncertainty, intense emotions, and physical illness in children), disruption of normal home routines, changes in relationships, and role conflict.

Kreamer (1989) investigated coping strategies of critical-care family members. Common coping strategies used by family members included seeking social support, positive reappraisal, planful problem solving, and self-control. Families tended to perceive their family members as more severely ill than objective measures indicated.

Koller (1991) found that the need to know the patient's prognosis was identified as most important by critical-care family members. Although hope was the most commonly used method of coping, confrontation and optimism were described as most useful and effective overall. Nursing interventions described by family members as helpful include the provision of information and emotional support and the competence and manner of nurse.

While the research just described included an indepth presentation of methodologies and results, the cultural composition of subjects from whom data were collected is missing. Thus the applicability of these findings to culturally diverse families is unknown.

A limited amount of transcultural research has been conducted in this area. Coutu-Wakulczyk and Chartier (1990) used a translated version of the CCFNI with French-speaking critical-care family members to begin to examine family needs in a French-Canadian context. In this study, the most important needs identified by family members were honestly answered questions, assurance of the best possible care, and hope. This research enhanced our understanding of family needs in relation to culture. In a follow-up study conducted in both French and English, Rukholm and associates (1991) found that situational anxiety and family needs were significantly related.

Nurse Perceptions and Responses

Nurses are only moderately accurate in their assessments of critical-care family needs. Using the CCFNI, Kleinpell and Powers (1992) compared family and nurse perceptions of family needs and the degree to which the needs were met. Family members and nurses identified many similar important needs, including the need to have questions answered honestly, the need to be called at home about changes in the patient's condition, and the need to know why things were done for the patient. However, family members indicated that some needs were more important and less satisfactorily met than what the nurses perceived, including the need to know the occupational identity of the staff members, directions as to what to do at the patient's bedside, and having friends for support.

When comparing family members' perceptions and nurses' assessments of the most and least important needs, Forrester and associates (1990) detected statistically significant differences for 50 percent of the critical-care family needs. Further, Murphy and associates (1992) explored the relationship between the empathy of intensive-care unit nurses and their ability to accurately assess the needs of critical-care family members. Using the CCFNI, they found that the more empathetic the nurses were, the more accurately they were able to assess family members' needs. Length of nursing experience negatively affected the nurse's ability to assess family members' needs accurately. Research also suggests that nurses' perceptions of critical-care family needs were influenced by units worked, length of time practicing in critical care, educational preparation, and time in nursing (O'Malley et al., 1991).

Reider's research (1989) suggested that satisfaction of family needs was not related to family adjustment. However, family coping, seeking spiritual support, and passive appraisal were positively related to family adjustment. Age of the family member and age of the patient also were related to family adjustment, with more difficult adjustments for younger family members and pediatric patients. Trauma cases were associated with lower levels of family adjustment.

Critical-care nurses can provide social support to family members through family assessment, counseling, referral, and support groups. Families must be an integral part of the hospitalization experience. Strategies that may be helpful in achieving this include formulating a staff-led family support group and family committee, instituting a family visitation contract, and developing nurse expertise in family care (Smith et al., 1991). Although not empirically tested, it is generally believed that such support will influence the ability of family members to provide support to the patient and thereby influence a positive recovery from critical illness (Halm, 1992).

In a quasi-experimental study to examine the effectiveness of support groups for critical-care family members, Halm (1990) found that subjects who attended a support group to share feelings and experiences in coping with illness had a statistically significant reduction in anxiety compared with subjects who received standard bedside support from nurses during visiting hours. These findings suggest that interventions may be helpful in reducing anxiety associated with the crisis of critical illness in the family system. Conversely, Watson's research (1991) found no statistically significant differences in the extent to which family members perceived their needs as being met between a group receiving usual nursing interventions, a group receiving support interventions, and a group receiving informational interventions. As with research into the needs of family members of patients in critical care, the cultural composition of these intervention research subjects is unknown. The studies, while valuable, do little to advance our ability to work with culturally diverse patients and families. Yet there is a real need to create an environment for acutely ill patients and their family members that provides and allows for well-balanced, humanistic, and thoughtful patient care (Clement, 1988). To provide such care, critical-care nurses must have the ability to address cultural needs of patients.

Culturally Congruent Care

When nurses do not understand the dynamics of a particular situation, a cycle of distrust may develop. The nurse may assist the patient and family members without understanding and taking into account their culture. Patients and family members, who may not understand the dominant culture, may begin to feel stressed, estranged, and vulnerable and may withdraw or lash out. The nurse may become hurt and angry when the care is not well received or appreciated. Thus a cycle of distrust and antagonism develops.

However, misconceptions, inaccurate perceptions, distrust, and antagonism need not occur with individuals from different cultures. If nurses acknowledge cultural differences and incorporate cultural sensitivity into their practice of critical-care nursing, patients and their families may experience increased well-being. Assessment skills may be honed to ensure an adequate understanding of the patient so that appropriate care may be delivered. In addition, practices may be modified and delivered in a way that is compatible with the patient's culture. Cases observed in a variety of clinical settings are described below to illustrate these points.

Cultural Assessment

Most nurses practicing in the United States provide care to some people whose cultural beliefs and values are different from their own. It is unrealistic to expect any nurse to have full knowledge of the beliefs, lifestyles, and health practices of the many cultural groups for whom she or he provides care. However, in order to provide nursing care that is congruent with the patient's own lifestyle and cultural values, the nurse must incorporate transcultural concepts into nursing practice. The critical-care nurse, who must remain technically competent, is no exception. Transcultural concepts should not replace other aspects of nursing care. Instead, these concepts should be integrated into the everyday practice of critical-care nursing. The nursing assessment provides an ideal entry point for transcultural concepts.

Several parts of the nursing assessment process used in critical-care settings are meaningless when taken out of cultural context. This is particularly true for a neurologic assessment, which cannot be interpreted without some knowledge of the patient's culture. Consider the following example.

Case Study 9-1

Mrs. Christiansen, an elderly woman who appears to fit within the dominant culture, is admitted to the intensive-care unit after a craniotomy. A thorough neurologic assessment is a high priority. As part of the assessment to determine level of consciousness, the nurse asks Mrs. Christiansen, "Who's the president?"

The nurse is surprised when Mrs. Christiansen responds with an unfamiliar name. The nurse repeats the question and is further concerned when Mrs. Christiansen's curt response is the same. "Furthermore," Mrs. Christiansen indignantly adds, "Everyone knows that."

Upon investigation, the nurse learns that the name mentioned by Mrs. Christiansen is that of the president of the Mormon Church. Mrs. Christiansen is a Mormon (member of the Church of Jesus Christ of Latter-Day Saints), and she has responded from her primary field of reference. The president of her church is far more important in her daily life than is the president of the United States.

Mrs. Christiansen's response indicates considerable mental awareness and is the most correct and culturally specific answer for her. However, if the nurse had not recognized the cultural values held by Mrs. Christiansen, the assessment would have been incorrect and might even have been the basis for unwarranted treatment.

In this example, both the nurse and the patient are ethnocentric. Because the patient looks the same and speaks the same language as the nurse, the nurse assumes that the patient's frame of reference is the same as her own. The possibility of a subculture is not considered. At the same time, the client assumes that her religion is known and understood by the nurse.

The second case study demonstrates the seriousness of the ramifications of conducting a nursing assessment out of cultural context.

Case Study 9-2

A nurse working in a busy intensive-care unit is assigned to Mr. Samir, a middle-aged man who has undergone extensive abdominal surgery for a tumor. Mr. Samir is described in the nursing report as "confused, combative, and speaking incoherently."

The nurse conducts a thorough physical assessment, notes that Mr. Samir's wrist and arm restraints are in place, and then asks a few questions for the neurologic assessment. Mr. Samir does not respond in English; the nurse, who has traveled in the Middle East, is surprised to hear what sounds like Arabic.

The nurse learns later that Mr. Samir is Palestinian and that his primary language is Arabic. Although he was labeled confused and disoriented, he is actually alert and oriented; he became combative because he did not understand what was happening to him. The physical restraints served as an additional stressor and further delayed his recovery.

Mr. Samir has been in the intensive-care unit for over 24 hours. Had an assessment that incorporated cultural information been conducted earlier, the confusion could have been avoided or at least minimized.

Clearly, this example emphasizes the importance of recognizing cultural influences when providing nursing care. Unfortunately, the nurses demonstrated ethnocentrism and cultural blindness, assuming that their way was the only way. They were unaware of any other explanations for their diagnosis of Mr. Samir's confusion, and Mr. Samir suffered as a result of these cultural stumbling blocks. He was needlessly traumatized in an already stressful situation caused by his diagnosis, surgery, isolation, vulnerability, and role change. He undoubtedly suffered from the stress of culture shock as a result of his treatment, since it made little sense to him.

No cultural assessment was conducted with Mr. Samir on admission to the hospital or the critical-care unit. Certainly, assessing the airway and obviating life-threatening situations must take priority. However, although completion of a full assessment at the time of admission to a critical-care unit may be unrealistic, a cultural assessment that provides information about the patient's primary language should be completed as soon as possible. Family assistance is often helpful. Unfortunately, regrettable situations such as Mr. Samir's exist partly because transcultural concepts have not been well integrated into the daily practice of nursing.

Acknowledging Differences

Patients and families benefit from cultural sensitivity and modification of nursing practices in many ways. Consider the following example.

Case Study 9-3

Mr. Nyun is a 28-year-old refugee from Vietnam. He has a mother, a wife, one child, and two cousins in the United States. The family is closely knit and lives together. Mr. Nyun suffered massive trauma in a motor vehicle accident, including head trauma, multiple fractures, and a pneumothorax. He was placed in an intensive-care unit for several weeks and saw his family infrequently during that time.

After his condition stabilized, he was transferred to an intermediate, step-down unit where visiting hours were more liberal. In addition to other treatments, it is recognized that an adequate nutritional intake is essential for wound healing to take place. However, Mr. Nyun refuses virtually all the foods offered to him. His family is encouraged to spend mealtimes with him, but even this strategy does not significantly increase food intake.

Discussion among nurses and other health care providers focuses on enteral feedings, since oral intake is so limited. As one last effort, nurses discuss the feasibility of incorporating food from Mr. Nyun's home into his diet. Some staff members are skeptical of the plan, fearing that Mr. Nyun's condition will deteriorate further if he consumes what they fear to be improperly prepared or preserved native food. The staff members discuss their concerns but ultimately agree to the plan. Mr. Nyun's wife and mother are encouraged to bring favorite meals from home.

When incorporated in this manner, the family is pleased to participate. The microwave oven on the unit is used to heat the dishes. Mr. Nyun's appetite improves, and his family believes they are making a significant contribution to his recovery. In addition, the complications of enteral feedings are avoided.

In this example, a number of key concepts may be identified. First, Mr. Nyun was isolated from his family for 2 weeks in a critical-care unit. During that time, he experienced many of the vulnerabilities described previously. As a result, Mr. Nyun developed a lack of trust in the nursing staff and a sense of antagonism toward them. When Mr. Nyun was transferred, the nurses may have displayed cultural insensitivity by reporting Mr. Nyun as "uncooperative."

In an ethnocentric and culturally blind fashion, the hospital menu offered only "American" food. The food was unappealing and unacceptable to Mr. Nyun. Presumably, the food was equally unacceptable to his family. Thus even family involvement at meal time did not significantly increase his food consumption.

Several nurses, however, attempted to understand Mr. Nyun's cultural system rather than imposing their own. They demonstrated cultural relativism when they suggested that both his wife and mother be involved in food preparation. Family involvement in the healing process was essential. The role of the family was preserved.

Because food was made more congruent with his cultural values and preferences, Mr. Nyun was able to ingest sufficient nutrients for healing. Obviously, he benefited physically from this change. In addition, Mr. Nyun may have developed increased trust in the scientific/medical system of health care delivery, which could increase the likelihood of his adhering to the prescribed regimen and follow-up treatment.

Cultural Care

Most critical-care nurses recognize the spiritual needs of patients and appropriately contact priests, rabbis, ministers, and other clergy. Other nursing practices also may require modification based on a patient's religious and cultural background. The following case study demonstrates the benefits to families that may result when nursing care is modified based on transcultural concepts.

Case Study 9-4

Mr. Claw, a 57-year-old Native American, was critically ill with severe, intractable cardiomyopathy. Death appeared imminent. His family arrived from their home on the tribe's reservation. They appeared at the critical-care unit with a huge eagle wing, an important symbol of strength in their culture.

The staff was concerned. As in many critical-care units, hospital policy dictated the restriction of items permitted in the unit. A staff meeting was held. Despite evidence to the contrary, several

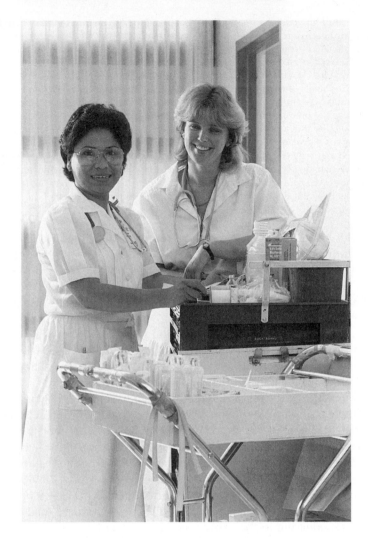

Incorporating individuals with a variety of racial, ethnic, and cultural backgrounds in the planning of care may facilitate the administration of culturally specific and appropriate care. (Reprinted by permission of Lutheran General Health System, Parkridge, Illinois.)

nurses felt that the wing was dirty or contaminated with insects and thus should not be permitted in the unit. One ecologically minded nurse morally objected to the eagle wing, since it obviously had been obtained from protected wildlife.

After considerable discussion, a consensus was reached. The wing was placed in a prominent but out-of-the-way place on top of the cardiac monitor. This greatly pleased the family, allowing them to feel more comfortable with Mr. Claw's care and the hospital staff. When Mr. Claw died a few days later, the eagle wing was carefully carried from the intensive-care unit by the family, who thanked the staff for allowing Mr. Claw to die with the eagle wing present. Knowing that he had died in a culturally appropriate manner, even in the midst of technology, brought solace and comfort to Mr. Claw's family.

In this example, several cultural stumbling blocks (as discussed in Chap. 1) may be identified. First, ethnocentrism and paternalism are evident in the initial response to the eagle wing. Second, stereotyping and prejudice existed; the opinion that the eagle wing must be dirty is an example of these. Third, cultural conflict was displayed by the ecologically minded nurse, who objected to the presence of the wing on moral grounds.

In addition, cultural sensitivity was demonstrated. The nurses recognized that his culture contributed to Mr. Claw's uniqueness as an individual. They accepted the eagle wing as an important symbol and eventually facilitated its placement at Mr. Claw's bedside. Lastly, the nurses ultimately acted as client advocates, enabling Mr. Claw to have the type of care desired by his family. Although the effects on Mr. Claw of incorporating transcultural concepts into his care are unknown, the family clearly experienced a heightened sense of well-being as a result.

A final case study demonstrates the importance of understanding family roles when providing culturally congruent care in a critical-care setting. In addition, this case demonstrates the results of an open attitude and asking questions rather than making false assumptions.

Case Study 9-5

Mrs. Trudeau, a 42-year-old woman from Trinidad, was in the terminal stages of leukemia. Because of her need for intensive care, she was placed on a step-down unit. Although her husband visited daily with clean nightgowns and food from home, he failed to offer emotional support and solace to his wife.

The nurse staff was appalled and had difficulty interacting with Mr. Trudeau. In fact, some nurses had difficulty even being polite to him. Yet Mrs. Trudeau, although depressed, did not seem concerned by what the staff perceived as a lack of support.

Finally, a nurse asked Mrs. Trudeau about her husband's behavior. Mrs. Trudeau explained that in their culture, his behavior was quite appropriate. He was expected to provide physically for her, but emotional support was to come from female relatives, particularly sisters.

Because no sisters were present to provide emotional support, Mrs. Trudeau felt isolated. Nursing staff and hospital volunteers became surrogate sisters and provided much support to Mrs. Trudeau. With an understanding of the cultural dynamics, the staff members also were able to support Mr. Trudeau during his wife's illness and after her death.

This example demonstrates the serious consequences of judging without understanding. In an ethnocentric manner, nurses assumed that they understood the dynamics of the situation. In addition, they sent a paternalistic message to the Trudeaus: "We know what's best for you." This was communicated to Mr. Trudeau through their avoidance of him when he visited his wife. Perhaps through behavior modification, the nurses hoped to moderate what they considered to be a negative behavior.

Fortunately, the behavior was questioned by one nurse. Cultural variations in the husband-wife role were acknowledged and addressed. Rather than imposing the roles advocated by the dominant society, the nurses accepted the roles used by the Trudeaus. Mr. Trudeau's visits were welcomed, and emotional support was provided to Mrs. Trudeau by female nurses and volunteers, addressing the culturally specific need for female support.

Summary

The critical-care environment is sometimes viewed as contrary to the humane treatment of critically ill patients and their families. For patients and their family members, hospitalization in a critical-care setting can be a frightening and dehumanizing experience as they are confronted with stressors that disrupt normal family functioning. The nurse is the pivotal person to positively affect family coping (Kupferschmid et al., 1991).

To diminish the negative aspects of both the critical illness and the environment, specific strategies to foster more culturally appropriate care are needed. Transcultural concepts can facilitate the shift, creating an environment where healing and recovery are possible. It is undesirable for nurses to stereotype based on culture or use a "cookbook" approach when dealing with people of different cultures. However, a knowledge of the general concepts presented in this text will assist the nurse in caring for people from diverse cultures. Within critical-care practice, nurses must begin by recognizing their own beliefs and values. Incorporating a cultural assessment into routine nursing practice is essential. Modifying nursing care practices to fit patients' special values and health needs also must be accomplished. Only in this fashion will professional nursing care be provided to vulnerable critically ill patients and their families.

Learning Activities

1. Arrange for a tour of a critical-care unit. Observe the critical-care unit. What aspects of the environment are most pleasing or disturbing for you? How do you believe your culture influences your response to the unit?
2. Look around the unit. What attempts have been made to personalize the patient bedside?
3. What are the visiting hours of the unit? How might these hours affect families from a variety of cultures?
4. Are families present at the bedside? What are they doing?
5. Talk to the nurses. Do they provide care to people from a variety of cultures? How is a cultural assessment included in the care they provide? How do they obtain an interpreter if needed?
6. Spend some time in the critical-care family waiting area. Talk to several family members. What do they view as their most pressing need while their family member is critically ill? What assistance for coping are they receiving, and from whom? What additional support would they like to receive? How do these responses vary by cultural group?

References

Ahrens, T. (1991). *Critical Care Certification Preparation and Review*. East Norwalk, CT: Appleton and Lange.

Alspach, J. G. (1991). *Core Curriculum for Critical Care Nursing*. Philadelphia: W. B. Saunders.

Artinian, N. T. (1991). Strengthening nurse-family relationships in critical care. *AACN Clinical Issues in Critical Care Nursing, 2*(2), 269–275.

Bernstein, L. P. (1990). Family-centered care of the critically ill neurologic patient. *Critical Care Nursing Clinics of North America, 2*(1), 41–50.

Caine, R. M. (1991). Incorporating CARE into caring for families in crisis. *AACN Clinical Issues in Critical Care Nursing, 2*(2), 236–241.

Clement, J. M. (1988). The need for and effects of touch in ICU patients. In B. S. Heater and B. AuBuchon (Eds.), *Controversies in Critical Care Nursing*, Rockville, MD: Aspen.

Clifford, C. (1986). Patients, relatives and nurses in a technological environment. *Intensive Care Nursing, 2*(2), 67–72.

Coutu-Wakulczyk, G., and Chartier, L. (1990). French validation of the critical care family needs inventory. *Heart and Lung, 19*(2), 192–196.

Donney, B. M., Guzzetta, C. E., and Kenner, C. V. (1992). *Critical Care Nursing: Mind-Body-Spirit.* Philadelphia: J. B. Lippincott.

Engli, M., and Kirsivali-Farmer, K. (1993). Needs of family members of critically ill patients with and without acute brain injury. *Journal of Neuroscience Nursing, 25*(2), 78–85.

Forrester, D. A., Murphy, P. A., Price, D. M., and Monaghan, J. F. (1990). Critical care family needs: Nurse-family member confederate pairs. *Heart and Lung, 19*(6), 655–661.

Halm, M. A. (1990). Effects of support groups on anxiety of family members during critical illness, *Heart and Lung, 19*(1), 62–71.

Halm, M. A. (1992). Support and reassurance needs: Strategies for practice. *Critical Care Nursing Clinics of North America, 4*(4), 633–643.

Hickey, M. (1990). What are the needs of families of critically ill patients? A review of the literature since 1976. *Heart and Lung, 19*(4), 401–415.

Kinney, M. R., Packa, D. R., Andreoli, K. G., and Zipes, D. P. (1991). *Comprehensive Cardiac Care.* St. Louis: Mosby–Year Book.

Kinney, M. R., Packa, D. R., and Dunbar, S. B. (1988). *AACN's Clinical Reference for Critical-Care Nursing.* New York: McGraw-Hill.

Kitt, S., and Kaiser, J. (1990). *Emergency Nursing: A Physiological and Clinical Perspective.* Philadelphia: W. B. Saunders.

Kleinpell, R. M., and Powers, M. J. (1992). Needs of family members of intensive care unit patients. *Applied Nursing Research, 5*(1), 2–8.

Koller, P. A. (1991). The family needs and coping strategies during illness crisis. *AACN Clinical Issues in Critical Care Nursing, 2*(2), 338–345.

Kreamer, C. L. (1989). The Relationship of Family Functioning, Family Demographics, and Severity of Illness to Family Coping with the Crisis of Critical Illness. Unpublished doctoral dissertation, The University of Texas at Austin.

Kupferschmid, B. J., Briones, T. L., Dawson, C., and Drongowski, C. (1991). Families: A link or liability? *AACN Clinical Issues in Critical Care Nursing, 2*(2), 252–257.

Leininger, M. M. (1991). *Culture Care Diversity and Universality: A Theory of Nursing.* New York: National League for Nursing Press.

Leininger, M. (1978). *Transcultural Nursing: Concepts, Theories and Practices.* New York: John Wiley & Sons.

Leske, J. S. (1986). Needs of relatives of critically ill patients: A follow-up. *Heart and Lung, 15*(2), 189–193.

Leske, J. S. (1991). Overview of family needs after critical illness: From assessment to intervention. *AACN Clinical Issues in Critical Care Nursing, 2*(2), 220–228.

Leske, J. S. (1988). Selected Psychometric Properties of the Critical Care Family Needs Inventory. Unpublished doctoral dissertation, The University of Wisconsin, Milwaukee.

Malloy, C., and Hartshorn, J. (1989). *Acute Care Nursing in the Home. A Holistic Approach.* Philadelphia: J.B. Lippincott.

McLaughlin, E. G. (1990). *Critical Care of the Burn Patient.* Rockville, MD: Aspen.

Mims, B. C. (Ed.) (1990). *Case Studies in Critical Care Nursing.* Baltimore: Williams & Wilkins.

Molter, N. C. (1979). Needs of relatives of critically ill patients: A descriptive study. *Heart and Lung, 8*(2), 332–339.

Murphy, P. A., Forrester, D. A., Price, D. M., and Monaghan, J. F. (1992). Empathy of intensive care nurses and critical care family needs assessment. *Heart and Lung, 21*(1), 25–30.

Norris, L. O., and Grove, S. (1986). Investigation of selected psychosocial needs of family members of critically ill adult patients. *Heart and Lung, 15*(2), 194–199.

O'Malley, P., Favaloro, R., Anderson, B., et al. (1991). Critical care nurse perceptions of family needs. *Heart and Lung, 20*(2), 189–201.

Price, D. M., Forrester, D. A., Murphy, P. A., and Monaghan, J. F. (1991). Critical care family needs in an urban teaching medical center. *Heart and Lung, 20*(2), 183–188.

Puntillo, K. A. (1991). *Pain in the Critically Ill.* Rockville, MD: Aspen.

Reider, J. A. (1989). The Relationship of Family Needs Satisfaction and Family Coping Strategies to Family Adjustment During the Critical Illness of a Family Member. Unpublished doctoral dissertation, Catholic University of America.

Reizian, A., and Meleis, A. I. (1986). Arab-Americans' perceptions of and responses to pain. *Critical Care Nurse, 6*(6), 30–37.

Rukholm, E., Bailey, P., Coutu-Wakulczyk, G., and Bailey, W. B. (1991). Needs and anxiety levels in relatives of intensive care unit patients. *Journal of Advanced Nursing, 16*(8), 920–928.

Smith, K., Kupferschmid, B. J., Dawson, C., and Briones, T. L. (1991). A family-centers critical care unit. *AACN Clinical Issues in Critical Care Nursing, 2*(2), 258–268.

Stanton, D. J. (1991). The psychological impact of intensive therapy: The role of nurses. *Intensive Care Nursing, 7*(4), 230–235.

Titler, M. G., Cohen, M. Z., and Craft, M. J. (1991). Impact of adult critical care hospitalization: perceptions of patients, spouses, children, and nurses. *Heart and Lung, 20*(2), 174–182.

Watson, L. A. (1991). Comparison of the Effects of Usual, Support, and Informational Nursing Interventions of the Extent to Which Families of Critically Ill Patients Perceive their Needs Were Met. Unpublished doctoral dissertation, University of Alabama at Birmingham.

Wooley, N. (1990). Crisis theory: A paradigm of effective intervention with families of critically ill people. *Journal of Advanced Nursing, 15*(12), 1402–1408.

10

Transcultural Aspects of Pain

Patti Ludwig-Beymer

Introduction

Pain, a universally recognized phenomenon, is an important area of consideration in nursing practice. Pain is the most frequent and compelling reason for seeking health care (Kim, 1980) and is a common result of many diagnostic, surgical, and treatment procedures. The management of pain is particularly important in nursing because nurses often encounter people either experiencing or anticipating pain. Nurses are in an ideal position to assess pain and to take action to alleviate it.

Pain is a very private experience and is influenced by cultural heritage. Culture has long been recognized in nursing practice and research as a factor that influences a person's expression of and reaction to pain (Villarruel and de Montellano, 1992). Expectations, manifestations, and management of pain are embedded in a cultural context. The definition of pain, like that of health or illness, is culturally influenced. Thus understanding culture is critical when dealing with clients in pain.

Definitions of Pain

Definitions of pain are quite diverse, partly because of the complex nature of pain and partly because of the many different existing perspectives on pain. The term *pain* is derived from the Greek word for "penalty," which helps to explain the long association between pain and punishment in Judeo-Christian thought. Pain has been defined as an unpleasant sensory and emotional experience arising from actual or potential tissue damage or described in terms of such damage (U.S. Department of Health and Human Services, 1992). Yet pain is much more variable and modifiable than previously believed. Variations within and among people and cultures have been identified. Stimuli

Margaret M. Andrews and Joyceen S. Boyle: TRANSCULTURAL CONCEPTS IN NURSING CARE.
SECOND EDITION. © 1995 J.B. Lippincott Company.

that would produce intolerable pain in one person may be embraced by another. For example, in some cultures, initiation rites and other rituals involve procedures generally associated with severe pain. However, participants reportedly feel little or no pain (Melzack and Wall, 1983).

Pain perception, then, cannot be defined simply in terms of particular kinds of stimuli. Rather, pain is a highly personal experience that depends on cultural learning, the meaning of the situation, and other factors unique to the individual. Perhaps the most comprehensive definition of pain has been proposed by McCaffery (1979): "Pain is whatever the experiencing person says it is, existing whenever he says it does." The meaning of painful stimuli for individuals, the way individuals define their situation, and the impact of previous personal experiences all help determine the experience of pain.

Measurement of Pain

In terms of pain measurement, it is generally believed that humans normally experience similar sensation thresholds. However, pain perception thresholds, pain tolerance, and encouraged pain tolerance may vary considerably among individuals. Sensation threshold, pain threshold, pain tolerance, and encouraged pain tolerance are defined and related research results are presented below.

Sensation Threshold

Sensation threshold refers to the lowest stimulus that results in tingling or warmth. Research suggests that most people, regardless of cultural background, have a uniform sensation threshold. For example, Sternbach and Tursky (1965) measured sensation thresholds in American-born women from Irish, Italian, Jewish, and "Old American" (third-generation) ethnic groups. They found no differences in the amount of stimulation needed to produce a detectable sensation.

Pain Threshold

Pain threshold refers to the point at which the individual reports that a stimulus is painful. Cultural background appears to have some effect on this measure of pain. For example, Hardy, Wolff, and Goodell (1952) found that levels of heat reported as painful by people of Mediterranean origin were described merely as warm by northern Europeans. Clark and Clark (1980) used electric shock to measure pain. They found that Nepalese porters and Western guests were equally sensitive to electric shock. However, the Nepalese required higher intensities before describing the stimuli as painful.

Pain Tolerance

Pain tolerance is the point at which the individual withdraws or asks to have the stimulus stopped. Cultural background appears to have a strong effect on pain tolerance levels. A number of studies examining pain thresholds have been conducted, and several studies have compared pain responses across racial groups, with mixed results. Chapman and Jones (1944) compared pain responses of southern African Americans, northern European Americans, Russian Jewish Americans, and Italian Americans using radiant heat technique. They found that northern European Americans had the highest pain perception threshold and pain reaction threshold. Italian Americans tended to vocalize their pain, while African Americans did not verbally express their pain.

Meehan and Stoll (1954) compared Native Alaskan Indians, Eskimos, and Anglo-Americans using radiant heat technique. They found that whites had the highest and Eskimos the lowest pain thresholds, but the results were not statistically significant. Last, Merskey and Spear (1964) compared white and black medical students in England. Inflicting pain through a pressure algometer, they found no statistically significant differences between the two groups in pain threshold or reaction time.

Researchers also have looked at pain responses in persons of various religions backgrounds. Lambert, Libman, and Poser (1960) found no significant differences between pressure pain in Jewish and Protestant groups. Poser (1963; cited by Wolff and Langley, 1977) also found no differences between Jewish and Roman Catholic groups in Canada.

The generalizability of these findings to clinical settings is questionable. It is unlikely that individuals experiencing pain due to illness or injury will respond in the same manner as people experiencing short episodes of controllable pain induced in a laboratory setting. However, the studies do provide some support for the idea that attitudinal factors influence the pain responses of various cultural groups.

Differences in pain tolerance may reflect different attitudes toward pain. For example, in clinical studies, Zola (1966) and Zborowski (1969) found major cultural differences in tolerance of pain. Yet clinical pharmacologic studies generally neglect cultural and psychosocial effects on pain, such as culture group membership, socioeconomic status, and treatment expectations. Too often, health care providers are interested in the physical and somatic basis of pain to the exclusion of psychological and cultural components.

Encouraged Pain Tolerance

Encouraged pain tolerance is the amount of painful stimuli an individual accepts when encouraged to tolerate increasingly higher levels of stimulation. Again, cultural differences have been documented. Early anthropologic studies remarked on the large amount of pain tolerated by members of the so-called primitive tribes. Wissler (1921), for example, described the Sun Dance "self-torture" ceremonies of the North American Plains Indians. Each participating young man had incisions made in his chest; skewers were then passed through the incisions and attached to the top of the sacred Sun Dance pole. As part of the ceremony, the man danced until his skin was torn from the skewers. The elders then inspected the wounds, cut away any dangling skin and ended the ceremony. As a result of participating in this ceremony, the man gained esteem and was admitted into the band of warriors.

Clearly, this situation was very painful; there is no reason to believe that these young men were physiologically different from anyone else. However, they somehow modified and tolerated the pain because the ceremony was accepted and encouraged by the culture. The euphoria of progressing to warrior, the increased esteem obtained, the trust of the elders, and many other factors appear to have altered the experience of pain.

As described above, pain perception thresholds, pain tolerance, and encouraged pain tolerance vary. Culture is one variable that influences the perception and toleration of pain. Because other factors also play a role in pain perception, the nurse should not expect all clients to react in the same fashion to painful stimuli.

Expressions of Pain

In addition to expecting variations in pain perception and tolerance, the nurse also should expect variations in the expression of pain. According to Festinger's (1954) theory of social comparisons, everyone wants to test the validity of his or her judgments and opinions of the outside world. Individuals tend to turn to their social environments for validation of their experiences. Since pain is a private, ambiguous situation, comparisons with others in the culture group help determine what reactions are appropriate.

A first important comparison group is the family, which transmits cultural norms to children. For example, in their study of adult fears of dental care, Shoben and Borland (1954) found that the experiences and attitudes of one's family were the most important factors determining whether one would react with anxiety to dental treatment, avoid it for a long time, or be uncooperative in the dental chair.

In addition to family influence, it has long been recognized that emotional factors abate the severity of pain or abolish it entirely, even in cases of extensive physical injury. Beecher (1956), for example, found that wounded soldiers, for whom a wound meant an honorable release from danger, were less in need of analgesics that civilians with comparable wounds, for whom a wound represented a largely unwelcome disturbance in their normal lives.

Perhaps the greatest contribution to our understanding of cultural responses to pain and the subjective nature of the pain experience has been made by Zborowski (1952, 1969). An anthropologist, Zborowski studied 103 patients on a Veterans Administration Hospital medical-surgical unit using a variety of qualitative methods including questionnaires, unstructured interviews, and direct observations. Data were collected from four cultural groups: Irish Americans, Italian Americans, Jewish Americans, and Old Americans (defined as third-generation Americans).

Zborowski compared pain interpretation, significance of pain, and other specific aspects of the pain experience, such as intensity, duration, and quality, across the four cultural groups. He found that Irish Americans had difficulty describing and talking about pain, showed little emotion with pain, deemphasized the pain, and withdrew socially when experiencing pain. Italian Americans were expressive in their pain and preferred the company of others when in pain. They tended to request immediate pain relief by any means possible and were generally happy when the pain was relieved. Like the Italian Americans, the Jewish Americans preferred company while in pain, sought relief from pain, and freely expressed their pain through crying, moaning, and complaining. However, the Jewish-American men were skeptical and suspicious of the pain and were concerned about the implications of the pain. The Old Americans were precise in defining pain, displayed little emotion, and preferred to withdraw socially when in pain.

Zborowski suggested that patterned attitudes toward pain behavior exist in every culture. Appropriate and inappropriate expressions of pain are thus culturally prescribed. Zborowski maintained that cultural traditions dictate whether to expect and tolerate pain in certain situations as well as how to behave during a painful experience. In addition, cultural groups expect individuals to conform to these culturally prescribed rules and norms. Despite some methodologic flaws, Zborowski's research remains the classic study of cross-cultural pain responses.

More recent studies have substantiated Zborowski's findings. Zola (1983) compared Italian-American and Irish-American men and women experiencing pain. The findings indicated that the Irish Americans tended to deny pain. Italian Americans tended to admit to pain and presented significantly more symptoms than the Irish Americans. Cluster analysis revealed that the variable most consistently correlated with pain response and illness behavior was the individual's cultural background.

Abu-Saad (1984) studied Arab-American, Asian-American, and Latin-American children. Descriptors of pain varied by cultural group. Arab-American children used such words as *sore, uncomfortable*, and *tingling* to describe the pain. Asian-American children described the pain as *scary, paralyzing*, and *cold*. Latin-American children used such words as *hitting, terrible*, and *sickening* to describe pain. Children from all three cultures agreed that when in pain they felt miserable/awful and scared. Arab-American and Latin-American children frequently indicated "feeling sick to their stomach" when experiencing pain, while Asian-American children felt "like being lost." Arab-American and Asian-American children often reported feeling nervous, embarrassed, or angry when in pain, while Latin-American children reported feeling bad when in pain.

Other researchers have examined pain responses in a variety of cultural groups with conflicting results. In a study of episiotomy pain, Flannery, Sos, and McGovern (1981) reported no significant differences in pain response among African-American, Anglo-Saxon Protestant-American, Irish-American, Italian-American, and Jewish-American women. Weisenberg and associates (1975) compared pain anxiety and pain attitudes in African-American, Anglo-American, and Puerto Rican dental patients. While no significant between-group differences were noted in the amount of pain or the number and types of symptoms experienced, anxiety levels were significantly different. Puerto Rican patients were more anxious than the other two groups and preferred to deny, eliminate, or not deal with the pain. The Anglo-Americans reported less anxiety and were most willing to face and deal with the pain.

Perkoff and Strand (1973) identified variations in the presentation of symptoms of acute myocardial infarction. White men were more likely to report chest pain, whereas black men were more likely to describe dyspnea. Studying patients after acute myocardial infarction, Neill (1993) found no statistically significant differences in sensory, affective, evaluative, or pain intensity measures among Yankee, Irish, Italian, Jewish, and black men. However, black men in the study were more likely to present with shortness of breath than were men from the other groups.

Rather than comparing cultures, several studies have examined a single cultural group. Calatrella (1980) found that Mexican Americans rarely acknowledge signs and symptoms of pain because they consider lack of stamina a sign of weakness. However, these individuals may moan while in pain, because this is seen as an acceptable expression of pain and may be used in an attempt to relieve the pain.

Reizian and Meleis (1986) found that Arab Americans had a present-time orientation to pain similar to Zborowski's findings with Italian Americans. The Arab Americans tended to focus on the immediacy of the pain. Pain was viewed as unpleasant, to be avoided or controlled at all costs. Responses were private and reserved for immediate family members, with families often overseeing and making decisions about the care.

When responses were shared with family but not with health care professionals, conflicts could arise. In addition, different pain episodes resulted in different responses. Some pain, such as labor pain, induced loud moans, groans, and screams. Arab Americans often used metaphors and analogies to describe pain.

While these studies are interesting, it is important to emphasize the great variation within cultures. Differences exist among individuals in any culture in terms of pain perception and expression. Nurses should avoid stereotyping or assuming that an individual will respond to pain in a certain way based on culture (see Table 10-1).

Nursing Subculture: Views and Attitudes About Pain

Although the population of the United States is composed of people whose ancestors immigrated from many counties, social customs and practices in society at large and particularly in health care have been dominated by white Anglo-Saxon Protestants.

Table 10-1. Cultural influences in the nursing care of clients with pain: A case study

	Culturally Insensitive	Culturally Congruent
History	Mr. Varrow is a 45-year-old man admitted to the hospital with abdominal pain.	Mr. Varrow is a 45-year-old man admitted to the hospital with abdominal pain.
Nursing assessment	Ms. Smith, the nurse assigned to Mr. Varrow, attempts to perform her admission assessment. Mr. Varrow begins to moan and cry. Ms. Smith is both uncomfortable and annoyed with Mr. Varrow's behavior. She leaves the room abruptly, stating, ''I'll be back later to do your assessment.''	Ms. Smith, the nurse assigned to Mr. Varrow, enters his room and introduces herself. She explains that she will be asking a few questions that will make his hospitalization more comfortable. Mr. Varrow begins to cry and moan. Ms. Smith states, ''I know you're in pain and this is difficult for you.'' Mr. Varrow states, ''It hurts so much, but I'll try to cooperate.'' The nurse assesses Mr. Varrow's abdomen and then asks Mr. Varrow how he would handle this pain at home.
Client reaction	Mr. Varrow is unaware of why the nurse has become so irritated with him. He does not like to be left alone and would prefer some distraction from the pain. As Ms. Smith's absence lengthens, Mr. Varrow begins to feel anxious, abandoned, hurt, and angry. He wonders if anyone will take care of him.	Mr. Varrow indicates, ''My wife would make me some herbal tea. It helps to calm me down. Then she would sit with me.'' Since the nurse knows that Mr. Varrow is permitted a liquid diet, she encourages him to call his wife and have her bring some tea from home. Mrs. Varrow is pleased to participate in the care. Later, after his tea, Ms. Smith talks to Mr. Varrow about his condition. Mr. Varrow is more relaxed, and Ms. Smith completes her assessment. As she leaves the room, she hears Mr. Varrow whisper to his wife, ''I think I'll be all right here.''
Analysis	The nurse expects the client to respond to pain in a stoic manner. When it becomes obvious that the client will not behave in the expected way, the nurse is uncomfortable and retreats from the situation. The client is abandoned to handle his pain alone. A negative nurse-client relationship has been established. The client may lose faith in the nurse and the health system in general and may reject the care offered by the nurse.	The nurse accepts the client and his expression of pain. She doesn't embarrass or demean him as a result of his response. As a result, some of his anxiety is alleviated, possibly decreasing pain perception. The nurse encourages family involvement and herbal tea, two strategies that have been used by the client at home. These strategies make the hospital environment more tolerable for the client and foster a relationship of trust between client and nurse. As a result, the client feels cared for rather than abandoned.

Regardless of their ethnic backgrounds, most individuals have been somewhat influenced by these dominant values and beliefs.

Silent suffering is probably the most valued response to pain in the United States (McCaffery, 1979). The majority of nurses in the United States are white, middle-class women who have been socialized to believe that self-control is better than open displays of strong feelings. It has been suggested that nurses as a subculture may be socialized, even more than most individuals, to place a high value on self-control in response to pain. One explanation for this is that nurses, because of the nature of their professional activities, must learn to control their feelings and function well under pressure and thus expect the same behavior from others (Benoliel and Crowley, 1974).

Research studies support the belief that these values are internalized by nurses. In a study of 52 white nurses, Acheson (1988) found that the nurses reported their own behavior while experiencing pain as "stoic" and "nonverbal." Further, they indicated a minimal use of analgesics when personally experiencing pain.

Partly as a result of the nursing subculture, nurses often expect people to be objective about the very subjective experience of pain. In clinical practice, nurses may expect a person experiencing pain to report it and give a detailed description of it but to display few emotional responses to the pain. When in pain, nurses expect people to stay calm and avoid complaining, screaming, and crying.

In addition, nurses may deny the pain that they observe in others. In a study of the biases of health care professionals, Baer, Davitz, and Lieb (1970) found that social workers tend to infer the greatest degree of pain, while physicians and nurse infer less pain. The researchers speculated that individuals who are in frequent contact with people in pain may protect themselves from becoming overwhelmed by denying the pain.

Davitz and Davitz (1981), who have extensively studied nursing attitudes toward pain, found that ethnic background of the client is an important determinant for inference of suffering due to both physical and psychological distress by U.S. nurses. Nurses viewed Jewish and Spanish clients as suffering most and Oriental, Anglo-Saxon, and Germanic clients as suffering least. In addition, Davitz and Davitz found that nurses who inferred relatively greater client pain tended to report their own experiences as more painful than nurses who inferred less client pain. In general, U.S. nurses with eastern European, southern European, or African backgrounds tended to infer greater suffering than did nurses with northern European backgrounds. Years of experience, current position, and area of practice were unrelated to inferences of suffering.

In a larger study, Davitz and Davitz (1975) examined the relationship between the degree of client suffering inferred by the nurse and the national background of the nurse. The researchers collected data from nurses in Belgium, England, India, Israel, Japan, Korea, Nepal, Nigeria, Puerto Rico, Taiwan, Thailand, Uganda, and the United States. Nurses were asked to infer physical and psychological pain for clients described in brief case studies. Analysis of the data from all 13 countries confirmed the assumption that attitudes are in part socially learned responses. Nurses from these cultures differed markedly. Korean nurses inferred the highest level of psychological distress, followed by Puerto Rican and Ugandan nurses; Nepalese, Taiwanese, and Belgian nurses inferred the least amount of psychological distress. Korean nurses also inferred the greatest amount of physical pain, followed by Japanese and Indian nurses; nurses from Belgium, the United States, and England inferred the least amount of physical pain.

In a separate study, Acheson (1988) found that nurses' inferences of client suffering varied by the client's culture. Using vignettes that described Native American, Southeast Asian, white American, and Mexican-American clients, nurses were asked to infer physical pain, psychological distress, and intervention choices. Nurses tended to infer the greatest physical pain for Southeast Asian clients, followed closely by Mexican-American clients. Inferences of pain for Native American and white American clients were identical. In addition, a statistically significant relationship was found between the level of pain inferred and the choice of intervention.

These findings provide dramatic support for the belief that one's perspective is important in making inferences about another person's experiences and that culture constitutes an important part of one's perspective. Significant differences in nurse perceptions were found in these studies. Perception is a crucial component of pain assessment and forms the basis of subsequent decisions about pain management.

According to McCaffery and Ferrell (1992), undertreatment of pain has been identified as a problem for over 20 years. The Agency for Health Care Policy and Research issued guidelines related to acute pain management in "recognition of the widespread inadequacy of pain management" (U.S. Department of Health and Human Services, 1992, p. 4). Even the lay press describes the U.S. culture as one "that prizes the stiff upper lip: no pain, no gain" (Allis, 1992, p. 61).

Several studies (Cohen, 1980; Jacox, 1979; Teske, Daut, and Cleeland, 1983) suggest that nurses' perceptions of pain do not coincide with those of patients, resulting in increased suffering for patients. Rankin and Snider (1984) found that 58 percent of nurses have the goal of reducing rather than eliminating pain. Sixty-seven percent of the patients in the study continued to have moderate pain despite interventions. Dudley and Holme (1984) found that nurses tended to infer a greater degree of psychological distress than physical distress from pain. This may lead to inappropriate interventions, such as psychological support without other pain interventions. Client dissatisfaction with pain control also has been documented in research conducted in Kenya (Ngugi, 1986).

In addition, administration of analgesia may differ by cultural group, with medications withheld from less vocal clients. For example, Streltzer and Wade (1981) studied postcholecystectomy pain in whites, Hawaiians, and Asians. They found that nurses limited the amount of analgesia given to all groups, with significantly fewer analgesics given to Japanese, Filipino, and Chinese patients, the least vocal group in this study.

Applying Transcultural Nursing Concepts to People in Pain

While it is beyond the scope of this chapter to present all of the various pain management techniques, five helpful strategies for dealing with the client in pain are described below: identifying personal attitudes, establishing an open relationship, establishing nurse competence, assessing pain, and clarifying responsibility. Transcultural concepts are integrated into these strategies. When these strategies are not employed, culturally insensitive care may be the result, as summarized in Table 10-1.

Identifying Personal Attitudes

Nurses bring their own attitudes about pain to each client interaction (Douglas, 1991). To have empathy for others, nurses must understand and confront their own personal beliefs (Martinelli, 1987) about pain and suffering. Each nurse must confront her or his own beliefs; therefore, it is helpful for individual nurses to identify how they view, express, and manage their own pain. Nurses also must identify beliefs they have regarding client expression of pain. The Learning Activities at the end of this chapter will assist nurses in this process. For example, is a nurse truly nonjudgmental, or does the nurse prefer the patient to express pain stoically? Identifying personal cultural beliefs is the first step in recognizing how these beliefs may interfere with truly therapeutic nurse-client relationships.

Establishing an Open Nurse-Client Relationship

An effective and supportive nurse-client relationship must be established. The quality of the relationship may be as important as the pain-relieving skills used. The nurse should strive to create a relationship with the client that is characterized by genuineness, empathy, warmth, and respect. These caring behaviors constitute the essence of transcultural nursing. A positive relationship incorporates respect for the client and avoids stereotyping.

Respect Clients as Individuals. It is essential for nurses to respect clients as unique individuals. Recognition that culture is an important aspect of individuality is also critical. For example, nurses must recognize that clients hold a variety of beliefs about pain. In addition to recognizing the existence of different perspectives on pain, nurses must acknowledge that clients are entitled to their own beliefs and values.

Respect the Client's Response to Pain. Although personal values and cultural expectations differ, nurses must accept the right of clients to respond to pain in the way they deem appropriate. Clients should never be made to feel ashamed of their responses to pain, even if the responses are not congruent with what nurses consider typical. Nurses need to remember that there is a wide variety of pain expressions, with none of the expressions inherently good or bad.

The nurse who is aware of cultural differences and understands clients in terms of cultural backgrounds will respond effectively and appropriately to their needs. Such a nurse will not be disturbed by the emotional expressiveness of a client whose culture expects and encourages open expression of pain. Similarly, the sensitive nurse will not mistake the stoic attitude of a client from another culture for lack of pain.

Never Stereotype a Person Based on Culture. Culture should never be used as a basis to stereotype an individual. Intragroup differences in pain perception and expression have been well documented in pain research (Wolff and Langley, 1977). When providing care, the nurse should take into account many aspects of the experience, including the pain itself, the client's culture, the psychological aspects of the situation, and additional needs of the client. There are a great many expressions of pain within each culture, and nurses must anticipate and accept these variations.

Nurse Competence

Benoliel and Crowley (1974) describe the importance of establishing nurse competence to clients. Clients should feel comfortable with both the technical and interpersonal skills of nurses. The way nurses present themselves and their care may greatly influence their reception. For example, Neufeld (1970) reported that the status of the person who suggests that a treatment will be effective influences the extent to which subjects believe the suggestion. In Neufeld's research, hypothetical treatments supposedly endorsed by ninth-grade students and by nurses' aides were found to be much less effective in increasing pain tolerance than the same endorsements supposedly given by physicians.

Part of establishing interpersonal competence involves being available to the client who is experiencing pain. This may involve staying with the client, providing privacy to the client, or using ordinary touch as an adjunct to pain relief. Research suggests that nurses often provide "instrumental touch," such as dressing changes and technology-related touch. However, "caring touch" is essential for comforting clients, generating warmth, decreasing anxiety, diminishing pain, and creating a bond (Mulaik et al., 1991).

In addition, nurses should not assume that they are the only people available to clients in pain. Discussions with the client and family and involvement of family members in the care may be helpful (Gropper, 1990). Friends, volunteers, and other health care providers also may be used to provide care. The ideal caregiver is at least partially determined by culture. For example, a member of a particular culture may prefer a caregiver of the same gender. These restrictions should be respected and honored as much as possible.

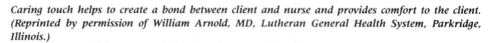

Caring touch helps to create a bond between client and nurse and provides comfort to the client. (Reprinted by permission of William Arnold, MD, Lutheran General Health System, Parkridge, Illinois.)

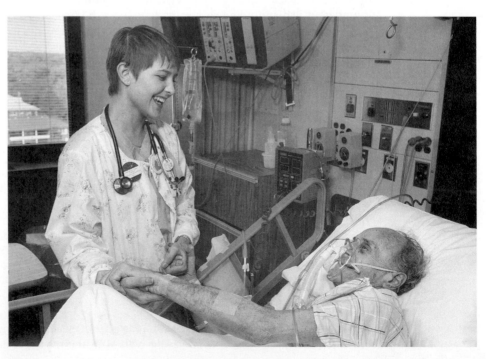

Assessing Pain

Nurses obtain the most useful results when they approach pain assessment not as a task but as an important interaction with the client (Thiederman, 1989). It is essential for nurses to believe clients when they say they are in pain. The single most reliable indicator of the existence and intensity of pain is self-report (National Institute of Health, 1987). In practice, however, nurses tend to use other, less reliable measures for assessing pain. For example, in one study, five of the six top factors identified by nurses as useful in assessing the patient's degree of suffering were found to be influenced by culture. These factors include facial expression, position and movement, vocalization, request for relief, and verbalization. The danger in using these measures alone is that clients who do not exhibit expected signs of distress may be overlooked by nurses (Oberst, 1978). Neither vital signs nor behavior can substitute for a self-report (Beyer, McGrath, and Berde, 1990).

When people in pain realize that the existence of their pain is not believed by others, they experience stress and increased pain intensity. Nurses need to try to understand how the client is experiencing pain and convey that understanding to the client. Since the word *pain* has so many different meanings and refers to such a variety of sensations, clarifying clients' experience of pain will be helpful for both nurses and clients.

The nurse is responsible for knowing the person's pain history and established coping mechanisms (Copp, 1990). A number of pain assessment tools have been developed and summarized (U.S. Department of Health and Human Services, 1992). Although they have different formats, they are meant to assess the same type of information. Cultural sensitivity (as described in Chap. 1) must always be a component of pain assessment.

The assessment of pain has three major objectives. First, it allows the nurse to understand what the client is experiencing. Second, it evaluates the effect the experience of pain is having on the client. Third, it sometimes allows for a determination of the physical nature of the phenomenon that has resulted in the pain (Fagerhaugh and Strauss, 1977). The first two objectives are described in the next two subsections. The third objective falls primarily within the domain of medicine rather than nursing, and is therefore not addressed.

Understanding the Experience. To understand what the client is experiencing, the nurse seeks information about the location, duration, intensity, and type of sensation. The main task is to facilitate communication about what is being experienced. Many clients are able to use numbers to describe and rank their pain. Other clients may use poker chips, drawings, or words to describe their pain (Tesler et al., 1991).

The nurse must remember that pain expressions will vary among clients and even with the same client in different situations. For example, stress resulting from fear of cancer may result in an increased expression of pain. Variations also must be acknowledged within cultures.

Clients experiencing chronic pain may display less intense nonverbal behavior relative to the pain they feel than clients experiencing acute pain. The absence of nonverbal pain behaviors such as grimacing and squinting, however, does not signify the absence of pain (Teske, Daut, and Cleeland, 1983). In addition, the nurse must remember that pain expressions will vary among clients and even with the same client in different situations. Variations also must be acknowledged within cultures.

Evaluating the Effect. Often the most difficult aspect of pain assessment is evaluating the effect the experience is having on the client. At the most fundamental level, the nurse should avoid dictating to clients what effect the pain "should" be having on them. Instead, the meaning of the experience should come from the clients.

An assessment of actual responses to pain should include gathering data on what a particular behavior means. For example, although Mexican-American women in pain may moan, the crying out with pain does not necessarily indicate that the pain is severe, that the woman is out of control, or that the nurse should intervene. Instead, it may be used to express and relieve discomfort (Calvillo and Flaskerud, 1991).

A baseline understanding of the client and his or her response to pain is essential. The nurse needs to assess the type of interventions desired by the client. For example, does the client want traditional interventions, nurturing behaviors, psychological support, physical interventions, or a combination of these interventions? The role of the family or social support network in providing these interventions also should be assessed (Calvillo and Flaskerud, 1991). Children, too, should be asked about their preferred coping strategies for managing pain (Abu-Saad, 1984).

Clarifying Responsibility

Responsibilities in pain relief should always be clarified with clients so that they know what they can do to achieve relief. For example, a member of a particular cultural group may consider it inappropriate to complain of pain. The client may need permission to request pain relief. A simple statement such as "Please tell me when your pain returns" may be all that is needed. This will allow the client to feel in control of the situation and involved in pain management. In addition, the nurse should assess how the client ordinarily copes with pain. This will identify some potentially effective therapeutic techniques, outlined later in this chapter. Above all, the nurse must be open to alternative forms of treatment.

Nurse-client collaboration is essential in pain management. Too often nurses approach a situation as if they had all the answers. Clearly, this attitude is not helpful. Instead, the client should be involved, actively setting goals. The client should not be left alone to manage the situation. Similarly, the client should not be managed by the health team without his or her input. Instead, health professionals and clients should work together to meet the challenge of pain.

Alternative Practices

A number of practices have been used for centuries in the management of pain. Unfortunately, the predominant biomedical system has adapted very few of these techniques, often restricting its practice to medication and biostimulation techniques. On a positive note, the National Institutes of Health have created an Office of Alternative Medicine and are funding research projects to test the effectiveness and efficacy of these nontraditional treatments (National Institutes of Health, 1993). Research suggests that unconventional medicine is currently being used by 34 percent of the population in the United States (Eisenberg et al., 1993). The topic of alternative therapies is also receiving increased attention in nursing practice and literature (Andreola, Steefel, and O'Sullivan, 1993).

This section is not designed to prepare the nurse to deliver the alternative practices described. Instead, it is meant to sensitize the nurse to the many options available to clients. In addition, the nurse and the client may choose together to use some of the techniques described below and summarized in Table 10-2, including relaxation techniques, distraction, imagery, cutaneous stimulation, therapeutic touch, herbal remedies, religious rituals, biofeedback, and acupuncture/pressure.

Relaxation Techniques

Many relaxation techniques have been demonstrated to result in physiologic changes. These changes act to reduce the damaging effects of stress and promote a sense of physical, mental, and spiritual well-being. Some of the relaxation methods most widely taught include Benson's relaxation response, transcendental meditation, autogenic training, progressive relaxation, hypnotic suggestion, and yoga. All these techniques result in an altered state of consciousness and produce a decrease in sympathetic nervous system activity. Each technique requires a calm and quiet environment, a comfortable position, a mental device or image (such as a mantra sound), and a willingness to let relaxation happen.

Benson's Relaxation Response. This relaxation technique is a simple procedure that does not require a change in lifestyle. The method was developed by Harold Benson (1976).

Table 10-2. Alternative methods of pain control

Method	Benefit

Relaxation techniques
  Benson's relaxation response
  Transcendental meditation
  Autogenic training
  Progressive relaxation
  Hypnosis
  Yoga
	Reduces stress and promotes a sense of well-being through reducing muscle tension and providing individual with method for increased control

Distraction	Shields individual from awareness of pain through use of techniques such as singing, conversation, or play
Music therapy	Decreases anxiety, promotes relaxation, and distracts individual from awareness of painful stimuli
Guided imagery	Decreases awareness of intensity of pain by focusing thoughts on a place or activity that is particularly pleasing to the individual
Cutaneous stimulation	Reduces intensity of pain
Therapeutic touch	Promotes client's utilization of self-healing potential
Topical salves and balms	Provides relief for superficial pain
Herbal remedies	Nourishes body with natural ingredients
Religious rituals	Promotes healing of whole person
Biofeedback	Provides client with information about body function, including muscle tension, to overcome pain syndrome

Acupuncture/acupressure	Targets selected peripheral nerves (acupoints) to achieve analgesia
	  Acupuncture through needle insertion at acupoints
	  Acupressure through application of pressure at acupoints

Relaxation is achieved through six basic steps: sit quietly, close eyes, deeply relax all muscles, breathe through nose, continue for 20 minutes, and allow relaxation to occur at its own pace.

Transcendental Meditation. This type of meditation was originally developed by the Maharishi Mahesh Yogi, an Indian scholar and teacher. The technique, which is taught individually, involves the use of a specific mantra during the meditation.

Autogenic Training. Autogenic training emphasizes passive attention to the body. The training, which was first recognized within the biomedical model in 1910, incorporates elements of hypnotism, spiritualism, and various yogic disciplines. Luthe and Schultz (1970) have written a handbook that includes a training system of meditative exercises. This form of systematized relaxation training has been used with some success to treat pain.

Progressive Relaxation. Progressive relaxation, originated by Jacobson (1964), is probably the most widely used relaxation technique today. The method teaches the client to concentrate on various gross muscle groups in the body by first tensing and then relaxing each group.

Hypnosis. This technique was introduced into Western medical practice in the 18th century by Mesmer. A hypnotic state may be induced either by a hypnotist or by the client (autohypnosis). Hypnosis is based on the power of suggestion and the process of focusing attention. It has been used as an adjunct to other pain-relieving therapies and has been found to be helpful in dentistry, surgery, and childbirth, as well as malignancies. Although hypnosis cannot change organic lesions that are causing pain, it can be used to reduce the discomfort of a wide range of conditions.

Yoga. Yoga techniques have been employed within the Hindu culture for thousands of years. Yoga involves the practice of both physical exercise (hatha yoga) and meditation (raja yoga). The correct performance of yoga results in deep relaxation without drowsiness or sleep.

All these techniques may be clinically useful, especially in conditions caused by sympathetic nervous system activity. The interventions have been particularly helpful in the management of pain such as migraine headache.

Distraction

Distraction from pain is a kind of sensory shielding in which one is protected from the pain sensation by focusing on and increasing the clarity of sensations unrelated to the pain. Most nurses are probably not aware of the extent to which clients use distraction because clients do not readily share this information with the health care team. Research conducted in Kenya suggests that 59 percent of clients engage in diversional activities to assist their coping with pain (Ngugi, 1986).

While some nurses believe that "real" pain cannot be relieved by distraction, clinical and research findings suggest that distraction may be a potent method of pain relief, usually by increasing the client's tolerance for pain (McCaffery, 1990; Miller,

Hickman, and Lemasters, 1992). Distraction appears to place the pain at the periphery of awareness. The pain is no longer the center of attention, although it still exists. When clients use distraction, they can at least partially avoid thinking about the pain.

Imagery

Imagery techniques for physical healing date back hundreds of years (Samuels and Samuels, 1975). In health care, guided imagery has been used for pain relief. Guided imagery involves using one's imagination to develop sensory images that decrease the intensity of pain or that become a nonpainful or pleasant substitute for pain. During guided imagery, the client is alert, concentrating intensely and imagining sensory images (McCaffery, 1979). Research suggests that pleasant imagery can effectively reduce the perception of postoperative pain (Daake and Gueldner, 1993). Music therapy is being used with increased frequency to augment imagery and other relaxation techniques (Coverston, 1993).

Cutaneous Stimulation

Cutaneous stimulation reduces the intensity of pain or makes the pain more bearable. Types of cutaneous stimulation for pain relief include massage/pressure, vibration, heat or cold application, topical application, and transcutaneous electrical nerve stimulation (TENS). Stimulation need not be applied directly to the painful site to be effective (McCaffery, 1990)

Therapeutic Touch

Therapeutic touch is derived from the ancient art of laying on hands but has no religious basis. According to Kreiger (1975, 1981), it is a conscious, intentional act that involves an actual energy transfer from the nurse-healer to the client to stimulate the client's own healing potential. It may be employed for a variety of problems, including pain. Research has documented the effectiveness of therapeutic touch in reducing tension headache pain (Keller and Bzdek, 1986).

Herbal Remedies

Herbalism, a specialty in the area of naturopathy, involves the belief that the body is nourished by natural ingredients. Further, proponents of herbalism believe the even if the body is exposed to disease-causing organisms, it can be strengthened through natural living, including exercise, fresh air, medication, and the use of unrefined foods. Herbal treatments have been used in China since at least 3000 B.C., and over 700 herbs were used for healing in Egypt in 1550 B.C. (Moore et al., 1980). Although adherence to herbalism diminished in the West, interest is currently increasing, as exemplified by the popularity of herbal teas.

The nurse should be sensitive to the desire of clients to use natural substances to enhance their health, cure their disease, or relieve their pain. Many of the herbs used have a physiologic effect and may result in comfort for the client who is experiencing pain.

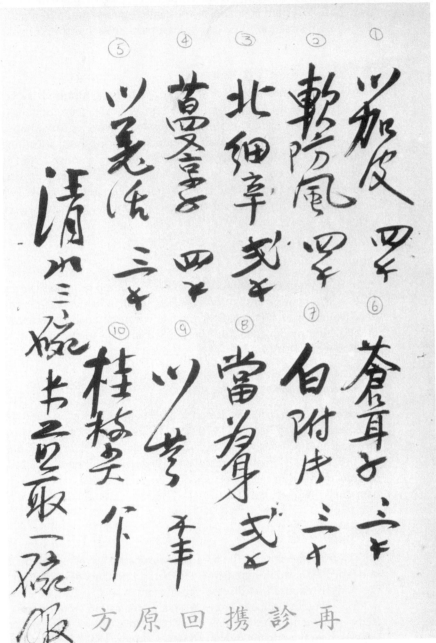

Herbal remedies are being used to enhance health, cure disease, and relieve pain. Above is a Chinese herbal prescription to treat some symptoms of lupus.

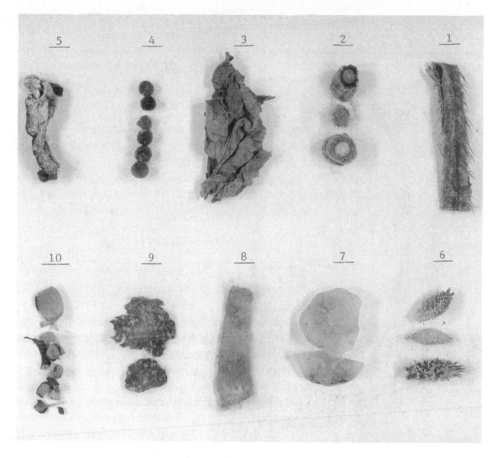

Above are the ten herbs named in the prescription on the facing page. The client brews the herbs into a tea and then drinks it on an empty stomach.

Religious Rituals

Nurses deal with a variety of religious rituals daily. For example, Catholic clients in pain may wish to pray the rosary or attend mass, whereas Jewish clients experiencing pain may ask to speak to a rabbi. Clients of many Christian denominations may actively seek healing through prayer and other rituals. Christianity has included the notion of healing through divine intervention since its inception.

In addition to recognizing Western religious rituals, nurses must be sensitive to non-Western religious rituals. A religious ritual for the purpose of healing or pain relief, for example, may be conducted by a shaman. In this context, the illness or pain is viewed as a disorder of the total person, involving all parts of the individual, as well as relationships to others. The shaman focuses on strengthening or stimulating the client's own natural healing powers. The ritual typically includes the shaman, the client, family members, and other members of the cultural group. The client is the focus of the group, with attention and resources devoted to him or her. Thus the healing ritual may improve the client's sense of self-worth (Frank, 1974).

Clients should be encouraged to use their religious practices as they desire to help in pain management. In addition, privacy should be provided. For example, the client may require a private room for a religious ritual, and this need should be respected. Various amulets and charms also should be respected and incorporated into the care provided.

Biofeedback

Biofeedback comprises a wide variety of techniques that use instrumentation to provide a client with information about changes in bodily functions of which the person is usually unaware. Clients are taught to manipulate and control their degree of relaxation and tension by way of biofeedback training using electroencephalography (EEG) or electromyographic muscle potential (EMG). Since these methods give precise feedback information immediately and continuously, they are often an effective way to reduce tension.

Acupuncture/Acupressure

Acupuncture. Acupuncture, believed to have been practiced for at least 3000 years, is a method of preventing, diagnosing, and treating pain and disease by the skilled insertion of special needles into the body at designated locations and at various depths and angles. According to Chinese thought, life energy, or *ch'i*, constantly flows and energizes humans through a pattern known as *meridians*. *Ch'i* may be intercepted at various acupoints throughout the body.

Acupuncture has been used as an alternative to other forms of analgesia for many minor surgical procedures in China. It also has been used in the treatment of pain in a variety of other countries. There are no simple explanations for the mechanisms that underlie the analgesia-producing effects of acupuncture. However, research has documented the release of endorphins into the vascular system during acupuncture, contributing to pain relief (O'Sullivan, 1993). Acupuncture and acupressure have been used to manage various types of pain, including labor (Beal, 1992).

Acupressure. Acupressure involves a deep-pressure massage of the appropriate acupoints. Self-help books are available to teach clients this technique (Chan, 1974; Kurland, 1977; Thie, 1973; Warren, 1976).

As seen in this brief overview, a number of alternative practices may be used to assist clients in the management of pain. Some practices involve only the nurse and the client. Other techniques involve different types of healers, family members, and significant others. Nurses who are familiar with these techniques will feel more comfortable suggesting, observing, participating in, or performing a variety of healing practices. An example of using some of these practices to provide culturally congruent care is presented in Table 10-2.

Summary

Pain has been experienced throughout the ages. Sophisticated pharmacologic interventions do not necessarily relieve pain, which people define, express, cope with, and manage in a variety of ways. Culture is a major influence in this process.

Traditionally a Chinese practice, acupuncture has gained acceptance in the United States and Canada. Research reveals that the procedure produces an analgesic effect because it causes the release of enkephalin, a naturally occurring endorphin that has opiate-like effects. The practitioner shown here is using moxibustion (heat) to enhance the therapeutic effects of acupuncture.

Nurses practicing in the United States come in contact with people from a variety of cultural backgrounds. In addition, nurses encounter clients experiencing pain in virtually every clinical setting. Recognizing cultural differences in beliefs about pain and suffering can prevent misunderstandings and lead to more sensitive, effective, and professional care.

Learning Activities

1. Think about the last time you experienced pain. Describe it. How intense was the pain? What do you think caused the pain? Did you want others to know about it? How did you respond to the pain? Did you want to be alone or with other people? What treatments did you use for the pain? Did you worry about the pain?

2. Ask five of your friends or relatives what treatments they use when they have a headache. Be sure to ask about folk remedies and who taught them to use a particular treatment. Identify similarities and differences compared with the treatments you use.

3. Think about one of the clients in pain for whom you have provided care. How did that client respond to pain? How did you help the client? How would you modify your practice based on what you've learned in this chapter?

4. Identify three times you have encouraged (or have seen others encourage) a client to accept more pain. What words were used? How was family involved? What was the

ultimate outcome? Did you realize you were applying principles of encouraged pain tolerance?

5. Select several clients with different cultural backgrounds. Assess their pain using several different techniques. Which technique is most helpful? Are your clients able to use numbers to describe their pain? Can they draw pictures or use colors to describe their pain? What words do they use to describe their pain?

References

Abu-Saad, H. (1984). Cultural group indicators of pain in children. *Maternal-Child Nursing Journal, 13*, 187–196.

Acheson, E. S. (1988). Nurses' Inferences of Pain and the Decision to Intervene for Culturally Different Patients. Doctoral Dissertation, The University of Texas at Austin.

Allis, S. (October 19, 1992). Less pain, more gain. *Time Magazine*, 61–64.

Andreola, N. M., Steefel, L., and O'Sullivan, C. (1993). A different way: A look at alternative therapies. *Nursing Spectrum, 6*(18), 7–9.

Baer, E., Davitz, L. J., and Lieb, R. (1970). Inferences of physical pain and psychological distress in relation to verbal and nonverbal patient communication. *Nursing Research, 19*, 388.

Beal, M. W. (1992). Acupuncture and related treatment modalities: II. Applications to antepartal and intrapartal care. *Journal of Nurse-Midwifery, 37*(4), 260–268.

Beecher, H. K. (1956). Relationship of wound to pain experienced. *Journal of the American Medical Association, 161*, 1609.

Benoliel, J. Q., and Crowley, D. M. (1974). *The Patient in Pain: New Concepts*. New York: American Cancer Society.

Benson, H. (1976). *The Relaxation Response*. New York: Avon Books.

Beyer, J. E., McGrath, P. J., and Berde, C. V. (1990). Discordance between self-report and behavioral pain measures in children age 3–7 years after surgery. *Journal of Pain and Symptom Management, 5*, 350–356.

Calatrella, R. L. (1980). The Hispanic concept of illness: An obstacle to effective health care management? *Behavioral Medicine, 7*(11), 23–28.

Calvillo, E. R., and Flaskerud, J. H. (1991). Review of literature on culture and pain of adults with focus on Mexican-Americans. *Journal of Transcultural Nursing, 2*(2), 16–23.

Chan, P. (1974). *Finger Acupressure*. Los Angeles: Price, Stern, Sloan.

Chapman, W. P., and Jones, C. (1944). Variations in cutaneous and visceral pain sensitivity in normal control subjects. *Journal of Clinical Investigations, 23*, 81–91.

Clark, W. C., and Clark, S. B. (1980). Pain responses in Nepalese porters. *Science, 209*, 410–412.

Cohen, F. L. (1980). Postsurgical pain relief: Patients' status and nurses' medication choices. *Pain, 9*(1), 265–274.

Copp, L. A. (August 1990). The spectrum of suffering. *American Journal of Nursing*, 35–39.

Coverston, C. (1993). The therapeutic use of music during childbirth. *Pro Re Nata, 2*(3), 14.

Daake, D. R., and Gueldner, S. H. (1993). The use of imagery instruction as a measure to control postsurgical pain. *Search, 16*(2), 4–6.

Davitz, L. J., and Davitz, J. R. (1975). How do nurses feel when patients suffer? *American Journal of Nursing, 75*, 1505.

Davitz, J. R., and Davitz, L. J. (1981). *Influences of Patients' Pain and Psychological Distress*. New York: Springer-Verlag.

Davitz, L. J., Sameshima, Y., and Davitz, J. (1976). Suffering as viewed in six different cultures. *American Journal of Nursing, 76*, 1296.

Douglas, M. K. (1991). Cultural diversity in the response to pain. In K. A. Puntillo (Ed.), *Pain in the Critically Ill*. Rockville, MD: Aspen.

Dudley, S. R., and Holm, K. (1984). Assessment of the pain experience in relation to selected nurse characteristics. *Pain, 18*(2), 179–186.

Eisenberg, D. M., Kessler, R. C., Foster, C., et al. (1993). Unconventional medicine in the United States: Prevalence, costs, and patterns of use. *New England Journal of Medicine, 328*(4), 246–252.

Fagerhaugh, S. Y., and Strauss, A. (1977). *Politics of Pain Management: Staff-Patient Interactions*. Menlo Park, CA: Addison-Wesley.

Festinger, L. (1954). A theory of social comparison processes. *Human Relations, 7*, 117–140.

Flannery, R. B., Sos, J., and McGovern, P. (1981). Ethnicity as a factor in the expression of pain. *Psychosomatics, 22*, 39–50.

Frank, J. D. (1974). *Persuasion and Healing*. New York: Schocken Books.

Gropper, E. I. (1990). Your Jewish patients in pain. *Advancing Clinical Care, 5*(5), 39–40.

Hardy, J. D., Wolff, H. G., and Goodell, H. (1952). *Pain Sensations and Reactions*. Baltimore: Williams & Wilkins.

Jacobson, E. (1964). *Self-Operations Control: A Manual of Tension Control*. Chicago: National Foundation for Progressive Relaxation.

Jacox, A. K. (1979). Assessing pain. *American Journal of Nursing, 79*(5), 859–900.

Keller, E., and Bzdek, V. M. (1986). Effects of therapeutic touch on tension headache pain. *Nursing Research, 35*(2), 101–105.

Kim, S. (1980). Pain: Theory, research and nursing practice. *Advances in Nursing Science, 2*, 43–59.

Krieger, D. (1975). Therapeutic touch: The imprimatur of nursing. *American Journal of Nursing, 75*, 784.

Krieger, D. (1981). *Foundations of Holistic Health Nursing Practices: The Renaissance Nurse*. Philadelphia: J.B. Lippincott.

Kurland, H. D. (1977). *Quick Headache Relief Without Drugs*. New York: Ballantine Books.

Lambert, W. E., Libman, E., and Poser, E. G. (1960). The effect of increased salience of a membership group on pain tolerance. *Journal of Personality, 38*, 350–357.

Luthe, W., and Schultz, J. H. (1970). *Autogenic Therapy: Medical Applications*. New York: Grune & Stratton.

McCaffery, M., and Ferrell, B. R. (August 1992). Does the gender gap affect your pain-control decisions? *Nursing*, 48–51.

McCaffery, M. (1979). *Nursing Management of the Patient with Pain*, 2d ed. Philadelphia: J. B. Lippincott.

McCaffery, M. (1990). Nursing approaches to nonpharmacological pain control. *International Journal of Nursing Studies, 27*(1), 1–5.

Martinelli, A. M. (1987). Pain and ethnicity. *AORN Journal, 46*(2), 273–281.

Meehan, J. P., and Stoll, A. M. (1954). Cutaneous pain threshold in Native Alaskan Indian and Eskimo. *Journal of Applied Psychology, 6*, 297–400.

Melzack, R., and Wall, P. D. (1983). *The Challenge of Pain*. New York: Basic Books.

Mersky, H., and Spear, F. G. (1964). The reliability of the pressure algometer. *British Journal of Social and Clinical Psychology, 3*, 130–136.

Miller, A. C., Hickman, L. C., and Lemasters, G. K. (1992). A distraction technique for control of burn pain. *Journal of Burn Care and Rehabilitation, 13*(5), 576–580.

Moore, L. G., Van Arsdale, P. W., Glittenberg, J. E., and Aldrich, R. A. (1980). *The Biocultural Basis of Health*. Prosect Heights, IL: Waveland Press.

Mulaik, J. S., Megenity, J. S., Cannon, R. B., et al. (1991). Patients' perception of nurses' use of touch. *Western Journal of Nursing Research, 13*(3), 306–323.

National Institutes of Health (1993). Exploratory grants for alternative medicine. In *National Institutes of Health Guide for Grants and Contract*, vol. 22, no. 12. Bethesda, MD: NIH.

National Institutes of Health (1987). The integrated approach to the management of pain. *Journal of Pain and Symptom Management, 2*, 35–44.

Neill, K. M. (1993). Ethnic pain styles in acute myocardial infarction. *Western Journal of Nursing Research, 15*(5), 531–547.

Neufeld, R. W. J. (1970). The effect of experimentally altering cognitive appraisals on pain tolerance. *Psychonomic Science, 2*, 106.

Ngugi, E. N. (1986). Pain: An African perspective. *Nursing Practice, 1*(3), 169–176.

Oberst, M. (1978). Nurses' inferences of suffering: The effects of nurse-patient similarity and verbalization of distress. In M. Nelson (Ed.), *Clinical Perspectives in Nursing Research*. New York: Teachers College Press.

O'Sullivan, C. (1993). Profile of a nurse acupuncturist. *The Nursing Spectrum, 6*(18), 9.

Perkoff, G. T., and Strand, M. (1973). Race and presenting complaints in myocardial infarction. *American Heart Journal, 85*(5), 716–717.

Rankin, M. A., and Snider, B. (1984). Nurses' perception of cancer patients' pain. *Cancer Nursing, 7*(2), 149–155.

Reizian, A., and Meleis, A. I (1986). Arab-Americans' perceptions of and responses to pain. *Critical Care Nurse, 6*(6), 30–37.

Samuels, M., and Samuels, N. (1975). *Seeing with the Mind's Eye: The History, Techniques and Uses of Visualization*. New York: Random House.

Shoben, E. J., and Borland, L. (1954). An empirical study of the etiology of dental fears. *Journal of Clinical Psychology, 10*, 171–174.

Sternbach, R. A., and Tursky, B. (1965). Ethnic differences among housewives in psychophysical and skin potential responses to electric shock. *Psychophysiology, 1*, 241–246.

Streltzer, J., and Wade, T. C. (1981). The influence of cultural group on the undertreatment of postoperative pain. *Psychosomatic Medicine, 43*(5), 397–403.

Teske, K., Daut, R. L., and Cleeland, C. S. (1983). Relationship between nurses' observation and patients' self-reports of pain. *Pain, 16*, 289–296.

Tesler, M. D., Savedra, M. C., Holzemer, W. L., et al. (1991). The word-graphic rating scale as a measure of children's and adolescents' pain intensity. *Research in Nursing and Health, 14,* 361–371.

Thie, J. (1973). *Touch for Health.* Marina Del Ray, CA: De Vorss.

Thiederman, S. (June 1989). Stoic or shouter, the pain is real. *RN,* 49–50.

U.S. Department of Health and Human Services (February 1992). *Acute Pain Management: Operative or Medical Procedures and Trauma.* Rockville, MD: Agency for Health Care Policy and Research, Public Health Service, U.S. Department of Health and Human Services.

Villarruel, A. M., and de Montellano, B. O. (1992). Culture and pain: A Mesoamerican perspective. *Advances in Nursing Science, 15*(1), 21–32.

Warren, F. (1976). *Freedom from Pain Through Acupressure.* New York: Frederick Fell.

Weisenberg, M., Kreindler, M. L., Schachat, R., and Werboff, J. (1975). Pain: Anxiety and attitudes in black, white and Puerto Rican patients. *Psychosomatic Medicine, 37,* 123–135.

Wissler, C. (1921). The sun dance of the Blackfoot Indians. *American Museum of Natural History Anthropology Papers, 16,* 223–270.

Wolff, B. B., and Langley, S. (1977). Cultural factors and the response to pain. *Culture, Disease, and Healing.* New York: Macmillan.

Zborowski, M. (1952). Cultural components in response to pain. *Journal of Social Issues, 8,* 16–30.

Zborowski, M. (1969). *People in Pain.* San Francisco: Jossey-Bass.

Zola, I. K. (1966). Culture and symptoms: an analysis of patients' presenting complaints. *American Sociological Review, 31,* 615–630.

11

Culture and the Community

Joyceen S. Boyle

Introduction

An understanding of culture and cultural concepts enhances the nurse's knowledge and facilitates culturally relevant nursing care in the community setting. Currently, many nurses practice in diverse settings with clients from a wide variety of cultural backgrounds. With the changing environment for health care, many nurses will function in a community setting with clients and families to maintain health and to promote wellness. In this chapter, the terms *community nursing* and *community health nursing* are used interchangeably. Whether the nurse is employed as a community health nurse in a health department or practices in another community-based setting, the ability to provide culturally competent care is necessary. The practice of nursing in a community setting requires that nurses be comfortable with clients from diverse cultures and the contexts in which they live. Nurses use cultural data to develop successful nursing interventions; cultural knowledge is used in conducting a community assessment and helps to identify high-risk groups and to develop interventions that are consistent with the community's values.

Culturally Competent Nursing Care in Community Settings

The use of cultural concepts in community health nursing practice should begin with a careful assessment of the client and family in their home environment. Cultural data that have implications for care are collected from the client and family during the assessment phase. Pertinent data are discussed with the family in order to develop mutually shared nursing goals. Community health nurses frequently encounter clients and families who must change behaviors and living patterns to maintain health or to

Margaret M. Andrews and Joyceen S. Boyle: TRANSCULTURAL CONCEPTS IN NURSING CARE, SECOND EDITION. © 1995 J.B. Lippincott Company.

promote wellness. Nursing interventions based on cultural knowledge help clients and families adjust more easily and assist nurses to work effectively and comfortably with all clients, especially those from different cultural backgrounds. An appreciation of cultural factors enhances family support of the client and the family's acceptance of nursing goals that have been developed collaboratively with the client and family. A major focus is to help the client and family plan and cope with the changes in activities of daily living.

Cultural data are important in the care of all clients; however, in community health nursing, they are a prerequisite to successful nursing interventions. Community health nursing is practiced in a community setting, often in the home of the client, and frequently requires a more active participation in the care plan on the part of the client and family. Culturally competent nursing care requires that the nurse understand the family lifestyle, the family value system, and health and illness behaviors. As a general rule, health maintenance and health promotion require behavioral changes on the part of the client, and cultural data aid in identifying clients' specific attitudes, values, and behavioral patterns (Bauwens and Anderson, 1992). Nurses often monitor clients with chronic diseases over a long period of time, and the nursing interventions must include aspects of counseling and education as well as anticipatory guidance directed toward helping clients and families adjust to a chronic condition on a long-term basis (see Chap. 7). Nursing care must take account of the diverse cultural factors that will motivate clients to make successful changes in behavior, since many opportunities for health improvement require lifestyle and behavioral changes.

Transcultural nursing practice improves the health of the community as well as the health of individual clients. From a community standpoint, an understanding of culture and cultural concepts will increase the skill and abilities of the nurse to work with diverse groups within the community. Identification of high-risk groups and appropriate community-based strategies to reduce health risk requires considerable knowledge about cultural and ethnic groups and their place within the community. Nurses who have knowledge of and an ability to work with diverse cultures are able to devise effective community interventions to reduce risks that are consistent with the community, group, and individual values.

A Framework for Providing Transcultural Care with the Community

A distinguishing and important aspect of community nursing practice is the nursing focus on the community as the client (Williams, 1992; Clark, 1992). Effective community health nursing practice must reflect accurate knowledge of the causes and distribution of health problems and of effective interventions that are congruent with the values and goals of the community (Institute of Medicine, 1988). A cultural framework for community nursing practice can enhance nurse-community interactions in the following ways:

1. A cultural framework for nursing care helps the nurse to identify subcultures within the larger community and to devise community-based interventions that are specific to health and nursing needs. In the multicultural society of the United States, it is not unusual to find communities that are composed of several distinguishable cultural groups. It is common to hear of "the black community" and "the Hispanic commu-

nity," both of which are framed within still another larger community. Many diverse cultural groups, especially if they are poor, have readily identifiable health concerns (Heckler, 1985a, 1985b). Proposed interventions must be congruent with the needs, resources, and values of specific cultural groups. Interventions that are successful in one subgroup may fail with another subgroup of the same community. A cultural framework facilitates a view of the community as a complex collective yet allows for diversity within the whole as well.

2. Cultural concepts often are useful in identifying and analyzing various components of the community such as the social structure and religious and political systems. How individuals organize themselves to meet group and individual needs is important information for community health nurses because this understanding may enable nurses to provide other needed services. An assessment of whether social institutions such as churches and schools, as well as the health and political system, are responsive to the needs of all citizens sometimes pinpoints critical needs and identifies gaps in care. Cultural traditions within a community often determine the structure of community support systems as well as how resources are organized and distributed.

3. A cultural framework is essential to the community health nurse's identification of the values and cultural norms of a community. Although values are universal features of all cultures, the types and expressions vary widely even within the same community. Norms provide direction for living up to one's values. Values often serve as the foundation for a community's acceptance and use of health resources or a group's participation in community-based intervention programs to promote health and wellness.

The emphasis on the health of the community is not new. Some four decades ago, Paul (1955) observed that

> If you wish to help a community improve its health, you must learn to think like the people of that community. Before asking a group of people to assume new health habits, it is wise to ascertain the existing habits, how these habits are linked to one another, what function they perform, and what they mean to those who practice them [p. 1].

Cultural Issues in Community Nursing Practice

The material presented in this section will assist nurses to be aware of cultural factors that affect health, illness, and the delivery of nursing care. A number of cultural assessment tools or guides are available that provide comprehensive frameworks to guide the nurse in the assessment of cultural factors in the care of individuals, families, and groups (Leininger, 1991; Spector, 1991) (see also Appendix A, Andrews/Boyle Transcultural Nursing Assessment Guide).

Cultural Views of Individuals and Families

When assessing individuals and families, the community health nurse should carefully examine the following:

1. Family roles, typical family households and structure, and dynamics in the family, particularly communication patterns and decision making
2. Health beliefs and practices related to disease causation, treatment of illness, and the use of indigenous healers or folk practitioners
3. Patterns of daily living, including work and leisure activities
4. Social networks, including friends, kin, and significant others, and how they influence health and illness
5. Ethnic, cultural, or national identity of client and family, e.g., identification with a particular group, including language
6. Nutritional practices and how they relate to cultural factors and health
7. Religious influences on well-being, health maintenance, and illness, as well as the impact religion might have on daily living and taboos arising from religious beliefs that might influence health status or care
8. Culturally appropriate behavior styles, including what is manifested during anger, competition, and cooperation, as well as relationships with health professionals, relationships between genders, and relations with groups in the community

A cultural assessment of individuals and families includes all the preceding factors. This list is by no means exhaustive but is presented as a guide for community health nurses to assess cultural aspects of individuals and families.

Cultural Views of the Community

Obviously, many of the factors that are important in the cultural assessment of individuals and families are equally important in a cultural assessment of the community. Bauwens and Anderson (1992) provide a list of pertinent cultural factors to be evaluated in the community nursing assessment. Some of their suggestions as well as others are presented below.

1. Existing influences that divide people into groups within the community (These factors might be ethnicity, religion, social class, occupation, place of residence, language, education, sex, race, and age.)
2. Conditions that lead to social conflict and/or social cohesion among community residents
3. Attitudes toward minority groups, youth and the elderly, males and females, or other identifiable groups
4. Neighborhoods communities and their distinguishing characteristics
5. Formal and informal channels of communication between health providers and members of the community
6. Barriers that may be the result of differences in cultural beliefs and practices
7. Political orientation in the community (attitudes toward authority, ability to use political bases to solve health problems)
8. Patterns of migration in or out of a community and effect on health care services
9. Presence of culturally specific conditions or "folk diseases"
10. Availability of social/community networks that could be mobilized to solve problems

Role of the Family in Transmitting Cultural Beliefs and Practices: A Context for Health and Illness

Cultural values shape human health behaviors and determine what individuals will do to maintain their health status, how they will care for themselves and others who become ill, and where and from whom they will seek health care. Families have an important role in the transmission of cultural values and learned behaviors that relate to both health and illness. It is in the family context that individuals learn basic ways to stay healthy and to ensure the well-being of one's self and family members.

One of the commonalties shared by members of functioning families is a concern for the health and wellness of each individual within the family, since the family has the primary responsibility for meeting the health needs of its members. The community health nurse not only must assess the health of each family member but also must define how well the family can meet family health needs. Just how well families function in relation to this will determine how, when, and where interventions will take place, by whom, and what the specific approach will be to the family. A cultural orientation assists the nurse in understanding cultural values and interactions, the roles that family members assume, as well as the support system available to the family to help them when health problems are identified.

The family is usually a person's most important social unit and provides the social context within which illness occurs and is resolved and within which health promotion and maintenance occur. Some studies have suggested that it is the family that defines health and illness and what to do about each condition as well as deciding whether to seek health care or to follow professional health advice (Danielson, Hamel-Bissell, and Winstead-Fry, 1993). A community health nurse can recognize and use the family's role in promoting and maintaining health. This requires an appreciation of the family context in health and illness and how this varies among diverse cultures.

Cultural Diversity Within Communities

The United States has many diverse cultures as a result of the history of immigration by a variety of cultural and ethnic groups to this country as well as the indigenous populations of Native Americans and Hawaiians. Although broad cultural values are shared by most people in this country, a rich diversity of cultural orientations does exist, including those with considerable variations in health and illness practices.

Subcultures in the United States. *Subcultures* are fairly large aggregates of people, who, although members of a larger cultural group, have shared characteristics that are not common to all members of the culture and which enable the subculture to be thought of as a distinguishable group (Saunders, 1954). Obviously, there can be diversity within each subculture also. Hispanic culture as a group includes Mexican Americans, Puerto Ricans, Cubans, and Central and South Americans, and there is diversity within each of these groups as well.

Certain geographic areas of the country such as Appalachia can be singled out as subcultures. Persons born and reared in the South or in New York City often can be identified by their language and mannerisms as members of a distinct subculture. We used to believe that the United States had a "melting pot" culture in which new arrivals gave up their former language, customs, and values to become Americans. It is now pretty much agreed that the "melting pot" notion may not be an appropriate analogy, at least not for everyone.

Refugee and Immigration Populations. The United States has grown and achieved its success as a nation of immigrants and foreigners. Immigration is a continuing phenomenon in the United States; for example, Spector (1991) pointed out that since 1972, more than 10 million legal immigrants have come to this country. Bauwens and Anderson (1992) observed that most recent immigrants and refugees are unacculturated to prevailing American norms of health beliefs or behaviors. Many arrive with scant economic resources and must learn English and become economically self-sufficient as quickly as possible. Certain factors such as settlement patterns or living near friends or family, communication networks, social class, and education have helped many immigrants maintain their cultural traditions. In addition to the legal entrance of immigrants and refugees, many other persons seeking political asylum have entered the United States, such as Central Americans and Haitians. Often, those seeking asylum or those who enter the country illegally are at considerable risk for health and social problems; in addition to language and employment barriers, they have few economic resources; some have experienced rapid change and traumatic life events, their coping abilities have been overwhelmed, and there are few resources available to assist them. Research Box 11-1 discusses the mental health risks and problems encountered by illegal immigrants.

Research Box 11-1. Immigrants as a High-Risk Population

Aroian, K. A. (1993). Mental health risks by illegal immigrants. *Issues in Mental Health Nursing, 14,* 379–397.

Immigrants are a high-risk population because they are confronted with many adaptive challenges related to extensive changes in lifestyle and environment. Most study participants reported difficulties and distress associated with the illegal immigrant experience. Further data analysis revealed that conflicting reports about the illegal immigrant experience reflect the complexity of the immigration phenomenon. A young individual who is willing to work without job security may find the experience adventuresome, whereas another person may find the same experience very stressful. Positive aspects included opportunity for monetary benefit. Negative aspects included difficulty finding work, exploitation by employers, and uncertainty about the future. The findings sensitize mental health professionals to the difficulties experienced by illegal immigrants and provide direction for clinical interventions with this high-risk group.

Refugee Resettlement. Of particular interest to community nurses and other public health officials has been the resettlement of Southeast Asian refugees throughout the United States as public and voluntary agencies were charged with responsibility for that task. Refugees came from South Vietnam, Cambodia, and Laos. There is tremendous variation among these Southeast Asian refugees based on sociocultural factors such as ethnic group, socioeconomic status, religion, geographic residence, gender, degree of urbanization, and time of migration (Lipson and Meleis, 1985; Montero, 1978; Muecke, 1983).

Unfortunately, from the beginning of the resettlement movement, many Americans, including health professionals, did not comprehend the ethnic, linguistic, and sociocultural variations among refugees, and as could be predicted, this caused many problems. Language barriers necessitated the use of interpreters, a practice that was neither familiar nor comfortable for most health professionals prior to the arrival of the Southeast Asian refugees. In retrospect, the concern for communicable diseases such as tuberculosis and parasitic infections in the refugee population was probably over-emphasized. However, one of the most difficult barriers faced by community health nurses in providing health and nursing care to Southeast Asian refugees was the difference in health beliefs and practices. To further complicate this situation, the traumatic events associated with fleeing their homeland disrupted the refugees' family and social support systems, adding to the cultural shock associated with their introduction to American culture. Although Southeast Asian refugee resettlement has now been limited, selected numbers continue to arrive in the United States.

In addition to Southeast Asians, nurses working in community settings in various geographic areas of the country encounter Afghans, Guatemalans, Salvadorans, Mexicans, Haitians, and others. While there are no firm guidelines for working with refugee populations, there are skills and attitudes that community health nurses can strive to develop. Range (1984) suggested the following for those persons interested in intercultural health work:

1. Listening skills, including being alert for different communication skills such as nonverbal behaviors
2. Careful observation and data collection
3. Patience, not always expecting the client or family to make the changes or adjustments
4. Flexibility, openness to change, and a willingness to learn from others
5. Ability to take risks and to try new things, e.g., a willingness to make a home visit to a family when you cannot pronounce their name correctly and when you know that language will be a barrier and you will feel uncomfortable at times
6. An awareness of your own values and cultural assumptions
7. A sense of humor
8. An ability to identify cultural resources in the community
9. Recognition that the reasons for your feelings of frustration (or the noncompliance on the part of your clients) may be cultural in origin

Maintenance of Traditional Values and Practices

An important aspect of transcultural nursing is the collection of cultural data and the assessment of traditional values and practices and how they are maintained over time. Earlier, in Chap. 1 of this text, the processes of assimilation and acculturation were defined briefly as those ways in which individuals and cultural groups adopt and change over time. Yet, at the same time, both individuals and groups may be resistive to some changes and retain many traditional cultural traits. Because traditional health beliefs and practices influence health and wellness, it is important for the nurse to understand the degree to which the client and family adhere to traditional health values and how these values affect the nursing goals. Unless community health nurses understand traditional health beliefs and practices of their clients and communities, they may intervene at the wrong time or in an inappropriate way.

A number of factors influence a client's or a family's likelihood of maintaining traditional health beliefs and practices:

1. The length of time in the United States
2. The size of the ethnic or cultural group with which an individual identifies and interacts
3. Age of the individual (As a general rule, children acculturate more rapidly than adults.)
4. The ability to speak English and communicate with members of the majority culture
5. Economic and education status (For example, if the family economic situation necessitates that an Afghan woman work outside the home, she may learn English more quickly than if she remains within the household.)
6. Health status of family members (If individuals/families seek health care in this country, they begin to "learn the system," so to speak. This does not mean that they comply with all health advice by any means, but the exposure to the system should decrease anxiety and confusion.)
7. Individuals and groups who have distinguishing ethnic characteristics may be more isolated because of discrimination and thus may retain traditional values related to health beliefs and behaviors.

Culture and Community

Traditionally, community nurses have conducted community nursing assessments to determine the health and nursing needs of the community at large and to identify groups within the community who have special health concerns. Quite frequently the high-risk groups identified in the community assessment are diverse cultural groups, and cultural barriers can impede the delivery of health and nursing services to these special populations.

Access to Health and Nursing Care for Diverse Cultural Groups

Diverse cultural groups, especially those who are poor, face special problems in accessing health and nursing care. Access to care is often determined by economic and geographic factors. Heckler (1985b) called attention to the long-standing and persistent burden of death, disease, and disability experienced by minority groups in this country. All health care indicators such as life span, infant mortality rates, maternal mortality, immunization levels, and others indicate that the health needs of poor minorities are greater than those of the European-American population in general. More specifically, some surveys have indicated that 1 in 11 black persons reported not seeing a doctor for economic reasons, compared with 1 in 20 whites. Blacks were less likely to have health insurance, with 32.2 percent of blacks in poor health going without a doctor's care (Blendon et al., 1989).

It has long been recognized that poverty or economic deprivation and health status are intertwined. Certain cultural groups have faced discrimination and poverty, and their ability to access care has been compromised. Besides economic status and discriminatory factors that limit access to care, geographic location plays an important role. Most rural areas lack medical personnel and the variety of health facilities and services that are available to urban populations. For example, Navajo Indians, living in sparsely settled reservations in the western part of the United States, often must travel long distances over primitive roads to obtain health care services (Szymanski and Szymanski, 1988).

Sensitivity to Cultural Practices in Community Nursing Settings

Another common and rather significant factor that limits access to health services is a lack of understanding on the part of clients of how to use health resources; this lack of understanding may be due in part to cultural factors. Often this lack of understanding means that members of diverse cultural groups are less able to adequately cope with health problems than other members of the community. Nurses can develop a sensitivity to these kinds of problems and help to alleviate them. Some access problems may be related to poverty. Mosley (1977) identified some factors that create barriers between nurses and the poor; community health nurses must be sensitive to these and other factors when planning and implementing health programs or other community-based services. Some important factors that nurses must take into account for culturally sensitive community-based care are shown in Box 11-1.

The need for nurses to be sensitive toward culturally different clients is increasing as we become more aware of the complex interactions between health care providers and clients and how these interactions might affect the client's health. The community health nurse must be able to identify and meet the cultural needs of clients and families; in addition, nurses must take into account social and cultural factors on a community level as well in order to respect cultural values, mobilize local resources, and develop culturally appropriate health programs and services.

Community Nursing Interventions: Cultural Knowledge in Health Maintenance and Health Promotion

Leininger (1978) suggested that cultural groups have their own culturally defined ways of maintaining and promoting health. Pender (1987) stated that "health promoting behaviors can be understood only by considering persons within their social, cultural, and environmental contexts" (p. 16). Community health nurses who have direct access to clients in the context of their daily lives should be especially aware of the importance of cultural knowledge in promoting and maintaining health. The range of cultural influences on health maintenance and promotion is considerable. Major cultural components can be identified that have application to health maintenance and promotion.

Family Systems. Because the family is the basic social unit, it provides the context in which health promotion and maintenance are defined and carried out by family

---

Box 11-1. Factors to Consider in the Nursing Care of Low-Income Clients

---

1. Lack of finances
2. Different value orientations
3. The humiliation of a "means test" to establish eligibility for care
4. Lack of bilingual personnel or staff members or the lack of interpreters to assist clients and providers
5. Fragmentation of care that depersonalizes care and often results in confusion on the part of the client
6. Operational features in the provision of services such as inconvenient locations or hours that preclude clients from accessing care
7. A lack of understanding, trust, and commitment on the part of health care providers
8. A lack of personnel or facilities (For example, because of staff shortages or inadequate facilities, health providers are unable to provide personalized services.)

Mosley, D. Y. (1977). *Nursing Students' Perceptions of the Urban Poor* (Publication No. 23-1694). New York: National League for Nursing Press. Reprinted by permission.

---

members. The nurse can recognize and use the family's role in altering the health status of a family member and in supporting lifestyle changes. This requires an appreciation on the part of the nurse of the role of the family in diverse culture groups. African-American families, for example, may demonstrate interchangeable roles for males and females, extended ties across generations, and strong social support systems, all of which can be tapped by a community health nurse to activate health and wellness in families (Lafargue, 1980; Spector, 1991; Andrews and Bolin, 1993).

Coping Behaviors. Culturally diverse clients often have distinct behaviors to cope with illness as well as to maintain and promote health. These behaviors may be traced to the health-illness paradigms that were discussed earlier in Chap. 1. Beliefs about hot and cold, yin and yang, harmony and balance may underlie actions to prevent disease and to maintain health. Community health nurses who understand cultural values and beliefs of clients can assess clients' understanding of health and illness; these assessment data serve as the basis for planning health guidance and teaching strategies that focus on incorporating cultural beliefs and practices in the nursing care plan.

Lifestyle Practices. Cultural influences have a significant impact on such health-promoting factors as diet, exercise, and stress management. Community health nurses should assess the implications of diet planning and teaching to clients and family members who adhere to culturally prescribed practices concerning foods. There are particular food preferences that some cultural groups believe maintain or promote health. Certain foods often are restricted during an illness episode, just like there are "sick foods"—those special dishes served to an ill person such as the proverbial chicken soup. Cultural preferences determine the style of food preparation and consumption, frequency of eating, time of eating, and eating utensils.

Nurses who work with culturally different clients must evaluate patterns of daily living as well as culturally prescribed activities prior to suggesting forms of physical activity or exercise to clients. Exercise is often defined in terms of white middle-class values. Not everyone has access to the tennis court at a local country club; in addition, many individuals would not feel comfortable in such surroundings.

Another aspect of lifestyle that is important to understand in order to successfully promote health and wellness is the manner in which culturally different clients manage stress. Stress management is learned from childhood through our parents, our social group, and our cultural group. Many cultural groups tend to express psychological distress through somatic symptoms. Flaskerud (1989) suggests that culture has a powerful influence on emotion and that different or alternative modes of expressing distress can be observed in other cultural groups. Some of these are illustrated in Box 11-2.

Health Care Practitioners and Cultural Issues

Kleinman (1980) suggested that the health care system in the United States can be divided into three overlapping sectors, popular, professional, and folk. Families and individuals vary greatly in the manner in which they choose and combine the use of these health systems (Ailinger, 1977; Chen-Louie, 1983; Hautman and Harrison, 1982).

As the community health nurse gathers data about clients' health practices, customs, and family support, she or he should ask the client about health concerns and where the client has gone for care in the past, as well as how illness symptoms have been treated. Many culturally diverse clients—if they feel comfortable in the presence of the

---

Box 11-2. Some Cultural Alternatives in Expressing Emotion and Distress

1. Emotional expression of distress is discouraged.
2. The use of special rituals helps individuals express distress and emotions (e.g., funeral rites).
3. A belief in spirit possession or the evil eye offers a variety of ways to express affect, bring to light sources of conflict, and mobilize support from others.
4. The performance of certain religious rites expresses and channels emotions.
5. A state of illness may be used to express psychosocial distress (somatization).

Adapted from Flaskerud, J. H. (1989). Transcultural concepts in mental health nursing. In J. S. Boyle and M. M. Andrews (Eds.), *Transcultural Concepts in Nursing Care*. Glenview, IL: Scott, Foresman/Little, Brown. Reprinted by permission.

nurse and trust has been established—will report a combination of the use of popular, folk, and professional systems. In addition, clients of the majority culture frequently use alternative systems of care; this fact may be overlooked in the nursing assessment because the nurse assumes that since the family is white or "Anglo" and middle class, they exclusively use the professional sector.

Communication and Culture

Andrews (1993) observed that both verbal and nonverbal communication is important in community health nursing, and both are influenced by the cultural background of both the nurse and the client. In part, nursing is an interpersonal process, and the use of interpersonal techniques, including communication skills, is very important if care is to be effective. The ability of the nurse and a client to communicate with each other through the use of the same language is basic to the success of nursing interventions. However, even when clients speak English, their cultural background influences the expression of emotions and the methods of communicating symptoms or distress, as well as their reactions to health professionals.

The Importance of Language

Language differences can hamper the therapeutic relationship between nurses of one culture and clients of another, and even if they speak the same language, they may do it differently. The use of slang words, colloquial phases, medical terminology, or other regional mannerisms in language may pose communication barriers between health care professionals and clients. The need for nurses to be able to communicate successfully with non-English-speaking or limited-English-speaking clients is important. For example, Muecke (1970) noted the tendency of nurses to avoid clients who could not speak English.

Language differences can be bridged partially in a number of ways. On a short-term basis, the nurse can ask family members who are fluent in English to interpret for the client, although this poses some difficulties. If children are used to assist the nurse, their maturity level and attention span must be considered. In addition, the parent who is the client may be unwilling to discuss certain subjects in front of the child. Often health care facilities can help solve language barriers by registering bilingual staff members at a central place or by employing interpreters to assist professionals in communicating with clients. This may require careful scheduling of activities so that clients, interpreters, and health professionals are all ready to attend to certain tasks at the same time.

Ideally, if nurses or other health professionals live and work in areas where there are large numbers of Spanish-speaking clients, attempts should be made to become fluent in Spanish. If health professionals work with Southeast Asian refugees who represent groups with distinct languages, the nurse should make a special effort to learn to say common expressions for greeting one another and other familiar and frequently used terms. In workings with clients who do not speak English, the nurse should conscientiously attempt, even in English, to emphasize gestures and words and to focus on nonverbal behaviors.

Nonverbal Communication

Muecke (1970) observed that health professionals (or other persons for that matter) unconsciously communicate when they are with another person. Body posture, the space between persons, facial expressions, touch, body gestures, and other mannerisms all give signals of some sort to other persons. Flaskerud (1989) defined a number of differences in nonverbal communication that are culturally determined. For example, self-disclosure or those factors which a client might feel comfortable in discussing with a health professional may vary by culture. For example, European Americans generally are much more open and willing to discuss private and family matters quite freely with friends, acquaintances, and even strangers. Hispanic clients may be very uncomfortable at the thought of revealing what is considered to be a private family matter. Some cultural groups (e.g., some Native Americans) value self-restraint and are uncomfortable if pressed for information or what might be considered "small talk." Asian cultures value politeness, and individuals from those cultural groups often agree with the physician or the nurse not because they *really* agree with him or her, but because they do not want to hurt his or her feelings by disagreeing.

Other factors such as eye contact and body gestures are important methods of nonverbal communication and can be easily misinterpreted by someone from another culture. For example, eye contact may be considered rude in the Native American culture, and exposing the bottom of one's foot is thought to be obscene by some Asian and Arabic groups.

Gestures differ by culture and are important nuances to be understood by health professionals. Touching a Southeast Asian infant on the head may violate taboos that consider the head sacred because it is believed the soul resides there. On the other hand, not touching the head of a Hispanic baby may cause the evil eye, or *mal ojo*, and bring on a serious illness. Stance and body posture are other forms of nonverbal communication that must be assessed and understood within a cultural framework. For example, in some cultural groups, women are expected to keep their heads bowed and to assume a subservient position.

The use of courtesy titles and epithets and formality of address are other aspects of cultural influences on language and communication styles that should be understood by nurses who work with other cultural groups. Generally speaking, European Americans are rather informal and frequently offend others by using first names or ignoring appropriate titles (i.e., "Bill" or "White" versus "Mr. White"). It is always appropriate, even when working with clients of the same culture group, to explore the preferred form of address with the individual client.

Working with Interpreters

Many health departments and community agencies employ interpreters to assist the health professionals who work with refugees, immigrants, or migrant populations. Although many interpreters have some background in health work, many others do not and thus have difficulty in translating and interpreting medical words or symptomatology. It is helpful to meet with the interpreter prior to the encounter with the client to explain the purpose of the visit, the information sought, the teaching content of the visit, and the health goals in general. Often, however, because of time constraints, this is not possible. The following list presents some general guidelines for community health nurses who use interpreters in clinics and/or making home visits:

1. The usual guidelines or protocols for contact with clients still apply. For example, the nurse should introduce herself or himself and make certain the client knows the name of the interpreter too.
2. The nurse should communicate with the client and family, not with the interpreter.
3. Culturally appropriate eye contact, gestures, and body language toward the client and family are important factors to enhance rapport and understanding.
4. Speak only a few sentences at a time, and ask the interpreter to translate for you. This can be a very time-consuming process but is essential for intercultural understanding. In turn, ask that the client speak slowly and allow for adequate translation back to you.
5. Remember that as a health professional or, more specifically, a community health nurse, it is your responsibility to be assured that the client understands what has been said; this means that he or she can repeat what was said back to you for clarification and verification. It also means that the client and family members have an opportunity to ask questions.
6. Be prepared to experience some frustration in working with interpreters and clients who do not speak English or who do not speak it well. These client encounters always take more time and call for creativity and cultural openness on the part of the nurse.

Cultural Assessment

A cultural assessment may be directed toward individual clients to assess their cultural needs (Leininger, 1991) (see also Chap. 2). Individual cultural assessments are accomplished through the use of the nursing process. In community health nursing, the community is considered the client, and several schema have been proposed to help nurses assess the community (Tinkham and Voorhies, 1977; Clark, 1992; Goeppinger and Schuster, 1992). A community nursing assessment requires gathering relevant data, interpreting the data base (including problem analysis and prioritization), and identifying and implementing intervention activities for community health (Goeppinger and Schuster, 1992). Although the community nursing assessment focuses on a broader goal, such as an improvement in the health status of a group of people, an important factor to remember is that it is the characteristics of people that give every community its uniqueness. These common characteristics that influence norms, values, religious practices, educational aspirations, and health and illness behavior are frequently determined by shared cultural experiences. Thus adding the cultural component to a community nursing assessment strengthens the assessment base.

Components of the Cultural Assessment

Orque (1983) developed an ethnic/cultural system framework to assess components of clients' cultural profiles. Leininger (1978) presented assessment domains within which to seek data to understand culture. Later, Leininger (1991) developed a tool to assess clients' cultural patterns by broadly looking at lifeways. Inherent in most definitions of culture is the notion of *shared* cultural backgrounds or *a way of life*. Thus the concept of culture may be more easily applied to a community or group of persons than to an individual. An overview of selected cultural components is presented in Table 11-1. These components can be used to assess diverse cultural groups within a community.

An Overview of Selected Cultural Assessments

Cultural Assessment: Native American (Navajo)

1. Family and kinship systems

   - Often an extended family that consists of an older woman and her husband and unmarried children, together with married daughters and their husbands and unmarried children.
   - The Navajo have many unique categories of relatives.
   - Descent is traced through the mother.

Table 11-1. Components of the cultural assessment

Cultural Component	Description
Family and kinship systems	Is the family nuclear, extended, or "blended"? Do family members live nearby? What are the communication patterns among family members? What is the role and status of individual family members? By age and gender?
Social life	What is the daily routine of the group? What are the important life-cycle events such as birth, marriage, death, etc.? How are the educational systems organized? What are the social problems experienced by the group? How does the social environment contribute to a sense of belonging? What are the group's social interaction patterns? What are its commonly prescribed nutritional practices?
Political systems	Which factors in the political system influence the way the group perceives its status vis-à-vis the dominant culture, i.e., laws, justice, and "cultural heros"? How does the economic system influence control of resources such as land, water, housing, jobs, and opportunities?
Language and traditions	Are there differences in dialects or language spoken between health care professionals and the cultural group? How do major cultural traditions of history, art, drama, etc. influence the cultural identity of the group? What are the common language patterns in regards to verbal and nonverbal communication? How is the use of personal space related to communication?
World view, value orientations, and cultural norms	What are the major cultural values about human nature and man's relationship to nature and to one another? How can the groups' ethical beliefs be described? What are the norms and standards of behavior (authority, responsibility, dependability, and competition). What are the cultural attitudes about time, work, and leisure?
Religion	What are the religious beliefs and practices of the group? How do they relate to health practices? What are the rituals and taboos surrounding major life events such as birth and death?
Health beliefs and practices	What are the group's values, attitudes, and beliefs regarding health and illness? Does the cultural group seek care from indigenous health (or folk) practitioners? Who makes decisions about health care? Are there biologic variations that are important to the health of this group?

- Head of household is the husband, although the wife has a voice in decision making.
- Children are highly valued.
- There is prestige with age as long as the elderly person can function independently.

2. Social life

- The earth and nature are valued; the individual should be in harmony with nature; this thought is interwoven with daily activities.
- Life-cycle events are marked by special rituals; for example, the blessingway takes place shortly after the birth of a child.
- Like many other indigenous people, the Navajo suffer high rates of alcoholism, suicide, and homicide.
- Tribal and family ties are strong and contribute to a sense of belonging to a social group.
- Educational opportunities are often limited because of an inferior school system.
- Diet is often high in carbohydrates and fats; staple foods are corn, mutton, and fried bread.

3. Political systems

- The system of tribal government was imposed by Anglos.
- Poverty and high rates of unemployment are overriding concerns.
- The extended family has an economic as well as a social function.
- Control of resources (land, water) has been problematic given the role of the U.S. government.
- Improving housing, sanitation, and work opportunities are major goals.
- A major problem is that of making deteriorated lands productive in an underpopulated region.

4. Language and traditions

- Most of the younger Navajo speak English. Reading, writing, and speaking English are taught in all the schools. Many elderly Navajo speak little or no English.
- There are many homonyms in the Navajo language, words that have identical sounds but different meanings. The Navajo language is very specific.
- Periods of silence during communication show respect.
- Nonverbal communication is a high art form among the Navajo, and there may be little eye contact.
- There is a lack of need for personal space.
- The group has a history of oppression from the white dominant group.
- The "Long Walk" (a forced move of 300 miles to Ft. Sumner in 1863) was a major calamity for the Navajo and remains a poignant chapter in cultural history that enforces Native American culture and identity.

5. World view, value orientations, and cultural norms

- The basic nature of human beings is neither good nor bad; both qualities exist in each person.
- Nature is more powerful than human beings.
- Individual success is not valued as highly as providing security to the extended family.

- The traditional Navajo views on the relationship of human beings with other human beings are both individualistic and collateral.
- The integrity of the individual must be respected. There is respect for the choice of an individual (even a child's decision is respected).
- There is also pressure for a Navajo to consider the extended family's welfare when making decisions.
- Time orientations are not strict; work and productivity are valued.

6. Religious ideology

- Religion enters every phase of the traditional Navajo life, and an important emphasis is on curing illness.
- There are many important Navajo ceremonies that may be used with illness; theology and medicine are difficult to separate in traditional Navajo culture.
- Earth and nature are a part of the Navajo's cosmology, and health is viewed as harmony with the universe.

7. Health beliefs and practices

- Health is a reflection of a correct relationship between human beings and the environment. Health is associated with good, blessing, and beauty, all that is valued in life.
- All ailments, both physical and mental, are believed to have supernatural aspects. The Navajo frequently use both their traditional health care system, including traditional health care practitioners, and the modern health care system.
- There are two major types of traditional health care practitioners; the first is the diviner or diagnostician. Different methods, such as star gazing or hand trembling, are used to identify the cause of an illness. Then, once the cause of the illness is determined, the individual seeks the second kind of practitioner, the singer, who provides the treatment that counters the cause of disease and restores harmony.
- Different types of ceremonials as well as herbal medicines and traditional remedies may be used.

(Adapted from Boyle, Szymanski, and Szymanski, 1993; Szymanski and Szymanski, 1988; and Kluckhohn and Leighton, 1974.)

Cultural Assessment: Mexican American

1. Family and kinship system

- The traditional Mexican-American family is an extended family with "fictive kin" (*compadrazgo*) or strong godparent relationships.
- Courtesy and respect toward the elderly and adults are emphasized.
- Mexican Americans are family oriented, with the father viewed as the head of the household and others in the family subordinate to him.
- Females are usually subordinate to males; there may be a strong mother-son relationship.
- Traditionally, the family is important in Mexican-American culture and is characterized by a close-knit kin group.

2. Social life

- Social life revolves around the family and family activities.
- Children are greatly valued, and extended family members play an important role in everyday activities.
- Many Mexican Americans have retained their cultural food practices. Staples are rice, beans, corn, and chilies.
- There is diversity in the cultural identification of Mexican Americans due to a number of factors. Many have faced discriminatory policies in terms of employment, education, and access to health care.

3. Political systems

- There may be diversity in ethnic/cultural identification.
- Because of geographic closeness of Mexico, there is considerable movement of Mexican Americans back and forth between the United States and Mexico; many still have relatives and/or family members in Mexico.

4. Language and traditions

- A large percentage of this cultural group speaks Spanish, although dialects may differ. Language barriers have presented problems in obtaining health care services.
- Many Mexican Americans share the cultural traditions (history, art, literature) of the majority culture; others may be more bicultural.
- Communication styles, particularly self-disclosure, may vary from the dominant culture.
- The use of personal space also differs, with Mexican Americans generally needing less personal space than members of the majority culture.
- Touch is a strong form of expression among members of the same sex.

5. World view, value orientation, and cultural norms

- There is great diversity among Mexican Americans depending on acculturation, length of time in the United States, frequency of visits to Mexico, and other factors.
- Present time orientation is most common.
- Lineal and collateral relationships are usually found in Mexican-American cultural groups; for example, lines of authority (patron-peon or boss-worker) may be reflected in the Mexican-American family, where the father is the dominant authoritarian figure.
- Modesty, privacy, and confidentiality are valued in this cultural system.
- Generally speaking, Mexican Americans do not adhere to the the work ethic of the majority culture.
- There is a tendency to view life events as the "will of God."
- Fatalism is often seen in Mexican-American culture.

6. Religious ideology

- About 85 to 90 percent of Mexican Americans are Catholic and may turn to religious practices to overcome illness (Monrroy, 1983).
- Health is viewed as harmonious relationships between the social and spiritual realms.
- During illness, dying, and/or death, religious activities or rituals are frequent.

- Because of religious beliefs, family planning methods may not be acceptable.
- Illness may be viewed as a punishment from God and can be prevented by correct behavior.
- Disruptions or difficulties in social relationships or cultural rules may be deleterious to an individual's mental or physical well-being.

7. Health beliefs and practices

- The diversity within this group calls for careful assessment, since Mexican Americans may recognize a number of scientific disease categories and folk concepts of illness.
- Rubel (1966) identified two major categories of folk illness in traditional Mexican-American culture, the natural illnesses and those caused by evil supernatural forces. The first category includes four common folk diseases: *molera caida* (fallen fontanel), *empacho* (indigestion infection), *mal ojo* (evil eye), and *susto* (fright). The second category includes illnesses that can be traced to witchcraft.
- A wide variety of folk practitioners may be used; the most common one is a *curandero*, who uses theories of hot and cold, strong and weak, traditional remedies, and herbal medicines to treat illnesses. Other practitioners are *parteras* (lay midwives), *sobadors* (bonesetters or masseuses), and spiritualists.

(Adapted from Clark, 1992; and Martinez, 1993.)

Using Cultural Knowledge in Primary, Secondary, and Tertiary Preventive Programs

Nurses working in community settings use two health-related concepts that are usually identified with the practice of community health nursing. The first concept is that of *community as client*, or a *population-focused practice*; this concept was discussed briefly in the first sections of this chapter. The second concept of importance to community nurses is that of *levels of prevention*. Preventive care, consisting of primary, secondary, and tertiary activities, is directed toward high-risk groups or aggregates within a community setting. *Primary prevention* is comprised of those activities which prevent the occurrence of an illness, a disease, or a health risk. *Secondary prevention* involves the early diagnosis and appropriate treatment of a condition or disease. *Tertiary prevention* focuses on rehabilitation and/or the prevention of recurrences or complications. The major aim of community-based preventive programs is not to seek to prevent illnesses in specific individuals, but rather to seek to reduce the risk for the population at large. As long as preventive actions are directed toward a given population rather than toward individuals, there is a chance of altering the general balance of forces so that although not all will benefit, many will have a chance to avoid illness. This last section of this chapter discusses the use of cultural knowledge to plan community nursing interventions for diverse cultural groups at the primary, secondary, and tertiary levels of prevention.

Primary Prevention: Prenatal Services in a Mexican-American Community

Greener (1989) observed that "all cultures recognize pregnancy as a special transition period, and many have particular customs and beliefs that dictate activity and behavior during pregnancy" (p. 97). For some time now, it has been recognized that adequate prenatal care helps to reduce infant mortality. With this in mind, public health agencies have tried to improve maternal and infant services to high-risk populations. The March of Dimes Birth Defects Foundation (1982) noted that Hispanic women not only tend to begin receiving prenatal care later in their pregnancies than European-American women but also make fewer visits for such care. Heckler (1985a) reported that only 58 percent of Mexican-American mothers begin prenatal care in the first trimester, less than for African Americans or non-Hispanic women. Heckler noted that the neonatal mortality rate appeared good for Mexican-American babies, but there is a concern that the rate is artificially low due to underreporting. Risk factors of pregnancy include age (both extremes), parity, and low socioeconomic status. Many women of Mexican-American origin fall in these categories; a high-risk group of great concern is the pregnant adolescent. A program of primary prevention would focus on preventing infant mortality and other health problems in Mexican-American mothers and their infants. Nursing care must be broadly focused, providing some specific services but also helping clients access other resources in the community. Information can be provided on an individual basis, or other means such as media campaigns can be geared to the Mexican-American community, informing women of available services and how to access them. Culturally related factors that might prevent Mexican-American women from obtaining care early in their pregnancies would include the factors discussed below.

Access to Care. There are various reasons why Mexican Americans might not seek care during pregnancy. Cost is often a factor, and in many areas of the country, Mexican Americans have tended to belong to poorer socioeconomic groups (Kay, 1978; Heckler, 1985a, 1985b). The community health nurse can provide information about community resources and help clients access care early in pregnancy by referral to appropriate agencies.

Cultural Views about Modesty. Any prenatal program that serves Mexican-American women may be underutilized unless consideration is given to some Mexican-American women's extreme modesty and resistance to examinations by male health care providers. The use of female nurse-practitioners and midwives is ideal for this population. In addition, some consideration should be given to incorporation of the traditional *parteras* (lay midwives) into the preventive educational services if deemed appropriate.

Language Barriers. It is absolutely essential in a prenatal program for a Mexican-American population that the majority of health care professionals in the program be bilingual. If this is impossible, interpreters must be employed to facilitate the professional services. All prenatal classes should be offered in Spanish and English. This sometimes means that two classes must be offered concurrently; many Mexican-American women speak predominantly either Spanish and English and would choose the class where they could understand the language. The availability of health education material in Spanish is critical to reinforce teaching and anticipatory guidance.

Cultural Views of Motherhood and Pregnancy. There is some evidence to indicate that women of Mexican-American culture may adhere to different value orientations and cultural views of motherhood and pregnancy (White, 1985). The Mexican-American culture traditionally values motherhood, and young women are encouraged to prepare themselves for this role. In most traditional cultures, motherhood is the appropriately defined role for women, and there are few alternatives. White (1985) found that self-image during pregnancy may differ in Mexican-American women from that found in the dominant culture. Pregnant Mexican-American women viewed their growing body as feminine, softening, and beautiful. Community health nurses are in important positions to help pregnant women prepare for motherhood and associated responsibilities. Understanding and reinforcing the approved cultural views of pregnancy may be helpful for clients in that trust and mutual goal setting can develop more rapidly.

Traditional Pregnancy-Related Folk Beliefs of Mexican Americans. Many Mexican Americans adhere to traditional beliefs and practices related to pregnancy and childbirth. Traditionally, children are greatly valued and desired soon after marriage. Like many other cultures, Mexican Americans consider pregnancy, birth, and the immediate postpartum period as a time of great vulnerability for women and their newborns. Koster (1986) noted that pregnant women frequently deal with this time of crisis by consulting with or being advised and cared for by respected older women such as an *abuela* or grandmother. Some traditional beliefs and practices related to pregnancy and childbirth are shown in Box 11-3.

Changing High-Risk Behaviors in Pregnant Mexican-American Women. Certain high-risk behaviors during pregnancy, such as smoking, using drugs, alcohol consumption, and poor nutritional habits, should be targeted by the community health nurse for change.

Box 11-3. Selected Beliefs and Practices of Pregnancy and Childbirth in Traditional Mexican-American Culture

Avoid strong emotions such as anger and fear during pregnancy.

Cool air is dangerous during pregnancy and should be avoided.

Bathe often during pregnancy; be active so that the baby will not grow too big and hinder delivery.

Eat a nutritious diet; "give in" to food cravings.

Massage is helpful to place the baby in the right position for birth.

Don't raise your arms above your head or sit with your legs crossed during pregnancy because it will cause knots in the umbilical cord.

Moonlight should be avoided during pregnancy, especially during an eclipse, because it will cause a birth defect.

After delivery, a 40-day period known as *la dieta* or *cuarentena* is observed. Activities and certain foods are restricted.

Chamomile tea will relieve nausea and vomiting in pregnancy.

Heartburn can be treated with baking soda.

Laxatives and purges may be used to "clean" the intestinal tract.

Although there is no set rule of thumb, a Mexican-American mother-to-be may respond to suggestions for change if she is convinced that her behavior will cause harm to her baby. Family and social support groups found in Mexican-American culture also can be helpful and supportive to expectant mothers wanting to make lifestyle changes.

Prenatal services should go beyond the birth of the baby to include information about breast feeding and family planning services. Traditionally, it has been assumed by some health professionals that family planning services would not be accepted in a Mexican-American population because of religious opposition and *machismo*—the need of the male to prove his manhood by having children or the belief in the biologic superiority of men. However, Monrroy (1983) suggested that Mexican-American men as well as women are interested in family planning and are concerned about the number of children that they could support.

Strategies for promoting breast feeding should be identified and encouraged. For example, educational levels, family experiences with breast feeding, husband's attitude, the need to return to work, and feelings of embarrassment have been associated with infant feeding choices among Mexican-American women (Young and Kaufman, 1988). These factors need to be explored with individual women in order to help Mexican-American women make choices best suited for them.

Mexican-American Cultural Networks. Traditionally, the family is very important in Mexican-American culture, and nursing care should be family-focused. Ties often go beyond the family to a wide network of kin. Bauwens and Anderson (1992) observed that a Mexican American is expected to turn first to the family for help; if preventive services are to be effective, they must tap these kinds of cultural networks to ensure the support of community residents in preventive programs in their neighborhoods that involve family members, neighbors, or friends.

Secondary Levels of Prevention: Type II Diabetes and Ute Indians

Non-insulin-dependent diabetes (NIDD), or type II diabetes, is seen commonly among some Native Americans, and certain tribes have extremely high rates of the disease. By all accounts, the high rate of diabetes in Native American groups is a leading and devastating health problem. This health problem was discussed in more detail in Chap. 5.

Cultural Views of Diabetes. The reasons for the epidemic of type II diabetes among some Native Americans are not clear. It is believed that some Native American tribes have an underlying genetic propensity for the disease that is triggered by changes in dietary practices, a sedentary lifestyle, and increasing obesity (Neel, 1962; West, 1978).

Because of the high rate of diabetes on some reservations, numerous secondary preventive services that focus on early diagnosis and treatment have been instigated. Many of these secondary prevention programs have been modeled after programs that have been successful with white middle-class Americans. Some culturally related beliefs and practices that mitigate against the success of these programs have been identified. Other culturally related factors that could influence the success of secondary preventive programs for diabetes among some Native Americans are shown in Box 11-4.

Box 11-4. Beliefs and Practices Related to Diabetes Found in Some Native Americans

Nutritional practices:

Diets high in calories, carbohydrates, and fats.

Sharing communal meals is a common and valued cultural practice.

High incidence of obesity in some groups.

Food preparation often adds fats and calories.

Snack foods (potato chips, carbonated beverages, prepackaged pastries) are common.

High intake of alcohol seriously compromises the treatment of diabetes.

Activity levels/fitness practices:

Sedentary lifestyles have become common.

Many reservations lack recreational facilities.

Formal exercise activities are associated with the white man's culture and are not thought to be appropriate for Native Americans.

Beliefs and values related to diabetes:

Ideal body image favors a heavier physique, and weight gain is considered normal; thinness is a cause for worry and concern.

Concept of "control of one's body," i.e., weight, glucose levels, blood pressure, may conflict with values and norms of Native American culture. Native American clients may be uncomfortable with comparison of individual performance against others or against the norms and standards of medical care.

Many Native Americans are uncomfortable with the discussion of "private body functions" such as urine testing in a public situation.

Illness is a personal and unpleasant topic, and Native American clients may be uncomfortable when asked to talk about it.

Diabetes is a white man's disease; Native Americans did not have diabetes until the white man came.

The term *diabetic* may be offensive to some, and the label *diabetic clinic* might discourage clients from seeking health care services.

White health professionals may be viewed with some suspicion and distrust given the past history of cultural contact between whites and Native Americans.

Because diabetes is so common in some tribal groups, there is a fatalism about developing the disease, especially if a family member already has diabetes.

Readers are cautioned that validation of beliefs and practices should always take place with individual clients and families, and stereotyping (thinking that all Native Americans are the same) should be avoided.

Culturally Appropriate Nursing Interventions at the Secondary Level of Prevention. Nursing interventions at the secondary level of prevention should focus on the implementation of healthful lifestyle changes that ultimately will decrease the complications of diabetes. Most of these are related to what health professionals call *diet* and *exercise*, but what is more appropriate for Native American culture is a focus on *health* and a *healthy lifestyle*.

Emphasize health and a healthy lifestyle rather than negative factors such as control of diabetes, prevention of complications, weight reduction, and exercise. The choice of words, as well as the emphasis, is important. For example, when teaching the client and family about diabetic diets, the nurse can substitute the word *nutrition* for *diet*, thus removing the negative perceptions and leading to a nursing plan that emphasizes substitution rather than deprivation. *Substituting* fruits for candy bars and packaged pastries, whole grains for potato chips or doughnuts, and vegetables for sugared snacks will improve nutritional status and lead to a healthier lifestyle. Special traditional foods, even fried bread, can be eaten on special occasions, and other types of bread can be substituted during regular meals. Tom-Orme (1984) suggested that desirable weight can be computed on the basis of a large body frame, and clients can be evaluated by their individual progress rather than by fixed norms.

Health education can be oriented toward individual clients and directed toward the family rather than provided in an impersonal clinic situation. Physical activities that are culturally congruent can be encouraged, and again, the value of health and a healthy lifestyle should be stressed over exercise and weight reduction. Physical activities that are congruent with overall lifestyle and cultural context will be easier to incorporate into daily living situations.

Kinship and Community Support for Programs of Secondary Prevention. Usually, the Native American family system is an extended family that includes several households of closely related kin. Primeaux and Henderson (1981) observed that "to be poor in the [Native American] . . . world is to be without relatives." Family structure becomes exceedingly important during times of crisis, since family members are a source of support, comfort, assistance, and strength. The importance of cultural ties with kin and other members of the reservation community always must be considered in planning for early diagnosis and treatment programs. It is in this context (family and community) that clients are encouraged and supported not only to seek care but also to instigate lifestyle changes that are congruent with cultural practices and that will enhance the health status of all members of the family and, ultimately, the tribal community.

Tertiary Levels of Prevention: Hypertension and African Americans

Significance of the Problem. African Americans are a highly heterogeneous group and display considerable variation in health beliefs and behaviors. For the most part, this section will discuss a more traditional, rural African-American culture, and the reader is advised to validate beliefs and behaviors with individual clients and communities.

Hypertension is a major risk factor for heart disease and stroke. Mean blood pressure levels are higher in African Americans than in European Americans, with a marked excess in African Americans. Heckler (1985a) stated that "hypertensive blacks were at least as likely as whites of the same sex to be treated with antihypertensive medication and nearly as likely to have their blood pressure controlled" (p. 110). Heckler also noted that from 1968 to 1982, stroke mortality in blacks declined 50 percent, and coronary heart disease also decreased dramatically. Hypertension control has certainly been one of the factors responsible for this improvement; it is critical that efforts to treat hypertension in the African-American population be continued. Unfortunately, appropriate care often has been complicated by limited access to care, discrimination, and poverty.

Tertiary prevention seeks to reduce disability and to prevent complications from developing. A major aim of nursing care when implementing tertiary activities is to help clients adjust to limitations in daily living, to increase coping skills, to control symptoms, and in general, to minimize the complications of disease by reducing the rate of residual damage in a given population. Cultural factors that should be considered in tertiary prevention programs for African Americans are shown in Box 11-5.

Using Cultural Knowledge in Tertiary Prevention. Community nurses have demonstrated competence in the management of community hypertension programs. While these programs are vital to the early diagnosis and management of hypertension, they also include a component that focuses on helping clients manage a chronic disease, an aspect of tertiary prevention. In addition, community health nurses are in the advantageous position of assessing clients and families in their own homes and neighborhoods. This provides an understanding of the daily life situation faced by clients that other health care professionals often lack. It is this understanding that community health nurses can bring to bear when helping clients with tertiary preventive activities.

Summary

Cultural concepts related to community health nursing practice have been discussed. A framework for providing culturally sensitive nursing care has been introduced to help nurses provide care to individuals and groups with diverse cultural backgrounds. This framework helps nurses use cultural knowledge in assessing, planning, and implementing nursing care. This chapter has explored the role of the family in transmitting beliefs and practices of health and illness. Cultural diversity within communities was addressed, and various subcultures within the United States, including refugees and immigrants, were discussed.

Cultural concepts were explored as they relate to the community at large. Major health care systems and practitioners were described. Concepts related to communication and culture were examined as they relate to community health nursing practice. Cultural assessments were described as integral components of a community nursing assessment. Selected cultural assessments of Navajo (Native American) and Mexican-American clients were presented as examples to provide cultural data to assist nurses in providing culturally sensitive nursing care to individuals and groups.

Preventive care in the community is of particular importance to community health nursing. The use of cultural knowledge in primary, secondary, and tertiary levels of

Box 11-5. Cultural Factors to Consider in Planning Tertiary Prevention for a Traditional African-American Population

Language:
African-American communication concepts/patterns can be identified and used in community education programs.

Cultural health beliefs:
Good health comes from good luck.

Health is related to harmony in nature.

Illnesses are classified as "natural" or "unnatural."

Illness may be God's punishment.

Maintenance of health is associated with "reading the signs," i.e., the phase of the moon, seasons of the year, position of the planets.

Cultural health practices:
Use of herbs, oils, powders, roots, and other home remedies may be common.

Cultural healers:
Older woman ("old lady") in the community who has a knowledge of herbs and healing

Spiritualist who is called by God to heal disease or solve emotional or personal problems

Voodoo priest/priestess who is a powerful cultural healer who uses voodoo, bone reading, etc. to heal or bring about desired events

Root doctor who uses roots, herbs, oils, candles, and ointments in healing rituals

Time orientation:
May be present time oriented, which makes preventive care more difficult to implement and maintain.

Nutritional practices:
Soul food takes it name from "a feeling of kinship" among African Americans and may be served at home, provided at church dinners, or served at homestyle restaurants.

Diets may reflect traditional rural southern foods such as greens, grits, corn bread, chick peas, etc.

Economic status:
African Americans account for a large number of those persons in the lower socioeconomic strata in American society.

Educational status:
High aspirations for education, but socioeconomic status and other complex factors limit educational opportunities.

Box 11-5 *(continued)*

Family and social networks:
Often strong extended family networks with a sense of obligation to relatives.

Self-concept:
The importance of race has been a continual issue for the self-identity of African Americans.

Impact of racism:
Unfortunately, racism is still present, and a negative perception of the African American's skin color by health professionals will seriously interfere with efficacious health care.

Religion:
African-American churches have tremendous influence on daily life of their members because they serve as a source of spiritual and social support.

The African-American church acts as a caretaker for the cultural characteristics of African-American culture (Roberson, 1985).

Biologic variations:
There is a high incidence of lactose intolerance and lactase deficiency; this has implications for diet planning if African-American clients cannot tolerate milk or milk products.

There is a higher prevalence of hypertension among African Americans than among European Americans.

Sickle cell anemia is more common among African Americans.

Adapted from Bloch, B. (1983). Nursing care of black patients. In M. S. Orque, B. Bloch, and L. S. A. Monrroy (Eds.), *Ethnic Nursing Care: A Multicultural Approach*, pp. 81–113. St. Louis: CV. Mosby; and Andrews, M. M., and Bolin, T. (1993). The African American community. In J. M. Swanson and M. Albrecht (Eds.), *Community Health Nursing: Promoting the Health of Aggregates*, pp. 443–458. Philadelphia: W. B. Saunders.

---

prevention was introduced. Examples of cultural diversity and levels of prevention were described to illustrate how cultural knowledge can be used in community health nursing practice.

Learning Activities

1. Assess sociocultural factors and their impact on health care for a subcultural group within your community.
2. Conduct a community cultural assessment of a cultural group within your community.
3. Develop a program plan or intervention that has components of primary, secondary, and tertiary prevention.
4. Attend religious services at a church, temple, synagogue, or place of worship for a religion different from your own.

5. Inquire about translation or interpreter services at a local hospital or health care agency. Which languages or linguistic groups are accommodated? What plans are in place to provide care to clients when interpreters are not available?
6. Identify alternative health care practitioners within your community. Which subcultures do they serve?

References

Ailinger, R. (1977). A study of illness referral in a Spanish-speaking community. *Nursing Research, 26,* 53–56.

Andrews, M. M. (1993). Cultural diversity and community health nursing. In J. M. Swanson and M. Albrecht (Eds.), *Community Health Nursing: Promoting the Health of Aggregates* (pp. 371–406). Philadelphia: W. B. Saunders.

Andrews, M. M., and Bolin, L. (1993). The African-American community. In J. M. Swanson and M. Albrecht (Eds.), *Community Health Nursing: Promoting the Health of Aggregates* (pp. 433–458). Philadelphia: W. B. Saunders.

Aroian, K. J. (1993). Mental health risks and problems encountered by illegal immigrants. *Issues in Mental Health Nursing, 14,* 379–397.

Bauwens, E., and Anderson S. (1992). Social and cultural influences on health care. In M. Stanhope and J. Lancaster (Eds.), *Community Health Nursing: Process and Practice for Promoting Health*, 3d Ed. (pp. 91–108). St. Louis: C. V. Mosby.

Blendon, R. J., Aiken, L. H., Freeman, H. E., and Corey, C. R. (1989). Access to medical care for black and white Americans. *Journal of the American Medical Association, 261*(2), 278–281.

Bloch, B. (1983). Nursing care of black patients. In M. S. Orque, B. Bloch, and L. A. Monrroy (Eds.), *Ethnic Nursing Care: A Multicultural Approach* (pp. 81–113). St. Louis: C. V. Mosby.

Boyle, J. S., Szymanski, M. T., and Szymanski, M. E. (1993). Improving home health care for the Navajo. *Nursing Connections, 5*(4), 3–13.

Chen-Louie, T. (1983). Nursing care of Chinese-American patients. In M. S. Orque, B. Bloch, and L. S. Monrroy (Eds.), *Ethnic Nursing Care: A Multicultural Approach* (pp. 183–218). St. Louis: C. V. Mosby.

Clark, M. J. (1992). Cultural influences on community health. In M. J. Clark (Ed.), *Nursing in the Community* (pp. 281–337). Norwalk, CT: Appleton & Lange.

Danielson, C. B., Hamel-Bissel, B., and Winstead-Fry, P. (1993). *Families, Health and Illness: Perspectives on Coping and Intervention.* St. Louis: C. V. Mosby.

Flaskerud, J. H. (1989). Transcultural concepts in mental health nursing. In J. S. Boyle and M. M. Andrews (Eds.), *Transcultural Concepts in Nursing Care.* Glenview, IL: Scott, Foresman.

Goeppinger, J., and Schuster, G. F., III (1992). Community as client: Using the nursing process to promote health. In M. Stanhope and J. Lancaster (Eds.), *Community Health Nursing: Process and Practice for Promoting Health*, 3d Ed. (pp. 253–276). St. Louis: C. V. Mosby.

Greener, D. L. (1989). Transcultural nursing care of the childbearing woman and her family. In J. S. Boyle and M. M. Andrews (Eds.), *Transcultural Concepts in Nursing Care.* Glenview, IL: Scott, Foresman.

Hautman, M. A., and Harrison, J. K. (1982). Health beliefs and practices in a middle-income Anglo-American neighborhood. *Advances in Nursing Science, 4*(3), 49–63.

Heckler, M. M. (1985a). *Report of the Secretary's Task Force on Black and Minority Health, Vol. 1: Executive Summary.* Washington: U.S. Department of Health and Human Services.

Heckler, M. M. (1985b). *Report of the Secretary's Task Force on Black and Minority Health, Vol. 2: Crosscutting Issues in Minority Health.* Washington: U.S. Department of Health and Human Services.

Henderson, G., and Primeaux, M. (1981). *Transcultural Health Care.* Menlo Park, CA.: Addison-Wesley.

Institute of Medicine, Committee for the Study of the Future of Public Health, Division of Health Care Services (1988). *The Future of Public Health.* Washington: Academy Press.

Kay, M. A. (1978). The Mexican American. In A. Clark (Ed.), *Culture, Childbearing, Health Professionals.* Philadelphia: F. A. Davis.

Kleinman, A. (1980). *Patients and Healers in the Context of Culture.* Berkeley, CA.: University of California Press.

Kluckhohn, C. & Leighton, D. (1974). *The Navaho.* Cambridge, MA: Harvard University Press.

Koster, V. A. (1986). Abuelas: Traditional and Transitional Involvement in Childbirth. Unpublished master's thesis, University of Utah, Salt Lake City, Utah.

LaFargue, J. P. (1980). A survival strategy: Kinship networks. *American Journal of Nursing, 80*(9), 1636–1640.

Leininger, M. (1978). *Transcultural Nursing: Concepts, Theories and Practices.* New York: John Wiley & Sons.

Leininger, M. (1991). Leininger's acculturation health care assessment tool for cultural patterns in traditional and nontraditional lifeways. *Journal of Transcultural Nursing, 2*(2), 40–42.

Lipson, J., and Meleis, A. I. (1985). Culturally appropriate care: The case of immigrants. *Topics in Clinical Nursing, 7*(3), 48–56.

March of Dimes Birth Defects Foundation (1982). Hispanics less likely to get early prenatal care. *Maternal/Newborn Advocate,* September (2), 4.

Martinez, R. A. (1993). Cultural influences in the community: The Mexican American community. In J. M. Swanson and M. Albrecht (Eds.), *Community health nursing: Promoting the health of aggregates* (pp. 407–420). Philadelphia: W. B. Saunders.

Monrroy, L. S. (1983). Nursing care of Raza/Latino patients. In M. S. Orque, B. Bloch, and L. S. Monrroy (Eds.), *Ethnic Nursing Care: A Multicultural Approach* (pp. 115–148). St. Louis: C. V. Mosby.

Montero, D. (1978). *The Vietnamese Refugees in America: Patterns of Socioeconomic Adaption and Assimilation.* College Park, MD.: Institute of Urban Studies, University of Maryland.

Mosley, D. Y. (1977). *Nursing Students' Perceptions of the Urban Poor* (Publication No. 23-1694). New York: National League for Nursing.

Muecke, M. A. (1970). Overcoming the language barrier. *Nursing Outlook, 18*(4), 53–54.

Muecke, M. A. (1983). Caring for Southeast Asian refugee patients in the USA. *American Journal of Public Health, 73*(4), 431–438.

Neel, J. V. (1962). Diabetes mellitus: A "thrifty" genotype rendered detrimental by progress. *American Journal of Human Genetics,* 14, 353–362.

Orque, M. S. (1983). Orque's ethnic/cultural system: A framework for nursing care. In M. S. Orque, B. Bloch, and L. A. Monrroy (Eds.), *Ethnic Nursing Care: A Multicultural Approach* (pp. 5–48). St. Louis: C. V. Mosby.

Paul, B. (1955). *Health, Culture and Community.* New York: Russell Sage Foundation.

Pender, N. J. (1987). Health and health promotion: Conceptual dilemmas. In M. E. Duffy and N. J. Pender (Eds.), *Proceedings of a Wingspread Conference: Conceptual Issues in Health Promotion* (pp. 7–23). Indianapolis: Sigma Theta Tau International, Honor Society of Nursing.

Primeaux, M., and Henderson, G. (1981). American Indian patient care. In G. Henderson and M. Primeaux (Eds.), *Transcultural Health Care* (pp. 239–254). Menlo Park, CA: Addison-Wesley.

Range, M. (1984). Preparation for international nursing: Ivory tower vs. trial and error. In M. M. Andrews and P. A. Lugwig (Eds.), *Proceedings of an International Conference: Nursing Practice in a Kaleidoscope of Cultures* (pp. 57–65). Salt Lake City: The University of Utah College of Nursing.

Roberson, M. H. B. (1985). The influence of religious beliefs on health choices of Afro-Americans. *Topics in Clinical Nursing, 7*(3), 57–63.

Rubel, A. J. (1966). *Across the Tracks: Mexican-Americans in a Texas City.* Austin: University of Texas Press.

Saunders, L. (1954). *Cultural Differences and Medical Care: The Case of the Spanish-Speaking People of the Southwest.* New York: Russell Sage Foundation.

Spector, R. E. (1991). *Cultural Diversity in Health and Illness,* 3d Ed. New York: Appleton-Century-Crofts.

Szymanski, M. T., and Szymanski, M. E. (1988). Home Health Care for the Navajo. Unpublished master's project, University of Utah, Salt Lake City, Utah.

Tinkham, C. W., and Voorhies, E. F. (1977). *Community Health Nursing: Evaluation and Practice,* 2d Ed. New York: Appleton-Century-Crofts.

Tom-Orme, L. (1984). Diabetes intervention on the Uintah-Ouray reservation. In J. Uhl (Ed.), *Proceedings of the Ninth Annual Transcultural Nursing Conference* (pp. 27–38). Salt Lake City: Transcultural Nursing Society.

West, K. (1978). *Diabetes in American Indians: Advances in Metabolic Disorders.* New York: Academic Press.

Williams, C. A. (1992). Community-based population-focused practice: The foundation of specialization in public health nursing. In M. Stanhope and J. Lancaster (Eds.), *Community Health Nursing: Process and Practice for Promoting Health,* 3d Ed. (pp. 244–252). St. Louis: C. V. Mosby.

White, V. (1985). The Experience of Pregnancy among Hispanic Women. Unpublished master's thesis, University of Utah, Salt Lake City, Utah.

Young, S. A., and Kaufman, K. (1988). Promoting breast feeding at a migrant health center. *Journal of the American Public Health Association, 78*(5), 523–525.

Suggested Readings

Refugee Health

Aroian, K. J. (1990). A model of psychological adaptation to migration and resettlement. *Nursing Research,* 39(1), 5–10.

Aroian, K. J. (1992). Sources of social support and conflict for Polish immigrants. *Qualitative Health Research, 2*(2), 178–207.

Aroian, K. J. (1993). Mental health risks and problems encountered by illegal immigrants. *Issues in Mental Health Nursing, 14,* 379–397.

Laffrey, S. C., Meleis, A. I., Lipson, J. G., et al. (1989). Assessing Arab-American health care needs. *Social Science and Medicine, 29,* 877–883.

Lipson, J. G. (1991). Afghan refugee health: Some findings and suggestions. *Qualitative Health Research, 1,* 349–369.

Lipson, J. G. (1993). Afghan refugees in California: Mental health issues. *Issues in Mental Health Nursing, 14,* 411–423.

Lipson, J. G., and Omidian, P. (1992). Afghan refugees in California: Health issues. *Western Journal of Medicine, 157,* 271–275.

Muecke, M. A. (1983a). Caring for Southeast Asian refugee patients in the USA. *American Journal of Public Health, 73*(4), 431–438.

Muecke, M. A. (1983b). In search of healers—Southeast Asian refugees in the American health care system. *Western Journal of Medicine, 139*(6), 835–840.

Muecke, M. A. (1987). Resettled refugee's reconstruction of identity: Lao in Seattle. *Urban Anthropology, 16*(3–4), 273–289.

Muecke, M. A. (1992). Mother sold food, daughter sells her body: Prostitution and cultural continuity. *Social Science and Medicine, 35*(7), 891–901.

Thompson, J. L. (1991). Exploring gender and culture with Khmer refugee women: Reflections on participatory feminist research. *Advances in Nursing Science, 13*(3), 30–48.

12

Religion, Culture, and Nursing

Margaret M. Andrews
Patricia A. Hanson

Introduction

Frequently, in addition to cultural heritage, religion plays a vital role in a client's perception of health and illness. An integral component of culture, religious beliefs may influence a client's explanation of the cause(s) of illness, perception of its severity, and choice of healer(s). In times of crisis, such as serious illness and impending death, religion may be a source of consolation for the client and family and may influence the course of action believed to be appropriate.

The purposes of this chapter are to explore the meaning of religion in clients' lives, examine the ways in which religious beliefs can be incorporated into nursing care, and describe the health-related beliefs and practices of selected religious groups in North America.

Dimensions of Religion

Religion is complex and multifaceted in both form and function. Religious faith and the institutions derived from that faith become a central focus in meeting the human needs of those who believe. "Not a single faith fails to address the issues of illness and wellness of disease and healing, of caring and curing. Stated more positively, most faiths were born as, at least in part, efforts to heal" (Marty, 1990, p. 14). Consequently, the influence of religion on health-related matters requires a few preliminary remarks.

First, it is necessary to identify specific religious factors that may influence human behavior. No single religious factor operates in isolation, but rather each exists in combination with other religious factors. Faulkner and DeJong (1966) have proposed

Margaret M. Andrews and Joyceen S. Boyle: TRANSCULTURAL CONCEPTS IN NURSING CARE,
SECOND EDITION. © 1995 J.B. Lippincott Company.

five major dimensions of religion: experiential, ritualistic, ideological, intellectual, and consequential.

The *experiential* dimension recognizes that all religions have expectations of members and that the religious person will at some point in life achieve direct knowledge of ultimate reality or will experience religious emotion. Every religion recognizes this subjective religious experience as a sign of religiosity. The *ritualistic* dimension pertains to religious practices expected of the followers and may include worship, prayer, participation in sacraments, and fasting. The *ideological* dimension refers to the set of beliefs to which a religion's followers must adhere in order to call themselves members. Commitment to the group or movement as a social process results in and members experience a sense of belonging or affiliation. The *intellectual* dimension refers to specific sets of beliefs, explanations, and the cognitive structuring of meaning. Members are expected to be informed about the basic tenets of the religion as well as to be familiar with sacred writings or scriptures. The intellectual and the ideological are closely related because acceptance of a dimension presupposes knowledge of it. The *consequential* dimension refers to religiously defined standards of conduct and includes religious proscriptions that specify what followers' attitudes and behaviors should be as a consequence of their religion. The consequential dimension governs people's relationships with others.

Obviously, each religious dimension has a different significance when related to matters of health and illness. Different religious cultures may emphasize one of the five dimensions to the relative exclusion of the others. Similarly, individuals may develop their own priorities related to the dimensions of religion. This affects the nurse providing

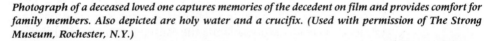

Photograph of a deceased loved one captures memories of the decedent on film and provides comfort for family members. Also depicted are holy water and a crucifix. (Used with permission of The Strong Museum, Rochester, N.Y.)

care to clients with different religious beliefs in several ways. First, it is the nurse's role to determine from the client or from significant others the dimension or combinations of dimensions that are important so that the client and nurse can have mutual goals and priorities. Second, it is important to determine what a given member of a specific religious affiliation believes to be important. The only way to do this is to ask either the client or, if the client is unable to communicate this information personally, a close family member.

Third, the nurse's information must be accurate. Making assumptions about clients' religious belief systems on the basis of their cultural or even religious affiliation is imprudent and may lead to erroneous inferences. The following case study illustrates the importance of verifying assumptions with the client.

Case Study 12-1

Observing that a patient was wearing a star of David on a chain around his neck and had been accompanied by a rabbi upon admission, a nurse inquired whether he would like to order a kosher diet. The patient replied, "Oh, no. I'm a Christian. My father is a rabbi, and I know it would upset him to find out that I have converted. Even though I'm 40 years old, I hide it from him. This has been going on for 15 years now."

The key point in this anecdote is that the nurse validated an assumption with the patient before acting. Furthermore, it should be noted that not all Jewish persons follow a kosher diet or wear a star of David.

Fourth, even when individuals identify with a particular religion, they may accept the "official" beliefs and practices in varying degrees. It is not the nurse's role to judge the religious virtues of clients but rather to understand those aspects related to religion which are important to the client and family members. When religious beliefs are translated into practice, they may be manipulated by individuals in certain situations to serve particular ends; that is, traditional beliefs and practices may be altered. Thus it is possible for a Jewish person to eat pork or for a Catholic to take contraceptives to prevent pregnancy. Although some find it necessary to label this as an exceptional or accidental occurrence, such a point of view tends to ignore the fact that change can and does occur within individuals and within groups. Homogeneity among members of any religion cannot be assumed. Perhaps the individual once embraced the beliefs and practices of the religion but has since changed his or her views, or perhaps the individual never accepted the religious beliefs completely in the first place. It is important for the nurse to be open to variations in religious beliefs and practices and to allow for the possibility of change. Individual choices frequently arise from new situations, changing values and mores, and exposure to new ideas and beliefs. Few people live in total social isolation, surrounded only by those with similar religious backgrounds.

Fifth, ideal norms of conduct and actual behavior are not necessarily the same. The nurse is frequently faced with the challenge of understanding and helping clients cope with conflicting norms. Sometimes conflicting norms are manifested by guilt or by efforts to minimize or rationalize inconsistencies. For example, in the case cited in Chap. 4, the Jehovah's Witness' mother allows her husband to make the decision about their child's transplant surgery because she knows that his choice will be different from that allowed by her professed, "ideal" beliefs.

Sometimes norms are vaguely formulated and filled with discrepancies that allow for a variety of interpretations. In religions having a lay organization and structure, moral decision making may be left to the individual without the assistance of members of the church hierarchy. In religions having a clerical hierarchy, moral positions may be more clearly formulated and articulated for members. Individuals retain their right to choose regardless of official church-related guidelines, suggestions, or even religious laws; however, the individual who chooses to violate the norms may experience the consequences of that violation, including social ostracism, public removal from membership rolls, or other forms of censure.

Religion and Nursing Care

For many years, nursing has emphasized a holistic approach to care in which the needs of the total person are recognized. Most nursing textbooks fail to provide as much information for nurses about meeting spiritual needs as about meeting the other types of needs. Providing spiritual care to culturally diverse clients is a subject about which little has been written. Since nurses desire to provide holistic health care, addressing spiritual needs becomes essential (Robinson, 1994).

Religious concerns evolve from and respond to the mysteries of life and death, good and evil, and pain and suffering. Although the religions of the world offer various interpretations of these phenomena, most people seek a personal understanding and interpretation at some time in their lives. Ultimately, this personal search becomes a pursuit to discover a god or some unifying truth that will give meaning, purpose, and integrity to existence (Cluff, 1986; Ebersole and Hess, 1994).

Before spiritual care for culturally diverse clients is discussed, an important distinction needs to be made between religion and spirituality. *Religion* refers to an organized system of beliefs concerning the cause, nature, and purpose of the universe, especially belief in or worship of God or gods; *spirituality* is born out of each person's unique life experience and his or her personal effort to find purpose and meaning in life.

The goal of spiritual nursing care is to assist clients in discovering their own god or unifying truth, the ultimate reality that gives meaning to their lives in relationship to the illness that has precipitated the need for nursing care. Spiritual nursing care promotes clients' physical and emotional health as well as their spiritual well-being. When providing care, nurses must remember that the goal of spiritual intervention is not, and should not be, to impose religious beliefs and convictions.

Although spiritual needs are recognized by many nurses, spiritual care is often neglected. Among the reasons that nurses fail to provide spiritual care are the following: (1) they view religion as a private matter, (2) they feel that spirituality is a private matter concerning only an individual and his or her creator, (3) they are uncomfortable about their own religious beliefs or deny having spiritual needs, (4) they lack knowledge about spirituality and the religious beliefs of others, (5) they mistake spiritual needs for psychosocial needs, and (6) they view meeting the spiritual needs of clients as a family or pastoral responsibility, not a nursing responsibility (Ellerhorst-Ryan, 1985; Fish and Shelly, 1988; Marty, 1990; Robinson, 1994; Shelly and John, 1983).

Spiritual intervention is appropriate if the nurse cares about clients' spiritual well-being as much as about their biologic, physical, and psychosocial health and if the nurse recognizes that the balance of physical, psychosocial, and spiritual dimensions is essential to overall good health. Nursing is an intimate profession, and nurses routinely inquire without hesitation about very personal matters such as hygiene and sexual habits. The spiritual realm also requires a personal, intimate type of nursing intervention (Fish and Shelly, 1988).

In 1971, the White House Conference on Aging defined the spiritual dimension as pertaining to "man's inner resources, especially his ultimate concern, the basic value around which all other values are focused, the central philosophy of life, which guides a person's conduct, the supernatural and nonmaterial dimensions of human nature." The spiritual dimension encompasses the person's need to find satisfactory answers to questions about the meaning of life, illness, or death (Ebersole and Hess, 1994; Moberg, 1971; Numbers and Amundsen, 1986).

In 1978, the Third National Conference on the Classification of Nursing Diagnoses recognized the importance of spirituality by including "spiritual concerns," "spiritual distress," and "spiritual despair" in the list of approved diagnoses. Because of practical difficulties, these three categories were combined at the 1980 National Conference into one category, "spiritual distress," defined as "disruption in the life principle which pervades a person's entire being and which integrates and transcends one's biological and psychosocial nature" (Kim and Moritz, 1981). Moberg (1981) acknowledges the multidimensional nature of spiritual concerns and defines these as "the human need to deal with sociocultural deprivations, anxieties and fears, death and dying, personality integration, self-image, personal dignity, social alienation, and philosophy of life."

Spiritual Care and the Phenomenon of Nursing

As discussed in Chap. 2, cultural assessment includes assessment of the relationship among religious and spiritual issues as they relate to the health care status of the client. In the case of integration of health care and religious/spiritual beliefs, the focus of the nursing plan is to help the client maintain his or her own beliefs in the face of the health care crisis and to use those beliefs to strengthen coping patterns. In the event that the religious beliefs are contributing to the overall health problem (i.e., guilt, remorse, expectations, etc.), the nurse can be therapeutic by asking questions that clarify the problem and nonjudgmentally supporting the client's problem solving. Summarized in Box 12-1 are guidelines for assessing spiritual needs in culturally diverse clients.

Religion and Childhood Illnesses

Religion is especially important to clients during periods of crisis. In a broad sense, any hospitalization or serious illness can be viewed as stressful and therefore has the potential to develop into a crisis situation. Nurses may find that religion plays an especially significant role in situations involving the serious illness of a child and in circumstances that include dying, death, or bereavement.

Illness during childhood may be an especially difficult clinical situation. Children as well as adults have spiritual needs that vary according to their developmental level and the religious climate that exists in the family. Parental perceptions about the illness of the child may be influenced in part by religious beliefs. For example, some parents may believe that a transgression against a religious law is responsible for the congenital anomaly in their offspring. Other parents may delay seeking medical care because they believe that prayer should be tried first.

Box 12-1. Assessing Spiritual Needs in Culturally Diverse Clients

---

Environment:
- Does the client have religious objects, such as a Bible, prayer book, devotional literature, religious medals, rosary or other type of beads, photographs of historic religious persons or contemporary church leaders (e.g., pope, church president), paintings of religious events or persons, religious sculptures, crucifixes, objects of religious significance at entrances to rooms (e.g., holy water founts, a *mezuzah*, or small parchment scroll inscribed with an excerpt from the Bible), candles of religious significance (e.g., Pascal candle, menorah), shrine, or other?
- Does the client wear clothing that has religious significance (e.g., head covering, undergarment, uniform)?
- Are get-well greeting cards religious in nature or from a representative of the client's church?
- Does the client receive flowers or bulletins from his or her church?

Behavior:
- Does the client appear to pray at certain times of the day or before meals?
- Does the client make special dietary requests (e.g., kosher diet, vegetarian diet, or diet free from caffeine, pork, shellfish, or other specific food items)?
- Does the client read religious magazines or books?

Verbalization:
- Does the client mention God (Allah, Buddha, Yahweh), prayer, faith, church, or religious topics?
- Does the client ask for a visit by a clergy member or other religious representative?
- Does the client express anxiety or fear about pain, suffering, or death?

Interpersonal relationships:
- Who visits? How does the client respond to visitors?
- Does a priest, rabbi, minister, elder, or other church representative visit?
- How does the client relate to the nursing staff? To his or her roommate(s)?
- Does the client prefer to interact with others or to remain alone?

Spiritual Care: The Nurse's Role, 3d Ed., by Judith Allen Shelly and Sharon Fish. © 1988 by InterVarsity Press, Christian Fellowship of the USA. Used by permission of InterVarsity Press, P.O. Box 1400, Downers Grove, IL 60515.

The nurse should be respectful of parents' preferences regarding the care of their child. When parental beliefs or practices threaten the child's well-being and health, the nurse is obligated to discuss the matter with the parents. It may be possible to reach a compromise between which parental beliefs are respected and provision of the necessary care. On rare occasions, it may become a legal matter. Religion may be a source of consolation and support to parents, especially those facing the unanswerable questions associated with life-threatening illness in their children.

Nursing Care for the Dying or Bereaved Client and Family

All Americans do not mourn alike. Mourning is cultural behavior, and we live in a multicultural society. But the way we are raised dictates patterns we regard as proper or natural. Just as we celebrate holidays or marriages differently, we also mourn differently. The mourning customs of others may seem unusual when compared to your tradition, but like yours, they help people cope with death.

Memory and Mourning, American Expressions of Grief, Strong Museum, 1994

Nurses inevitably focus on restoring health or fostering environments in which the client returns to a previous state of health or adapts to physical, psychologic, or emotional changes. However, one aspect of *care* that is often avoided or ignored, though it is every bit as crucial to clients and their families, is death and the accompanying dying and grieving processes. Death is indeed a universal experience, but one that is highly individual and personal. While each person must ultimately face death alone, rarely does one person's death fail to affect others.

There are many rituals, serving many purposes, that people use to help them cope with death. These rituals are usually determined by cultural and religious orientation. Situational factors, competing demands, and individual differences are also important in determining the dying, bereavement, and grieving behaviors that are considered socially acceptable (Kalish and Reynolds, 1981).

The role of the nurse in dealing with dying clients and their families varies according to the needs and preferences of both the nurse and client, as well as the clinical setting in which the interaction occurs. By understanding some of the cultural and religious variations related to death, dying, and bereavement, the nurse can individualize the care given to clients and their families.

Nurses are often with the client through various stages of the dying process and at the actual moment of death, particularly when death occurs in a hospital, nursing home, extended-care facility, or hospice. The nurse often determines whom to call, and when, as the impending death draws near. Knowing the religious, cultural, and familial heritage of a particular client as well as his or her devotion to the associated traditions and practices may help the nurse determine whom to call when the need arises.

Religious Beliefs Associated with Dying

Universally, people want to die with dignity. Historically, this was not a problem when individuals died at home in the presence of their friends and families. Now, when more and more people are dying in institutions (hospitals, nursing homes, and extended-care facilities), ensuring dignity throughout the dying process is a more complex task. Once death is seen as a problem for professional management, the hospital displaces the

In order to preserve traditions associated with death and burial practices, some Chinese Americans prefer to use Chinese funeral directors, such as this one located in New York City's Chinatown.

home, and specialists with different kinds and degrees of expertise take over for the family (Madan, 1992).

The way in which people commemorate death tells us much about their attitude and philosophy of life as well as death. While it is beyond the scope of this book to explore the philosophical and psychological aspects of death in detail, some points will be made that relate to nursing care.

A nurse may or may not actually participate in the rituals associated with death. When people die in the United States and Canada, they are usually transported to a mortuary, where the preparation for burial occurs.

In many non-Anglo cultural groups, preparation of the body has in the past been very important. While many cultural groups have adopted the practice of letting the mortician prepare the body, there are some, particularly new immigrants, who want to retain their native customs. For example, for certain Asian immigrants, it is customary for family and friends of the same sex to wash and prepare the body for burial or cremation (Mayor, 1984; Green, 1989a–d).

If a person dies in an institution, it is common for the nursing staff to "prepare" the body according to standard procedure. Depending on the cultural practices of the family, this may be objectionable—the family may view this washing as an infringement on a special task that belongs to them alone. If the family is present, the nurse should ask family members about their preference. If ritual washings will eventually take place at the mortuary, the nurse may carry out the routine procedures and reassure the family that the mortician will comply with their requests, if these have in fact been verified.

North American funeral customs have been the topic of study in lively discussions. The initial preparation of the body has been described in the following way (Kalish and Reynolds, 1981, p. 65):

> After delivery to the undertaker, the corpse is in short order sprayed, sliced, pierced, pickled, trussed, trimmed, creamed, waxed, painted, rouged and neatly dressed . . . transformed from a common corpse into a beautiful memory picture. This process is known in the trades as embalming and restorative art, and is so universally employed in the United States and Canada that the funeral director does it routinely without consulting the corpse's family. He regards as eccentric those few who are hardy enough to suggest it might be dispensed with yet no law requires, no religious doctrine commends it, nor is it dictated by considerations of health, sanitation or even personal daintiness. In no part of the world but in North America is it widely used. The purpose of embalming is to make the corpse presentable for viewing in a suitably costly container, and here too the funeral director routinely without first consulting the family prepares the body for public display.

This extensive preparation and attempt to make the body look "alive" or "just as he used to" or "just as if he were asleep" may reflect the fact that Anglo-Americans have been less in contact with death and dying than other cultural groups. The Anglo-American group is a culturally bound ethnic group, and the avoidance of death may reflect cultural and religious differences. For example, if a patient has died and a family member does not want to see the body until the mortician has "fixed it up," this request needs to be respected, regardless of the personal beliefs of the nurse.

Funeral Practices

By their very nature, people are social beings who need to develop social attachments. When these social attachments are broken by death, people have a need to bring closure to the relationships. The funeral is an appropriate and socially acceptable time for the expression of sorrow and grief. Although there are some mores that dictate acceptable behaviors associated with the expression of grief, such as crying and sobbing, the wake and funeral are generally viewed as times when members of the living social network can observe and comfort the grieving survivors in their mourning and say a last goodbye to the dead person.

Customs for disposal of the body after death vary widely. Muslims have specific rituals for washing, dressing, and positioning the body. In traditional Judaism, cosmetic restoration is discouraged, as is any attempt to hasten or retard decomposition by artificial means. As part of their lifelong preparation for death, Amish women sew white burial garments for themselves and for their family members (Ross, 1984; Klassen, 1986; Wenger, 1991). Faithful Mormons are dressed in their "temple clothes" for burial. Burial clothes and other religious or cultural symbols may be important items for the funeral ritual. If such items are present in the institution, the nurse should ensure that they go with the family or to the funeral home.

Believing that the spirit or ghost of the deceased person is contaminated, some Navaho are afraid to touch the body after death. In preparation for burial, the body is dressed in fine apparel, adorned with expensive jewelry and money, and wrapped in new blankets. After death, the Navaho believe that the structure in which the person died must be burned (Nagel, 1991).

Funeral arrangements vary from short, simple rituals to long, elaborate displays. Among the Amish, family members, neighbors, and friends are relied on for a short, quiet ceremony. Many Jewish families use unadorned coffins and stress simplicity in burial services. Some Jews fly the body to Jerusalem for burial in ground considered to be holy. Regardless of economic considerations, some groups believe in lavish and costly funerals.

Attitudes Toward Death

In some cultures, people believe that particular omens such as the appearance of an owl or a message in a dream warn of approaching death. Breaking a taboo may be believed to cause death, and the nurse may be seen as the responsible agent. For example, Ross (1984) reports an incident in which a nurse removed a necklace and its curative attachments from an elderly Native American woman in order to keep them in a safe place with other valuables (Halfe, 1989).

Voodoo beliefs and practices are still known to exist in North America. Incidents of sudden death or minor injuries following hexing have been attributed to the power of suggestion and to total social isolation, which have been thought to trigger fatal physiologic responses and sensitization of the autonomic nervous system.

Acceptance of sudden, violent death is difficult for family members in most societies. For example, suicide is strictly forbidden under Islamic law. In the Filipino culture, suicide brings shame to the individual and to the entire family. Many Christian religions prohibit suicide and may impose sanctions even after death for the "sin." For example, a Catholic who commits suicide may be denied burial in blessed ground or in a Catholic cemetery. In some religions, a "church funeral" is not permitted for a suicide victim, requiring the family to make alternative arrangements. This harsh imposition of religious law can further add to the grief of surviving family members and friends.

The Northern Cheyenne believe that suicide or any death resulting from a violent accident disturbs the individual's spiritual balance. This disharmony is termed *bad death* and is believed to render the spirit earthbound in its wanderings, thus preventing it from entering the spirit world. A bad death occurs unexpectedly and violently, leaving the victim without a chance to settle affairs or to say good-bye.

> A "bad death" is "bad" because evil caused it, which leaves the soul of the dead unrestful, unfulfilled, and desirous of returning to the living out of a longing for what has been taken away. The soul returns to the living, although not out of malevolence, to visit loved ones. It is on these visits that the dead can bring a form of *ka:cim mumkidag*

(staying—Indian—sickness), to the living—hence their dangerousness [Kozak, 1991, p. 214].

In addition to exploring Tohono O'odham (Papago) categories of death, Kozak looks at the larger causes of the increase in violent deaths, arguing "that shifting mortality trends indicate shifts in other aspects of society" (Kozak, 1991, p. 211). Increased deaths are tied to declining economic conditions on the reservation, where jobs have disappeared.

> . . . the O'odham's economic transition has meant either migrating away from family and friends to find work or remaining on the reservation at home usually to confront extreme unemployment and welfare dependency. Neither option is considered satisfactory or desirable. The social-psychological side effects of these economic transformations are highlighted, in an inverse relationship in alcohol and drug abuse, violence, and a general increase in dependency [Kozak, 1991, p. 213].

Among the Tohono O'odham, there has been a notable increase in violent deaths, particularly for young males, since 1955. The majority of these violent deaths are the result of motor vehicle accidents and are marked by the Tohono O'odham people with roadside death memorials or shrines. Death memorials provide a place for the dead to go without bringing harm to the living and a place for the living to go to help the dead to a proper afterlife. Suicides and homicides are also sometimes commemorated with death memorials. A good death among the Tohono O'odham comes at the end of a full life, when a person is prepared for death.

Deaths from nonviolent but untimely causes can be equally difficult for the patient, family, and friends. Cancers and chronic diseases may give the patient and family time to "prepare" for the death, but the death still occurs and must be dealt with.

The Tohono O'odham's categories of "good" and "bad" deaths have implications for research on excess deaths. Accidents, homicide, and suicide produce bad deaths; in Tohono O'odham eyes, these are deaths that should not occur, deaths that should be avoided if possible. "Bad" deaths are excess deaths. If the medical community's concern is with eliminating excess deaths, it also must be concerned with the larger cultural, social, and economic context in which these deaths occur. Other causes of death, while still important, may affect a people to a much lesser degree. Diabetes mellitus, for example, most often affects people of more advanced years and, because of its slow progress, allows them to prepare for death. This is still an excess death by Western medical standards, but it is not a "bad" death (see Hickey and Hall, 1993; Huttlinger et al., 1992; Nelson et al., 1990; Sugarman et al., 1990; Sugarman, 1991; Tom-Orme, 1988; Wiedman, 1989).

Buddhism has a holistic approach to death. To the Buddhist way of thinking, illness is inevitable and is a consequence of events and actions taken. These may not necessarily be in this life but also can be in previous lives. The belief is in the cause and effect of events in this life as in previous lives. There is an acceptance of death, which means that the choice has been made to anticipate the grief and accept the inevitability of death. This does not mean resignation or the denial of conventional medicine. It does mean moving peacefully into the next existence from the presence of loving family and friends (Chapman, 1991).

A Native American explains that beliefs and practices surrounding the death of a family member vary widely from tribe to tribe.

The Death of a Child

Although there is a great deal written about children's conceptions of death, cross-cultural studies have not yet been reported. Children develop a concept of death through innate cognitive development, which has significant cultural variations, and through acquired notions conveyed by the family, which vary according to the family's cultural beliefs. Thus it is unsafe to assume that all children, regardless of their family's culture, will develop parallel concepts of and reactions to death (Eisenbruch, 1984a; Corrine et al., 1992).

Most children's initial experience with death occurs with the loss of a pet rather than a person. Because of reduced childhood mortality and delayed adult mortality, Western children are much less exposed than they used to be to family death and tend to be sheltered from the experience. The current lack of direct exposure of children to death is both a class phenomenon and a cultural one.

In many societies of the Western world, children are considered precious, valued, and vulnerable; they are protected and often the first to be saved in emergencies. In less developed societies, by contrast, parents are less likely to see most of their children grow into adulthood because of a very high infant mortality rate. As a result, a child's life is viewed as less valued and precious than an adult's, but it is still viewed as valuable to the parents and other loved ones. Regardless of the sociocultural situation, each society has a special view of the significance of the child and his or her death as it affects the bereaved family.

African-American culture in the northeastern United States contains many elements brought from former homelands. The decorations on this child's grave, common in some parts of the South, also can be found in Africa and the Caribbean. Originally, survivors believed the deceased would need objects from daily life in the next world. (Used with permission of The Strong Museum, Rochester, N.Y.)

Awareness of Dying

The issue of whether individuals should be made aware of their impending death has been debated extensively by physicians, nurses, and others. In the Kalish and Reynolds (1981) study, 71 percent of Anglos, 60 percent of African Americans, 49 percent of Japanese Americans, and 37 percent of Mexican Americans favored telling clients that they were dying. Each cultural group believed the physician was the most appropriate person to communicate the information, while a family member was the second most appropriate choice. However, individual preferences should be respected.

Bereavement, Grief, and Mourning

Bereavement is a sociologic term indicating the status and role of the survivors of a death. *Grief* is an affective response to a loss, while *mourning* is the culturally patterned behavioral response to a death. What differs between races and cultural groups is not so much the feelings of grief but their forms of expression or mourning.

Different family systems may alleviate or intensify the pain experienced by bereaved persons. Ross (1984) suggests that in the typical nuclear Anglo family, the death of a member leaves a great void because the same few individuals fill most of the roles. By contrast, cultural groups in which several generations and extended family members commonly reside within a household may find that the acute trauma of bereavement is softened by the fact that the familial role of the deceased is easily filled by other relatives (Ross, 1984).

Although nurses frequently encourage clients and their families to express their grief openly, many people are reluctant to do so in the institutional setting. The nurse often sees the family at a time when members are still in shock over the death and are responding to the situation as a crisis rather than expressing their grief. Three-fourths of the African Americans, Japanese, and Anglos stated they would try hard to maintain control of their emotions in public, while less than two-thirds of Mexican Americans were concerned with the public expression of grief. When asked about crying, either publicly or privately, 88 percent of Mexican Americans, 71 percent of the Japanese, 70 percent of the Anglos, and 60 percent of the African Americans indicated that this was acceptable, particularly in private.

When asked who would be sought for comfort and support in time of bereavement, these groups most frequently named a family member or a member of the clergy. In an institutional setting, a nurse who has been with the patient and family throughout the dying process may be surprised at the time of death when the grieving persons turn to other family members, and the nurse is "left out."

While the experience of grief is a universal phenomenon, a nurse should recognize that the expression of grief is strongly influenced by cultural factors. For example, mourning may vary according to the lines of emotional attachment. In matrilineal societies, a woman may be expected to grieve for male members of her maternal family, such as fathers and brothers, but not for her spouse.

It is not uncommon for a surviving spouse to have a serious illness within the year following the death. Although the exact reasons for this are unknown, the stress of losing a spouse seems to render the surviving partner more vulnerable to illness. Caring for a person who is not only seriously ill but also mourning a death requires added sensitivity by the nurse to the patient's emotional needs.

Some mourning rituals are highly structured and lengthy, while others are relatively simple and short. In the Jewish tradition, there are five successive stages of mourning that extend for a year and include practices that influence virtually every aspect of life. The examination of the following four ethnic groups is intended to provide the nurse with insight into specific cross-cultural bereavement behaviors.

Spanish-Speaking Groups. With 17.4 million members, the Spanish-speaking represent the second largest cultural group in the United States (U.S. Census Bureau, 1990). Of these, 59 percent are of Mexican origin, 15 percent Puerto Rican, 6 percent Cuban, and 20 percent other Hispanic origin. While little is known about specific bereavement patterns of each group, the Puerto Ricans have been studied, and the resulting information may help the nurse to empathize with the client from this cultural group. However, the nurse should not generalize for all members of the group, nor assume that mourning will be the same for other Hispanic groups.

Many Puerto Ricans believe that a person's spirit will not be free to enter the next life if that person has left something unsaid before death. For this reason, it is important for friends and family to complete their relationships with a dying person. With sudden death, such closure is obviously impossible, but in the case of chronic illness, those close to the dying client should be given the privacy necessary to accomplish this task. Atypical grief may arise when grieving Puerto Ricans feel that the relationship has not been properly completed (Eisenbruch, 1984b).

Following the death, the family meets together to comfort one another and to pray for the dead. The wake offers a mechanism for mobilizing community support and for the expression of grief. With the predominant religion being Roman Catholic, religious rituals such as masses, rosaries, and novenas are observed to benefit both the deceased and the surviving family members. In North America, time restrictions for wakes are often imposed by funeral directors, but traditionally, they last for several days.

Grief is sometimes expressed in a syndrome called *el ataque*, which is characterized by seizure-like behavior, hyperkinetic episodes, a display of aggression, and sometimes stupor. Such behavior is accepted and socially sanctioned within the Puerto Rican culture as a way for bereaved persons to discharge anger. Anglo-American nurses, however, may view this behavior as aberrant. In keeping with beliefs about *machismo*, in which males in general are raised to keep all feeling of suffering inside, bereaved Hispanic men are often unreceptive to grief counseling and may resent being told by the nurse "it's okay to cry." Economic stress may add a burden to the bereaved. Many Puerto Rican families wish to accompany the body of the deceased to Puerto Rico for burial. The family, community, and church may provide financial assistance, but the economic necessity of returning to work after only 3 days of mourning may interfere with the ability to grieve.

Kalish and Reynolds (1981) found that for Mexican Americans, the family protective network is prominent. Of all groups studied, the Mexican Americans were the most likely to want to protect both the dying and the bereaved, such as small children who might have difficulty with the death. Mexican Americans often rally around the hospitalized client and take turns in shifts of vigil. They tend to encourage the open expression of feelings of anguish and grief (Eisenbruch, 1989b).

Urban African Americans. The way people handle the problems surrounding death indicates the way in which they deal with life. There are very few new resources available to an individual who faces critical illness or death. The decision-making process used to cope with life-threatening illness is likely to be similar to the process used during other times in the individual's life.

With the help of the media, the belief has been perpetuated that blacks have more contact than whites with death, particularly violent deaths and accidents. Bereaved African Americans (and Anglo-Americans) are likely to rely on friends, church members, neighbors, and other nonrelatives when faced with the death of a loved one (Kalish and Reynolds, 1981; Jacobs, 1990). African Americans are less likely to express their grief overtly and publicly. Patterns of coping with death will vary widely among urban blacks, depending more than in many other ethnic groups on the educational and socioeconomic background of the bereaved.

One stereotype is that when faced with a crisis, blacks, because of a closely knit supportive family network, can look after themselves. But the extended family does not predominate among either rural or urban blacks. With a preponderance of female-headed, single-parent family units, it is unrealistic to expect the bereaved to rely solely on the family for the needed support.

Besides the cultural idiom of bereavement, blacks may experience different modes of death. Fewer whites die violently than do blacks. Those who survive violence often end up relying on the biomedical system for help over an extended period of time.

Ethnic Chinese and Related Groups. Included in this group are not only people from China but also ethnic Chinese from all of Southeast Asia. Even though many Chinese Americans have been assimilated into Western society, the attitudes toward death in classic Chinese society have pervaded. In general, Chinese Americans tend to be stoic and fatalistic when faced with terminal illness and death (Lecso, 1987).

Traditional Chinese society recognized that the family was the basic social unit and codified the concept in laws of degrees of kinship. *Wu-fu*, meaning "the five kinds of clothing," defines degrees of relationships and determines the severity of mourning in terms of closeness of the deceased to the mourner.

The Chinese traditionally follow a system of double burial. The initial burial in a coffin lasts for 7 years, after which time the remains are exhumed and stored in an urn for years or decades more. Reburial in an elaborate tomb marks the second burial, after which time the deceased is able to have a beneficial effect on descendants (Watson, 1982). Many Chinese Americans are unaware of these traditional customs (Eisenbruch, 1984b). They have adopted an American Christian religion while maintaining non-Christian cultural beliefs related to death, dying, and burial. In such cases, it is especially critical to know whom to call in the event of an emergency and particularly at the time of death.

Southeast Asian Refugees. During recent years, Southeast Asian refugees have developed into an important cultural group in the United States and Canada. Included in the group are at least five distinct categories: Vietnamese, Kampucheans, Hmong, Lao, and Lao-Theung.

Refugees are particularly vulnerable to the stress of bereavement; many have already suffered the loss of close family members as a result of the war in Southeast Asia, and the refugee experience is itself a stressful event. Furthermore, traditional mourning practices must be modified in the United States due to cultural differences. Major differences in mourning among the subgroups of Southeast Asians exist and include the following: the color of mourning clothes and the duration for which they are worn, the commemorative celebration on the anniversary of the death, and marriage of the deceased person's spouse and children.

When the bereaved are unable to carry out meaningful traditional rituals, their stress may be amplified while the cultural mechanisms for support are impeded. Some traditional Vietnamese practices include preparation of the body by family members, including placement of a coin in the deceased person's mouth to help the spirit at various stages of its journey and use of special divination when choosing the grave site. American morticians are usually unwilling or unable to comply with requests of this nature because, for example, rigor mortis has set in by the time the body reaches the funeral home, making opening the mouth difficult. Furthermore, cemeteries have specific regulations about grave sites, some of which are governed by zoning, health, and sanitation laws. Thus bereavement codes of the immigrant may violate laws of the host country.

Social and religious practices among the refugees from Southeast Asia vary markedly. The Vietnamese and ethnic Chinese may be Mahayana or Theravada Buddhist, and the Hmong and other hill tribes are usually animist in their beliefs (Eisenbruch, 1984b). Each group has its own ritual prescriptions and proscriptions. The nurse should become aware of differences and avoid stereotyping all Southeast Asians in order to prevent embarrassing errors that could lead to further distress for the client and family.

Summary of Beliefs Related to Death and Dying

The contemporary bereavement practices of various cultural groups discussed here demonstrate the wide range of expressions of bereavement. Each group reflects practices that best meet its members' needs. Once nurses understand this, they can better appreciate their role in promoting a culturally appropriate grieving process. Conversely, hindering or interfering with practices that the client and family find meaningful can disrupt the grieving process. Bereaved people can develop physical and psychological symptoms and may succumb to serious physical illnesses, leading even to death. Even if bereavement was regarded as a "universal" stressor, the magnitude of the stress and its meaning to the individual vary significantly cross-culturally. For example, one Western misconception is that it is more stressful to mourn the death of a child that the death of an older or more distant relative. Yet cross-cultural studies show that emotional attachments to relatives vary significantly, because they are not based on Western concepts of kinship (Eisenbruch, 1984b).

Although traditional funeral and postfuneral rituals have benefited both bereaved persons and their social groups in their original settings, the influence of the contemporary Western urban setting is unknown. It is likely that most individuals have assimilated U.S. and Canadian practices to varying degrees. Nurses should obtain information from individual clients in a caring manner, explaining that they need it in order to provide culturally appropriate nursing care.

Religious Trends in the United States and Canada

The United States and Canada are cosmopolitan nations to which all the major and many of the minor faiths of Europe and other parts of the globe have been transplanted. With an influx of refugees from Southeast Asia, many Eastern religions have become increasingly prevalent. With such a complex mosaic of religions, no one has succeeded in enumerating all the denominations. According to the *1990 Yearbook of American and Canadian Churches*, there are 358,194 congregations representing more than 1200 different religious denominations. As discussed, a wide range of beliefs frequently exists within many religions, a factor that adds complexity. Some religions have a designated spokesperson or leader who articulates, interprets, and applies theological tenets to daily life experiences, including those of health and illness. These include a Jewish rabbi, a Catholic priest, and a Lutheran minister. Some churches rely more heavily on individual conscience, whereas others entrust decisions to a group of individuals or to a single person vested with the ultimate authority within the church he (or rarely she) represents (e.g., pope, president).

Although it is impossible to address the health-related beliefs and practices of any religion adequately, the following section offers a brief overview of some select groups, listed in alphabetical order. Appendix C, "Significant Cultural Events and Holidays," provides a calendar guide to religious and nonreligious holidays that are celebrated in the United States and Canada. (See also Research Box 12-1.)

Listing of Select Religions

Baha'i International Community

The Baha'i Faith is an independent world religion. It has members in approximately 340 countries and localities and represents 1900 ethnic groups and tribes. Membership: North America, 363,000; worldwide, 5.4 million

Beliefs and Religious Practices

The writings that guide the life of the Baha'i International Community comprise numerous works by Baha'u'llah, prophet-founder of the Baha'i Faith. Central teachings are the oneness of God, the oneness of religion, and the oneness of mankind. Baha'u'llah proclaimed that religious truth is not absolute but relative, that Divine Revelation is a continuous and progressive process, that all the great religions of the world are divine in origin, and that their missions represent successive stages in the spiritual evolution of human society.

For Baha'is, the basic purpose of human life is to know and worship God and to carry forward an ever-advancing civilization. To achieve these goals, they strive to fulfill certain principles:

1. Fostering of good character and the development of spiritual qualities, such as honesty, trustworthiness, compassion, and justice.
2. Eradication of prejudices of race, creed, class, nationality, and sex.
3. Elimination of all forms of superstition hampering human progress and achievement of a balance between material and spiritual aspects of life. An unfettered search for

Research Box 12-1. Selected Studies on Religion, Health, and Culture

A question that may be asked about religious beliefs and health is, "Do religious beliefs have a positive effect on the health of practicing members?" Included here is a review of selected studies that address this question.

Jedrychowski, W., Tobiasz-Adamczyk, B., and Gradzidiewicz, P. (1985). Survival rates among Seventh-Day Adventists compared with the general population in Poland. *Scandinavian Journal of Social Medicine, 13*(2), 49–52.

The purpose of this study was to compare the survival rates among Seventh-Day Adventists with those of the general population in Poland. Results showed that the Seventh-Day Adventists had a longer life expectancy than the general population. While there was a difference in life expectancy between males and females in the general population, that difference did not exist among the Seventh-Day Adventists.

Beeson, W. L., Mills, P. K., Phillips, R. L., et al. (1989). Chronic disease among Seventh-Day Adventists, a low-risk group. *Cancer, 64*(3), 570–581.

This article reports the rationale, methodology, and description of the Adventist Health Study. This study followed 34,198 non-Hispanic white, Seventh-Day Adventists over a 6-year period (1977–1982). Extensive baseline data were collected from this population. A total of 20,702 records were reviewed for evidence of cancer and cardiovascular disease. Analysis showed that 1406 incidents of cancer were found, and 2716 deaths from all causes were identified. The researchers did not draw a conclusion as to whether Seventh-Day Adventists were in fact at low risk for cancer and cardiovascular disease.

Fraser, G. E., Beeson, W. L., and Phillips, R. L. (1991). Diet and lung cancer in California Seventh-Day Adventists. *American Journal of Epidemiology, 133*(7), 683–693.

The main purpose of this study is to report results of the Adventist Health Study related to the effects of individual food items on risk of lung cancer. Special emphasis was given to the difference between foods frequently consumed by vegetarians and nonvegetarians. Results indicated that only fruit consumption showed clear associations with lung cancer, in that people who consumed more fruit (all types) had a significantly lower ($p = 0.006$) incidence of lung cancer. Foods containing substantial beta-carotene content showed no consistent associations.

(continued)

Research Box 12-1 *(continued)*

Linsted, K. D., Tonstad, S., and Kuzma, J. W. (1991). Self-report of physical activity and patterns of mortality in Seventh-Day Adventist men. *Journal of Clinical Epidemiology, 44*(4–5), 355–364.

This study reports the results of the Adventist Mortality Study that provides 26-year follow-up for 9484 males who initially completed a lifestyle questionnaire in 1960. Self-reported physical activity and all-cause and disease-specific mortality were compared. Moderate activity was associated with protective effect on cardiovascular and all-cause mortality in the analyses completed. As a result of the data collected, a model was used to predict the age at which there is a crossover risk. For moderate activity, this age was 95.6 years for all-cause mortality and 91.5 years for cardiovascular mortality.

Watson, J. S. (1991). Religion as a cultural phenomenon, and national mortality rates from heart disease. *Psychological Reports, 69*(2), 439–442.

The researcher hypothesized that mortality rates from heart disease are a function of the nation's dominant religious tradition, with predominantly Catholic countries having lower rates than predominantly Protestant countries. Results showed an inverse relationship between Catholic countries and Protestant countries, with Catholic countries having a statistically significant lower incidence of heart disease.

Burkhardt, M. A. (1993). Characteristics of spirituality in the lives of women in a rural Appalachian community. *Journal of Transcultural Nursing, 4*(2), 12–18.

This qualitative study reports the results of research investigating how women in rural Appalachia experience and describe spirituality in their daily lives. Characteristics described by the five subjects in this study included belief in God or greater source, prayer/meditation, and a sense of relationship or connectedness with others, nature, and oneself. The dominant theme that emerged relative to these relationships was that of self-reliance or inner strength. Spirituality for these women relates to the whole of life and is relational.

truth and belief in the essential harmony of science and religion are two aspects of this principle.

4. Development of the unique talents and abilities of every individual through the pursuit of knowledge and the acquisition of skills for the practice of a trade or profession.
5. Full participation of both sexes in all aspects of community life, including the elective, administrative, and decision-making processes, along with equality of opportunities, rights, and privileges of men and women.
6. Fostering of the principle of universal compulsory education.

Baha'is may not be members of any political party but may accept nonpartisan government posts and appointments. They are enjoined to obey the government in their respective countries and, without political affiliation, may vote in general elections and participate in the civic life of their community.

The Baha'i administrative order has neither priesthood nor ritual; it relies on a pattern of local, national, and international governance, created by Baha'u'llah. Institutions and programs are supported exclusively by voluntary contributions from members.

The Baha'i International Community has consultative status with the United Nations Economic and Social Council and with the United Nations Children's Fund. It is also affiliated with the United Nations Environment Program and with the United Nations Office of Public Information.

The World Center of the Baha'i Faith is in Israel, established in the two cities of Haifa and 'Akka. The affairs of the Baha'i International Community are administered by the Universal House of Justice, the supreme elected council, situated in Haifa.

Holy Days. Extending from sunset to sunset are Baha'i holy days, feast days, and days of fasting. These holy days are not contraindications to medical care or surgery.

Sacraments. Although the Baha'i Faith does not have sacraments in the same sense that the Christian church does, it does have practices that have similar meanings to members. These practices include the recitation of obligatory prayers and participation in observance of holy days and the Nineteen-Day Fast, which is mandatory for all Baha'is between the ages of 15 and 70 years. Exceptions are made for illness, travel away from home, and pregnancy. Fasting occurs from sunrise to sunset for an entire Baha'i month, which consists of 19 days.

Religion and Healing. With an attitude of harmony between religion and science, Baha'is are encouraged to seek out competent medical care, to follow the advice of those in whom they have confidence, and to pray.

Diet, Medications, and Procedures. The use of alcoholic beverages and narcotic drugs is prohibited except by prescription. There are no restrictions against the use of blood, blood products, or vaccines if advised by health care providers.

Surgical Procedures. Amputations, organ transplantation, biopsies, circumcision, and amniocentesis are permitted if advised by health care providers.

Controversial Issues Related to Health Care

Birth Control. Baha'is believe that the fundamental purpose of marriage is the procreation of children. Individuals are encouraged to exercise their discretion in choosing a method of family planning.

Baha'u'llah taught that to beget children is the highest physical fruit of man's existence. The Baha'i teachings imply that birth control constitutes a real danger to the foundations of social life. It is against the spirit of Baha'i law, which defines the primary purpose of marriage to be the rearing of children and their spiritual training. It is left to each husband and wife to decide how many children they will have. Baha'i teachings state that the soul appears at conception. Therefore, it is improper to use a method that produces an abortion after conception has taken place (e.g., intrauterine device). Methods that result in permanent sterility are not permissible under normal circumstances. If situations arise that justify sterilization (e.g., removal of cancerous reproductive organs), those called on to make the decision would rely on the best medical advice available and their own consciences.

Abortion. Members are discouraged from using methods of contraception that produce an abortion after conception has taken place (e.g., intrauterine device). A surgical operation for the purpose of preventing the birth of an unwanted child is strictly forbidden.

Baha'i teachings state that the soul comes into being at conception. Abortion and surgical operations for the purpose of preventing the birth of unwanted children are forbidden unless circumstances justify such actions on medical grounds. In this case, the decision is left to the consciences of those concerned, who must carefully weigh the medical advice they receive in the light of the general guidance given in the Baha'i writings.

Artificial Insemination. Although there is no specific Baha'i writing on artificial insemination, Baha'is are guided by the understanding that marriage is the proper spiritual and physical context in which the bearing of children must occur. Couples who are unable to bear children are not excluded from marriage, since marriage has other purposes besides the bearing of children. The adoption of children is encouraged.

Eugenics and Genetics. The Baha'is view scientific advancement as noble and praiseworthy endeavor of humankind. Baha'i writings do not specifically address these two branches of science.

Social Activities (Dating, Dancing). Baha'is strive for high standards of conduct in both their private and public lives; this includes chastity before marriage; moderation in dress, language, and amusements; and complete freedom from prejudice in their dealings with peoples of different races, classes, creeds, and orders.

The Baha'i Faith forbids monastic celibacy, noting that marriage is fundamental to the growth and continuation of civilization. The function of dating is to afford individuals an opportunity to become acquainted with each other's character. Those contemplating marriage are encouraged to engage in some form of work and service together, a practice intended to promote assessment of their own maturity and readiness for marriage as well as to improving their knowledge of the character and values of the prospective marriage partner.

Substance Use. Alcoholic beverages and drugs are forbidden unless prescribed by a physician. Tobacco use is strongly discouraged.

Religious Support System for the Sick

Visitors. Individual members of local and surrounding communities assist and support each other in time of need.

Title of Religious Representatives. Religious titles are not used.

Church Organizations to Assist the Sick. Individual members of local communities look after needs.

Issues Related to Death and Dying

Prolongation of Life (Right to Die). Since human life is the vehicle for the development of the soul, Baha'is believe that life is unique and precious. The destruction of a human life at any stage, from conception to natural death, is rarely permissible. The question of when natural death has occurred is considered in light of current medical science and legal rulings on the matter.

Euthanasia. Same as above.

Autopsy. Acceptable in the case of medical necessity or legal requirement.

Donation of Body. Baha'is are permitted to donate their bodies for medical research and for restorative purposes.

Disposal of Body. Local burial laws are followed. Cremation is prohibited.

Burial. Unless required by state law, Baha'i law states that the body is not to be embalmed. Cremation is forbidden. The place of burial must be within 1 hour's travel from the place of death. This regulation is always carried out in consultation with the family, and exceptions are possible.

Buddhist Churches of America

Buddhism is a general term that indicates a belief in Buddha and encompasses many individual churches. In 1993, there were 554,000 Buddhists in North America. Worldwide membership is 309 million.

The Buddhist Churches of America is the largest Buddhist organization in mainland United States. This group belongs to the largest subsect of Jodo Shinshu Buddhism (Shin Buddhism), Honpa Hongwanji, which is the largest traditional sect of Buddhism in Japan. The Jodo Shinshu sect was started by Shinran (1173–1263) in Japan. The headquarters of Jodo Shinshu Buddhism are in Kyoto, Japan. The group of churches in Hawaii is a different organization of Shin Buddhism, called Honpa Hongwanji Mission of Hawaii. There are numerous Buddhist sects in the United States, including Indian, Sri Lankan, Vietnamese, Thai, Chinese, Japanese, Tibetan, and so on.

Buddhism was founded in the 6th century B.C. in northern India by Gautama Buddha. In the 3rd century B.C., Buddhism became the state religion of India and spread from there to most of the other Eastern nations. The term *Buddha* means "enlightened one."

At the beginning of the Christian era, Buddhism split into two main groups: Hinayana, or southern Buddhism, and Mahayana, or northern Buddhism. Hinayana retained more of the original teachings of Buddha and survived in Sri Lanka (formerly Ceylon) and southern Asia. Mahayana, a more social and polytheistic Buddhism, is strong in the Himalayas, Tibet, Mongolia, China, Korea, and Japan.

Beliefs and Religious Practices

Buddha's original teachings included *Four Noble Truths* and *Noble Eightfold Way*, the philosophies of which affect Buddhist response to health and illness. *Four Noble Truths*

Buddhist woman lights incense in remembrance of deceased ancestors during the Chinese New Year celebration.

expounds on suffering and is the foundation of Buddhism. The truths consist of (1) the truth of suffering, (2) the truth of the origin of suffering, (3) the truth that suffering can be destroyed, and (4) the way that leads to the cessation of pain.

Noble Eightfold Way gives the rule of practical Buddhism, which consists of (1) right views, (2) right intention, (3) right speech, (4) right action, (5) right livelihood, (6) right effort, (7) right mindfulness, and (8) right concentration. *Nirvana*, a state of greater inner freedom and spontaneity, is the goal of all existence. When one achieves *Nirvana*, the mind has supreme tranquility, purity, and stability (Hinnells, 1984).

Although the ultimate goals of Buddhism are clear, the means of obtaining those goals are not religiously prescribed. Buddhism is not a dogmatic religion, nor does it dictate any specific practices. Individual differences are expected, acknowledged, and respected. Each individual is responsible for finding his or her own answers through awareness of the total situation.

Holy Days. Special holy days occur on January 1 and 16, February 15, March 21, April 8, May 21, July 15, September 1 and 23, and December 8 and 31. Although there is no religious restriction for therapy on these days, they can be highly emotional, and a Buddhist patient should be consulted about his or her desires for medical or surgical intervention then.

Sacraments. Buddhism does not have any sacraments. A ritual that symbolizes one's entry into the Buddhist faith is the expression of faith in the Three Treasures (Buddha, Dharma, and Sangha).

Religion and Healing. Buddhists do not believe in healing through a faith or through faith itself. However, Buddhists do believe that spiritual peace and liberation from anxiety by adherence to and achievement of awakening to Buddha's wisdom can be important factors in promoting healing and the recovery process.

Diet, Medications, and Procedures. There are no prescriptions in Buddhism for any of these things. Buddha's teaching on the middle path may apply here; he taught that extremes should be avoided. What may be medicine to one may be poison to another, so generalizations are to be avoided. Medications should be used in accordance with the nature of the illness and the capacity of the individual. Whatever will contribute to the attainment of Enlightenment is encouraged.

Surgical Procedures. Treatments such as amputations, organ transplants, biopsies, amniocentesis, and other procedures that may prolong life and allow the individual to attain Enlightenment are encouraged.

Controversial Issues Related to Health Care

The immediate emphasis is on the person living now and the attainment of Enlightenment. If practicing birth control or having sterility testing will help the individual attain Enlightenment, it is acceptable.

Buddhism does not condone the taking of a life. The first of Buddha's Five Precepts is abstention from taking lives. Life in all forms is to be respected. Existence by itself often contradicts this principle (e.g., drugs that kill bacteria are given to spare a patient's life). With this in mind, it is the conditions and circumstances surrounding the patient that determine whether abortion, therapeutic or on demand, may be undertaken.

Religious Support System for the Sick

Title of Religious Representative. Priest.

Issues Related to Death and Dying

Prolongation of Life (Right to Die). If there is hope for recovery and continuation of the pursuit of Enlightenment, all available means of support are encouraged.

Euthanasia. If life cannot be prolonged so that the person can continue to search for Enlightenment, conditions may permit euthanasia.

Donation of Body or Parts. If the donation of a body part will help another continue the quest for Enlightenment, it may be an act of mercy and is encouraged.

Autopsy and Disposal of Body. The body is considered but a shell; therefore, autopsy and disposal of the body are matters of individual practice rather than of religious prescription. *Burial.* Burials are usually a brief graveside service after a funeral at the temple. Cremations are common.

Addendum. The headquarters of the Buddhist Churches of America are located at 1710 Octavia Street, San Francisco, California 94109 (Telephone: (415) 776-5600). Additional material is available at the Buddhist Bookstore of the Buddhist Churches of America Headquarters.

Catholicism (According to the Roman Rite)

With a North American membership of approximately 96 million and a worldwide membership of more than 1 billion, some 32 rites exist within Catholicism. Of these, the Roman Rite is the major body.

Beliefs and Religious Practices

Holy Days. Catholics are expected to observe all Sundays as holy days. Sunday or holy day worship services may be conducted anytime from 4:00 P.M. on Saturday to Sunday evening. In addition, there are 7 days set aside for special liturgical observance: Christmas (December 25), Solemnity of Mary, Mother of God (January 1), Easter Sunday (Feast of the Resurrection of Jesus from the Dead), Ascension Thursday (The Lord's Ascension Bodily into Heaven—observed 40 days after Easter), Feast of the Assumption (August 15), All Saints Day (November 1), and the Feast of the Immaculate Conception (December 8).
Sacraments. The Roman Catholic Church recognizes seven sacraments. These are Baptism, Reconciliation (formerly Penance, or Confession), Holy Communion or Eucharist, Confirmation, Matrimony, Holy Orders, and Anointing of the Sick (formerly Extreme Unction).
Religion and Healing. In time of illness, the basic rite is the Sacrament of the Sick, which includes anointing of the sick, communion, if possible, and a blessing by a priest. Prayers are frequently offered for the sick person and for members of the family. The Eucharist (a small wafer made of flour and water) is often given to the sick as the food of healing and health. Other family members may participate if they wish to do so.

Diet, Medications, and Procedures

Diet (Foods and Beverages). The goods of the world have been given for use and benefit. The primary obligation people have toward foods and beverages is to use them in moderation and in such a way that they are not injurious to health. Fasting is recommended as a valued discipline, in moderation. There are a few days of the year when Catholics have an obligation to fast or to abstain from meat and meat products. Catholics fast and abstain on Ash Wednesday and Good Friday, and abstinence is required on all the Fridays of Lent. The sick are *never* bound by this prescription of the law. Healthy persons between the ages of 18 and 62 years are encouraged to engage in fasting and abstinence as described.

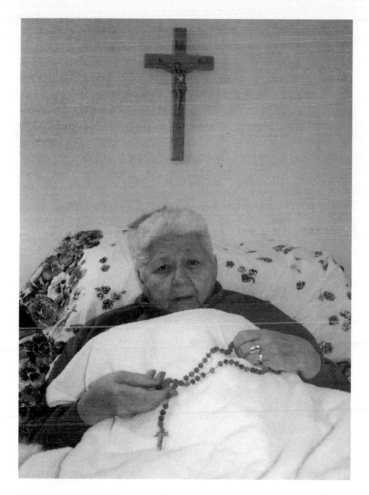

This Roman Catholic home care patient uses rosary beads as an aid in the recitation of prayers. The crucifix (cross with a figure of Jesus) hung above the bed is a religious symbol found in many Catholic homes.

Medications. As long as the benefits outweigh the risk to the individual, judicious use of medications is permissible and morally acceptable. The Church has traditionally cited the "principle of totality," which states that use of medications is allowed as long as the medications are used for the good of the whole person.

Blood and Blood Products. As above.

Amputations. A major concern is the risk of mutilation. Amputation is acceptable if consistent with the "principle of totality."

Organ Transplants. The transplantation of organs from living donors is morally permissible when the anticipated benefit to the recipient is proportionate to the harm done to the donor, provided that the loss of such organ(s) does not deprive the donor of life itself nor of the functional integrity of his or her body.

Biopsies. Permissible.

Circumcision. Permissible.

Amniocentesis. The procedure in and of itself is not objectionable. However, it is morally objectionable if the findings of the amniocentesis are used to lead the couple to decide on termination of the pregnancy or if the procedure injures the fetus.

Controversial Issues Related to Health Care

Birth Control. The basic principle is that the conjugal act should be one that is love-giving and potentially life-giving. Only natural means of contraception, such as abstinence, the temperature method, and the ovulation method, are acceptable. Ordinarily, artificial aids and procedures for permanent sterilization are forbidden. Birth control (an-ovulents) may be used therapeutically to assist in regulating the menstrual cycle.

Abortion. Direct abortion is always morally wrong. Indirect abortion may be morally justified by some circumstances (e.g., treatment of a cancerous uterus in a pregnant woman). Abortion on demand is prohibited. The Church teaches the sanctity of all human life, even the unborn, from the time of conception.

Sterility Tests. Use of such tests for the purpose of promoting, not misusing sexuality, is permitted.

Artificial Insemination. Although debated heavily, traditionally this has been looked on as illicit, even between husband and wife (Lawler, 1987).

Eugenics and Genetics. Objectionable. This violates the moral right of the individual to be free from experimentation. It also interferes with God's right as master of life and man's stewardship of his life. Some genetic investigations to help determine genetic diseases may be used, depending on their ends and means (McMannus, 1993).

Social Activities (Dating, Dancing). The major principle is that Sunday is a day of rest; therefore, only unnecessary servile work is prohibited. The 7 holy days are also considered days of rest, although many persons must engage in routine work-related activities on some of these days.

Substance Use. Alcohol and tobacco are not evil per se. They are to be used in moderation and not in a way that would be injurious to one's health or that of another party. The misuse of any substance is not only harmful to the body but also sinful.

Religious Support System for the Sick

Visitors. Although a priest, deacon, or lay minister usually visits a sick person alone, he or she may invite the family or other significant people to join in prayer. In fact, that is most desirable, since they, too, need support.

The priest, deacon, or lay minister will usually bring the necessary supplies for administration of the Eucharist or administration of the Sacrament of the Sick (in the case of a priest). The nursing staff can facilitate these rites by ensuring an atmosphere of prayer and quiet and by having a glass of water on hand (in case the patient is unable to swallow the small wafer like host). Consecrated wine can be made available but is usually not given in the hospital or home. The nurse may wish to join in the prayer. Candles may be used, although not if the patient is on oxygen. The priest, deacon, or lay minister will usually appreciate any information pertaining to the patient's ability to swallow. Any other information the nurse believes might help the priest or deacon respond to the patient more caringly and effectively would be appreciated.

Catholic laypersons of either sex may visit hospitalized or home-bound elderly or sick persons. Although they may not administer the Sacrament of the Sick or the Sacrament of Reconciliation, they may bring Holy Communion (the Eucharist).

Titles of Religious Representatives. Father (priest), Mr. or Deacon (deacon), Sister (Catholic woman who has taken religious vows), Brother (Catholic man who has taken religious vows).

Environment During Visit by Religious Representative. Privacy is most conducive to prayer and to the administration of the sacraments. In emergency cases, such as cardiac or respiratory arrest, medical personnel will need to be present. The priest will use an abbreviated form of the rite and will not interfere with the activities of the health care team.

Church Organizations to Assist the Sick. Most major cities have outreach programs for the sick, handicapped, and elderly. More serious needs are usually handled by Catholic Charities and other agencies in the community or on the local parish level. Organizations such as the St. Vincent DePaul Society may provide material support for the poor and needy as well as some counseling services, depending on the location. The Catholic Church owns and operates hospitals, extended-care facilities, orphanages, maternity homes, hospices, and other health care facilities. It is usually best to consult the pastor or chaplain in specific cases for local resources (Bainbridge, 1991).

Issues Related to Death and Dying

Prolongation of Life (Right to Die). Members are obligated to take ordinary means of preserving life (e.g., intravenous medication) but are not obligated to take extraordinary means. What constitutes extraordinary means may vary with biomedical and technological advances and with the availability of these advances to the average citizen. Other factors that must be considered include the degree of pain associated with the procedure, the potential outcome, the condition of the patient, economic factors, and the patient's or family's desires (Green, 1992a and b).

Euthanasia. Direct action to end the life of patients is not permitted. Extraordinary means may be withheld, allowing the patient to die of natural causes.

Autopsy. This is permissible as long as the corpse is shown proper respect and there is sufficient reason for doing the autopsy.

Donation of Body. The principle of totality suggests that this is justifiable, being for the betterment of the person doing the giving.

Disposal of Body. Ordinarily, bodies are buried. Cremation is acceptable in certain circumstances, such as to avoid spreading a contagious disease.

Burial. Since life is considered sacred, the body should be treated with respect. Any disposal of the body should be done in a respectful and honorable way.

Christian Science (Church of Christ, Scientist)

Christian Science accepts physical and moral healing as a natural part of the Christian experience. Members believe that God acts through universal, immutable, spiritual law. They hold that genuine spiritual or Christian healing through prayer differs radically from the use of suggestion, willpower, and all forms of psychotherapy, which are based on use of the human mind as a curative agent. In emphasizing the practical importance

of a fuller understanding of Jesus' works and teachings, Christian Science believes healing to be a natural result of drawing closer to God in one's thinking and living.
Membership. The church does not keep membership data; 3000 congregations worldwide.

Beliefs and Religious Practices

Holy Days. Besides the usual weekly day of worship (Sunday), other traditional Christian holidays are observed on an individual basis. Wednesday evenings are observed worldwide as times for members to gather for testimony meetings.
Sacraments. Although sacraments in a strictly spiritual sense have deep meaning for Christian Scientists, there are no outward observances or ceremonies. Baptism and holy communion are not outward observances but deeply meaningful inner experiences. Baptism is the daily purification and spiritualization of thought, while *communion* refers to finding one's conscious unity with God through prayer (Christian Science Publishing Society, 1974).
Religion and Healing. Viewed as a by-product of drawing closer to God, healing is considered proof of God's care and one element in the full salvation at which Christianity aims. Christian Science teaches that faith must rest not on blind belief but on an understanding of the present perfection of God's spiritual creation. This is one of the crucial differences between Christian Science and "faith healing" (Christian Science Publishing Society, 1974; Green, 1992a).

The practice of Christian Science healing starts from the Biblical basis that God created the universe and man "and made them perfect." Christian Science holds that human imperfection, including physical illness and sin, reflects a fundamental misunderstanding of creation and is therefore subject to healing through prayer and spiritual regeneration.

An individual who is seeking healing may turn to Christian Science practitioners, members of the denomination who devote their full time to the healing ministry in the broadest sense. In cases requiring continued care, nurses grounded in the Christian Science faith provide care in facilities accredited by the mother church, the First Church of Christ, Scientist, in Boston, Massachusetts. Individuals also may receive such care in their own homes. Christian Science nurses are trained to perform the practical duties a patient may need while also providing an atmosphere of warmth and love that supports the healing process. No medication is given, and physical application is limited to the normal measures associated with hygiene. *The Christian Science Journal*, a monthly publication, contains a directory of qualified Christian Science practitioners and nurses throughout the world.

Before they can be recognized and advertised in *The Christian Science Journal*, practitioners must have instruction from an authorized teacher of Christian Science and provide substantial evidence of their experience in healing. There are some 4000 Christian Science practitioners throughout the world. Practitioners who speak other languages also may be listed in appropriate editions of *The Herald of Christian Science*, which is published in 12 languages.

The denomination has no clergy. Practitioners are thus lay members of the Church of Christ, Scientist, and do not conduct public worship services or rituals. Their ministry is not an office within the church structure but is carried out on an individual basis with those who seek their help through prayer. Both members and nonmembers are welcome to contact practitioners by telephone, by letter, or in person for help or for information.

Christian Science practitioners are supported not by the church but by payments from their patients. Their ministry is not restricted to local congregations but worldwide. Many insurance companies include coverage of payments to practitioners and Christian Science nursing facilities in their policies. Despite such superficial resemblances with the health professions, the work of Christian Science practitioners involves a deeply religious vocation, not simply alternative health care. Practitioners do not employ medical or psychological techniques.

The term *healing* applies to the entire spectrum of human fears, griefs, wants, and sin, as well as to physical ills. Practitioners are called on to give Christian Science treatment not only in cases of physical disease and emotional disturbance but also in family and financial difficulties, business problems, questions of employment, schooling problems, theological confusion, and so forth. The purpose of prayer, or Christian Science treatment, is to deal with these interrelated and complex problems of establishing God's law of harmony in every aspect of life. When healings are accomplished through perception and living of spiritual truth, they are effective and permanent. Physical healing is often the manifestation of a moral and spiritual change (Christian Science Publishing Society, 1978; Skolnick, 1990; Gundersen, 1990).

Ordinarily, a Christian Science practitioner and a physician are not employed on the same case, because the two approaches to healing differ so radically. During childbirth, however, an obstetrician or qualified midwife is involved. Given that bone setting may be accomplished without the use of medication, a physician is also employed for repair of fractures if the patient requests this medical intervention. In the case of a contagious or infectious disease, Christian Scientists observe the legal requirements for reporting and quarantining affected individuals. The denomination recognizes public health concerns and has a long history of responsible cooperation with public health officials.

Christian Scientists are not arbitrarily opposed to doctors. They are always free to make their own decisions regarding treatment in any given situation. They generally choose to rely on spiritual healing because they have seen its effectiveness in the experience of their own families and fellow church members, experience that goes back over 100 years and in many families for three or four generations. Where medical treatment for minor children is required by law, Christian Scientists strictly adhere to the requirement. At the same time, they maintain that their substantial healing record needs to be seriously considered in determining the rights of Christian Scientists to rely on spiritual healing for themselves and their children. They do not ignore or neglect disease, but they seek to heal it by the means they believe to be most efficacious (Fox, 1984).

Diet, Medications, and Procedures

Diet. No restrictions.

Medications. Christian Scientists ordinarily do not use drugs. Immunizations/vaccines are acceptable only when required by law.

Blood and Blood Products. Ordinarily not used by members.

Amputations. A Christian Scientist who has lost a limb might seek to have it replaced with a prosthesis.

Organ Transplants. Christian Scientists are unlikely to seek transplants and are unlikely to act as donors.

Biopsies. Christian Scientists do not normally seek biopsies or any sort of physical examination.

Circumcision. This is considered an individual matter.

Amniocentesis. Christian Scientists are unlikely to seek this type of procedure.

Controversial Issues Related to Health Care

Birth Control. Matters of family planning are left to individual judgment.

Abortion. Since abortion involves medication and surgical intervention, it is normally considered incompatible with Christian Science.

Artificial Insemination. This is unusual among Christian Scientists.

Eugenics and Genetics. Christian Scientists are opposed to compulsory programs in this field.

Social Activities (Dating, Dancing). Members are encouraged to be honest, truthful, and moral in their behavior. Although every effort is made to preserve marriages, divorce is recognized. The Christian Science Sunday School teaches young people how to make their religion practical in daily life as related to school studies, social life, sports, and family relationships.

Substance Use. Members abstain from alcohol and tobacco; some abstain from tea and coffee.

Religious Support System for the Sick

Christian Scientists have their own nurses and practitioners (see section on Religion and Healing).

Title of Religious Representative. No special religious titles are used. Although each branch church elects two Readers for Sunday and Wednesday services, Christian Scientists are a church of laymen and laywomen.

Church Organizations to Assist the Sick. Benevolent homes staffed by Christian Science nurses; visiting home nurse service.

Issues Related to Death and Dying

Prolongation of Life (Right to Die). A Christian Science family is unlikely to seek medical means to prolong life indefinitely. Family members pray earnestly for recovery of a person as long as the person remains alive.

Euthanasia. This is contrary to the teachings of Christian Science.

Donation of Body. Most Christian Scientists feel that they can make their particular contribution to the health of society and of their loved ones in ways other than this.

Disposal of Body. This is left to the individual family to decide.

Burial. The form of burial and burial service is decided by the individual family.

Addendum. A wide variety of books and journals are published by the Christian Science Publishing Society, Boston, Massachusetts. Most major cities have Christian Science Reading Rooms, which carry these publications and which are staffed by church members, who are available to provide additional information.

The Church of Jesus Christ of Latter-Day Saints (Mormonism)

Membership. The Church of Jesus Christ of Latter-Day Saints, commonly known as Mormonism, has a North American membership of 6.5 million and a worldwide membership approaching 9 million.

Beliefs and Religious Practices

Holy Days/Special Days. Sunday is the day observed as the Sabbath in the United States. In other parts of the world, the Sabbath may be observed on a different day; in Israel, for example, Mormons observe the Sabbath on Saturday.

Sacraments (Commonly Called Ordinances)

Ordinances of Salvation

Elders of the Church of Jesus Christ of Latter-Day Saints (Mormons) lay hands on the head of a sick child to give a blessing for healing. (Original picture copyright © by The Church of Jesus Christ of Latter-Day Saints. Used by permission.)

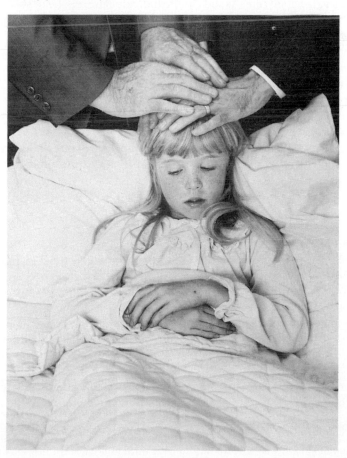

1. Baptism at the age of accountability (8 years or after); never performed in infancy or at death; always by immersion.
2. Confirmation at the time of baptism to receive the gift of the Holy Ghost.
3. Partaking of the sacrament of the Lord's Supper at Sunday sacrament meetings.
4. Endowments.*
5. Celestial marriage.*
6. Vicarious ordinances.*

Ordinances of Comfort, Consolation, and Encouragement

1. Blessing of babies.
2. Blessing of the sick.
3. Consecration of oil for use in blessing of the sick.
4. Patriarchal blessings.
5. Dedication of graves.

After being deemed worthy to go to a temple, a Mormon will wear a special type of underclothing, called a *garment*. While in a health care setting, the garment may be removed to facilitate care. As soon as the individual is well, he or she is likely to want to wear the garment again (elderly may not wish to part with the garment in the hospital). The garment has special significance to the person, symbolizing covenants or promises the person has made to God.

Religion and Healing. Mormons believe that the power of God can be exercised in their behalf to bring about healing at a time of illness. The ritual of blessing of the sick consists of one member (Elder) of the priesthood (male) anointing the ill person with oil and a second Elder "sealing the anointing with a prayer and a blessing." Commonly, both Elders place their hands on the individual's head. Faith in Jesus Christ and in the power of the priesthood to heal, requisite to the healing use of priesthood, does not preclude medical intervention but is seen as an adjunct to it. Mormons believe that medical intervention is one of God's ways of using humans in the healing process.

Diet, Medications, and Procedures

Diet. Mormons have a strict dietary code called the *Word of Wisdom*. This code prohibits all alcoholic beverages (including beer and wine), hot drinks (i.e., tea and coffee, although not herbal tea), and tobacco in any form.

Fasting to a Mormon means no food or drink (including water), usually for a 24-hour period. Fasting is required once a month on the designated fast Sunday. Pregnant women, the very young, the very old, and the ill are not required to fast. The purpose of fasting is to bring oneself closer to God by controlling physical needs. Ideally, the person will donate the price of what has not been eaten to the church to be used to care for the poor.

Medications. There is no restriction on the use of medications or vaccines in Mormon Church doctrine. It is not uncommon to find many members of the Mormon Church

---

*These ordinances occur in temples. Temples are sacred places of worship that are accessible only to observant Mormons, who are "worthy" to enter them as deemed by their local religious leaders.

using herbal folk remedies, and it is wise to explore in detail what an individual may have done or taken to help himself or herself.

Blood and Blood Products. There is no restriction on the use of blood or blood components.

Surgeries/Procedures. Surgical intervention is a matter of individual decision in cases of amputations, transplants, and organ donations (both of donor and recipient). Biopsies and resulting surgery are also a matter of individual choice.

Circumcision of infants is viewed as a medical health-promotion measure and is not a religious ritual.

Amniocentesis is a matter of individual choice. However, even if the fetus is found to be deformed, abortion is not an option unless the mother's life is in danger.

Controversial Issues Related to Health Care

Birth Control. According to Mormon belief, one of the major purposes of life is procreation; therefore, any form of prevention of the birth of children is contrary to church teachings. Exceptions to this policy include ill health of mother or father and genetic defects that could be passed on to offspring.

Abortion. Abortion is forbidden in all cases except when the mother's life is in danger; even in these circumstances, abortion would be looked on favorably only if the local priesthood authorities, after fasting and prayer, receive divine confirmation that the abortion was acceptable.

In the event of pregnancy resulting from rape, the church position is that the child should be born and put up for adoption if necessary rather than be aborted. The final decision rests with the mother. No official church sanction would be employed if she chose to abort the child.

Abortion on demand is strictly forbidden.

Sterility/Fertility Testing. Since bearing children is so important, all measures that can be taken to promote having children are acceptable.

Artificial Insemination. Acceptable if the semen is from the husband.

Social Activities (Dating, Dancing). The Mormon Church has a wide variety of activities for its youth and encourages group activities until young people are at least age 16.

Young men are highly encouraged to perform "missions" for the church for 2 years at their own expense. The earliest this can be is at age 19 years. Women may go on missions when they are 21, but marriage is more strongly emphasized for them.

Substance Use. Alcohol, tea, coffee, and tobacco are forbidden. In recent years, "recreational drugs" also have been considered forbidden substances.

Religious Support System for the Sick

Visitors. Mormonism has a highly organized network, and many church representatives are likely to visit a hospitalized member, including the bishop and two counselors (leaders of the local congregation), home teachers (two men assigned to visit the family each month), and visiting teachers (two women assigned to visit the female head of household each month). Friends within the local congregation also can be expected to visit.

Title of Religious Representative. A variety of titles are used for members of the Mormon hierarchy. The term *Elder* is generally acceptable regardless of a man's position, and the term *Sister* is acceptable for women.

Environment Needed for Health-Related Rituals. To perform a blessing of the sick, the Elders performing the blessing need privacy and, if possible, quiet. They generally bring a vial of consecrated oil with which to anoint the person. If they want to perform a Sacrament of the Lord's Supper, they usually bring what they need with them. Bread and water are used for this ordinance.

Church Organizations to Assist the Sick. The Relief Society is the Mormon organization for helping members. It is organized by the women of the church, who work closely with priesthood leaders to determine general needs of members, including use of the church-run welfare organization. Church members who are in need may receive local help, such as child care for children when parents are ill or hospitalized and money for medical expenses.

Issues Related to Death and Dying

Prolongation of Life (Right to Die). Whenever possible, medical science and faith healing are used to reverse conditions that threaten life. When death is inevitable, the effort is to promote a peaceful and dignified death. Mormons firmly believe that life continues beyond death and that the dead are reunited with loved ones; therefore, the belief is that death is another step in eternal progression (Green, 1992a and b).

Euthanasia. Life and death are in the hands of God, and humans must not interfere in any way.

Autopsy. Permitted with the consent of the next of kin and within local laws.

Disposal of Body Parts. Organ donation is permitted; it is an individual decision.

Burial. Cremation is discouraged but not forbidden; burial is customary. Graves are dedicated by a local priesthood member.

Hinduism

The Hindu religion may be the oldest religion in the world. There are over 719 million Hindus worldwide, with a North American following of approximately 1.3 million members.

Beliefs and Religious Practices

No common creed or doctrine binds Hindus together. There is complete freedom of belief. One may be monotheistic, polytheistic, or atheistic. The major distinguishing characteristic is the social caste system.

The religion of Hinduism is founded on sacred, written scripture called the *Vedas*. Brahman is the principle and source of the universe and the center from which all things proceed and to which all things return. Reincarnation is a central belief in Hinduism.

Life is determined by the law of *karma*. According to karma, rebirth is dependent on moral behavior in a previous stage of existence. Life on earth is transient and a burden. The goal of existence is liberation from the cycle of rebirth and redeath and entrance into what in Buddhism is called *Nirvana* (a state of extinction of passion).

The practice of Hinduism consists of roles and ceremonies performed within the framework of the caste system. These rituals focus on the main socioreligious events of birth, marriage, and death. Hindu temples are dwelling places for deities to which people bring offerings. There are numerous places for religious pilgrimage (Naidoo, 1989; Madan, 1992).

Holy Days. Based on a lunar calendar:

1. Purnima (day of full moon)
2. Janamasthtmi (birthday of Lord Krishna)
3. Ramnavmi (birthday of Rama)
4. Shivratri (birth of Lord Shiva)
5. Naurate (nine holy days occurring twice a year, in about April and October)
6. Dussehra
7. Diwali
8. Holi

Religion and Healing. Some Hindus believe in faith healing; others believe illness is God's way of punishing a person for his or her sins.

Diet, Medications, and Procedures

Diet. The eating of meat is forbidden because it involves harming a living creature.
Medications. Acceptable.
Blood and Blood Products. Acceptable.
Amputations. Persons who lose a limb are not outcasts from society. Loss of a limb is considered due to "sins of a previous life."
Organ Transplants. Donation and receipt of organs are both acceptable.
Amniocentesis. Acceptable, although not often available.

Controversial Issues Related to Health Care

Birth Control. All types acceptable.
Abortion. No Hindu policy exists on abortion, either therapeutic or on demand.
Artificial Insemination. No religious restriction exists; not often practiced owing to lack of availability.
Social Activities (Dating, Dancing). Strictly limited by caste system.
Substance Use. No restrictions

Religious Support System for the Sick

Title of Religious Representative. Priest.
Church Organizations to Assist the Sick. None; help is provided by family and friends within the caste.

Issues Related to Death and Dying

Prolongation of Life (Right to Die). There is no religious custom or restriction. Life is seen as a perpetual cycle, with death considered just one more step toward *Nirvana*.
Euthanasia. Not practiced.
Autopsy. Acceptable.
Donation of Body or Parts. Acceptable.
Disposal of Body. Cremation is most common. Ashes are collected and disposed of in holy rivers.
Burial. As described above under "Disposal of Body." Fetus or newborn is sometimes buried.

Islam

Islam is a monotheistic religion founded between A.D. 610 and 632 by Mohammed. Followers of Islam are called *Moslems* or *Muslims*. Current U.S. membership is 2.6 million, with worldwide membership of 950 million.

Mohammed, revered as the prophet of Allah (God), is seen as succeeding and completing both Judaism and Christianity. *Islam* means submission to the will of Allah. Good deeds will be rewarded at the last judgment; evil deeds will be punished in hell.

Beliefs and Religious Practices

Islam has five essential practices, or "Pillars of Faith." These are (1) bearing witness to one true God and acknowledging Mohammed as his messenger (*shahada*), (2) praying five times daily: dawn, noon, afternoon, sunset, and night, facing Mecca, Saudi Arabia, Islam's holiest city (*salat*), (3) giving alms to the needy and for communal purposes (*zakat*), (4) fasting from dawn until sunset throughout Ramadan, the ninth month of the Islamic lunar calendar (*saum*), and (5) making one pilgrimage to Mecca if able to do so (*hajj*).

The sources of the Islamic faith are the *Qur'an* (Koran), which is regarded as the uncreated and eternal Word of God, and *Hadith* (tradition), regarded as sayings and deeds of the prophet Mohammed.

Various sects of Islam have developed. When Mohammed died, a dispute arose over the leadership of the Muslim community. One faction, the Sunni, derived from the Arabic word for "tradition," felt that the caliph, or successor of Mohammed, should be chosen, as Arab chiefs customarily are, by election. Therefore, they supported the succession of the first four, or the rightly guided caliphs who had been Mohammed's companions. The other group maintained that Mohammed chose his cousin and son-in-law, Ali, as his spiritual and secular heir and that succession should be through his bloodline. In A.D. 680, one of Ali's sons, Hussein, led a band of rebels against the ruling caliph. In the course of the battle, Hussein was killed, and with his death began the Shi'a, sometimes called the Shi'ite movement, whose name comes from the word meaning "partisans of Ali." The Shi'a and Sunni are the two major branches of Muslims, with the Sunni constituting about 85 percent of the total. The Sunni are found in Lebanon, the West Bank, Jordan, and throughout Africa, whereas the Shi'a are located in Iran, Iraq,

Yemen, Afghanistan, and Pakistan. The Shi'a and the Sunni also have different rituals, practices, and structural and political orientations.

Holidays and Special Observances. Days of observance in Islam are not "holy" days but days of celebration or observance. The Muslims follow a lunar calendar, so the days of observance change yearly.

Each Muslim observance has its own significance. They are listed here in the same order in which they occur in the Muslim lunar calendar, and their standard Arabic names are used. However, the Arabic spellings for the names of the holidays may vary, or local names may be used.

Muharam 1 Rasal-Sana (or New Year): The first day of the first month, celebrated much the same as the first day of the year is celebrated throughout the world.

Muharam 10 Ashura (the 10th of the first month): A religious holiday through which pious Muslims may fast from dawn to sunset. For Shi'ite Muslims, this is a special day of sorrow commemorating the assassination of the prophet's grandson, Hussein.

Rabi'i 12 Maulid al-Nabi: The birthday of the prophet Mohammed. In some regions this holiday goes on for many days, a time of festivities and exchange of gifts.

Rajab 27 Lailat al-Isra wa al Miraj (literally, "The Night of the Journey and Ascent"): Commemorates Mohammed's night journey from Mecca to the al-Aqsa mosque in Jerusalem and his ascent to heaven and return on the same night.

Sh'ban 14: This is the 14th night of the 8th month of Sh'ban. It is widely celebrated by pious Muslims, sometimes called the "Night of Repentance." It is treated in many parts of the Muslim world as a New Year's celebration.

Ramadan (the 9th month of the Muslim year): This entire month is devoted to meditation and spiritual purification through self-discipline. It is a period of abstinence from food, drink, and physical pleasure. The fast is an obligation practiced by Muslims throughout the world unless they are old, infirm, traveling, or pregnant. The fast is from sunup to sundown.

Ramadan 27 Lailat al-Qadir (next to the last night of the fasting month): This is simply called the "Night of Power and Greatness," and it is by custom a very special holy time. It is the night that commemorates when revelation was first given to Mohammed.

Shawwal 1 "Id ad-Fitr": This is called the "Lesser Feast" because it begins immediately after the month-long Ramadan feast. It is perhaps Islam's most joyous festival, marking as it does the month of abstinence and the cleansing of the believer. It usually lasts for 2 or 3 days. Families and friends visit each others' homes, new clothes and presents are exchanged, and sweet pastries are a favorite treat.

Dhu al-Hijjah 1–10: Muslims, if they are able, are obliged to undertake a pilgrimage to Mecca at least once in their lifetime. This journey, called the *hajj*, is performed during the last month of the Muslim calendar, *Dhu al-Hijjah*.

Dhu al-Hijjah 10: All Muslims, whether they are on the pilgrimage or at home, participate in the feast of the sacrifice, *Id al-Adha*, which marks the end of the *hajj* on the tenth of *Dhu al-Hijjah*. The feast is the "Feast of the Sacrifice," called the "Greater Feast," and is observed by the slaughtering of animals and distribution of the meat. In some places this is done individually. The meat is shared equally among the family and the poor. Sometimes the slaughtering takes place in public areas, and the meat is then distributed.

Sacraments. None.

Religion and Healing. Faith healing is not acceptable unless the psychological health and morale of the patient are deteriorating. At that time, faith healing may be employed to supplement the physician's efforts.

Diet, Medications, and Procedures

Diet. Eating pork and drinking intoxicating beverages are strictly prohibited. In all cases, moderation in one's life is expected.

Fasting during the month of Ramadan is one of the pillars of Islam. Children (boys 7 years old; girls 9 years old) and adults are required to fast. Pregnant women, nursing mothers, and the elderly, as well as anyone whose physical condition is so fragile that a physician recommends that he or she not fast, are exempt from fasting but are expected to fast later in the year or to feed a poor person to make up for the unfasted Ramadan days.

Medications. There are no restrictions as far as medications are concerned. Even items normally forbidden are permitted if prescribed as medicine.

Blood and Blood Products. No restrictions.

Amputations. Acceptable; no restrictions.

Organ Transplants. Acceptable for both donor and recipient.

Biopsies. Acceptable; no restrictions.

Circumcision. No age limit is fixed, but circumcision is practiced on male children at an early age. For adult converts, it is not obligatory, although it is sometimes practiced.

Amniocentesis. Available in many Islamic countries; used by "progressive" doctors and expectant parents only. Used only to determine the status of the fetus, not the sex of the child; this is left in the hands of God.

Controversial Issues Related to Health Care

Birth Control. All types of birth control are generally acceptable in accordance with the law of "what is harmful to the body is prohibited." Family physician's advice on method of contraception is required. Husband and wife should agree on the method.

Abortion. No official policy on abortion, either therapeutic or on demand. There is a strong religious objection to abortion, though.

Artificial Insemination. Permitted only if from husband to his own wife.

Eugenics and Genetics. No official policy exists. Different Islamic schools of thought accept differing opinions.

Substance Use. Alcohol is strictly forbidden.

Religious Support System for the Sick

Church Organizations to Assist the Sick. None; family and friends provide emotional and financial support.

Issues Related to Death and Dying

Prolongation of Life (Right to Die). The right to die is not recognized in Islam. Any attempt to shorten one's life or terminate it (suicide or otherwise) is prohibited.

Euthanasia. Not acceptable.

Autopsy. Permitted only for medical and legal purposes.

Donation of Body Parts or Body. Acceptable; no restrictions.

Disposal of Body. It is important in Islam to follow prescribed burial procedure. Under conditions that cause fragmentation of the body, sections of the burial ritual may be omitted.

Burial. Burial of the dead, including fetuses, is compulsory. The five steps of the burial procedure consist of

1. *Ghasl El Mayyet*: Rinsing and washing of the dead body according to Muslim tradition. Muslim women cleanse a woman's body; Muslim men, a man's body.
2. *Muslim*: After being washed three times, the body is wrapped in three pieces of clean white cloth. The Muslim word for "coffin" is the same as that for "Muslim."
3. *Salat El Mayyet*: Special prayers for the dead are required.
4. The body should be processed and buried as soon as possible. The body should always be buried so that the head faces toward Mecca.
5. *Burial of a fetus*: Prior to a gestational age of 130 days, a fetus is treated like any other discarded tissue. After 130 days, the fetus is considered a fully developed human being and must be treated as such.

Jehovah's Witnesses

Membership. North American, 1,485,426; worldwide, 4,709,889.

Beliefs and Religious Practices

Many Americans have at one time or another encountered "ministers" of the Watch Tower Bible and Tract Society, known as Jehovah's Witnesses. The name *Jehovah's Witnesses*, the name that members prefer, is derived from the Hebrew name for "God" (Jehovah) according to the King James Bible. Thus, *Jehovah's Witnesses* is a descriptive name, indicating that members profess to bear witness concerning Jehovah, his Godship, and his purposes. Every Bible student devotes approximately 10 hours or more each month to proselytizing activities.

Holy Days. Although Witnesses do not celebrate Christmas, Easter, or other traditional Christian holy days, a special observance of the Lord's Supper is held. Witnesses and others may attend this important meeting, but only those numbered among the 144,000 chosen members (Revelations 7:4) may partake of the bread and wine as a symbol of the death of Christ and the dedication of God. This memorial of Christ's death should take place on the day corresponding to Nisan 14 of the Jewish calendar, which occurs some time in March or April. These elite members will be raised with spiritual bodies (without flesh, bones, or blood) and will assist Christ in ruling the universe. Others who benefit from Christ's ransom will be resurrected with healthy, perfected physical bodies (bodies of flesh, bones, and blood) and will inhabit this earth after the world has been restored to a paradisiacal state (Backman, 1983; Singelenberg, 1990; Green, 1992b).

Sacraments. No sacraments are observed.

Religion and Healing. The practice of faith healing is forbidden. However, it is believed that reading the scriptures can comfort the individual and lead to mental and spiritual healing.

Diet, Medications, and Procedures

Medications. To the extent that they are necessary, medications are acceptable.

Blood and Blood Products. Blood in any form and agents in which blood is an ingredient are not acceptable. Blood volume expanders are acceptable if they are not derivatives of blood. Mechanical devices for circulating the blood are acceptable as long as they are not primed with blood initially. In some cases, children have been made wards of the court so that they could receive blood when a medical condition mandating blood transfusion was life-threatening.

The determination of Jehovah's Witnesses to abstain from blood is based on scriptural references and precedents in the history of Christianity. Courts of justice have often upheld the principle that each individual has a right to bodily integrity, yet some physicians and hospital administrators have turned to the courts for legal authorization to force blood to be used as a medical treatment for an individual whose religious convictions prohibit the use of blood (Sugarman et al., 1991).

Surgical Procedures. Although surgical procedures are not in and of themselves opposed, administration of blood during surgery is strictly prohibited (Smith, 1986).

Amputations. There is no church rule pertaining to the loss of limbs or the amputation of body parts.

Organ Transplants (Donor and Recipient). If they are a violation of the principle of bodily mutilation, transplants are forbidden. However, this is usually an individual decision. Blood may not be used in this or any surgery.

Biopsies. Acceptable.

Circumcision. Individual decision.

Amniocentesis. Acceptable.

Controversial Issues Related to Health Care

Birth Control. Sterilization is prohibited because it is viewed as a form of bodily mutilation. Other forms of birth control are left up to the individual.

Abortion. Both therapeutic and on demand abortions are forbidden.

Sterility Tests. This is an individual decision.

Artificial Insemination. This is forbidden both for donors and for recipients.

Eugenics and Genetics. Jehovah's Witnesses do not condone any activities in these areas; they are considered to interfere with nature and therefore are unacceptable.

Social Activities (Dating, Dancing). Youth are encouraged to socialize with others of their own religious background.

Substance Use. Members abstain from the use of tobacco and hold that drunkenness is a serious sin. Alcohol used in moderation, however, is acceptable.

Religious Support System for the Sick

Visitors. Individual members of congregation, including elders. Visitors pray with the sick person and read scriptures. Since members do not smoke, it is preferred that patients be placed in rooms with nonsmokers.

For Jehovah's Witnesses, blood and agents in which blood is an ingredient are strictly prohibited. A pamphlet entitled **Jehovah's Witnesses an** **the Question of Blood** *provides further information on this impor* *religious belief.*

Title of Religious Representative. If male, Mr. or Elde
are not generally used.
Church Organizations to Assist the Sick. Indiv
needs.

Issues Related to Death and Dying

Prolongation of Life (Right to Die). The
prolong life is a matter of individual c
Euthanasia. This practice is forbidden.
Autopsy. An autopsy is acceptable only if it is re
from the body. Man's spirit and body are neve

Donation of Body. This practice is forbidden.

Disposal of Body. This is a matter of individual preference.

Burial. Burial practices are determined by local custom. Cremation is permitted if the individual chooses it.

Addendum. Jehovah's Witnesses are opposed to saluting the flag, serving in the armed forces, voting in civil elections, and holding public office. These prohibitions are related to belief in a theocracy that is in harmony with New Testament Christianity. Governed by a body of individuals, members united with the theocracy are to dissociate themselves from all activities of the political state and give full allegiance to "Jehovah's organization." This practice is related to the belief that Jesus Christ is King and Priest and that there is no need to hold citizenship in more than one kingdom. Members also refrain from gambling.

A pamphlet entitled *Jehovah's Witnesses and the Question of Blood* may be obtained free of charge by contacting the World Headquarters for the Jehovah's Witnesses at 117 Adams Street, Brooklyn, NY 11201

Judaism

Judaism is an Old Testament religion that dates back to the time of the prophet Abraham. Worldwide there are approximately 18 million Jews. U.S. membership consists of approximately 7 million members.

Beliefs and Religious Practices

Judaism is a monotheistic religion. Jewish life historically was based on interpretation of the laws of God as contained in the Torah and explained in the Talmud and in oral tradition.

Anciently, Jewish law prescribed most of the daily actions of the people. Diet, clothing, activities, occupation, and ceremonial activities throughout the life cycle are all part of Jewish religious life.

Jewish Culture and Traditions. Today, there are at least three schools of theological thought and social practice in Judaism. The three main divisions include Orthodox, Conservative, and Reform. There is also a fundamentalist sect, called *Hasidism.* Hasidic Jews cluster in metropolitan areas and live and work only within their Jewish communities.

Any person born of a Jewish mother or anyone converted to Judaism is considered a Jew. All Jews are united by the core theme of Judaism, which is expressed in the *Shema,* a prayer that professes a single God.

Holy Days. The Sabbath is the holiest of all holy days. The Sabbath begins each Friday 18 minutes before sunset and ends on Saturday 42 minutes after sunset or when three stars can be seen in the sky with the naked eye (Charnes and Moore, 1992).

Other holy days are

1. Rosh Hashanah (Jewish New Year)
2. Yom Kippur (Day of Atonement, a fast day)
3. Succot (Feast of Tabernacles)

4. Shmini Atzeret (8th Day of Assembly)
5. Simchat Torah
6. Chanukah (Festival of Lights, or Rededication of the Temple in Jerusalem)
7. Asara B'Tevet (Fast of the 10th of Tevet)*
8. Fast of Esther*
9. Purim
10. Passover
11. Shavuot (Festival of the Giving of the Torah)
12. Fast of the 17th of Tammuz*
13. Fast of the 9th of Ave (Commemoration of the Destruction of the Temple)*

Holy days are very special to practicing Jews. If a condition is not life-threatening, medical and surgical procedures should not be performed on the Sabbath or on holy days.

Preservation of life is of greatest priority and is the major criterion for determining activity on holy days and the Sabbath. If a Jewish patient is hesitant to receive urgent and necessary treatment because of religious restrictions, a rabbi should be consulted (Pearl, 1990; Weiss, 1988).

Sacraments. Circumcision is performed on all Jewish male children on the 8th day following birth. This may be done by a ritual circumciser (*mohel*), by the child's father, or by a pediatrician. Circumcision must be delayed if medically contraindicated. Failure to be circumcised carries no "eternal" consequences should the child die.

Religion and Healing. Medical care from a physician in the case of illness is expected according to Jewish law. There are many prayers for the sick in Jewish liturgy. Such prayers and hope for recovery are encouraged (Davis, 1991).

Diet, Medications, and Procedures

Diet. The dietary laws of Judaism are very strict; the degree to which they are observed varies according to the individual. Strictly observant Jews never eat pork, never eat predatory fowl, and never mix milk dishes and meat dishes. Only fish with fins and scales are permissible; shellfish and other water creatures are prohibited.

Kosher is a Jewish word that means "properly prepared." All animals must be ritually slaughtered to be kosher. This means that the animal is to be killed by a *shochet*, quickly, with the least possible pain. More colloquially, many people think *kosher* refers to a type of food. If a patient asks for kosher food, it is important to determine what he or she means.

Medications. There are no restrictions when medications are used as a part of therapeutic process.

Blood and Blood Products. There is a prohibition in Judaism against ingesting blood (e.g., blood sausage, raw meat). However, this does not apply to receiving blood transfusions.

Controversial Issues Related to Health Care

Birth Control. It is said in the Torah that Jews should be fruitful and multiply; therefore, it is a *mitzvah*, or good deed, to have at least two children. Since the Holocaust of World

---

* Not observed by liberal/Reform Jews.

War II, it has been increasingly acceptable to have more children to replace those who were lost. It is permissible to practice birth control in traditional and liberal homes (Forsythe, 1991).

In the past, contraception was limited to the female; vasectomy was prohibited. Currently, Judaism permits contraception by either partner, although Hasidic and Orthodox Jews rarely employ vasectomy.

Abortion. Although therapeutic abortion is always permitted if the health of the mother is jeopardized, traditional Judaism frowns on abortion on demand; liberal Judaism permits it with strong moral admonition (i.e., it is not to be used as a means of birth control). The fetus, although not imbued with the full sanctity of life, is a potential human being and is acknowledged as such.

Sterility Testing. Permissible when the goal is to enable the couple to have children.

Artificial Insemination. Permitted under certain circumstances. A rabbi should be consulted in each individual case.

Eugenics and Genetics. Jews have an understandable aversion to genetic engineering because of the experimentation carried on during the Nazi era. At the same time, eugenics are permitted under a limited range of circumstances. The Jewish belief in the sanctity of life is a guiding factor in rabbinical counseling.

Social Activities (Dating, Dancing). Like all ethnic groups, Jews tend toward endogamy. Social activities that might lead to marriage outside the faith are discouraged. However, it is recognized that a significant number of individuals in Jewish society will seek partners outside. When this occurs, every effort is made to bring the non-Jewish partner into Judaism and to keep the Jewish partner a member and part of Jewish society.

Substance Use. The guideline is moderation. Wine is a part of religious observance and is used as such. Drunkenness is not a sign of a good Jew. Historically, Jews well connected with their faith have had a low incidence of alcoholism.

Religious Support System for the Sick

Visitors. The most likely visitors will be family and friends from the synagogue. To visit the sick is a *mitzvah* of service (an obligation, a responsibility, and a blessing). There are many Jewish social service agencies to help those in need. The Jewish Federation and the Jewish Community Service are two large organizations that provide services to fulfill a variety of needs.

Title of Religious Representative. The formal religious representative from a synagogue is the rabbi. A visit from the rabbi may be spent talking, or the rabbi may pray with the person alone or in a *minyan*, a group of 10 adults 13 years of age or older. If the patient is male and strictly observant, he may wish to have a prayer shawl (*tallit*), a cap (*kippa*), and *tefillin* (special symbols tied onto the arms and forehead). If the patient's own materials are not at the hospital, it may be necessary to ask that they be brought. Prayers are often chanted. If possible, privacy is desirable.

Issues Related to Death and Dying

Prolongation of Life (Right to Die). A person has the right to die with dignity. If a physician sees that death is inevitable, current measures should not be stopped, but no new therapeutic measures that would artificially extend life need to be initiated (Perlin, 1990).

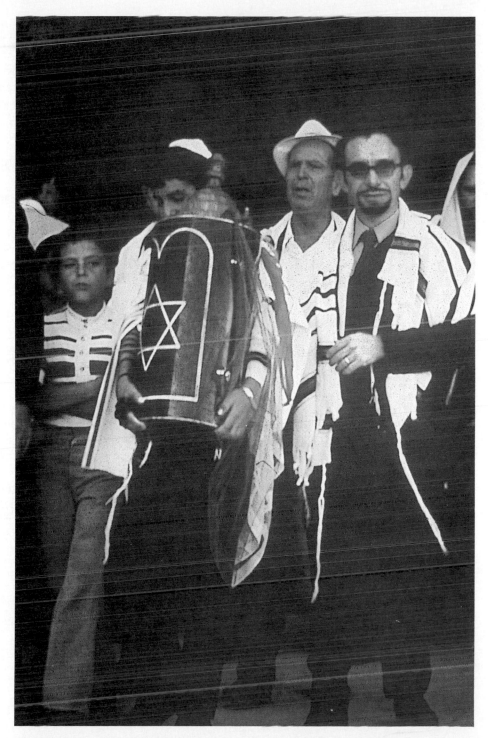

After a period of rigorous religious study, Jewish boys are accepted into the adult congregation at a ceremony called a bar mitzvah. A similar ceremony for Jewish girls is called a bat mitzvah.

Euthanasia. Prohibited under any circumstances. It is regarded as murder. However, in the administration of palliative medications that carry the calculated risk of overdose, the amelioration of pain is paramount.

Autopsy. Permitted only in special circumstances. A decision for autopsy would be made by the physician and family in consultation with the rabbi. Usually autopsy is limited only to essential organs or systems. Needle biopsy is preferred. All body parts must be returned for burial.

Donation of Body Parts. This is a complex matter according to Jewish law. If it seems necessary, consultation with the rabbi is needed.

Burial. The body is ritually washed following death, if possible by members of the *Chevra Kadisha* (Ritual Burial Society). This is usually done at a funeral home. Following death in an institution, a nurse may wash the body for transport to the funeral home. Ritual washing then occurs later. Human remains, including a fetus at any stage of gestation, are to be buried as soon as possible. Cremation is not in keeping with Jewish law.

Addendum. Additional information can be obtained from Synagogue Council of America, 432 Park Avenue South, New York, NY 10016 (Phone: (212) 686-8670).

Mennonite Church

Membership. United States, 260,000.

Beliefs and Religious Practices

Holy Days. The Mennonites observe the religious days of the traditional Christian churches. Observance places no restrictions on health-related procedures on these days.

Sacraments. Mennonites observe Baptism and Holy Communion as official church sacraments. Patients will request sacraments as necessary. Neither sacrament is believed necessary for salvation.

Religion and Healing. Healing is believed to be a part of God's work in the human body through whatever means He chooses to use, whether medical science or healing that comes in answer to specific prayer. There is no religious ritual to be applied unless the patient asks for one in whatever way is personally meaningful. Sometimes anointing of oil is practiced.

Diet, Medications, and Procedures

No specific guidelines or restrictions.

Blood and Blood Products. Acceptable; no restrictions.

Surgical Procedures. No restrictions.

Controversial Issues Related to Health Care

Birth Control. All types of contraception are acceptable. The choice is left to the individual.

Abortion. Therapeutic abortions are acceptable. Mennonites generally believe that on demand abortion must be decided according to the specifics of individual cases. The church has chosen to avoid making a ruling that must be followed unquestionably. The individual must follow her own conscience and learn to live with the consequences. Some parts of the Mennonite Church have adopted statements opposing abortion on demand.

Artificial Insemination. The church does not have regulations regarding artificial insemination. The individual conscience and point of view of the patient need to be respected. Usually, artificial insemination is sought only if husband and wife are donor and recipient, respectively.

Eugenics and Genetics. The church accepts scientific endeavor as a valid activity that needs to respect all God's creation. The concerns of eugenics and genetics in its future potential have not been fully confronted. Mennonites believe that God and humans work together in caring for and improving the world.

Social Activities (Dating, Dancing). No restrictions.

Issues Related to Death and Dying

Prolongation of Life (Right to Die). The church does not believe that life must be continued at all cost. Health care professionals should decide whether to take heroic measures on the basis of the patient's individual circumstances and the emotional condition of the family. When life has lost its purpose and meaning beyond hope of meaningful recovery, most Mennonites feel that relatives should not be censured for allowing life-sustaining measures to be withheld.

Euthanasia. Euthanasia as the termination of life by an overt act of the physician is not condoned.

Autopsy. Acceptable; no restrictions.

Donation of Body. Acceptable; no restrictions.

Disposal of Body. Per local law and custom.

Burial. Burial practices follow local customs and legal requirements.

Addendum. Mennonites believe that each person is responsible before God to make decisions based on his or her understanding of the Bible. For this reason, there are a minimum of official statements or regulations. Even when these are to be found, they are perceived by members as guidelines rather than proclamations to supplant individual responsibility. It also should be noted that the Mennonite faith encompasses a wide spectrum of cultural circumstances, which are more responsible for variations among individual Mennonites than is the basic theology, which is relatively uniform. It is therefore necessary to ascertain individual preferences and to work with patients on a one-on-one basis rather than stereotyping according to religious affiliation.

Native American Churches

Differentiating Native American health care practices from their religious and cultural beliefs is much more difficult than with the other religions presented in this chapter. Native Americans represent 2 million people and more than 500 tribal units within North America. Each group has individual beliefs and practices, yet they maintain a similar nonprescriptive attitude toward health care.

There is in the United States today a specific religion called the *Native American Church* or *Peyote Religion*. Encompassing members of many tribes, its focus is on the revival of Native American culture and beliefs.

When trying to support a Native American in physical or psychological crisis, the nurse needs to remember a number of seemingly unrelated facts. First, the non-Westernized Native American belief about disease is not necessarily based on symptoms. Disease may be attributed to intrusive objects, soul loss, spirit intrusion, breach of taboo, or sorcery. Disease also may be attributed to natural or supernatural causes (Vogel, 1970). Second, the Native American may embrace an organized, Christian religion, as well as be a member of a particular Native American tribe. Native Americans also balance "modern theories of disease" with long-standing tribal beliefs or customs. Therefore, during illness and particularly hospitalization, Native Americans may ask to see a priest or minister as well as a tribal healer. Visits from these persons will likely be spiritually supportive in nature, although the form of the support may vary greatly.

The spiritual basis for much of Native American belief and action is symbolized by the number 4. This number, which pervades much Native American thought, is seen in the extended hand, which means life, unity, equality, and eternity. The clasped hand symbolizes *unity*, the spiritual law that binds the universe.

It is this unity upon which decisions should be made. Questions about abortion, use of drugs, giving and receiving blood, right to life, euthanasia, and so on do not have

With more than 500 Native American tribes, health-related religious beliefs and practices vary widely. In general, Native Americans embrace holistic practices in which health of mind, body, and spirit is integrally interrelated. (Map available in 16" × 20" full color from Cherokee Publications, P.O. Box 430, Cherokee, N.C. 28719. Used here by permission.)

dogmatic "yes" or "no" answers; rather, answers are based on the situation and the ultimate unity/disunity that a decision would produce.

To the Native American, everything is cyclical. Communication is the key to learning and understanding, understanding brings peace of mind, peace of mind leads to happiness, and happiness is communicating. Other guidelines also function in groups of four (Steiger, 1975). Four guidelines toward self-development are

1. Am I happy with what I am doing?
2. What am I doing to add to the confusion?
3. What am I doing to bring about peace and contentment?
4. How will I be remembered when I am gone, in absence and in death?

The four requirements of good health are

1. Food
2. Sleep
3. Cleanliness
4. Good thoughts

The four divisions of nature are

1. Spirit
2. Mind
3. Body
4. Life

The four divisions of goals are

1. Faith
2. Love
3. Work
4. Pleasure

The four ages of development are the

1. Learning age
2. Age of adoption
3. Age of improvement
4. Age of wisdom

The four expressions of sharing are

1. Making others feel you care
2. An expression of interest
3. An expression of friendship
4. An expression of belonging

Unity, the great spiritual law, also can be expressed in four parts:

1. Going into the silence in spirit, mind, and body
2. The union through which all spirituality flows
3. A goal toward communicating with all things in nature
4. Recognized through sense, emotions, and impressions

In concert with the belief in the interconnectedness of all things, natural remedies in the form of herbal medicine are often used. (It is interesting to note that Native American folk medicine and herbal remedies provided the forerunners of many of today's pharmaceutical remedies.) Herbal treatments are still used today and may be requested by Native American patients in a Western medical setting.

A nurse caring for a Native American client should be careful to obtain a careful and complete history, including a list of whatever native remedies have been tried. The patient may not know the names of herbs used in treatment, and the tribal medicine man or woman may need to be consulted.

Respecting the concept that religion, medicine, and healing are inseparable to the Native American, one must be sensitive to the fact that asking for names of native medicines or descriptions of healing practices tried in an attempt to cure the person before his or her entrance into the Western medical system is not just simply obtaining a history but also entering into the realm of what might be not only private but also very sacred. The nurse must use care and sensitivity and show deep respect for the information received.

Seventh-Day Adventists

Membership. Worldwide, 7.5 million; North American, 783,000.

Beliefs and Religious Practices

Seventh-Day Adventists believe that because the body is the temple of God, it is appropriate to abstain from any food or beverage that could prove harmful to the body. Since man's first diet consisted of fruits and grains, the church encourages a vegetarian diet. However, not all members follow such a diet.

Holy Days. The 7th day (Saturday) is observed as the Sabbath, from Friday sundown to Saturday sundown. The Sabbath is the day that God blessed and sanctified. It is a sacred day of worship and rest. Saturday worship services are held, as are weekly evening prayer meetings (usually midweek).

Sacraments. There are three church ordinances: (1) Baptism by immersion, (2) the Ordinance of Humility, and (3) the Lord's Supper or Communion. There is no requirement for a final sacrament at death.

Rituals at Time of Birth. None.

Rituals at Time of Death. Anointing, if requested, by individual or family member.

Religion and Healing. The church believes in divine healing and practices anointing with oil and prayer. This is in addition to healing brought about by medical intervention.

Since 1865, the church has maintained chaplains and physicians as inseparable in its institutions.

Diet, Medications, and Procedures

Diet. Although the church encourages a vegetarian diet, some members prefer to eat meat and poultry. Based on a passage in Leviticus, Chap. 11, Verse 3, nonvegetarian members refrain from eating foods derived from any animal having a cloven hoof that chews its cud (e.g., meat derived from pigs, rabbits, or similar animals). Although fish with fins and scales are acceptable (e.g., salmon), shellfish are prohibited. Consumption of some birds is prohibited, but common poultry such as chicken and turkey are acceptable. Fermented beverages are prohibited.

Fasting is practiced, but only when members of a specific church elect to do so. Practiced in degrees, fasting may involve abstention from food or liquids. Fasting is not encouraged if it is likely to have adverse effects on the individual.

Medications. Adventists operate one of the world's largest religiously operated health systems, including a medical school. Physical medicine and rehabilitation are emphasized and recommended along with therapeutic diets. There are no restrictions on the use of vaccines.

Blood and Blood Products. No restrictions.

Amputations. No restrictions.

Organ Transplants and Donation of Organs. No restrictions.

Biopsies. No restrictions.

Circumcision. No restrictions.

Amniocentesis. No restrictions.

Controversial Issues Related to Health Care

Birth Control. This is an individual decision; the church prohibits cohabitation except between husband and wife.

Abortion. Therapeutic abortion is acceptable if the mother's life is in danger and in cases of rape and incest. On demand abortion is unacceptable, since Adventists believe in the sanctity of life.

Artificial Insemination. If between husband and wife, there is no objection.

Eugenics and Genetics. Although the church views this as an individual decision, it upholds the principle of responsibility in dealing with children.

Social Activities (Dating, Dancing). Dancing is not encouraged as a form of recreation or social activity. Members are encouraged to date other members or persons holding similar beliefs and values.

Substance Use. Abstinence from the use of fermented beverages and tobacco products.

Religious Support System for the Sick

Visitors. At the request of the sick person or the family, the pastor and elders of the church will come together to pray and anoint the sick person with oil.

Title of Religious Representative. Doctor, Pastor, Elder.

Church Organizations to Assist the Sick. There is a worldwide Seventh-Day Adventists health system, which includes hospitals and clinics.

Issues Related to Death and Dying

Prolongation of Life (Right to Die). Although there is no official position, the church has traditionally followed the medical ethics of prolonging life.
Euthanasia. As above.
Autopsy. Acceptable.
Donation of Entire Body or Parts. Acceptable.
Disposal of Body. No directives or recommendations.
Burial. No specific directives concerning burial; this is an individual decision.

Addendum. The Seventh-Day Adventists church is opposed to the use of hypnotism in the practice of medicine or under any other circumstance.

Unitarian/Universalist Church

Membership. Worldwide, Unitarian Universalist membership is 200,599, with a North American membership of 199,472.

Beliefs and Religious Practices

Unitarianism was officially organized in 1774 in England. This organization occurred after a long history of debate and dissension regarding the nature of God, particularly regarding the trinitarian concept, which existed in various forms in the Catholic and Protestant religions.
Holy Days. No religious holy days are celebrated. Members come from various cultural and religious backgrounds and observe special days according to their own heritage and desire.
Sacraments. Normal milestones of life (birth, marriage, death) may be celebrated religiously. Although it is uncommon, puberty and divorce may include religious observances.

Unitarian/Universalism does not believe in a need for sacraments. Baptism of infants and occasionally of adults is sometimes performed as a symbolic act of dedication. The Lord's Supper is administered in some congregations.
Religion and Healing. Faith healing is considered largely superstitious and wishful thinking. Members believe in use of the empirical method, reason, and science to facilitate healing.

Diet, Medications, and Procedures

Diet. No restrictions.
Medications. No restrictions.
Blood and Blood Products. No restrictions.
Amputations. No restrictions.
Organ Transplants. No restrictions.
Biopsies. No restrictions.

Circumcision. Viewed as a health practice, not a religious one.

Amniocentesis. No restrictions; encouraged if medical evaluation deems it necessary.

Controversial Issues Related to Health Care

Birth Control. Strongly favor all types as a human right.

Abortion. Both therapeutic and on demand abortions are acceptable. Strongly favor the right of the mother to decide.

Sterility Testing. Acceptable; more research is encouraged.

Artificial Insemination. Both donation and receipt are acceptable. Strongly favor this as a human right.

Substance Use. No restrictions. Use according to reason.

Issues Related to Death and Dying

Prolongation of Life (Right to Die). Favor the right to die with dignity. "Personhood" is sacred, not the spark of life.

Euthanasia. Members tend to favor nonaction, including withdrawal of technical aids when death is imminent or when the patient has made a written request in advance.

Autopsy. Recommended.

Donation of Body. Acceptable.

Disposal of Body/Burial. Cremation is most common. Donation to a medical school for study is not uncommon. Burial of a fetus is rare.

Funeral. Memorial service in the church or at home without the body present is customary.

Learning Activities

1. Visit a church not of your own belief system and interview a member of the clergy or an official church representative about the health-related beliefs of that religion. Discuss with him or her the implications of those beliefs for someone hospitalized for an acute illness or a chronic illness. Inquire about the ways in which nurses can be of most help to hospitalized members of this religion.

2. Interview members of various religions about their beliefs about health and illness. Compare these interviews with the published beliefs or official statements from these religions. Discuss the implications of the differences (if any) that you found.

3. Interview fellow students, classmates, or co-workers (if you are employed) about what they know about health beliefs of various religions, especially those religions most often encountered among the patients you work with. Make a poster or prepare a presentation comparing the results of your interviews with the official beliefs of those religions. Share this information with your classmates.

4. Interview four or more members of the same religious group who are of various ages (i.e., children, teenagers, young adults, middle-aged, and elderly). Ask them about their religious beliefs and how they affect their health. Compare the results, commenting on similarities and differences.

5. If you have thought about the preceding exercises in terms of physical health, consider each of the questions from the perspective of mental health and spiritual health.

References

Backman, M. V. (1983). *Christian Churches of America*. New York: Charles Scribner & Sons.

Bainbridge, W. (1991). Dying east, dying west. *Nursing Standard, 6*(6), 22–23.

Becerra, R. M., Karno, M., and Escobar, J. I. (Eds.) (1982). *Mental Health and Hispanic Americans: Clinical Perspectives*. New York: Grune & Stratton.

Chapman, A. (1991). The Buddhist way of dying. *Nursing Praxis in New Zealand, 6*(2), 23–26.

Charnes, L. S., and Moore, P. S. (1992). Meeting patients' spiritual needs: The Jewish perspective. *Holistic Nursing Practice, 6*(3), 64–72.

Christian Science Publishing Society (1974). *Questions and Answers on Christian Science*. Boston: Christian Science Publishing Society.

Christian Science Publishing Society (1978). *What Is a Christian Science Practitioner?* Boston: Christian Science Publishing Society.

Cluff, C. B. (1986) Spiritual intervention reconsidered. *Topics in Geriatric Rehabilitation, 1*(2), 77–82.

Corrine, L., Bailey, V., Valentine, M., et al. (1992). The unheard of voices of women: Spiritual intervention in maternal-child health. *Maternal Child Nursing, 17*(3), 141–145.

Davis, D. S. (1991). Dealing with real Jewish patients. *Journal of Clinical Ethics, 2*(3), 211–212.

Ebersole, P., and Hess, P. (1994) *Toward Healthy Aging*. St. Louis: C. V. Mosby.

Eisenbruch, M. (1984a). Cross-cultural aspects of bereavement: I. A conceptual framework for comparative analysis. *Culture, Medicine, and Psychiatry, 8*, 283–309.

Eisenbruch, M. (1984b). Cross-cultural aspects of bereavement: II. Ethnic and cultural variations in the development of bereavement practices. *Culture, Medicine, and Psychiatry, 8*, 315–347.

Ellerhorst-Ryan, J. (1985). Selecting an instrument to measure spiritual distress. *Oncology Nursing Forum, 12*(2), 93–99.

Faulkner, J. E., and DeJong, C. F. (1966). Religiosity in 5D: An empirical analysis. *Social Forces, 45*, 246–254.

Fish, S., and Shelly, J. (1988). *Spiritual Care: The Nurse's Role*, 3d Ed. Downer's Grove, IL: Intervarsity Press.

Forsythe, E. (1991). Religious and cultural aspects of family planning. *Journal of the Royal Society of Medicine, 84*(3), 177–178.

Fox, M. (1984). Conflict to coexistence: Christian Science and medicine. *Medical Anthropology, 8*(4), 292–301.

Green, J. (1989a). Death with dignity: Buddhism. *Nursing Times, 85*(9), 40–41.

Green, J. (1989b). Death with dignity: Christian Science. *Nursing Times, 88*(4), 32–33.

Green, J. (1989c). Death with dignity: Hinduism. *Nursing Times, 85*(6), 50–51.

Green, J. (1989d). Death with dignity: The Mormon Church. *Nursing Times, 88*(6), 44–45.

Green, J. (1992a). Death with dignity: Christianity. *Nursing Times, 88*(3), 25–29.

Green, J. (1992b). Death with dignity: Jehovah's Witnesses. *Nursing Times, 88*(5), 36–37.

Gundersen, E. S. (1990). Christian Science nursing. *South Dakota Nurse, 32*(2), 6–8.

Halfe, L. B. (1989). The circle: Death and dying from a native perspective. *Journal of Palliative Care, 5*(1), 37–41.

Hickey, M. E., and Hall, T. R. (1993). Insulin therapy and weight change in Native American NIDDM patients. *Diabetes Care, 16*, 364–368.

Hinnels, J. R. (1984). *The Penguin Dictionary of Religions*. New York: Penguin Books.

Huttlinger, K., Krefting, L., Drevdahl, D., et al. (1992). Doing battle: A metaphorical analysis of diabetes mellitus among Navajo people. *American Journal of Occupational Therapy, 46*, 706–12.

Jacobs, C. F. (1990). Healing and prophecy in the black spiritual churches: A need for reexamination. *Medical Anthropology, 12*(4), 349–370.

Kalish, R. A., and Reynolds, D. K. (1981). *Death and Ethnicity: A Psychocultural Study*. New York: Baywood.

Kim, M., and Moritz, D. (Eds.) (1981). *Proceedings of the 3rd and 4th National Conferences: Classification of Nursing Diagnosis*. New York: McGraw-Hill.

Klaassen, W. (1986). The Anabaptist tradition. In R. L. Numbers and D. W. Amundsen (Eds.), *Caring and Curing*. New York: Macmillan.

Kozak, D. L. (1991). Dying badly: Violent death and religious change among the Tohono O'odham. *Omega 23*, 207–216.

Lawler, R. D. (1987). Moral reflections on the new technologies: A Catholic analysis. *Women and Health, 13*(1–2), 67–77.

Lecso, P. A. (1987). Buddhist teachings on suffering and withholding care. *Journal of the American Geriatric Society, 35*(12), 1131.

Madan, T. N. (1992). Dying with dignity. *Social Science Medicine, 35*(4), 425–432.

Marty, M. M. (1990). Health, medicine, and the faith traditions. In *Healthy People 2000: A Role for America's Religious Communities.* Emory University: The Carter Center and the Park Ridge Center.

Mayor, V. (1984). The Asian community: The family, bereavement, and dietary beliefs. *Nursing Times,* June 6, 40–42.

McManus, R. J. (1993). Medicine and ethics at the crossroad: A Roman Catholic perspective. *Rhode Island Medicine, 76*(2), 79–81.

Moberg, D. (1971). *Spiritual Well-Being* (pp. 1–3). Washington: White House Conference on Aging.

Moberg, D. (1981). Religion and the aging family. In P. Ebersole and P. Hess (Eds.), *Toward Healthy Aging* (pp. 349–351). St. Louis: C. V. Mosby.

Nagel, J. K. (1991). Unresolved grief and mourning in Navajo women. *American Indian and Alaska Native Mental Health Research, 2*(2), 32–40.

Naidoo, T. (1989). Health and healthcare: A Hindu perspective. *Medicine & Law, 7*(6), 643–647.

Nelson, R. G., Sievers, M. L., Knowler, W. C., et al. (1990). Low incidence of fatal coronary heart disease in Pima Indians despite high prevalence of non-insulin dependent diabetes *Circulation, 81*, 987–995.

Numbers, R. L., and Amundsen, D. W. (1986), *Caring and Curing.* New York: Macmillan.

Pearl, A. J. (1990). Get yourself a new heart: Judaism and the organ transplantation issue. *Canadian Medical Association Journal, 143*(12), 1365–1369.

Perlin, E. (1990). Jewish medical ethics and the care of the elderly. *The Pharos, 53*(3), 2–5.

Robinson, A. (1994). Spirituality and risk: Toward an understanding. *Holistic Nursing Practice. 8*(2), 1–7.

Ross, H. M. (1984). Societal/cultural views regarding death and dying. *Topics in Clinical Nursing, 3*(3), 1–16.

Shelly, J. A., and John, S. D. (1983). *Spiritual Dimensions of Mental Health.* Downer's Grove, IL: Intervarsity Press.

Singelenberg, R. (1990). The blood transfusion taboo of Jehovah's witnesses: Origins, development and function of a controversial doctrine. *Social Science Medicine, 31*(4), 515–523.

Skolnick, A. (1990). Christian Scientists claim healing efficacy equal if not superior to that of medicine. *Journal of the American Medical Association, 264*(11), 1379–1381.

Slotkin, J. S. (1975). *The Peyote Religion.* New York: Octagon Books.

Smith, E. B. (1986). Surgery in Jehovah's Witnesses. *Journal of National Medical Association, 78*(7), 668–669.

Steiger, B. (1975). *Medicine Talk.* New York: Doubleday & Co.

Sugarman, J., Churchill, L. R., Moore, J. K., and Waugh, R. A. (1991). Medical, ethical, and legal issues regarding thrombolytic therapy in the Jehovah's Witnesses. *American Journal of Cardiology, 68*(15), 1525–1529.

Sugarman, J. R. (1991). Hypoglycemia associated with hospitalizations in a population with a high prevalence of non-insulin dependent diabetes mellitus. *Diabetes Research and Clinical Practice, 14*, 139–148.

Sugarman, J. R., Hickey, M., Hall, T., et al. (1990). The changing epidemiology of diabetes mellitus among Navajo Indians. *The Western Journal of Medicine, 153*, 140–145.

Tom-Orme, L. (1988). Chronic disease and the social matrix: A Native American diabetes intervention. *Recent Advances in Nursing, 22*, 89–109.

Vogel, V. J. (1970). *American Indian Medicine.* Norman, OK: University of Oklahoma Press.

Watson, J. L. (1982). Of flesh and bones: The management of death pollution in cantonese society. In M. Bloch and J. Parry (Eds.), *Death and the Regeneration of Life.* Cambridge: Cambridge University Press.

Weiss, D. W. (1988). Organ transplantation, medical ethics and Jewish law. *Transplantation Proceedings, 20*(1), 1071–1075.

Wenger, A. F. Z. (1991). Culture specific care and the old order Amish. *IMPRINT,* April–May, 80–85.

Wiedman, D. W. (1989). Adiposity or longevity: Which factor accounts for the increase in type II diabetes mellitus when populations acculturate to an industrial technology? *Medical Anthropology,* 11, 237–253.

13

International Nursing and Health

Margaret M. Andrews

Introduction

Throughout this text the emphasis has been largely on U.S. and Canadian cultures and subcultures. This chapter will provide an overview of *international nursing*, a term that is sometimes used interchangably with *transnational nursing*. The purposes of this chapter are to examine international nursing as a clinical specialty within the profession, provide a brief overview of the world's state of health, identify ways that nurses prepare for international nursing, suggest guidelines to consider when choosing an international sending agency, and identify selected health care agencies that send U.S. and Canadian nurses abroad.

> International health is like a distant exotic place: difficult to reach, replete with unfamiliar tribal customs, strangely alluring, perhaps a bit dangerous; but with the prospect that the journey there would be immensely worthwhile [Basch, 1990].

There are many reasons for incorporating international nursing content into the curriculum and providing clinical learning opportunities whereby other parts of the world can be experienced by nurses and nursing students. According to International Council of Nurses President Margretta Styles (1993), when the year 2000 arrives, it will mark the beginning of the "International Century." This new century will be a time when political alignments and technology combine to encourage mobility and interchange and an era when national borders are less obvious and obstructive. Nurses must increasingly see themselves as part of a global community in which problems, solutions, resources, and opportunities are shared (Fagin, 1990; Styles, 1993).

Margaret M. Andrews and Joyceen S. Boyle: TRANSCULTURAL CONCEPTS IN NURSING CARE. SECOND EDITION. © 1995 J.B. Lippincott Company.

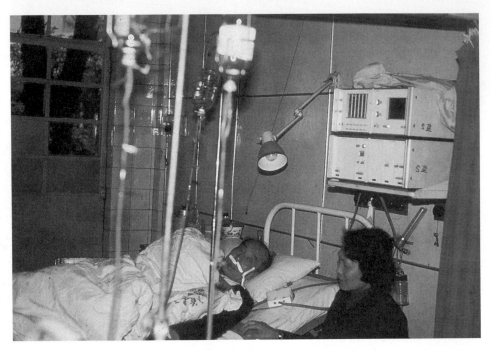

Intensive-care unit in the People's Republic of China.

Historical Overview

Nursing is indisputably among the oldest and most universal human activities. Until the 19th century, nursing was carried on by families for their own members, by religious orders committed to the care of the sick, and in the large public institutions built for the care of the sick poor, by untrained persons from the lower socioeconomic class. As a result of the contributions of Florence Nightingale during the 19th century, modern nursing was born, and an era in which highly trained nurses traveled to all parts of the globe to practice their profession began.

Florence Nightingale and International Nursing

By age 29, Florence Nightingale had begun her nursing-related foreign travels as she journeyed to the Institution of Deaconesses at Kaiserwerth, Germany, a trip that she subsequently would make many times. Critical of the English hospital system, Nightingale encouraged international nursing education by targeting farmers' daughters to become trained as nurses using the Kaiserwerth model. Many young English women heeded the call and traveled to Germany for formal educational preparation in the art and science of nursing (Brown, 1988; Uhl, 1992).

As English fatalities in the Crimean War escalated, military leaders agreed to allow Nightingale and her companions to travel to Scutari, which is located on the southwest border of the Black and Aegean seas. In Scutari, Nightingale organized the Barrack Hospital for casualties of the battles of Balaclava, Sebastopol, and Inkerman, as well as for those soldiers who fell victim to cholera. Following the Crimean War, the 36-year-old Nightingale rested briefly in Paris before returning to England, where she received a heroine's welcome for her wartime efforts to save the lives of wounded and sick soldiers. Shortly after her return to England, Nightingale again traveled and studied hospitals throughout Europe, where she was recognized as an expert on primary prevention and hospital procedures. Nightingale's hospital reforms reached beyond Europe to India, where she concluded that healthier living would result in increased longevity (Brown, 1988; Nightingale, 1859; Uhl, 1992).

At age 39, Nightingale published *Her Notes on Hospitals* (1859), in which she advocated improved hospital construction and physical maintenance to reduce deaths during hospitalization. In 1860, Nightingale founded a school of nursing at London's Saint Thomas Hospital, thus marking the beginning of both modern professional nursing and nursing education. Virtually all nursing education programs in the world today are modeled on the English pattern or one of two others that evolved from it: the French and the U.S. patterns.

Graduates of the Saint Thomas Hospital Nursing School were known as "Nightingale Nurses" and were prepared to train others. Nightingale nurses accepted positions where they could teach and promote the high standards of nursing care advocated by Nightingale, and hospitals from all over the world sought Nightingale nurses to start new schools of nursing. As early as 1867, Nightingale nurses were found in Australia, and throughout the 1880s, they were at work in Canada, Sweden, Germany, and most of the large hospitals in the United Kingdom and the United States (Brown, 1988; Uhl, 1992).

North American Nurses Abroad

Early in the development of U.S. and Canadian nursing history, nurses prepared in the Nightingale tradition traveled abroad, often motivated by religious and/or moral convictions. In 1885, Linda Richards became the first U.S. nurse on record to engage in international nursing when she went to Japan under the auspices of the American Board of Missions to establish a school of nursing. With the creation of the World Health Organization in 1948 and the proliferation of technical assistance programs, nurses have become increasingly involved in international health. Today, nurses have many opportunities to go abroad for the purposes of travel, research, education, consultation, and service in virtually all clinical practice specialty areas.

The World's Health

In analyzing the overall status of the world's health, the nurse rapidly realizes that there is wide variation in the quality of health care and in access to services for many of the world's people. There are substantive differences between and within countries, and socioeconomic status is among the major factors in determining an individual's health and his or her access to health care services. At the 1978 International Conference on Primary Health Care held in Alma-Ata (in the former Union of Soviet Socialist Republics), leaders from 134 World Health Organization member nations declared that the health status of hundreds of millions of people in the world was unacceptable. In 1981, the Thirty-Fourth World Health Assembly adopted the global strategy of "Health for All by the Year 2000" and identified *primary health care* as keystone in improving global health (Hirschfeld, 1992).

Primary Health Care

Both the World Health Organization (WHO) and the International Council of Nurses (ICN) state that

> primary health care is essential to health care made universally acceptable to individuals and families in the community by means acceptable to them, through their full participation and at costs the community and country can afford. It forms an integral part both of the country's health system, of which it is the nucleus, and of the overall social and economic development of the community [WHO, 1978, p. 2].

As conceived by the World Health Organization, primary health care includes five basic principles. The first is universal coverage, with care provided according to need. The second advocates a range of services—promotive, preventive, curative, rehabilitative, and terminal—that are provided in community-based settings as well as in hospitals. The third principle addresses the need for services to be effective, culturally acceptable, affordable, and manageable. The fourth principle advocates that communities be involved in primary health care and that self-reliance be encouraged while dependence is reduced. The fifth principle reaffirms that health must be related to other sectors of development. Comprising the largest sector of the global health care work force are nurses and midwives, whose role in primary health care is crucial (Holleran, 1992; Hirschfeld, 1992). Beyond the scope of this chapter is a review of the many primary health care programs that have been established by United Nations member countries and an evaluation of the effectiveness of the "Health for All by the Year 2000" program. In general, however, the outcomes have been quite favorable (Gudmundsen, 1989; Mangay-Maglacas, 1989, 1992).

Global Health Care Problems

According to Dr. Hiroshi Nakajima, director general of the World Health Organization, each year 50 million people die throughout the world, with 46.5 million deaths due to illness and disease. Of the 140 million babies born each year, almost 4 million die within hours or days from perinatal causes. More than 500,000 women die each year from causes related to pregnancy and childbirth (Nakajima, 1993; WHO, 1992).

On the positive side, some childhood diseases—measles, poliomyelitis, pertussis (whooping cough), and neonatal tetanus—are decreasing as a result of immunization programs. It should be noted that the cost of vaccines to accomplish this was less than $1 per child (Gunby, 1992). The incidence of cardiovascular diseases in most developed countries (except those in eastern Europe) has decreased in recent years due to health education and promotion efforts around the world. Infant and child mortality rates and the overall death rate are continuing to decrease globally, and life expectancy is increasing worldwide (Nakajima. 1993; WHO, 1992).

In analyzing global health, nations are frequently categorized as *less developed countries* (LDCs, or agricultural, nonindustrialized nations) or *more developed countries*

Life expectancy for women, infants, and children is significantly increased as a result of improved standards of living and immunization programs.

(MDCs, or industrialized nations), terms that are admittedly subjective and relative. For example, although the United States and Canada are categorized as MDCs, there are underdeveloped sections in which poverty-stricken people live in substandard housing with poor or absent sanitary facilities. Conversely, China, Mexico, and other nations classified as LDCs have rich cultural histories that predate the founding of the United States and Canada by many centuries. In all LDCs there is a small segment of the population that is very affluent. Recognizing these paradoxes, the categorization is still useful in examining general patterns of global health care.

Major Health Problems in Less Developed Countries

The World Health Organization estimates that 80 percent of illness in LDCs could be avoided if safe drinking water were available. As a result of unsafe water and other environmental conditions, *infectious and parasitic diseases* account for almost one-half of all deaths in LDCs. Tuberculosis, acute respiratory infections, diarrheal diseases (e.g., cholera, amebic dysentery), malaria, and sexually transmitted diseases are prevalent in most LDCs. Although not necessarily life-threatening, the most common infections in the LDCs are roundworm (*Ascaris*), hookworm (*Ancylostoma*), and whipworm (*Trichuris*). The protozoan *Giardia lamblia* is distributed worldwide, affecting almost 1 in every 3 people (Nakajima, 1993; WHO, 1992).

Every year, about 3.5 million new cases of *cancer* occur in LDCs, making it the second leading cause of death. Two-thirds of all cancers are attributable to lifestyle and

According to the World Health Organization, 80 percent of disease in less developed countries could be eradicated if people had clean water to drink. Many families rely on children to transport (carry) water from public water sources to their homes.

environment, and at least one-third are preventable. As the life expectancy continues to increase and the chronic conditions associated with increasing life expectancy are manifested, cancer incidence rises. Although worldwide life expectancy is 65 years, the majority of LDCs still have a life expectancy below 50 years (notable exceptions are Argentina, Cuba, Singapore, and Sri Lanka, where a life expectancy of 70 or more years is enjoyed) (Gunby, 1992; Nakajima, 1993; WHO, 1992).

Ranked *third* as a cause of mortality in LDCs is *circulatory diseases* (including heart attack and stroke). One of the most prevalent risk factors associated with circulatory diseases is diabetes mellitus, a condition that is increasing everywhere in the world (WHO, 1992).

The *fourth* leading cause of death in LDCs is *perinatal problems*, largely due to (1) lack of prenatal health care resulting from inadequate access to maternal-child health care, (2) insufficient numbers of obstetricians, nurse-midwives, and trained lay birth atten-

Despite primary prevention programs, such as blood pressure screening, vascular diseases are a leading cause of death in many countries of the world.

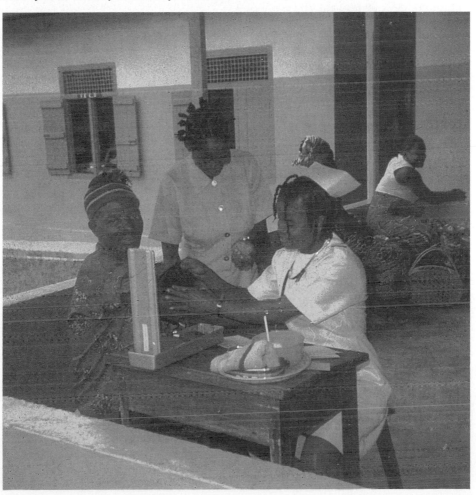

dants, and (3) cultural beliefs and practices about childbearing (e.g., cultural prohibitions against blood transfusions) and child rearing (e.g., ritual circumcision with nonsterile instruments for both males and females). In a regional analysis of global health care trends, sub-Saharan Africa has the highest birth and death rates, 45 births and 14 deaths per 1000 population (WHO, 1992).

The *fifth* leading cause of mortality in LDCs is *accidents*. Interrelated with overpopulation and crowding in large urban centers, motor vehicle accidents, often involving pedestrians or bicycle riders, are growing at alarming rates. In some countries, the government's lack of involvement in establishing and monitoring motor vehicle safety standards, testing and licensing operators of motor vehicles, developing and enforcing traffic regulations, and maintaining safe roadways has been a contributing factor. Drownings, burns, industrial mishaps, and household accidents also claim large numbers of victims (Badran, 1993; Henry and Nagelkerk, 1992; Mangay-Maglacas, 1992; Nakajima, 1993; WHO, 1992).

Occupational hazards are often responsible for the high incidence of accidental injuries in many parts of the world.

Major Health Problems in More Developed Countries

In many MDCs, the trend for noncommunicable diseases is generally downward, but *cancer, cardiovascular diseases, chronic bronchitis*, and *diabetes* are increasing. Antismoking campaigns in many MDCs are bringing positive results in the fight against lung cancer, but for men only. Among women, death rates from lung cancer are increasing rapidly and are now three times greater than they were 35 years ago. Vascular disease (including heart attacks and strokes) and motor vehicle accidents, although declining, are still major causes of death. Suicide in MDCs has increased steadily and is 50 percent higher than it was 35 years ago. Japan leads the world with the highest life expectancy at 79 years and the lowest infant mortality rate at 4 per 1000 live births (WHO, 1992).

Infant and Children's Health

Summarized in Table 13-1 are the infant mortality rates reported by the United Nations for selected countries. It should be noted that more than one-half of the LDC population is 15 years of age or under. Fifty percent of children from LDCs are vaccinated against polio, measles, tetanus, and whooping cough compared with 5 percent 15 years ago when the WHO Expanded Program on Immunization began. Forty percent of the world's unimmunized children live in China, India, Indonesia, or Nigeria. Vaccine research and development will lead to improved products to fight typhoid, shigella, cholera, and leprosy as the year 2000 approaches (Henry and Nagelkerk, 1992; Mangay-Maglacas, 1989, 1992; WHO, 1992). (See Research Box 13-1.)

HIV/AIDS Pandemic

The World Health Organization estimates that at least 10 to 12 million adults and children worldwide have become infected with the *human immune virus* (HIV) since the start of the pandemic. Approximately 2 million of those have developed *acquired immune deficiency syndrome* (AIDS), a condition that afflicts people in both MDCs and LDCs. In the world as a whole, heterosexual intercourse has rapidly become the dominant mode of transmission of the virus. As a result, the LDCs already hold as many newly infected women as men, and the MDCs are approaching equal incidence in men and women. Homosexual transmission has remained significant in North America, Australia, Asia, and Northern Europe, although even in these areas heterosexual transmission is showing the fastest rate of increase. WHO estimates that by the year 2000, cumulative totals of 30 to 40 million men, women, and children will have been infected and 12 to 18 million will have developed AIDS (Mangay-Maglacas, 1989, 1992; Nakajima, 1993; Vatre, 1992; WHO, 1992).

Nearly 90 percent of the projected HIV infections and AIDS cases for this decade will occur in the LDCs. In sub-Saharan Africa, where more than 6 million adults already are infected, the situation is critical. As many as one-third of pregnant women attending some urban antenatal clinics are HIV-infected. As a result, WHO estimates that 5 to 10 million HIV-infected children will have been born by the year 2000 (Mangay-Maglacas, 1989, 1992; Nakajima, 1993; Upvall, 1993a; Vatre, 1992; WHO, 1992).

Table 13-1. Infant mortality rates, 1985–90

Country	Infant mortality rate (IMR) per 1,000	Country	Infant mortality rate (IMR) per 1,000
Asia		Central Africa Rep.	104
Afghanistan	172	Chad	132
Bangladesh	119	Congo	73
Cambodia	130	Côte d'Ivoire	96
China	32	Egypt	65
India	99	Ethiopia	137
Indonesia	75	Gabon	103
Iran	52	Gambia	143
Iraq	69	Ghana	90
Israel	12	Guinea	145
Japan	5	Guinea-Bissau	151
Korea, North	28	Kenya	72
Korea, South	25	Lesotho	100
Malaysia	24	Liberia	142
Pakistan	109	Madagascar	120
Philippines	45	Malawi	150
Sri Lanka	28	Mali	169
Syria	48	Mauritania	127
Thailand	28	Mauritius	23
Vietnam	64	Morocco	82
		Mozambique	141
		Niger	135
Europe		Nigeria	105
Albania	39	Rwanda	122
Austria	11	Senegal	87
Belgium	10	Sierra Leone	154
Bulgaria	16	Somalia	132
Czechoslovakia	15	South Africa	72
Denmark	7	Sudan	108
Finland	6	Tunisia	52
France	8	Tanzania	106
Greece	17	Zaire	83
Hungary	20	Zambia	80
Ireland	9	Zimbabwe	66
Italy	11		
Malta	10	**America, North**	
Netherlands	8	Canada	7
Norway	7	Mexico	43
Poland	18	United States	10
Portugal	15		
Romania	22	**America, Central and South**	
Spain	10	Argentina	32
Sweden	6	Bolivia	110
Switzerland	7	Brazil	63
United Kingdom	9	Chile	20
Yugoslavia	25	Colombia	40
		Costa Rica	18
Oceania		Ecuador	63
Australia	8	El Salvador	64
New Zealand	11	Guatemala	59
		Guyana	56
Africa		Honduras	69
Algeria	74	Nicaragua	2
Angola	137	Panama	23
Benin	90	Paraguay	42
Botswana	67	Peru	88
Burkina Faso	138	Suriname	33
Burundi	119	Uruguay	24
Cameroon	94	Venezuela	36
Cape Verde	44		

United Nations Department of International Economic and Social Affairs, Statistical Office, 1991.

Research Box 13-1. Pregnancy Practices Among the Maasai of Kenya

Mpoke, S., and Johnson, K. E. (1993). Baseline survey of pregnancy practices among Kenyan Maasai. *Western Journal of Nursing Research, 15*(3), 298–313.

Two public health nurses studied the pregnancy practices of the Kenyan Maasai culture, a pastoral, nomadic group inhabiting large areas of the Rift Valley (located in both Kenya and Tanzania). The purpose of the study was to assess present practices surrounding pregnancy and childbirth reported by the Maasai within the context of what is known about their traditional practices. Two-hundred and six Kenyan Maasai mothers participated in the study. The pregnant woman's diet is restricted during the first 6 months of pregnancy to avoid weight gain (believed to make delivery difficult and dangerous). Blood drawn from the jugular vein of cows is given to women for excessive bleeding.

Sixty-one percent ($n = 129$) of Maasai mothers delivered at home, while the remainder ($n = 54$) had their babies at a hospital. Of the women who delivered at home, 71 percent indicated that a traditional birth attendant had assisted with the delivery, with the remainder reporting assistance from a cowife, mother, healer, nurse, husband, or no assistance. Although the majority (70 percent) of traditional birth attendants reportedly did nothing, some put the mother in delivery position (5 percent), eased the baby's head out (15 percent), massaged the mother with fat, assisted with delivery of the placenta, and/or performed an episiotomy with a fingernail. Mothers report that a razor blade was used to cut the cord in 93 percent of home deliveries.

Results indicate that there is a trend for Maasai practices surrounding motherhood to move from traditional to more contemporary ways, especially when there are pregnancy complications. Although antenatal care is available for pregnant women, it is not always readily accessible. The researchers report that the results of this study will be used for planning health services that will maximize the strengths of both traditional and modern systems to reduce maternal and child morbidity and mortality.

The World's Nurses

Although there is no valid statistical information on nursing/midwifery personnel because of classification problems and lack of established information systems, it is estimated that there are 40 million worldwide to care for the world's estimated 5.4 billion people. Although the population of the United States accounts for approximately 5 percent of the world population, 25 percent of the world's nurses are in the United States. Two-thirds of the world's nurses and midwives live in the MDCs (5 million in Europe; 2.5 million in the United States and Canada). Table 13-2 summarizes the number of physicians and nurses/midwives in selected regions of the world. During the past decade, there has been a steady increase in international exchanges by U.S. and Canadian nurses, a trend that is likely to continue.

In addition to a lack of uniformity in classifying nursing and midwifery personnel, there are significant discrepancies in roles and functions, standards of performance, and quality of care by nurses in various parts of the world. In the eastern Mediterranean region, for example, there are 22 different categories of nurse, many having the same functions and responsibilities, though they come from widely different educational backgrounds. The scope of practice for nurses varies widely from country to country. In parts of Africa and Asia, nurses may prescribe medications, perform essential primary surgeries, suture wounds, and plaster fractures. In some cases, apprenticeship training occurs, with on-the-job skill development and clinical instruction being supervised by staff nurses working in the unit (Davis, 1992; Devereaux, 1993; Gudmundsen, 1989; Mangay-Maglacas, 1989, 1992; Masipa, 1991).

Educational Preparation for Nurses

Each country has special educational programs, and curricula vary widely in content, length, standards, and evaluation criteria. General education required to enter the nursing program ranges from 6 to 13 years, and the length of the nursing program varies from 1 to 4 years. There are general and specialty programs at the basic level of education. Post-basic educational programs in nursing vary widely in length and usually prepare nurses as specialists in clinical practice, education, or administration. In some nations, post-basic education prepares nurses in specialties not recognized in North America, such as dental and veterinary nursing (Mangay-Maglacas, 1989, 1992).

International Council of Nurses (ICN)

Founded nearly 100 years ago, the International Council of Nurses (ICN) has more than 110 national nurses associations joined together through ICN. Both the American Nurses Association (ANA) and the Canadian Nurses Association (CNA) are members of ICN and serve as vehicles for promoting and facilitating internationalism within their respective countries. The major objectives of the International Council of Nurses are to help nurses make a difference in the health care system and to be a strong and positive social force in upgrading health care. ICN works collaboratively with WHO and other international health organizations to solve global health care problems and to facilitate a high level of caring practices for nurses throughout the world. Every 4 years, when as many as 10,000 to 15,000 nurses from around the world attend ICN's congress, nursing

The world's nurses (clockwise from top left): Nigeria, Russia, China, and Hong Kong.

Table 13-2. Number of physicians and nurses in selected parts of the world

World region	Total (thousands)		Total (thousands)	
	Physicians	Nurses*	Physicians	Nurses*
Africa	109	448	2.4	9.9
Latin America	234	294	7.3	9.7
North America	458	1,164	18.2	51.1
East Asia	749	1,545	6.3	13.2
South Asia	445	871	3.2	6.2
Europe	1,021	2,025	21.1	54.8
Oceania	32	153	14.2	67.6
Former USSR	996	NA	36.5	NA
World Total	4,044	6,501	9.1	14.8

* And midwives.
NA = not available.
Data from Basch, P. (1990). *Textbook of International Health*, p. 316. New York: Oxford University Press.

students hold an assembly. At the Madrid Assembly in 1993, an International Student Committee was created, which will provide an avenue for increased involvement by nursing students from around the world (Holleran, 1992; Styles, 1993; Vatre, 1992).

International Nursing as a Specialty

There is currently a spirited professional debate about whether *international nursing*, a term that is sometimes used interchangeably with *transnational nursing*, is a specialty, a framework through which some aspect of nursing is delivered, or transcultural nursing practiced across international boundaries (Andrews, 1988; 1992; Chmielarczyk, 1991; Dawes, 1986; DeSantis, 1987, 1988; Leininger, 1981, 1990, 1992, 1993; Lindquist, 1990; Luna, 1992; May and Meleis, 1987). In referring to specialization within nursing, Peplau (1965) states that at first, particular nurses move in a direction of special interest, which presents as an immediate opportunity or need. Their focus becomes narrowed to one part of a larger field, thus allowing for greater depth in developing that part. Henkle (1979) elaborates the definition of nursing specialty as follows:

1. There is a unique body of knowledge and skills specific to a particular field.
2. This body of knowledge and skills is built on a theoretical base.
3. This body of knowledge and skills can be identified and taught to professionals who possess a broad knowledge and skill base in nursing.

The most closely related specialty is transcultural nursing, which, as indicated in Chap. 1, is sometimes used synonymously with cross-cultural, intercultural, or multicultural nursing. It is the opinion of this author, however, that the focus of international (or transnational) nursing extends beyond those areas of concern in transcultural nursing or the recognized nursing specialties and subspecialties.

International nursing is a specialty because it consists of a unique body of knowledge with specific problems and domains of practice not shared by other recognized

In many African nations, a staff nurse (**right, wearing a belt**) *provides clinical instruction for nursing students* (**left**).

nursing specialties. The following are some of the unique characteristics of international nursing not shared by other recognized nursing specialties: challenges related to understanding health care delivery systems and nurse practice regulations in other countries; learning about the nursing role and clients' expectations of nurses; working with counterparts who ultimately bear responsibility for nursing practice, education, and research in their nations; functioning safely with unfamiliar equipment, supplies, and medications; confronting ethical dilemmas having complex transnational components; working with limited health care resources (in some LDCs); collaborating with health care team members representing categories that may not exist in the United States or Canada; learning about tropical illnesses and other health care problems unfamiliar in the nurse's country of origin (including cultural definitions of health and illness, culture-bound syndromes); understanding and effectively working with political, social, economic, and cultural systems unlike those in the nurse's homeland; identifying and effectively using health care resources in the host country; and solving problems related to visas, immunizations, licenses, insurance, and other necessities in a foreign country (Andrews, 1988, 1992; Andrews and Fargotstein, 1986; DeSantis, 1987, 1988; Gudmundsen, 1989; Lindquist, 1990; Lubanga, 1993; Leininger, 1990; May and Meleis, 1987; Upvall, 1993b). Instead of expending energy on debating whether international nursing is a specialty, the time has come to explore ways in which curricularly sound educational programs can prepare nurses to practice in the "International Century."

International Nursing as a Career

As with other careers, international nursing has benefits and drawbacks. Travel is stimulating, but living abroad has many challenges. For example, Leininger (1989) reports that one hospital in Saudi Arabia has nurses representing more than 60 different cultures. In Sweden and Denmark, nurses care for many political refugees from countries about which they often have little knowledge. In many parts of the world, nurses find themselves providing care for refugees whose culture and language are often unfamiliar. In order to be successful in the international arena, the nurse needs a high degree of dedication, exceptional technical knowledge, and facility in informal diplomacy.

The total number of persons whose primary professional focus is international health is unknown, despite efforts by nurses and others to gather the data. An estimated 9000 U.S. health professionals are working in the international health field. Of these, 3800 are considered "long term," i.e., employed for 1 year or more; 1700 are short term, usually consultants; and 3200 are volunteers. Of the total, the largest category is nurses, followed by physicians and administrators. Most professionals do not follow lifelong careers in international health care but devote an average of about 12 years beyond professional education (Baker, Weisman, and Piwoz, 1984; Basch, 1990).

International Nursing: A Two-Way Street

When reflecting on their international experiences, most nurses who have spent substantial periods of time abroad indicate that they have learned *from* the exchange as well as contributed to improved health for the people in the host country. Research on this subject reveals that nurses identify gaining increased knowledge in the following areas: cultural awareness, alternative health care delivery models (e.g., England's hospice care, elder care in Scandinavian countries), ways to include family members in the nursing care, conservation of resources, nonbiomedical nursing interventions (e.g., therapeutic use of music, therapeutic massage, meditation to reduce anxiety and pain), and increased political awareness (Andrews, 1985, 1986, 1992; Masipa, 1991; Meleis, 1984).

Preparation for International Nursing

Nurses often ask about academic qualifications and experience necessary for international health work. There is, in fact, no identified international health career pattern for U.S. or Canadian nurses, in the sense that such a career existed (and to some degree still

International nursing is a two-way street in which the U.S. or Canadian nurse both learns from and contributes to the health care of the people in other countries. Author (right) with Nigerian counterpart in a school of nursing.

exists) in the colonial powers (England, France, Germany, the Netherlands, and other European nations) that have had vast overseas administrative responsibilities.

How do U.S. and Canadian nurses prepare to go abroad? What types of formal academic and continuing education are appropriate, useful, and helpful?

Academic Preparation

Addressing the need for formal educational preparation for international nursing, Leininger captures the urgency of the task (1981, p. 371):

> Time is running out to help nurses in international consultations and work without having transcultural knowledge and skills. . . . Tourism and television are not enough.

Formal education, by well-prepared educators, and application of the principles of transcultural nursing in the health care setting are indeed the ultimate goal; culturally sensitive caring to promote health and well-being.

With increasing frequency, U.S. and Canadian nurse-educators are recognizing the importance of incorporating international nursing into the curriculum of baccalaureate, master's, and doctoral programs and in providing continuing education courses with an international focus. Nurses and nursing students are expressing an increased interest in international nursing and are traveling, studying, and working abroad in greater numbers each year (Andrews, 1988, 1992; DeSantis, 1987; Frisch, 1990; Gudmundsen, 1989; Martin, 1992; Paillet-Kelson, 1992). Nursing students are seeking information about the appropriate ways in which to become prepared for the practice of nursing in other countries and are choosing programs that have internationalized their curriculum (Lindquist, 1986, 1990). In a study by Mooneyhan and associates (1986), 13 percent of NLN-accredited schools reported courses specifically designed to teach international aspects of nursing and health care.

As the nurse prepares for international/transnational health care, he or she may wonder, "How can I ever learn all I need to know about a culture so I won't appear foolish or alienate clients?" First of all, recognize that it is impossible to learn all there is to know about another culture, regardless of how many years spent living in the country. By definition, the nurse will always be perceived as an outsider, stranger, or foreigner (Gao and Gudykunst, 1990; Gudykunst and Hammer, 1988).

Research on international health care indicates that most U.S. and Canadian nurses work with more than one culture, often rotating back and forth between an international assignment and a position in the United States or Canada. Nonetheless, there are still skills and attitudes that nurses can develop. The following is a list of attributes that the Peace Corps (Gudmundsen, 1989) seeks in its volunteers (and it has been widely adopted by corporations, hospitals, and other groups sending their staff overseas):

1. Listening skills, including listening for the nonverbal
2. Careful observation
3. Patience, not always expecting "them" to do the adjusting
4. Flexibility, openness to change and to learn from others
5. Ability to take risks, try new things, development of "emotional muscle"
6. Awareness of one's own values and cultural assumptions
7. Sense of humor
8. Ability to identify cultural resources in the community
9. Recognition that the reasons for one's feelings of frustration (or noncompliance on the part of clients) may be cultural in origin.

Summarized in Box 13-1 are the ways in which U.S. and Canadian nurses can prepare for international nursing, in addition to formal academic coursework.

Patterns of Cultural Adjustment

Whenever people are immersed in another culture, they will go through a period of *cultural adjustment*. One of the more well known patterns of cultural adjustment is the

---

Box 13-1. Preparation for International Nursing

Reading about the culture, politics, economics, religions, and health care of the country

Reviewing scholarly and popular literature about the culture

Talking with host nationals living in the United States or Canada

Eating foods from the country (ethnic restaurants, practicing with chopsticks)

Contacting consulate or embassy of country to be visited

Contacting U.S. or Canadian government offices for information

Language studies

Watching documentaries/travel films

Visiting the country as a tourist prior to taking a professional position

---

W model. Many variations on this theory exist, but the general pattern has been well documented in intercultural communications research. It is one of the few concepts agreed on by most professionals involved in cross-cultural education (see Gao and Gudykunst, 1990; Gudykunst and Hammer, 1988; Pillette, 1989). Figure 13-1 illustrates the theory.

Cultural Adjustment

There are five stages of cultural adaptation illustrated as the points on a W; this pattern may depend on the length of stay and the purpose of being in the other culture. The five stages are

1. *Excitement*, or the *honeymoon period*, which is characterized by enthusiasm resulting from the newness and sense of adventure.

Figure 13-1. The W model of cultural adjustment.

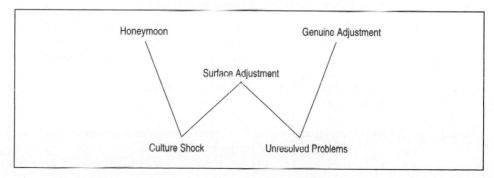

2. *Culture shock*. The excitement is gone. Things are not "like back home"; social cues and relationships are difficult; there are feelings of alienation and homesickness and a temporary dislike of the host culture.
3. *Surface adjustment*. During this stage, the nurse is beginning to catch on; things are starting to make sense; rudimentary language (more accurate communication) skills are acquired, and the nurse is able to communicate some basic ideas and feelings, making some relationships in the local culture; the nurse begins to feel more comfortable.
4. *Frustration* and a deeper level of *unresolved problems* arise; the assignment period in the culture may seem very long, and the nurse may experience feelings of boredom, frustration, and isolation.
5. *Genuine adjustment* is characterized by acceptance of the new culture as just another way of living; the nurse may not always approve of cultural practices but understands the differences and begins to peel back some of the rich layers of the culture. The nurse has established genuine, real relationships with people in the host country.

All nurses experience the components identified in the cultural pattern when living in an unfamiliar culture. Some may decide that trying to adjust is too difficult and return home at the early "cultural shock" stage. Being aware that there is a pattern to feelings and reactions to the new culture is one step in making the nurse more effective in the international setting. Clients from other nations experience similar cultural patterns when they enter the United States or Canada. Shorter in duration, a phenomenon known as *reentry shock* can be expected when the nurse returns home. Reentry shock consists of feelings of general dissatisfaction, criticism for lifeways of his or her home country, and free-floating anxiety.

Refugees

Although most nurses visit another culture with the knowledge that they will, at some point, return home, some refugees can never return home. Therefore, what nurses may see in these people is not only culture shock but a genuine process of grieving over the loss of their homeland, for these clients may be suffering the permanent loss of an integral part of their being, their physical culture (Muecke, 1992). In addition, migration and resettlement require psychological adaptation. In a study by Aroian (1990), loss and disruption, novelty, occupational adjustment, language accommodation, and subordination were described as predominant aspects of migration and resettlement.

International Studies on Campuses

In 1987, the American Council on Education examined international studies at colleges and universities across the United States and gathered information about study abroad programs (see Lachat and Zerbe, 1992; Martin, 1992), internationally oriented majors and minors, and the role of international studies in general education. With a response rate of 74 percent (400 of the 541 institutions), the following is a partial summary of the final report:

- Three-quarters of all 4-year colleges and universities require at least one course with some international content.
- Nearly half (47 percent) require courses in Western history or civilization.

- One-third of 4-year institutions reported having a foreign language requirement for admission to the college; two-thirds require some or all students to study a foreign language before they graduate.
- Less than 5 percent of 2-year institutions have a foreign language requirement for admission; 1 of 8 have a language requirement for an associate degree.
- Study abroad programs are operated by two-thirds of 4-year institutions and one-eighth of 2-year colleges.

International Students in Schools of Nursing

Perhaps the great untapped resource in U.S. and Canadian nursing programs is the international student. According to Mooneyhan et al. (1986), more than one-half of NLN-accredited programs have international students studying at their institutions. The citizenship of international students includes those from Southeast Asia and Africa most frequently, followed by those from the Caribbean or Mediterranean area and then South America and Europe (Mooneyhan et al., 1986). Nationally, there are 356,000 international students attending U.S. colleges and universities. The exact number of international students majoring in nursing is unknown.

Those schools most likely to have international nursing students are universities or 4-year colleges having a graduate program. International students are more likely to be found attending the larger-sized schools, irrespective of whether they are private or public. International students are enrolled at all levels of educational preparation (Mooneyhan et al., 1986).

In the next section, the nurse will be given guidelines for making decisions about going abroad and choosing sending agencies that are congruent with their philosophical beliefs.

Going Abroad

Motivation

Before choosing a sending agency, it is essential to examine one's motivation for going abroad. In studies of U.S. nurses engaging in international consultation, several reasons motivating nurses have been identified, including enjoyment of people from other cultures, interest in travel, moral convictions, religious beliefs, financial rewards, personal invitation by host country counterparts, cross cultural exchange of ideas, professional commitment, and service to those in need. Identifying motivation and determining the goal(s) and purpose(s) for the international experience will facilitate selection of the appropriate type of position and sending agency (Andrews, 1985, 1986, 1988, 1992; Horsley, 1991).

Length of Time Abroad

Related to the motivation for going abroad is the length of time that the nurse plans to spend overseas. Before contacting potential sending agencies, it is important to determine a time commitment, stated in terms of days, weeks, months, or years. Opportunities for short-term international experiences (less than 6 months) vary widely and are likely to require tradeoffs in benefits provided by the agency. Travel/study programs usually assume that the applicant is willing to pay part or all of the expenses for the trip. Long-term international experiences offer a wide variety of opportunities, with contracts varying according to the agency's needs and resources.

Geographic Region

If a particular region is preferred, this must be matched with the sending agency's activities and projects. Some agencies specialize in a particular region, whereas others have programs on virtually every continent. The following reasons may motivate the nurse to choose a particular region or country: (1) political stability of the country, (2) personal/emotional reasons such as a significant other living in the area, and/or (3) matching host country needs with the expertise of the nurse.

Although global politics may shift rapidly, the Middle East, South Africa, and certain parts of Central and South America have a reputation for volatile politics, including anti-U.S. demonstrations. Personal safety is of concern, and careful research should be conducted before accepting an assignment in a politically unstable area. State Department reports, information provided by the sending agency, informal discussions with recently returned visitors to the country, and current news sources may provide the necessary information to determine the safety of the area.

Reasonable Expectations of Sending Agencies

Although specific details will vary according to the sending agency, Box 13-2 is intended to provide guidelines for asking questions. Sending agencies expect questions and recognize that interviewing is a two-way process.

Negotiating a Contract

The preceding discussion has focused on some aspects that are reasonable to expect in a contractual agreement with a sending agency. Before signing the contract, it is important to study the details carefully and to discuss any unclear matters with the agency representative. A written job description should accompany the contract along with a statement detailing the conditions surrounding contract termination by either the nurse or the sending agency.

Choosing an International Sending Agency

Because there are many agencies that send nurses abroad, it is beyond the scope of this chapter to provide an exhaustive list. Appendix D lists the names and addresses of selected agencies that engage the services of nurses for health-related projects. Not included in the listing are a wide variety of church-related organizations, universities, foundations, private industries, study/travel groups, professional nursing associations, and the U.S./Canadian military.

Nurses may affiliate with a variety of sponsoring agencies. Sponsorship may be through a U.S. or Canadian organization or through the host country (ministry of health, university, hospital, school of nursing, public health agency, or other). International agencies, such as the World Health Organization, also engage the services of

---

Box 13-2. Guidelines for Choosing an International Sending Agency

---

Salary/stipend:

What is the salary/stipend in U.S. or Canadian dollars?

If any portion is paid in local currency, what is the exchange rate?

What has been the history of fluctuation in the exchange rate during the past 2 years?

What is the cost of living compared with the salary/stipend?

What is the average cost for housing, food, transportation, and utilities in the host country?

Can local currency be exchanged for U.S. dollars? Can U.S. or Canadian dollars be used to purchase local currency?

Can salary earned in the country be taken out of the country? If so, by what means? Bank transfer? Cashier's check?

What length of time is usually required for bank transactions? International transfers? Local banking needs?

To which government(s) are taxes owed? What is the rate of taxation? How, when, and where should tax statements be processed/filed?

Travel to host country assignment:

Is round-trip airfare paid by agency? Are spouse and/or dependents sent or eligible for discounted fares?

Is there a payback clause for early contract termination?

Who makes travel arrangements? Is a confirmation by the ticket holder required?

How frequently are return trips to the United States or Canada allowed/paid for by the agency?

Housing and moving:

Does the agency provide housing? In an expatriate community or in a neighborhood inhabited by host country nationals?

What is the type of housing provided? Is there central heating and/or air conditioning, running water, toilet and bathing facilities, window screens?

What type of energy is used? What is the average monthly cost?

Is there a reliable source of electricity available? If not, is there a generator?

Is the housing furnished or unfurnished?

What are the conditions of the move? By what means (air, surface, sea)? Is travel and household insurance included? Amount of coverage provided? Who is responsible for packing?

What household goods and commodities are reasonable to expect locally? At what cost?

Does the agency have special arrangements for shipping items such as regular mail pouch service, agency deliveries, etc?

If housing allowance is given, are family members included?

(continued)

Box 13-2 *(Continued)*

Local transportation:
Are vehicles available to staff for job-related travel? For personal use after hours and on weekends?

What is the cost of gasoline? Maintenance of a vehicle? Does the agency employ a mechanic? Are reliable local mechanics available? Are replacement parts for vehicles available?

Does the agency provide car loans? What are the terms? Is there a waiting list for vehicle purchases? If so, how long? What is the average price for a vehicle?

What are local regulations on drivers' licenses, automobile insurance?

If vehicles are not available, what methods of local transportation are used by agency staff? Cost? Availability? Safety?

Are women permitted to drive vehicles? If not, is a driver provided by the agency? During what hours/times?

Insurance benefits:
What type of health, life, disability, and retirement insurance is available? Are family members included?

In case of illness, what is the agency policy concerning treatment? What health care facilities may be accessed for personal and family health care?

If local hospitals are used, what is the quality of care compared with the United States? What type of pediatric care is available locally for dependent children?

Is paid leave and/or airfare to the United States granted for health care emergencies? For compassionate leave?

Vacations and holidays:
What U.S., Canadian, and local holidays does the agency recognize?

What is the length and frequency of vacation/holiday absences? Are there limitations to travel during vacations?

In politically volatile areas, are more frequent vacations permitted/encouraged?

Does the agency have an informal or formal network allowing for vacationing staff to vacation at reduced cost?

Do staff offer hospitality to other agency members while traveling? Is it expected that all staff reciprocate by housing agency members during vacations and/or job-related travel?

Orientation program:
What is the length, location, and nature of the agency orientation?

Are language studies required? Where do language studies occur? Who pays for classes?

Are local interpreters available? Are there any gender-related or age-related factors to consider when using an interpreter?

Does the orientation include study of the political, economic, social, cultural, religious, and health related aspects of the host country?

Who is the U.S./Canadian ambassador to the host country? Where is the U.S./Canadian embassy located?

In case of natural disaster or political unrest, what is the emergency evacuation plan for expatriates?

nurses for consultation and clinical practice. Joint sponsorship, though relatively un-common, also may occur. For example, some religious groups have both international and national organizations that may elect joint sponsorship.

Summary

With increasing frequency, U.S. and Canadian nurses are traveling, studying, research-ing, consulting, teaching, administering, and practicing nursing abroad. The decision to engage in an international interchange requires much thought and planning. Philo-sophical congruence with the sending agency or organization, selection of geographic area of interest, length of time available, and matching background with host-country needs are factors that interplay with the desire to go abroad.

Many U.S. and Canadian nurses are relatively naïve about negotiating a contract with a sending agency. An overview of reasonable questions to pursue with the agency has been provided, including discussions of salary/stipend, travel to the assignment site, housing and moving expenses, local transportation, insurance coverage, vacation and holiday leave, and orientation policies. The names and addresses of selected health-related sending agencies are listed.

Learning Activities

1. Identify someone who has recently moved to the United States or Canada from another country. After reviewing the section of the chapter dealing with cultural adjustment, ask the person to tell you about his or her experiences since arriving. How does the response compare with the W model? What is your assessment of the stage of cultural adjustment the person is experiencing?
2. Identify a foreign-born nurse and ask him or her to describe the health care delivery system in his or her country of origin. Compare and contrast the U.S./Canadian health care delivery system with that of the country you have chosen.
3. Select a country (other than your own), and examine the professional and lay health care systems. You may find it helpful to conduct a library search to identify relevant articles, books, and audiovisual materials available on the topic.
4. Watch your local television guide for programs on international health. Choose one program and critically review its contents in terms of accuracy, caliber of sources used, presence/absence of reporting biases, clarity of presentation, effectiveness in conveying the message(s), and identification of intended audience (e.g., adults, high school students, etc.).
5. If you learned that you would be leaving next month for Kenya to work as a staff nurse in the outpatient department of a clinic, how would you prepare yourself?
6. If the opportunity presents itself, participate in a travel/study abroad program at your college/university. What information will you need to plan for your trip? Where will you go to obtain the necessary information?

References

Andrews, M. M. (1985). International consultation by United States nurses. *International Nursing Review, 32*(1), 50–54.

Andrews, M. M. (1986). U.S. nurse consultants in the international marketplace. *International Nursing Review, 33*(2), 50–55.

Andrews, M. M. (1988). Educational preparation for international nursing. *Journal of Professional Nursing, 4*(6), 430–35.

Andrews, M. M. (1992). Cultural perspectives on nursing in the 21st century. *Journal of Professional Nursing, 8*(1), 7–15.

Andrews, M. M., and Fargotstein, B. P. (1986). International consultation: A perspective on ethical issues. *Journal of Professional Nursing, 2*(5), 302–308.

Aroian, K. J. (1990). A model of psychological adaptation to migration and resettlement. *Nursing Research, 39*(1), 5–10.

Badran, I. G. (1993). Accidents in the developing world. *World Health Organization, 46*(1), 14–15.

Baker, T. D., Weisman, C., and Piwoz, E. (1984). United States health professionals in international health work. *American Journal of Public Health, 74*(5), 438–441.

Basch, P. F. (1990). *Textbook of International Health.* New York: Oxford Press.

Brown, P. (1988). *People Who Have Helped the World: Florence Nightingale.* Waterford, Herts, UK: Exley.

Chmielarczyk, V. (1991). Transcultural nursing: Providing culturally congruent care to the Hausa of Northwest Africa. *Journal of Transcultural Nursing, 3*(1), 15–19.

Davis, C. F. (1992). Culturally responsive nursing management in an international health care setting. *Nursing Administration Quarterly, 16*(2), 36–39.

Dawes, T. (1986). Multicultural nursing. *International Nursing Review, 33*(5), 148–150.

DeSantis, L. (1987). Principles of transnational co-operation in nursing. *International Nursing Review, 34*(3), 67–71.

DeSantis, L. (1988). The relevance of transcultural nursing to international nursing. *International Nursing Review, 35*(4), 110–112, 116.

Devereaux, G. (1993). Making the most of things . . . nursing overseas. *Nursing Times, 89*(1), 44–46.

Fagin, C. M. (1990). Nursing leadership: Global strategies. *Conference Overview: International Nursing Development: Consensus on Solutions.* NLN Publication Number 41-2341. New York: National League for Nursing Press.

Frisch, N. C. (1990). An international nursing student exchange program: An educational experience that enhanced student cognitive development. *Journal of Nursing Education, 29*(1), 10–12.

Gao, G., and Gudykunst, W. B. (1990). Uncertainty, anxiety, and adaptation. *International Journal of Intercultural Relations, 14,* 301–317.

Gudmundsen, M. A. (1989). Building and infrastructure for international health promotion and disease prevention: The Peace Corps fellows program. *Journal of Professional Nursing, 5*(4), 172, 236.

Gudykunst, W. B., and Hammer, M. R. (1988). Strangers and hosts: An extension of uncertainty reduction theory to intercultural adaptation. In Y. Y. Kim and W. B. Gudykunst (Eds.), *Cross-Cultural Adaptation.* Newbury Park, CA: Sage.

Gunby, P. (1992). 1992 could be pivotal year in efforts to improve health of people everywhere. *Journal of the American Medical Association, 267*(1), 15–23.

Henkle, E. (1979). International nursing: A specialty? *International Nursing Review, 26*(2), 170–73.

Henry, B. M., and Nagelkerk, J. M. (1992). International nursing research. *Annual Review of Nursing Research, 10,* 207–230.

Hirshfeld, M. J. (1992). Challenges from the World Health Organization. *Nursing Administration Quarterly, 16*(2), 1–2.

Holleran, C. (1992). International affairs: Perspective of the International Council of Nurses. *Nursing Administration Quarterly, 16*(2), 1–3.

Horsley, M. R. (1991). Transcultural travel tips for the nurse abroad. *Imprint, 38*(2), 107–112.

Lachat, M. F., and Zerbe, M. B. (1992). Planning a baccalaureate clinical practicum abroad. *International Nursing Review, 39*(2), 53–55.

Leininger, M. (1981). Transcultural nursing: Its progress and its future. *Nursing and Health Care, 9,* 365–371.

Leininger, M. M. (1989). Transcultural nursing: A worldwide necessity to advance nursing knowledge and practice. In J. McCloskey and H. Grace (Eds.), *Nursing Issues.* Boston: Little, Brown.

Leininger, M. (1990). *Ethical and Moral Dimensions of Care.* Detroit: Wayne State University Press.

Leininger, M. M. (1992). Editorial: Globalization of transcultural nursing: A worldwide imperative. *Journal of Transcultural Nursing, 4*(2), 2–3.

Leininger, M. M. (1993). Editorial: International Council of Nursing and Transcultural Nursing Society: Alike or different? *Journal of Transcultural Nursing, 5*(1), 2–3.

Lindquist, G. J. (1986). Programs that internationalize nursing curricula in baccalaureate schools of nursing in the U.S. *Journal of Professional Nursing, 2*(3), 143–150.

Lindquist, G. J. (1990). Integration of international and transcultural content in nursing curricula: A process for change. *Journal of Professional Nursing, 6*(5), 272–279.

Lubanga, N. (1993). The legacy of apartheid in a changing South Africa. *Nursing and Health Care, 14*(10), 512–519.

Luna, L. J. (1992). Educational strategies in a transcultural setting. *Nursing Administration Quarterly,* *16*(2), 39–41.

Mangay-Maglacas, A. M. (1989). Close encounters in international nursing: The impact on health policy and research. *Journal of Professional Nursing, 5*(6), 305–314.

Mangay-Maglacas, A. M. (1992). Nursing research in developing countries: Needs and prospects. *Journal of Advanced Nursing, 17*(3), 267–270.

Martin, R. (1992). International exchange programs and recruitment. *Nursing Management, 23*(7), 111–112.

Masipa, A. (1991). Transcultural nursing in South Africa: Prospects for the 1990s. *Journal of Transcultural Nursing, 3*(1), 3–4.

May, K. M., and Meleis, A. I. (1987). International nursing: Guidelines for core content. *Nurse Educator, 12*(5), 36–40.

Meleis, A. I. (1984). Preparation for international nursing: Ivory tower versus trial and error. In M. M. Andrews and P. A. Ludwig (Eds.), *Nursing Practice in a Kaleidoscope of Cultures,* (pp. 38–47). Salt Lake City: University of Utah.

Mooneyhan, E. L., McElmurrary, B. J., Sofranko, M. S., and Campos, A. B. (1986). International dimensions of nursing and health care in baccalaureate and higher degree nursing programs in the United States. *Journal of Professional Nursing, 2*(2), 82–90.

Muecke, M. (1992). Nursing research with refugees. *Western Journal of Nursing Research, 14*(6), 703–720.

Nakajima, H. (1993). The state of the world's health. *World Health Organization, 3,* 3–5.

Nightingale, F. (1859). *Her Notes on Hospitals.* London: Parker.

Paillet-Kelson, M. (1992). Education nurses for practice in Europe. *Nursing Standard, 6*(19), 32–34.

Peplau, H. (1965). Specialization in professional nursing. *Nursing Science, 8,* 24–27.

Pilette, P. C. (1989). Recruitment and retention of international nurses aided by recognition of phases of the adjustment process. *Journal of Continuing Education in Nursing, 20*(6), 277–281.

Styles, M. M. (1993). The world as classroom. *Nursing and Health Care, 14*(10), 507.

Uhl, J. E. (1992). International Affairs: Nightingale The international nurse. *Journal of Professional Nursing, 8*(1), 5.

Upvall, M. J. (1993a). HIV/AIDS Prevention in Zanzibar: The role of nursing education. *Nursing and Health Care, 14*(10), 524–527.

Upvall, M. J. (1993b). Therapeutic syncretism: A conceptual framework of persistence and change for international nursing. *Journal of Professional Nursing, 9*(1), 56–62.

Vatre, N. J. (1992). International Affairs: Global issues for nurses and nursing. *Journal of Professional Nursing, 8*(5), 259.

World Health Organization. (1978). *Primary Health Care—Report of the International Conference on Primary Health Care.* Geneva: WHO.

World Health Organization (1992). *Eighth Report on the World Health Situation.* Geneva: WHO.

Appendix A

Andrews/Boyle Transcultural Nursing Assessment Guide

Cultural Affiliations

With what cultural group(s) does the client report affiliation (e.g., American, Hispanic, Navajo, or combination)? To what degree does the client identify with the cultural group (e.g., "we" concept of solidarity or as a fringe member)?

Where was the client born?

Where has the client lived (country, city) and when (during what years)? *Note*: If a recent relocation to the United States, knowledge of prevalent diseases in country of origin may be helpful. Current residence? Occupation?

Values Orientation

What are the client's attitudes, values, and beliefs about developmental life events such as birth and death, health, illness, and health care providers?

Does culture affect the manner in which the client relates to body image change resulting from illness or surgery (e.g., importance of appearance, beauty, strength, and roles in cultural group)? Is there a cultural stigma associated with the client's illness (i.e., how is the illness or client condition viewed by the larger culture)?

How does the client view work, leisure, education?

How does the client perceive change?

How does the client perceive changes in lifestyle relating to current illness or surgery?

Margaret M. Andrews and Joyceen S. Boyle: TRANSCULTURAL CONCEPTS IN NURSING CARE, SECOND EDITION. © 1995 J.B. Lippincott Company.

How does the client value privacy, courtesy, touch, and relationships with individuals of different ages, social class (or caste), and gender?

How does the client view biomedical/scientific health care (e.g., suspiciously, fearfully, acceptingly)? How does the client relate to persons outside of his or her cultural group (e.g., withdrawal, verbally or nonverbally expressive, negatively or positively)?

Cultural Sanctions and Restrictions

How does the client's cultural group regard expression of emotion and feelings, spirituality, and religious beliefs? How are dying, death, and grieving expressed in a culturally appropriate manner?

How is modesty expressed by men and women? Are there culturally defined expectations about male-female relationships, including the nurse-client relationship?

Does the client have any restrictions related to sexuality, exposure of body parts, certain types of surgery (e.g., amputation, vasectomy, hysterectomy)?

Are there any restrictions against discussion of dead relatives or fears related to the unknown?

Communication

What language does the client speak at home? What other languages does the client speak or read? In what language would the client prefer to communicate with you?

What is the fluency level of the client in English—both written and spoken use of the language? Remember that the stress of illness may cause clients to use a more familiar language and to temporarily forget some English.

Does the client need an interpreter? If so, is there a relative or friend whom the client would like to interpret? Is there anyone whom the client would prefer did not serve as an interpreter (e.g., member of the opposite sex, a person younger/older than the client, member of a rival tribe or nation)?

What are the rules (linguistics) and modes (style) of communication? How does the client prefer to be addressed?

Is it necessary to vary the technique of communication during the interview and examination to accommodate the client's cultural background (e.g., tempo of conversation, eye contact, sensitivity to topical taboos, norms of confidentiality, and style of explanation)?

How does the client's nonverbal communication compare with that of individuals from other cultural backgrounds? How does it affect the client's relationship with you and with other members of the health care team?

How does the client feel about health care providers who are not of the same cultural background (e.g., black, middle-class nurse and Hispanic of a different social class)?

Does the client prefer to receive care from a nurse of the same cultural background, gender, and/or age?

What are the overall cultural characteristics of the client's language and communication processes?

Health-Related Beliefs and Practices

To what cause(s) does the client attribute illness and disease (e.g., divine wrath, imbalance in hot/cold or yin/yang, punishment for moral transgressions, hex, soul loss, pathogenic organism)?

What are the client's cultural beliefs about ideal body size and shape? What is the client's self-image vis-à-vis the ideal?

What name does the client give to his or her health-related condition?

What does the client believe promotes health (eating certain foods, wearing amulets to bring good luck, sleep, rest, good nutrition, reducing stress, exercise, prayer, rituals to ancestors, saints, or intermediate deities)?

What is the client's religious affiliation (e.g., Judaism, Islam, Pentacostalism, West African voodooism, Seventh-Day Adventism, Catholicism, Mormonism)? How actively involved in the practice of this religion is the client?

Does the client rely on cultural healers (e.g., curandero, shaman, spiritualist, priest, minister, monk?) Who determines when the client is sick and when he or she is healthy? Who influences the choice/type of healer and treatment that should be sought?

In what types of cultural healing practices does the client engage (use of herbal remedies, potions, massage, wearing of talismans, copper bracelets or charms to discourage evil spirits, healing rituals, incantations, prayers)?

How are biomedical/scientific health care providers perceived? How does the client and his or her family perceive nurses? What are the expectations of nurses and nursing care?

What comprises appropriate "sick role" behavior? Who determines what symptoms constitute disease/illness? Who decides when the client is no longer sick? Who cares for the client at home?

How does the client's cultural group view mental disorders? Are there differences in acceptable behaviors for physical versus psychological illnesses?

Nutrition

What nutritional factors are influenced by the client's cultural background? What is the meaning of food and eating to the client?

With whom does the client usually eat? What types of foods are eaten? What is the timing and sequencing of meals?

What does the client define as food? What does the client believe comprises a "healthy" versus an "unhealthy" diet?

Who shops for food? Where are groceries purchased (e.g., special markets or ethnic grocery stores)? Who prepares the client's meals?

How are foods prepared at home [type of food preparation, cooking oil(s) used, length of time foods are cooked, especially vegetables, amount and type of seasoning added to various foods during preparation]?

Has the client chosen a particular nutritional practice such as vegetarianism or abstinence from alcoholic or fermented beverages?

Do religious beliefs and practices influence the client's diet (e.g., amount, type, preparation, or delineation of acceptable food combinations, e.g., kosher diets)? Does the client abstain from certain foods at regular intervals, on specific dates determined by the religious calendar, or at other times?

If the client's religion mandates or encourages fasting, what does the term *fast* mean (e.g., refraining from certain types or quantities of foods, eating only during certain times of the day)? For what period of time is the client expected to fast?

During fasting, does the client refrain from liquids/beverages? Does the religion allow exemption from fasting during illness? If so, does the client believe that an exemption applies to him or her?

Socioeconomic Considerations

Who comprises the client's social network (family, friends, peers, and cultural healers)? How do they influence the client's health or illness status?

How do members of the client's social support network define caring (e.g., being continuously present, doing things for the client, providing material support, looking after the client's family)? What is the role of various family members during health and illness?

How does the client's family participate in the promotion of health (e.g., lifestyle changes in diet, activity level, etc.) and nursing care (e.g., bathing, feeding, touching, being present) of the client?

Does the cultural family structure influence the client's response to health or illness (e.g., beliefs, strengths, weaknesses, and social class)? Is there a key family member whose role is significant in health-related decisions (e.g., grandmother in many African-American families or eldest adult son in Asian families)?

Who is the principal wage earner in the client's family? What is the total annual income? (*Note*: This is a potentially sensitive question.) Is there more than one wage earner? Are there other sources of financial support (extended family, investments)?

What insurance coverage (health, dental, vision, pregnancy) does the client have?

What impact does economic status have on lifestyle, place of residence, living conditions, ability to obtain health care? How does the client's home environment (e.g., presence of indoor plumbing, handicap access) influence nursing care?

Organizations Providing Cultural Support

What influence do ethnic/cultural organizations have on the client's receiving health care [e.g., Organization of Migrant Workers, National Association for the Advancement of Colored People (NAACP), Black Political Caucus, churches such as African-American, Muslim, Jewish, and others, schools including those which are church-related, Urban League, community-based health care programs and clinics].

Educational Background

What is the client's highest educational level obtained?

Does the client's educational background affect his or her knowledge level concerning the health care delivery system, how to obtain the needed care, teaching-learning, and any written material that he or she is given in the health care setting (e.g., insurance forms, educational literature, information about diagnostic procedures and laboratory tests, admissions forms)?

Can the client read and write English, or is another language preferred? If English is the client's second language, are materials available in the client's primary language?

What learning style is most comfortable/familiar? Does the client prefer to learn through written materials, oral explanation, or demonstration?

Religious Affiliation

How does the client's religious affiliation affect health and illness (e.g., life events such as death, chronic illness, body image alteration, cause and effect of illness)?

What is the role of religious beliefs and practices during health and illness? Are there special rites or blessings for those with serious or terminal illnesses?

Are there healing rituals or practices that the client believes can promote well-being or hasten recovery from illness? If so, who performs these?

What is the role of significant religious representatives during health and illness? Are there recognized religious healers (e.g., Islamic imams, Christian Scientist practitioners or nurses, Catholic priests, Mormon elders, Buddhist monks)?

Cultural Aspects of Disease Incidence

Are there any specific genetic or acquired conditions that are more prevalent for a specific cultural group (e.g., hypertension, sickle cell anemia, Tay Sachs, G6PD, lactose intolerance)?

Are there socioenvironmental diseases more prevalent among a specific cultural group (e.g., lead poisoning, alcoholism, HIV/AIDS, drug abuse, ear infections, family violence)?

Are there any diseases against which the client has an increased resistance (e.g., skin cancer in darkly pigmented individuals, malaria for those with sickle cell anemia)?

Biocultural Variations

Does the client have distinctive physical features characteristic of a particular ethnic or cultural group (e.g., skin color, hair texture)? Does the client have any variations in anatomy characteristic of a particular ethnic or cultural group [e.g., body structure, height, weight, facial shape and structure (nose, eye shape, facial contour), upper and lower extremities]?

How do anatomic and racial variations affect the physical examination?

Developmental Considerations

Are there any distinct growth and development characteristics that vary with the client's cultural background (e.g., bone density, psychomotor patterns of development, fat-folds)?

What factors are significant in assessing children of various ages from the newborn period through adolescence (e.g., expected growth on standard grid, culturally acceptable age for toilet training, introducing various types of foods, gender differences, discipline, socialization to adult roles)?

What is the cultural perception of aging (e.g., is youthfulness or the wisdom of old age more highly valued)?

How are elderly persons handled culturally (e.g., cared for in the home of adult children, placed in institutions for care)? What are culturally acceptable roles for the elderly?

Does the elderly person expect family members to provide care, including nurturance and other humanistic aspects of care?

Is the elderly person isolated from culturally relevant supportive persons or enmeshed in a caring network of relatives and friends?

Has a culturally appropriate network replaced family members in performing some caring functions for the elderly person?

Appendix B

Resources in Transcultural Health and Nursing

American Nurses' Association
600 Maryland Avenue, S.W.
Suite 100 West
Washington, DC 20024
(202) 554-4444

Asian-Pacific Islander Nurses Association
C/O College of Mount Saint Vincent
6301 Riverdale Avenue
Riverdale, NY 10471
(718) 405-3354

Association of Black Nursing Faculty in Higher Education
5823 Queens Cove
Lisle, IL 60532
(708) 969-3809

Canadian Nurses Association
50 Driveway
Ottawa, Ontario K2P 1E2
(613) 236-4547

Chi Eta Phi Sorority, Inc.
3029 13th Street, N.W.
Washington, DC 20036
(202) 232-3858

Council on Nursing and Anthropology
C/O Dr. Mildred Roberson
Nursing Department
Southeast Missouri State University
Cape Girardeau, MO 63701

Margaret M. Andrews and Joyceen S. Boyle: TRANSCULTURAL CONCEPTS IN NURSING CARE, SECOND EDITION. © 1995 J.B. Lippincott Company.

Native American Nurses Association
927 Treadale Lane
Cloquet, MN 55720
(218) 879-1227

National Association of Hispanic Nurses
1501 16th Street, N. W.
Washington, DC 20036
(202) 387-2477

National Black Nurses Association
P.O. Box 1823
Washington, DC 20012-1823
(202) 393-6870

Philippine Nurses Association of America, Inc.
489 Morris Avenue
Boonton, NJ 07005
(908) 647-0180 Beeper 195

Transcultural Nursing Society
c/o Madonna University
College of Nursing and Health
36600 Schoolcraft Road
Livonia, MI 48150-1173
(313) 591-8358

U.S. Department of Health and Human Services
U.S. Public Health Service
Indian Health Service
Parklawn Building
5600 Fishers Lane
Rockville, MD 20852-9788
(301) 443-4242

U.S. Department of Health and Human Services
U.S. Public Health Service
Office of Minority Health
P.O. Box 37337
Washington, DC 20013-7337
(800) 444-6472

Appendix C

Significant Cultural Events and Holidays

This calendar is a guide to religious and nonreligious holidays that are celebrated in the United States and Canada. The list is not exhaustive but is given to encourage the reader to be aware of the many holidays and festivals that are reflective of the great mixture of religious and cultural groups that exist in North America.

Key to Religious Groups and Nonreligious Holidays

A	= African American	J	= Jewish
B	= Buddhist	Ja	= Jain
Ba	= Baha'i	M	= Mormon
C	= Christian (general)	O	= Eastern Oxthodox Christian
Ci	= Civic holiday	P	= Protestant
H	= Hindu	RC	= Roman Catholic
I	= Islam	S	= Sikh

January

1 New Year's Day   Ci
  Feast of St. Basil   O
6 Epiphany   C
7 Nativity of Jesus Christ   O

3rd Monday   Martin Luther King, Jr., Birthday Observance   Ci

February

Black History Month (U.S.)
8   Scout Day   Ci
14   Valentine's Day   Ci
Midmonth   President's Day (U.S.)   Ci

Other holidays that often occur in February according to the Lunar Calendar

Chinese New Year
Ramadan (30 days)   I
Nehan-e (Death of Buddha)   B
Vasant Panchami (Advent of Spring)   H, Ja
Ash Wednesday   C
Purim   J

March

Women's History Month (U.S.)

17   St. Patrick's Day   C
25   Annunciation   C

Other holidays that often occur in March according to the Lunar Calendar

Eastern Orthodox Lent begins   O
Idul-Fitr (End of Ramadan)   I
Higan-e (First Day of Spring)   B
Naw-Ruz (Baha'i and Iranian New Year)   Ba
Palm Sunday   RC, P
First Day of Passover (8 days)   J
Holi (Spring Festival)   H, Ja
Maunday Thursday   RC, P
Good Friday   RC, P
Easter   C, RC, P, M
Mahavir Jayanti (Birth of Mahavir)   Ja

April

16   Yom Ha'atzmaut (Israel Independence Day)   J

Other holidays that often occur in April according to the Lunar Calendar

Hanamatsuri (Birth of Buddha)   B
Yom Hashoah (Holocaust Remembrance Day)   J, Ci
Baisakhi (Brotherhood)   S
Huguenot Day   P
Ramavani (Birth of Rama)   H
Palm Sunday   O
Holy Friday   O
Easter   O

May

5   Cinco de Mayo (Mexico and some U.S. locations)
13   Ascension Day   RC, P
23   Victoria Day (Canada)   Ci
30   Memorial Day   Ci

Other holidays that often occur in May according to the Lunar Calendar

Shavuot   J
Idul-Adha (Day of Sacrifice)   I
Pentecost   RC, P

June

9   Ascension Day   O
12   Anne Frank Day
14   Flag Day (U.S.)   Ci
24   Nativity of St. John the Baptist   RC, P

Other holidays that often occur in June according to the Lunar Calendar

Muharram   Islamic New Year
Ratha-yatra   Hindu New Year

July

1   Canada Day (Canada)   Ci
4   Independence Day (U.S.)   Ci
24   Pioneer Day   M

Other holidays that often occur in July according to the Lunar Calendar

Obon-e   B

August

6   Transfiguration   C
     Hiroshima Day   Ci
15   Feast of the Blessed Virgin Mary   RC, O

September

1st Monday   Labor Day (U.S.)   Ci
15   National Hispanic Heritage Month (30 days)   Ci
17   Citizenship (U.S. Constitution)   Ci
19   San Gennaro Day   RC
25   Native American Day   Ci

Other holidays that often occur in September according to the Lunar Calendar

Higan-e (First Day of Fall)   B
Rosh Hashanah (Jewish New Year, 2 days)   J

October

12   Columbus Day (U.S.)   Ci
     Thanksgiving Day (Canada)   Ci

24   United Nations Day   CI
31   Reformation Day   P
      Halloween   RC, Ci

Other holidays that often occur in October according to the Lunar Calendar

Dusserah (Good over Evil)   H, JA
Yom Kippur (Atonement)   J
Sukkot (Tabernacles)   J
Shemini 'Azeret (end of Sukkot)   J
Diwali, or Dipavali (Festival of Lights)   H, Ja

November

1   All Saints Day   RC, P
11   Veterans Day   Ci
25   Religious Liberty Day   Ci

1st Tuesday   Election Day (U.S.)   Ci
4th Thursday   Thanksgiving Day (U.S.)   Ci

Other holidays that often occur in November according to the Lunar Calendar

Baha'u'llah Birthday   Ba
Guru Nanak Birthday   S

December

6   St. Nicholas Day   C
8   Feast of the Immaculate Conception   RC
10   Human Rights Day   Ci
12   Festival of Our Lady of Guadalupe (Mexico, Hispanic)
25   Christmas   C, RC, P, M, Ci

Other holidays that often occur in December according to the Lunar Calendar

Bodhi Day (Enlightenment)   B
Hanukkah (Jewish Festival of Lights: 8 days)   J
Kwanzaa (7 days)   A

Appendix D

Selected Agencies Sending Nurses Abroad

U.S. Government Agencies

Action/Peace Corps
Recruiting Office
P-301
Washington, DC 20526

U.S. Agency for International Development (USAID)
Recruitment Branch, Room 111SA2
515 22nd Street, NW
Washington, DC 20523

U.S. Department of Defense
The Pentagon
Washington, DC 20330

U.S. Department of State
General Recruitment Division
Recruitment Branch
Washington, DC 20520

Canadian Government Agency

Canadian Council for International Development (CETA)
170 Laurier Avenue West
Suite 900
Ottawa, Ontario K1P 5V5
(819) 997-5456

U.S. Private Agencies

American Red Cross
17th and D Streets, NW
Washington, DC 20006

Amdoc/Option Agency
3550 Afton Road
San Diego, CA 92702

American Medical International
9465 Wilshire Boulevard, Suite 307
Beverly Hills, CA 90212

Care
660 First Avenue
New York, NY 10016

Concern
P.O. Box 1790
Santa Ana, CA 92702

Direct Relief International
P.O. Box 30820
Santa Barbara, CA 93130

HCA International Company
P.O. Box 550
Department N87-887
Nashville, TN 37202

International Liaison
124 Massachusetts Avenue, NW
Washington, DC 20005

International Voluntary Services, Inc.
1424 16th Street
Washington, DC 20036

Lalmba Association
7685 Quartz
Golden, CO 80403

Medicine and Public Health: Develop Assistance Abroad
200 Park Avenue
New York, NY 10003

Project HOPE
The People-to-People Health Foundation, Inc.
Division of Nursing
Education and Personnel Department
Carter Hall
Millwood, VA 22646

Thomas Dooley Foundation
442 Post Street
San Francisco, CA 94102

Westinghouse Health Systems
P.O. Box 866
Columbia, MD 21044

Whittaker International Services Company
Medical Careers Center
P.O. Box 12029
Arlington, VA 22209

Canadian Nongovernment Agency

Canadian Council for International Cooperation
1 Nichols Street, Third Floor
Ottawa, Ontario K1N 7B7
(613) 236-4547

Provides a listing of 130 nongovernment agencies in a directory called *ID Profiles*

International Organizations

International Council of Nurses (ICN)
Box 42
1211 Geneva 20
Switzerland

Pan American Health Organization
Nursing Section, Health Services Division
525 23rd Street, NW
Washington, DC 20037

World Health Organization (WHO)
Avenue Appia
1211 Geneva
Switzerland

Information Clearinghouses

An information clearinghouse has current reports on the types of nurses that are needed for specific countries but does not usually provide placement services.

American Council of Voluntary Agencies for Foreign Service, Inc.
Technical Assistance Clearinghouse
200 Park Avenue
New York, NY 10003

American Nurses' Association*
2420 Pershing Road
Kansas City, MO 64108

Canadian Nurses Association*
50 Driveway
Ottawa, Ontario K2P 1E2
(613) 236-4547

Friends of World Nursing
P.O. Box 1049
San Diego, CA 92112-1049

International Liaison, Inc.
1234 Massachusetts Avenue, NW
Washington, DC 20005

National Council for International Health (NCIH)†
1701 K Street, NW, Suite 600
Washington, DC 20006

*The ANA and CNA will send a letter of introduction to the national nurses' association of any country the nurse plans to visit.
†NCIH is a membership organization that provides a computerized listing of health-related international employment opportunities and a directory of U.S.-based agencies involved in international health assistance.

Index

Ableism, 263
Abnormality, mental health nursing and, 255–258
Abortion
  Baha'is and, 374
  Catholics and, 380
  Christian Scientists and, 384
  culturally sensitive fertility counselling and, 118
  Hindus and, 389
  Jehovah's Witnesses and, 394
  Jews and, 398
  Mennonites and, 400–401
  Mormons and, 387
  Muslims and, 392
  Seventh-Day Adventists and, 405
  Unitarian/Universalists and, 407
Abuela, 343
Academic preparation of nurses for international nursing, 422, 426–428
Acatalascmia, 150
Acceptance, promoting feelings of, 278
Access to health and nursing care, 330–333
Accidents
  of adolescent, 162–163
  in less developed countries, 418
Acculturation, 37
Achieved characteristics, identification through, 210
Achievement concept, childbirth and, 107
Acquired immunodeficiency syndrome (AIDS)
  in adolescent, 162
  mental health nursing and, 276–278

  worldwide, 419
  refugees and, 194
Activity
  postpartum, 112–113
  pregnancy and, 104–105
Activity-centered society, 139
Acupuncture/acupressure for pain, 318, 319
Adaptation, culture and, 10
Adolescent, 123–179. *See also* Child
  alcoholism in, 164
  bicultural or tricultural, 161
  communicating with, 160–162
    cultural variations in, 161
    jargon and, 161
    nonverbal, 160–161
  cultural identification of, 162
  death of, 162
    homicide in, 163
    suicide in, 163–164
  development of, 157–159
  growth spurt of, 129
  health care of, 162–166
    special needs in, 159–160, 162–166
  middle adulthood and rearing of, 184
  nursing care of
    application of cultural concepts to, 169–175
    evaluation of plan for, 169
    transcultural, 166–169
  pregnancy in, 165–166
  subculture of, 159
  substance use and abuse by, 164
    drugs in, 165

Adolescent *(cont.)*
  tasks of, before entering adulthood,
      157–158
  unintentional injuries in, 162–163
Adrenal hyperplasia, 150
Adulthood
  acceptance of physiological changes in, 184
  civic responsibility and, 183–184
  maturity as criterion of, 182
  psychosocial development during, 183–185
  social responsibility and, 183–184
Adultism, 263
Advocacy in mental health nursing, 253, 268
Aesthetic paradigm, 18
Afghans, refugee resettlement and, 329
African Americans
  adolescent
    homicide of, 163
    pregnancy in, 165
    suicide of, 163
  child-rearing practices of, 130
  cultural values and, 63
  culture-bound syndromes in, 80
  culture care meanings and action modes of,
      63
  culture values in folklore and literature of,
      58
  death, dying, and grieving of, 366
  dying and bereavement and, 368
  healers and, 30
  health beliefs and customs of, 24, 25,
      247–248, 249–250
  HIV/AIDS prevention program and,
      276–278
  mourning rituals of, 368
  nursing care for
    hypertension risks and, 239
    meanings of, 63
    mental health, 264
    prenatal care and, 342
    tertiary levels of prevention and, 346–347,
        348–349
  perceptions of
    infant cry, 130
    kin utilization in pregnancy, 102
  prejudice against, 262
  as subcultural group, 14
Age. *See also* Child; Elderly; Infant
  chronological definitions of, 209–210
  functional definitions of, 206–209
Ageism, 263
Agencies sending nurses abroad, 432–435,
      451–454
Agenesis of teeth, 89
Age-stratification theory, 214
Aging. *See also* Elderly; Older Population;
      Older Woman
  alienation among elderly, 227
  American attitudes toward, 229
  chronological definitions of, 209–210
  common features of, 204–205
  cross-cultural responses to, 210–216,
      229–232

social support systems and, 213–216
  socioeconomic status and, 211–212
  sources of care and, 212–213
cultural forces affecting, 204
developmental aspects of, 216–223
  achieving tasks and, 220–223
  needs and, 217–218
  self-actualization and integrity in,
      217–220
in cultural groups, 214
functional definitions of, 206–209
societal definitions of, 209–210
AIDS. *See* Acquired immunodeficiency
      syndrome
Albinism, 150, 151
  ocular, 150
Alcoholism, 92
Alcohol use
  in children and adolescents, 164
  hypertension and, 242
  in Native Americans, 265
  subcultural differences in, 164, 265
Alienation among elderly, 227
Alkaptonuria, 150
Alterations in lifestyle, chronic illness and,
      237–252. *See also* Chronic illness
Alternative practices
  in health care delivery, 426
  in pain management, 312–318
American Council on Education recommenda-
      tions on international studies, 430
American Nurses' Association (ANA), 6
  international nursing and, 422
Amish
  adolescent, 158–159
  case study of, 169–173
  clothing of, 81
  extended family in, 169–173
  funeral customs of, 361–362
  nursing plan of care in, 171–172
  pregnancy in, 103
Amniocentesis
  Catholics and, 380
  Christian Scientists and, 384
  Hindus and, 389
  Jehovah's Witnesses and, 394
  Mormons and, 387
  Muslims and, 392
  Seventh-Day Adventists and, 405
  Unitarian/Universalists and, 407
Amniotic fluid, 90
Amputations
  Catholics and, 379
  Christian Scientists and, 383
  Hindus and, 389
  Jehovah's Witnesses and, 394
  Muslims and, 392
  Seventh-Day Adventists and, 405
  Unitarian/Universalists and, 406
Amyloidosis, 150, 151
ANA (American Nurses' Association), 6
  international nursing and, 422
Andrews/Boyle Transcultural Nursing Assess-
      ment Guide, 439–444

Anemia, 92, 93
Anglo-Americans
    alcoholism in, 164
    attitudes of
        toward death, 361, 362
        toward public expression of grief, 366
    cultural values and, 63
    cultural values in folklore and literature of, 58
    cultural care meanings and action modes, 63
    nursing care of, 63
    perceptions of infant cries of, 130
    proverbs and values of, 59
Animist mourning rituals, 369
Anointing of the Sick in Catholicism, 378, 381
Anorexia nervosa, 257
Antepartum period, 102–103
Anthropology and nursing, synthesis of, 4
Apocrine sweat glands, 89
Apology in communication, 269
Appalachian Americans, 220–223, 327
Appearance, biocultural variations in, 81
Art and practice of healing, 29–33
Arthritis, 92
Artificial fertility control, 116–119
Artificial insemination
    Baha'is and, 374
    Catholics and, 380
    Christian Scientists and, 384
    Hindus and, 389
    Jehovah's Witnesses and, 394
    Jews and, 398
    Mennonites and, 401
    Mormons and, 387
    Muslims and, 392
    Seventh-Day Adventists and, 405
    Unitarian/Universalists and, 407
Asara B'Tevet, 397
Ascribed characteristics, identification through, 210
Asian Americans
    expectations of, for chronic disease survival, 154–155
    mental health nursing and, 266–267
    prejudice against, 262
    as subcultural group, 14
Asian cultural traditions in funeral preparations, 361
Aspartylglycosaminuria, 150
Assessment
    of attitudes towards health, 244–250. *See also* Health belief systems
    cultural. *See* Cultural assessment
    developmental, 196–197
    dietary
        guide for, 441–442
        self, 73
    of elderly, 223–228
    neurological, 293
    nutrition, 441–442
    organizations providing cultural support and, 443

of pain, 311–312
    nurse national background and, 307
    self
        dietary, 73
        elderly and, 213
    of spiritual needs, 358
Asthma, 92
Ataque el, 367
Ataxia-telangiectasia, 150
Atharva-Veda, 145
Atonement concept, childbirth and, 107
Attitudes
    for international nursing and health, 428
    of mother toward health and illnesses, 126
    parental, child behavior and, 126
    toward death, 362–364
Autopsy
    Buddhists and, 378
    Hindus and, 390
    Jehovah's Witnesses and, 395
    Jews and, 400
    Mennonites and, 401
    Mormons and, 388
    Muslims and, 392
    Seventh-Day Adventists and, 406
    Unitarian/Universalists and, 407
Ayurvedic medicine, 145

Bacteriuria, 101
Bad air, blood, and wind, 144
Bad death, 362–363
Baha'i International Community, 370–375
Balance concept of health, 249. *See also* Yin/Yang theory
    of Asian Americans, 266
Bar mitzvah, 397, 398, 399
Barriers
    in communication and service delivery to older person, 230, 231
    in cross-cultural communication, 67
    cultural, 189–192
    language, in preventive care, 342. *See also* Communication; Language
Basic needs. *See* Needs
Bat gio, 149
Bat mitzvah, 399
Bedtime routine, 132
Bed types and preferences, 133
Behavior
    child
        influences on, 123–124, 126
        parental attitudes and, 126
    coping. *See* Coping patterns
    cultural standards for adult, 182
    cultural variations in, 81
    elderly and
        culturally acceptable nursing care and, 230–232
        illness in, 211
    in health and illness, 34–35
        lifestyle changes and, 242–244
    of Mexican Americans in pregnancy, 343–344
    norms of conduct and, 355–356

Behavior *(cont.)*
    reason as controlling force in, 41
    sex differences in, 138
    in sick roles, 34, 35, 67
Beliefs, cultural. *See* Cultural beliefs and
        practices
Benson's relaxation response in pain manage-
        ment, 313–314
Bereavement, 359–369. *See also* Dying and
        bereavement
    cultural practices related to, 361–364
Beverages and foods. *See* Diet
Bicultural adolescent, 161
Bilingual interpreters. *See* Interpreters
Biocultural aspects of disease, 92–93
Biocultural variations, 80–90
    assessment guide for, 444
    in body proportion, height, and weight,
        81–82
    childhood disorders and, 149–152
    in ears, 88
    erythema and, 84–85
    in eyes, 87–88
    general appearance in, 81
    in hair, 87
    jaundice and, 83–84
    laboratory tests and, 90
    in mammary venous plexus, 89
    in mouth, 88
    in musculoskeletal system, 85, 86–87
    pallor and, 84
    petechiae and, 85
    secretions and, 89–90
    in skin, 82–83
    in teeth, 88–89
    in thorax, 85
Biofeedback for pain, 318
Biologic variations
    in fertility, 116
    pregnancy and, 101
    tertiary prevention planning and, 349
Biomedical health paradigm, 23–26, 33
Biophysiologic data categories, 55
Biopsy
    Catholics and, 379
    Christian Scientists and, 384
    Jehovah's Witnesses and, 394
    Muslims and, 392
    Seventh-Day Adventists and, 405
    Unitarian/Universalists and, 406
Birth. *See* Childbirth
Birth control, 116–119
    Baha'is and, 373–374
    beliefs about, 166
    Catholics and, 380
    Christian Scientists and, 384
    Hindus and, 389
    Jehovah's Witnesses and, 394
    Jews and, 397–398
    Mennonites and, 400
    Mormons and, 387
    Muslims and, 392
    Seventh-Day Adventists and, 405
    Unitarian/Universalists and, 407

Black Americans. *See* African Americans
Black English, 161
Blended family, 124
Blood and blood products
    Christian Scientists and, 383
    Hindus and, 389
    Jehovah's Witnesses and, 394
    Jews and, 397
    Mormons and, 387
    Muslims and, 392
    Seventh-Day Adventists and, 405
    Unitarian/Universalists and, 406
Blood as indicator of health status, 195
Bloom syndrome, 150
Body image, 75–76
Body language in communication, 67
Body proportion, biocultural variations in,
        81–82
Bone length, 81–82
Bonesetters, 341
Bottlefeeding, 114
Breastfeeding, 114
    Haitian beliefs about, 196
Bronchitis, 93
    in developed countries, 418
Brujo, 24
Buddhism, 375–378
    approach of, to death, 363
    mourning rituals of, 369
Burial clothes, 361–362
Burial customs, 361–364
    of Baha'is, 375
    of Buddhists, 378
    of Catholics, 381
    of Christian Scientists, 384
    double burial in, 368
    of Hindus, 390
    of Jehovah's Witnesses, 396
    of Jews, 400
    of Mennonites, 401
    of Mormons, 388
    of Muslims, 393
    of Seventh-Day Adventists, 406
    of Unitarian/Universalists, 407
Burning, Southeast Asian folk healing prac-
        tices and, 148

Caída de la mollera, 24, 144
Cambodians, refugee resettlement and, 329
Canadian Nurses' Association (CNA), 422
Cancer, 93
    in less developed countries, 416–417
    in more developed countries, 418
Cao gio, 148
Cardiovascular diseases, 93
    in less developed countries, 417
    in more developed countries, 418
Care, meaning of, to client, 280
Care, concept of, 41, 42
Careers
    in international nursing and health, 426
    performance in, in middle adulthood, 183

Caregivers
family as, 225–228
multiple, 136
in pain management, 310
Carencia de agua, 144
Caring
concept of, 41–42
culture-specific, care of elderly and, 230–232
as essence of nursing, 42, 43
Leininger's model on cultural diversity and universality in, 43, 44
transcultural dimensions of, 41–42
study of, 42–44
as universal phenomenon, 5
Cartesian dualism, 25
Catholicism, 378–381
in Hispanic Americans, 265
suicide and, 362
Cerumen, 88
Change
allowing for, 174
culture and, 16–19, 20–21
dietary, 78
Chanukah, 397
Characteristics, achieved or ascribed, 210
Cheyenne attitudes toward suicide, 362
Child, 123–179. *See also* Adolescent; Childhood diseases and disorders
abuse of, 145
folk healing *versus*, 145–149
age and development of, 128
Amish case study and, 169–173
attitudes toward touching of, 69
communication with, 160–162
death of, 365
family and culture and, 123–128
growth and development of, 128–140. *See also* Growth and development
health of
international nursing and, 419, 420, 421
problems with, 162–166
promotion of, 140, 141, 142
illness in, 142–157
abuse *versus* folk healing and, 145–149
biocultural influences and, 149–152
chronic, 152–154
culturally perceived causes of, 153–154
disability and, 152–154
expectations for survival after, 154–155
social roles and, 155–157
Jehovah's Witness case study and, 173
nursing care of
cultural concepts in, 169–175
evaluating plan of, 169
planning of, 169–175
transcultural, 166–169
Childbearing woman, 99–122
birth and. *See* Childbirth
fertility control and, 116–119
infant care and, 113–116
postpartum, 111–113
pregnancy and, 100–107

Childbirth
beliefs and customs surrounding, 107–111
father participation in, 108, 109
at home, 107, 110–111
perceived normalcy in, 110
positions for, 110
weight at, 128
Childhood diseases and disorders. *See also* Child
biocultural influences on, 149–152
Chinese expectations in, 154–155
hereditary predisposition and, 152
international nursing and, 414, 419
mortality rates from, 414
religion and, 357–359
Child-rearing practices, 138–140
Chinese
culture-bound syndromes in, 80
expectations of, for chronic disease, 249
in child, 154–155
healers and, 30
mental health care of, 266–267
mourning rituals and, 368
Chloride excreted by sweat glands, 89
Choices about care, 34–35
Cholecystitis, 93
Cholestasis-lymphedema, 151
Cholesterol, serum, 90
Christian religions, suicide and, 362. *See also* Religion
Christian Science, 381–384
The Christian Science Journal, 382
Chronic illness, 237–252
coping behaviors in, 244–250
health beliefs and, 246–249
traditional healers and other health practices in, 249–250
cultural expectations for survival in, 154–155
hypertension as, 238–239
African Americans and increased risk for, 239
risks for, 239
lifestyle changes in, 239–242
cultural and behavioral factors and, 242–244
diet and exercise, 241–242
family support systems and, 243–244
medication regimens in, 240–241
in middle adulthood, 186–192
in Native Americans, 186–192
psychological factors and, 227
Church of Christ, Scientist, 381–384
practitioners in, 382–383
Church of Jesus Christ of Latter-Day Saints, 385–388. *See also* Mormons
Circulatory diseases
in less developed countries, 417
in more developed countries, 418
Circumcision, 115–116
Catholics and, 379
Christian Scientists and, 384
Jehovah's Witnesses and, 394
Jews and, 397

Circumcision *(cont.)*
  Mormons and, 387
  Muslims and, 392
  Seventh-Day Adventists and, 405
  Unitarian/Universalists and, 407
Civic responsibility, 183–184
Classism, 263
Cleanliness, cultural attitudes toward, 56
Cleft lip, 150
  and cleft palate, 88
Cleft uvula, 88
Client
  goals and expectations of, 280–281
  meaning of care to, 280
  use of term, 37
Climate, childhood disorders and, 152
Clinical decision-making, transcultural nursing
      care and, 92–94
Clothing
  adolescent preoccupation with, 159
  for burial, 361–362
  cultural variations in, 81
Clubfoot, 151
CNA (Canadian Nurses' Association), 422
Cognitive mode of child-rearing, 138
Cohabitation family, 124
Coining, folk healing and, 148
Colitis, 93
Collaboration in pain management, 312
Collecting information about cultures, 272
Colleges, international studies in, 430–431
Communal family, 124
Communication. *See also* Language
  assessment guide for, 440–441
  body and paralinguistic cues in, 62
  community nursing and, 334–336
  cross-cultural, 62–72
    with family members and significant
      others, 62–65
    introductions in, 65
    language in, 70–72
    nonverbal, 67–69
    nutrition and, 73–78
    overcoming barriers in, 67
    sex/gender considerations in, 69
    space, distance, and intimacy in, 65–67
  mental health nursing and, 268–270
  mistakes in, 269
  nonverbal, 62
    adolescent and, 160, 161
    cross-cultural, 67–69, 334, 335
  open, establishing, 278–279
  redirection in, 269
  verbal, 62
Communication recovery skills, 269
Communion, Catholicism and, 378
Community
  as client, 341
  components of, 325
  cultural assessment and views of, 326
  cultural diversity in, 327–329
  health of, 325
  nursing care and. *See* Community nursing
  sense of, in family, 244

Community-based health education programs,
    142
Community-based health resources, 198
Community health representative, 189
Community nursing, 323–352
  assessment tools for, 325, 439–444
  communication and, 334–336
  cultural groups and, 330–333
  cultural issues in, 325–330
    health care practitioners and, 333–334
  high-risk groups and, 324, 328
  interventions in, 331–333
    at secondary level of prevention, 346
  nursing care in, 323–324
    framework for, 324–325
  primary prevention in, 341–344
  secondary prevention in, 344–346
  sensitivity to cultural practices in, 331, 332
  settings for, 324
  terminology in, 323
  tertiary prevention in, 346–347, 348–349
Compadres, 265
Compadrozgo, 339
Competence and excellence in transcultural
    nursing care, 54
Compliance
  definition of, 240
  level of, 91
  motivation for, 238–239
  with treatment, 35
Complications, tertiary levels of prevention of,
    347
Comprehensive theory of nursing care, 52, 92,
    94
Conflicts
  cultural, 41
  of norms, 174
Congenital anomalies, religious beliefs and,
    357
Conja, 25
Conjuring, 264
Constipation in child, 135
Consumers of mental health care, 273
Contraception, 116–119. *See also* Birth control
Contracts in international nursing, 432
Conversion disorders, 145
Coping patterns
  of Appalachian Americans, 220–223
  in chronic illness, 244–250. *See also* Chronic
    illness
  developmental tasks in elderly and,
    220–223
  of family of critical patient, 291
  in health promotion and maintenance, 332
  in pain, 311
Cosmic paradigm, 18
Counseling, peer, 276
Critical Care Family Needs Inventory, 290,
    291, 292
Critical care nursing, 297–300
  antagonism and distrust in, 293, 294, 295
  culturally congruent care in, 292–297
    acknowledging differences in, 294–295

cultural assessment skills in, 293–294
  cultural care in, 295–297
  distrust and antagonism in, 293, 294, 295
  family issues in, 290–292
  misconceptions in, 293, 294, 295
  patient vulnerability and, 288–290
  separation from family and significant others
    in, 288–290
  stress and, 289–290
Cross-cultural communication. *See* Communi-
    cation, cross-cultural
Cross-cultural experiences, 40
Cross-cultural psychiatry, 258
Cross-cultural research, on growth and devel-
    opment, 129–130
Crowding in less developed countries, 418
Cuarentena, la, 111
Cuban-Americans, perceptions of infant cries
    of, 130
Cuban refugees, 193
Cues in communication, 62
Cultural adjustment
  genuine, 430
  in international nursing and health,
    428–431
  stages of, 429–430
Cultural affiliations, assessment guide for, 439
Cultural aspects of disease incidence, assess-
    ment guide for, 443
Cultural assessment, 55, 439–444
  collecting information in, 272
  of community, 326
  for community nursing, 325, 326, 439–444
  components of, 336–341
  critical care and, 293–294
  cultural norms in, 337, 338–339, 340
  family in, 337–338, 339
    views of, 325–326
  of health beliefs and practices, 337, 339, 342
    guide for, 441
  of individual and family, 325–326
  kinship in, 337, 338, 339
  language in, 337, 338, 340
  of Mexican Americans, 339–341
  of Mormons, 293
  of Native Americans, 337–339
  nursing content in, 55
  nursing process in, 55
    transcultural perspective of, 42–44
  political systems in, 337, 338, 340
  of religious affiliation, 337, 339, 340–342
    guide for, 443
  skills in, 20–21, 55
  of social life, 337, 338, 340
  of socioeconomic considerations, 442
  traditions in, 337, 338, 340
  of values orientation, 337, 338, 340
    guide for, 439–440
  of variations, 20–21
  world view in, 337, 338, 340
Cultural barriers, 189–192
Cultural beliefs and practices, 17–18. *See also*
    Health belief systems

of Haitian refugees, 194–196
health-related
  assessment guide for, 441
  in pregnancy, 104–105, 106
  maintenance of, over time, 329–330
  mental health nursing and, 259–260
  parental, 124
  psychiatric disorders in, 255
  role of family in transmitting, 327
  superstitions and, 259
  voodoo in. *See* Voodoo beliefs and practices
Cultural blindness, 38
Cultural building blocks, 39–40
  elderly in, 224
Cultural characteristics and concepts, 11–12
Cultural code, 69
Cultural competence, 40–41, 54
Cultural conflict, 41
Cultural context
  choices about care in, 34–35
  elderly adult nursing care and, 210–216
  self understanding and, 271
Cultural data categories, 55
Cultural diversity in community, 327–329
Cultural encounters, 37
Cultural events, significant, 447–450
Cultural food practices, 76–78
Cultural groups. *See also* Culture
  access to health and nursing care by,
    330–331
  in United States, 12–16
Cultural imposition, 39
Cultural knowledge
  in health maintenance and promotion,
    331–333
  in tertiary levels of prevention, 347
Cultural manifestations, guide for assessment
    of, 20–21
Culturally competent nursing care, 40–41, 54
Culturally congruent nursing care decisions,
    274
Cultural networks, 198
Cultural norms. *See* Norms
Cultural paradigm, dominant, 18
Cultural relativism, 40
Cultural sanctions and restrictions, 440
Cultural sensitivity, 39
Cultural stereotyping, 124, 125
Cultural stumbling blocks, 37–39
Cultural support, organizations providing, 443
Cultural symbols, 6
Cultural values and culture care meanings,
    63–64
Cultural value orientations, 12, 13, 55–62
  meaning of, to nursing care, 62, 63–64
Culture
  assessment. *See* Cultural assessment
  conflict of, 39
  defined, 9, 10
  and food. *See also* Foods
  free will or free agency, 139
  mental health nursing and, 272–274
  of nurse, 271

Culture *(cont.)*
personality of, 12
phenomenon of, 8–19, 20–21
change and, 16–19, 20–21
characteristics and concepts in, 11–12
definitions in, 9, 10
United States cultural groups and, 12–16
values and, 11–12, 13
psychiatric misdiagnosis and, 257
religious dimensions in, 353–356. *See also*
Religion
study of, 19
values of, 55–62, 63–64
variations in
assessment of, 20–21
chronic care model and, 227–228
elderly and, 210–216, 229–232
in health and illness behavior, 35
in pregnancy, 99–100
Culture-bound syndromes, 79–80, 257, 258
international nursing and, 425
Culture care accommodation and/or negotiation, 52, 92, 94
mental health nursing and, 274, 275
Culture care preservation and/or maintenance,
52, 92–94
mental health nursing and, 274–275
Culture care repatterning and/or restructuring,
52, 92, 94
mental health nursing and, 274, 275
Culture shock, 39, 430
Culture values in folklore and literature, 58
Cupping in folk healing, 148
Curanderola, 24, 30, 142, 143, 144, 249, 257,
341
Curricula, international nursing content in,
411, 428
Cutaneous stimulation for pain, 315
Cyanosis, 83
Cystic fibrosis, 150, 151, 152
Cystinuria, 150

Data-gathering
categories of, 55
nursing process and, 174–175
ongoing, 174–175
Death. *See also* Dying and bereavement
attitudes toward, 362–364
awareness of, 366
bad, concept of, 362–363
of child, 365
common practices related to, 361–364
perinatal, 414
preparation and disposal of body after,
361–362
Deception, cultural attitudes toward, 56
Decision making
family in
extended, 127
primary caretaker or, 64–65
influences on, 34
transcultural nursing care and, 92–94
Defensiveness, 269
Dehydration, *mal ojo* and, 143

Delusions, 257
Demography, mental health problems and,
260
Depression
elderly adults and, 227
labeling differences and, 257
as mental health problem, 257, 259
Deshidratación, 144
Determinism, 23–25, 139
Developmental considerations
assessment guide for, 444
elderly and, 220–223
refugee experience and, 192–199
Diabetes mellitus, 93
in more developed countries, 418
Native American view of, 187
pregnancy and, 101
secondary levels of prevention in, 344–346
Diagnoses, nursing, transcultural perspectives
on, 50–52, 51
*Diagnostic and Statistical Manual of Mental Disor-
ders (DSMMD)*, 258
Diagnostician, 339
Diet. *See also* Foods
of Baha'is, 373
of Buddhists, 377
Catholics and, 378
of Christian Scientists, 383
client preferences in, 73–75
in health promotion and maintenance,
332–333
Hindus and, 389
hypertension and, 241–242
Jews and, 397
lifestyle changes in chronic illness and,
241–242
of Mormons, 386
Muslims and, 392
postpartum, 112
promoting change in, 78
promotion of healthy, 190, 198
in secondary level of prevention, 346
self-assessment of, 73
of Seventh-Day Adventists, 405
Unitarian/Universalists and, 406
Dieta, la, 111
Differences, acknowledgment of, 294–295
Discrimination, 38. *See also* Prejudice
and health care access, 331
against older adults, 230–231
Disease
cardiovascular or circulatory, 93, 417, 418
chronic. *See* Chronic illness
cultural assessment of incidence of, 443
definitions of, 21
elderly adults and, 210–216
hereditary predisposition toward, 152
mental, 254–255
parasitic or infectious, 416
prevalence of, 92, 93
prevention of, 141
socioeconomic status and, 160
susceptibilities to specific, 149–152
use of term of, 18

Dislocation of hip, 151
Dissociative disorders, 145
Distance zone in cross-cultural communication, 65–67
Distraction techniques for pain, 314–315
Distress, cultural alternatives in expressing, 333
Diversity
    acknowledgement of, 274
    affirmation of, 279–280
Diviner, 339
Dominant cultural paradigms, 18
Dominant values orientation, 12
Double burial, 368
Double set of standards, 270
Doulas, 78
Down's syndrome, 87
Drinking water, safe, 415–416
Drug abuse, 165. *See also* Substance use
    communication and, 161
Dubin-Johnson syndrome, 151
Dwarfism, 150
Dyggve-Melchoir-Clausen syndrome, 151
Dying and bereavement, 359–369. *See also* Death
    African Americans and, 368
    awareness of, 366
    children and, 365
    funeral practices and, 361–362
    grief and mourning in, 366–369
    nursing care in, 359–369
    religious beliefs associated with, 359–361
    Southeast Asians and, 368–369
    Spanish-speaking groups and, 367
Dynamics of culture. *See* Culture
Dysautonomia, familial, 150
Dysphoria as concept of chronic illness, 247

Ears
    anomalies of, 151
    biocultural variations in, 88
Ecchymotic lesions, 85
Eccrine sweat glands, 89
Economic deprivation and health care access, 331, 332
Educational background, assessment guide for, 443
Educational preparation for international nursing and health, 422, 426–428
Education programs, community-based, 142
Egocentric interactive pattern, 262, 263
Elder, Mormonism and, 385, 386, 388
Elderly, 203–234. *See also* Aging
    achieving integrity and, 219–220
    American attitudes toward, 205–210, 229
    assessment of, 223–228
    care for
        comprehensive approach to, 225–228
        guidelines for appropriate, 228–232
        interventions and, 223–228
        Middle Eastern attitudes toward, 267
        social support systems and, 213–216
        sources of, 212–213, 230–232

cultural definitions of, 228, 229
cultural forces affecting, 204
developmental aspects of, 216–223
    achieving tasks in, 219–223
disease patterns among, 211
energy use in, 217–218
folk health practices among, 212–213
illness among
    behavior and, 211
    cross-cultural variations in, 210–216
    cultural explanations of, 204
    response to, 211
    self-assessment of, 213
individual intervention with, 227
living arrangements of, 207–209
multidimensional nursing analysis of, 225–228
needs of
    basic, 217
    beyond basic needs, 217–218
socioeconomic status of, 211–212
theories of aging and, 205–206
transcultural nursing studies of, 220–223
Elimination, 134–135
Elitism, 263
Ellis-van Creveld disease, 150
Emotions
    in child-rearing, 138
    cultural alternatives in expressing, 333
Empacho, 24, 144, 341
Empowerment, 199, 253, 276
Energy, elderly and, 217–218
Entrant status of refugee, 193
Environment, 19–21
    mental health problems and, 259
Erythema, biocultural variations in, 84–85
Espiritualista, 24, 228
Ethnic groups, 12, 13
    childhood disorders and, 152
    death, dying, and grieving and, 360–361
    preservation of heritage of, 224–225
    theoretical perspectives on aging in, 214
Ethnicity, mental health nursing and, 262–264
Ethnocentrism, 38, 40, 263
Ethnonursing, 7
Ethnopharmacology, 90–91
    level of compliance and, 91
    perception of side effects and, 91
Ethnoreligious subcultures, 64
Eucharist, Catholicism and, 378
Eugenics and genetics. *See* Genetics, eugenics and
Euthanasia
    Baha'is and, 375
    Buddhists and, 377
    Catholics and, 381
    Christian Scientists and, 384
    Hindus and, 390
    Jehovah's Witnesses and, 395
    Jews and, 400
    Mennonites and, 401
    Mormons and, 388
    Muslims and, 393

Euthanasia *(cont.)*
    of Seventh-Day Adventists, 406
    Unitarian/Universalists and, 407
Evil eye, 23, 24, 69, 105, 143, 257
    dehydration and, 143
Excitement period in cultural adjustment, 429
Exercise, promotion of
    chronic illness and, 241–242
    community nursing and, 332, 333
    middle-aged adult and, 188, 190–191, 198
    in secondary level of prevention, 346
Expectations
    of client, 280–281
    of family of critical care patient, 290–291
Experiences
    cross-cultural, 40
    in cultural relativism, 40
    group
        Appalachian Americans and, 220–223
        elderly and, 220, 227
    learning from international nursing, 426
    refugee, 192–199
    religious, 354
        pain and, 303
    sharing, 277–278
Explanatory model, 247, 269–270. *See also*
        Folk medicine
Extended family, 124, 126–128
    adolescent and, 169–173
    lifestyle changes and, 243
    of Mexican Americans, 339
    of Native Americans, 346
Eyes
    biocultural variations in, 87–88
    in communication, 67, 68

Facial expressions in communication, 67
Facial hair care, adolescents and, 168
Factor XI deficiency, 150
Faja, 113
Falling out, 257
Familiar references, separation from, 289
Familism, 62
Family
    adolescents in, 123–138
    bereavement in, 359–369. *See also* Dying
        and bereavement
    blended, 124
    as caregivers
        in Asian American values, 266–267
        in Nicaraguan immigrants, 224–228
    children in, 123–138
        care and relationships of, 136–138
    cohabitation, 124
    communal, 124
    communication with, 62–65
    critical care nursing and, 290–292, 297
    in cultural assessment, 325–326, 337–338,
        339
    cultural expectations and, 19
    of dying patient, 359–369. *See also* Dying
        and bereavement
    elderly and, 208–209

essence of, 64
extended. *See* Extended family
fear of touching and, 288
gay, 124
health promotion and maintenance in,
    331–332
    international nursing and, 426
Hispanic Americans' attitudes toward,
    223–228, 265–266
interchangeable roles in, 243
lifestyle disruptions in, 243
    elderly and, 227
Nicaraguan immigrant multigenerational,
    223–228
nuclear, 124
obligations in, 244
refugees and, 192–199
sense of community in, 244
separation from, vulnerability and, 288
single-parent, 124
as social unit, 62
solidarity among generations of, 219
supportive and assistive functions of
    Amish and, 169–173, 170
    lifestyle alterations and, 227, 243–244
    Native Americans and, 189–192
in transmitting cultural beliefs and practices,
    327
Family constellations, 124
Family planning, 116–119
Fasting
    Judaism and, 397
    Mormons and, 386
    Seventh-Day Adventists and, 405
Fatalism, 139, 267
    in Latin culture, 245
Father, infant care and, 113
Fear
    of cold air and water in postpartum period,
        112
    of pain in labor and delivery, 110
    of touching, 288
    of unknown, 289–290
Feast of the Sacrifice, 391
Feelings of acceptance, promotion of, 278
Fertility
    biological variables in, 116
    control of, 116–119
Fetus, burial customs for, 393
Filipino culture, suicide and, 362
Flag display, Jehovah's Witnesses and, 396
Folk healers. *See* Traditional practitioners
Folklore, cultural values in, 58
Folk medicine
    African Americans and, 264
    as alternative to Western medicine, 31,
        249–250
    appeal of, 267–268
    child abuse *versus*, 145–149
    elderly and, 212–213, 228
    as explanatory model, 247
    of Haitian refugees, 194–196
    of Mexican Americans, 343

practitioners of, 30–33
   Southeast Asian, 148–149
   Western medical beliefs coexisting with, 33, 142
Fontanel, fallen, 24, 144
Foods. *See also* Diet
   body image and, 75–76
   in critical care nursing, 295
   culture and, 73–75, 76
   in health promotion and maintenance, 332–333
   religion and, 76–78
Frailty, population, 203
Free will or free agency culture, 139
Freud's study of role relations, 129
Friendships, middle adulthood and, 185. *See also* Relationships
Frustration period in cultural adjustment, 430
Funeral practices, 361–362

Garment of Mormon, 386
Gaucher disease, 150
Gay family, 124
Gender
   in cross-cultural communication, 69
   and roles in middle adulthood, 185
Generalizations, mental health problems and, 260
Generations, solidarity among, 219
Generativity, 196
Genetics, 149–152
   Baha'is and, 374
   Catholics and, 380
   childhood disorders and, 149–152
   Christian Scientists and, 384
   diabetes in Native Americans and, 186–192
   eugenics and, 384
      Baha'is and, 374
      Catholics and, 380
      Jehovah's Witnesses and, 394
      Jews and, 398
      Mennonites and, 401
      Muslims and, 392
      Seventh-Day Adventists and, 405
   pregnancy and, 101
   traits and disorders by population or ethnic group, 150–151
Genuine cultural adjustment, 430
Geographic areas
   childhood disorders and, 152
   health care access and, 331
   subcultures and, 14–15, 327–328
Ghasl El Mayyet, 393
Ghost illness and ghost possession, 144, 145
Glaucoma, 150
Global health care problems, 414–415
Glycogen storage disease, 150
Goals
   for community nursing, 323–324
   and expectations of client, 280–281
   for spiritual nursing care, 356
Godparents, 265

Going abroad, 431–435
   expectations of sending agencies and, 432
   geographical region and, 432
   length of time of, 431–432
   motivation for, 431
   negotiating contract before, 432
   sending agency in, 451–454
      choice of, 432–435
G6PD, 93
G6PD deficiency, 150, 151, 152
Granny midwives, 107
Greater Feast, 391
Greeks, culture-bound syndromes in, 80
Greetings, forms of, 65–66
Grief, 366–369. *See also* Dying and bereavement
Group experience
   Appalachian Americans and, 220–223
   elderly and, 220, 227
Group history, 220
Group loyalty, 56
Growth and development, 128–140
   child-rearing practices and, 138–140
   cross-cultural research on, 129–130
   elimination and, 134–135
   menstruation and, 135–136
   nutrition and, 131–132
   parent-child relationship and, 136–137
   relationships with other family members and, 137–138
   sex roles and, 138
   sleep and, 132–134
Guatemalans, refugee resettlement and, 329

Hair
   biocultural variations in, 87
   care of, 167–168
Haitian Americans
   cultural values and, 63
   culture-bound syndromes of, 80
   culture care meanings and action modes of, 63
Haitian refugees, 192–199
   background and context of, 193–194
   developmental assessment and nursing interventions for, 196–197
   health-related crises in, 192–199
   new ways of coping for, 197–199
   resettlement of, 329
   traditional health beliefs of, 194–196
Hajj, Islam and, 390
Hallucinations, 257
Harmony. *See also* Yin/Yang theory
   communication and, 66
   as concept of health, 249
   in relationships, 266
Hasidism, 396
Healers, 24, 25, 31–33, 249, 250
   nursing care and, 78–79
   scope of practice and, 30
Healing, 249–250
   art and practice of, 29–33
   Christian Scientists and, 383
   methods of, 29–33
   organic or nonorganic method of, 27, 29–33

Healing systems
  choices of, 32–33
  types of, 31
Health
  assessment of attitudes towards, 244–250.
    See also Health belief systems
  biocultural variations in, 80–90. *See* Bio-
    cultural variations
  of community, 325
  definitions of, 21
  situational crises in, 186–199
    chronic illness onset and, 186–192
    refugees and, 192–199
  world. *See* World health status
Health behavior, 34–35
Health belief systems, 22–29, 246–249. *See*
    also Cultural beliefs and practices
  in African Americans, 247–248
  healing art and practice and, 29–33
  paradigms in
    biomedical, 23–26
    holistic, 26–29
    magico-religious, 22–23
    scientific, 23–26
  in prediction of health and illness behaviors,
    34–35
  sick role behavior and, 34
  United States and, 33
Health care
  access to, 330–333
  elderly and sources of, 212–213
  global problems of, 414–415
  international. *See* International nursing and
    health
  primary, international nursing and, 414
  as system, 31
  transcultural, resources in, 445–446
Health care practitioners
  community nursing cultural issues and,
    333–334
  in intercultural work, 329
  in international health field, 426
  nonverbal communication of, 335
Health care professionals. *See* Health care
    practitioners
Health care providers, personal relations and
    communication with, 66
Health education programs, community-based,
    142
"Health for All by the Year 2000," 413–414
Health information, lay sources of, 31–32
Health maintenance. *See* Health promotion
Health orientations in United States, 33
Health problems
  in less developed countries, 415–418
  in more developed countries, 419
Health professionals. *See* Health care
    practitioners
Health promotion
  cultural knowledge in, 331–333
  in HIV/AIDS prevention program, 276
  nursing intervention and, 188
  in pregnancy, 102

studies relating to, 141
  use of term of, 18
Health-related beliefs and practices, assessment
    guide for, 441
Health-seeking behavior, factors influencing,
    34–35
Health status, lifestyle and, 239
Heart disease, 93
Height, biocultural variations in, 81–82
Help/health-seeking process, 34–35
Hematocrit, 90
Hemoglobin, 90
  abnormalities of, 101, 150–152
Hemoglobin C disease, 150, 152
Hemoglobin E disease, 150, 151
Hemoglobinopathies, 150, 151, 152
Hemophilia, 150
Hepatitis, 93
The Herald of Christian Science, 382
Herbalist, 30
Herbal medicine, 29–33
  Native Americans and, 404
  pain remedies and, 315, 316–317
  tertiary prevention planning and, 348
Hereditary predisposition to disease, 152. *See*
    also Genetics
Heterosexism, 263
Hexing as health belief, 25
High blood as health belief, 25
Hinduism, 388–390
Hip, dislocation of, 151
Hispanic, term of, 265
Hispanics. *See also* Latin culture; Spanish-
    speaking groups
  adolescent homicide of, 163
  culture-bound syndromes in, 80
  diversity in, 327
  drug abuse in, 165
  healers and, 30
  magico-religious paradigm and beliefs of, 23,
    24
  mental health nursing and, 265–266
  as subcultural group in United States, 14
History
  of international nursing and health,
    412–413
  in pain assessment, 311
HIV. *See* Human immunodeficiency virus
Hmong, mourning rituals and, 368–369
Holidays
  foods and, 74
  significant, 447–450
Holistic, term of, 18, 27
Holistic health paradigm, 26–29
Holistic health practices, 33
Holistic nursing care
  culture care accommodation of, 52, 92, 94
  spiritual care in, 356
Holy days
  of Buddhists, 377
  of Catholics, 378
  of Christian Scientists, 382
  of Hindus, 389

of Jehovah's Witnesses, 393
of Jews, 396–397
of Seventh-Day Adventists, 404
of Unitarian/Universalists, 406
Home birth, 107, 110–111
Homicide
adolescent and, 163
Native Americans and, 265
Honeymoon period in cultural adjustment, 429
Honpa Hongwanji sect of Buddhism, 375
Hoodoo, 264
Hospitalization
critical care nursing and, 290. *See also*
Critical care nursing
for psychiatric illness, 274
Hot/cold theory, 29
of Haitians, 195–196
in postpartum period, 111
in Spanish-American folk medicine, 266
Hougan, 30
Human immunodeficiency virus
mental health nursing and, 276–278
pandemic, in world, 419
refugees and, 194
Human machine in biomedical model, 26
Human response patterns, 51
Humor in communication, 269
Hyperpigmentation, oral, 88
Hypertension, 238–242, 246. *See also* Chronic
illness
diet in, 241–242
early detection and treatment of, 238
inactivity and, 242
and motivation in absence of symptoms,
240
nursing care of, 238–239
questions for client with, 246
risks for, 239
tertiary levels of prevention and, 347,
348–349
traditional treatment of, 250
Hypnosis, pain management and, 314

Ichthyosis vulgaris, 151
ICN (International Council of Nurses), 411,
414, 422–424
Id al-Adha, Islam and, 391
Ideology
mental health nursing and, 276–278
religion and, 354
Illness
attitudes toward, 244–250
family, 327
biocultural variations in, 80–90. *See also*
Biocultural variations
in children and adolescents, 142–157
biocultural influences on, 149–152
folk healing *versus* child abuse in,
145–149
special health care needs in, 159–160
chronic, in middle adulthood, 186–192
elderly client perspectives on, 230
sociological perspective on, 22
use of term of, 18

Illness behavior, 34
determinants of, 35–36
elderly and, 211
Imagery for pain, 315
Immigrants, 328–329
elderly among, 206–207
refugees as, 192–199
Immunity, genetic composition and, 151
Immunization programs, 414, 419
Incorporation rites, 36
Individuality, allowing for, 173–174
Infants
care of
beliefs surrounding, 113–116
cultural approaches to, 114–115
father and, 113
carrying practices for, 116, 117
feeding of, by Haitians, 196
international nursing and, 419, 420, 421
mortality rates of, 414, 419, 420
in Japan, 419
sex of, 105
Infarction, myocardial, 93
Infections
international nursing and, 416, 419
urinary tract, 101
Influenza, 93
Information collection, 272
Intellectual dimension of religion, 354
Intensive care units, nursing in. *See* Critical
care nursing
Interactions, personal space requirements and,
65–66
Interactive processes, mental health problems
and, 260–262
Intermarriage, childhood disorders and,
151–152
International Council of Nurses (ICN), 411,
414, 422–424
International nursing and health, 411–437
as career, 426
educational preparation for, 422, 426–428
Florence Nightingale and, 412–413
going abroad and, 431–435
history of, 412–413
International Council of Nurses and, 411,
414, 422–424
international students in schools of nursing
and, 431
international studies on campuses and,
430–431
learning from experiences of, 426
nurse classification and numbers in,
422–424
patterns of cultural adjustment in, 428–431
preparation for, 426–428
refugees and, 426, 430
skills and attitudes for, 428
as specialty, 424–426
terminology in, 411
world health status and, 413–419, 420, 421
global health care problems in, 414–415
HIV/AIDS pandemic in, 419

International nursing and health *(cont.)*
  infant and children's health in, 419, 420, 421
  major problems in, 415–419
  primary health care in, 414
International Society for the Prevention of Child Abuse and Neglect (ISPPCAN), 145
International Student Committee, 424
International students in schools of nursing, 431
International studies on campuses, 430–431
Interpersonal relationships. *See* Relationships
Interpreters, 335–336
  bilingual, 70, 71
  in communication with adolescent, 160–161
  functioning without, 72
  use of, 71–72
Interpreting, styles of, 71
Interventions in nursing care. *See* Nursing care, interventions in
Intimacy in cross-cultural communication, 65–67
Ischemic heart disease, 93
Islam, 390–393
  funeral customs and, 361
  suicide and, 361
"Isms," 262, 263
ISPPCAN. *See* International Society for the Prevention of Child Abuse and Neglect (ISPPCAN)

Japanese
  culture-bound syndromes in, 80
  culture values in folklore and literature of, 58
  death, dying, and grieving and, 366
Jargon, teenage, 161
Jaundice, biocultural variations in, 83–84
Jehovah's Witnesses, 393–396
  case study of, 173
Jehovah's Witnesses and the Question of Blood, 396
Jodo Shinshu sect of Buddhism, 375
Joseph disease, 151
Journal of Transcultural Nursing, 6
Judaism, 396–400
  culture values in folklore and literature in, 58
  funeral customs and, 361
  funeral practices in, 361
  mourning stages in, 367

Kadisha, Judaism and, 400
Kafias, 81
Kampucheans, mourning rituals and, 368–369
Karma, 139, 388
Kenya, pregnancy practices of Maasai in, 421
Kinship
  in cultural assessment, 337, 338, 339
  in factors affecting health and illness, 224, 226–227
  in secondary level of prevention, 346

Kippa, Judaism and, 398
Kissing, patterns of, 66
Knowledge
  cultural
    in health maintenance and promotion, 331–333
    in tertiary levels of prevention, 347
  mental health nursing and, 254
Koran, 390
Koreans
  culture-bound syndromes in, 80
  pregnancy in, 103–104
Kosher, 397
Krabbe disease, 151

Labor and delivery
  beliefs and customs surrounding, 107–111
  pain of, fear and anxiety about, 110
  positions for, 110
Laboratory tests, biocultural variations in, 90
Lactose intolerance, 93, 150, 151
Language
  acquisition of, 10
  as barrier in preventive care, 342
  in critical care nursing, 293–294
  in cross-cultural communication, 70–72, 334
  in cultural assessment, 337, 338, 340
  of distress, 256
  in mental health nursing, 268
Lao-Theung, mourning rituals and, 368–369
Laotians
  mourning rituals and, 368–369
  refugee resettlement and, 329
Latin culture. *See also* Hispanics
  beliefs about chronic illness of, 248, 249
  drug abuse in youths of, 165
  fatalism in, 245
  obligations in, 243–244
Latino, term of, 265
Law of *karma,* 139
Lay midwives, 78, 341
Learning
  of cultural beliefs, 10
  from experiences in international nursing, 426
  in preparation for international nursing, 422, 426–428
Lecithin/sphingomyelin ratio, 90
Leininger's Sunrise Model, 43–44
Leininger's theory of culture care diversity, 43, 44, 92, 94
  applications of, 52
Leisure activities, middle adulthood and, 185
Lesbian mothers, 114
Less developed countries, 414
  major health problems of, 415–418
Lesser Feast, 391
Leukodystrophy, metachromatic, 151
Leukoedema, 88
Levels of prevention, 341–347. *See also* Prevention

Life expectancy, 415, 417
  in Japan, 419
Lifestyle
  alterations in
    chronic illness and, 237–252. See also
      Chronic illness
    diet and, 241–242
    exercise and, 242
    family support systems and, 243–244
  cultural and behavioral factors in, 242–244
    coping behaviors and, 244–250
    family support systems and, 243–244
    health beliefs and, 246–249
    medication regimen and, 240–241
    traditional healers and health practices
      and, 249–250
  in health promotion and maintenance,
    332–333
  health status and, 239
  in secondary level of prevention, 346
Limb girdle muscle dystrophy, 150
Lip, cleft, 88, 150
Literature, cultural values in, 58
Lom phit dyan, 113
Loss of spouse, stress of, 366. See also
  Bereavement
Low blood as health belief, 25
Low-income clients
  factors in nursing care for, 332
  and health care access, 331
Loyalty to group, 56
Lung cancer, 418
Lymphedema, 151

Maasai of Kenya, pregnancy practices of, 421
Magico-religious health paradigm, 18, 22–23,
  24–25
Mahabharata, 144
Major health problems in world, 415–419
Mal ojo, 23, 24, 69, 105, 143, 257, 341
  dehydration and, 143
Malnutrition, 131–132
Mal puesto, 24
Mammary venous plexus, biocultural varia-
  tions in, 89
Mariel boat lift, 193
Masseuses, 341
Matrescence, 99
Maturity as criterion of adulthood, 182
Meal patterns, culture and, 73–75
Meaning
  and experiences in cultural relativism, 40
  of illness, cultural aspects of, 287
Measles, 152
Mecca, 390
Mechanic's model of illness behavior, 35
Mechanism as thought process in scientific
  paradigm, 25
Medication
  chronic illness and, 240–241
  side-effects of, 241
Mediterranean fever, 150, 151
Melanin content in skin, 83

Melting pot metaphor, 14–15, 327–328
Mennonite Church, 400–401
Menstruation
  children and adolescents and, 135–136
  cultural beliefs about, 117–118
Mental health care. See also Mental health
    nursing
  consumers of, 273
  services giving, 274
Mental health nursing, 253–285
  challenges of categories in, 260–268
    African Americans and, 264
    appeal of alternative systems in, 267–268
    Asian Americans and, 266–267
    ethnicity and, 262–264
    Hispanic Americans and, 265–266
    Middle Eastern groups and, 267
    Native Americans and, 265
  communication and, 268–270
  culture and, 259–260, 272–275
  guidelines for, 278–281
  ideologic conflict in, 276–278
  mental illness and mental disease in,
    254–255
  needs, beliefs, and practices and, 259–260
  normality and abnormality in, 255–258
  self understanding in, 270–272
  themes in, 253–254
Mental illness, 254–255
  history of attitudes toward, 253
  misdiagnosis or overdiagnosis in, 257
  rates of, 272
Metachromatic leukodystrophy, 151
Metaphors, 17
  in symbolism, expressions of, 17
Methemoglobinemia, 150
Mexican Americans. See also Hispanics; Latin
    culture
  child-rearing practices of, 130
  chronic illness in child and, 154
  communication with, 334
  cultural values and, 63
  cultural care meanings and action modes of,
    63
    assessment of, 339–341
    attitudes toward seeking care in, 342
    death, dying, and grieving and, 366, 367
    meanings of nursing care in, 63
    mourning rituals and, 367
    networks in, 344
    views of, toward motherhood and preg-
      nancy, 342–344
  extended family of, 339
  folk medicine of, 343
  language barriers of, 342
  prenatal care and, 342
Mexican refugee resettlement, 329
Middle adulthood, 181–201
  aging parents and, 184–185
  career performance in, 183
  child-rearing in, 184
  cultural influences on, 181–183
  friendships in, 185
  gender roles in, 185

Middle adulthood *(cont.)*
  health-related situational crises in, 185–199
    chronic illness and, 186–192
    refugees and, 192–199
  leisure activities in, 185
  Native Americans and, 186–192
  parental role in, 184–185
  physiological changes in, 184
  psychosocial development and, 183–185
  refugee experience and, 192–199
  terminology of, 181
Middle Eastern groups, mental health nursing
    and, 267
Midwives
  granny, 107
  lay, 78
Minority group, definition of, 12
Mitzvah, 397, 398, 399
Mobility, cultural variations in, 81
Modernization theory, 214
Modesty
  client sense of, 68
  cultural views of, 342
Mohammed, 390–393. *See also* Muslims
Mohel, 397
Mojo, 264
Molera caida, 341
Mongolian spots, 82–83
Moral orientation, 14
Moral paradigm, 18
More developed countries, 414–415
  major health problems in, 419
Mormons, 385–388
  in case history of cultural assessment, 293
  funeral practices of, 361
Morquio syndrome, 150
Mortuary, 361–362
Motherhood
  cultural views of, 342–343
  U.S. expectations of, 99–100. *See also* Child-
    bearing woman
Mother's attitude toward health and illnesses,
    126
Motivation
  for compliance, 238–239
  for going abroad, 431
Mourning, 366–369. *See also* Dying and
    bereavement
  cultural practices related to, 361–364
Mouth, biocultural variations in, 88
Multigenerational families of Nicaraguan
    immigrants, 223–228
Multiple caretakers of child, 136
Muneco, 105
Musculoskeletal system, biocultural variations
    in, 85, 86–87
Music therapy in labor care, 108
Muslims, 390–393
  observances of, 391
  rituals and funeral customs of, 361
  suicide and, 361
Myocardial infarction, 93

Nakajima, Dr. Hiroshi, 414
NANDA. *See* North American Nursing Diag-
    nosis Association (NANDA)
National Conference on the Classification of
    Nursing Diagnoses recognition of spiri-
    tual concerns, 357
Native American Church, 402
Native Americans
  adolescent
    homicide of, 163
    pregnancy in, 165
    suicide of, 163
  alcoholism in, 164
  case study of, 187–192, 295–296
  chronic illness and, 186–192, 249
  cooperation and, 264
  cultural assessment of, 337–339
  cultural values and, 63
  culture-bound syndromes in, 80
  culture care meanings and action modes of,
    63
  culture values in folklore and literature of, 58
  diabetes in, 186–192
  family support systems and, 189–192
  funeral customs of, 362–363, 364
  mental health nursing and, 265
  nursing care meanings to, 64
  pregnancy and
    adolescent, 165
    perceptions of kin utilization in, 102
  prejudice against, 262
  religions and, 401–404
  secondary levels of prevention in, 344–346
  spiritual symbols of, 402
  as subcultural group in United States, 14
  suicide and, 362–363
Naturalistic paradigm, 18
Natural methods of contraception, 116–117
Natural phenomena, 17
Navajo Americans
  burial preparation and funeral customs of,
    362
  supernatural aspects of illness and, 339
Needs
  of adolescent for special health care,
    159–160, 162–166
  critical care and, 290–291, 292, 295
  of elderly, 217–218, 228
  mental health nursing and, 259–260
  in pregnancy for assistance, 102–103
  spiritual. *See* Spirituality and religion
Negative beliefs and pregnancy, 105–106
Negotiating contract before going abroad, 432
Nephrosis, congenital, 150
Nervous breakdown, 257
Networks, cultural, 198
Neural tube defects, 150
Neurasthenia, 257
Neurological assessment, 293
Nicaraguan immigrants
  case study of, 223–224
  client perspective and, 224–225
  ethnic heritage of, 224
  lay medicine of, 224

multidimensional nursing analysis for, 225–228
multigenerational families of, 223–228
religious needs and, 224
Niemann-Pick disease, 150, 151
Nightingale, Florence, 412–413
Night of Power and Greatness, 391
Night of Repentance, 391
Nirvana, 376, 388
Noble Eightfold Way, 376
Non–English-speaking clients, 70–71. *See also* Interpreters
Non–insulin-dependent diabetes, 344–346
Nontraditional medical practices, 33. *See also* Folk medicine
Nonverbal communication
    adolescent and, 160, 161
    cross-cultural, 67–69, 334, 335
Normality, mental health nursing and, 255–258
Norms, 11
    community nursing and, 325
    of conduct and behavior, 355–356
    conflicts of, 174
    in cultural assessment, 337, 338–339, 340
North American Indians. *See* Native Americans
North American Nursing Diagnosis Association (NANDA), 50–52
North India Indians, culture-bound syndromes in, 80
Nuclear family, 124
Nudity, physical examination and, 161–162
Nurse-client relationships, pain relief and, 309. *See also* Relationships
Nurses
    classification and numbers of, in world populations, 422–424
    comfort level of, with cultural groups, 58–62
    competence of, 309–310
    critical care, perceptions and responses of, 291–292
    cultural background of, 58
    involvement of, in family system, 66
    national background of, assessment of pain and, 307
    professional, 37
    self-understanding in, 270–272
    spiritual intervention and, 356–357
    supportive and assistive functions of, for elderly, 227
Nursing
    anthropology and, 4
    concepts in, 36–42
        central, 7
    international. *See* International nursing and health
    socialization process into, 37
    spiritual care and phenomenon of, 357, 358
    theories of. *See* Theoretical foundations of transcultural nursing
    transcultural. *See* Transcultural nursing
    transnational, 424

Nursing care
    access to, 330–333
    caring concepts in, 41–42
    community, 323–352. *See also* Community nursing
    comprehensive approach to, elderly client and, 225–228
    culturally competent, 40–41
    dying or bereaved client and, 359–369. *See* Dying and bereavement
    for elderly, summary of, 228
    interventions in
        community nursing and, 331–333, 346
        developmental assessment and, 196–197
        with elderly, 213–216, 223–228
        Haitian refugees and, 196–197
        health promotion strategies and, 188
        learned from international nursing, 426, 427
        planning of, 213–216
    meaning of, to client, 280
    meaning of cultural values to, 62, 63–64
    pain considerations in, 301
    prevailing paradigm for, transcultural critique of, 50
    spiritual, 356–357
    transcultural, 49–96. *See* Transcultural nursing
    use of term of, 18
Nursing care plan
    for child and adolescent, implementation of, 169–175
    evaluation of, 169
Nursing content in cultural assessment, 55
Nursing diagnoses, transcultural perspectives on, 50–52, 53
Nursing framework, transcultural, 7–8
Nursing process
    application of, 169–175
    in cultural assessment, 55
        transcultural perspective of, 42–44
Nursing specialties
    definition of, 424–425
    international nursing and health as, 424–426
Nursing subculture, pain issues and, 306–308
Nutrition
    assessment guide for, 441–442
    children and adolescents and, 131–132
    culture and, 73–78

OAA (Older Americans Act), 230
Obesity, hypertension and, 242
Objective materialism, 26
Ocular albinism, 150
Oguchi disease, 150
Older Americans Act (OAA), 230
Older population, projections and challenges for, 203–204. *See also* Aging; Elderly
Older woman or old lady as healer, 30
    in tertiary prevention planning, 348
Ongoing data-gathering, 174–175
O'odhams from Papago, 363

Open-ended questions, 269
Oral hyperpigmentation, 88
Orderliness, 56
Ordinances, Mormonism and, 386
Orem's self-care theory, transcultural view of, 53–54
Organ donations
  Baha'is and, 375
  Buddhists and, 377
  Catholics and, 379
  Christian Scientists and, 384
  Hindus and, 389, 390
  Jehovah's Witnesses and, 394, 396
  Jews and, 400
  Mennonites and, 401
  Mormons and, 388
  Muslims and, 392, 393
  Seventh-Day Adventists and, 405, 406
  Unitarian/Universalists and, 406, 407
Organic method of healing, 27, 29–33
Organizations providing cultural support in assessment guide, 443
Osteopetrosis, malignant, 150
Otitis media, 93
Overcoming barriers. *See* Barriers
Overpopulation in less developed countries, 418

Pain, 301–322
  acupuncture/acupressure for, 318, 319
  alternative practices for, 312–318, 319
  applying transcultural concepts to persons in, 308–312
    identifying personal attitudes and, 308–309
    nurse competence and, 309–310
    open nurse-client relationships and, 309
  assessment of, 311–312
  biofeedback for, 318
  case study of, 306
  clarifying responsibility and, 312
  critical care nursing and, 287
  cultural differences in attitudes toward, 303, 304–306
  cutaneous stimulation for, 315
  definitions of, 301–302
  denial of, by medical staff, 307
  distraction techniques for, 314–315
  evaluating effect of, 312
  expressions of, 304–306
  herbal remedies for, 315, 316–317
  imagery for, 315
  measurement of, 302–304
  nurse background and perception of, 307
  nursing subculture and, 306–308
  relaxation techniques for, 313–314
  religious experiences and, 303
  religious rituals for, 317–318
  signs and symptoms of, 305
  silent suffering in, 307
  therapeutic touch for, 315
  threshold of, 302, 303
    tolerance of, 302–303
      encouragement in, 303–304
    views and attitudes toward, 306–308
Pain threshold, 302, 303
Pain tolerance, encouraged, 303–304
Palate, cleft, 88, 150
Palestinian, case study of, 294
Pallor, biocultural variations in, 84
Pandemic HIV/AIDS in world, 419
Paradigms, 17–18
  biomedical, 23–26, 33
  dominant cultural, 18
  of health/illness causation, 22–29
  holistic, 18, 26–29
  magico-religious, 18, 22–23
  scientific, 18, 23–26
Parasitic diseases, 416
Parenthood
  cultural expectations for, 9–10
  mental health care and patterns in, 259
  middle adulthood and, 184
Parents
  attitudes of, child behavior and, 124
  beliefs or practices of, in care of child, 357–359
  of disabled and chronically ill child, 156–157
  relationships of, with child, 136–137
Paroxysmal polyserositis, 150
Parteras, 78, 107, 341
Passover, 397
Patrescence, 99
Peace Corps, 428
Peer counselors, 276
  sexual information and, 165–166
People, concept of, in transcultural nursing, 34–36
Perceptions
  of critical care nurses, 291–292
  of infant cry, 130
  of need for assistance in pregnancy, 102–103
  of pain, 307
    stereotypes and, 309
  of side effects of drugs, 91
  of symptoms, 256–257
Perinatal deaths, 414
Perinatal problems in less developed countries, 417–418
Personal activities, involvement of nurse in, 66
Personality of culture, 12
Personal space requirements, 65–66
Petechiae, biocultural variations in, 85
Peyote Religion, 402
Phenomena
  of nature, 17
  normal or abnormal, 256
Phenylketonuria, 150, 151, 152
Physical appearance, biocultural variations in, 81
Physical environment, 19
Physicians, number of, in selected parts of world, 424

Physiology
  acceptance of changes in, 184
  in data categories, 55
  low-income African Americans and, 248
Piaget's theories of growth and development, 129
Pinching in folk healing practices, 149
Pneumonia, 93
Political stability, 432
Political systems in cultural assessment, 337, 338, 340
Pollution, postpartum period and, 111
Polycystic liver disease, 150
Polyserositis, paroxysmal, 150
Population-based practice, 341
Population frailty, 203
Population projections, 203–204, 253
Postpartum period, 111–113
Posttraumatic stress disorder, 257
Pova, 148
Poverty
  factors in nursing care and, 332
  and health care access, 331
  mental health problems and, 259
  of refugees, 196–198
Practitioners, health care. *See* Health care practitioners
Pregnancy
  activity during, 104–105
  avoidance of, 116–119
    beliefs about, 166
  biologic variations in, 101
  cultural variations in, 100–107, 101–107
    health-related beliefs or practices and, 104–105, 106
  cultural views of, 342–343
  kin utilization in, 102
  Maasai of Kenya practices and, 421
  Mexican American beliefs and practices in, 343
  nurse reaction to superstition and, 105
  perceptions of need for assistance in, 102–103
  prescriptive beliefs and, 105, 106
  restrictive beliefs and, 105, 106
  taboos in, 105, 106
  validation of femaleness and, 166
Prejudgment, mental health problems and, 260–262
Prejudice, 38. *See also* Discrimination
  mental health problems and, 260–262
  against refugees, 197–198
Prenatal care, 104, 342
  classes in, 104
  in Mexican Americans, 343–344
Prescriptive beliefs, pregnancy and, 105, 106
Prevention
  primary, 341–344
    elderly and, 203
    international nursing and, 414
  secondary, 344–346
    in community nursing, 344–346
    elderly and, 203

studies relating to, 141
  tertiary, 346–347, 348–349
    elderly and, 203
Priest or priestess as healer, 25, 30
Primary prevention
  in community nursing, 341–344
  elderly and, 203
  international nursing and, 414
Principle of totality, Catholicism and, 379
Privacy, client sense of, 68
  critical care nursing and, 289
Problems
  major health
    in less developed countries, 415–418
    in more developed countries, 419
  mental health. *See* Mental health nursing
    statement of perceived, 268
Professional sector of health care system, 32
Progressive relaxation for pain, 313–314
Projections of population, 203–204, 253
Prolongation of life or Right to Die
  Baha'is and, 375
  Buddhists and, 377
  Catholics and, 381
  Christian Scientists and, 384
  Hindus and, 390
  Jehovah's Witnesses and, 395
  Jews and, 398
  Mennonites and, 401
  Mormons and, 388
  Muslims and, 392
  Seventh-Day Adventists and, 406
  Unitarian/Universalists and, 407
Proportions, body, 81–82
Proverbs, 59
Pseudocholinesterase deficiency, 150
Psoriasis, 93
Psychiatric disorders, resources for, 255. *See also* Mental health nursing; Mental illness
Psychological data categories, 55
Psychomotor development tests, 128
Psychosocial development during adulthood, 183–185
Puerto Ricans
  adolescent pregnancy in, 165
  bereavement, grief, and mourning of, 367
  culture values in folklore and literature of, 58
Pujos, 142
Punishment, illness as, 248, 264
Puranas, 144
Purim, 397
Pyruvate kinase deficiency, 150

Qur'an, 390

Rabbi, 398
Race, childhood disorders and, 152
Racism, 38, 263
  tertiary prevention planning and, 349
Ramadan, 391, 392
Reason as controlling force in behavior, 41
Reductionism, 25

Reentry shock, 430
Refugees
    international nursing and health of, 426, 430
    resettlement of, 329
        family in, 192–199
        health problems of, 193–194
        situational crises of, 192–199
Reintegration rites, 36
Relationship-oriented society, 139
Relationships. *See also* Nurses
    compliance and, 240–241
    culture and, 10–11
    with family of child and adolescent, 136–138
    harmonious, 266
    middle adulthood and, 185
    pain relief and, 309
Relaxation techniques for pain, 313–314
Religion, 353–409. *See also* Spirituality and
        religion
    assessment guide for, 443
    Baha'is and, 370–375
    bereavement and, 359–369. *See also* Dying
        and bereavement
    Buddhists and, 375–378
    Catholics and, 378–381
    childhood illness and, 357–359
    Christian Scientists and, 381–384
    in cultural assessment, 337, 339, 340–342
    cultural theories and food and, 76–78
    death and dying and, 359–369. *See also*
        Death; Dying and bereavement
        beliefs about, 359–361
    denominations in United States, 370–407
    dimensions of, 353–356
    family planning and, 118
    of Haitian refugees, 195
    Hindus and, 388–390
    Muslims and, 390–393
    Jehovah's Witnesses and, 393–396
    Jews and, 396–400
    Mennonites and, 400–401
    Middle Eastern concept of, 267
    Mormons and, 385–388
    Native Americans and, 265, 401–404
    nursing care and, 356–357, 358
        for dying, 359–369. *See also* Dying and
            bereavement
    in rituals for pain, 317–318
    selected studies on, 371–372
    Seventh-Day Adventists and, 404–406
    spirituality and, 356
    subcultures and, 64
    tertiary prevention planning and, 349
    trends in, in United States and Canada, 370
    Unitarian/Universalists and, 406–407
    verification of assumptions in, 355
Religious holidays, 447–450
    foods and, 74
Renal disease, 93
Research
    cross-cultural, on growth and development,
        129–130
    on international health care, 428

Resistiveness, 269
Resources in transcultural health and nursing,
    445–446
Respect in nurse-client relationship, 309
Response patterns, 51
Responsibility in pain management, 312
Restrictions
    of postpartum period, 111–113
    pregnancy and, 105, 106
Retinoschisis, 150
Retirement, repercussions of, 209–210
Richards, Linda, 413
Right to Die. *See* Prolongation of life or Right
    to Die
Riley-Day syndrome, 150
Rites
    in expressing emotion and distress, 333
    of passage, 36
Rituals, 35–36
    coping with death through, 359–361
    in expressing emotion and distress, 333
    mourning, 366–369
    religion and, 354. *See also* Religion
Roles
    cultural definition of, 10–11
    of family
        in critical care nursing, 297
        in transmitting cultural beliefs and prac-
            tices, 327
    Freud's study of, 129
    responsibilities and, 10–11
    sick, 34, 35, 67
    in society, 10–11
Root medicine, 249, 264
    in tertiary prevention planning, 348
Rosh Hashanah, 396
Rubeola, 152

Sabador, 24, 30
Sacrament of the Sick, 381
Sacraments
    of Baha'is, 373
    of Buddhists, 377
    of Catholics, 378
    of Christian Scientists, 382
    of Jews, 397
    of Mormons, 385–386
    of Seventh-Day Adventists, 404
    of Unitarian/Universalists and, 406
Safe drinking water, 415–416
Safety in international nursing, 432
Salat, 390
Salat El Mayyet, 393
Salvadorans, refugee resettlement and, 329
Saris, 81
Saum, 390
Schizophrenia, 257
Schools of nursing, international students in,
    431
Scientific paradigm, 18, 23–26
Secondary prevention
    in community nursing, 344–346
    elderly and, 203

Second burial, 368
Secretions, biocultural variations in, 89–90
Seeking treatment, 35
Self-assessment, dietary, 73
Self-care theory of Orem, 53–54
Self-determination or self-actualization, 217, 218
Self-development, Native American guidelines for, 403
Self-understanding, mental health nursing and, 270–272
Sending agencies in international nursing, 432–435, 451–454
Sensation threshold, 302
Sense of community, 23
Sensitivity
    to cultural practices in community nursing settings, 331, 332
    in mental health nursing, 254
Separation
    anxiety from, 136
    from familiar references, 289
    from family and significant others, vulnerability and, 288
    rites of, 36
Serum cholesterol, 90
Serum transferrin, 90
Seventh-Day Adventists, 404–406
Sex differences
    behavior and, 138
    in cross-cultural communication, 69
Sexism, 263
Sex of infant, folk prediction of, 105
Sex roles in child and adolescent, 138
Sexual activity in adolescent, 165–166
Sexual information, peer counselors and, 165–166
Sexual relations in pregnancy, 113. See also Contraception
Shahada, 390
Sharing of cultural beliefs, 10
Sharing experiences and exercises, 277–278
Shavuot, 397
Shema, 396
Shi'ite Islamic movement, 390
Shin Buddhism, 375
Shmini Atzeret, 397
Shochet, 397
Shock, culture or reentry, 430
Sickle cell anemia, 93, 150, 151, 152
Sickle cell trait, 101
Sickness, sociological perspective and, 22
Sick role behavior, 34, 35, 67
Side effects of medication, 241
    perception of, 91
Significant others
    communication with, 62–65
    separation from, 288
Silence in communication, 67, 68
Silent suffering in pain, 307
Simchat Torah, 397
Sin, illness as punishment for, 248, 264

Single-parent family, 124
Sizism, 263
Sjögren's-Larsson syndrome, 151
Skills
    communication recovery, 269
    for international nursing and health, 428
    in mental health nursing, 254
Skin
    biocultural variations in, 82–83
    care of child and adolescent, 168–169
    color of, 82
Sleep
    children and adolescents and, 132–134
    restriction of, in hospital, 289
Smoking
    adolescent, 162
    hazards of, in more developed countries, 418
Sobadors, 341
Social activities
    Baha'is and, 374
    Catholics and, 380
    Christian Scientists and, 384
    in cultural assessment, 337, 338, 340
    of elderly, 206–209
    Hindus and, 389
    involvement of nurse in, 66
    Jehovah's Witnesses and, 394
    Jews and, 398
    Mennonites and, 401
    Mormons and, 387
    Muslims and, 392
    Seventh-Day Adventists and, 405
Social classification, mental health problems and, 260–262
Social environment, 19
    mental health problems and, 259
Social harmony, communication and, 66
Socialization process into nursing, 37
Social norms, 34
Social paradigm, 18
Social responsibility, adulthood and, 183–184
Social stratification, 274
Social support for family of critical-care patient, 292
Society
    diverse, 253
    psychiatric disorders in, 255
    roles in, 10–11
Sociocentric interactive pattern, 262, 263
Socioeconomic status
    assessment guide for, 442
    childhood disease and, 160
    elderly adults and, 211–212
Sociological data categories, 55
Solidarity among generations, 219
Somatization, 145, 333
Southeast Asians
    culture-bound syndromes in, 80
    expectations of, for chronic disease, 249
    folk healing practices of, 148–149
    health during pregnancy and, 101
    mourning rituals and, 368–369

Southeast Asians *(cont.)*
  as refugees
    communication with, 334
    dying and bereavement and, 368–369
    resettlement of, 329
Space, functional use of
  by Anglo-American nurses, 66
Spanish-speaking groups. *See also* Hispanics;
      Latin culture; Mexican Americans
  communication with, 334
  dying and bereavement in, 367
Specialties
  definition of, 424
  international nursing and health as,
      424–426
Spirit protector, 195
Spiritualists, 25, 30, 249, 264, 341
  tertiary prevention planning and, 348
Spirituality and religion, 356–357. *See also*
      Religion
  assessment of, 358
  comprehensive care and, 228
  critical care nursing and, 295
  of elderly, 228
  Nicaraguan immigrants and, 224
  phenomenon of nursing and, 357, 358
Spiritual symbols, 402
Sponsorship in international nursing, 432–435
Spouse, loss of, 366
Stability, political, 432
Standards
  double set of, 270
  of performance, 14
Status change, 36
Stealing, cultural attitudes toward, 56
Stereotyping, 39
  child behavior and, 124, 125
  mental health problems and, 253, 260–262,
      273
  in pain perception and responses, 309
Sterility/fertility testing
  Catholics and, 380
  Jehovah's Witnesses and, 394
  Jews and, 398
  Mormons and, 387
  Unitarian/Universalists and, 407
Stimulation, cutaneous, for pain, 315
Stranger anxiety, 136
Stress
  death of spouse and, 366
  management of, 332, 333
  vulnerability and, 289–290
Structure of body, biocultural variations in,
      81–82
Subcultures, 12
  of adolescent, 159
  diversity in, 327
  ethnoreligious, 64
  as framework for community nursing,
      324–325, 327–328
  geographic areas and, 327–328
  nursing, pain issues and, 306–308
  regional, 14–16
  in United States, 14–16, 327–328

Substance use. *See also* Drug abuse
  Baha'is and, 374
  Catholics and, 380
  Christian Scientists and, 384
  Hindus and, 389
  Jehovah's Witnesses and, 394
  Jews and, 398
  Mormons and, 387
  Muslims and, 392
  Seventh-Day Adventists and, 405
  Unitarian/Universalists and, 407
Succot, 396
Suicide
  in adolescent, 163–164
  attitudes toward, 362
  in more developed countries, 418
  in Native Americans, 265
Sunni Islamic sect, 390
Supernatural aspects of illness, 339
  Navajo Americans and, 339
Supernatural entities as protectors, 195
Superstition
  versus health beliefs, 259
  pregnancy and, 105–107
Support groups
  for family of critical-care patient, 292
  in secondary prevention programs, 346
Support systems
  cultural assessment guide for, 443
  for elderly, 213–216
    culturally acceptable, 230–232
    intervention planning and, 213–216
Surface adjustment, cultural, 430
Susceptibilities to specific diseases and disor-
      ders, 149–152
Susto, 24, 142, 257, 341
Sweat glands, 89
Symbolic environment, 19–21
Symbols, spiritual, 402
Symptoms
  defined, 79
  mental health nursing and, 256
  perceptions of, 256–257
  transcultural nursing care and, 79–80

Taboos, 35
  in attitudes toward death, 362
  in pregnancy, 105, 106
Tallit, 398
Taveez, 139
Taxonomy of North American Nursing Diag-
      nosis Association (NANDA) diagnoses,
      50–52
Tay-Sachs disease, 150, 152
Technology, critical care nursing and, 287, 288
Teeth
  absence of, 89
  biocultural variations in, 88–89
  eruption of, 128
Tefillin, 398
Temple garments, 81
Tertiary prevention
  in community nursing, 346–347, 348–349
  elderly and, 203

Thalassemia, 150, 151, 152

Theoretical foundations of transcultural nursing, 3–47
  concept of people in, 34–36
  culture phenomenon in, 8–19, 20–21
    change and, 16–19, 20–21
    cultural characteristics and concepts and, 11–12
    definition of culture and, 9, 10
    U.S. cultural groups and, 12–16
    value formation and, 11–12, 13
    value orientations and, 11–12, 13
  environment concept in, 19–21
  foundation of, 34–36
  framework for, 7–8
    environment in, 19–21
  health concept in, 21–23
    belief systems and, 22–29
    healing art and practice and, 29–33
    U.S. health orientations in, 33
  nursing concept in, 36–42
  perspective of, 4–8, 9
  perspectives on, 52–54
  transcultural caring concepts study in, 42–44

Theories of aging in ethnic groups, 214

Therapeutic touch, in pain management, 310, 315

Therapeutic touch for pain, 315

Thin blood, 25

Third National Conference on the Classification of Nursing Diagnoses recognition of spiritual concerns, 357

Thorax, biocultural variations in, 85

Thrifty gene hypotheses, 187

Time, cultural attitudes toward, 56

Time and experiences in cultural relativism, 40

Time as dominant force, 273

Time concept, 289

Tohono O'odham from Papago, 363

Torsion dystonia, 150

Touch, therapeutic, in pain management, 310, 315

Touch as healing gesture for child and adolescent, 169

Touch in communication, 67, 68–69

Trachoma, 93

Traditional healers, nursing care and, 78–79

Traditional health beliefs
  appeal of, 267–268
  of Haitian refugees, 194–196
  maintenance of, over time, 329–330

Traditional practitioners, 24, 25, 30, 249–250. *See also* Folk medicine

Traditions, in cultural assessment, 337, 338, 340

Tradition sharing by elderly, 219–220
  disruptions of, 227

Transcendental meditation, 314

Transcultural caring concepts, study of, 42–44

Transcultural communication
  personal introductions and, 65

Transcultural conflict, minimization of, 11

Transcultural nursing, 49–96
  assumptions and propositions basic to, 5–6
  biocultural variations in. *See* Biocultural variations
  body of knowledge in, 6–7
  clinical decision-making and nursing actions in, 92–94
  conceptual framework in, 7
  critique of prevailing nursing paradigm in, 50
  cross-cultural communication in, 62–72
    with family members and significant others, 62–65
    introductions in, 65
    language in, 70–72
    nonverbal, 67–69
    overcoming barriers in, 67
    sex/gender considerations in, 69
    space, distance, and intimacy in, 65–67
  cultural assessment in, 55
  cultural competence, cultural competencies, and excellence in, 54
  culture values in, 55–62, 63–64
  defined, 6
  development and current status of, 4–7
  disease prevalence and, 92, 93
  environment and, 19–21
  ethnopharmacology in, 90–91
  evaluation of, 94
  framework for, 7–8
    environment in, 19–21
  international nursing and, 424
  model for, 5, 7–8
  nursing actions in, 92–94
  nutrition and, 73–78
  and perspectives, 4–8, 9
    on nursing diagnoses, 50–52
    on nursing theories, 52–54
  resources in, 445–446
  symptoms in, 79–80
  theoretical foundations of, 9
  traditional healers in, 78–79

Transcultural Nursing Society, 44

Transferrin, serum, 90

Transition rites, 36

Transnational nursing, 424

Travel abroad, 431–435
  geographical region and, 432
  length of time of, 431–432
  motivation for, 431
  negotiating contract before, 432
  sending agencies in, 432, 451–454
    choice of, 432–435

Treatment, determinants in Seeking and compliance with, 35

Tricultural adolescent, 161

Trinidadian, case study of, 297

Trisomy 21, 87

Truth, cultural attitudes toward, 56

Tuberculosis, 93, 152

Type II diabetes. *See* Diabetes mellitus

Tyrosinase positive albinism, 150, 151

Tyrosinemia, 150

Ulcers, 93
Umbilical cord, care of, 116
Unani prophetic medicine, 145
Unclean drinking water, 415–416
Understanding
    of goals and expectations of client, 280–281
    in pain assessment, 311
Undertaker, 361–362
Unitarian/Universalist Church, 406–407
United States
    cultural groups in, 12–16
    health orientations in, 33
    population changes in, 253
    religious denominations in, 370–376. *See also* Religion
    subcultures in, 14–16, 327–328. *See also* Subcultures
    value orientations in, 14
Unity, spiritual symbols of, 402–404
Universities, international studies in, 430–431
Unknown, fears of, 289–290
Urinary tract infections, 101
Ute Native Americans. *See also* Native Americans
    case study of, 187–192
    secondary levels of prevention in, 344–346
Uvula, cleft, 88

Vaccines, 414, 419
Value systems, comparison of, 15
Values, 11–12, 13
    community nursing and, 325, 327
    culture and formation of, 11–12, 13
    dominant 20th century, 15
    elderly adult and alienation from, 227
    functions of, 11–12
    of nurses, nursing process and, 42
Value orientations
    assessment guide for, 439–440
    common, 11–12, 13, 16
    in cultural assessment, 337, 338, 340
    mastery as, 14
    in United States, 14
Vedas, 388
Venous plexus, mammary, 89
Ventouse, 148
Ventricular septal defects, 151, 169–173
Vietnamese
    case study of, 294–295
    mourning rituals and, 368–369
    refugee resettlement and, 329

Vitiligo, 83
Vocal cues in communication, 67
Voodoo beliefs and practices, 25, 30, 195, 249, 264
    in attitudes toward death, 362
    tertiary prevention planning and, 348
Vulnerability of client, 288–290

Wake, 367
Weight
    biocultural variations in, 81–82
    loss of, cultural beliefs about, 188
Werdnig-Hoffman disease, 151
Western medical beliefs
    coexistence of, with traditional health beliefs, 142
    in curing ghost illness, 145
    faulty assumptions of, 33
White Anglo-Saxon Protestant as subcultural group in United States, 13
White House Conference on Aging, 357
Whites, culture-bound syndromes in, 80
White Shell Woman Way, 105, 116
WHO (World Health Organization), 413–414
    sponsorship in international nursing by, 432
Witchcraft, 25
W model of cultural adjustment, 429
Word of Wisdom, 386
Work-centered society, 139
World Health Assembly, 413
World Health Organization (WHO), 413–414
    sponsorship in international nursing by, 432
World health status, 413–419, 420, 421
    global health care problems in, 414–415
    HIV/AIDS pandemic in, 419
    infant and children's health in, 419, 420, 421
    major health problems in, 415–419
    primary health care in, 414
World view of health, 17–18
    in cultural assessment, 337, 338, 340
    in symbolism, expressions of, 17–18
Wu-fu, 368

Yerbera, 30
Yin/yang theory, 27–28, 29, 249
    of Asian Americans, 266
    in postpartum period, 111
Yoga, pain management and, 314
Yom Kippur, 396